WORLD POLITICS 91/92

Twelfth Edition

Annual Editions

A Library of Information from the Public Press

Editor

Suzanne P. Ogden
Northeastern University

Dr. Suzanne Ogden is Professor and Chair of Political Science at Northeastern University, and Associate in Research at the Fairbank Center for East Asian Research at Harvard University. She has lived in Hong Kong, Taiwan, Mexico, and Honduras, and has traveled extensively throughout the People's Republic of China, Southeast Asia, Japan, Central America, and Europe. Dr. Ogden is the author of *China's Unresolved Issues: Politics, Development, and Culture* (2nd ed.) (Prentice Hall, 1992); *Global Studies: China* (4th ed.) (Dushkin Publishing Group, Inc.); numerous articles on Chinese foreign policy, politics, and higher education; and senior editor on *China's Search for Democracy: The Student and Mass Movement of 1989* (M. E. Sharpe, Inc., 1991). At Northeastern University, she teaches courses on international relations, Chinese politics, and Japanese politics. She is currently a member of the Board of Directors for the Center for International Politics and Administration at Northeastern.

Cover illustration by Mike Eagle

The Dushkin Publishing Group, Inc.
Sluice Dock, Guilford, Connecticut 06437

This map has been developed to give you a graphic picture of where the countries of the world are located, the relationship they have with their region and neighbors, and their positions relative to the superpowers and power blocs. We have focused on certain areas to more clearly illustrate these crowded regions.

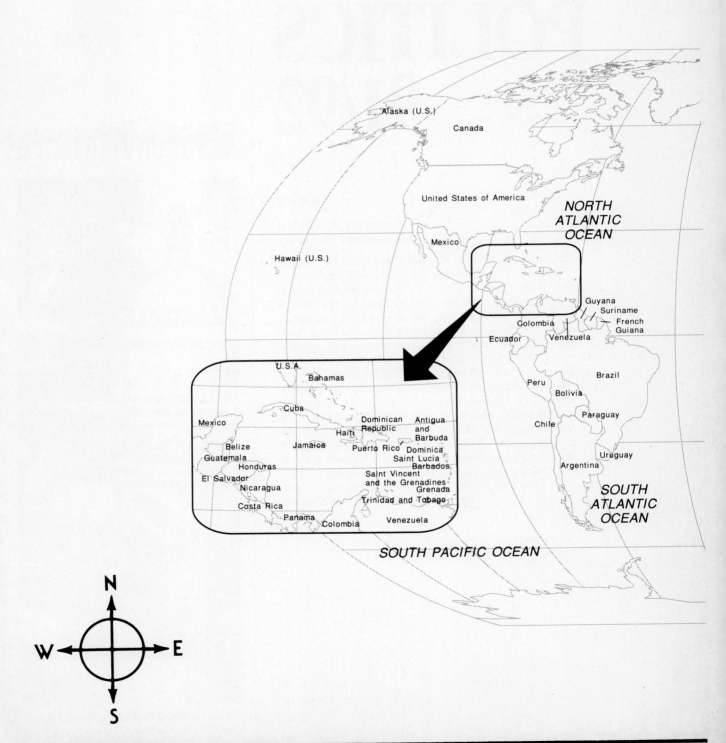

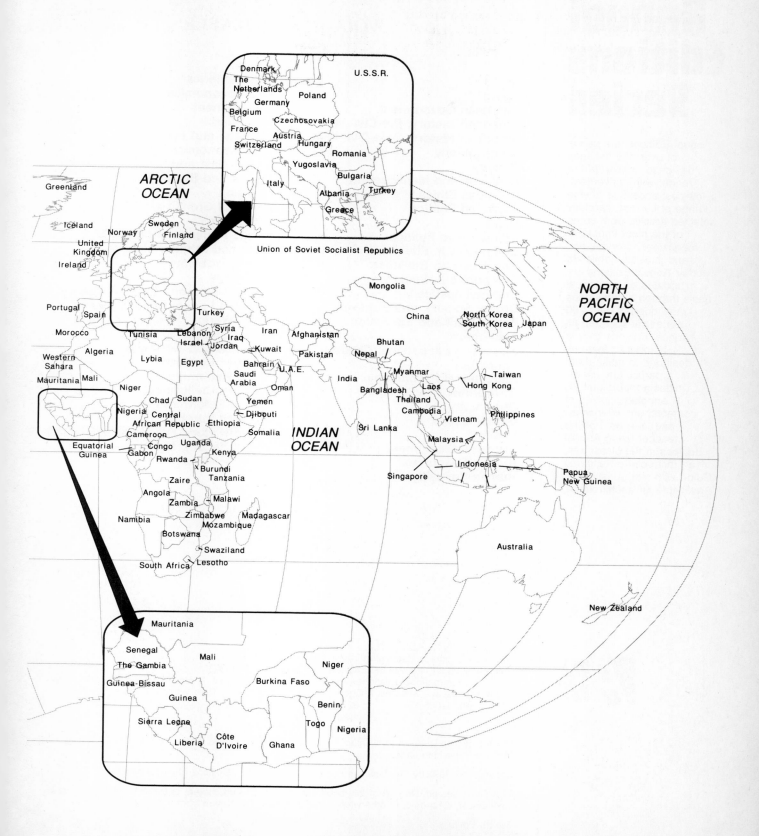

Denmark
The Netherlands
Germany
Belgium
Poland
France
Czechosovakia
Switzerland
Austria
Hungary
Italy
Yugoslavia
Romania
Bulgaria
Albania
Turkey
Greece
U.S.S.R.

Union of Soviet Socialist Republics

Greenland

ARCTIC OCEAN

Iceland
Norway
Sweden
Finland
United Kingdom
Ireland
Portugal
Spain
Turkey
Morocco
Tunisia
Lebanon
Syria
Iraq
Iran
Afghanistan
Mongolia
China
North Korea
South Korea
Japan
Israel
Jordan
Kuwait
Pakistan
Bhutan
Nepal
Algeria
Lybia
Egypt
Bahrain
U.A.E.
India
Myanmar
Taiwan
Hong Kong
Western Sahara
Mali
Saudi Arabia
Oman
Laos
Mauritania
Niger
Chad
Sudan
Yemen
Bangladesh
Thailand
Cambodia
Vietnam
Philippines
Nigeria
Central African Republic
Djibouti
Ethiopia
Sri Lanka
Malaysia
Equatorial Guinea
Cameroon
Uganda
Somalia
INDIAN OCEAN
Singapore
Indonesia
Papua New Guinea
Gabon
Congo
Rwanda
Kenya
Burundi
Tanzania
Zaire
Angola
Zambia
Malawi
Namibia
Zimbabwe
Madagascar
Mozambique
Botswana
Swaziland
Australia
South Africa
Lesotho

NORTH PACIFIC OCEAN

New Zealand

Mauritania
Senegal
Mali
The Gambia
Niger
Guinea-Bissau
Burkina Faso
Guinea
Benin
Sierra Leone
Togo
Nigeria
Liberia
Côte D'Ivoire
Ghana

The Annual Editions Series

Annual Editions is a series of over fifty volumes designed to provide the reader with convenient, low-cost access to a wide range of current, carefully selected articles from some of the most important magazines, newspapers, and journals published today. Annual Editions are updated on an annual basis through a continuous monitoring of over 200 periodical sources. All Annual Editions have a number of features designed to make them particularly useful, including topic guides, annotated tables of contents, unit overviews, and indexes. For the teacher using Annual Editions in the classroom, an Instructor's Resource Guide with test questions is available for each volume.

VOLUMES AVAILABLE

Africa
Aging
American Government
American History, Pre-Civil War
American History, Post-Civil War
Anthropology
Biology
Business and Management
Business Ethics
Canadian Politics
China
Comparative Politics
Computers in Education
Computers in Business
Computers in Society
Criminal Justice
Drugs, Society, and Behavior
Early Childhood Education
Economics
Educating Exceptional Children
Education
Educational Psychology
Environment
Geography
Global Issues
Health
Human Development
Human Resources
Human Sexuality

Latin America
Macroeconomics
Management
Marketing
Marriage and Family
Microeconomics
Middle East and the Islamic World
Money and Banking
Nutrition
Personal Growth and Behavior
Psychology
Public Administration
Race and Ethnic Relations
Social Problems
Sociology
Soviet Union and Eastern Europe
State and Local Government
Third World
Urban Society
Violence and Terrorism
Western Civilization,
   Pre-Reformation
Western Civilization,
   Post-Reformation
Western Europe
World History, Pre-Modern
World History, Modern
World Politics

Library of Congress Cataloging in Publication Data
Main entry under title: Annual Editions: World Politics. 1991/92.
        1. International relations—Addresses, essays, lectures. 2. United States—Foreign relations—Addresses, essays, lectures. I. Ogden, Suzanne P., comp. II. Title: World Politics.
ISBN 1-56134-035-9   327".05

Twelfth Edition

Manufactured by The Banta Company, Harrisonburg, Virginia 22801

Editors/ Advisory Board

EDITOR

Suzanne P. Ogden
Northeastern University

ADVISORY BOARD

Valerie Assetto
Colorado State University

William Chittick
University of Georgia

David Dickson
Northeastern University

Paul Dyster
Catholic University

Peggy Falkenheim
University of Western Ontario

Dennis R. Gordon
Santa Clara University

Elizabeth Hanson
University of Connecticut

Chun-tu Hsueh
University of Maryland
College Park

Asad Husain
Northeastern Illinois University

William D. Jackson
Miami University

John A. Jacobsohn
West Virginia University

Edward Lavalle
Capilano College

Helen Purkitt
United States Naval Academy

Hans P. Ridder
California State University
Long Beach

John T. Rourke
University of Connecticut
Storrs

Bernard Schechterman
University of Miami

Iqbal Sing
North Carolina State University

James Stegenga
Purdue University

Primo Vannicelli
University of Massachusetts
Boston

Shirley Washington
Ohio University

W. Marvin Will
The University of Tulsa

Members of the Advisory Board are instrumental in the final selection of articles for each edition of Annual Editions. Their review of articles for content, level, currentness, and appropriateness provides critical direction to the editor and staff. We think you'll find their careful consideration well reflected in this volume.

STAFF

Ian A. Nielsen, Publisher
Brenda S. Filley, Production Manager
Roberta Monaco, Editor
Addie Raucci, Administrative Editor
Cheryl Nicholas, Permissions Editor
Diane Barker, Editorial Assistant
Lisa Holmes-Doebrick, Administrative Coordinator
Charles Vitelli, Designer
Shawn Callahan, Graphics
Meredith Scheld, Graphics
Libra A. Cusack, Typesetting Supervisor
Juliana Arbo, Typesetter

To the Reader

In publishing ANNUAL EDITIONS we recognize the enormous role played by the magazines, newspapers, and journals of the *public press* in providing current, first-rate educational information in a broad spectrum of interest areas. Within the articles, the best scientists, practitioners, researchers, and commentators draw issues into new perspective as accepted theories and viewpoints are called into account by new events, recent discoveries change old facts, and fresh debate breaks out over important controversies.

Many of the articles resulting from this enormous editorial effort are appropriate for students, researchers, and professionals seeking accurate, current material to help bridge the gap between principles and theories and the real world. These articles, however, become more useful for study when those of lasting value are carefully *collected, organized, indexed,* and *reproduced* in a *low-cost format,* which provides easy and permanent access when the material is needed. That is the role played by *Annual Editions.* Under the direction of each volume's *Editor,* who is an expert in the subject area, and with the guidance of an *Advisory Board,* we seek each year to provide in each ANNUAL EDITION a current, well-balanced, carefully selected collection of the best of the public press for your study and enjoyment. We think you'll find this volume useful, and we hope you'll take a moment to let us know what you think.

Annual Editions: World Politics 91/92 is aimed at filling a void in materials for learning about world politics and foreign policy. Among the dozens of textbooks and anthologies available today, this accessible compilation of readings brings together major, current problems concerning relations among nations in an easily understandable language.

The articles are chosen for those who are new to the study of world politics. The objective of this compilation is to stimulate interest in learning about issues that often seem foreign, remote, and irrelevant, but which actually have profound consequences for economic well-being, security, and even survival.

International relations can be viewed as a constant flow of actions and reactions that produce new situations calling for further actions. The readings in this volume convey the complexities and the interdependence of international relations in the world at this time. The interdependence of relationships means that events in places as far away as Japan, the Middle East, South Africa, and Latin America affect the United States, just as America's actions, and inactions, have significant repercussions for other states. International events proceed at such a rapid pace, however, that often what is said about international affairs today may be outdated tomorrow. This collection of articles about international events provides the most up-to-date commentaries available.

This twelfth edition of *World Politics 91/92* is divided into eight units. The first five units focus on the major actors in the world: the United States, the Soviet Union, Western Europe, Canada, Japan, Eastern Europe, China, and the Third World. In the Third World unit, the focus is on those countries which have drawn considerable international attention in the past year. After presenting the major actors and analyses of their current foreign policy issues and concerns, the book turns to three broad areas of concern to international relations: the international political economy; the arms race, arms control, and disarmament; and international organization and international issues. In each unit, a variety of political perspectives is offered to make readers more aware of the complexities of the problems in international relations, and to stimulate them to consider alternative perspectives on seemingly straightforward issues.

I wish to thank my colleagues and the previous users of *Annual Editions: World Politics* who have taken time to comment on this collection of articles. Please continue to provide feedback to guide the annual revision of this anthology by filling out the article rating form on the last page of this book.

Suzanne P. Ogden
Editor

Contents

Unit 1

The United States

Four selections review the dynamics of the role of the United States as a world power. They discuss American relationships with different segments of the world.

Unit 2

The Soviet Union

Five articles discuss the present state of the Soviet Union's recent economic and political reforms.

The concepts in bold italics are developed in the article. For further expansion please refer to the Topic Guide, the Index, and the Glossary.

Unit 3

American Allies: Western Europe, Canada, and Japan

Nine selections review the current state of America's
allies, focusing on Western Europe, Canada, and
Japan.

Unit 4

The Disintegrating Socialist World: Eastern Europe and the People's Republic of China

Six articles consider the world's socialist states and their relationships with the Soviet Union. The articles examine the latest developments in China and Eastern Europe.

Unit 5

The Newly Industrialized Countries and the Less Developed Countries

Ten selections review the current state of the Third World by focusing on Africa, Asia, Latin America, and the Middle East.

The concepts in bold italics are developed in the article. For further expansion please refer to the Topic Guide, the Index, and the Glossary.

Unit 6

The International Political Economy: Aid, Investment, Trade, and Finance

Four articles examine the international political economy. Topics include the Third World debt and the importance of worldwide economic growth.

Unit 7

The Arms Race, Arms Control, and Disarmament

Four selections discuss the current state of the arms race by considering the future of deterrence, world military expenditures, and the changing role of nuclear power.

Unit 8

International Organization and International Issues

Four articles discuss the influence of nationalism and international organizations on world peace.

The concepts in bold italics are developed in the article. For further expansion please refer to the Topic Guide, the Index, and the Glossary.

Topic Guide

This topic guide suggests how the selections in this book relate to topics of traditional concern to students and professionals involved with the study of world politics. It can be very useful in locating articles that relate to each other for reading and research. The guide is arranged alphabetically according to topic. Articles may, of course, treat topics that do not appear in the topic guide. In turn, entries in the topic guide do not necessarily constitute a comprehensive listing of all the contents of each selection.

TOPIC AREA	TREATED IN:	TOPIC AREA	TREATED IN:
Africa	25. Black Africa 26. African Famine	**Debt and International Finance**	25. Black Africa 29. New and Improved South America 30. Latin America 35. Emperor's New Clothes 36. From Geopolitics to Geo-Economics 38. Toffler's Next Shock
Arms Control and Disarmament	14. NATO's Identity Crisis 36. From Geopolitics to Geo-Economics 39. STARTing Over 40. Goodwill Missions for Castoff Missiles 41. Is the Soviet Union Prepared for Peace? 42. Missile Mania	**Democracy**	5. Crisis in the Soviet Union 6. New World Disorder? 7. Brzezinski on Breakup of USSR 44. Nationalism
Asia	27. Hong Kong	**Europe**	1. Finding America's Place 4. U.S. Foreign Policy and Europe 6. New World Disorder? 10. Europe's Extremes 11. Several Germanys Since 1871 13. A United Germany 14. NATO's Identity Crisis 17. American-Japanese-European Relations 20. Two Faces of Eastern Europe 22. Eastern Europe on Edge 43. Stirrings of History 44. Nationalism
Canada	15. The Two Canadas		
China	19. Reforming the Nonreforming Regimes 23. Crises in Communist Reform 24. Domestic Roots of China's Post-Tiananmen Foreign Policy 27. Hong Kong		
Cold War	1. Finding America's Place 3. Coping With Victory 4. U.S. Foreign Policy and Europe 14. NATO's Identity Crisis 46. What Next?	**Germany**	6. New World Disorder? 10. Europe's Extremes 11. Several Germanys Since 1871 13. A United Germany 14. NATO's Identity Crisis
Communism's Collapse	5. Crisis in the Soviet Union 6. New World Disorder? 7. Brzezinski on Breakup of USSR 8. Russia vs. Soviet Union 9. Toward a New Russian Federation 14. NATO's Identity Crisis 19. Reforming the Nonreforming Regimes 20. Two Faces of Eastern Europe 22. Eastern Europe on Edge 23. Crises in Communist Reform 41. Is the Soviet Union Prepared for Peace? 44. Nationalism 46. What Next?	**Gorbachev**	8. Russia vs. Soviet Union 39. STARTing Over
		Hong Kong	27. Hong Kong
		IMF and The World Bank	25. Black Africa

TOPIC AREA	TREATED IN:	TOPIC AREA	TREATED IN:
Japan	1. Finding America's Place 16. Don't Write Off Japan 17. American-Japanese-European Relations 18. Japan As Competitor	**Soviet Union (cont'd)**	14. NATO's Identity Crisis 39. STARTing Over 40. Goodwill Missions for Castoff Missiles 41. Is the Soviet Union Prepared for Peace? 46. What Next?
Latin America	39. New & Improved South America 30. Latin America	**United States**	1. Finding America's Place 2. Look Homeward 3. Coping With Victory 4. U.S. Foreign Policy and Europe 6. New World Disorder? 14. NATO's Identity Crisis 17. American-Japanese-European Relations 30. Latin America 39. STARTing Over 40. Goodwill Missions for Castoff Missiles 46. What Next?
Middle East	31. Crisis of Leadership 32. Revolution, Reform, or Regression? 33. Brotherly hate 34. Baghdad Formally Agrees		
NATO	14. NATO's Identity Crisis		
Soviet Union	3. Coping With Victory 4. U.S. Foreign Policy and Europe 5. Crisis in Soviet Union 6. New World Disorder? 7. Brzezinski on Breakup of USSR 8. Russia vs. Soviet Union 9. Toward a New Russian Federation *(continued)*		

The United States

The "revolution of 1989," which changed the face of Eastern Europe, also changed the entire fabric of the confrontation between the two major superpowers and their allies. As one Communist regime after another crumbled in Eastern Europe while the Soviet Union stood quietly on the sidelines, Americans wondered what ideology would fill the vacuum of anticommunism, the ideology that had motivated American foreign policy since World War II.

For a brief period in 1990, the United States groped for new values to fill the ideological vacuum. It wondered how the United States would affect, and be affected by, the emerging "new world order." How should it reshape its relationships with its former enemies and new friends? How could it best use the "peace dividend" garnered from the disarmament accompanying "the end of the cold war"? Would its former Communist enemies become valuable trade partners or just new aid recipients? Could it prevent the Soviet Union from itself collapsing into a quagmire of ethnic and nationalist rivalries? How could it address the deterioration of its relationship with Japan and its potentially adversarial relationship with the European Community of 1992? What would the collapse of "the enemy" mean for the role of the United States in a world where economic power now seemed more important than military power?

This relatively pleasurable period of speculation about how the United States could fit into, and lead, a newly shaped world was abruptly interrupted on August 2, 1990, by Iraq's invasion of oil-rich Kuwait. It is impossible to raise here the dozens of viewpoints expressed about how the United States and its allies could have avoided what turned out to be an utterly catastrophic war for Iraq. Indeed, as the oil fields of Kuwait continue to burn, as civil insurrection plagues Iraq, and as U.S.-led coalition forces remain tied down in the Middle East, this short but brutal war has not turned out to be such a clear "victory" for the United States, or for anyone else either. One thing is very clear: The concept of "compromise," the notion of "negotiation"—these simply were not a part of the vocabulary of President George Bush, or of President Saddam Hussein. And one thing is very unclear: Would the United States ever have committed some 500,000 U.S. troops to the Middle East to eject the Iraqi aggressor from Kuwait if the Soviet Union had remained a major military threat and if the cold war had not seemingly come to an end in 1989? This is a moot point, but it does raise the question of how the United States would have prioritized its commitment to a military conflict in the Middle East had the cold war with the U.S.S.R. been unresolved. It also highlights the problem the United States now faces: Who, or what, will be the next enemy? Not knowing the answer, how do we address our security needs?

As a result of the war with Iraq, the "peace dividend" has not yet materialized. Instead, the United States has found itself in the position of chasing after its allies to pay their promised share of the costs of the war—a share promised reluctantly by Germany and Japan, and only under much pressure from Washington. The remarkable fuss over this issue has further eroded an already deteriorating relationship with Japan, the major ally of the United States in East Asia. With the United States already blaming Japan for its imbalance of trade, with Japan in turn blaming the United States for overspending and thereby creating its own indebtedness, and with no real effort on either side to accommodate the other, the relationship is likely to fester until both sides realize how crucial it is to sustain good relations. Whether we *like* each other or not matters far less than whether we can work together for mutual benefit.

In the international economic arena, the United States remains the world's greatest economic power; but relative to the past, it has declined. In this arena, many argue that the United States has purposefully engineered its own relative decline in economic power by fostering the growth of the economic power of other states. Indeed, it has been a central tenet of U.S. policy in the post–World War II era to strengthen the economic power of its allies and even of its former enemies, Germany and Japan, to the point that they could stand economically independent of the United States. It is much to the credit of the United States that it has succeeded in doing so. Their growth did not, however, come at the expense of growth in the United States, for the American economy has continued to grow throughout the postwar period, albeit at a slower rate than that of Western Germany, Japan, and the "newly industrialized countries" (NICs) of East Asia.

To the extent that the United States' declining economic power has been purposeful, U.S. leaders should be applauded. But to the extent that its decline since the 1960s comes from internal weaknesses—an educational system that fails to train a literate and competent work force, a culture undermined by drugs and a lack of commitment to the public good, an unwillingness on the part of the government and the people to curb consumption (resulting in massive international indebtedness and inadequate funds for investing in domestic economic growth), and wastefulness—it must be viewed with grave concern. First-rate powers have declined to second- and third-rate powers within a few generations. It is essential not only for America's economic health, but also for its international leadership, that effective policies be undertaken to turn this downward spiral around, for an abdication of its right to lead in the international economic arena is undercutting its ability to lead in the political and diplomatic arenas as well.

In short, the United States faces formidable tasks at this point in history. Among other tasks, it must rescue itself from economic decline; reshape its policy of "containment" and the "cold war" to account for the loss of its main enemy, the U.S.S.R., build more constructive relationships with its Central and South American neighbors that can serve as the basis for resolving issues other than through the use of military force, and determine how it will restructure its economic aid programs to promote democratization in the newly non-Communist regimes of Eastern Europe while sustaining aid to the less developed countries and such traditional allies as Israel.

President Bush and Congress have taken some initial steps along this road. They have offered substantial economic aid packages to certain Eastern European governments in hopes that these additional resources will make the transition from centralized command economies to free market economies, with the attendant transitional problems of massive inflation and unemployment, more palatable to their peoples, and hence, less destabilizing. In recognition of the multiple crises Gorbachev faces within the Soviet Union, the United States has tried to remain supportive of him, without tying up the future of Soviet-American relations completely with one man. But in many ways, the importance of the Soviet-American relationship has been eclipsed by other events, other trends, other issues. If, as Paul Kennedy argues, the rise and fall of great powers is determined by uneven rates of economic and technological development, and if such issues as AIDS, the environment, and drugs are becoming so threatening to *all* countries that international cooperation will be essential to escaping catastrophe, the relationship between the two superpowers matters much less. Indeed, with the United States barely able to pay its bills, and with the Soviet Union barely able to feed its people, it is hard to think of the two countries as superpowers.

To conclude, does it really matter that, in relative terms, the United States has lost power? In a world of complex interdependence, the issue no longer is one of *control* but of *harmony* and *mutual benefit*, of fitting into a complex whole in a positive way rather than attempting to dominate it, of expanding the opportunities and resources available for all rather than possessing them. The world has simply become too complex and too interdependent for any one country to control it, or to have its way at the expense of others. In the non-zero-sum sort of world that has evolved, the United States may perhaps only succeed by helping others to succeed as well, by becoming far more internationalist in its orientation than ever before.

Looking Ahead: Challenge Questions

Given the collapse of Communist regimes in Eastern Europe, is there a need to maintain NATO forces in Europe? In what country/countries would you position them? What purpose would they serve? Do you think that war among the countries of Eastern Europe is more or less likely than when the Soviet Union dominated them through the Warsaw Pact? What should the role of the United States be if war breaks out within Eastern Europe? As part of its military disengagement from Europe, should the United States turn the position of commander of NATO forces over to a Western European state? Why or why not? What does a "neutralized" Germany mean for the United States, for the U.S.S.R., and for Eastern and Western European states?

In what ways might the United States restore its leadership role, if not its power to control, in the technological, economic, diplomatic, military, and political arenas? What advice would you give the president or the Congress as to how to restore this leadership? Since responsibilities of a sometimes overwhelming nature come with leadership, are we necessarily prepared, and do we really want, to be considered the world's leaders in each of the above-mentioned arenas? Why or why not?

FINDING AMERICA'S PLACE

Michael J. Brenner

MICHAEL J. BRENNER *is a professor of international affairs at the University of Pittsburgh.*

The approach of the millennium finds Americans filled not with dread of an apocalypse but with hope for a new age of peace. The apparent end of the Cold War has done more than lift the specter of a nuclear holocaust. It has given new spirit to the old belief that the vocation of nations includes working in harmony for the common good. This pervasive optimism has been inspired by the epochal changes in Europe. There, the twin notions that war is on the verge of obsolescence and that states share an overriding community of interest are regaining wide currency as the expression of a progressive logic at work in the world.

These are captivating ideas; and, indeed, events are offering much that is new and positive. But there is reason to question the claim that humans are destined to transcend interstate conflict and to judge as premature the heralding of a dramatic break from the past. The retreat of communism in Eastern Europe, along with the fading Soviet threat, certainly requires a different model from that of the postwar period. Likewise, the United States needs to rethink the terms of its engagement in a world where the mission of organizing the defense of free nations is no longer compelling. The risk is that Americans will succumb to the too-comfortable belief that the world is reshaping itself according to American principles and desires, thereby satisfying a yearning for validation of America's past tenure as world leader.

There are two revelations being proclaimed that frame an emerging world view at once seductive and misleading. According to the first, the dissolution of the communist system and its successors' pronounced devotion to the free market and liberal politics are the first signs that modern societies will find natural equilibrium in the kind of political and economic system known in the West. This view announces the rediscovery of a teleology in the world social order that points to liberal welfare-capitalism as the culmination and realization of modernity's intrinsic qualities. The other revelation is that constructive engagement is becoming the norm in international affairs. The end of the ideological antagonism that was the mainspring of the Cold War purportedly clears the way for pragmatic cooperation—and the eclipse of power politics.

Both of these notions have special appeal in the United States, where they are an antidote to the dispiriting talk of American decline. After a period of suspended emotion tinged with disbelief, events in the East are acting as a tonic for the U.S. body politic. A sense of triumph is displacing gloomy thoughts of lost economic prowess and a fading mastery of foreign relations. The values embodied in the American system seem to be confirmed as virtuous by the emulation of peoples freeing themselves from communist orthodoxy. The Cold War appears less like a stale struggle between two morally ambiguous powers and more like the contest between truth and untruth that Americans originally thought it to be. Its peaceful resolution on U.S. terms now promises to open the way to concord and cooperation.

But does the West's apparent victory over communism and the dissipating Soviet threat settle the issue of how the United States should involve itself in the world, especially in Europe? Is the debate over decline and its consequences drained of all practical significance? Is the United States now free to retrench, to in-

Reprinted with permission from *Foreign Policy* 79 (Summer 1990), pp. 25-43. Copyright © 1990 by the Carnegie Endowment for International Peace.

vest its political energies as well as its resources in its own domestic affairs, and to do so without any serious cost to its foreign interests or to world order? In sum, is the call to duty stilled by America's successes?

Despite these successes, formidable political tasks lie ahead that must engage the United States if a stable new European order is to emerge. Liberal values and economic growth must be fostered in the new regimes of Eastern Europe, the two military blocs must be reconstituted into a pan-European security system, and a collective accommodation must be made to the power of a reunified Germany. This agenda suggests a U.S. role quite different from the one to which Americans are accustomed, one now requiring the talents of a facilitator and the earnest virtue of an underwriter rather than the fortitude of a protector. In attempting this adjustment to a more modest, if still valued, place in the affairs of Europe, the United States will be relearning the lesson that there is more to conflict than war and more to politics than conflict.

In Eastern Europe, economic well-being is vital to a stable change of systems. The achievement of viable democracies hinges on it; the construction of durable structures linking Eastern and Western Europe will be indirectly influenced by it. Liberal, market-oriented reform, whatever its exact trajectory, is certain; its success, however, is not. The declarations of faith in liberal economics by the new regimes arguably puts them on the same track that led to prosperity in the West. But the process is neither inexorable nor the goal self-fulfilling. Outside support, material and moral, will be a determinant of what economic reform achieves in Eastern Europe.

Indisputable is the central position of economic conditions in the communist world's transformation. To put it simply, people want a better life and the West seems to show them how to get it. The image, as one observer put it, is of a popularity contest between Marxism and McDonald's. However crude, the formulation contains a kernel of ironic truth. Marxism, the great philosophy of materialism, is failing, in large part because it could not deliver the goods. The god that ruled Eastern Europe filled neither stomachs nor souls. Communist governments lost whatever vestige of support they had and sealed their fates with an embarrassing inability to satisfy material wants.

In materialism, Eastern Europe may have found its political salvation. Western values are prevailing there as much because of their iden-tification with economic success as because of a social logic that ineluctably links prosperity with liberal political principles. As a consequence, a good measure of economic well-being is necessary for the stabilization of democratic institutions in Eastern Europe. If these countries are to become the prosaic, post-ideological, and conflict-averse societies for which the Western liberal democracies are the model, they must first become prosperous. If they fail economically, liberalism may be discredited throughout the region. The alternative may be recrudescent autocracy and nationalist strife that together could disturb the structure of security in Europe. Hence the West's stake in the success of these countries is not just altruistic or prideful. Engagement with the fledgling democracies to the East is dictated by foreign-policy realism.

This elementary truth was recognized early in Western Europe and belatedly accepted in Washington. U.S. allies saw that stabilizing the changing regimes of Eastern Europe through economic assistance is central to the geopolitical task of reconciling the two parts of the Continent. Arms reductions and the neutering of the two military alliances address the regional security question only in its starkest form. Security, understood in its fullest sense, rests on removing the sources of instability and threat. That is the goal of economic diplomacy toward the USSR and its former clients that rightly sees development as the pivot for the broad process of liberalization in domestic and foreign policy. It is a *political* undertaking in which U.S. involvement is essential to success and that will test the U.S. capacity for diplomatic engagement without the prerogatives of unquestioned leadership.

Stepping Aside

It is the West Europeans, not the Americans, who have stated the theme and led in trying to channel the forces of change in Eastern Europe. They have been more active on the political front and in the economic domain, working both individually and jointly through the European Community (EC). Bilateral diplomacy, with West Germany in the forefront, is important across the region. But it is the move toward a common EC strategy that has the widest long-run implications. The increasingly forthcoming policies emanating from Brussels carry the potential for redesigning Europe's political architecture in ways that alter not only the relationship between Eastern and Western Europe, but also the U.S. contribution to the collective diplomacy of building a new continental security system.

The focusing of initiative and responsibility on the West Europeans has come with Washington's blessing, which has been given through a series of pragmatic steps. In June 1989 at the G-7 summit meeting in Paris, President George Bush surprised and pleased his partners by seconding a proposal of West German Chancellor Helmut Kohl that the EC secretariat coordinate food aid to Poland and serve as the clearinghouse on economic aid to Eastern Europe generally. It was a sensible move. As a practical matter, the Europeans are better placed—by virtue of geography, history, and their larger economic presence in the region—to take the lead.

These practical considerations notwithstanding, the food initiative was unprecedented in two respects. First, Washington yielded primary responsibility on a sensitive question of East-West relations to its allies. Second, EC institutions were granted the operational authority to orchestrate a common external policy with obvious political content.

Uncharacteristic American deference to a West European lead is equally evident in the relative contributions of financial aid to Eastern Europe. The largest U.S. commitment is for $938 million in mixed loans and credits over three years to Poland and Hungary. This sum, a modest fraction of the aggregate Western assistance now planned, is itself substantially greater than the initial amounts Bush offered during his much-publicized July 1989 visits to Warsaw and Budapest, a very modest $115 million and $30 million respectively. Those amounts were raised to current levels only under strong congressional pressure.

The same pattern of burden sharing—which departs strikingly from postwar experience—more recently has taken institutional form in the design of an East European development bank. (Its official name, the European Bank for Reconstruction and Development, harks back to the Marshall Plan.) The bank's mission of providing loans, credits, and technical assistance is to be backed by a $12 billion fund subscribed mainly by the 24 leading members of the world's liberal trading community. Based on a French concept, the plan has been adopted and supported by the EC. The Community's four largest members—West Germany, Great Britain, France, and Italy—each will take an 8.5 per cent share in the bank, as will Japan; the U.S. stake will be 10 per cent. Thus, the United States will provide only one-

tenth of the capital for the most far-reaching program to concert support for Eastern Europe's economic development—one intended to consolidate long hoped-for political change in the region. As a fraction of gross domestic product, the British, French, German, and Italian contributions are several times larger than that of the United States. America's participation will be only slightly greater than that of Japan, whose stake in the region is at the margin of its political and economic interests.

A small stake means small influence on bank policies. That was already evident in the dispute between Washington and its allies over the eligibility of the Soviet Union to participate in the project. Isolated in its stubborn resistance to a Soviet role, Washington learned that its already diminished power to define common Western positions is further limited on economic matters in the absence of a predominant (in this case, even substantial) resource commitment. The incident also demonstrated that the habit of presuming the prerogatives of leadership on issues of dealing with the USSR dies hard. That was all the more striking given the Bush administration's otherwise ready acceptance of a more assertive Western Europe.

The nominal reasons for this disproportion are the omnipresent U.S. budgetary constraints. More is involved, however, than arithmetic. An administration dedicated to maintaining leadership in European affairs would find the additional money. The decision not to do so conforms to a growing belief in senior circles of the Bush administration (not least in the White House itself) that the United States has an interest in encouraging the West Europeans to shoulder a heavier political and economic load in the Atlantic partnership. Specifically, the administration would like to see the EC move beyond its purely economic vocation. Washington welcomes the deepening of integrative ties that expand the capacity for collective diplomatic action. Bush, in a notable speech in Leiden in July 1989, unequivocally supported a stronger, united Europe as a natural evolution within the alliance. It would be, in his words, "the product of true partnership 40 years in the making." He reinforced the message in consultations with NATO leaders after the 1989 Malta summit when he called for an intensified move toward Community integration so that Europe might better undertake the delicate task of erasing the divide between East and West. While reaffirming America's position as a European power, Bush made clear that the United States does not visualize itself as the arbiter of Europe's future.

A watershed has been crossed in the Atlantic partnership. Unheralded and without fanfare, an unmistakable shift of responsibilities is taking place. After decades of discussion about a European pillar, about a devolution of power onto America's allies, about burden sharing and multilateralism, the foundations of the alliance are finally being displaced. It is a development no less consequential for the absence of a formal announcement or the coining of an apt phrase to memorialize it.

Resistance to giving the United States a formal voice in Community affairs is strong, and Washington's leverage is weakening.

In Washington, the prevailing view pictures a United States actively engaged in revamping Europe's defense structures and playing a central role in the search for answers to the German puzzle, while having only a subsidiary place in the construction of a new economic and political regime in Europe. It follows that as the first of these tasks is accomplished and the second moves toward resolution, American presence and influence will wane even further. This transfer of responsibilities for managing the Atlantic community's affairs onto the West European allies could reflect an intelligent reading of the new strategic environment. Growing capabilities in Western Europe juxtaposed with resource limitations in the United States support a more balanced transatlantic partnership. But does it meet the sterner test of serving U.S. interests and obligations in the political reconstruction of a continental system?

On questions of armaments and alliance structures, the United States still has exceptional responsibilities and continues to exert its leadership. This was evident with Washington's initiative at the February 1990 meeting of NATO and Warsaw Pact foreign ministers at Ottawa, where it promoted the Two plus Four formula for negotiation of German reunification. The United States had to overcome resistance from the British and French, as well as from the Soviets, who unrealistically sought the reverse sequence in the hope of strengthening the hand of the World War II victors. American assertiveness at Ottawa stands in sharp contrast to its readiness to take a back seat to its allies in dealing with Eastern Europe.

U.S. policy is running on two tracks simultaneously. One, expressing a keen sense of limits and impelled by financial constraints, points to retrenchment and devolution. It governs thinking about current and future participation in the campaign to promote prosperous democracies in Eastern Europe. The other, keyed by continuing great power obligations, dictates activism on German reunification and the immediate security problem that it creates in central Europe. These approaches may clash in two respects:

First, to use fully its acknowledged authority as facilitator and underwriter of a German settlement, the United States may have to do more to establish its bona fides as a player in the political drama of Eastern Europe. In all likelihood Washington will be called upon to perpetuate its stake and involvement in Europe's strategic structures: U.S. power denies Washington the luxury of a relaxed, relatively unengaged position in the politics and economics of half the Continent. Second, domestic reform and external security policy are interlaced in both the Soviet Union and Eastern Europe. They are also part of a complex exchange of reciprocal influences across borders as well as across policy spheres. At one extreme, this means that the domestic fortunes of East Europeans can have a bearing on Soviet security thinking. The outcome of the East Europeans' movement toward liberalization will figure in the Soviets' ongoing calculation of the risks and opportunities in proceeding with reform of their own internal structures. Progress in that bold enterprise, in turn, could determine the fate of an enlightened leadership in the Kremlin that sees the future of Soviet society tied to constructive engagement with the West. These are linkages that might be overlooked by a U.S. approach that combines a passive role in the politics of reform with an active role as architect of security arrangements.

The picture is complicated by Washington's policy in a third sphere of its dealings with Europe: defining the terms of the U.S. relationship with an EC pointed toward full integration. Economic anxieties already seem to be coloring the Bush administration's perspective on the EC, and this is understandable. Western Europe's prospects look brighter than those of the United States and could be enhanced through economic ties with the East. The EC is beginning to receive advances on the benefits of full market integration in 1992, and West European growth rates are projected to outpace those of the United States. The opening of Eastern Europe's markets and cheap labor to economic enterprise from Western Europe could widen the gap in prospective economic performance.

The risk to U.S. economic interests posed by current trends has not gone unnoticed in official Washington. Secretary of State James Baker broached the issue in a December 1989 Berlin address outlining his blueprint for a new European order. Baker proposed that "the institutional and consultative links" between the United States and the EC be strengthened significantly. They would be part of what he called "a new architecture for a new era." Baker's ploy is designed to protect U.S. trade interests by getting a foot in the Community door before its domestic arrangements are fully settled.

Implicit in the Baker proposal is the exchange of a continued U.S. military presence in Europe (something all Community governments still desire) for a privileged relationship with the EC. It is aimed at ensuring that, as the single market forms, an American voice is heard and American interests are taken into account. The proposal was greeted by polite noises in Brussels and quiet applause in London. It is likely to lead to some useful arrangements for routine consultations. But resistance to giving the United States a formal voice in Community affairs is strong, and Washington's leverage is weakening. The deal is almost certain to be spurned for reasons that highlight the dilemma of an American strategy that, given its economic preoccupations, is lowering the U.S. profile in Europe, even while the United States continues to conduct itself as alliance leader on security issues.

Western Europe today is far more self-confident and self-reliant than at any time since World War II. Catering to Washington is out of date and out of order. Economic success and bright prospects of competing on the same footing with the United States are one reason. The desire to develop the Community into a united force with a common set of political and economic policies is another. There is also the drastically reduced military threat. Defense used to be Washington's long suit in dealing with the West Europeans. It is not the trump it once was. The West Europeans no longer feel a compelling need for U.S. military protection, and they remain confident that the United States will not make a precipitous departure from the Continent. The United States can still offer Europe two things, both of which con-

tribute to the political construction of Western Europe and are also to America's advantage. One is the full engagement of its moral authority with some reasonable commitment of its material resources to foster democracy in Eastern Europe. Washington is clearly dubious on this score. The other is American initiative in framing a settlement of the German Question and American readiness to act as a guarantor of the eventual terms. Here the United States has not been shy about asserting itself. Today, however, U.S. policy exhibits a dual personality: confident and encouraging on some things, passive and vaguely anxious on others.

The administration's preferences on the distribution of roles with its West European partners is a case of belief reinforced by apparent necessity. The dulled appetite for U.S. leadership outside the realm of military security accurately expresses the sentiment prevailing in the American public. Policy choices cannot fail to be colored by a national mood that is preoccupied with domestic concerns and that has already psychologically banked the peace dividend from the Cold War's demise. The notion of a natural progression to the process of liberalization in the USSR and Eastern Europe is very congenial to this frame of mind. It relieves Americans of the need for strenuous exertion and satisfies through rhetoric alone the sense of obligation to act on behalf of the newborn democracies. The presence of others willing to take the lead reinforces the disposition to limit American involvement. It taps the popular feeling that if American leadership is not wanted, there is no need for substantial participation.

To its credit, the Bush administration recognizes that the success of reform in Eastern Europe is not a sure thing. It knows that economic forces there need political facilitation, if not generous financial aid, if the liberal revolution is to be realized. But its thinking falls short by projecting a fuzzy image of America's place in the overall project of bridging East and West.

Building on Mutual Interests

The paramount tasks of diplomacy in Europe today and in the foreseeable future are political. The forces of liberalization at work in Eastern Europe cannot by themselves create a stable system of political security and economic cooperation—certainly not with the two Germanys lurching toward reunification. Defining such a system and giving institutional form to common purposes will be an arduous process that demands all the political resources of both West and East. It is not certain to achieve a complete or wholly satisfactory conclusion for all participants. For the United States the challenge is twofold. It must amend the form and method of its involvement in Europe to match the changing diplomatic environment, and it must do so in a way that strikes a politically acceptable balance between underengagement and overextension.

The Soviet Union and the West are engaged in collective political management of historic proportions. It is inspired by a radical purpose: the reconciliation of Eastern and Western Europe in a reconstituted international system built on mutual interest. Equally radical, interest is defined mainly in terms of economic welfare. That mutuality exists in principle. To realize it in fact depends on building a consensus on forms as well as purposes and on composing divergent priority scales. The difficulties are manifest in dealing with the overlapping problems associated with the newly autonomous, liberalizing regimes of Eastern Europe and the move toward German reunification.

The breakup of communist hegemony without any serious challenge from Moscow creates an opportunity for continental conciliation; it also exposes the Soviet Union's vulnerability as a partner in the project. All parties are in basic agreement on the East Europeans' right to political self-determination. Yet there remain differences in outlook. The Soviet leadership would like to see a continuation of economic collaboration and a modicum of political kinship, avoiding what Soviet President Mikhail Gorbachev has called, in reference to a united Germany, "moral, political, and economic damage." Satisfying the Soviets on that score will not be easy. Ironically, the West's efforts at knitting ties with Eastern Europe could compound the problem. Success may widen the gap in public philosophy and material well-being between the more progressive states of Eastern Europe and a Soviet Union where liberal reform and economic performance lag behind.

The West, while acknowledging the reasonableness of the Soviet concern, does not place so high a value on the future compatibility of the USSR and the new governments of Eastern Europe. Stability is the common denominator —stability of interstate relations in the region and domestic stability to the extent that it is a precondition of the former. Even on this count a discrepancy exists that is rooted in differ-

ences of circumstance as much as interest. Stability means anything but the status quo. With the tide of change running strongly in favor of liberal democracy and free-enterprise economics, an inescapable asymmetry separates the Soviet Union from the West. A deteriorating economy, accompanied by the erosion of communism's ideological authority, has exposed the Soviet system's weakness in comparison to the flourishing societies of the West. This distressing comparison has been given a stunning geopolitical dimension in the collapse of communist rule in Eastern Europe. The resulting insecurity leaves the Soviet leadership in an awkward position: It must seek from the West comity and practical help in meeting its internal development needs while it fears that its own power and external influence will erode further in the process. This intrinsic dilemma of reform could qualify the USSR's commitment to an all-European settlement. Specifically, it raises the possibility of the USSR as an inhospitable neighbor to the new East European democracies if Moscow feels itself marginalized by a new continental system.

The Soviet Union and the West are engaged in collective political management of historic proportions.

Reconciling the USSR with the inescapable loss of status and power is not a Soviet problem alone: It is a concern for all parties with a stake in a stable European order. But finding a solution is akin to squaring the circle. Certainly, it would be unrealistic—as well as unjustified— to compensate for the dissolution of the Eastern camp by suspending or diluting the West's continued interest in unified action. The zero-sum contest for advantage that has dominated interbloc relations in the postwar era will have to be superseded without a forced depoliticization of Western institutions. The West needs a delicate, patient diplomacy that stresses the logic of reconciliation and coalescence but that avoids mounting an intolerable threat to a Soviet Union engaged in its own perilous reform process. The United States, as the architect of the West's institutional identity and still its titular leader, cannot avoid a key role in that diplomatic endeavor.

There is little the United States can do directly to alleviate Soviet worries about being shortchanged in the merger of Eastern and Western Europe. The USSR's grave maladies

1. THE UNITED STATES

are beyond the ability of either the United States or the EC to remedy. However, two aspects of the situation do fall within the province of American influence: devising a viable format for German reunification and reshaping the two military alliances into instruments for political cooperation.

Germany is at the heart of the Soviet predicament, for obvious reasons. History encourages a focus on the military side of security. Even a peaceable, united Germany would have the weight—if not necessarily the will—to dominate the political and economic affairs of Europe. That is an unsettling prospect for the USSR. The Soviets have no good alternatives, only unsatisfactory variations on two competing conceptions of a single Germany: a neutral, unaligned state or a Germany that remains a member of the Atlantic alliance. Official Soviet policy urges the former. But the prospect of a Germany outside the existing alliance structures is not reassuring either. It could be a dangerously unpredictable element in the new security equation that detracts from established structures of cooperation.

Any security framework for a single German state must assuage legitimate Soviet anxieties without, somehow, either cutting its connection to NATO entirely or running the incalculable risks of nonalignment. The precise means for doing so are now in negotiation, but the broad contours of an agreement are becoming discernible. It has three features: (1) NATO and the Warsaw Pact would subscribe jointly to the settlement terms and assume some responsibility as guarantors; (2) a pan-European structure centered on the Conference on Security and Cooperation in Europe (CSCE) would be created to put the continental seal of approval on the accord and provide another layer of collective oversight; and (3) German membership in NATO would continue, though qualified by restrictions on the deployment of foreign forces and, perhaps, on command structures (accompanied by substantial reductions in German troop levels). An agreement along these lines would be designed to allow Germany's Western partners to remain a stabilizing influence on German security policy while institutionalizing the Soviet (and East European) interest in containing German power.

America's Essential Role

This tricky course can only be navigated with the active involvement of the United States. The United States must be the crucial underwriter of a European settlement because it will remain the ultimate counter to latent Soviet military power. The United States also provides reassurance to all parties as the only "European" power that does not harbor a visceral fear of Germany and, therefore, can maintain a relationship of frankness and goodwill without taint of mistrust. (A recent sign of this is Bush's ability to hold Kohl's feet to the fire on the Polish border question without evoking recrimination.) Finally, the United States retains a unique standing among the countries of Western Europe. It enjoys a reserve of respect for its civic decency and goodwill for its unstinting dedication to Europe's liberty. Further, the United States is in a position to provide encouragement to a still unaccomplished European Community. For the EC, despite its economic achievements, is facing its own identity crisis in seeking to affirm a collective political personality while struggling to accommodate an expanded Germany and a new association with its Eastern neighbors. The value of Washington's continued promotion of European unity is now heightened, inseparable from the common, overarching goal of solidifying the Continent's political structure.

This American role as underwriter in a European settlement presumes, in the first instance, a continuation of the U.S. defense commitment. But the need for a physical military presence on the Continent clearly will decline sharply. As NATO's mission shifts from a military to a political one, a corresponding change in the nature of the American presence in Europe will follow. In the short run, the retention of troops in Germany will be needed as a concrete statement of Washington's readiness to act as a guarantor of that nation's responsible behavior. However, this can be only an interim arrangement at best. The Soviets can be expected to press harder for clearing a united Germany of foreign troops as their own military presence becomes less and less tenable. But above all, it is delusory to think that a proud Germany, exultant in its newfound nationhood, would tolerate perpetual "occupation."

The more enduring, and important, U.S. contribution to reconciling Europe with a united Germany will be its continued political participation in the affairs of the Continent. That would both reassure Germany's neighbors (East and West) and cement Germany's affiliations with the wider Atlantic community of liberal democracies. It would be a prime element in the larger strategy of institutionalizing Germany's international responsibilities and accountability. The EC, for a time a reoriented NATO, and a renewed CSCE all will be part of a compact that sanctions a single German state while bonding it to its neighbors and economic partners. This would be the tangible expression of West German Foreign Minister Hans Dietrich Genscher's concept of a "European Germany."

The prominent U.S. place in the organs of Atlantic cooperation is integral to its underwriting role in Europe. Collaboration among Atlantic partners, in turn, is still an asset in the interlocking challenges of conciliation with the USSR, encouragement of liberal reform in Eastern Europe, and accommodation of a unified Germany. A Cold War-era solidarity is not needed or wanted. But a healthy mechanism for political consultation and collective diplomatic action is needed. NATO, the one organization that joins solely the United States and Western Europe, is the obvious candidate. The Bush administration has made clear its wish that NATO be the prime instrument of Western strategy. But NATO may not be able to overcome its organizational character as a military alliance or its image as a Cold War relic (an image prevalent, among other places, in German public opinion). As a cost-effective vehicle for Western cooperation it is perhaps nearing the end of its natural life. A mix of organizational instruments looks to be the order of the future.

What counts is function, not form. Realistically, new frictions will arise in the Western camp. While objectives are held in common, notable differences exist between methods and priorities. The Federal Republic of Germany (FRG), preoccupied with the tasks of unification and the enlarged responsibilities of statehood, risks slowing European integration. That risk exists despite agreement in April 1990 on a Franco-German plan to speed the political integration of the European Community. With the timetables for Europe 1992 and German reunification now badly out of sync, concerns that Germany may dominate its EC partners economically are growing. The French, along with other Europeans, remain committed to their vision of a fully integrated EC endowed with formal powers of policymaking. But France realizes how uncertain is the goal of anchoring the FRG so securely in a network of Community institutions as to ensure that any German entity would lack the full powers of sovereignty.

The French and British responses to the challenge of German reunification have been predictably divergent, adding further complication to maintaining the EC's identity and direction. Paris is now promoting a grand European confederation associated with the CSCE that parallels its architectonic plans for the Community. London, equally disquieted by the prospect of a Germany that may loosen its NATO ties and looms as an economic superpower, still places stock in the Atlantic alliance as the main instrument for keeping Germany oriented toward the West and for constraining its power. Great Britain therefore is resisting the Franco-German call for developing the EC into a "political union."

The United States can make a valuable contribution to harmonizing these divergent perspectives, or at least to keeping them in proportion. But it will not be through the exercise of tutelary authority of bygone days when common policies were fashioned under American supervision. The mere suggestion of that would aggravate tensions—it runs against growing sentiment that a uniting Western Europe should be more assertive in shaping its own destiny. Rather the United States can be an effective honest broker, helping ease the strains placed on the bonds of unity by radical change in Europe's strategic geography.

The two roles—of honest broker and facilitator within the alliance and of underwriter for a Europe-wide settlement—are companion. Both derive from America's singular authority, an attribute that owes more to its status than its power. The United States brings to the great questions of European construction a unique blend of traits. It is an interested party with a relatively detached perspective. The United States is of Europe but not in Europe. Further, it retains a good measure of its moral authority —not only in the West as leader of the postwar alliance, but more broadly as the amalgam of European societies and the repository of common values now in ascendance throughout the Continent.

The United States also has credibility in Soviet eyes as a force for stability. After a period of oscillating between a vision of a European home without a resident extracontinental cousin and a vision that accommodates an American presence, Gorbachev has recognized that a prominent place for the United States in Europe's political affairs is a net advantage. With his position seriously weakened by internal problems, and the unexpected totality of

1. THE UNITED STATES

communism's disintegration in Eastern Europe, he cannot afford to hazard bets on his ability to profit from continent-wide political flux. Better the perpetuation of the relatively benign influence of the United States than the risks of disorder—and their potential for generating less benign forces. The American political presence therefore is welcomed as a facilitator of orderly transition in European affairs by former enemies as well as allies.

The influence afforded the United States by virtue of its unique status is substantial but fragile. It is defined by circumstances. Unlike military power, political influence cannot be gauged in static quantities. It resides largely in the intangibles of relations among governments and societies. To be effectively used, American policy must observe a fine awareness of the difference between command-style leadership and those other, more subtle roles. Those roles can be undermined by absent-minded reversions to the proprietary style of the past. They are equally vulnerable to signs that the United States is yielding to a self-interested parochialism (e.g., by injecting trade matters into discussions of security cooperation) or that it is too readily finding refuge in domestic preoccupations when the engagement of American resources is inconvenient (as in the parsimonious approach to aiding Eastern Europe).

Another condition for changing roles successfully—and thereby maintaining political effectiveness—is to develop an aptitude for statecraft. The hallmark of today's policy field is fluidity, not threat; it features the collective management of systemic change, not the challenge of confrontation. It penalizes episodic engagement. The requisite statecraft will be particularly difficult to cultivate and sustain in the absence of a clear and compelling goal that justifies this new form of U.S. internationalism. The fading of the communist challenge is putting in doubt the accustomed rationale for long-term foreign policy engagements. For many, it is seen as the final curtain on the long drama of containing Soviet power, especially because its demise is accompanied by the embrace of America's own most cherished values. The easy next step is to assume that the affairs of Europe will order themselves, bypassing politics and bringing with it a welcome surcease from America's foreign-policy labors. In truth, the momentous events in Europe carry their own political obligations. However different from the obligations the United States bore in the Cold War, they too have a claim on America's resources and resolve.

Look Homeward

Michael Vlahos

Michael Vlahos is director of the Center for the Study of Foreign Affairs, U.S. Department of State. The views expressed here are those of the author and do not necessarily reflect those of the U.S. government.

As WE RUSH to embrace the new world, we have little time to reflect on what we leave behind. We should, because we haven't left it yet. We are in a transition, a bridge time; we sense a new reality, but still live in the old. And when we talk—about change, the future, America's purpose—we speak in the old language. Its powerful codewords still rule our subconscious. Most of us have only known this reality, this paradigm. When we think of beginnings, trying to imagine a new creation, we describe it with the slogans of the late 1930s and 1940s, when this old world was being built. That reality grew out of the received truths and myths of world war, prelude and postlude: Munich, Hitler-Stalin, the Bomb, Berlin. When Charles Krauthammer and Patrick Buchanan speak, as they have recently in these pages, it is with the passions of another time. They replicate the great argument in the drama that made that world: and suddenly, it is internationalism versus isolationism all over again. But only the language, the imagery.

Fifty years ago, the terms of debate hinged on the needs of America against the survival of the civilized world. Abstention from the world balance of power was then our national norm. Surely, the world was in trouble; but in saving the world, what would be left of us? And could it even be saved?

Today, engagement is the norm. The world has, arguably, been saved. The Krauthammer-Buchanan exchange, however, is not just the old debate reversed. It is not, after all, the existential question reprised: to engage or to abstain. The era we are now departing has changed that forever. How?

When the postwar paradigm found its liturgy in NSC–68, world engagement meant a protracted, Manichaean struggle, at the end of which a U.S. global culture would triumph. The Free World would become one world, with the U.S.-bequeathed United Nations as its government.

Well folks, it didn't quite turn out that way. The Manichaean part may indeed be over, but the world looks nothing like what the paradigm-creators expected back in the 1940s. Democracy is catching, but not as Americanism. They are not our little eaglets. Our world government-to-be has been forever despoiled, and our allies now emerge— the EC and Japan—as equal world powers. This frets us because, along the way, we developed a taste for superpower. This is the unnamed, latent thought in today's debate about national purpose: what began as a crusade is ending as the lament of godhead lost. "We are still a superpower!" comes the cry. But the inner theme is loss.

Krauthammer turns Wilsonianism into frank imperialism, and he is up-front: "universal dominion." There is no better restatement of the postwar vision of a U.S. global culture, except now one supposes it is to be forced on others, not embraced by them. Has he asked the EC and Japan if they want to abridge their new-found integrity as world players to suit yet another ploy for U.S. domination? Will the Third World applaud our plan to gradually use their dependency to suck them into subservience? Buchanan wrestles mostly with the loss of U.S. power, responding both that it doesn't matter and that it isn't happening. To reassure himself he quotes Nakasone's condescending scrap for U.S. face-saving: "The twenty-first century will also be the American century."

Why do they both spend so much time worrying about our place in the world? You see, it really doesn't matter what we want. The world is going its own way, no matter how earnest our entreaties to the contrary. And much more important, America is going its own way too. World change unlocks change here, long repressed by the needs of global mission. What we—the beltway insiders, the archons of the Washington clubs, the fatted scions of an old power establishment—really fear is the loss of our social ranking, of our special imperial trusteeship when empire is gone. Will we still be important? What will happen to the imperial city now?

BEFORE WE ponder our own fate, let's look at what is really happening in the world. In our rhetoric, global crusade always announced its own eventual disestablishment. Kennedy spelled out the vision when he called for a "world safe for diversity." We simply assumed that this would be one-dimensional diversity: native garb and music, American democratic values—this is the "multipolar" world for which we waited. To turn early Christian theology about the nature of God just a bit, we looked to "one world, many operators."

The new world reality, however, is one of many worlds; or more correctly, a pantheon of many realities. In spite of the power and the glory of U.S. culture, the decolonized went their own way. Europe and Japan stuck by us. . . had they any choice? They were strategic dependents helpless in the face of raw evil. Now the evil mask is torn away, and both EC-Europe and Japan are moving toward self-realization. They are already our rough equal as economies; the recognition that they are full-fledged world powers is not far away. We remain warrior chieftain only through the transition.

After the transition, we may imagine a power balance built around three world powers—North America (USCAN), the EC, and Japan. These centers will drive the world economy, and will retain some measure of collegiality. They will also be engaged in ferocious competition—in which economic scrimmage over advantage in trade and technology will be the new game on the playing field of national security. It should be a time of great global economic growth; but however much we keep to fraternal handshakes, this competition will be the greatest challenge to the American way of life in the early twenty-first century. Europe and Japan will no longer be allies save in name.

Three great powers (a tier down from world powers) will cluster in Asia: Russia, China, and India. They will have roughly equivalent GNPs, science and technology, and military power. Russia may be more advanced but less martially inclined if it sheds restive republics; if it clings to empire, its army will be bigger, but its economy weaker. Indian growth will be steady; China should surge if it gets a popular new dynasty.

Other culture areas will remain diffuse, with some regional powers dominating and others competing: for example, South Africa will dominate Niger-Kordofanian Africa, and Indonesia the Austronesian; while the Arab-Islamic world will find no leader among sullen rivals.

The United States and Canada will come closer than ever through free trade union, and eventually pull in Mexico. USCAN will have no rival in its world, and will be free to move flexibly and forcefully in others. After the transition, we should be disentangled from our overseas "trip wires" (as Buchanan suggests). So unencumbered, our strategic freedom of action will grow.

But this is all surface image. What are we doing? What are we all about? The answer to America's national purpose is to be found right here at home. Our approach to the world has always reflected our domestic agenda. This was just as true for the postwar era as any other. As we debate the course of world change, we forget that our old global mission mirrored a domestic paradigm, created by FDR and sustained by a coherent party system and political establishment. It was a political model for America built on the bedrock premise of big government, or better yet, a crusading state that would lead America and the world to the Promised Land.

This vision's time is past. Its political establishment has lost the pulse of its own people. (Need we belabor the Democrats in their agony?) And the vision's promise itself gave out more than a decade ago. Failure in Vietnam was, after all, only the foreign reflection of a gathering failure of big government's domestic mobilization, its Great Society.

Americans today feel that this nation has lost its way. We see a welter of single issues burning in the political ether—from abortion to racism and its cures, to drugs, education, and the environment. With the S&L crisis, we talk about a failure of government, and now two-thirds of Americans want length of congressional service limited. With abortion, we rage over moral decay versus yet further encroachment of government on individual liberty. With drugs, we are like helpless penitents scourging ourselves, in the face of a social plague that our great system cannot cure. With education, we are perplexed by a vast federal octopus actually abetting a decline in knowledge and skills among our youth. With the environment, many see the American Garden itself despoiled. Different vantages, same judgment: America corrupted. But these are only the fragments of visions of America yet to be patterned. They are like the tiny pieces of a mosaic, each expressing an intense part of the whole, linked by a pattern seen only from a distance. We do not yet have the distance.

When it comes to foreign policy, many Americans also feel that our own needs have been postponed by the claims of the great struggle, that we have sacrificed so long for others only to find ourselves weakened and astray. This is the unspoken content of the codeword "peace dividend," of cartoons showing Germany and Japan as the real postwar victors, of so many lamentations about national decline. Our foreign policy musings today are shot through with domestic melancholy.

In fact, it is almost irrelevant to talk about America's purpose when it is right here in front of us. The American idea is today at risk, and continuing an empty world crusade could kill it. Who are we? What do we stand for? What kind of society are we building? Renewing ourselves must come before any foreign relations: it must be our first priority. And world change that (for awhile) banishes old threats not only allows, but encourages, America to remake itself.

THIS BRINGS US full circle to the foreign policy debate inside the beltway about America's purpose. The debaters are out of touch with the people they serve. The observer might even infer that we have come merely to serve ourselves. Accret-

ing over half a century, Washington has become something both aberrant and unexampled in American eyes: an imperial metropole. The purpose for which it was established—internal as well as imperial state mobilization—no longer lives. But the great city does, resented as it is by the rest of the U.S. This city and its establishment live to defend a fading reality, thus its inner debate cannot really address America's future course.

This truth must not be lost: What we do in the world for the good must come from a collective vision, strong and new within us. In the fifty years since our last Big Change (as Max Lerner calls it), the elite has become comfortable in, and dependent upon, our perpetual starring role: "United States, Superpower." The role became the end in itself, and for many it still is.

"Superpower" doesn't matter. The greatness of the American idea does. The urgent task ahead is one of remaking, reinterpreting. Choosing an American agenda for a new century outweighs all foreign claims. We simply cannot speak to the world until we can speak to ourselves.

What does this suggest for our actual approach to the world? First we must ditch the old debate of the 1930s and 1940s. The point now is not isolationism versus internationalism: we are strong today, not beaten down and afraid as we were in 1935. We could hardly be isolationists now if we tried. But no matter how hard we push, we cannot bring to life the universal spell of an American global culture. An opposite force is sweeping the world: cultures repressed by Free World universalism (especially in Europe and Japan) are finding themselves again.

And they will be at best associates, not friends. The basis for trust will not pass the bar of the end of our postwar reality. We may have no enemies, but we will have no real allies either. Yes, they have imbibed a "democratic spirit" that we have spread. But once it is *their democracy*, it ceases to look to us for inspiration, and its political forms become more referent to native traditions. Arguably, as culture areas go their own way, so increasingly will their politics.

The practical foreign policy debate we should be having is how to deal with a time of parallel realities. The old paradigm is fading but it's not yet dead. Paradoxically, its claim on our passions is all the more wrenching (a death grip?) in its ending time. The new world reality still awaits the event to call it forth.

During the transition, we must try to imagine the next frame of reference while our day-to-day, operational energies are screwed to the task of gradually deconstructing the postwar world. This is the key to understanding the transition we are now in and the new world to come. The issues that seize us today are ones involving merely the managing of transition. They are not preparing us for what's ahead.

The transition period will demand the utmost of us: vigilance, forbearance, strength. We must see to the dismantling of Soviet (and then American) power in Europe, and stand guard as the Soviet slide works its way of imperial decline. When this transition ends, the new geopolitics can become American strategic opportunity. In it,
- What kind of challenges and threats do we face?
- How do we define national interest and responsibility?
- What military capabilities will be needed to defend us?

First, the security challenges we will face after the transition (post–2000) will be more moderate, if still significant. A national competition over technology will begin to describe a new balance of power with our former allies (the EC and Japan). Great powers and regional powers will fret and jostle. Economic bargaining will drive power diplomacy. Now there is no denying that the spirit of the age has turned against war; as in other true postwar times, we can expect war as a legitimate political tool to be in hiding for at least a decade. That peacetime bloom will darken, however, and the world of the next century will again find uses for military force, and in places, like space, where there are no earthly battle rules and precedents.

Second, national interest and responsibility should be to ourselves first, and then to the promotion of a kind of global collegiality. We may wish to intrude ourselves at will (by sea, air, and space) in local potboilers, but we will intervene on the ground very selectively. U.S. interests will remain global, and we should stay interested in all that happens affecting the global balance. But we will have the flexibility and relative strategic distance to choose when and how to get involved, if at all. In a pluralistic world where there are many powers, in which we may have no sworn enemies but also few real friends, a strategy of selective engagement gives the United States (or USCAN) the most leverage and the best chance to achieve our broader national goals through mediation rather than intervention.

Third, we must keep the high ground. We will need non-nuclear, high-technology, low-manpowered forces that we can bring to bear to support a strategy of global selective engagement. Our current advantage over all others in space and naval systems must be the focus of future American national security. Dominance in space and in the oceans will also support us in international technology competition; it will in effect be our insurance against the worst consequences of "multipolarity."

Let's face it: we cannot control world change to suit us; we cannot keep as our own the old world we've grown to like. The new world gives us room, however. The U.S. will not mature to be just another standard, historical cookie-cutter power on the scene. We will draw strength from the energies released in our renewal, and continue to offer ourselves to the world. We can still, if we seize its primacy as our new mission, do best by looking again at ourselves, and the idea that made us.

Now that the United States and its allies have prevailed in the Cold War, the West must think seriously—and quickly—about how to avoid squandering the opportunities at hand

COPING WITH VICTORY

JOHN LEWIS GADDIS

John Lewis Gaddis is a professor of history at Ohio University.

ONE DAY IN SEPTEMBER OF 1946 AN AS YET LITTLE-KNOWN George F. Kennan found himself trying to explain to State Department colleagues what it was going to be like to deal with the Soviet Union as the other great power in the postwar world. Traditional diplomacy would not impress Stalin and his subordinates, Kennan insisted: "I don't think we can influence them by reasoning with them, by arguing with them, by going to them and saying, 'Look here, this is the way things are.' " They weren't the sort to turn around and say, "By George, I never thought of that before. We will go right back and change our policies."

But by last year leaders of the Soviet Union and Eastern Europe were saying something very much like that. Once confident of having mastered the "science" of politics and history, the successors to Lenin and Stalin have had to acknowledge that the system those "founding fathers" imposed on Russia after the First World War and on its neighbors after the Second World War simply has not worked. They have now in effect turned to the West and said, "Tell us what to do. We will go right back and change our policies."

We have witnessed one of the most abrupt losses of ideological self-confidence in modern history. The once impressive façade of world communism no longer impresses anyone: those who lived for so long under that system have at last, like Dorothy in *The Wizard of Oz*, looked behind the curtain; they have found there, frantically pulling the levers, pumping the bellows, and pontificating into the speaking tubes, a few diminutive and frightened humbugs. As a result, Eastern Europe has come to resemble the stage set for *Les Misérables*, but with the revolutionaries this time winning. And most remarkably of all, it is the leader of the Soviet Union itself—the

current chief wizard, if you will—who seems to be playing simultaneously the roles of Dorothy and Jean Valjean.

The resulting situation leaves the United States and its allies—preoccupied so recently with visions of American decline—in a position of great and unexpected influence. For not only have we prevailed, by peaceful means, over our old Cold War adversaries; it is also the case that for the first time in more than a century there is no clear challenger to the tradition of liberal democratic capitalism according to which this country and much of the rest of the West organizes itself. We are at one of those rare points of leverage in history when familiar constraints have dropped away; what we do now could establish the framework within which events will play themselves out for decades to come.

Unfortunately we are almost certainly not up to this task. There exists in the West something we might call the dog-and-car syndrome: the name refers to the fact that dogs spend a great deal of time chasing cars but very little time thinking about what they would actually *do* with a car if they were ever to catch one. Our leaders are not all that different: they pour their energy vigorously into the pursuit of victory, whether in politics or in war, but when victory actually arrives, they treat it as if it were an astonishing and wholly unforeseen development. They behave like the senator-elect in Robert Redford's movie *The Candidate* when he takes an aide aside at the victory celebration and asks incredulously, "What do we do now?"

If history is any guide, what we will probably do is fritter away the fruits of victory by failing to think through what it is we want victory to accomplish. The Athenians defeated the Persians in the fifth century B.C. only to defeat themselves through their own subsequent ambition and arrogance. The Turks spent centuries trying to take Constantinople for Islam only to see world power passing at the moment of their triumph, in 1453, to secular European states for whom the question of which faith ruled the "Eastern Rome" meant very little. The British drove the French from North America in 1763 but then alienated their own colonists, who in turn drove them out of their most valuable possessions on that continent. Victory in the First World War brought only dissension and disillusionment among the victors, and a purposeful urge for revenge among the vanquished. An even more decisive victory in the Second World War produced a long, costly, and nerve-wracking Cold War for those who won, and the mutually reinforcing benefits of peace and unprecedented prosperity for those who lost.

This depressing pattern of victories gone awry is almost enough to make one wish we were commemorating Cold War defeat. It certainly ought to make us think seriously, and rather quickly, about how not to squander the opportunities that now lie before us.

WE SHOULD BEGIN BY RECALLING THAT THE COLD War was a new kind of great-power rivalry, one in which the possibility of going to war always existed, but in which the necessity for doing so—at least in a form that would pit the Soviet Union and the United States *directly* against each other—never arose. As a result, that conflict took on the paradoxical character we associate with the name history has given it: the Cold War contained most of the anxieties, animosities, and apocalyptic exhortations that one tends to find in "hot" wars, but without the rubble or the body count. In time people became so used to this situation that some, myself included, began using the equally paradoxical term "long peace" to characterize it. Whatever the merits of the label, the importance of what it describes ought not to be minimized: a great-power competition carried on without great-power war is a distinct improvement over the way most such rivalries have been handled in the past.

But we also need to remember that the long peace grew out of a relationship between two superpower adversaries. If they are no longer to be adversaries—or if one of them is no longer to be a superpower—then the conditions that gave us the long peace will change. We need to make sure as we put the Cold War behind us that we do not also jettison those principles and procedures that allowed it to evolve into the longest period of great-power rivalry without war in the modern era. If a long peace was in fact the offspring of the Cold War, then the last thing we should want to do, in tossing the parent onto the ash heap of history, is to toss the child as well.

We will need a strategy that does not waste time and energy trying to turn back irreversible changes, but also one that is imaginative enough to find ways, within the limits of what is possible, to preserve the stability the Cold War has given us. The very concepts we employ in thinking about international affairs grew out of the now antiquated circumstances of superpower rivalry: if all we do is to apply old categories of thought to the new realities we confront—if we limit ourselves to trying to teach

new dogs old tricks—we could find our approach to world politics to be as outdated as was the approach that certain now-defunct Marxist regimes took toward their own internal affairs prior to 1989.

The following are some new issues we will face as we seek to extend the long peace beyond a Cold War the West has now won. Old answers will not suffice in dealing with them.

SHOULD WE WELCOME THE DECLINE AND POSSIBLE BREAKUP OF THE SOVIET UNION?

THE MOST ASTONISHING FACT FACING US AS THE 1990s begin is that we can no longer take for granted the continued existence of the USSR as the superpower we have known throughout the Cold War. Its economy is in ruins; its government is unsure of its own authority; its leaders confront nationalist pressures far more deeply rooted than the "socialist" values the Soviet state has been trying to implant for more than seven decades. There are those in the West who welcome these developments as the consummation of a wish long and devoutly held. Second thoughts, one hopes, will produce more-mature reflections.

Among them should be the realization that it takes two to tango, and that the United States has no particular reason to want to conclude the bipolar superpower dance that has been going on since 1945. For by comparison with the multipolar international systems that preceded it, Cold War bipolarity has served the cause of peace remarkably well: the First and Second World Wars arose from failures of communication, cooperation, and common sense among several states of roughly equal strength, not from situations in which two clear antagonists confronted each other. The relative simplicity of postwar great-power relations may well have made possible their relative stability, and a situation in which the Soviet Union is no longer such a power would mean an end to that arrangement. War might not result, but instability, volatility, and unpredictability almost certainly would.

It is also worth noting that military hardware does not simply vanish into thin air as a nation's position in the world declines, or as its internal authority crumbles. The means by which a new war could start—and indeed, with nuclear weapons, the means by which we ourselves could be destroyed—will remain in the hands of whoever rules the Soviet Union. If that country should break apart, these lethal instruments might well come under the control of competing factions whose caution with respect to their use might not exceed the intensity of the rivalries that exist among them.

We confront, then, an apparent paradox: now that we have won the Cold War, our chief interest may lie in the survival and successful rehabilitation of the nation that was our principal adversary throughout that conflict. But a historian would see nothing odd in this: Napoleon's conquerors moved quickly to reintegrate France into the international community after 1815; Germany and Japan received similar treatment after their defeat in 1945. It was the failure to arrange for Germany's reintegration after the First World War, some scholars have argued, that led to the Second World War. Power vacuums are dangerous things. Solicitude for a defeated adversary, therefore, is not just a matter of charity or magnanimity; it also reflects the wise victor's calculated self-interest, as confirmed by repeated historical experience.

But to say that the United States should seek the survival and rehabilitation of the Soviet Union is not to say that we should do so in its present form. That country's future is in question today not because anyone has attacked it but because its own internal structure has proved unworkable. If the USSR is to recover, it will have to change that structure; the only question is how. And although the Soviet people themselves will, in the end, decide that question, we in the West are not without influence in the matter: consider the regularity with which Soviet officials now solicit our advice.

Americans have long questioned the wisdom of trying to maintain multinational empires against the will of their inhabitants. The collapse of the Russian, Ottoman, and Austro-Hungarian empires during the First World War vindicated that skepticism, as did the dismantling of the British, French, Dutch, and Portuguese empires after the Second World War. Soviet officials have argued, of course, that the analogy is imperfect, that their non-Russian republics are not colonies at all but rather constituent parts of the USSR, linked to it by their own free will. But the French used to insist, with equal lack of credibility, that Algeria was part of France itself and content to remain so. A mother country's claims of filial devotion do not establish its existence.

The French experience also shows how close a state can come to destroying itself by trying to hang on to an empire for too long. It would hardly strengthen the Soviet Union to have several simultaneous insurgencies going on within its borders; just one, in Algeria, was enough to persuade that most imperious of modern statesmen, Charles de Gaulle, that imperial devolution had its advantages. France's position in the world has hardly declined since then, and many of its former colonies have chosen to maintain economic, linguistic, and cultural ties with their former ruler—as have many of Great Britain's—even as they have broken political ties. Denying autonomy ensures the absence of allegiance; allowing it at least leaves possibilities open.

A Russia that embraced a De Gaulle solution would remain a great power: even if the Russian federal republic alone were all that survived under Moscow's rule, it would still control 76 percent of the land area and 52 percent of the population of the present USSR. Bloated boundaries have never provided very much security in a nuclear age in any event, but with nationalism rampant and with the means of suppressing it no longer effective, they are certain in the future to provide even less.

It would appear to make sense, therefore, for the United States to favor as much of a breakup of the Soviet Union as would be necessary to leave it with a reasonably contented as opposed to a disaffected population, *precisely because we should want to see that state survive as a great power*. And who knows: in a post–Cold War world Kremlin leaders might actually acknowledge the sincerity of our motives in taking such a position (although we should probably not count on that).

WHAT IS GOING TO BE LEFT FOR NUCLEAR WEAPONS TO DETER?

AS AREAS OF AGREEMENT IN SOVIET-AMERICAN relations have expanded, the occasions on which either side has felt the need to deter the other have become rare, and that trend has in turn raised the possibility of getting by with far fewer nuclear weapons and delivery systems than each side has now. Reductions have already begun, and there is every reason to think that they will continue.

We and the Russians would do well, though, to resist the temptation to abolish nuclear weapons altogether, or even to reduce our stockpiles to a level approximating that of the next largest nuclear power. The reason for this is simple: nuclear weapons have played a major role in bringing about the evolution from Cold War to long peace. They have made each side think twice before taking action that might risk war; they have served as a kind of crystal ball into which statesmen can look to see what the consequences of a future conflict will be, and that vision has induced caution.

Nuclear weapons also sustained Soviet-American bipolarity beyond the time that it might otherwise have been expected to last. Given the Soviet Union's chronic economic difficulties, its claim to superpower status would have lost credibility long ago had that country not possessed a tremendous nuclear arsenal. But because of the stability that bipolarity brings, it is not at all clear that the world would have been a more peaceful place had the USSR become an "ordinary" power.

The relationship between nuclear weapons and superpower status is, to be sure, poorly understood. No one has ever been quite certain how to define just what a superpower is, apart from this characteristic of having a large number of nuclear weapons. But no one has ever been quite certain either just how nuclear weapons made the United States and the Soviet Union superpowers in the first place. What we do know is that the caution nuclear capabilities encourage and the bipolarity they sustain have created the framework for a reasonably stable international order. It might be best not to inquire too deeply into how.

Witch doctors, after all, produce their cures largely by psychological effect: their powers evaporate if examined too closely. The psychological effects that nuclear weapons have provided may well have cured the great powers of a very dangerous illness indeed, which was their propensity to rush blindly into wars without considering the consequences. We would do well to accept this result gratefully, and without challenging too directly the means by which it has been brought about.

It would be to the advantage of the United States and the Soviet Union, therefore, to retain their nuclear superiority over the rest of the world, albeit at much reduced levels, and with maximum cooperation to avoid surprises and accidents. But we might well rethink targeting doctrines, for as the physicist Freeman Dyson has wisely observed, just because a nation has nuclear weapons does not mean that it has to point them at anyone in particular. Their purpose, rather, should be to maintain a healthy fear of incautious action on the part of everyone, and a healthy respect for a major method by which we have achieved a long peace. If that fear and that respect come from the contemporary technological equivalent of rattling bones and chanting incantations around a campfire, then so be it.

HOW WILL NATO, THE WARSAW PACT, AND A REUNIFIED GERMANY FIT TOGETHER?

IF THE SOVIET UNION AND THE UNITED STATES ARE no longer to confront each other as adversaries, then the original purpose of NATO and the Warsaw Pact—deterring military attack—will have passed away. It is worth recalling, though, that these alliances had secondary purposes as well: both were intended to overcome old nationalist rivalries in Europe; both were instruments by which the superpowers sought to integrate those portions of Germany that they controlled into those parts of Europe that fell within their influence. The two alliances served as stabilizers in that they brought a certain order and predictability to Europe; and although that stability was not always based on justice— witness Soviet behavior in Eastern Europe—it did secure peace for almost half a century on a previously warprone continent.

But with self-determination triumphant among former Soviet satellites and with German reunification imminent, we will soon confront a task quite unfamiliar to our generation (although not to those of our parents and grandparents), which is cartographic revision: the map of post–Cold War Europe is not going to be the one to which we have become accustomed since the end of the Second World War. Soviet-American rivalry, it is now apparent, simply suppressed nationalism in Europe; it did not end it, and it will not take long for the effects of resurgent nationalism, both in reality and on maps, to manifest themselves. Europeans are entering uncharted territory, and in such circumstances it may be wise to hold on to what is familiar, even if it is a bit out of date.

We should therefore seek to preserve the secondary stabilizing functions of NATO and the Warsaw Pact, even as their original deterrent purposes disappear. It is always easier to modify existing institutions than to create new ones; preserving the Cold War alliances but shifting their roles could ensure that resurgent European nationalism does not, in these new and volatile circumstances, once again get out of control.

One way to accomplish this might be for a reunified Germany to link itself to both alliances at the same time. Such a solution would have seemed ludicrous when NATO and the Warsaw Pact confronted each other as Cold War adversaries, but is it so implausible in a post–Cold War era? People have learned to live with stranger things: consider what happened to Germany itself, and to its former capital, in the years that followed the Second World War. If one keeps in mind that we are talking about a world in which once-competitive alliances have taken on the common task of preserving the stability Europe achieved during the Cold War—and if we remember that stability will be the prerequisite for any Europe-wide economic integration—then it might well be possible to persuade both East and West Germans that reunification would best proceed under the sponsorship of both alliances, and perhaps even with the continued stationing of at least a token number of Russian and American troops on German soil.

Cooperation between NATO and the Warsaw Pact to bring about the orderly reunification of Germany would have additional advantages as well. It would provide a new basis for legitimizing the Pact in the eyes of Eastern Europeans, who have tended to see that organization until now—with good reason—only as an instrument of Soviet oppression. With that legitimacy, the Warsaw Pact could then take on another useful function, which would be that of mediating potentially dangerous disputes in Eastern Europe and the Balkans, in much the way that NATO has successfully managed the long-standing antagonism between Greece and Turkey: the bitter conflict between Hungarians and Romanians over Transylvania is only one of several unresolved issues in that part of the world which ought to remind us of how easily self-determination can lead to conflict. A reinvigorated Warsaw Pact could also help sustain at least a semblance of superpower bipolarity in Europe: NATO will probably survive whatever happens, but it is not clear what the effect on European stability will be if that alliance lacks a viable counterpart.

The old meaning of sovereignty will not suffice in dealing with the resurgence of nationalism in Europe: too many Europeans—and non-Europeans as well—have suffered from its excesses to be denied an interest in seeing to it that old evils do not return. The Cold War experience, for all its danger, illogic, and injustice, provided a valuable opportunity for Europeans to mature, to put away those irresponsible practices that dragged their continent into war twice during the first half of this century. Keeping NATO and the Warsaw Pact around for a while— even if their role resembles that of nursemaids more than that of warriors—might be the best way to reassure all concerned that this process of becoming wise will continue.

SHOULD WE HELP TO REPAIR THE DAMAGE MARXISM HAS CAUSED?

ECONOMIC DISTRESS OBVIOUSLY ENCOURAGES PO-
litical instability: as Paul Kennedy, the Yale historian, has pointed out, uneven rates of economic and technological development are what
cause great powers to rise and fall. If one accepts the argument that the United States and its allies should want
Russia to remain a great power, then it would hardly
make sense to welcome an economic collapse there or in
Eastern Europe, however misguided the policies were
that produced that prospect.

But the West has an ideological as well as a material interest in wanting to see *perestroika* succeed: the cause of
democracy throughout the world can only prosper if that
ideology—and not Marxist authoritarianism—provides
the means by which the USSR and its neighbors at last
achieve economies capable of satisfying the needs of
their peoples. And if the emergence of even partly democratic institutions inside the Soviet Union makes the
prospect of war less likely—there is strong historical evidence that democracies tend not to fight each other—
then that would be an important reinforcement for the
role nuclear deterrence has already played in discouraging the incautious use of military force.

Few people today remember that a similar combination of geopolitical and ideological motives impelled Secretary of State George C. Marshall in 1947—at Kennan's
suggestion—to offer to include the Soviet Union and
Eastern Europe in the plan for economic assistance that
came to bear Marshall's name. Stalin, with characteristic
shortsightedness, rejected the idea, and the Marshall
Plan went on to become a program for the rehabilitation
of Western Europe—one that was so successful that editorial pages ever since have resounded with calls for its
revival, however dissimilar the circumstances might be
to those that existed at the time of its creation.

Now, though, the way is open to implement Marshall's
original vision. For although it lies beyond the power of
anyone in the West to ensure the success of economic reforms in either the Soviet Union or Eastern Europe,
those countries are already asking the United States to
provide much of the training and technology without
which failure will be certain. We will need to think carefully about just what we can do, and how we should do it.

One thing is apparent at the outset: any new aid program for the Soviet Union and Eastern Europe will have
to be multinational in character. The United States is
well beyond the point at which it can take on a burden of
this magnitude by itself, as it did in 1947. Fortunately,
though, it can now enlist the very considerable resources
and skills of former recipients of Marshall Plan aid in Europe, notably West Germany, and also those of Japan, another past beneficiary of American assistance. All these
states have cause to welcome an integration of Soviet and
Eastern European economies with those of the rest of the
world; none of them has any good reason to want to see
perestroika fail.

A multinational aid program would have several advantages over older, unilateral forms of aid. It would maximize the resources available while minimizing the burden on an already overstretched American economy. It
would be less susceptible than past foreign-aid programs
to the charge that it serves the political interests of a particular state; it would also be less vulnerable to the volatility of domestic politics in any one state. It would soak
up surplus products and capital from two large-scale exporters of these commodities—Germany and Japan—
whose success in exporting has periodically strained their
relationship with the United States. And such a program
might also help to heal political differences that still exist
between Japan and the Soviet Union and that might well
exist between a reunified Germany and the Soviet
Union.

We might also consider encouraging corporate rather
than government sponsorship for at least a major portion
of this assistance, where profitability and propriety make
it feasible. Corporate management could provide faster
action and greater efficiency than would otherwise occur;
it might also be more sensitive than official initiatives to
those market forces in the Soviet Union and Eastern Europe whose emergence we want to encourage. Some such
activity is already under way, most conspicuously with a
project that surely marks a turning point of some kind in
the history of our times: I refer to the recent and long-
awaited opening of McDonald's in Moscow, a project that
will be particularly interesting to watch because of the
corporation's decision to develop its own network of
farms, processing plants, and training centers inside the
USSR. The resulting contest is sure to be a titanic one,
and whether Russia will overwhelm McDonald's or
McDonald's will overwhelm Russia is far from clear.
But the fact that it is taking place at all can only warm
the heart of anyone who has ever been to the Soviet
Union and felt the urge to shout, out of sheer exas-
peration: "What this country needs is a good service
economy!"

WHAT HAPPENS AFTER GORBACHEV?

NO ONE, NOT EVEN THE CURRENT LEADER OF
the Soviet Union, is indispensable (although
he comes about as close as any person in recent memory). The frailties that flesh—or a
political career—is heir to can only increase with the passage of time; we in the West must be prepared for the
moment when the most imaginative Soviet leader since
Lenin is no longer on the scene. To fail to do this—to assume that everything that is happening hinges on Gorbachev alone—would in itself be to fall into an outmoded
way of thinking.

There is at least one reason to think that the post–Cold
War era will continue into the post-Gorbachev era: it is

1. THE UNITED STATES

the fact that the roots of the long peace were in place well before Gorbachev came to power. Whatever their dissimilarities, neither Stalin nor Khrushchev nor Brezhnev wanted a war with the United States; the likelihood of such a conflict has declined steadily over the years, regardless of whether tyrants, reformers, or stagnationists ruled in the Kremlin. It is true that Soviet domestic and foreign policies are harder to separate today than they once were: an abandonment of *perestroika* or a crackdown on dissent would obviously undermine Moscow's improved relations with the West, just as the Tiananmen Square massacre undermined Beijing's. But a return to all-out Cold War seems unlikely, if for no other reason than that today's Soviet Union would have to compete in it from a severely weakened geopolitical, ideological, and economic position.

The West's strategy, therefore, ought to be to do nothing to undermine Gorbachev's authority, but not to be wholly dependent upon it either. Because the forces that have ended the Cold War are deeply rooted—and because the problems that beset the Soviet Union will remain after Gorbachev leaves the scene—we have some basis for confidence that the initiatives he has taken to deal with both domestic and foreign-policy issues are not going to disappear after he does.

T HE NAMES THAT WE ATTACH TO THINGS—WHICH in turn determine the categories we use in thinking about them—are only representations of reality; they are not reality itself. Reality can shift, sometimes more rapidly than the names we have devised to characterize it. Concepts like "communism," "capitalism," "deterrence," "credibility," and "security" only approximate the conditions we confront; but words like these tend to take on a life of their own, thereby constraining imagination. One sees the argument made even today that Communist parties running command economies will never give up power, despite overwhelming evidence that this is exactly what is happening. We need to avoid letting the categories that exist in our minds blind us to what our eyes are seeing.

At the same time, though, there is at least one thing to be said in favor of retaining old names, even as one accommodates to new realities. Cloaking change in the appearance of continuity is a time-honored technique of political leadership, for it allows those at the top to alter their thinking and shift their policies without seeming to be inconsistent. Cloaking change in the garb of continuity eases transitions; it can be a way of making revolution look like evolution, which is sometimes a useful thing to do. We should not, therefore, do away entirely with the terminology of the Cold War, or even with all the institutions that reflect that terminology; but we should welcome the opportunity slowly but steadily to shift the meanings we attach to them.

W HO IS IT THAT WE HAVE DEFEATED IN THE COLD War? It is not the Russian people, whom we never saw as enemies, and toward whom we bear no ill will. It is not the Soviet Union, for we should want to see that state survive as a great power. It is not communism, because that doctrine has proved so malleable over the years that it has long since lost any precise meaning. It is certainly not Gorbachev and the current Soviet government, who have had the wisdom to recognize reality and the courage to adjust to it. It is not even the Cold War, because that experience brought us the long peace. Indeed, it is odd that there should be so much talk of victory and so little specificity as to at whose expense it actually came.

It might help clarify things if we recall what appears to be a recurring competition in human affairs between coercive authority and individual autonomy, between what the sociologist John A. Hall has referred to as the forces of power and those of liberty. The tension is as old as recorded history, and it will no doubt be with us as long as history continues. But power and liberty are rarely precisely balanced: one or the other predominates most of the time, with only occasional shifts back and forth.

The century has not, on the whole, been kind to liberty. The forces of authoritarianism overcame those of autonomy in most parts of the world most of the time during this period: witness the respective triumphs of fascism, communism, and all the varieties of dictatorship that lay between. It appeared until quite recently to be the fate of most people to have most of their lives managed for them, to lack the means of controlling their own affairs.

What happened in the revolutionary year 1989 was that liberty suddenly found itself pushing against an open door. The balance swung away from power with breathtaking speed; the authoritarian alternatives that have dominated so much of twentieth-century history were revealed to be, for the most part, hollow shells. We have good reason to hope that liberty will flourish in the next few years as it has not in our lifetime; and it is in that context that the real nature of the West's "victory" in the Cold War becomes clear. For it was authoritarianism that suffered the real defeat, and in that sense all of us—including our old Cold War adversaries—have won.

But history will not stop with us, any more than it did with all the others—Marx and Lenin among them—who thought they had mastered its secrets. The triumph of liberty will almost certainly be transitory; new forces will eventually arise that will swing the balance back to power once again. It is not clear at the moment, though, where they will come from, or when they will arrive. It would be prudent to be on the lookout for them; it would be wise to be prepared for their effects. But the fact that the forces of resurgent power are not yet in sight—that we have the luxury of at least some time to savor the liberties that all of us, Russians included, have won—ought to be an occasion for ecumenical, if wary, celebration.

U.S. Foreign Policy and Europe, 1990–2000

Catherine McArdle Kelleher

Catherine McArdle Kelleher is a visiting fellow in the Brookings Foreign Policy Studies program and a professor of public policy and director of the Center for International Security Studies of the School of Public Affairs at the University of Maryland, College Park. Her current research focuses on the role of a unified Germany in post-Cold War European security.

A fter close to a half-century of stability, American foreign policy toward Europe is in for a dramatic change. Gone, suddenly, is the organizing principle of anticommunism in both its political and ideological senses. Eastern Europe is no longer a bloc in any conceivable sense of the term; the Soviet Union may still be a formidable adversary, but only as an ordinary and increasingly limited great power. Western Europe is increasingly integrated, self-reliant, and prosperous, and potentially more a competing than an allied bloc. And German unification and its consequences are now out of our control and were not in our gift, yet will be central to our continuing political, economic, and security relations with all of Europe.

Much of the new challenge comes from our undisputed past success. But celebration of the blessings wrought by containment will do little to prepare Americans, both elite and electorate, for the evolution of a successful European policy in the decade of the 1990s. What is needed is revolutionary: a new definition of basic American interests in Europe that allows us to overcome past habits of easy political dominance and ram-

pant NATO-ism; that permits us to cope with both uncertainty and instability without fear; and that encourages unprecedented levels of security and cooperation with all of Europe, including the Soviet Union. The challenge for the United States will be to participate meaningfully in the emergence of a new, if somewhat untidy, Europe that, by choice and circumstance, no longer fits the post-1945 American definition of Europe as part of "us." Opposition will come not only from international competitors and detractors, but also from broadly based domestic critics sunk in the gloom of "America's decline," attracted by the Pacific's promise, or overwhelmed by the unfinished agenda at home.

The choices to be made in the coming transformation of America's European policy are in some ways reminiscent of the choices and bargains of 1946–47. The war just ended is cold, not hot; yet the scope and implication of our choices are at least as great, and the sense that we must learn from the mistakes of the past war is just as potent. Popular enthusiasm for peace, for change, and for peace dividends is certainly on the same scale. There are crucial differences, however. The United States is now both better prepared and less able to make these choices on its own. The list of winners and losers with whom the United States must deal is decisively different. The importance of active usable military power, nuclear and conventional, for the setting of balances or the calculation of future advantage has undergone a fundamental reevaluation. So too has the role of national economic power or national financial independence.

1. THE UNITED STATES

America's perspective on Europe over the past 45 years, though now being overturned, still sheds light on the ways in which the United States will view Europe over the next several decades. At least it helps to clarify the questions to be asked now. The answers may come later.

The Postwar Policy Context

The most novel aspect of American foreign policy in the postwar period was the new definition of Europeans as somehow immutably part of "us." In contrast to the stark separationist views of the 1920s and 1930s, American leaders and pundits came to view Europeans as "most like us," a people to be defended as we defend ourselves, a kindred people with whom to share the benefits and the risks of the international order established after the defeat of fascism. It was, of course, only Western Europe, NATO Europe plus a few respectable others, that was at issue. Eastern Europe largely drifted from view.

It is this sense of the United States and Europe as being kindred and incorporated that is now subject to the greatest pressures for change. The problem is not the revolutionary changes in Eastern Europe, or in Germany, or the overblown debate over burden sharing in the Iraq action. For both policy elites and the general public, the surface identity of American and European interests is still intact; in every vital area, cooperation still far outweighs conflict and continuing mutual irritation. But emerging from American and European discussions is a powerful new sense of inevitable Atlantic disengagement, of European identity, and eventual American autarky. Basic Atlantic consensus and long-term European-American cooperation no longer seem as relevant or compelling conceptions for the future.

Three Postwar American Images of Europe

The perception of Europe and Europeans that emerged in the early postwar period perhaps said more about American goals and motives than it did about reality, much less about European perceptions of the same cluster of international factors. But it also presented to the American public both good and real reasons for Europe to be the central focus of postwar American foreign policy.

The first and dominant perception was of Europe as both the prize and the price of the postwar political and ideological struggle with the Soviet Union. The security of a devastated Europe from both internal subversion and external pressure became the acid test of America's determination to make the world truly safe for democracy. The existence of a Europe "like us" was a precondition to the establishment of an international order con-

Emerging from American and European discussions is a powerful new sense of inevitable Atlantic disengagement, of European identity, and eventual American autarky.

ducive to American political and economic interests. In the language of Bretton Woods, democratic, capitalist European systems, tied inextricably to an international economic order led by the United States, were ultimately in America's best interest. The cost of postwar European reconstruction was high; but from this perspective the Marshall Plan was simply the down payment on a future of common benefit and continuing American growth.

Another part of Europe's price was a strategy involving both containment of the Soviet Union and extension of an American security guarantee of Western Europe. The American military guarantee provided the shield behind which those "like us" could restore and then maintain functioning political systems that would avoid the ideological quarrels and fatal social divisions that led to the triumph of fascism. Soviet military strength was overwhelming, whatever the Soviet intention. American nuclear weapons balanced, first, Soviet conventional numbers and, then, Soviet nuclear forces themselves. The critical factor was continued American military superiority and increasingly, for many, a direct permanent military presence in Europe so we would not have "to fight our way back in again."

A central secondary task was the reform and then rehabilitation of the West Germans in ways that ensured both future stability in the European balance and the maximum use of German resources in deterrence and defense. Most Americans had considerable respect for German ingenuity and industriousness, once the initial horrors of World War II had passed. German participation in the defense of the West was "natural" so long as an integrated framework could be constructed against German military power. The struggle for German hearts and minds — first against the traditions of Marxism, then against Soviet blandishment — was seen as the centerpiece of American efforts to spread democracy and create an international (or at least Atlantic) system favorable to basic American values.

Through the 1960s, European and American interests continued to be seen as congruent if not identical, over both the long and short haul. Atlantic defense cooperation and economic coordination were seen as reflecting the basic identity of interests among democratic industrial states. Détente made the necessary connection between economic interests and containment less obvious during the 1970s. The struggles during the 1980s over intermediate-range nuclear forces (INF) also tested the relationship. Yet both the deployment and the agreement to eliminate INF demonstrated the basic "rightness" and resolve of the Atlantic strategy. Tough decisions had been taken and implemented; the Soviet Union had won neither its games in Europe nor the opportunity, probably, to return to the field.

The second significant American perspective on postwar Europe was the necessity of "doing it right." Having twice rescued Europe from chaos and conflict of its own making, this time the United States would ensure that peacemaking worked, that the Europe it had twice restored with its expeditionary forces would be rebuilt on a stable democratic basis into a zone of peace.

Central to this perspective was the concept of a regional security system. Superficially, the task was to mobilize European resources against the Soviet Union. Yet, for at least the first postwar decade, a goal of almost equal importance was the design of a lasting regional balance: a system that would allow for the necessary rearmament of Germany (recognized by many American leaders as unavoidable as early as 1948), while also catering to France and Britain's need for firm guarantees against a German resurgence. Direct continuous American involvement was not foreseen as necessary for all time; even into the mid-1950s, President Eisenhower spoke of an interim overseas deployment of no longer than perhaps seven or eight years. The overwhelming preference of policymakers, liberal and conservative alike, was a Europe strong enough and united enough to organize its own defenses, with the U.S. role decreasing to one of general leadership, especially in nuclear matters, and of an emergency fire brigade.

By the mid-1960s, the image of "doing it right" had become focused on the unity of NATO. The health of the Alliance and the loyalty of the national members became surrogate tests for how well Europe's interwar problems of stability and cooperation had been resolved. Also, NATO became the framework for the coordination of Western interests, the symbol for Americans of the continued maintenance of the new Europe they had helped to construct and were now destined to lead. The Alliance was not perfect. It called for continuing American sacrifices in the interest of European security that were never reciprocated or appreciated. NATO clearly needed a new system of burden sharing and better consultation on American strategic preferences. But it was a working organization, of great value for concerting policies in ways that bilateral channels did not allow, and with a military structure of impressive deterrent strength.

Just as NATO was attaining, especially for conservatives, the symbolic status of man's last best hope, the

The United States must find a new organizing principle for its policy toward Europe. Anticommunism and anti-Sovietism are no longer policy lodestars.

unanimity of support for it began to crumble. During the 1960s, Senator Mike Mansfield's successive resolutions on American troop withdrawals coincided with the defection of the French from the integrated military organization. As the 1960s passed, numerous liberals joined with scattered conservative critics to question the need for continuing massive American involvement and the need for the United States to play global policeman, especially in a Europe strong enough to fight for its own interests. Liberals also worried that the United States had been trapped into answering the wrong questions in its concern for stability and the European balance. Defining the primary task of U.S. foreign policy as the avoidance of nuclear war and the stabilization of relations with the Soviet Union, these critics argued that NATO was a critical significant bond, but that it was neither paramount nor immutable in the calculation of American, or even European, interests. The approach was now "globalist," with NATO only one of many instruments.

The third American perspective on postwar Europe was a critical assessment of the role played by particular European states in global politics. The issue arose when European states pursued what they saw as their interests in defiance of what the United States saw as being in the general Western interest. Over time, the specifics varied, but the general thrust of the American critique was that individually, if not as a group, the Europeans gave paramount weight to narrow, short-term political gains and to national economic interests. The issues ranged from arms sales to preferential trading and investment policies; the forum was most often the Middle East but also Latin America, Africa, and Southeast Asia. But consistently from the 1950s through the 1980s the charge was the same: the Europeans were insular, recalcitrant, or soft — and always in the rear.

The Present Policy Context: 1990–2000

This review of postwar American perspectives on Europe dramatizes the stark shifts in context that have occurred since 1989, the radically new policy world that the United States will have to deal with in the Europe of the 1990s and beyond, and the inevitability of a wholesale transformation of the U.S. perspective on Europe. As new images of Europe evolve over the coming months and years, it is imperative to recognize the fundamental changes in Europe that will affect American policy calculations.

The first is that the United States must find a new organizing principle for its policy toward Europe. Anticommunism and anti-Sovietism are no longer policy lodestars. Although still a nuclear superpower, the Soviet Union will be more of an ordinary state, anxious to remain in the European economic and political game. It may still revert to hostility, but a more likely outcome seems internal economic absorption and political fragmentation. The Eastern European security zone is gone forever, and the pressures for lower budgets and lower force levels, no matter who is in power, are probably inescapable.

In the post–Cold War era, the United States must be prepared to deal with a new Europe, one that will resist being seen as part of us. Whether organized as an extended European Community or as pan-Europe spanning East and West, Europe will demand its own identity, which the United States will still influence but be able neither to determine nor to deny. Security concerns defined in traditional military terms will be fewer — in a pattern more like that of late 19th-century Europe than the Europe of the past 40 years. The United States may participate in defining the boundaries of this new Europe and in sketching out a role for itself that goes beyond NATO partnership. But it will have a smaller, less continuously central share in the emerging economic and political structures that constitute the new European order — an outcome that may be the result of European priorities or congressional action or both.

For the United States, perhaps the hardest adjustment will be to form a new relationship with the Federal Republic of Germany, the key actor in all the future European circles. The postwar German-American relationship has gone through a number of phases: Germany as pupil; Germany as key NATO ally; Germany as America's strategic partner in the ending of the Cold War. But unification signals the end of political constraint and most of postwar security dependency and thus a Germany less affected by American choices and preferences. A united Germany will have a larger agenda, a more assertive, confident tone, and a far more critical approach to the United States and its Western European partners. It has stronger political and economic interests in stabilizing Eastern Europe — if only to guard against migrations westward. It has a special relationship with the Soviet Union, at least until 1994–95, when Soviet troops are withdrawn from German soil, and probably beyond.

Much of American adaptation to this new Germany will take place in a familiar channel, NATO. As the United States has demanded since the Berlin Wall's fall, a united Germany will be a member of NATO and hold significant military forces to a present maximum of 370,000 troops. But as reflected in both NATO's London Summit declaration and the German-Soviet agreements of July 1990, German unification itself transforms NATO. This will be the time for changes in personnel (fewer forces even as a ceiling, perhaps a German Supreme Commander for NATO) as well as in strategy (the shift from larger active forces and static forward defense at the inner-German border to smaller, highly mobile, perhaps multinational units and a policy of force regeneration should unlikely war threaten). There will be few, if any, nuclear weapons on German soil in the future, given the expressed preferences of both East and West Germans. And over the next decade, NATO forces stationed in Germany will also shrink — with an American contingent of 50,000 to 75,000 troops by the end of the 1990s now widely discussed.

To the ire of many in Congress, some in Germany will see NATO's value strictly as a means of transition to a European security order. They may envisage evolution from a NATO European pillar or from the European Community (EC) or from either under the broader pan-European scope of a newly institutionalized Conference on Security and Cooperation in Europe (CSCE). In all cases, there may still be a role for the United States — and perhaps for the Soviet Union as well. But the role may be far more that of a guarantor of European choices, the nuclear protector of ultimate resort — not the leader or shaper of European security even against the residual threats of ethnic or nationalist violence or a disintegrating Soviet Union.

Moreover, military security will probably be seen as less pressing than economic stabilization and security, especially vis-à-vis Eastern Europe. Economic status and competitiveness will be the measure of day-to-day European power, with Germany most able to gain its preferences inside and outside the Community. Without a regularized link to post-1992 Europe, the United States will find itself more of an outsider, more dependent on the intervention and assistance of others for access than at any time in the postwar period. And without full involvement in the redevelopment and reshaping of the Eastern economies, Washington may find its policy preferences far less relevant to the daily policy concerns of a new German economic superpower or a new European economic "pole."

One aspect of the new Europe that Americans will find rewarding will be the increasing emphasis placed on democratic rule as the critical standard for bilateral and multilateral relationships. The new emphasis will emerge not only because of the guarantees of stability and noninterference that democracies generally provide, but because the most powerful states — Germany, the EC members, and the United States itself — believe that democratic rule will best safeguard their interests. Democratization may well prove a tough, exclusionary test for the new Europe. Much of the Balkans will become marginal; a military-dominated Greece or Turkey will be consigned to secondary European status. For a Soviet Union or Soviet republics that cling to bureaucratically authoritarian structures or for an Eastern European country that returns to the popular authoritarianism of the 1930s, the result will be lesser status and perhaps ultimately a lesser share in the European game.

Over the next decade, the United States thus will confront a Europe only somewhat like us, with a variety of organizations and structures that have overlapping responsibilities, ambitions, and memberships. Almost certainly included will be a European Community with expanded powers, functions, and membership; a NATO in decline but viable at least as a transitional element; and a CSCE as a new overarching umbrella with specific functions for arms control and perhaps crisis containment and peacekeeping. Most but not all will involve roles sometimes equal, sometimes secondary for the United States. The meshing of these various organizational activities and the political and economic compromises they represent will be the major challenge of the second half of the 1990s.

Goals for Future Policy

What minimum foreign policy goals should the United States pursue toward a Europe that is moving in ways still not totally discernible but clearly revolutionary? From the vantage point of 1990, four interrelated goals, while limited in nature, are certainly preferable to simple reaction or muddling through. At the least, these goals should help identify future changes that are risk-laden or politically troublesome. At a maximum, they will serve as benchmarks for American elites and publics concerned about short-term outcomes and the long-term future.

The first goal is to ensure the continued well-being of the existing zone of economic and political peace that the United States has helped create since 1945. Basically a defensive goal, it aims to secure through extension the success achieved through the economic, security, and political structures built up since 1945. The evolution of this zone of peace does not itself provide for the "inevitability" of either NATO or the European Community in its present structural configuration. But it provides strong incentives to preserve them at least as transitional structures. And any new European frameworks must incorporate guarantees to safeguard and extend their principal outcomes — regular, cooperative, transparent relations within overarching mediating structures that are viewed by national electorates as normal, predictable, and preferable to past competition and conflict — or to future instability.

Maintaining this zone is in the basic interest of the United States whatever the ultimate European framework. If the new Europe is a more potent economic competitor or far less tied to U.S. security guarantees, a Europe open to the free flow of trade and ideas is still a critical cornerstone in the type of international political order that the United States requires in 1990 — perhaps even more than it did in 1945. As economic competition grows between Europe, Japan, and the United States into the 21st century, a free economic zone will be of even greater significance for U.S. interests.

The second minimum goal is to preserve for the United States a role vis-à-vis all basic European structures that is legitimate in the eyes of all European players and *not* dependent on the good will of Germany or any other "strategic partner." This aim runs somewhat contrary to the present Bush administration strategy that posits the centrality of a preserved NATO and the strategic partnership with a reuniting Germany — almost to the exclusion of any other option. It is not a basic American interest to cling to any particular structure, much less to an emphasis on purely military cooperation to the detriment or exclusion of far more important economic and political coordination and policy development. To ensure American access across the spectrum of European policy areas, the United States must not merely react to evolution within the Community or to new forms of cooperation with Eastern Europe, but actively participate in their creation. Such a strategy is both a hedge against the future and an opportunity to underline the continuing stake the United States has in Europe.

Carrying out that strategy will require considerable American flexibility and a critical reeducation of Americans, both policymakers and publics, about possible European outcomes. The American postwar preference has been for decisionmaking in Washington to flow through clear-cut and mutually reinforcing channels of influence. Typically, the United States has relied on strong, semi-exclusive partnerships, first with Britain and then with the Federal Republic; strong multilateral organizations of friendly major actors, such as the G-7 group; and well-defined structures for multilateral diplomacy and integrated functional action — principally NATO, but also the Coordinating Committee for Multilateral Export Controls (COCOM) and the International Monetary Fund. At best, the United States must strive now for multiple channels of influence but without the assurance either of a continuing commanding role or of easy policy coordination. To do this with grace will be hard; to do it effectively, still harder.

As the U.S. role in Europe changes, so too does the part the Soviet Union will play in Europe's future. In some respects, the Soviet script is more certain, given its geopolitical location, its economic dependency on Europe, and the political uncertainty about its future nature and actions that will absorb much of Europe's political calculation. But even a minimum American role in Europe should be more positive, given both enormous American assets and newfound flexibility. In the short run, the United States will be the primary reassurer of a new Germany against a gathering of its enemies; it will also provide the balance wheel that all Europeans, East and West, seem to want for now. For the longer term, the United States may be more an available partner, an honest broker, and, only occasionally, a makeweight in a German-led Europe or a hedge against residual threats of ethnic unrest, Soviet reversals, or political collapse in Eastern Europe or, more likely, the Soviet Union.

The third minimum goal is to foster the orderly political transition of both united Germany and the Soviet Union to their new European roles. This must be a primary goal for the United States, even though American efforts will be neither exclusive nor determining. To many, American images of Europe have always been too pro-Bonn or German-centric. But it is now more essential than ever that the United States reinforce a democratic Germany — the new kind of democratic Germany — as the new king of democratic as well as economic Europe. A continuing American military presence, so long as it remains wanted by the Germans and other Europeans, remains useful. And American participation, on more equitable terms and in more cooperating or coordinating modes, will be essential.

It may not be particularly easy to sustain a constructive relationship with a newly assertive Germany, flush with the success of its unification triumphs. Germany will undoubtedly be more self-absorbed, less willing (and able) to contribute to the transatlantic common good, and determined to stabilize its Eastern neighbors, whatever America's views. Mutual irritations will grow, and there will be many temptations to rehearse the German past to constrain the German future. But the United States will still have a unique fostering role to play despite policy differences and diverging areas of primary economic commitment. The United States may have to do for Germany what Britain did for the United States in the late 19th century — help without obvious support or direct interference, consult at the grand level with tolerance and flexibility for the inevitable clashes and irritations. And it should do so gladly — and for its own long-run benefit.

The focus of the U.S.-Soviet relationship will be far less defined and probably far more concerned with continuing strategic questions. Washington will probably play a less important role in Soviet economic and political restructuring, whether reform or disintegration, than will Germany and the other major West European states. It will certainly play a smaller part in democratizing Eastern Europe. U.S. reluctance to be actively involved reflects both present economic limitations and the self-concerns of American domestic politics. But it also signals continuing American ambivalence about

America must strive now for multiple channels of influence but without the assurance either of a commanding role or of easy policy coordination. To do this with grace will be hard; to do it effectively, still harder.

the extension of Europe eastward and the risks of involvement with those even now "not quite like us."

But, as it will for Germany, the United States should play a facilitating, structuring part in involving even a rump Soviet Union in Europe, especially in all-European security and economic arrangements. It is not in the U.S. strategic interest to allow, much less encourage, the marginalization of the Soviet Union in European affairs. Rather, the United States should actively support Soviet participation in multilateral solutions to pressing regional problems ranging from environmental degradation to ethnic unrest to the safety of remaining nuclear weapons. It should also promote Soviet acceptance of the standards of behavior, responsibility, and internal political compromise that have prevailed in Western Europe since the late 1950s. And in the short run the United States can provide legitimacy for the constraints on military capabilities that affect European security arrangements that the Soviet Union (and the United States) will have to accept.

The final goal is to maintain, if not extend, political and economic access within Europe and to Europe. This goal not only reflects America's own interests; it also represents an exercise of influence the United States should seek on behalf of the have-nots in Europe and throughout the rest of the world. The principal economic gatekeepers will clearly be European — the Community, the deutsche mark bloc, or Germany itself. But the "outsiders" must have an effective voice for access and transparency across all international areas. The United States is uniquely positioned to meet that need, even though both its incentives and capabilities to do so are far less today than they were during the 1960s or 1970s.

This last goal involves a wide range of possible activities; the specifics will depend on how Europe's institutions develop. At a minimum, it will involve American pressure against European protectionism and excessive Eurocentric self-absorption. At a maximum, it might involve the development of joint American-European ventures in the interest of specific development goals, requirements of regional security, or hedges against environmental dangers. At the core will be the education of the democratic electorate, American and European, about international responsibility and a recasting of the limits and obligations of state sovereignty and economic power.

Domestic Goals to Support a New Policy toward Europe

These new foreign policy goals toward Europe will require several critical developments at home. The domestic situation is more familiar and needs less analytic development. But it is crucial to the process of transforming American foreign policy toward both major and minor European players and to the risks and opportunities that will develop from 1990 until 2000.

The loss of the Cold War lodestar of American foreign policy in Europe must not lead to the invention of a new "threat": the German economic and political menace, the European Community as "devil," the German-Soviet relationship as minefield, or even instability (read "change") as a "bad thing."

The necessary restructuring and drawdown of American military forces because of budgetary pressures and the changing strategic environment must not lead to mindless withdrawals of forces in the interest of fiscal savings and the politically driven retention of domestic bases. Nor should it lead, in the longer term, to neglect of the continuing need for other kinds of military forces to do long-term force regeneration in the case of a renewed major military threat in Europe; eventually to secure minimum deterrence in both the conventional and the nuclear arena; or to assist in peacekeeping around Europe's periphery as well as around the world.

Finally, evolution of a Europe creating its own identity and securing its own economic competitiveness must not fuel either a return to outdated isolationist ten-dencies or a backlash of protectionist, exclusionist policies to punish European efforts to drive competitive bargains in trade or in financial or monetary cooperation. The domino effect of such American actions is a real possibility. In the long run, so, too would be the increasing self-marginalization of the United States.

Conclusion

Much may happen to derail the fundamental assumptions made in this essay about the future of American-European relations in the 1990s. Developments in the Soviet Union are the obvious uncertainty. The critical obstacles may be the effects of a rapidly, radically fragmenting Soviet Union and the induction of a chain reaction along its periphery, especially in what has been Eastern Europe. There is still room in the short run for British and French intransigence and for the collapse of the hopeful revolutions in Eastern Europe in the face of economic failures and political vacillation. German unification will run myriad risks, not the least of which is the short-run education and incorporation of a surprisingly xenophobic East German population that has a self-centered economic agenda and an immature political sense. There is always the possibility, but not the probability, of American neo-isolationism.

The United States faces a decade of great challenge and of great opportunity to cooperate in, not create, a new Europe. It will require immense moderation and restraint, a recasting of many of the truisms and lessons of prewar European-American relations, and a reformulation of some, but not all, of the images of Europe the United States has developed since 1945. It will mean adjusting to the new economic competition with Europe (and Japan) with greater equanimity than till now, and downgrading the significance of military power in our foreign policy generally and with regard to Europe in particular. And, it will mean a steadfast insistence on America's continuing stake in an evolving Europe, begun in our own image and now assuming new responsibilities in the liberal international order we have given so much to create.

The Soviet Union

At this time in history, the Soviet Union faces so many critical challenges simultaneously that it is almost unimaginable it can successfully address them all. Failure in any one area could provide the context for a succession of failures in other areas and, ultimately, to the collapse of Mikhail Gorbachev's leadership. A downward spiral has already begun not only in the economic arena where *perestroika* has failed to deliver its promises of greater productivity, but also in even greater demands for democracy. This has mushroomed into literally hundreds of demonstrations in Moscow against Gorbachev's government, and into demands for secession that Gorbachev has used military force to halt.

Ironically, Gorbachev's "new thinking" has provided tolerance for the very ideas that threaten to undo him. Boris Yeltsin, president of the Russian Republic, has been steadily gathering public support at Gorbachev's expense. Yet Yeltsin also has his detractors; and were he to succeed Gorbachev, it is not at all clear that he would be any more successful in reshaping the Soviet Union. Still, Gorbachev has allowed his rival to challenge his power because in his mind, without a revolution in thinking, which to him means the entire process of modernization and democratization, the Soviet Union would degenerate still further along the lines it had followed for decades, until it was truly a "Third World country with nuclear weapons."

Gorbachev has been unstinting in his criticism of communism in the Soviet Union. An impoverished interpretation of Communist doctrine and inept execution of Communist policies has, in his view, led to stagnation, a corrupt and incompetent corps of bureaucrats, and the elimination of whatever idealism might have existed in earlier generations. Soviet youths are interested in drugs, rock and roll, and sex, not in building a new society. Older generations have seen one leader after another fail—and witnessed the political reprisals taken against those who carried out the policies of a leader later proven wrong. Gorbachev, in their view, might be just one more of those leaders. If they wait long enough, he will be replaced, and a new leader, with different ideas, will usurp his role. Yeltsin seems ripe for the role.

The working class, for whose interests the Communist revolution theoretically occurred, are apathetic, lack initiative, have little pride in what they produce or in the Soviet Union, and have had the work ethic undermined by cradle-to-grave paternalistic state policies. Unfortunately, the very incentives that the workers demand if they are to produce more cannot be given to them *until* they produce more. There simply are no incentives, in the form of high-quality consumer goods, to hand out. And unlike the Chinese and the peoples of Eastern Europe, who have lived under communism for some 40 years, the Soviet peoples—having lived under communism for more than 70 years—have little memory of capitalism and free markets. They seem to worry more that the government will no longer take care of their most basic needs *under a capitalist system* than that the government under communism will soon be unable to take care of them at all.

In this respect, the Bush administration has been conciliatory toward the Soviet Union: It is willing to take away many of the impediments to American trade in high technology goods with the Soviet Union, to encourage businessmen to engage in joint ventures with the Soviets, and even to consider giving the Soviets greater access to Western markets by permitting them to join GATT (General Agreement on Tariffs and Trade). Membership in GATT would mean that the high tariffs on Soviet imports would gradually be removed, thereby making Soviet goods more competitive. These plans are for the purpose of encouraging Gorbachev to continue his policies of liberalization at home and disengagement abroad. The United States has much to lose if Gorbachev and his policies fail.

The gravest problem embodied in the economic reforms promised by *perestroika* lies in the transition from a centralized "command economy" to a market economy, where the forces of supply and demand, not state bureaucrats, would determine prices, the allocation of resources, labor, and materials, and the distribution of goods. As Poland and China have both experienced, this transition is likely to be accompanied by nearly intolerable levels of inflation and unemployment, factors that themselves may be politically destabilizing. Further, the bureaucrats responsible for implementing these economic reforms are the very individuals who have the most to lose, for when the market takes over the allocation of resources and distribution of goods, the bureaucrats lose their control over them—the greatest source of their patronage (and corruption). Thus far, these economic reforms have failed to produce the intended results. Goods, including food, have become increasingly difficult to buy. In fact, the Soviet economy is in such steep decline that it is unable to bring home the 300,000 Soviet troops stationed in what was formerly East Germany—there simply are no jobs, housing, or food for them. The government has even been reduced to accepting gifts of food from foreign governments to help it feed its people.

Introducing political reforms that will democratize the Soviet Union is an important ingredient of Gorbachev's policies. In 1989, Gorbachev permitted unprecedented elections to the Congress of People's Deputies—and then allowed the whole country to watch on national television the live broadcast of this extraordinary congress, including speeches of all those who criticized Gorbachev and the Soviet Union Communist party (SUCP). In February 1990, Gorbachev announced that Article 6 of the Soviet Constitution, guaranteeing the Communist party a dominant leadership role, should be removed and that a multiparty system should be tolerated. Thereafter, the Communist party would only have as much power as it *earned* in free elections. This has now happened, but so far Yeltsin, as the major leader of the opposition, has been unable to muster enough support to challenge the leading role of the SUCP.

Another entrée on Gorbachev's menu of problems is the threat of secession by the fifteen republics within the multinational U.S.S.R. In December 1989, Lithuania became the first of the republics to abolish the SUCP's leading role and rewrote its constitution to allow for a multiparty system—a move denounced by Gorbachev. In the summer of 1990, Gorbachev responded with a boycott of goods to and from Lithuania, and later used force to contain efforts by secessionists to take over buildings controlled by the central governments of the U.S.S.R. Demands for greater autonomy from Lithuania, Azerbaijan—and even from

the Russian Republic itself—have furthered the pressures on Gorbachev to find an appropriate solution; if any republic succeeds in gaining greater autonomy, an avalanche of pressures from the other republics will follow. Serious nationality unrest in Moldavia, Transcaucasia, the Baltics, and Georgia, combined with labor strikes, create a sense that Moscow is no longer in charge.

Foreign policy is, however, Gorbachev's prize. It is he who has taken the lead in bringing about the disarmament of the two superpowers, beginning with his bold gesture in 1988 of unilaterally announcing the withdrawal of 50,000 troops and 500 tactical nuclear weapons from Eastern Europe, and the withdrawal of tens of thousands of troops from the Sino-Soviet border. He has also been willing to allow the verification measures necessary for the withdrawal by both NATO and the Warsaw Pact of intermediate-range nuclear missiles stationed in Europe, and to put relentless pressure on the United States to continue with both nuclear and conventional disarmament. And it is, of course, Gorbachev who lanced the boil of communism in Eastern Europe. Without his willingness to lend military support to the decaying Communist regimes of Eastern Europe, they were overthrown almost overnight. Only Gorbachev had the power to halt this process—and he chose not to use it. During the air war of the U.S.–led coalition forces against Iraq in early 1991, Gorbachev tried to find a diplomatic solution to the war that would prevent a land war. Although the United States accused him of meddling, Gorbachev at least tried to resolve the crisis. And, perhaps most important for the United States, he supported the United Nations resolutions to the very end.

Some would argue that the Soviet withdrawal from Afghanistan, from support of the Vietnamese-controlled puppet regime in Cambodia, and indeed, from support of Communist regimes throughout the world, as well as all of Gorbachev's seemingly generous gestures toward disarmament, merely reflect the disastrous economic situation in which the Soviet Union found itself. But if that is the case, they why did it not happen under the already disastrous economic situation of the preceding 20 years? Gorbachev as a leader must be given credit for his understanding of the failure of communism, for his willingness to take the political risks involved in introducing both political and economic reforms, for disengaging the Soviet Union from the

role of spreading communism throughout the world, and for his sensitivity to the demands of the various interest groups within the Soviet Union.

Is it likely that the Soviet Union would, were it to regain its economic strength, relaunch its aggressive pursuit of world power? The evidence suggests that it, like the democratic industrialized states of the West and Japan, will find it more in its interest to use economic, financial, and diplomatic tools to achieve its ends, that its national interest will become intertwined with the national interests of dozens of other states, and together they will function as an integrated whole. In short, the growing interdependency of all states means that their individual "national" interests are best served by greater integration into a larger community, not by military aggression. As Gorbachev proclaimed, a "Europe without enemies" is possible, and he has already contributed significantly to this end.

Looking Ahead: Challenge Questions

Why are the countries of Eastern Europe so concerned that the Soviet Union's efforts at democratization and economic restructuring succeed? What do these countries fear might happen if the Soviet Union fails to achieve these goals? How can you explain this extraordinary turn of events: that countries brutally oppressed by the Soviet Union since the late 1940s began to wish it well within weeks of the overthrow of their own Communist regimes?

What kinds of concerns does the Soviet Union have about a united Germany? Does it favor a neutral Germany over a Germany tied to NATO? Can the Soviet Union tolerate NATO troops in what was East Germany? What advantage does the Soviet Union see in acquiescing to the unification of Germany? What might it have lost if it had continued to oppose it?

What kinds of benefits does the Soviet Union hope to receive from its new relationship with the industrialized countries of the West and Japan? Why does it want to encourage this new relationship, rather than continuing to fear the West? Is the West likely to reward the Soviet Union for its steps toward political liberalization and the end of its dominance in Eastern Europe? What might halt the trend toward liberalization in the Soviet Union?

Crisis in the Soviet Union—the historical perspective

Dominic Lieven

When one stands back from the dramas now occurring almost daily in the Soviet Union and attempts to see the problems facing the Soviet government in broader historical perspective, optimism is difficult. The burden weighing down Mikhail Gorbachev seems beyond the capacity of the human frame to bear. Three basic tasks face him. He has to transform a political system rooted in fear and inertia into one based on consent. He also has to replace the oldest and most deeply rooted Stalinist economy on earth. Finally, he is presiding over the last of the great European empires on the eve of its own era of decolonisation. Singly, any of these tasks would tax the ability of any great statesman. Together, feeding off each other, they are formidable.

The attempt to move from despotism to democracy through a species of revolution from above is reminiscent of Spanish politics after Franco's death. The world rightly applauded the skill and courage of Adolfo Suarez and King Juan Carlos as they surmounted the considerable obstacles in their path. But Suarez and the King had a clear model before them from the start, namely multiparty liberal democracy. They personally had no ideological doubts about this goal, and nor did the bulk of the Spanish elite.

Gorbachev's case is different. Even now his commitment to multiparty democracy is equivocal, and what is true of him is even truer of most members of the Communist Party elite. Ideological doubts still matter greatly, for the Soviet Union is the founder and leader of the anti-capitalist and anti-parliamentary camp. Accepting multiparty democracy is a tremendous reversal of ideological nostrums, quite apart from the fact that to many Russian nationalists the wholesale borrowing of Western political models is offensive. It has, after all, always been one of the strengths of Soviet Communism that it upheld the idea of a 'separate path' for Russia distinct from European models, a concept very dear to both conservatives and many radicals in pre-revolutionary Russia.

Nor are Russian society or the Russian people as fertile a ground for liberal democracy as the Spain which Franco bequeathed to his successors. The distinction between Francoist authoritarianism and even the crumbling totalitarianism of Brezhnev is an important one. In Spain a civil society existed and merely awaited crowning with a political edifice. In Russia society was still struggling to regain even a degree of autonomy from the state. Moreover, Russian society had been much more isolated from the modern world than was the case in Spain. The very strong collectivist and egalitarian values of the pre-revolutionary village, strengthened by the revolution and Communist rule, not merely survived but had gone unchallenged for 70 years. Popular resentment of the allocation of wealth and status through the market was likely to be intense. The flexibility, hard work, insecurity and risk entailed in a capitalist economy would not be taken kindly.

At which point politics shades into economics and the problems of transforming the Stalinist economy loom before us. Because the Soviet Union is the world's oldest socialist society, both the institutions and the values underpinning the socialist economy are uniquely deeply rooted. In Poland or China, for instance, peasant farmers have always dominated agriculture. In all the former Soviet satellites capitalism existed in living memory. Not so in the Soviet Union, where most people's experience of private enterprise is confined to the Brezhnevite black market. The furtive, half-criminal entrepreneur, concerned only with quick profits, is the product of this species of capitalism, and he is often in evidence in the new cooperative sector. He is not the best advertisement for capitalism. There are huge technical problems involved in moving from a planned economy to a competitive market one. There are also severe social and political problems, sometimes reminiscent of the clash between capitalism and established aristocratic and religious values in early modern Europe.

On top of all this comes the question of decolonisation. To some extent it is right to say that the Soviet Union is *sui generis*, not merely a Russian variant on the general European imperial theme. A solid land mass, it is far easier to consolidate and defend than the maritime empires of the past. Russians even now are just over half the population, and Russia's human, natural and industrial resources are a firmer basis for empire than was the case with metropolitan England, France or the Netherlands. Socialist beliefs and values potentially provided a source of unity unparalleled in other colonial empires, where one nation ruled openly over others. It was even argued that the economic relations between Russia and the other republics were not based on exploitation and that this in itself was enough to deny the Soviet Union the title of Empire.

Some of these arguments are more convincing than others. It is important that the Soviet Union is a contiguous land mass, that it is militarily formidable, and that no neighbour is likely to be brave enough to provide bases for 'national liberation' movements operating on Soviet soil. Up to 1985 geopolitical realities were a big factor in generating acquiescence in Soviet power even among peoples who hated Moscow's rule. The inertia and fear bred of memories of Stalinist terror and contemporary experience of a still ruthless and all-pervading police state were also of vital importance. Despotism finds it much easier to govern Empire than does liberal democracy. Under Brezhnev overt nationalism seemed both futile and suicidal.

Ideology, however, was losing ground as the realities of the modern world exposed the inadequacies of Marxist-Leninist tenets and as the corrupt, hypocritical forms taken by Soviet life exposed the Kremlin's boasting as fraudulent. How could one take pride in belonging to an Empire so visibly in a mess and so quickly falling behind its major international rivals? How could one deny the reality of imperialism as Russian immigrants were encouraged to pour into the Baltic and as a disastrous cotton monoculture was imposed on Central Asia? To create a truly Soviet man, the regime needed to last for much more than seven decades. Russo-Soviet culture needed to be as superior to that of non-Russians as Rome's was to those of its tribal subjects. The Soviet Union needed to be totally cut off from the anti-imperial currents dominating the outside world. The regime itself needed to remain unbending rather than periodically tearing at its own entrails by denouncing first the two decades of Stalinist dictatorship and then the 18 years of Brezhnevism—in other words, the bulk of Soviet history.

Here, though, was the rub. The price of Empire was the denial to Russians of political and civil rights. With non-Russians less than half the population and divided into innumerable groups, the greatest threat to Empire was always likely to come from the Russians' own revolt against despotism. In its last years Tsarism had, after all, been weakened by national minorities' discontent, and the spread of revolution after March 1917 was quickened by nationalist movements: but the key to the Romanovs' overthrow was revolt on the streets of Russia. The same realities exist today. For Russians the price of liberty must be secession for those republics whose people do not consent to Moscow's rule.

The present nationalities crisis was not initially, however, set in motion by a Russian revolt but rather by a process of reform initiated from above which undermined inertia, removed fear and created institutions through which national discontent could be mobilised effectively. Perhaps if the Politburo had been more knowledgeable about non-Russians and their suppressed resentments, less the prisoner of the regime's own propaganda, it would have been more cautious about releasing the brakes and embarking on reform.

But the political elite had also been paying a price for despotism, albeit not so severe a one as that demanded of the bulk of the Russian population. The younger generation of *apparatchiki* were often better educated and more aware of the outside world than Brezhnev and his cronies. Mikhail Gorbachev's law degree from Moscow University and his famous trip around France with Raisa as *obkom* (Regional Committee) First Secretary symbolise this fact. It was difficult for anyone with intelligence, patriotism and self-esteem not to make damaging comparisons between foreign and Soviet reality and to suffer from them in his pride. The persistence, courage and honesty with which reform from above has been pursued since 1985 illustrates that by no means all members of the ruling elite are devoid of patriotism, intelligence or desire to improve Soviet life. Still more important, the semi-totalitarian despotism which was so politically effective was an economic disaster. Having struggled ever since the Great Reforms of the 1860s to draw level with the Western industrial revolution, Russia had finally almost caught up by the 1960s, only to find itself hopelessly ill-equipped to compete in the new world of the scientific-technical revolution. In the short term, superpower status was at risk since economic might was a vital component of international influence. In the longer run economic failure would undermine defence, the regime's legitimacy and domestic political stability.

The radical reform initiated from above in 1985 has unleashed a popular revolution from below which threatens the survival of the Communist Party, Gorbachev and even the Soviet Union itself. Few could have predicted this in 1985 and, certainly, very few Western political scientists did so. Political loyalties among Western Sovietologists played a part here. The Right would seldom have accepted that the Soviet political elite could produce a leader as radical or honest as Gorbachev. The Left would usually have denied that discontent ran so deep or that Soviet society contained such glaring faults and weaknesses. The publication by the Soviet government itself of facts and opinions previously proclaimed as Cold War propaganda has been a shock to some.

The strong pressures in Western universities to subsume Soviet studies under more general concepts of political science, though often useful, exacted a toll since these concepts are frequently, though unavowedly, linked to Anglo-American political instincts and experience. Armed with these conceptions Sovietologists often radically underestimated the role of fear and coercion in politics, something which Leonard Schapiro and Hugh Seton-Watson, members of a less 'scientific' and more commonsensical older generation with personal experience of fascist and wartime Europe, never did. Brought up on a Brezhnevite era of 'small deeds' and conditioned to the idea that Soviet society, having surmounted some supposedly universal 'crisis of modernisation', now required management rather than radical leadership, most political scientists were unprepared either for the power still inherent in the General Secretary's position or the spectacular effects of Gorbachev's policy of liberalisation. Knowledge of Russian history was often superficial and sometimes deliberately shunned, but the 30 years of Soviet politics since Stalin's death was an insecure basis on which to make generalisations about a still relatively lawless and unsystematic political regime or to understand the fault-lines that lay beneath the surface of Brezhnevite political stability.

Yet, to do the Western observer justice, it was hard to predict that a Soviet leader would embark on changes that must undermine the postwar European order, Communist Party rule in the Soviet Union and even his country's territorial integrity. Both Russian and Soviet history taught that radical reform in the Russian heartland would undermine political stability in the borderlands where the regime's legitimacy was weak. The 1863 Polish rebellion and the 1956 Hungarian revolution were witness to this fact. Once Gorbachev embarked on his domestic liberalisation, it was always likely that he would have to allow the Soviet satellites to float free. To do otherwise was to commit the Soviet Union to a hopeless long-term strategy of permanent subsidy and periodic military intervention to uphold illegitimate regimes and inefficient economies: it was also to doom a reformist leader's reputation at home and abroad and to stretch Soviet finances beyond endurance. But, save in the short run, it was always very probable that democratisation in Poland and Hungary would destabilise the rest of Eastern Europe, especially East Germany, a state which was not a nation and which shared a common history, language and culture with a much larger and more powerful neighbour which was Europe's most successful example of capitalism.

Domestically, too, there was reason to fear that reform could not be stopped halfway. Many years ago Alexander Solzhenitsyn wrote that if only people spoke the truth the Soviet regime would collapse. To those who took his words even half seriously, *glasnost*'s loosing of the intelligentsia was very risky, especially since the regime had so many skeletons in the cupboard and had frozen so many potential conflicts through repression. When democratisation, embodied in semi-free parliamentary elections, was added to *glasnost* in 1989–90 the floodgates really risked opening. Clearly in 1985 Gorbachev had not anticipated that political reform would go anywhere near this far. He had radicalised himself in order to stay abreast of democratic currents whose strength he had not suspected. But it was vastly to his credit that, as democratic challenges to the authorities strengthened, Gorbachev's commitment to a law-governed state grounded in consent grew. In 1987, and even in 1988, the option of violent repression of discontent existed, but it was resolutely shunned.

The main victims of Gorbachev's reform policies have been conservative party *apparatchiki*, and it remains surprising that their opposition to his moves has been so ineffectual. Not entirely ineffectual, of course: the failure to introduce radical agricultural reform before this year must surely be owed to party bureaucrats' traditionally very strong commitment to the collective farm. In part the conservatives' failure was due to their lack of credible alternatives to Gorbachev's policies. Brezhnevism was unacceptable because it represented economic failure and corruption, which the austere Yegor Ligachev detests quite as much as does Gorbachev. Stalinism is also not an option, not only because it is morally unacceptable and dangerous to the elite itself (e.g., members of Ligachev's own family were killed by Stalin) but also because it has no solutions to contemporary economic problems.

Conservative *apparatchiki* were, however, also the victims of a party political culture which stresses monolithic unity and loyalty to the leader. Though Khruschchev's overthrow shows that this loyalty is less than absolute, Gorbachev did not repeat his predecessor's error of antagonising the Party elite without creating an alternative base of power for himself. By mobilising popular support against the apparatus and institutionalising this support through the Supreme Soviet, of which he was the president, Gorbachev greatly reduced his vulnerability to Party opponents. If indeed the long-predicted split in the Party occurs, conservatives may in time turn out to be its major beneficiaries. At present conservative *apparatchiki* are deeply unpopular, partly because they are still held responsible for the failings of an economy over which, in fact, they have decreasing control. Should the Party split and the apparatus crumble, conservatives will be freer to criticise the President and the soviets for their failure to reverse economic decline, reduce crime and halt the Union's disintegration. The anti-capitalist, egalitarian and collectivist traditions of the Russian masses should provide conservatives with plentiful mass support should an alliance between Gorbachev and the radicals attempt radical free-market policies.

If the Party apparatus has failed to block Gorbachev's reforms, why have we not heard more from the KGB and the army? The failure of these two major institutions to hamper the process of democratisation suggests that the Party General Secretary and his supporters in the Politburo are much more powerful than was believed by scholars who, in the 1970s, made influential claims that Soviet politics revolved around the conflict of various institutional interest groups, between which the Politburo and its leader were said to be mere arbiters and brokers. In addition, however, it is clear that, up to now, Gorbachev has made a deal with elements in the KGB, whose inner life and institutional interests have been much less affected by the process of democratisation than is the case with the Party apparatus and the army. If Gorbachev's solicitude for the KGB is in part owed to power-political considerations, it may well also reflect his desire not to undermine the braking mechanism of the unwieldy caravan he is attempting to bring safely down a perilously steep and winding road.

The KGB's inability to stop the reform process is also, however, conditioned by weaknesses deliberately built into the security police by the Soviet leadership. Ever since the police purged and terrorised the Party at Stalin's command, the Politburo has been careful to keep the KGB to heel. Above all, the security police has no large-scale paramilitary units at its disposal, for fear that its chief, like Beria in 1953, might dream of using his private army to seize power. To repress serious disorders on the streets, let alone to envisage a coup d'état, the KGB would need the support of the army.

Since 1985 the army has suffered blows which would have brought the tanks on to the streets in many countries: unilateral strategic arms cuts; withdrawal from East-Central Europe; a lost war in Afghanistan; unwilling involvement in preserving order on Soviet streets; General Rodionov's disgrace after the Tbilisi massacre; the collapse of the army's prestige in Soviet society; major difficulties in enforcing conscription; large-scale cuts in the officer corps; a major housing crisis and severe material deprivation for many officers and NCOs.

Military quiescence may owe a little to the fact that no sane general would wish to govern the Soviet Union in present circumstances. Moreover, though the 110,000 paratroops, marines and *Spetsnaz* (special commandos), in alliance with a KGB operation to 'take out' opposition leaders, could hold the streets of major Soviet cities for a time, it would not be long before uncontrollable violence erupted. The army's NCOs are mostly conscripts, while 38 per cent of its soldiers in 1988 were drawn from the Trans-Caucasus and Central Asia. Discipline is becoming a major problem, with 250,000 weapons 'lost' in 1989 alone. In all likelihood, a military-police coup would lead speedily to the breakup of both army and country.

Above all, however, the army has not intervened because of its traditional desire to distance itself from politics. The last successful military coup d'état in Russia was Peter Pahlen's overthrow of Paul I in 1801. In its present form the army dates from the 1860s and 1870s, when professionalisation transformed the old noble officer corps into a body of military experts resentful of civilian interference but anxious not to be involved in domestic politics. Since then the graduates of the General Staff Academy who dominate the army have always remained experts in very narrow military specialisations. They are strongly motivated by Russian patriotic values, but extremely naive and ignorant about anything political. Only in the event of the collapse of political authority in Russia and the disintegration of the Union is it likely that generals could be prevailed upon to take on the burdens of political responsibility. For their rule to be effective, however, they would have to delay their move until disintegration had created a powerful mood for order, authority and nationalism in the Russian masses.

For the present, the Soviet crisis must be mastered by political means. In both economy and government most problems stem from the fact that this is an era of transition in which traditional institutions and mechanisms are collapsing before new ones are in a position to replace them. The disciplines of the command economy have not yet, for instance, been replaced by those of a competitive market. Enterprises are, therefore, often able to charge monopoly prices for their produce and then dole out inflationary wage settlements to their workers as sweeteners. Since industrial prices are rising more quickly than state procurement prices for food, a scissors crisis reminiscent of the autumn of 1916 is in the offing. Radical policies to free prices would send the cost of food, transport and accommodation soaring, risking revolution on the streets. The desire of the Prime Minister, Nikolai Ryzhkov, to use the remaining levers of the command-administrative system temporarily to control production, distribution and prices is not totally without merit. But the institutions he is using today know that tomorrow they face abolition. The temptation to go slow or to sabotage reform policies is compelling.

The crumbling of the Communist Party apparatus is destroying the institution which, ever since the demise of Stalin, has formulated policy and acted as coordinator, supervisor and energiser of all the other bureaucracies through which Soviet life has been governed. A huge gap is opening up which a powerful executive presidency can only partly fill. The new legislatures cannot run day-to-day government business, lack experience, and contain neither the government placemen nor the Party discipline which gave structure to British parliaments in the pre- and post-1832 eras respectively. At the republican and regional levels the decline of the Party apparatus means power must devolve *faute de mieux* on the ministerial bureaucracy, whose cumbersome, ill-coordinated inefficiency is notorious. Time is required for a reordering of institutions and relationships, but confusion in government at a moment of mounting socio-economic crisis is alarming.

The worst immediate threat to the government comes from the spiralling down of the mechanism for the exchange and distribution of goods. Years of under-investment, combined with slackening labour discipline and the strikes and blockades in the Caucasus, are causing havoc on the railways. Production of raw materials and energy is beginning to decline, as is their transport, and factories are threatened with short-time working. As local democracy grows, power stations and polluting factories are closed down with effects which ripple through the economy. Pressures towards regional economic autarchy grow, with Leningrad only the best-known example of a city banning outsiders from its shops. Left unchecked, this process threatens the breakdown of the economy and the radicalisation of public opinion to the point where the country becomes ungovernable.

Pressures towards economic autarchy are greatly increased by the nationalities question. Even the most conservative republican leaderships are determined to wrest far greater control over local economic affairs from Moscow. It is, however, on the political rather than the economic front that the rise of nationalism causes the greatest worry. 60m people, more than one fifth of the total Soviet population, live outside their ethnic homeland, and if the Empire should actually disintegrate the potential for violent conflict is immense. Virtually every republic contains significant minorities, many of them burning with as strong a resentment of the local 'master race' as the latter feels towards Moscow. Almost all republican boundaries are potentially disputable.

Even in the Baltic republics, where nationalist movements are directed by the coolest heads, Lithuanians are disinclined to allow meaningful autonomy to their indigenous Polish minority. Very many Estonians would quite literally rather die than see Narva, with its immigrant Slav majority, ceded to Russia in the event of secession. If Latvia became independent, what would become of the large Russian majority in its capital, Riga? Yet if the process of dissolution becomes general, the Baltic's problems will seem small indeed. Already anarchy looms in Central Asia, where poverty and disease are creating a mood of despairing xenophobia, which was reflected in pogroms against a number of non-indigenous communities, Russians included, over the past nine months. Yet Central Asian Moslems are far from united, the biggest potential conflict in the area at present probably being between Uzbeks and Tajiks for possession of the ancient cities of Samarkand and Bokhara. Even this will seem small beer, however, should the rise of Ukrainian secessionism spark off a conflict

about the fate of the 11m Russians in the Eastern Ukraine. Ultimately out of disintegration there would emerge a Russian rump state which would annex Russian enclaves such as Narva, Northern Kazakhstan and the Eastern Ukraine, but the murderous and lasting instability which would follow the Soviet Union's collapse might well put even the results of British India's partition in the shade.

Are such gloomy scenarios bound to occur? Certainly not. Gorbachev has shown extreme skill in manoeuvring around difficulties, and in his new position as President he can be a source of stability amidst the agonising problems of an era of transition. The July 1990 Party Congress should transform the local party leadership, allowing for a *modus vivendi* with the local Soviets which can guarantee an orderly transfer of power from Party to state institutions. Should the Communist Party of the Soviet Union (CPSU) split, the radical rump would form the core of a reformist party incorporating democratic forces in the soviets. These in turn might provide the basis for a government sufficiently legitimate to introduce painful economic measures. The March 1990 legislation on property and individual enterprise offers a framework for an advance towards a market economy. So long as the present spiralling downwards of the economy can be halted, the possibility of an economic and political upturn in the mid-1990s is real. One can take comfort from the poor showing of the racist right in the March 1990 Russian elections and hope that the Soviet Union's appalling history of violence in this century will remain a powerful disincentive to taking political conflict to extremes.

Even the nationalities problem is not hopeless. Secession seldom makes economic sense, and its potential political costs are evident to many. At present, outright secessionism probably only commands a majority in the Baltic, Azerbaijan and Georgia. Equally, intelligent Russians understand that holding non-Russian republics within the Soviet Union against their will is in no one's interests. So long as time can be bought and nationalist, economic and institutional crises do not combine to make the Soviet Union ungovernable in the near future, then it is possible to look to partial solutions even for the nationalities problems.

Relations between the republics and Moscow must be treaty-based and differ from region to region. The Baltic must be allowed to float towards an independence covered by links no stronger than those binding the British Commonwealth. An 'historic compromise' with Kiev and Minsk must be concluded rather on the lines of that achieved between Vienna and Budapest in 1867: a common free trade zone and defence arrangements must be combined with maximum autonomy in all other matters. For the moment Russian rule must be maintained in Central Asia, for the alternative is utter chaos. In time, however, the Russians must seek to remove themselves from an area which will otherwise demand from them massive subsidies and peace-keeping forces, and whose huge, alien Moslem population will decisively influence the outcome of any genuinely democratic all-Union election by the year 2000.

All this is possible, and it is certainly in the interests of Russians, non-Russians and the rest of the world that the present Soviet crisis be surmounted peacefully and that a stable, prosperous regime in both politics and economics should emerge in this huge area of the world. Yet major doubts and fears are impossible to dispel. Let us hope that this is merely because the terrible events of this century are casting an unnecessarily gloomy shadow forwards, in the process distorting my true appreciation of contemporary prospects. If so, then it is perhaps the product of an historian's professional failing: his inability to forget the past.

The New World Disorder?

The Collapse of Eastern Europe: Moscow's View

Valentin Falin, Régis Debray, Abolhassan Bani-Sadr, Vytautas Landsbergis, Octavio Paz, Li Xianglu

Valentin Falin   *The head of the powerful International Department of the Soviet Communist Party, Valentin Falin is also a former ambassador to West Germany.*

In the following excerpts from a rare conversation with NPQ Editor Nathan Gardels at the International Department Central Committee offices – once the headquarters of world communism – Falin reviews the final collapse of communism in Eastern Europe and registers the strong Soviet opposition to NATO membership for a united Germany.

We were as surprised at the pace of what happened in Eastern Europe as the rest of the world was. The difference was that much of the rest of the world did not believe we were serious about the right of each nation to choose its own course. You heard our words, but in the depth of your mind you did not believe us.

Nonetheless, from the very beginning of "new thinking," we swore to ourselves that the right of national self-determination was not a declaration of words but a principle of practical policy. We were convinced that it could be no other way.

Despite Panama, we were determined not to step into Eastern Europe to prop up falling regimes. We are determined not to be pushed off this track, this principle.

We never made it a secret to anybody in the East German leadership that, whatever the developments, our forces were not stationed in the GDR to be a judge in domestic developments. They were there to fulfill a security mission for the Warsaw Pact.

Party As Victim | In Eastern Europe, the Communist Parties fell as a consequence of the emo-

tional reaction of the people against regimes of personal rule by the likes of Honecker and Ceausescu. But, to be historically correct, the Party itself was the first victim of personal rule in Eastern Europe.

Before these men could commit evil against the people, they had to commit it within the ranks of the Party. They deprived Party members of the right to speak, and of freedom of choice, turning them into instruments of their personal rule.

The main source of resistance to Ceausescu was from within the Party – Silviu Brucan, Ion Iliescu, Cornelio Minescu and others. In fact, Minescu had to refuse the position of chair of the National Council of Salvation because of health problems. Last spring, when he took a stand against the government over a bread riot in Brasov, he was beaten by Securitate thugs sent by Ceausescu.

On Humane, Democratic Socialism | The Communist Party can still play an important role in Eastern Europe. The idea, the social dream of communism, cannot be killed; it is the most fruitful idea of the 20th century.

The October Revolution took place in the Soviet Union, but the convictions from which it sprang took hold and transformed the whole world. The very term "social justice" was born with the October Revolution; anti-colonialism was born with the October Revolution.

Indeed, much of the social welfare state in the West developed in the historical context of a socialist alternative.

Social democracy and socialism do not exclude each other; they are different sides of the same crystal. However, social democracy permits exploitation of man by man. We are for democratic socialism, which presumes that each individual is born equal and thus must live equally, not subjugated by others. We believe in

From *NPQ*, New Perspective Quarterly, Vol. 7, No. 2, Spring 1990, pp. 22-26. Copyright © 1990 by the Center for the Study of Democratic Institutions.

equality, irrespective of talents and personal labor. One's life should not result from being born as a prince or as a beggar. No one should live off the social surplus unless he is engaged in the process of producing wealth.

We don't believe in equality and social justice in the formal sense alone, where every four years citizens are invited to the ballot box and otherwise just stand aside and watch.

Democratic socialism is an unceasing process of the popular participation of citizens through correspondent democratic institutions – in economic, social, and political life, including democracy in the work place.

The point now is not to create something like a 5th International, that is, a new communist international organization. What is central is that the common human interest be given priority over class and Party interests. The Party is an instrument to achieve consensus, not an end of power in itself.

World socialism is still an objective, as a solution to fundamental problems, but we can no longer impose our views. There simply is no other choice.

World socialism as a common approach must pass through many stages, and there will be differences before we can arrive at a higher stage of mutual action.

On East Germany | We did not hide it from Honecker, or anyone else, that changes were necessary. In 1989 alone, both in Moscow and Berlin, we put it to Honecker four times straight on the table: If the Party doesn't take the initiative, changes will go on in an organic way and you will be left out in the cold.

We told him that the GDR has more room to maneuver than the other Eastern European countries because of its relatively advantageous economic situation. But he didn't listen. He had been separated from reality and had failed to comprehend the world around him; he was so lost that neither our words nor those of Egon Krenz penetrated his consciousness. It caused alienation and bitterness between us.

After the 40th Jubilee Anniversary of East Germany's foundation as a state, Honecker was planning to remove Krenz from the Politburo in Berlin and send him to Leipzig. He had disagreed too often with Honecker.

Krenz's domestic fights with Honecker and

with the leadership circle were not a matter of knowledge to the Party. And, of course, they were not a matter of knowledge to the public. This knowledge was held only in a very narrow circle of people.

Krenz insisted that force and violence should not be used against demonstrators in Leipzig and other cities. Honecker insisted on using violence, though in the end, he was forced by events to support Krenz.

When the leadership was renovated, in a campaign for the replacement of the old Party officials in October of last year, Krenz was the engine. This fact was also known to few people.

On the Wall | Both Gorbachev and Yakovlev made it clear to East Germany's leaders that they did not consider the Berlin Wall "a pleasant decoration of the city" but a tragic tribute to times, now past, of fierce confrontation.

When I said in West Berlin early last year that it is not necessary to break the Wall, just make it easier to penetrate, Honecker fumed. When I said further that the Four Power Agreement was not the last word, Honecker called me "Mr." Falin instead of the usual "Comrade."

On Romania | Because Ceausescu was critical of the Soviet Union, hardly anybody in the West was critical of him. They just looked the other way. Our relations with him were worse than cool; although we maintained formalities, we didn't speak in any real terms.

We therefore expected that his end would come differently than that of other Party leaders in Eastern Europe. We knew there would be victims; we knew that a coup was inevitable because the regime was not only rotten but intransigent.

Even so, we did not foresee the extent of the bloody bacchanalia that finally came to pass.

When key critics of the regime, like Silviu Brucan, came to Moscow in November, we were asked to appreciate the fact that Romania had no other way out. We therefore watched the developments within the armed forces of Romania, and the growth of resistance to the regime from November through the end of the year, very closely.

On German Reunification | With respect to Germany, the very term "reunification" is doomed. It is burdened historically. There is one truth, which is very bitter for the Germans: The

2. THE SOVIET UNION

Second World War was initiated by Hitler under the slogan "unification of all the Germans" – including those that lived in Poland, the Soviet Union and elsewhere in Europe.

When we speak of the "German Question" today, however, what is at issue is not the matter of a unified state. We mean only one thing: There can never again be a situation where the threat of a new war emerges from German soil.

The Soviet Union was always opposed to splitting up Germany. At the time of Potsdam, we spoke of a demilitarized, de-Nazified and democratized Germany.

It was US President Harry Truman and his aides who pushed for the division of Germany. They very much wanted to turn the western

---

"It Is Wrong To Prod Us On."

The arduous and contradictory process underway in Eastern Europe was not just spontaneous; it was precipitated, above all, by the example—though not the export—of Soviet perestroika.

The Soviet Communists launched perestroika quite consciously. And, in the course of the process, our Party has been moving away voluntarily and deliberately from any formal claim to monopoly role.

Some say we are now lagging behind our fast-moving European neighbors. But would it not be reckless folly in so gigantic and contradictory a country as the Soviet Union to make the passage to a new order at one go? The Communist Party of the Soviet Union has been able to maintain a broad public consensus over decades. Previously, in the totalitarian climate, this consensus seemed to rest exclusively on suppression, fear, and the power of the state.

Today, everything appears to be far more complex. Conservatism is much more deeply rooted in the public consciousness than we thought. At the same time, centrifugal tendencies have grown stronger, with political pluralism asserting itself increasingly through, among other things, the emergence of various new movements, some of which have all the trappings of political parties.

In this setting, the CPSU is, for the majority of our society, an essential factor ensuring broad consensus on the transition toward democratic and humane socialism. The Party has been working out these concepts on its own initiative, and is maintaining a dialogue with a variety of currents. At the present stage, the CPSU is the only party that has enough potential to ensure the least painful passage from totalitarianism to rule of law and an open society.

The people who are in the party today have a wide range of views—from Nina Andrayeva [the Leningrad teacher who symbolizes the conservative viewpoint] to Yuri Afanasyev [the liberal historian], with a highly diverse spectrum of opinions in between.

Why is this? Is it because of inertia, a lack of multiparty experience, or because of a low level of political culture? These are all partial causes. But there is another, more weighty reason: Responsible politicians are aware that the redistribution and shifting of power must not destabilize the country. It is no abstract issue whether the Soviet Union remains a world power or shrinks, as some predict (and probably also wish), to the size of the Principality of Moscovy. That is not just an internal or regional problem. The danger of destabilizing a country that has 30,000 nuclear warheads and other weaponry is a global problem: The pace of change in the Soviet Union must also be viewed from the angle of its international responsibilities. It is wrong to prod us on.

Already, the most audacious forecasts have fallen short of the actual Soviet political reconstruction that has been achieved in the past year. And the present processes are continuing at a fairly rapid clip. But it is essential that the new power structures have time enough to take root before the old ones are torn down.

So far, this exceedingly difficult process is being controlled by the CPSU, which is doing its utmost to prevent the country from galloping past the stage of democracy into anarchy and chaos. That danger has obviously increased due to sharpening contradictions between the nationalities within the USSR. It is common knowledge that when a vacuum of power appears, it is instantly filled by extremists. This is hardly in the interests of the West, irrespective of the type of extremism that seizes power—neo-Stalinism or left radicalism.

Alexander Lebedev
Deputy Head of the Ideology Department,
Communist Party of the Soviet Union

portion of the country into a front-line bastion in the struggle against communism.

For us, a unified, but neutral Germany has never been a problem. Taking into account the reality of the existence of one German nation, we have never withdrawn the proposal for a neutral Germany, which dates to the 1950s. The problem has been with the West, which still does not find it acceptable.

Since the US will not permit the whole of Germany to be part of the Warsaw Pact, or to be neutral, it is difficult to speak about the reunification of Germany in any form – as a commonwealth, a community of treaties, as a special relationship or as an independent state.

The US insists that all of Germany should be a part of NATO. That is unacceptable to us. Moreover, Germany's alignment is not a matter that can be resolved by a vote of the German people, for there exists circumstances that are stronger than mutual national gravity. Resolution of this question must be a matter of international agreement. No one has cancelled the postwar agreements and the settled arrangement of forces in Europe. If the West sticks with the demand for NATO membership of all of Germany, then reunification will not be possible.

We have long held the position that the principle of German self-determination can be implemented only after a new postwar order has been achieved. Yet, 45 years after the end of the war, there still has been no peace treaty which defines this order.

Aside from belonging to two separate military pacts, the two Germanys also have very different economic structures. West Germany has a common market with Western Europe, but East Germany can't survive without the Soviet supply of raw materials. All the oil and the gas of East Germany, for example, comes from the Soviet Union. For such reasons, I find it hard to imagine how one can put together two things that cannot be put together in a narrow, national framework. Whatever pace change takes, German unity must only come after a greater integration of European stuctures as a whole.

Many in the West have argued that Soviet interests would be better served by a Germany contained by membership in the NATO Pact, and thus not free to act in a dangerous way unilaterally. I would put the argument differently.

Are the NATO countries in favor of the creation of a common European home where there would be common security – both military and ecological? Do they favor a common Europe where the dominant principle would be "good neighborhood" and nonconfrontation?

Do they want, as we do, the closest economic cooperation with no discrimination against anyone, where each nation will have its national apartment with windows facing the sunny side?

This common European home made up of a community of equals will be a complicated construction. But it is possible.

The possibility of a new home, however, rests on the assumption that the sound of the guns of war in Europe must not be heard again. In the end, the only real question is whether the NATO countries share this vision.

On USSR-China Relations | I was in China at the end of December, just after US NSC Advisor General Brent Scowcroft. Although there have been reports in some Chinese papers, attacking the USSR as "revisionist," I heard nothing of this from the Chinese leadership. They did not indicate to me that we had any difficulties now that we did not have last summer.

My impression from that trip is that, given the differing specific features of our two parties – due to national, historic and other circumstances – we have a good and solid basis for mutual understanding and cooperation.

There are no grounds for pessimism about the prospects of Chinese-USSR relations.

On Cuba and Fidel | With perestroika, many people wonder about our Party's relations with Cuba. Lets look at the map. For 30 years, Fidel Castro has lived under the conditions of economic blockade and of persistent animosity on the part of his northern neighbor.

When we understand this, we can understand Fidel much better. His emotions and his attitudes may be difficult to grasp from the luxury of an armchair in Moscow or Washington.

It is not with our own scales that we should judge the things that bother our Cuban comrades. As a matter of fact, the most unproductive part of our conversation at Malta with the US was on the Cuban trade embargo and Nicaragua.

I can attest that this was not through fault of the Soviet side, but resulted from the dogmatic, fixed positions of the US Administration.

BRZEZINSKI ON THE BREAKUP OF THE USSR

US policy should radically change, says a top former presidential adviser.
Washington should help the Soviet republics become independent nations,
and that will aid democracy, Yeltsin's Russia — and even Gorbachev.

Zbigniew Brzezinski

Zbigniew Brzezinski, National Security Adviser to President
Carter, foretold the collapse of communism in his most recent
book, "The Grand Failure: The Birth and Death of Commu-
nism in the 20th Century." He is professor of American
foreign policy at the Paul Nitze School of Advanced Interna-
tional Studies, Johns Hopkins University, and counselor at
the Center for Strategic and International Studies.

American policy toward the Soviet Union must adjust to a fundamentally important fact: The Soviet Union is ceasing to exist.

Even Mikhail Gorbachev concedes as much. As he put it recently, when addressing a gathering of Soviet Army officers in Odessa in mid-August, "The acute tension in relations between nationalities and the fate of our Union are of no less concern to all of us today than the economy. Indeed, the Soviet Union, in the form in which it has existed to date, has exhausted its possibilities. . . ."

The point of departure, therefore, for an American policy that promotes the democratic transformation of what today is still the Soviet Union must be the recognition of the centrality of the "national issue"—owing to the fact that half the Soviet population is not Russian but of other nationalities. The simple truth is that the national problem is the most difficult and potentially the most explosive issue that the Soviet Union confronts.

But one thing is clear already: The existing Soviet Union is doomed. Moreover, it will not be replaced with Gorbachev's favorite formula: a Union of Sovereign Socialist States. That formula seeks to diffuse, by reinterpreting the word "sovereign," the national aspirations of the non-Russians while retaining the "Union." It is therefore a formula increasingly repugnant to democratic Russians and non-Russians alike. To the former, it still condemns them to playing the imperial role that the democratic Russians increasingly recognize as the main impediment to their own freedom, and to the latter it is a camouflaged version of the noxious past.

That the national issue has grown to crisis proportions emerges with considerable force from even a casual reading of the Soviet press. For example, published reports on the annual conscription of young people for military service indicate that in Latvia only 54% showed up; in Estonia, only 40%; in Lithuania, only 33%; in Georgia, only 27%; and in Armenia, only 7%. Service in the Soviet Army is being viewed by the non-Russians as a colonialist obligation to be avoided.

Other recent press reports reflect the growing scale of nationally motivated violence in the different parts of the Soviet Union. In fact, regular fighting of a guerrilla type has been ongoing for some months in the Caucasus and in Central Asia. Numerous reports have spoken of sophisticated arms used in sustained guerrilla skirmishing and in outbursts of massive communal violence. Even such weapons as tanks, armored personnel carriers, and helicopters equipped with machine guns—either bought or seized by force—have been employed in combat.

Not surprisingly, casualties in some cases have been high. By mid-1990, probably several thousand people had perished in the course of escalating bloodshed. In just the Kirghiz town of Osh, for example, several hundred were killed in ethnic violence during last July. Earlier in the summer, the capital of Tadzhikistan, Dushambe, was for a while "liberated" from Soviet control by a nationalist uprising—until it was crushed by the Soviet Army. In many parts of the Soviet Union, martial law has had to be imposed, and the Soviet press reports that nationally motivated violence has already produced more than 600,000 homeless refugees.

Some of the communal violence has been extraordinarily brutal. Literaturnaya Gazeta reported in early August this year that victims in the violence in Osh had their "throats slashed and their blood drained (as they do when they slaughter sheep) . . . people killed and then burned to cinders; . . . noses and ears cut off and eyes plucked out; . . . a human head on a pole . . . a dozen horsemen, having tied up a beekeeper with iron wire, dragged him behind their horses and then finished him off . . .," etc. The article went on to say that as of the latest count 214 were officially listed as dead, but as many as 80 burial places had not yet been investigated, though it was evident that large numbers of bodies had been quickly interred.

Potentially even more lethal for the future of the Soviet Union is the growing sense of national self-assertiveness among the seemingly rather Russified Slavic republics of Byelorussia and the Ukraine. The Ukrainian Supreme Soviet earlier this summer passed a declaration of sovereignty,

From *World Monitor*, November 1990, pp. 30-33. Copyright © 1990 by Zbigniew Brzezinski. Reprinted by permission.

including a statement of Ukrainians' determination to create their own independent armed forces and to become "a permanently neutral state which is not a member of military blocs and adheres to three principles: not to produce, not to spread, and not to use nuclear weapons." The Byelorussian Supreme Soviet passed a similar resolution, and in addition it has called upon Byelorussians serving in the Soviet armed forces in Central Asia and the Caucasus to refuse to be involved in any Soviet military operations against non-Russian nationalist movements and to come home.

It is thus unlikely that there is much future for Alexander Solzhenitsyn's formula: a grand Slavic state uniting Russia, the Ukraine, and Byelorussia. Nationalism has become too contagious and is sweeping particularly the 50-million-strong Ukraine like wildfire. The western parts of the country—from Lvov to Kiev—are effectively in the hands of the nationalists, with traditional national flags displayed everywhere and with monuments to Lenin tumbling down. The eastern part is more Russified, but a Ukrainian leader scored a telling point when he said to me recently:

"You in the West have simply not grasped how intense the Ukrainian nationalist awakening has become. The fact that the eastern Ukrainians speak Russian is of no relevance. What language do the anti-English IRA members speak?!"

The declarations of independence by Lithuania, Latvia, Estonia, Georgia, and Armenia are but the beginning. It is only a matter of months before the other "Soviet" republics duplicate the process, thereby rejecting both the central domination of Moscow and its Leninist legacy. In Central Asia, the 50 million Muslims are increasingly asserting both their faith and their desire for an independent "Turkestan." Gorbachev's belated efforts to create a new constitutional framework are in fact accelerating the process.

But what will follow—and how the West should respond—is an immensely complex issue. One has to recognize, first of all, that this disintegrating empire embraces an international mosaic of more than 290 million people, 145 million of whom are not Russians and who are themselves at different levels of historical development and at different stages of national consciousness. Moreover, 65 million of the overall total live outside their ethnic homes. The potential for massive violence and grand chaos cannot be overestimated.

At the very minimum, this means that the United States should not become wedded to a single formula in defining its hopes for the Soviet future. Nor is it appropriate to seek to devise from the outside a prescription for solving the Soviet Union's national dilemmas. One has to recognize that this is a problem that the people who live in what is today called the Soviet Union will confront for many years to come. The solution will have to come from within, from them above all.

This much, however, is now clear: An imperial Russia—that is, the Russia inhabited by the 145 million ethnic Russians—cannot be a democratic Russia, and a democratic Russia will not be an imperial Russia. Moreover, an imperial Russia is bound to be a poor Russia because of the costs of maintaining a centralized empire. Thus for the Russians the choice is between autocracy and poverty on the one hand,

and democracy as well as perhaps prosperity on the other. It is no longer possible for the politically alert Russians to escape the fact that an imperial Russia would have to rule by force the politically awakened and now nationally self-conscious 145 million non-Russians. Coercion has its moral, economic, and political costs—and the Russians are becoming increasingly aware that they have had to pay an exorbitant price for having been an imperial nation.

No wonder then that more and more Russians, with Boris Yeltsin, president of the Russian Republic, leading the way, are beginning to state that the end of the Russian empire is the beginning of their own liberation. This represents a shift of truly historic dimensions in the Russian world outlook. It has profound implications for the outside world as well.

In effect, the West has to recognize that the processes of the democratization of Russia and of self-determination within the disintegrating Soviet Union are organically connected. This means that for the West to ignore the goal of self-determination for the non-Russian nations, just for the sake of maintaining relations with Moscow, is bound to conflict eventually even with the goal of Russia's own democratization. It follows, finally, that as a general principle US policy toward the Soviet Union must hence be committed to the goal of democratic self-determination.

These two words are linked very deliberately: "democratic self-determination." Not just self-determination at any cost by any ethnic group that seeks it, but a democratic self-determination. There are movements for self-determination in the Soviet Union which are extremist, which are intolerant, which are anti-Semitic, which are anti-democratic. They do not deserve our sympathy. But by and large, these are extreme and relatively isolated phenomena, and the more important aspect is that the movement toward self-determination in the Soviet Union tends to be related to the movement for the democratization of the Soviet Union.

In any case, the only alternative to democratic self-determination within the Soviet Union is some form of coercive maintenance of the existing imperial structure. In the context of fading Communist ideology, the emotional source for an attempt to preserve a coercive empire would have to be Great Russian chauvinism. This would mean an intensification of national conflicts with the non-Russians and the emergence of a chauvinistically intolerant, non-democratic Russia as the successor to Communist Russia. The consequence in effect would be two negative developments at the same time: the intensification of national conflicts, and the triumph of a nondemocratic Russian nationalism.

This is why American policy toward the Soviet Union henceforth has to operate on two levels. The US should continue to support Gorbachev to the extent that that is feasible and practicable. But the United States should not focus on Gorbachev exclusively. It should match support for Gorbachev's ambivalent top-down democratization of the Soviet Union with genuine and explicit support for the spontaneous and in many cases nationally motivated bottom-up democratization of the Soviet Union.

2. THE SOVIET UNION

Support for democratic self-determination is even essential in order to help Gorbachev himself. Gorbachev's proclaimed goal is the democratization of the Soviet Union. If that goal is serious and sincere, it has to mean the pluralization of the Soviet system. In turn, true pluralism has to entail authentic self-expression for those who seek self-determination on a national basis. Therefore, there is no conflict between sympathy for Gorbachev and support for those who express the yearning for democratic self-determination.

In brief, the United States should not favor exclusively Gorbachev's attempt at a guided democracy, but instead it should support genuine democracy. "Guided democracy" is democratization from the top down under controlled circumstances. Previous examples of guided democracy, such as Sukarno's Indonesia, have not proven to be very democratic. True democratization has to involve not only initiatives from the top down, but also spontaneous democratic aspirations from below. In a multinational system such as the Soviet one, it has to mean support of self-determination of democratic national movements.

What would a policy of support for democratic self-determination actually entail?

■ First, it would mean not only dealing directly with Gorbachev and supporting him, which he deserves because he has played a historically significant role in opening up the Soviet Union to change, but it also means helping in a variety of ways the mayors of the new democratic majorities in some key Soviet cities. Moscow, Leningrad, Lvov, Tallinn, Vilnius, Tbilisi, Yerevan, and others immediately come to mind. Americans have opportunities for city-to-city contacts. There are also opportunities for engaging in business opportunities on the urban level. That would help to institutionalize forces for pluralism from below.

■ Second, it means expanding relations, to the extent that that is practicable, with those Soviet republics that are themselves engaging in internal democratization on the republican level.

For example, Boris Yeltsin opposed Gorbachev's efforts to subdue the Lithuanians through an economic blockade. Moreover, he has embarked on a more ambitious and a more urgent democratization program than Gorbachev has dared to adopt. Under Yeltsin's leadership, the Russian people, who are enormously gifted and talented and who have suffered very much under Stalinism, are beginning to realize, perhaps for the first time in their long and difficult history, that having an empire is not a blessing but a curse.

As a result, to the extent feasible, the United States should deal with Yeltsin. The US should try to facilitate his reform program, and engage increasingly in direct and cooperative relationships with his government. He should be treated publicly in a manner that enhances his standing and buttresses him politically.

■ Third, the US should also expand relations with those Soviet republics that are in the process of quietly asserting their independence. This can be done through frequent consular visits and congressional delegations, and by encouraging American private business to channel its investments directly to such republics.

To the extent that it is possible, the US should therefore try to channel economic assistance and technical advice to the national republics, and particularly toward those republics that are willing to move more rapidly toward a market economy. It is important to note in this connection that the rejection of Moscow's control goes hand in hand with efforts to establish market economies on the local level, and clearly the encouragement of that process is in keeping with the goal of democratic pluralism. In fact, given the chaos that prevails today in Moscow, stable economic relations are more likely to be developed on the republic level than by negotiations with the disintegrating central bureaucracy. For American business, it is particularly noteworthy that a market economy is more likely to flourish at the national—the republic—level among the non-Russians than at the central level, because the Russians are culturally conditioned against free enterprise.

■ Fourth, Washington should directly provide tangible support and moral encouragement to those political movements in the disintegrating Soviet Union that are clearly democratic in character and that seek self-determination. The US has instrumentalities, such as Radio Free Europe/Radio Liberty and the National Endowment for Democracy, which have an excellent record in helping democratic movements in Eastern Europe. Activities designed to strengthen democratic movements for self-determination within the Soviet Union should therefore be expanded and more generously funded. Publicly, the US should state boldly its commitment to self-determination as an integral part of its commitment to human rights and indicate the US readiness to deal on a practical level with the self-emancipating republics.

It must be stressed that such a US policy would not be anti-Russian but anti-imperial. The US position should be that America favors democratic self-determination for all the nations of the Soviet Union. It is up to the peoples themselves to determine what kind of relationships they will wish to have in the future with each other and with Moscow.

In some cases, that may mean secession. But even if secession were to take place, it would not need to entail in every case the rupture of old relationships. One could envisage some current Soviet republics seceding and yet, even after secession, developing security and economic links with what remains of the existing Soviet Union.

The US should even *encourage* such cooperation because it would militate against ethnic violence. A loose economic confederation and perhaps a consultative league embracing some of the ex-Soviet states could eventually emerge in place of the existing Soviet Union.

In any case, we cannot currently predict the eventual outcome of the ongoing but inevitable dismantling of the Soviet Union. Nor is it proper for Washington to postulate any specific solution. But it is necessary for the US to support democratic self-determination within the Soviet Union as the central means of helping to transform the Soviet Union into a pluralistic and democratic society.

Russia vs. the Soviet Union

By declaring its independence from the Kremlin, the Russian heartland has destroyed the U.S.S.R., **Seweryn Bialer** *argues*

The Soviet Union, which claims sovereignty over one sixth of the globe and 290 million people, has virtually disintegrated. The dissolution of the political, economic and cultural ties between the center and the periphery, among the 15 republics and even *within* the Russian heartland itself, has achieved a momentum of its own that Mikhail Gorbachev cannot stop and is not willing, or does not know how, to accommodate.

All 14 non-Russian republics have declared their sovereignty and proclaimed the supremacy of their own authority over that of the Soviet government in Moscow, but Gorbachev is still clinging to the belief that power flows from the center to the periphery. He wants to reform the Union by delegating specific rights and greater autonomy to the republics, but the republics are insisting that *they* will delegate powers and rights to Gorbachev and his central government, if there is to be one. Gorbachev's political relevance and ultimately his survival now depend on what the republics will grant him. Unless, of course, he is willing and able to use massive violence.

With every passing week, the claims of sovereignty are becoming more radical and all-embracing. In all the Soviet republics, though in varying degrees, the claims of sovereignty now include:

■ Freedom to choose their own political systems and to draft their own constitutions and the radical diminution, or even eradication, of the central-government bureaucracies within the republics that were immune to local control.

■ Claims to all the land and property within their borders; the right to all natural and other resources, including labor, and, in some cases, the right to their own currency.

■ The end of Russification and the establishment of the native tongue as the official language of politics, business and education, not only for native speakers, but for everyone, including Russians.

■ Control of local police, with authority over border troops, secret police and intelligence (the KGB) left vague but with the Kremlin's authority already hotly disputed in some places.

■ The right to direct relations, particularly economic ties, with other countries.

■ Demands that local draftees into the Soviet Army must serve only on their own territory. Some republics already are forming their own armed forces.

The quest for sovereignty is no longer confined to the democratic and nationalist forces. The centrist and even conservative leaderships that remain dominant in many republics and are still the largest force in the Ukraine and Byelorussia have also embraced the principle. Their reasons vary, but the most decisive is probably political and pragmatic: In an atmosphere of growing nationalistic fervor, opposing greater sovereignty would mean losing influence even more rapidly. Other reasons are more deeply seated. The Russian-dominated central government treated the local Communist elites as "younger brothers" at best, stooges at worst.

These local elites do not want full independence because they are afraid to be left alone with their nationalist and democratic opponents — and with their neighbors. Yet they, too, may opt for independence if their people leave them no alternative or, ironically, if some new unifying authority in Moscow were so "progressive" that it endangered their conservative domination of their nations.

Trouble in the heartland. The most important declaration of sovereignty, however, has taken place not on the non-Russian periphery but in Russia itself, in the very heart of the Soviet Union. The Russian parliament's declaration of sovereignty is a revolutionary watershed. It has, in fact, destroyed the Soviet Union.

Russia *was* the Soviet Union. The Russian Republic was the first among the 15, and Russian authority and Soviet rule were synonymous. The Russians ruled the Soviet Union, while local non-Russian Communist elites ran the day-to-day affairs of their own regions. Each republic had its own Communist party; the Russians did not need a separate party because they ran the entire Communist Party of the Soviet Union.

Now there are two Moscows: Moscow of the Kremlin, the capital of the Soviet Union, where foreign dignitaries pay their respects to President Gorbachev, and Moscow the capital of the Russian Republic, housed in a white building a mile from the Kremlin's red walls. The Kremlin represents the past; its contract with the people has been terminated, or at least suspended. The capital of Russia represents the Russian people, but nobody else. The Moscow of the Kremlin still has all the accouterments and instruments of power, and it is still feared. But when it lost the homeland of the Russians, it lost both its legitimacy and its only power base.

Russia's declaration of sovereignty and its growing independence are sometimes attributed primarily to the ambitions of the leader of Russia, Boris Yeltsin, Gorbachev's most prominent opponent. But the roots and the meaning of the Russian position go much deeper. In the Russian language, there are two different words to identify Russia: *Rus,* the traditional and self-centered Russia, and *Rossiya,* the imperial, expansionist Russia. Bolshevism was nourished by the chauvinistic and imperial soul of Russia, which it in turn reinforced. But Bolshevism was a merciless enemy of Russia's culture, its religion, its democratic intelligentsia, its agrarian ethos and its preoccupation with Russia's own well-being.

The collapse of the messianic Bolshevik ideology; the demise of Russia as a superpower; the overwhelming sense of spiritual, cultural, economic and political catastrophe, and the exhaustion of the Russian nation have prompted Russia, for the first time in many centuries, to turn away from its imperium. Whether this will last is impossible to say, but its consequences are already historic.

The demise of Russian domestic imperialism and the disintegration of the Soviet Union would be relatively clean-cut were it not for another legacy of the imperial past reinforced by the 70 years of totalitarian Communism—the ethnic diversity of the republics. When Russia declared its independence from the Soviet Union, it called into question its own authority over significant parts of its own territory and population.

Some 25 million non-Russians are concentrated in separate administrative units called autonomous republics or regions within the Russian Republic. Motivated by the same emotions, passions and self-interests that have led the Soviet republics on their separatist paths, many of these units are in the process of declaring their sovereignty within Russia. In other words, the non-Russians in Russia are demanding exactly what Russia wants from the Soviet Union. But if they are treated as full partners and not as minorities within the Russian federative republic, they will be able to veto its programs and practically paralyze the work of the Russian government.

Further complicating things, non-natives, primarily Russians, sometimes account for 50 percent of the populations in these autonomous republics and regions. In the very center of the highly industrialized Urals, Bashkirs make up only about one fourth of the more than 4 million people in the Bashkir Autonomous Republic, which declared its independence from both the Soviet Union and Russia on October 13.

National time bombs are ticking in other republics, as well. Northern Kazakhstan is populated by Slavs; Kazakhs account for only 36 percent of the republic's 17 million people. The Russians living in the autonomous republics within the Russian Republic, and in the non-Russian republics, are unlikely either to accept domination by the non-Russians or to emigrate en masse. The reformers have not found a satisfactory solution to this dilemma, and the question of borders could provoke major—and perhaps violent—conflicts.

Even where national and ethnic aspirations are not at issue, executive power is collapsing at every level. The Soviet Union has become ungovernable, either as a whole or in parts. Rural areas want independence from urban centers, boroughs from cities, towns from regions, regions from republics, areas of extractive industries (oil, coal, gold, etc.) from everybody else. Executive power, whether it is in the hands of conservatives or democratic reformers, remains toothless and inchoate.

Unless this centrifugal trend is reversed, the fragmentation of the society, polity and economy will accelerate, with violence just around the corner. Not even the most radical market or democratic reforms will have a chance.

Is confederation next? Can a reformed Soviet Union, with a strong central authority, re-emerge? Probably not. The point of no return has been reached, even if Gorbachev's government stops simply reacting to events and begins trying to take command of the situation. At some point, a *confederation* of the national republics may emerge, but it is unlikely to include all 15 of the Soviet Union's present republics.

Yeltsin, the leader of the most powerful republic, and the most important figures around him now want an agreement with other republics to create some form of a federal authority. If the present impasse with the Gorbachev government persists, however, the republics will be forced to find their own ways to integrate and reform their economies. If that continues, the new ties among them will be formed in direct negotiations, not through Gorbachev's mediation.

The only other force available to hold together either parts of the union or a new confederation with a strong central government is the military, the only real instrument of mass power still in Gorbachev's hands. Force and intimidation can be effective against the power of ideas and of loosely organized social and political groups. But it is unclear whether the military can act and succeed, and whether it will act on its own. The authority of the Army and the KGB has declined significantly. The Army leadership has been unable to keep the national and political passions out of the armed forces, not only among draftees but also among the professional-officer corps. The mass mobilization of national fervor outside Russia, the rejection of the old order and the organization of large segments of workers (especially those in the oil and coal industries) inside Russia and the Ukraine, and the deterioration of the Army itself all have reached a level where the Army would be foolish to attempt a massive domestic crackdown.

The security forces, however, are becoming desperate, angry and frustrated as they see the rot spreading within their own ranks. They fear—realistically—that if the disintegration continues, the republics may stop drafting young men into the Soviet armed forces and start or accelerate the construction of their own military forces. If the military's very existence is at stake, one cannot exclude acts of desperation. In such a case its thrust will concentrate not on Lithuania or Georgia but on the Russian Republic, and particularly on the political forces in Moscow itself.

A much more likely scenario, however, is that the military and the KGB will join in actions initiated by Gorbachev that may get out of hand. To save what he believes can and must be saved, the Soviet leader is moving closer and closer to enlarging emergency presidential rule. If, as seems likely, decrees and orders continue to be ineffective, Gorbachev may show no more determination than he has so far, and let the disintegration continue apace. But he may consider this his last chance to restore a modicum of economic and social order. If so, his most likely option will be to suspend the Moscow and Leningrad soviets, and even the Russian parliament, and to put himself in charge.

But if these and other institutions refuse to comply with his orders, Gorbachev cannot continue without martial law. He may expect that people, tired of shortages, crime and chaos, will acquiesce when presented with the promise of order.

Nothing in these scenarios is inevitable. What is certain, however, is that the choices are becoming starker and the confrontations deeper. The democratic forces in Moscow are growing apprehensive, but whether central Soviet authority will end with a whimper or try to save itself with a bang remains to be seen.

SEWERYN BIALER, A LEADING SCHOLAR IN SOVIET AFFAIRS, IS BELFER PROFESSOR OF SOCIAL SCIENCES AND INTERNATIONAL RELATIONS AND DIRECTOR OF THE RESEARCH INSTITUTE ON SOCIAL CHANGE AT COLUMBIA UNIVERSITY

Toward a New Russian Federation

Recent changes in the Soviet Union have been nothing short of revolutionary. Almost as startling was how little scholars or journalists were prepared for them. Partly to blame was their "Copernican" approach to Soviet politics, a tendency, says Nicolai Petro, to look only at the top leadership. To understand the Soviet Union today, he argues, it is necessary to consider popular politics and the nation's emerging civil society. A new national consensus, based on traditional Russian values, may well provide the foundation for a future non-Soviet federation.

Nicolai N. Petro

Nicolai N. Petro is an International Affairs Fellow at the Council on Foreign Relations. Until June 1990 he was special assistant for policy at the U.S. Department of State's Office of Soviet Union Affairs. Born in Berlin, Germany, he received a B.A. (1980) and a Ph.D. (1984) from the University of Virginia. He is the author of The Predicament of Human Rights: The Carter and Reagan Policies *(1983) and editor of* Christianity and Russian Culture in Soviet Society *(1990). He is currently working on a book about the Russian response to perestroika.*

In just five years, much to the astonishment of professional Sovietologists, the Soviet Union has gone from being the world's most menacing superpower to a weak agglomeration of states uncertain of its very future. Why were most Moscow-watchers so ill-prepared for this dramatic transformation? The fault lies partly in what may be called their "Copernican" view of the Soviet Union, a view which has dominated the field since the 1960s. According to Copernican Sovietology, all political life revolves around the sun, and the sun most recently has been Mikhail Gorbachev. Copernican analysts tend to view the rest of society—at least everybody below the top Party leadership—as bit players, seemingly content to play out secondary roles in a well-worn script.

Such a perspective, as Moshe Lewin noted in *The Gorbachev Phenomenon* (1988), led to rather bizarre ideas about Soviet political reality: "A political system without a social one, a state floating over everything else, over history itself. Such a state submitted only to its own laws, was explainable in its own terms.... [W]hile change was posited as possible, it was conceived of as small variations within the unalterable framework: that such a state could undergo serious reform seemed unthinkable."

Most Copernicans also believed in a fundamental continuity between Russian and Soviet political culture. Scholars like Adam Ulam, Stephen Cohen, Robert V. Daniels, and the late Cyril Black argued that specifically Russian values lent support and stability to the regime. Identifying the ruled with the rulers, they saw little possibility of change coming from below. Harvard's Timothy Colton, in *The Dilemma of Reform in the Soviet Union* (1986), predicted that there would be no serious challenges to the regime's legitimacy for at least another decade because it was so firmly "moored in familiarity, past successes, and Russian nationalism."

It is not easy to escape Copernican thinking. Even today, the fate of reform in the Soviet Union is tied almost exclusively to the fate of Gorbachev. There are good reasons for this. Gorbachev is the prime instigator of perestroika and, as such, deserves enormous credit for initiating change

From *The Wilson Quarterly*, Summer 1990, pp. 114-122. *The Wilson Quarterly*, published by the Woodrow Wilson International Center for Scholars.

at the top of the political pyramid. But after giving Gorbachev his due, we must look beyond him. After all, Gorbachev's initial vision of perestroika was limited to a program of economic restructuring; glasnost was merely a convenient tool for breaking the resistance of recalcitrant factory managers. Public pressure forced him repeatedly to revise and expand his agenda.

During the past five years, in fact, Gorbachev found himself presiding over an expanding civil society with its own ideas about reform and openness, and with its own ideas about what the greater Russian federation should be. More than 60,000 informal social and political groups have sprung up around the country; at the same time, assorted nonpolitical groups concerned with ecological or historical preservation have increasingly been adopting their own political platforms and asserting themselves in areas where the Party is losing influence. This embryonic civil society has its own independent information outlets— more than 700 non-official publications in the Russian language alone. These groups, these movements, and these publications are now the driving force behind perestroika.

To understand what is going on in the Soviet Union, we need to develop a more "Newtonian" approach that takes into consideration not only the constituent parts of Soviet society but also culture, particularly literature, folk traditions, and religion. Only by looking at society and culture can we begin to comprehend the frustrations and aspirations of Soviet citizens who are rejecting communism and turning ever more insistently to traditional Russian values as a desirable foundation for a future Russian federation.

To be sure, ethnic Russians make up only half the population of the Soviet Union—a vast federation consisting of about 50 political units (including peoples with republic status, peoples with autonomous republic status, and peoples with autonomous region status). Nevertheless, Russian language and culture, or at least what historian Hugh Seton-Watson called a "mutilated" version of the latter, form the core of the Soviet federation. It is no coincidence that leaders of reform are often figures of cultural authority—writers, artists, editors—or, more to the point, that many of the more popular USSR People's Deputies, including actor Mark Zakharov and Academicians Dmitry Likhachev and Sergei Averintsev, have made traditional Russian values the centerpiece of their political proposals.

The questions of Russian cultural identity and Russian nationalism are matters of importance not only to Russians. If there is to be a nonviolent evolution toward greater autonomy for the Baltic, Central Asian, and other peoples, then the core of the Soviet Union—the "vast Slavic territory of Russia, Byelorussia, the eastern Ukraine, and northern Kazakhstan," as political scientist Martha Brill Olcott defined that core—must be confident of its cultural and national identity. Even Baltic independence leaders such as Virgilius Chepaitis and Lagle Park say that a healthy Russian nationalism should be encouraged.

To understand what Russians are striving to restore, one must first understand what they have lost. They have lost their history. Vladlen Sirotkin, a professor at the foreign ministry's diplomatic academy, is not alone in deploring the "nihilistic attitude toward the country's past" that has prevailed since the 1920s. At the end of that violently transformative decade, the doyen of Marxist historians, Mikhail Pokrovsky, declared that the very concept of "Russian history" was anti-revolutionary. Russia's religious heritage has been nearly destroyed: As many as 95 percent of the country's churches may have been demolished. Perhaps most devastating of all, Russia's national patrimony—a rich and vibrant peasant culture with all its traditions, crafts, legends, songs, and proverbs—was nearly extinguished by the forced collectivization that took the lives of millions during the 1930s. Historian Ksenia Mialo aptly compared Stalin's rural collectivization drive to the extermination of Inca civilization by the conquistadors.

The first openly to lament the destruction of peasant life, and thus to restore these events to the national memory, were the so-called "village prose writers." Novels such as Valentin Ovechkin's *A Difficult Spring* (1956), Efim Dorosh's *Village Diaries* (1958), and later Vasily Belov's *That's How Things Are* (1966) and Valentin Rasputin's *Mark You This* (1974) depicted the costs of precipitous industrialization and the uprooting of an entire way of life. The tremendous popularity of the village prose writers during the Brezhnev era (1964–82) owed largely to their championing authentic Russian values. Maurice Friedberg identified the best of these values as "hatred of war; an affirmation of Russian ethnic identity, nostalgia for a pastoral Russian past, a desire for a measure of privacy protected from state interference, a need for personal ethics, and a sense of compassion . . . ." As social critics appealing to Russian traditions and eternal human values, the village prose writers saw themselves, often correctly, as working in the tradition of the great 19th-century Russian writers such as Turgenev, Dostoyevsky, Tolstoy, Gogol, and Goncharov.

Their main concerns centered on the preservation of villages, religion, historical monuments, and the environment. Although they organized no political parties, their work aligned them with other individuals opposed to the policies of the regime. A notable example was the decade-long campaign waged by writers, scientists, historians, artists, and journalists to reverse the government's decision to divert major northern rivers into the country's arid south. Arguing that such an undertaking would destroy much of the northern Russian heartland, this spontaneous coalition eventually forced the government to shelve the project in 1987.

Such informal associations to preserve Russia's environment and its historical and religious monuments grew more common during the 1980s. Yet it was not until Gorbachev and glasnost that cautious supplication yielded to an active search for alternative Russian values and for more open ways of expressing them.

Many in the West view the re-emergence of Russian national self-awareness with justifiable concern. While sympathetic to the anguish caused by the Soviet destruction of Russian national heritage, foreign observers worry about the revival of anti-Semitism, imperialism, and anti-Western sentiment. The village writers themselves, notably Rasputin and Viktor Astafyev, have frequently been criticized for their anti-Semitism and for their insensitivity to other non-Russian nationalities. The crucial question, however, is whether such sentiments are shared by most Russian nationalists. If so, any future reforms based on Russian national values would clearly be odious to liberals both within the Soviet Union and abroad.

Discussion of anti-Semitism has certainly increased under glasnost. In such prominent literary journals as *Molodaya Gvardiya* (*The Young Guard*) and *Nash Sovremennik* (*Our Contemporary*), the issue of Jewish participation in the Russian Revolution and in the subsequent Party leadership has become virtually an editorial obsession. When *Nash Sovremennik* published an essay on "Russophobia" by dissident mathematician Igor Shafarevich, it brought the issue to a head.

Shafarevich, a friend of Aleksandr Solzhenitsyn, based much of his provocative essay on the ideas of Augustin Cochin, a 19th-century French historian who had argued that revolutions were caused by alienated "little nations" within the "larger nation." Just as Cochin blamed the French revolution on anti-national, self-contained groups like the Masons, so Shafarevich attributed the distinctive character of the Russian Revolution to the "Jewish element." Little matter that relatively few of the revolutionary leaders, and even fewer of the later Soviet leaders, were Jewish—or that the most famous, Trotsky, was exiled from Russia. Shafarevich got around such empirical deficiencies by claiming that the "Jewish element" meant not so much individual Jews as an iconoclastic Jewish spirit which had infected traditional Russia. Anticipating his critics, moreover, Shafarevich denounced as "Russophobes" all those who tarnish Russian nationalism by equating it with a resurgence of anti-Semitism. Nevertheless, it is hard to read his article and think that those who see such an equation are completely wrong.

What about the resurgence of imperialist chauvinism? Here again, one finds several nationalist groups, including the Association of Russian Artisans and Fatherland, that want the empire held together at any cost. In general, though, most nationalist groups believe that such unity is to be achieved not by force of arms but by establishing a new common bond—resting on vague, rather romanticized notions of common historical ties—among the various ethnic groups in the country. While all Russian nationalists pay lip-service to the principle of self-determination, some seem noticeably hesitant about implementing it. As more Soviet nationalities opt for secession, the distinction between those who support freedom over empire and those who do not will emerge.

A third concern is that Russian nationalism is anti-democratic and anti-liberal and thus poses a threat to the ascendancy of Western values. As it turns out, there are some Russian nationalists who oppose the introduction of free markets and a multi-party system on the grounds that they are not Russian. Many others fear more simply that at present such moves would produce greater anarchy and turmoil. While the former are anti-Western, the latter are looking for reassurance that a realistic alternative to anarchy exists, that political forces outside the Party can prevent chaos and even bloodshed.

Acknowledging the dark side of the Russian national revival, one must at the same time avoid blurring some important distinctions, a mistake that would be as serious as confusing the conservatism of a William Buckley or a George Will with the reactionary racism of the Ku Klux Klan. Indeed, the failure to distinguish between chauvinism and patriotism feeds the counter-accusation of "Russophobia."

2. THE SOVIET UNION

Russophobes, Shafarevich charges, fear a strong and nationally healthy Russia; they would rather see the country destroyed by communist rule or dismembered by national tensions before they would countenance any Russian national revival.

The debate over Russia's national revival is sensitive precisely because it touches so directly on the character and historical prospects of the Russian people. The polemic in the Soviet press over the recent publication of excerpts of Vasily Grossman's novel *Life and Fate* (published abroad in 1980) goes to the heart of the quarrel: Who should be blamed for the dismal failure of the Soviet Union? Socialist ideology, say the Russian nationalists. The backward economic and political traditions of Russia, say the radical reformers. The reformers read *Life and Fate* as an exposé of the crimes of Stalinist collectivization and the corruption of Lenin's idealism. But conservative nationalists are offended by the novel's depiction of Lenin as a well-intentioned liberal intellectual whose progressive impulses were thwarted by "Russia's thousand-year tradition of slavery." They were incensed that Soviet historian G. Vodolazov, in his preface to the novel, absolved Lenin of any blame for the events leading to Stalin's dictatorship. Wrote Vodolazov: "I believe that people who wish to assist humanity's progress should not be thinking about how to 'replay' October and Leninism, but about how to 'replay' the years 1929 and 1937, relying on the values of October and Leninism."

People like Grossman and Vodolazov follow in the footsteps of 19th-century Westernizers such as Alexander Herzen and Nikolai Chernychevsky. Although they reject the current political system, they are attracted to Western-style socialism. In the Soviet Union today they are known as "radical Westernizers," or "radical reformers," or "left radicals."

Many others charge that socialism—by which they mean communism—is itself largely to blame for the country's current crisis. Socialism, they claim, infected the Russian intelligentsia with disdain for all that was traditionally Russian. What is needed today, they argue, is to cast aside the present value system and to pick up what Ksenia Mialo calls "the broken thread to the past." Sharing many philosophical assumptions of the early 19th-century Slavophiles such as Ivan Aksakov and Yuri Samarin, these people today are variously referred to as "Russites," *vozrozhdentsy* (revivalists), "Russophiles," or "the Russian Party."

The philosophical differences between radicals and restorationists lead, as might be expected, to significant practical differences. Radicals tend to want a rapid introduction of free markets, while restorationists usually stress social guarantees. Radicals view the secession of republics as a step toward a healthy decentralization, while restorationists are fearful of the costs of fragmenting the empire. Radicals at times seem almost eager to dismantle the Soviet military; restorationists are concerned about security and foreign policy.

But these differences should not obscure the fact that both groups have learned to compromise and work together on key Soviet reform legislation. In the Supreme Soviet last year, they came together to repeal the electoral provisions that guaranteed a certain percentage of seats to the Communist Party; together, they are pushing for a new law on the freedom of the press that goes far beyond Gorbachev's proposed version of the law. On at least seven other occasions, radicals and conservatives working together have rejected Gorbachev-proposed legislation as too restrictive.

Both sides acknowledge that they need each other to promote changes in the system. The progressive deputy-mayor of Moscow, Sergei Stankevich, in a speech to the Supreme Soviet last fall, commented on how essential conservatism was to providing a balance of ideas in the new parliament. Likewise, Anatoly Salutsky, the arch-conservative commentator for *Literaturnaya Rossiya* (*Literary Russia*), has argued that today's Slavophiles and Westernizers are not opposing forces but complementary wings of a movement that is shaping a new Russian national consensus.

There is much about this new consensus that should be appealing to the West. Both radicals and restorationists share a belief in the rule of law, in a national revival based on Russian patriotic sentiment, and in an educational system resting not on ideological slogans but on a critical understanding of Russian and foreign history. Supporters of the consensus are likely to be wary of any foreign adventures that would further bleed the country. They are already skeptical of the value to Russia of many non-Slavic areas of the Soviet Union. In a remarkable public letter published this year, three prominent nationalist organizations warned that if tranquility did not return soon to the Caucasus, they would launch a campaign to remove Russian servicemen from the region. The reluctance of conservatives to use troops echoes earlier appeals by liberals not to use force to keep regions like Lithuania in the Soviet Union.

The new Russian consensus is not without historical precedent. A strand of turn-of-the-century Russian thought—represented by the religious philosophers Nikolai Berdyaev and Semyon Frank and the political economist Peter Struve—combined many of the same disparate elements. Although the earlier thinkers were, as the late Leonard Schapiro pointed out, "first and foremost nationalists and patriots," they "stood midway between Slavophiles and Westernizers. They accepted the Slavophile veneration of Russian national tradition, while rejecting their romantic idealization of innate Russian virtues as a substitute for the more usual civic virtues." For these people Schapiro employed the oxymoron "liberal conservative"—an epithet first used to describe Russia's most famous poet, Aleksander Pushkin. It applies equally well to many of the radicals and nationalists of today.

The liberal conservative consensus has found organizational expression in the more than 40 political groups active throughout the Russian federation. This broad spectrum of political opinion should not be confused with the factions that have developed within the Party itself, even though certain ideas are shared across the non-Party–Party divide. Party factionalists, whether reformers like the historian Roy Medvedev or conservatives like Egor Ligachev, still insist that the Communist Party remain the guiding force in Soviet society.

The Party, however, is rapidly losing its credibility. Over 10 million young people have abandoned the Communist Youth League since 1985. After local elections this past March, Party members were, for the first time in Soviet history, a minority among people's deputies elected to Russia's supreme legislative body. In large Russian cities like Moscow and Leningrad, Communists have relinquished power to the democratic opposition.

The establishment of pluralistic politics in rural Russian areas has been much slower. Nevertheless, Russia's political evolution seems clearly foreshadowed in the experiences of Eastern Europe and the Baltic States. And as in Eastern Europe, the new political parties, rather than the discredited remnants of the Communist Party, are likely to guide the country's future. Most of these parties fall into political categories analogous to those on the rest of the European continent.

• *The Social Democrats.* During the first days of perestroika, reformist intellectuals organized discussion clubs. A number of their political leaders—Yuri Afanasyev, Gavril Popov, Sergei Stankevich, the late Andrei Sakharov—eventually "graduated" to the influential Moscow Rostrum and the leadership of the Interregional Deputies Group in the USSR Supreme Soviet. The social-democratic groups see themselves as standing for a humanistic renewal of socialist values. They support the introduction of Western constitutional guarantees as well as radical economic reform, but they are rightly concerned about the extent of popular support for radical change. Even so, the social-democrat orientation appears to be the most active in Russian politics today, both within the Communist Party and as a separate party itself, the Social-Democratic Association. In recent local elections, social-democratic candidates won a majority of seats in over 20 large Russian cities, including Moscow, Leningrad, Gorky, and Sverdlovsk.

• *The Conservatives.* Last fall a number of the conservative groups moved beyond their strictly cultural preoccupations to form a political organization—the Bloc of Russian Public-Patriotic Movements—in order to counter the growing popularity of the social democrats. Before that, conservatives had been as reluctant to enter politics as social democrats had been to appeal to Russian patriotic sentiment. Both have abandoned their reluctance.

Most conservatives, rejecting Marxism-Leninism, see Russian patriotism and religion as the only alternative to decay. They are united by five common assumptions: the need for a moral and religious revival; skepticism about Western intellectual imports such as capitalism, pop culture, and especially Marxism; fear of unconstrained market competition and "windfall profits" (some, like Mikhail Antonov, propose a Japanese model, with the economy more closely attuned to native cultural traditions); the need to return land to the peasantry; and belief in the nobility of military service. But conservatives differ widely on how to resolve Russia's current problems. Some recommend radical decentralization and even Russia's secession from the Soviet Union; others see a strong centralized authority as the only thing preventing the country's collapse.

The conservatives have not done well at the polls. In direct confrontations with social democrats in last March's local elections, they were easily defeated. (Only 16 out of 65 conservative candidates in Moscow even made it to the run-off elections.) Their prospects are hampered by a lack of clarity about how to achieve a Russian revival, by a contradictory economic and political platform, and by ambivalent attitudes toward the Party's monopoly on power. In the not-too-distant future, conservatives are likely to split over the central political issue of the day: whether the Party is still a viable political force or simply a burden to the country. Those who support the Communist Party are likely to join forces with reactionaries within the Party such as Nina Andreyev and Egor Ligachev. Those who abandon the Party are likely to edge closer to the views of the Christian democrats.

• *The Christian Democrats.* Christian democrats are found in the middle of the political spectrum. Like the conservatives, they reject Marxism-Leninism and believe that Russian patriotism can contribute to promoting reform. But like the social democrats, their program includes an insistence upon the rule of law, a clear separation of church and state, and privatization of markets. Christian democrats, however, stress that all politics needs a firm moral foundation. Many of the Russian religious philosophers that they turn to, including Semyon Frank, Nikolai Berdyaev, and Father Sergei Bulgakov, had themselves been Marxists in their youth but later abandoned Marxism in favor of democracy and religion.

Christian democracy has no political precedent in pre-revolutionary Russia, but it is quickly finding a following. Three members of the newly elected Russian Supreme Soviet—among them noted human-rights activist Father Gleb Yakunin—recently joined the Russian Christian Democratic Movement. As André Louis, secretary-general of the Christian Democratic International, recently observed, "In the long run, I think Christian Democracy has its best opportunity in the Soviet Union. Christian Democrats there have come to political life out of religious conviction. In searching for a more fraternal and useful religion, they come to recognize the need for political activity." The movement's uncompromising rejection of communist ideology may be the best guarantee of its future success.

• *Extremist groups.* A number of small but vocal chauvinistic groups—Pamyat (Memory), Vityazi (Heroes), and Patrioty (Patriots)—go far beyond professing concern for Russia's revival and openly accuse "dark forces" and "foreign elements" of engaging in a conspiracy to destroy Russia. They typically identify these forces as people of Jewish origin and those who do their bidding.

Extremists of both the left and the right often form strange and paradoxical alliances. In Leningrad, Pamyat groups have received open help from two district Party organizations. In a recent interview, Elena Bonner, wife of the late Andrei Sakharov,

noted that the Leningrad KGB was protecting and promoting Pamyat.

Western concern about these groups stems from the fear that they may eventually have a decisive influence on national policy. Many of these organizations are actively seeking allies among disgruntled soldiers, workers, and Russian minorities in the outlying republics. In the event of a weakened and demoralized Soviet state—a "Weimar Russia"—such groups might seize power, unleashing a campaign against minorities (particularly Jews) and threatening military aggression abroad.

Such a turn of events is possible but highly unlikely. First of all, in the aftermath of the Afghan war, foreign military adventures have no popular constituency. We are witnessing in the Soviet Union today perhaps the most widespread peacetime rejection of military service in the 20th century. Not only are individuals in many parts of the country refusing to serve; a number of the country's leading universities are no longer offering the required courses in military indoctrination. Furthermore, given the country's dire economic straits, it would be almost impossible to mobilize support for a war—absent the immediate threat of foreign invasion.

For all the attention it receives in the Western and Soviet media, Pamyat has never attracted more than a few hundred people to its rallies (compared to nearly 200,000 for Democratic Russia rallies in Moscow this past February). It has failed to elect a single candidate to public office, either in national or local elections. In Moscow, the Pamyat candidate, Tamara Ponamareva, received five percent of the votes for, and 86.5 percent of the votes against, her candidacy.

Moreover, public opinion surveys report that the overwhelming majority of the population favors continued glasnost, despite doubts about the economic success of perestroika. And there is still reported to be strong support for expanding friendly contacts with the West. In one recent survey, for example, the only ministry to get a favorable rating was the ministry of foreign affairs, presumably because of its role in fostering better relations with the West.

Thus while there are dangers associated with the emerging Russian national consensus, notably authoritarianism and intolerance, there are good reasons for thinking that the Soviet Union has what S. Frederick Starr calls "a usable past." Star and other scholars—including James Billington, John Dunlop, Geoffrey Hosking, and Helen Carrere D'Encausse—have all pointed to the resurgence of interest in Russia's pre-revolutionary classical liberal heritage. It is a fragile flower in Russian history, they all acknowledge, but it exists.

The question is how to cultivate it in the present. The weakness of the Russian liberals in the past, according to émigré historian Nicholas Zernov, was their indifference to the more conservative traditions of the populace. This led first to their isolation, then to disillusion with liberalism, and finally to a fatal attraction to radicalism.

Today, however, particularly in the political arena, radicals and restorationists are consciously striving to build bridges, to wed the best elements of Western universalism and Russian particularism, rule of law and healthy patriotism. Their efforts embody Dostoyevsky's insistence that to "become a true Russian" means "to become a brother of all men, a *universal* man." The Democratic Russia coalition of People's Deputies is the most promising fruit of their labors. With over one-third of People's Deputies in the next Russian Supreme Soviet under its banner, the Democratic Russia coalition is likely to play a key role in the passage of legislation in the republic's supreme governing body.

The recent election of coalition leader Boris Yeltsin to the chairmanship of the Russian Supreme Soviet will only increase that likelihood. Yeltsin himself exemplifies the spirit of liberal conservatism: He champions the social-democratic agenda and greater independence for the republics while calling for the restoration of religious and other traditional Russian values. The Russian national consensus is also beginning to build momentum at the local level. There we are witnessing efforts to restore land tenure to peasants, to bring back pre-revolutionary symbols and place names, and to promote a more prominent role for religious organizations. With the election of local governments oriented toward radical economic reforms, the search for political alternatives is likely to proceed even more rapidly than before.

The thorniest issue facing supporters of the new national consensus is the question of other Soviet nationalities. Apart from the Slavic majority of Russians, Byelorussians, and Ukrainians, there are 19 other major nationalities and scores of smaller national and ethnic groups. How will the minorities abide an explicitly Russian federation? History provides a possible answer. During the 19th century, the word *rossiiskoe* (which suggests the broad multiethnic Russian national state) was as commonly used as the narrower term *russkoe* (meaning only ethnic Russians), a distinction roughly analogous to the difference between British and English. Today, a number of Russian political organizations are using *rossiiskoe* to broaden their appeal. But they will succeed only if their inclusiveness is backed up with real assurances: of mutually beneficial economic ties between the center and periphery; of full cultural and religious freedoms for all nationalities; and of the right of any people to independence. Treated fairly, non-Russian peoples will have good reasons for remaining within the federation, including a shared defense burden and a huge, established outlet for manufactured goods. It is worth remembering that Russians made up only half of the population of the empire during the 19th century; yet for most of that century—until restrictive nationalities policies were imposed by Tsars Alexander III and Nicholas II—ethnic frictions were minimal.

At its best, then, the emerging Russian consensus is one that both Western liberals and conservatives can be comfortable with. It promotes decentralization, political accountability, domestic tranquility, and international retrenchment. It is also an ideal that Russians themselves find increasingly attractive, preferring it to either the restoration of communism or the vagaries of Gorbachev's perestroika. Surveys by the Center for Public Opinion Study show that while three-quarters of ethnic Russians believe that "relying on their national roots" is an important consideration for Russia's salvation, a mere 14 percent now expect government to solve their problems. Nearly a third feel that they "must at last become free people and make the state serve [their] interests."

The combination of economic necessity and national revival is a powerful prod to the development of a healthy national self-conception. The best traditions of Russia's pre-revolutionary past may hold the key to Russia's post-revolutionary future.

American Allies: Western Europe, Canada, and Japan

- **Western Europe (Articles 10-14)**
- **Canada (Article 15)**
- **Japan (Articles 16-18)**

Economic issues, the war with Iraq, and the still-unfolding changes in Eastern Europe and the Soviet Union are deeply affecting the relationships between the United States and its allies of Western Europe, Japan, and Canada. As these relationships are redefined, all sides are anxious that the gains made in reducing the threat of war between the Communist and capitalist countries not be replaced by tensions generated by economic and political issues.

The U.S. defense relationship with Western Europe is being carefully reexamined in light of the dramatic changes in the Communist world, and also in the awareness that the next "enemy," one that threatens the interests of the Western alliance, may emerge far from Europe's frontiers. The collapse of the Communist regimes of Eastern Europe and the Soviet Union's movement away from communism muddy the issue of just who Western Europe's enemy is.

NATO cannot simply disappear overnight. It would be foolish to assume that a Soviet Union teetering on the edge of economic collapse and threatened by politically destabilizing civil violence and secession could not again become "the enemy." Insecure leaders often resort to violence, even to war. Popular discontent with Gorbachev's policies of *perestroika* is serious, and Gorbachev could lose power if he allows decisions to be made democratically. Further, there are still tens of thousands of nuclear weapons in the Soviet Union, and under circumstances of a complete breakdown of civil authority, these could fall into rebel hands, with an unpredictable outcome.

On the other hand, to continue to deploy forces on both sides at levels geared toward an imminent threat makes little sense in the present international context. Thus NATO's objectives, military strategy, and force levels must be rethought. Europeans have, however, been reluctant to increase their own conventional forces as an antidote to an unreliable nuclear defense, both because of the costs and also because of their doubts about whether conventional deterrence works.

The reduction of the U.S. military presence in Europe would indicate that, in the area of defense, "Atlanticism," the close partnership between the United States and the Western European states, appears to be giving way to "Europeanism"— Europe acting as a unit independent of the United States. The joining of European military forces with American forces in the war against Iraq, however, indicates that even beyond Europe, the United States and its Western European allies are willing to work together against a common enemy.

Nevertheless, Europeans still harbor deep anxieties about the possibility of the United States being decoupled from the defense of Europe. With intermediate-range nuclear missiles already being removed from Europe, and large numbers of American soldiers leaving the European theater, and with present conventional forces in NATO too weak to defend Western Europe against a Soviet attack with conventional forces, Europeans are concerned about the U.S. commitment to defend Western Europe from a conventional force attack. Once short-range and tactical nuclear weapons are removed from a re-

unified Germany, only the American "nuclear umbrella" provided by submarine-launched missiles and ICBMs stationed in the United States will provide for Europe's security. Western Europeans may well wonder whether the United States will be willing to endanger its own security by using its ICBMs to turn back a Soviet attack. Of course, with Gorbachev's decision to reduce Soviet conventional forces stationed in Eastern European countries to as low a level as NATO's, and with the dissolution of the Warsaw Pact, there is little likelihood that Soviet conventional forces could overwhelm those of Western Europe.

In the economic arena, the formation in 1992 of a truly united European Community, one in which virtually all trade, monetary, financial, and investment barriers will be eliminated *within* this community, but which would establish itself as a competitive economic giant vis-à-vis the U.S. and Japanese markets, has sent businessmen worldwide scrambling to position themselves favorably. Businessmen, not to mention governments, are concerned that the new, larger European Community will be more protectionist, and hence more impenetrable, than the present loose economic alliance among the European countries. Europeans insist that this will not be the case, but minimally, they will have a far larger internal market within which to trade than before. This in itself is likely to increase intra-European trade at the expense of international trade.

A reunified Germany is also an issue for Europe's economy. Even before unification in 1990, Germany was the most powerful economy within the European Economic Community. The fear of other Europeans was that Germany's reunification would make it even more powerful, to the point where it could completely dominate the European Community. But so far, history has indicated that their fears are unfounded. Thus far, if anything, the addition of the territory, people, and governmental responsibilities of the former East Germany has simply drained the former West Germany of its energy and strength.

Finally, the prospect of a European unity that encompasses some, or even all, of the formerly socialist states of Eastern Europe is something that must now be considered. A "super Europe" of states unified economically, politically, and militarily is now a possibility. And, if the Soviet Union has its way, a "Europe without boundaries" will include it, too.

The U.S. relationship with Canada is perhaps the most stable and positive of America's alliances. Cooperation between these bordering countries and a willingness to compromise when conflicts arise have characterized this relationship. Nevertheless, the built-in imbalance, with the United States dominating the relationship both militarily and economically, creates ambivalence on the part of the Canadians. Canada wants to be able to assert its national interests vis-à-vis the United States, particularly in cases such as acid rain and free trade. The two countries have accelerated their movement toward a Canadian-American free trade zone, a zone that might within a few years extend to include Mexico. The resulting North American "common market" would be more competitive with the new European

Community market than any one of the three countries would be operating as independent economies.

Of America's three major partnerships, it is the U.S.–Japan one that still seems to generate the most emotional response. Haunted by an ever-growing balance of trade deficit in Japan's favor, and by deep anti-Japan sentiments over the presumed damage that Japan's strong exports cause to the health of American industries, the relationship is in trouble both at the psychological level and on the balance sheet. It is the lack of reciprocity that distresses the outside world, for whereas Japan is free to invest and develop trade in most other countries, others are not equally free to do so in Japan. The hidden, nontariff barriers continue to thwart investment in Japan. While Japan had removed almost all tariffs on imports by 1991, thus allowing foreign goods to arrive on Japanese docks, the Japanese retail distribution system and bureaucratic regulations prevent these goods from actually being distributed through Japan's retail stores for purchase by the public.

With these tensions added to Japan's refusal to spend a larger percentage of its GNP on either social expenditures or the environment, and a growing reputation for "racism" and arrogance about its superiority as a culture and a nation, the rest of the world seems to be turning against Japan. Japan is well aware of the outside world's view of it as an "economic animal" and is desperately trying to improve its image. In particular, as of 1989, Japan became the world's largest economic aid donor. But Japan's refusal to send even support personnel to help the U.S.–led coalition forces in the war against Iraq—indeed, the unwillingness of even a dozen Japanese to *volunteer* to serve as support personnel (such as doctors) for the coalition forces, has set back the Japanese government's efforts to be considered a true friend. For its part, the Japanese people are irritated that once again, the United States requested them to violate their own American-written constitution, which prohibits Japan from engaging in war for an purpose other than self-defense. Further, the Japanese believe that it was the fault of the United States that it got itself into the war with Iraq. They argue that if the United States had seriously undertaken a new energy policy in the wake of the oil boycotts of the 1970s, it could have weaned itself from its dependence on oil from the Middle East. Of course, the Japanese who make this argument rarely acknowledge Japan's own nearly total reliance on oil from the Middle East.

In Asia, concerns have been growing that Japan, an economi-cally powerful industrial nation, might again become an engine of war, for although Japan spends only a minuscule amount above 1 percent of its total GNP on defense, it already has the sixth largest military in the world. Korea is particularly vocal about its suspicions, and officials from Taiwan, the People's Republic of China, and other Asian states have also voiced concern. This is in spite of the fact that Japan has literally been *forced* by the United States to spend more on defense for the purpose of "burden sharing" than it ever wanted to do.

Thus, Asian states are psychologically burdened with the remembrance of World War II and disturbed both by Japan's penetration of their economies and by Japan's defense buildup. In a sense, however, these fears of Japan are contradictory, as it would hardly make sense for Japan to become a military aggressor against those states that it has economically penetrated. War would endanger precisely what Japan wants: control over economic resources and assured markets for Japanese products abroad.

Looking Ahead: Challenge Questions

What makes some European states jittery about their future security in the new context of a decrease in both nuclear and conventional forces on both sides in Europe? How does German reunification affect the concept of European unity militarily, economically, and politically? If you owned a company that did business in Western Europe, how would you feel about the prospect of a unified Europe in 1992?

For what reasons might Canada, also occupying the North American continent, view international relations differently from its southern neighbor? Has the United States proven to be a reliable ally for the Canadians? Is the relationship a partnership or one of American dominance? In what direction is the relationship moving?

What are the key elements in the U.S.–Japan relationship? Are the psychological and economic issues of enough importance to endanger this alliance? If Japan were not an American military ally, with whom might it choose to ally? Is there a strong likelihood of Japan moving closer to the Soviet Union or the People's Republic of China? For what reasons? Is it likely, in your view, that Japan will decide in the near future to have a more independent military, one free of American dominance? Why or why not?

EUROPE'S EXTREMES

JEFFREY GEDMIN

Jeffrey Gedmin is a research associate at the American Enterprise Institute.

ONE WEST GERMAN COMMUNIST SAW it all coming: "the betrayal of the working class," when one day the "class enemy" would be given "free rein to turn communists out of office through elections." From the time Mikhail Gorbachev began the implementation of his sweeping reforms in the Soviet Union in 1985, Stalinist-run communist parties in Portugal, France, and West Germany sensed that it was not only their comrades in Eastern Europe who would be in for rocky times but also their own parties. Even moderate "Eurocommunists" in Italy and Spain must have suspected that revolution in Mother Russia would ultimately spell upheaval in their ranks.

Five years later, the evidence confirms their foreboding. While the Soviet-inspired demolition of communism in Eastern Europe has captured world attention, the nonruling communist parties in the West have not been far behind. Funding from Eastern Europe and the Soviet Union has dried up, membership has plummeted, and ideological disarray has left the few remaining faithful in tired confusion. Communism in Western Europe may soon be classified as a relic. That's the good news. But while Europe's communist left disappears, there are signs that a revitalizing extremist right may be waiting in the wings, ready to fill the vacuum in Europe's new politics.

WHAT'S LEFT OF THE LEFT

Prelude to the Collapse

It would be unfair to give Mikhail Gorbachev all the credit for the demise of Western Europe's communist parties. In the mid-1970s, a thriving "Eurocommunism" threatened to transform the political landscape of much of Western Europe. But as democratic capitalism prospered and Marxian solutions to social and economic problems began gradually to lose

currency with left-wing constituencies across the continent, Western Europe's communist parties entered a phase of steady decline. The left in general has shifted in Europe. As Seymour Martin Lipset has documented, virtually all of Europe's social democratic parties shifted toward the center in the 1980s.

Between 1976 and 1986, the Italian communist party (PCI), the world's largest nonruling communist party, watched membership sink from 2 million to 1.65 million. In 1976, when the Italian communists made impressive gains in the national government (they secured 228 seats in the 630-seat Chamber—only 34 less than the Christian Democrats—and 116 seats in the 315-seat Senate—only 19 less than the Christian Democrats), the PCI could also boast of communist mayors in five large cities, including Rome and Naples. By the time Gorbachev had settled into power, over a quarter of the PCI's national support had evaporated, and Bologna was the only large city that still had a communist mayor.

In Spain in 1977, the communist party (PCE) managed to capture 9.4 percent of the national vote, expanding its portion to 10.8 percent in the second parliamentary elections, held in March 1979. But since that time, the party has been on the skids. Following a poor performance in the 1982 general election, the communists disintegrated into three factions. In 1986, an emaciated PCE was able to attain only 4.6 percent in the country's national election. Similar downward trends can be found for communist parties in pre-Gorbachev France and West Germany. Only Portugal's communist party (PCP)—the most Stalinist of Western Europe—was able to remain stable throughout the mid-1980s, consistently garnering around 15 percent of the Portuguese vote.

Over the last five years, Gorbachev's *"glastroika"* and popular revolution in Eastern Europe have plunged Western Europe's communist parties, Portugal's now included,

IS THE RIGHT ON THE RISE?

From *The American Enterprise,* Vol. 1, No. 4, July/August 1990, pp. 38-44. *The American Enterprise,* published by The American Enterprise Institute.

into the throes of a deep identity crisis, accelerating a process of decline leading to disintegration. Ironically, it has been the so-called moderate Eurocommunist parties in Italy and Spain, parties that appeared to have the most in common with Gorbachev's concept of communist "renewal," that have crumbled most quickly.

The Moderates: Spain and Italy

For more than two decades, communist parties in Spain and Italy have pursued a public position of "moderation" in their quest to participate in government. Following the Soviet invasion of Czechoslovakia in 1968, the Spanish communists labored to project their independence from Moscow. In his book *"Eurocommunismo" y Estado*, published in 1977, communist party boss Santiago Carillo went so far as to challenge the very nature of the Soviet Union's system of socialism—a view that earned him Moscow's condemnation for alleged collaboration with "the interests of imperialism."

Where the Spanish communists left off, their comrades in Italy tirelessly pushed forward. Embodying the Eurocommunist commitment to the parliamentary democratic process—a commitment opponents frequently referred to as a tactical position of "postponed totalitarianism"—the Italian communist party has come to resemble, at least on paper, something not far from the British Labour Party or West Germany's Social Democrats. Since the 1970s, the PCI has officially repudiated violence as a means of attaining power, rejected democratic centralism (running the party entirely from above), accepted limited market mechanisms, and even approved of Italy's membership in NATO. Such enlightened Marxism won for Italy's communists Gorbachev's praise as the "precursors of *perestroika*."

Perhaps uninspired by the Kremlin's own example, however, Italians responded with apathy in the 1987 elections, leaving the PCI with its most serious defeat in more than two decades and its third consecutive drop at the polls since 1976. Further demoralized by communism's collapse in Eastern Europe in 1989, nearly one-half of the 1.2 million Italians holding communist party membership cards had failed to renew their membership by the beginning of this year. In regional elections held this spring, the PCI limped home with its worst showing in more than 30 years.

In response to the PCI's collapsing ranks, general secretary Achille Ochetto has scrambled to revamp the party's image, proposing that the communists change their name and discard the party's hammer-and-sickle symbol.

To avoid further isolation of his party, Ochetto also proposes that the PCI join a broad coalition of the left that includes Bettino Craxi's Italian socialists (PSI).

Militant communists, fearing an unfavorable balance of forces, emphatically reject Ochetto's risky campaign to salvage something of their party, accusing the general secretary of a sell-out when he champions the union of "Marxist and liberal culture." Nevertheless, according to recent opinion polls, Ochetto's reformist course—a direction that could eventually reduce the PCI to extinction—has the support of nearly two-thirds of the current party membership.

If the PCI splinters, antireformers, who deplore what they see as the abandonment of the party's identity, may move to form a new communist organization. To be sure, the PCI's antireformers won't give up easily. As the *Wall Street Journal* reported earlier this year, old-guard communists in one small farming town in northern Italy were locked in battle with local citizens who had audaciously suggested that the larger-than-life bronze bust of Lenin gracing the town's square be taken down. But even if such "Cro Magnon communists" (so described by a PCI spokesman in Rome) band together, that tiny party of antireformers would pale in comparison to the significant Italian communist movement that was able to capture between a quarter and a third of the national vote since the war.

In Spain, the story has been much the same. The Spanish communists currently claim 83,000 members, a far cry from the peak of 200,000 members the party reported in 1977, two years after Francisco Franco's death. Although the Spanish communists insist they "will not renounce Marxism," ideological confusion among rank-and-file members stemming from communism's collapse in the East and the PCE's reported desire to move toward collaboration with the country's socialist party brought secretary general Julio Anguita to concede this year that the 68-year-old party has begun to dissolve. In March, Anguita fatalistically observed at a meeting of party *apparatchiks* that "within a year at most, we shall have to change [our] symbols and . . . name." In autonomous regions such as Navarra and La Rioja, the process is already under way; disillusioned proletarians have begun to detach the hammer-and-sickle from signs and party flags.

The Recalcitrants: France, Portugal, and West Germany

Staunch Stalinists, such as long-time French communist party boss Georges Marchais and Álvaro Cunhal, who has led the Portuguese communist party for the last 48 years, have fought bitterly to keep *glasnost* from infecting their ranks.

Marchais still likes to maintain that he is "very close to Mikhail Gorbachev," despite the fact that Soviet publications like *Izvestia* have attacked the French communists for their unfashionable orthodoxy and intransigence. According to French press reports, the Soviet Embassy in Paris has even authorized active participation by its diplomats in meetings organized by opponents of the hard-liners.

In the 1986 and 1988 national legislative elections, the French communist party (PCF) captured 9.8 and 11.3 percent of the votes, respectively, roughly one-half of their support in the 1970s and their lowest totals since 1932. The beginnings of the PCF's current malaise can be traced at least in part to François Mitterrand's shrewd political manipulation of this domestic opponent.

In 1981, the PCF entered a coalition with Mitterrand's socialists in which the communists were able to obtain four ministries: civil service, transport, health, and education and vocational training. Caught in a trap undoubtedly laid by Mitterrand, the communists became partners in a government whose agenda they could not control but whose policies they were obliged to support. The last PCF minister left the Mitterrand government in the summer of 1984, leaving the French president to witness a prophecy come true. In 1972, Mitterrand, only two days after signing the Common Program with the PCF, had boasted that his party would "prove that out of five million communist electors, three million are quite capable of voting socialist."

Today, a frantic Marchais urges loyal supporters to fight on. The communist party boss decries reformers within the PCF's ranks as "liquidators" who, "duped" by events in Eastern Europe, "want us to stop being communists." But the liquidators appear to be gaining strength. Gorbachev enthusiasts, like French Central Committee member Charles Fiterman (who served as minister of transport and minister of state during the communist stint in the Mitterrand government), claim they have at least one-third of the PCF's membership on their side. The "restructurers" hope their own *perestroika* will engender a turnaround of the communists' declining fortunes.

If French communist reformers want a chance to save the party, however, they'll have to act quickly. Party statistics put current membership at 200,000 (compared to 710,000 claimed in 1985), but party insiders concede this figure may be doctored a little. Signatures on "humanitarian" petitions circulated at communist-sponsored rallies are frequently counted as PCF membership, and many old comrades, even the deceased, are still counted as vital members of the French communist movement. The Paris daily *Le Figaro* suggests that the number of actual PCF members may already have dwindled to 100,000.

In Portugal, 76-year-old hard-liner Cunhal has rejected the notion that the Portuguese communist party (PCP) be held responsible for the mistakes of others, insisting instead on what he calls the "solution of continuity." Facing sinking membership (199,000 currently claimed, with 28 percent having no regular ties to the PCP) and a decline in votes received in local elections (where the PCP is usually stronger than in national elections), the leadership clings to its Stalinist course. But party dissidents like Zita Seabra, who was one of a number of would-be reformers expelled from the party this year, continue to argue "in exile" for unlimited debate, acceptance of the multi-party system, and privatization of many of Portugal's means of production.

If Seabra and other reform-minded expellees prevail, it will likely signal the full-scale "social democratization" of Western Europe's most doctrinaire communist party. Meanwhile, a frail but militant Álvaro Cunhal digs in for a showdown that may never take place. Rumors are afloat that the general secretary's poor health, which was worsened by "deficient" treatment at a Moscow hospital in 1988, may soon force the PCP's fossilized Stalinist leader to step down.

Equally orthodox has been the leadership of West Germany's communist party (DKP), whose fate, it seems, was inextricably linked to Erich Honecker's Socialist Unity Party in East Berlin. During the course of East Germany's stunning popular revolution last fall, nearly 30,000 of West Germany's 58,000 communists turned in their membership cards. By Christmas, the DKP was forced to lay off the last of its estimated 500 paid employees. According to West German intelligence sources, the West German communists funded their activities with the 50–70 million West German marks ($29–41 million) they received each year from their comrades in East Berlin.

The West German communists never attained the success of communists elsewhere in Western Europe, receiving only 0.5 percent of the 1987 vote, for example. But support from East Berlin's regime allowed the DKP the opportunity to be at least a player in the Federal Republic's political system. Today, the handful of militants still remaining in the DKP struggle against further splintering and the absorption of their tiny party by the left wing of the Social Democratic Party (SPD) and the West German Greens.

As Western Europe's communist left

THE FRENCH COMMUNIST PARTY'S STATISTICS PUT CURRENT MEMBERSHIP AT 200,000 (COMPARED TO 710,000 CLAIMED IN 1985).... THE NUMBER OF ACTUAL PCF MEMBERS MAY ALREADY HAVE DWINDLED TO 100,000.

collapses, strident hold-outs from the Rhine to the Pyrenees, repulsed by the prospect of social democratization, may soon found new communist organizations whose size and influence are likely to remain modest for the foreseeable future. Other ex-communists may find a niche for themselves in lesser currents of militant environmentalism, radical feminism, or sundry other preoccupations of the left. In Italy, so many communists have already joined the country's two Green parties that Italians have unofficially dubbed the Greens the "Watermelons"—green on the outside, red on the inside.

In Britain, where the Communist Party has never exerted an overt influence on politics, the ranks and resources of the movement continue to flag. The Kremlin recently canceled half of its standing order for 12,000 copies of Britain's communist newspaper, the *Morning Star*, threatening the existence of the 23,500-circulation paper.

An Opening for the Extremist Right?

It seems premature to conclude, however, that the death of West European communism will spell the end of significant radical political movements in Europe. In the world of radicalism, psychology is infinitely more important than ideology. One might argue, for example, that for many Western communists, Marxist ideology has represented not just an alternative approach to organizing a society but also a defiant, antisocial act in itself. While there may be little space for political and social militancy on the left in the coming decade, there are already signs that in the very heart of Western Europe frustrated, alienated elements of European society have begun to find their expression in protest parties of the extreme right.

Extremist right-wing parties have been active in Italy, France, and West Germany for years. Italy's neofascist Italian Social Movement (MSI) was founded in 1946; Germany's National Democratic Party (NPD) in 1964. In France, Jean-Marie Le Pen's National Front, organized in 1972 on an anti-immigration program, was able to startle observers in 1984 by winning 10 of the 81 seats in the European Parliament. Nevertheless, the influence of extremist right-wing political parties has remained marginal. In Germany, the rise of Franz Schönhuber's *Republikaner*, a party some critics call neo-Nazi, could be the first sign of a change in this state of affairs.

Poor showings in two regional elections held this spring, together with the recent resignation of party chairman Franz Schönhuber, a former officer in Hitler's *Waffen-SS* (he became frustrated by the dominance

of "extremist functionaries" in the party), have taken some wind out of the *Republikaner*'s sails. But even if the *Republikaner* party falters, the *Republikaner* phenomenon shows signs of taking hold. With a platform that embodies a combination of ethnocentric nationalism, isolationism, and strong authoritarian tendencies, the *Republikaner* have reached a surprisingly diverse audience in West Germany. One-third of the party's current voters previously voted for the liberal SPD, and while the majority of *Republikaner* members are over the age of 50, according to party statistics nearly 70 percent of new recruits since January 1989 are under 30.

On the eve of German reunification, the *Republikaner* attempt to harness the anxiety of many Germans over their country's social and economic future. The *Republikaner* cast themselves as "the party of the little man," bent on protecting job security, providing affordable housing, and reinstating "law and order." But in doing so, the party aggressively exploits the issue of West Germany's 4.6 million immigrant workers, whose presence, according to the *Republikaner* platform, threatens the "property and social status of German citizens." The *Republikaner* have fared best in West Berlin—last year they captured 7.5 percent of the vote—where the foreign population is 10 percent of the city's two million total.

Winning 7.1 percent of the vote in the 1989 European parliamentary elections, the *Republikaner* believe—despite a drop in recent opinion polls—that they can attain the minimum 5 percent nationally required for representation in Bonn's *Bundestag* next December. And with an eye cast toward the first Pan-German elections, party activists have been exploring "fertile soil" in the present-day German Democratic Republic. In light of the multitude of socioeconomic problems East Germans will inevitably face in the process of reunification, it is conceivable that the *Republikaner* will do well in reaching a segment of East German society where, after 56 years of dictatorship, a residual authoritarian impulse may lead some frustrated voters to identify with the extremist *Republikaner* platform.

If the *Republikaner* manage to establish themselves at the national level, even if the party's support remained modest, Germany's system of proportional representation allows the opportunity for smaller parties to exert enormous influence. Rarely receiving more than 10 percent of the vote, for example, the Free Democrats have been able to serve in coalition governments in Bonn since the war, capturing important cabinet posts from economics to foreign affairs.

The prospects for right-wing extremists

in France and Italy appear favorable as well. Like the *Republikaner*, Le Pen's National Front and Italy's neofascist MSI are fueled by anti-immigration sentiment, opposition to European unification, and in some cases, latent anti-Americanism. In last year's European elections, the National Front received 11.7 percent of the vote, the Italian neofascists 5 percent.

In both countries, there is already some evidence that suggests the issue of "foreigners" is serving as a catalyst for the improved position of the extreme right. Italy's estimated 1.5 million non-European immigrants, convenient scapegoats for right-wing extremists in a country struggling with 11 percent unemployment, have been confronted by rising levels of isolated but well-organized racially motivated violence, according to Italian officials.

Italy's MSI, which received 5.9 percent of the last national vote in 1987, has undergone a process of political rehabilitation in recent years that may well place the extreme right-wing party in a position to profit from rising levels of racial conflict and an immigration debate that has only begun to heat up.

Perhaps no national party campaigns as vigorously on race as the extreme right-wing National Front. In France, where non-European immigrants represent 6.5 percent of the population (compared to 8 percent in West Germany and less than 3 percent in Italy), racial politics have been a source of tension for a number of years. With unemployment at 10 percent and many Frenchmen on edge over the economic threat—real or imagined—posed by German reunification, Le Pen has turned up the rhetoric, maintaining that his brand of racism is "French patriotism."

In May, the French National Assembly approved a bill, apparently aimed at Le Pen's National Front, that would bar anyone found guilty of inciting racial hatred from holding an elective office or a government job. (The bill also makes it a misdemeanor in France to engage in "revisionism"—the denial of the crimes of Nazi Germany. Le Pen was recently ordered by a French court to pay a fine for referring to the Nazi gas chambers as just a "detail in World War II history.") But this attempt to legislate morality is unlikely to fend off parties like the National Front in the long run if the preference of some voters indeed surges to the extreme right.

With 9.6 percent of the vote in 1988, France's system of majoritarian representation allowed Le Pen's party only a single deputy in the 577-seat National Assembly. But Le Pen's hate-mongering won him 14 percent of the vote in the 1988 presidential race, and this self-proclaimed protector of French interests will likely remain a force to be reckoned with.

It's ironic that in the aftermath of communism's collapse in the East, while so many observers have focused their attention on what some have called the specter of right-wing nationalism in the Soviet Union and Eastern Europe, racial conflict in Western Europe has begun to show signs of becoming less manageable than in the past. It's also true that the fragmented political landscapes of France and Italy have safely endured a certain amount of right-wing extremism since the war. Even in Germany, it remains to be seen whether the *Republikaner* can actually establish themselves as a national party with a future. But columnist Jim Hoagland is correct when he observed that Europe's new enemy is "the enemy within." With the scourge of communism disappearing in both East and West, Western Europe's democrats must hold the ship steady as the new Europe embarks on its course into the twenty-first century.

LIKE THE REPUPUBLIKANER, LE PEN'S NATIONAL FRONT AND ITALY'S NEOFASCIST MSI ARE FUELED BY ANTI-IMMIGRATION SENTIMENT, OPPOSITION TO EUROPEAN UNIFICATION, AND IN SOME CASES, LATENT ANTI-AMERICANISM.

Several Germanys Since 1871, but Today's Is 'Very Different'

Richard Bernstein

In 1871 when Germany was first unified under Otto von Bismarck, the way ahead was marked by his phrase "blood and iron." This time the slogan has been inappropriate.

There have been several Germanys over the 119 years since the country first became a single national unit, governed from Berlin. They have in turn stretched over widely varying territories, incorporated different peoples, erected different political systems, and, perhaps most significant, caused innumerable human tragedies.

Historians generally agree that the Germany about to come into being has never existed before, not in its precise territorial condition, not in its political makeup and not in its relation to the rest of the world.

"I think we're going to see a new Germany very different from anything that existed before 1945, but I hope quite continuous with what we have seen in West Germany since 1949," said Fritz Stern, a German historian at Columbia University. "In some ways the real test of whether the Federal Republic constitutes a historic break with the past will come now.

"If, as I hope, it can assimilate East Germany into its political culture, respecting the social and psychological needs of the East Germans but gradually winning them over to a free and democratic society, then the break with the past will be assured," Professor Stern said.

Another historian, James Sheehan of Stanford University, argues that the newness of the emerging Germany makes the word "reunification" inaccurate.

A Turning to the West

"To think of a reunification is to suppose that there is some natural entity out there called Germany that was separated and is now reunited," he said. "But this is, after all, a state that never existed in its current boundaries. And it's not only a matter of borders. My impression is that Germany never was before a Western European state and society. The eastern border has moved west, and, in a much more important and significant way, German allegiances have turned west."

Any country's relationship with its past is complicated and often troubled, but the place of the new Germany in its history has a special meaning given its colossally flawed, tragic nature. Historians, looking at two world wars and the holocaust, have identified certain fundamental themes of the German past, all of them related to the country's historic inability to satisfy its national aspirations and, at the same time, to remain peaceful and democratic. It is in this sense that the latest unification of Germany seems a departure from previous models, and a happy departure, historians say.

"The classic account of German history talks about the struggle for unity and freedom," Professor Sheehan said. "The liberal tradition within Germany always hoped that the two would turn out to be one and the same, but, in fact, the Germans seemed continually to have been confronted by the apparent need to choose one or the other."

Four Separate Periods

In all, German history since the first unification could be divided up into four separate periods, each of them seeming to be characterized by a different Germany. Each of the German incarnations gripped the geographical center of Europe. Every version of the German nation has also been at the heart of the overall contest that continued, in one form or another, right up to the end of the cold war.

The Germany forged in war and diplomacy by Bismarck stretched in the west from Alsace and Lorraine, seized in a war with France in 1870, to the territories of East Prussia, now parts of either Poland or the Soviet Union. Bismarck's Germany had some fundamental features that have endured throughout modern history. It had the largest population in Europe, outside Russia. It had the continent's most powerful economy. It had the most advanced system of social welfare in Europe.

Unlike the present day unified Germany, however, it was a highly militaristic state. Unlike France and Britain, which both made progress, however difficult and halting, toward genuine representative democracy, Germany, despite some democratic trappings, remained autocratic, controlled by the emperor and the chancellor in league with large, conservative landowners and industrialists. It was, moreover, highly nationalistic, yearning, as the phrase had it, for its "place in the sun."

Responsibility for the outbreak of World War I is a complicated question, much disputed by historians. But German militarism and expansionism certainly played a major, very likely decisive role. Professor Stern argues that the central element of German history at the time was a deep antagonism between the deeply conservative, authoritarian ruling classes and the growing Social Democratic Party in Germany that was both reformist and patriotic. This was an antagonism that explains the tragic violence of German history, the country's long failure to make peace with itself and the outside world.

"The antagonisms that existed after 1918 were, of course, profoundly sharpened by the defeat in World War I,

which the ruling classes and the military immediately tried to blame on domestic opponents—the infamous 'stab in the back' lie," Professor Stern said.

The Germany that remained after World War I, the second of the modern Germanys, was vastly changed in its size and extent from Bismarck's era, though internally, much remained unaltered. The last emperor, William II, abdicated and what came to be known as the Weimar Republic was formed two days before Germany surrendered. In the peace treaty imposed by the Allies, Germany gave back Alsace and Lorraine to the French. A newly reconstituted Poland got large portions of previous German territory, including a corridor to the sea and the mining territory of Upper Silesia.

Seeds of Further Conflict

The remaining antagonisms inside Germany, the belief that domestic traitors had been responsible for the defeat, the humiliation of the peace, which formally blamed Germany for the war, a crippling inflation and the impossibility of paying the huge indemnity imposed by the peace treaty all were seeds of further conflict.

The Weimar republic struggled on with a succession of Socialist-led coalition governments, but all of the conservative forces, the monarchist army officers, the large landowners, even the former police agents of old imperial Germany remained in place. There were armed bands of anti-democratic rightists and agitators, one of whom, Adolf Hitler, went to prison after staging an abortive revolt in Munich in 1923.

Hitler, who joined the newly formed National Socialist German Workers Party in 1920, came to power in 1933 in a free election, and, once again, the old German urge toward militarism and expansion was ascendent, combined with a virulent strain of racial supremacy and a vicious anti-Semitism whose final result was the destruction of six million European Jews.

Hitler's Third Reich lasted until the end of World War II, and pushed the German borders to their widest extent. Germany in 1942 stretched from its pre-1919 borders on the West to the border of the Soviet Union in the East, a state of imperial dimensions built on old Prussian power, but far larger than anything envisaged, or desired, by Bismarck. It included Austria, which Bismarck had forcibly excluded from his Prussian-controlled federation.

Borders Were Redrawn

After the German defeat in World War II, the borders were dramatically redrawn to what they will be in the newly unified Germany. The border of Poland was moved about 100 miles to the west to compensate it for Polish lands taken in the war by the Soviet Union. The former German territory of East Prussia was divided between Poland and the Soviet Union, so that old German cities like Danzig (now Gdansk) and Königsberg (now Kaliningrad), where Immanuel Kant lived, were German no longer. Germany itself, after the war, became divided into the western zones, occupied by France, Britain and the United States, and the eastern zone, occupied by the Soviet Union.

Thus, the united Germany formally constituted today, with its capital in Berlin, is only a portion of the historic Germany created first by Bismarck and expanded, briefly, by Hitler. Will it remain that way? Nobody, of course, can be sure; but historians, comparing the new Germany with past Germanys, cite important differences that suggest an end to the old German habit of autocracy and expansionism.

"The Germany that was created in 1866 did have a chance to bring together the elements of unity and freedom," said Professor Sheehan. "It failed for lots of reasons, but the most important was that it refused to accept its geopolitical limits. The disasters that Germany brought upon itself were disasters of overreaching itself.

"That underscores the important difference between now and the past," Professor Sheehan continued. "I think that the Germans have now recognized their limits and have become Europeans in a way that was never the case in the past."

Referring to the Thirty Years' War, Professor Stern said: "The 17th century for Germany was a disaster of unprecedented magnitude. That was followed by efforts at Enlightenment in the 18th century, but, since then, from 1914 to 1945—and, for the East Germans, from 1949 to 1989—the Germans went through devastation and hardship, which they also inflicted on others. I have to believe they will have learned from all that."

Germany: The Uncertain Colossus

A new nation faces delicate questions about its role in the world

Marc Fisher
Washington Post Foreign Service

BONN—As the inevitability of German reunification became clear this year, countries whose people still wince at the mention of Germany insisted that the united nation not be allowed to fall into the aggressive pattern that led it to wage world war twice this century.

The Germans, anxious for approval of their audacious rush to end the postwar division, acceded to nearly every foreign demand: They promised a smaller military, forswore nuclear weapons and—after some domestic wrangling—assured their neighbors of permanent borders.

But by midyear, the pressures on the reuniting nation had shifted. The financially pressed superpowers wanted Germany to take the lead in rebuilding Eastern Europe. The Soviet Union began to see Germany as its economic savior. The Western allies criticized Germany for being slow to do its part in the international effort in the Persian Gulf.

The new Germany, which last week became whole and fully sovereign for the first time since 1945, finds itself in an uncomfortable position: astride the center of Europe, simultaneously a potential threat and benefactor to troubled nations on all sides.

The Germans keep trying to calm foreign concern. After considerable delay, they came up with $2 billion for the gulf effort. They agreed to pay $10 billion to the Soviets, part in direct aid, part to support the 360,000 Soviet troops still stationed in East Germany.

But the truth is, the new Germany cannot entirely ease its neighbors' suspicions because neither the Bonn government nor the German people are yet certain of their country's global role.

"We are not a world power, and I consider it foolish to dream world-power dreams," Chancellor Helmut Kohl said after Soviet President Mikhail Gorbachev gave his surprise endorsement of German unity in July.

But this month, after some U.S. congressmen and other allies complained of Bonn's passivity in the gulf crisis, Kohl agreed that the united Germany faces new international responsibilities.

"The united Germany will carry greater weight," Foreign Minister Hans-Dietrich Genscher told the United Nations two weeks ago. "We will accept this responsibility in Europe and around the world."

After 40 years of successful democracy, will West Germany be replaced by a larger, more powerful country whose strong ties to the Soviet Union and economic and political dominance of Europe make the world wary? Or is the new Germany only a somewhat larger West Germany—a successful merchant with a shy diplomatic front, a limited military and a deep fear of getting involved?

Divided, Germany was the focus of the Cold War, playing host to the most destructive weapons and most concentrated collection of forces on the planet.

What happens to those forces in the coming years will help mold the future Germany. For now, a modified version of the status quo prevails. The reunified Germany will be a member of NATO, but the Soviet troops will remain, to be withdrawn over the next four years. NATO troops will not be stationed in former East German territory but will stay in the area that was West Germany.

United, Germany will be a country of nearly 80 million people with an economy almost double the size of France's. Even before unification, the West German GNP was $1.4 trillion, behind only the United States and Japan.

For the next few years, the new Germany will focus on retraining East German workers and updating the disastrous infrastructure it has inherited from the Communist regime. But the new Germany, stretching from France to Poland, will soon be poised to resume its historic role as the business backbone of Eastern Europe, reaching out to new

THE NEW GERMANY

Area: 137,743 square miles, more than half the size of Texas. It combines West Germany's 95,975 square miles with 41,768 square miles of East German territory.

Population: At least 77.6 million, 61 million from West Germany plus 16. 6 million in East Germany. Berlin, with 3 million residents, is the largest city and the united nation's capital, as stated in the treaty uniting the Germanys. Bonn will be the interim seat of government. The all-German parliament (to be elected Dec. 2) will decide if the seat of government stays in Bonn or moves to Berlin.

Economy: The most powerful in Europe. Restructuring East Germany's economy to bring it to Western standards may cost $775 billion. Unemployment in what is now East Germany could reach 2 million as formerly state-subsidized firms go bankrupt. Germany has pledged to pay more than $7 billion to the Soviet Union to pay for the withdrawal of the Soviet Army from East German territory within four years.

Government: A federal democracy, run by Chancellor Helmut Kohl, Vice-Chancellor and Foreign Minister Hans-Dietrich Genscher and President Richard von Weizsaecker. The three now hold those posts in West Germany.

History: East Germany and West Germany were founded in 1949 after the victorious World War II Allies divided Germany. West Germany was created from territory occupied by the United States, France and Britain. East Germany was composed of territory occupied by the Soviet Union. Germany was first united in 1871 under Kaiser Wilhelm I. The Weimar Republic replaced

the imperial government at the end of World War I. Nazi dictator Adolf Hitler replaced the parliamentary government in 1933 and ruled until his defeat in 1945.

markets with the East Germans' Communist-era contacts and the all-new industrial plants that West German companies plan for the former East Germany.

The fall of the Berlin Wall last November brought the curtain down on Germany's postwar probation; by endorsing unification, the countries that fought Nazi Germany recognized the success of West German democracy. That makes some Germans feel proud, but it has not clarified the debate over the new Germany's role in the world.

"Feelings of strength are not good for us Germans," says Oskar Lafontaine, the Social Democratic chancellor candidate whose campaign in the first all-German election includes a strong pitch against any expansion of German power.

"We really have no idea what we want to be," says Robert Leicht, a leading West German political essayist. "If any German had said at the end of 1989 that we want reunification and then a wider role, even a wider military role, the whole world would have seen this as an outrage. But now the economic interdependence of the world makes it impossible to stand aside."

"For 45 years, we've had a marvelous division of labor in the world," says Munich historian Michael Stuermer. "Others did the dirty work and we did the moralizing. Now we are a rich country with worldwide interests. Everyone knows that if civil war breaks out in the Soviet Union, Ger-

many would have to be in the forefront of containing it."

Until the gulf crisis, many Germans saw their united country playing no new role other than as passive model for the emerging democracies of Eastern Europe. Countries such as Czechoslovakia and Hungary already are using postwar West Germany as a guide, adopting elements of its success, such as a law that admits political parties to parliament only after they have won 5 percent of the vote—a way of preventing a paralyzing fragmentation of the body politic.

Kohl sees the conversion of East Germany's Communist system into a market economy as an object lesson to Eastern Europe. "If we cannot make a success out of reunification, who is likely to succeed anywhere else?" he says.

But in recent weeks, Germans have been forced to consider a much more active role for their emerging nation. "We're being pushed onto a track again where we have to act as a national state," says Theo Sommer, editor of the influential weekly Die Zeit. "But if we have learned any lesson, we must proceed through Europe, as one Europe."

The dream of European integration—not just in economics, but in some undefined political union—is stronger in Germany than almost anywhere else, in good part because of the discomfort many leading Germans feel about collapsing once more into a nationalist nightmare.

Although British Prime Minister Margaret Thatcher continues to resist giving up more national authority to the European bureaucracy in Brussels, Kohl and Genscher, who see eye to eye on little else, are adamant in their insistence that, as the foreign minister put it, "We want not a German Europe, but a European Germany."

That goal—a desire for unity beyond the common trade and customs zone that the European Community is scheduled to become at the end of 1992—has grown even more pressing to leaders in Bonn because of fear that East Germans will become a provincial and even nationalist strain as they struggle through years of unemployment and other transitional hardship.

West German officials are confident that, contrary to worries that the German obsession with unification will steal the momentum of European integration, German unity will actually boost the European process because, as one official says, "no one wants a dominant Germany."

Opinion polls show the West German population firmly behind their government's wish to ease the German burden by investing more heavily in a European melange. But when it comes to broadening their country's political and military global role, West Germans part company with their leaders.

The consensus among the political elite that unification brings new responsibilities has not broken through to the wider public in the West. The East Germans, focused on their own economic plight, are even more likely to back a neutralist path, polls show. Even the gulf crisis, which has so dominated public attention in the United States and other Western countries, remains a secondary story in the German media.

West Germany has the largest military in Europe outside of the Soviet Union, but the legacy of two world wars has created a public that strongly rejects participation by German troops in the Persian Gulf. A survey by the respected Allensbach Institute this month showed West Germans opposed by 53 percent to 32 percent to the constitutional change Kohl has proposed to allow German troops to take part in U.N. military actions. Only 24 percent said German troops should respond even if another country asks for help.

West German officials say the Nazi drive for world domination makes Germany deeply reluctant to send troops to the Middle East even if the role of the German military is broadened by constitutional amendment—a legal change many scholars call unnecessary. "You will not see German troops in any role anywhere near Israel or anywhere in the Balkans," one Bonn source says. "Our history simply will not allow it."

The strong anti-military strain in German society is part of a strong popular reluctance to expand the country's profile abroad. Guenter Grass, the West German novelist and opponent of reunification, says that a united Germany is "doomed to failure" because "our unified state filled the history books of the world with suffering, ruin, defeat, millions of refugees, millions of dead and a burden of crimes which we will never be able to throw off."

Grass's view, although a distinct minority in Germany, contributes to a broader belief that the newly sovereign Germany should no longer be the base for hundreds of nuclear weapons—part of a national tendency toward neutrality that worries Germany's NATO allies.

As Soviet troops pull out of East Germany—with Bonn paying for their transportation, job training and housing back home—popular pressure will rise for the United States to remove its nuclear weapons from West Germany, the former front line in the East-West confrontation. Germany already has declared the former East German territory to be a nuclear-free zone.

Lafontaine, Kohl's challenger, has called for the withdrawal of all U.S. nuclear weapons. Kohl's Christian Democrats, who are heavily favored to win renewed support in the December elections, dismissed Lafontaine's proposal as a step toward neutrality and reaffirmed their commitment to NATO.

U.S. and other Western diplomats here say they hope to maintain a nuclear presence in Germany by relying on a "no nukes, no troops" formula, an appeal to the many Germans who believe that a continued U.S. troop presence in their country is essential to their security, especially given the volatile state of the Soviet Union. Last week, the United States and the Soviet Union agreed in principle on a treaty to limit non-nuclear forces in Europe. Negotiations on limiting the number of troops are pending.

Despite smooth progress toward German unity and the relative ease of winning international agreement on unification, many West German leaders are wary of the future. The Soviet troops in East Germany remain a potential flashpoint; several hundred already have deserted, and officials here fear many more will be emboldened by the idea of being behind "enemy" lines after unification.

Only three months ago, some West German commentators spoke of an emerging Washington-Bonn-Moscow axis, a new structure for the post-postwar world in which the reunited Germany would take on political and perhaps military responsibilities commensurate with its size. Under this scenario, as the superpowers' financial might declined, the new Germany would outgrow the Nazi legacy and be more willing to lead. Its first task would be rebuilding East Germany and Eastern Europe; a united Western Europe would follow.

But the first world crisis since the unification juggernaut began less than a year ago has made that vision seem simplistic.

"The word 'axis' is wrong," says Oxford historian Ralf Dahrendorf, a longtime Germany observer. "There are two special relationships—Washington and Bonn, and Moscow and Bonn, with Britain and France disappearing somewhere. But you can be sure that Washington's dealings with Moscow won't be through Bonn. Germany's role expands, but we cannot yet know how. This is really the emergence of a Germany that no one understands."

In the West, the Bloom is Off the Rose

HAMBURG—In the first weeks after the Berlin Wall opened, East Germans, rushing over the border in their sad, sputtering Trabant automobiles and marveling at the riches in the shops, were embraced with more warmth than many West Germans thought their nation could muster.

Even big cities, including this one, laid out a small-town welcome, showering newcomers with money, advice, food, clothes and jobs.

That was before West Germans watched the East German government collapse, before they discovered that the country they had always heard described as the jewel of the East Bloc was really an economic relic, firmly fixed in the 1940s. It was before West Germans learned that the unexpected end of the 40-year division of their land could cost $775 billion over the next five years, enough to force even the most affluent nation in Europe to borrow money and, as the government in Bonn finally admitted this month, perhaps even to raise taxes.

Now, as the West German flag has become the banner of all Germany, a surprisingly large number of West Germans have approached the birth of a new nation with a combination of resignation, regret and nostalgia for their own country, which represented the rebirth of democracy after the Nazi disaster.

Last winter's euphoria is over; 29 percent of West Germans now oppose unification, according to a poll by the newsmagazine Der Spiegel. West German investment in the East is lagging far behind what the Bonn government had expected, largely because of continuing uncertainty about East German property laws. And even top aides to Chancellor Helmut Kohl now believe that, as one official says, "We went too fast. We both needed time. We are just too different."

> **Many West Germans greeted the birth of a new nation with resignation, regret and nostalgia for their own country.**

"This is worse than an old house we are taking over," says Michael Stuermer, a West German historian and adviser to Kohl. "It's a rotten piece of real estate, but we have to buy it because it's an old family heirloom. There will be no end to the cost of repairs. But it must be done."

The jubilation that last fall led to an outburst of pride and flag-waving that Germans had not permitted themselves since the early years of Nazi rule has been replaced by a more sober, businesslike attitude. When President Bush and Soviet President Mikhail Gorbachev both said they were too busy to accept invitations to attend last week's unification ceremonies, Kohl announced that instead of the proposed nationwide spectacle, the event would be "inward-looking."

The celebration may have been muted, but no one has given up on the ultimate success of unification. Rather, the process looks slower and much more complicated than many had first hoped. The potential profits and pride that could accrue to the West from bringing 16 million people into a high-tech consumer society have captured the imagination of many West Germans. The West is experiencing something of a unification boom. But as of last week, there is no more West Germany, and the new part of the united nation is not a happy sight.

East Germany emerged from its proud, bloodless revolution little more than a charity case. Last winter, the Hamburg city employment office had little trouble finding positions for arriving East Germans. But then word started trickling back from employers: East Germans got tired quickly—they weren't used to working a full day. They had to be taught everything from how to open a bank account to how to find an apartment. They did nothing they weren't told to do.

Klaus Koch, chief of Hamburg's employment office, has dealt with West German employers and their East German workers since last fall. "As more things got difficult here," he says, "as more things went crazy over there, with their ministers coming

and going, political nonsense, the costs going up and up, the taxes—well, people here lost all interest in East Germany."

Two-thirds of West Germans expect to have to make financial sacrifices, but only one-third say they are willing to do so, according to the Der Spiegel poll. And another survey found that two-thirds of West Germans expect unification to produce rising social tensions. Bonn officials say there was no choice. East Germany unraveled faster than anyone expected; industrial production there has plummeted by 42 percent in the past year. And East German voters made their preference for quick unification clear at the ballot box in March.

The East German hunger for Western goods has given the already-strong West German economy a boost. The German Institute for Economic Research predicts 4 percent economic growth this year with a 2 percent rise in employment. Nearly every major company plans to build plants or sell products in the East. Volkswagen broke ground in September for a $1.9 billion plant in Mosel, East Germany, where Europe's largest auto maker plans to produce 250,000 cars a year by 1995. In the first half of this year, the West German auto industry reported a 50 percent increase in new car orders over the first six months of 1989—a reflection of East Germans' desire to scrap their embarrassing Trabants and get something that can compete on the no-speed-limit West German highways.

Still, most of the plans remain just that. Many firms have postponed expanding to the East because East Germany failed to guarantee the finality of land purchases by Westerners or because the desperate shape of the East German infrastructure seemed daunting.

Last winter's benevolence has been replaced by an undercurrent of resentment against the struggling East Germans. A West German official complains that her nephew, the son of an ambassador, is angry because the Foreign Ministry is making his job search harder by deciding to hire East Germans. A Bonn landlord told her tenants she has found them a new and cheap gardener, but she will have to send a friend to watch over him because he is East German and therefore may steal.

For months after the Berlin Wall fell, Ruediger Loewe, a Munich television executive, did not visit his ancestral estate in East Germany even though his family has two sets of Meissen china buried on the grounds. "Of course we had to send them Christmas parcels every year," Loewe says. "But really, I feel no connection to them. We have so little in common."

"They are total strangers to me," says Angelika Volle, a political scientist in Bonn. "I don't know any East Germans. I know more Hungarians and Poles than I do East Germans. They don't know anything of Europe. My friends are British, French and American. I speak their languages. The East Germans don't. They've never traveled. They've never been confronted with being German and taking responsibility for what this country has done. We had all those painful discussions in our student days: What did your parents do in the Third Reich? What did we do to the Jews? The East Germans are just starting all that."

West Germans who have tried to reconnect with their cousins "over there" are sometimes frustrated, sometimes rewarded. "We used to have a bad conscience about them because they had a wall and we were rich," says Sybille Wehrle, 31, a West Berlin schoolteacher. "Now you meet them and you feel like the mother. They want you to teach them everything. So now people here feel free to say, 'Lousy Easties.'"

When Wehrle met some East German colleagues, she found the cultural gulf too deep. Her fellow teachers immediately addressed Wehrle using the informal German word for "you" and called her house the day after they first met. "That would never happen" in the more formal West, Wehrle says. She did not return the call.

Other West Germans rediscovered bonds that had weakened over two generations of forced separation. Monika Zimmermann, a West German, is the new editor of East Berlin's Neue Zeit, a daily newspaper now owned by the Frankfurter Allgemeine, one of the West's most successful papers. "West Germans really knew nothing of East Germany," she says. "Some just had this fear of socialism. Some wouldn't come over [to the East] because of all the unpleasantness you faced at the border. Then suddenly the whole world said we West Germans were the experts on East Germany. It wasn't true. The human contact between West and East was mostly between relatives, and it was forced. I have relatives in the West whom I don't see because I don't like them. But if you had relatives in the East, you had to send a Christmas basket—no question."

Now, building relationships driven by more than guilt, Zimmermann finds East Germans curious about her and hungry to connect with the West. "This is a poorly developed part of Germany," she says. "We have to give them the courage to make their own decisions, and then things work perfectly."

The clash between East and West can be ugly. Some East Germans accuse West German politicians and business people of being arrogant colonizers. Some West Germans call their cousins lazy workers incapable of thinking for themselves.

"In fact, we are not arrogant," says Theo Sommer, editor of Die Zeit, West Germany's most influential intellectual weekly. "We just know how things work. Maybe what they resent is that their way doesn't work."

The gap between the two societies has been exacerbated by a relentless West German assault on nearly every aspect of the East German system. After long and bitter debate, East Germany was allowed to keep its more liberal abortion law for an interim period of two years, but other than that, the East Germans lost almost every major dispute with Bonn.

West German politicians and TV commentators routinely ridicule East German leaders. The premier of Bavaria called them "hobby ministers." The Bonn government put out an instructional comic book for East Germans showing Ludwig Erhard, architect of West Germany's 1950s economic miracle, teaching a dog the basics of capitalism. The comic was quickly scrapped after criticism that it was insulting to East Germans.

Despite such lapses, many West Germans have faced unification with a sense of duty, turning considerable attention and resources to the mammoth tasks of rebuilding houses, roads and railways and installing telephone, energy and pollution control systems. They are doing the work in part because, as East German Prime Minister Lothar de Maiziere says, "it is their moral obligation." But they are also doing it to save what they have built since Germany surrendered in 1945, its cities and villages reduced to rubble. West Germany was the first German state in which democracy thrived, and West Germans, proud of that legacy, are worried that the addition of 16 million East Germans may threaten their political stability.

"They're more xenophobic than we are, condescending and even offensive to Poles and Russians," Sommer says. "The priority here is not to get back on the nationalist track."

Last fall, West Germans were thrilled by East German demonstrators' standing up to their government and chanting, "We are the people." But now, Sommer says, "We have to stand up for West Germany. The time will come when we say, 'We are also the people.' The tail can't wag the dog."

—Marc Fisher

A United Germany Shoulders New Responsibilities

HANS-DIETRICH GENSCHER

Hans-Dietrich Genscher is the Minister of Foreign Affairs for the Federal Republic of Germany. This article is adapted from a speech delivered to the Bundestag *September 20, 1990.*

Together with the original unification treaty, the treaty on the final settlement with respect to Germany (the result of the two-plus-four negotiations) signed in Moscow on September 12 has opened up the way to the unification of a free Germany. The signing of this treaty marks the end of Europe's post-war history. Not only does it present Germans with a new opportunity to make a comprehensive new beginning, but the treaty also points to a better future for all of Europe. The document expresses the desire for peace and terminates the

> *Germany confirms the rights and obligations arising from the treaty on the nonproliferation of nuclear weapons. The decision to reduce the united German armed forces to 370,000 is a significant contribution to the reduction of conventional forces in Europe.*

rights and responsibilities of the four powers (the United States, Britain, France and the Soviet Union) relating to Berlin and Germany as a whole. With the treaty in force, a united Germany regains full sovereignty over its internal and external affairs, including the right to belong to alliances. Thus, our objective not to encumber the united Germany with unresolved questions has been achieved. While the treaty on the final settlement still bears the signature of the representatives of the two German states, its ratification will be a task for the first all-German parliament.

The participating states of the Conference on Security and Cooperation in Europe (CSCE) already appreciate that the unification of Germany does not create new problems for Europe. Germans have confirmed the united Germany's responsibility for peace in the final settlement treaty. We have solemnly reaffirmed that only peace will emanate from German soil. We have confirmed that any acts intending to disturb the peaceful relations between nations are unconstitutional and should be subject to punishment.

Germany has thus declared to the world that it shall never employ any of its weapons except in accordance with the German constitution and the United Nations Charter. Furthermore, the united Germany will try to set a good example by reaffirming its renunciation of the manufacture, possession and control of nuclear, biological or chemical weapons. Germany confirms the rights and obligations arising from the treaty on the nonproliferation of nuclear weapons. The decision to reduce the united German armed forces to 370,000 within three to four years is a significant contribution to the reduction of conventional forces in Europe. It is hoped that Germany's example will be followed by others.

On October 3, 1990, the German people began once again to live in one democratic state for the first time in 57 years. While this was greeted with joy and gratitude, it was an occasion for reflection. When the darkness of fascism descended on Germany in 1933, Germany lost the respect and friendship of other nations. Conscious of the four powers' approval of our national unity, we commemorate the untold suffering which Germany brought on other nations. We commemorate the victims of the war and totalitarianism, and are united in the intention never to allow any of this to happen again. Our thoughts turn especially to the Jewish people. The united Germany will continue to be aware of its responsibility toward the Jewish people.

Trust Regained

We recognize that the trust of all nations accompanied us on the way to national unity. The establishment of a free political and social order in the Federal Republic of Germany, as well as our country's policy of peace and responsibility, has won back the trust of the other nations. We have returned to the community of democracies by joining the Council of Europe, the Western Alliance, and the European Community. The Treaties of Moscow and Warsaw, the Treaty with Czechoslovakia and the basic treaty with the German Democratic Republic laid the foundation for a new relationship with our Eastern neighbors and the relationship between the two German states during the period of national division. The path leading us out of the ruins of World War II has been a long one, yet it has led to the most peaceful and the most socially oriented state in our history.

The actions of men like Konrad Adenauer, Willy Brandt and Walter Scheel represent Germany's fundamental post-war foreign policy decisions. The Federal Republic's treaty policy, for instance, opened up the way to the Helsinki Final Act. Starting from the basis of the Moscow treaty, the German-Soviet declaration of June 13,1989 lent a new quality to German-Soviet relations. It was a major interim step on the road to the comprehensive treaty initialed in Moscow on September 12, 1990.

German unification opens up the historic opportunity for Germans to make a joint contribution to a peaceful, free and united Europe. In following the European path to national unity, Germany has achieved the goal embodied in the preamble of its Basic Law. The pledges made by France, the United States and Great Britain in the 1954 Convention on Relations between the three powers and the Federal Republic of Germany have been fulfilled.

Germany will exercise its full sovereignty with an awareness of its responsibility for peace. The sovereign, democratic and free Germany will be committed to the unity, stability and progress of Europe as a whole. Germany will also help Europe in its responsibility to shape a new global order. Indeed, the united Germany will have more weight with Europe. We know that the nations of Europe are concerned as to how the Germans will use it. There can be only one answer: with its greater weight, Germany will not seek more power but will act in awareness of the added responsibility imposed upon it.

Commitment to Peace

Policy of the united Germany will be determined by its commitment to peace and to the fundamental values enshrined in our Basic Law. Even in light of four decades of German post-war policy, our mandate today could not have been formulated more impressively than it was in the preamble to the Basic Law: to achieve the unity of Germany, to unite Europe and to serve world peace. This determines Germany's European calling—the responsibility for peace.

We shall continue our responsible policy in Europe. We wish to develop the European Community into a European union that will embrace political union as well as economic and monetary union. The quicker we achieve European union, the more we shall be promoting the unification of the whole of Europe. The European Community is a fundamental element of the one Europe of tomorrow.

Fundamental to the future of the European Community is a unique link between Germany and France. Ever closer Franco-German cooperation is the basis of German foreign policy. At their meeting in Munich on September 18, 1990, Chancellor Kohl and President Mitterand declared that "the achievement of German unification, which we jointly welcome, gives a new dimension and a broader horizon to our cooperation, the aim of which has been from the very outset to advance together the cause of European unification in all spheres."

Germany's contribution to this one Europe is also an investment in its European future. The major task of a European policy for stability is to sustain political, economic, social and ecological changes in Central and Eastern Europe; military factors will play an ever-decreasing role in this process. Germany has a special responsibility in this process due to our economic and political weight and our position at the center of Europe. Nonetheless, we are always aware that the Soviet Union is a part of Europe and that without it, one Europe cannot come about.

The "treaty on good neighborliness, partnership and cooperation" initialled in Moscow serves this great European aim. Not only does it establish a new, future-oriented basis for German-Soviet relations, it also underlines the central importance of these relations for the whole of Europe. This was reaffirmed at the meeting between Chancellor Kohl and President Gorbachev in the Caucasus in July 1990. The people of our two countries should also be included in these new-style relations. This applies equally to the Soviet soldiers who will leave the GDR within the next three to four years. Both states have set about bringing innovation to the whole of Europe.

Before us lie major opportunities for comprehensive, broad-based, future-oriented cooperation. Yet this cooperation is not only a German-Soviet matter. The Soviet Union is linking its future with Europe's destiny through its close cooperation with Germany – an EC member that is firmly anchored within the Western Alliance and represents one of the driving forces behind the CSCE process.

European Security

Germany also recognizes its greater responsibility for the future of Europe in its relations with Poland. The inviolability of the existing borders is a key element of a peaceful European order. As the treaty of September 12, 1990 confirms, Germany has no territorial claims against other countries. The united Germany will confirm the present German-Polish border in a treaty binding under international law as soon as possible. Through the Warsaw Treaty, we paved the way for reconciliation with the Polish people. German relations with Poland are a special expression of its European calling, and Germany therefore intends to lay the foundations for a new chapter of good neighborly relations between Germany and Poland in an additional comprehensive German-Polish treaty.

We will also help consolidate and institutionalize the CSCE process. This is the great European structural task for the next decade. In 1975, the 35 signatory states committed themselves to freedom, democracy and respect for human rights by signing the CSCE Helsinki Final Act. Developments since then have proved the expediency of that courageous decision. The summit conference due to be held in Paris on November 19 will

3. AMERICAN ALLIES: Western Europe

mark a new stage in the CSCE process and will set up the first joint institutions of the new, united Europe. A new, cooperative, peaceful order will be established throughout Europe by regular ministerial consultations, the creation of a center for the prevention of conflict and the development of a secretariat. With active German participation, the Conference for Security and Cooperation in Europe is developing step-by-step into a structure for European cooperation, security and stability.

The end of the East-West conflict and the changing relations between the states belonging to the two alliance systems pave the way for new cooperative security structures in Europe. Within the framework of this cooperative security policy, the Bundeswehr will continue to maintain peace, albeit under changed circumstances. The single German nation will have a single army, though the new federal states will have a different security status for the time being. This also means that Bundeswehr soldiers will be stationed next to Red Army soldiers. It is our wish that a new partnership and new trust will evolve from this.

Through a cooperative European security system institu-tionalized within the CSCE framework, the essential foundations for a new peaceful European order from the Atlantic to the Urals will have been laid. To achieve this, arms negotiations must catch up with the breathtaking pace of political developments. We will give them new impetus.

For Germany, greater responsibility means strengthening transatlantic relations. The Atlantic must not grow wider as the European Community acquires a stronger identity on the path towards European union. On the contrary: the two continents must grow even closer together. A transatlantic declaration between the European Community and the North American democracies will lend this bond a new quality. The Western Alliance, which redefined its future and its responsibility in the London declaration of June 6, 1990, links the United States and Canada with the newly evolving cooperative security structures in Europe. Furthermore, the elimination of the East-West conflict has opened up the prospect of a new global order. For decades, the division of Europe and the East-West conflict have tied up our energies. Now we want to use them together, for Europe and the world.

NATO'S IDENTITY CRISIS

NATO leaders have thought of seven reasons to stay in business, even though the communist threat has crumbled.

ECKHARD LÜBKEMEIER

Eckhard Lübkemeier is a research associate in the study group on security and disarmament issues at the Friedrich Ebert Foundation in Bonn, Germany. This article is adapted from a paper presented at a symposium sponsored by the Swedish Defense Research Establishment in Stockholm, June 1990.

At their London summit in July, NATO leaders celebrated the North Atlantic Alliance as "the most successful defensive alliance in history." NATO members indeed have a good reason for being pleased—the epic change in Europe's political and military landscape. The Cold War has ended without ever erupting, and the collapse of communist regimes and command economies in Central and Eastern Europe testifies to the strength of Western political ideas and economic structures.

But at its very moment of triumph, NATO faces an unprecedented identity crisis. Contrary to its leaders' recent claims, NATO has been predominantly a military alliance. Its main purpose has been to deter the Soviets and their communist allies. More tacitly, NATO also served to fetter West German military might. The crumbling Warsaw Pact and Moscow's "new thinking" on foreign policy—mutual security at radically reduced force levels—are undermining NATO's overt role. That process, in turn, will erode the viability of NATO's less obvious purpose, to restrain German military potential. Ironically, German unification, which increases concern about German power, is occurring at the same moment.

Thus, in its forty-first year, NATO is confronted with the question of whether it has outlived its usefulness. Is NATO still needed when the potential aggressor is turning into a partner? Or, as Strobe Talbott suggested, has the time come "to think seriously about eventually retiring the North Atlantic Treaty Organization?"[1]

At the July summit, Western leaders agreed that the alliance must change. Their new watchword is politicization, and they suggest that NATO's political role should grow as its military role declines. The particulars of this transformation have not been spelled out, but in general the formula is meant to indicate that functions other than containing the Soviet Union will become more important. What their relative importance will be is still a matter for conjecture.

Alliance leaders also stated in their London communiqué that, "as Europe changes, we must profoundly alter the way we think about defense." They adopted several guidelines which can be summarized as the "Four M Principles"—minimum deterrence (particularly with regard to substrategic nuclear forces), mobility, mobilizable conventional forces, and multinational forces. But implementing these principles may stir controversial discussions within the alliance in the future.

Nearly all NATO supporters reject the view that one of NATO's new missions is to render itself obsolete. The

3. AMERICAN ALLIES: Western Europe

NATO foreign ministers, meeting in Turnberry, Scotland, in June, said instead, "We see the CSCE [Conference on Security and Cooperation in Europe] process as an important framework for far-reaching reforms and stability and as a central element in the construction of a new Europe, along with other European institutions including the alliance itself. The function of the CSCE will be complementary to that of the alliance." Similarly, U.S. Secretary of State James Baker, in a June 3 interview on *Meet the Press*, favored giving the CSCE process a security component, "but only if it complemented the role of NATO, and did not, in any way, supplant it." West German Chancellor Helmut Kohl has made the same argument. An exception is West German Foreign Minister Hans-Dietrich Genscher who, at a March meeting of the Western European Union, publicly mused about "new European security structures" which eventually could absorb NATO and the Warsaw Pact.

NATO proponents have suggested seven principal elements—some new, some old—to NATO's future role.

■ **Keeping U.S. might as a counterweight.** Even after the Soviet Union makes deep conventional and nuclear cuts, it will remain the foremost military power in Europe. In an April 29 interview on *This Week with David Brinkley*, U.S. Defense Secretary Richard Cheney explained: "The U.S. is the counterweight, if you will, to the Soviet influence on the continent of Europe. And a presence by the U.S. there is crucial." President George Bush said in a May commencement address at Oklahoma State University, "As part of our global responsibilities, the foundation for America's peaceful engagement in Europe has been, and will continue to be, NATO."

This argument has two main flaws. It is true that the Soviet Union—or Russia, should the Soviet Union break up into independent republics—will remain a formidable military power. But military capabilities per se do not constitute a military threat. A state is a potential aggressor depending on its leadership and whether it is perceived as such by another state, when its military capabilities are seen as threaten-

ing because of suspicions about its political intentions. Although the United States, Great Britain, and France all have nuclear weapons that could destroy Germany, most Germans feel protected rather than threatened by these weapons.

In the past, the Soviet threat was the result of its military hardware combined with Europe's perception of its policy as expansionist and confrontational. Moscow's new cooperative foreign policy has caused this perception to change in a fundamental way. Still, it will take some time to overcome the Cold War legacy and establish the same level of mutual confidence between the Soviet Union and the West that the Western countries have achieved among themselves. Until then, Europe will need some kind of military counterweight to the Soviet Union.

In principle, this requirement could be met without NATO. If Western Europeans mustered the political will, their financial and technological resources would be sufficient to deploy an independent deterrent force. This has been true for some time, and the objection that Western Europe alone could not contain its gigantic Soviet (or Russian) neighbor has become even less convincing in an era of mutual disarmament and the withdrawal of the Red Army from Central Europe.

Still, an independent West European deterrent is neither likely nor desirable, for political reasons. Western Europe has not yet reached the requisite level of political integration. As the Soviet threat diminishes, one of the prime motives for developing a separate defense identity is disappearing with it. European security would not be served if additional barriers to associations with the Central and East European democracies were erected. Similarly, there is no need to dissolve the European alliance with the United States. Doing so would cause transatlantic tensions and irritations in the East and the West—a price that cannot be justified. Thus, in the short run NATO remains the best means of balancing Soviet military strength in Europe.

■ **Providing insurance against Eastern instability.** The radical changes occurring in the Soviet Union and in Central and Eastern Europe are fraught with risks and the possibility of setbacks. As President Bush said in

May, "Our enemy today is uncertainty and instability." British Foreign Minister Douglas Hurd expressed a similar sentiment in an address at the Konrad Adenauer Foundation in February: "NATO offers us the prospect of stability in a world which to the south and to the east of our part of Europe will certainly remain turbulent."

The risks associated with the collapse of the Cold War confrontation are real. Ethnic and religious conflicts and separatist movements have arisen. However, under the old order of communist dictatorships and the Brezhnev doctrine these disputes were simply suppressed. It was the West that always pointed out the order's fragility and the need to replace it with political systems based on popular consent.

Can NATO function as insurance against the uncertainty and instability in Central and Eastern Europe? There is little the alliance can do to prevent or contain ethnic, religious, or national conflicts. At a level above the immediate parties, the security aspects of these conflicts are best dealt with by dispute resolution mechanisms on a regional or CSCE-wide level. Beyond its classic function of deterring aggression against a member state, NATO's role is limited to supporting such conciliatory efforts.

Turmoil within the Soviet Union could have, of course, a much larger effect on Western security. Some commentators have postulated scenarios in which a major war in Europe is triggered by the disintegration of the Soviet Union. These scenarios are usually based on implausible, sometimes bizarre assumptions. Nevertheless, even the remote prospect of a violent dissolution of the Soviet Union is unsettling. The alliance would have to contain whatever danger such a process might cause. But this is not a new task; rather it is merely an extension of NATO's traditional mission of deterrence.

■ **Promoting security cooperation.** In his May commencement address, President Bush asserted that "as military threats fade, the political dimension of NATO's work—always there but seldom noticed—becomes more prominent." At the London summit, NATO leaders described one of these central political functions as establishing a cooperative security order characterized by mutual confidence, defensively oriented military forces, and CSCE institutions charged with verifying arms agreements or settling disputes within and between states. NATO, they said, is an essential component of this new security architecture.

NATO can play an important role in organizing common security in Europe. Moreover, it will have to promote its development, since NATO's public support could critically wane if it were perceived to be engaged in foot-dragging. In a sense NATO representatives are—legitimately—trying to make a virtue of necessity. But their argument is problematic.

In the past, the principal factor binding NATO members together was the political and military threat posed by the communist bloc. This threat is disappearing, and it is unlikely to be supplanted by an equally strong adhesive. Barring a conservative backlash in the Soviet Union, NATO's cohesion and its importance will diminish in the future.

The dissolution of the Warsaw Pact and the establishment of CSCE-wide security structures will intensify this development. For NATO's value is bound to decrease if security becomes a common, pan-European effort.

Nor can NATO simply regard the Warsaw Pact, with its present members, as its natural partner in creating new and larger security arrangements for Europe. States such as Hungary, Czechoslovakia, and Poland must be free to decide about membership in the Warsaw Pact. The West should not suggest that they play a role they may wish to relinquish.

■ **Guaranteeing a U.S. presence.** For political and military reasons, the United States should remain closely allied and militarily present in Europe, and NATO guarantees that coupling.

For a variety of reasons, all European states apparently want the United States to remain a "European" power. Even Moscow seems to share this view. In a May interview in *Izvestia*, Soviet Foreign Minister Eduard Shevardnadze said, "In the past, it was our goal to push the Americans out of Europe at all costs. . . . We no longer regard the United States as our opponent." And Secretary Baker told his *Meet the Press* interviewers, "The Soviet Union has told us that they support the idea of a continuing American presence in Europe as a force for stability."

It is also true that—as seen from Washington—NATO is the best guar-antee of a continued U.S. voice in European affairs. Moreover, the U.S. has always enjoyed a dominant position in NATO.

However, the United States has been engaged in Europe to protect its own interests, not for mere benevolence. NATO is an instrument to this end, but it need not be indispensable to the United States. New arms control agreements and the CSCE process will become increasingly relevant.

Whatever NATO's future role may be, Washington will probably have to contend with a loss of influence, for two reasons. One is that growing West European integration will allow the Europeans to deal with the United States on a more equal footing. The other is a decreasing demand for U.S. military, particularly nuclear, protection.

■ **Promoting the political transformation of Eastern Europe.** One of NATO's new missions, some argue, is to further the reform process in Central and Eastern Europe. Secretary Baker told the Berlin Press Club in December 1989, "NATO should also begin considering further initiatives the West might take, through the CSCE process in particular, to build economic and political ties with the East, to promote respect for human rights, to help build democratic institutions, and to fashion, consistent with Western security interests, a more open environment for East-West trade and investment."

NATO can and must help to maintain a stable security framework, which will ease the successful economic and political transformation of Central and East European states. And this task is not different from NATO's central mission of preserving Western security. But the alliance is ill-suited to becoming an economic and political development agency. The European Community, the European Council, and, once operations begin in spring 1991, the European Bank for Reconstruction and Development will assume these responsibilities.

■ **Containing German power.** Soviet proposals for a neutral united Germany, put forward before the Kohl-Gorbachev meeting in July 1990, were unanimously rejected by Germany's Eastern and Western neighbors, who want to see Germany firmly embedded in a larger international framework. Many NATO supporters want the alliance to continue its oversight role: "The aim should be a strong, steady NATO—the other main check on German power—but that is going to be harder to bring off."[2]

The issue of NATO control over German military power resurfaced in spring 1989, during the argument over the follow-on-to-Lance missile. Now, the prospect of German unification has intensified concerns about German military potential. Germany must accept the fact that its history and potential power inevitably raise these concerns, and continuing membership in NATO helps to alleviate them.

At the same time, the end of the Cold War means Germany will be less dependent on NATO's overt military role. Its political leadership and population will be less tolerant of NATO's covert mission because of the discriminatory status it assigns Germany. Disarmament and arms control agreements and a reduction in German military forces will reduce fears about Germany's military strength, as will German participation and integration in CSCE-wide institutions. The economic and technological potential of a united Germany will probably be the strongest in Europe. The best way to dilute German potential in a post–Cold War world is by deepening the process of integration within the European Community. As former Chancellor Willy Brandt told the Social Democratic Party in December 1989, "Those who are afraid of the German mark should be willing to join us in our efforts to create a strong ECU [European Currency Unit]."

■ **Countering external threats.** Beyond the NATO area there are new threats on the horizon, and some old threats are becoming more virulent. These include regional conflicts, terrorism, drug trafficking, and the proliferation of modern weapons technology, including missiles and nuclear, chemical, and biological weapons. Secretary Baker maintains that "intensified NATO consultations on these issues can play an important role in forming common Western approaches to these various threats."

But NATO's ability to meet out-of-area challenges will be much more circumscribed than Secretary Baker's statement suggests. NATO would, of course, defend against aggression from an extra-European power, should such a threat emerge. But in general, other institutions and mechanisms will figure more prominently on this front. For example, the Missile Technology Control Regime should do more than NATO to contain the proliferation of missile technology. And efforts to expand the geographic area to which the NATO treaty applies are likely to meet strong opposition. Anticipating such resistance, NATO's Supreme Allied Commander Europe, U.S. Gen. John R. Galvin, does not think "we can have a systematic arrangement for taking care of out of area questions within NATO. It will be ad hoc—that is my own view of it."[3] A case in point is Iraq's invasion of Kuwait. At their meeting on August 10, 1990, NATO foreign ministers strongly condemned the Iraqi aggression, but the United States failed to get a commitment to a more global scope for alliance responsibilities.

Is it time for NATO to retire? Not yet. NATO still has important roles to play—maintaining a counterweight to Soviet military potential; negotiating, implementing, and coordinating disar-

mament and arms control; participating in the creation of cooperative security structures; keeping the U.S. presence in Europe; and providing a security framework for German military power.

But NATO is not irreplaceable. For the future, two considerations must be kept in mind. First, Soviet "new thinking" has cleared the way for building a pan-European *security community*. Members of such a community regard security as a common good that cannot be enjoyed at the expense of other members. But members continue to deploy troops to protect themselves from other members they still do not fully trust. Under these circumstances, NATO will remain the most suitable Western instrument for organizing military protection from, and together with, the Soviet Union.

In the long run, the democratization of Central and Eastern Europe (including the Soviet Union or its former components), together with European regional cooperation, could lead to a pan-European *peace community*. As is the case in the West and in Scandinavia today, the only justification for armed

forces in such a community is to protect members from external threats. A sub-alliance, which NATO would become, is useless.

A European peace community is a very long way off. In the meantime, NATO should actively participate in building the European security community, although, in the process, it will lose importance as the Soviet Union turns into a political partner and as CSCE institutions progressively assume more of NATO's current functions.

The Atlantic Alliance has been a means to an end, not an end in itself. NATO did not create the Western community of values and interests; instead, it protected and promoted this community. As such it should play its part in developing the European peace community that would render it obsolete.

---

1. *Time* (Jan. 1, 1990), p. 40.
2. *Economist*, cited in the *International Herald Tribune* (Jan. 10, 1990), p. 4.
3. *ACE Output* (Brussels: Supreme Headquarters Allied Powers Europe, Public Information Office, June 1990), p. 33.

THE TWO CANADAS

Jeffrey Simpson

JEFFREY SIMPSON *is the national affairs columnist of the* Globe and Mail, *Canada's national newspaper. He is the author of four nonfiction books, the latest of which is* Spoils of Power *(1988).*

Twenty-five years ago, a royal commission investigating relations between English- and French-speaking Canadians warned that "Canada, without being fully conscious of the fact, is passing through the greatest crisis in its history." Those provocative words were intended to shock Canadians into examining themselves, their country, and the relations between the two founding peoples of Canada. Above all, they were written to awaken English-speaking Canadians to the new realities of an assertive, dynamic Quebec of the 1960s, a province throwing off its church-dominated and rural past, no longer content with its status within the Canadian confederation.

Today, despite myriad institutional and policy changes over the past two and a half decades designed to smooth relations between French- and English-speaking Canadians, the commission's words still aptly describe Canadian reality. Canada is now "passing through the greatest crisis in its history" in the aftermath of the June 1990 collapse of a constitutional accord desired by the French-speaking province of Quebec, but resisted, if the polls were correct, by a majority of English-speaking Canadians. The combined objections of two provinces and Canada's aboriginal communities ultimately defeated the pact.

The failure of the so-called Meech Lake accord (named after a small lake near Ottawa where the agreement was negotiated in 1987), and especially the bitter debate outside Quebec, has pushed support for Quebec independence, or at least increased sovereignty, to its highest levels ever. It has forced some Canadians to contemplate that at best their country faces radical changes, and at worst a split into two separate states.

Just as the royal commission of 1965 found many Canadians unaware of the linguistic and cultural tensions gnawing at their country, so today many Canadians—and certainly a majority of the English-speaking ones—have not fully grasped how and why the Meech Lake trauma left Canada so badly shaken. And if many Canadians themselves cannot yet comprehend what has happened to their country, imagine the difficulty for most Americans, who view Canada as a peaceful, solid, sensible northern neighbor whose standard of living, reputation for compromise, and social peace would make it an unlikely candidate for political dismemberment.

Matters are complicated because almost none of the traditional indices of discontent were or are present in the national crisis. The country's—including Quebec's—standard of living remains high. The political leadership is representative of all regions of the country; indeed, Quebec is slightly over-represented in the Conservative party government of Prime Minister Brian Mulroney, himself a Quebecker. No policies of the national government are considered so iniquitous or injurious in Quebec that the province should leave the country on their account. The country's national institutions are obliged by law to offer services in both French and English; and in an unparalleled pedagogical experiment, nearly a quarter of a million English-speaking schoolchildren are enrolled in French language-immersion programs in which all courses (except for English, of course) are taught in French.

And yet the threat to Canadian unity has never been more severe than in the aftermath of the collapse of Meech Lake. It is a crisis more insidious and subtle—and therefore more deeply rooted—than others Canada has faced in its often troubled history. It is a crisis of the heart and mind, a clash over symbols, a struggle for recognition and rights by newly empowered groups. It is a crisis that envenoms further what the French observer André Siegfried, a kind of de Tocqueville for Canada, called in 1907 the "fears and jealousies" between English- and French-speaking Canadians. It is a crisis of confidence about whether Canada, after 123 years as a federal state, is still worth the effort.

Meech Lake Demands

The Meech Lake accord was both cause and victim of these "fears and jealousies." To French-speaking Quebeckers, the accord symbolized the willingness of the rest of Canada to respect their province's distinctiveness. To a majority of English-speaking Canadians, Meech Lake represented yet another demand for concessions from a province perpetually unhappy within Canada. Meech Lake was described in Quebec, with good reason, as a set of minimalist demands for securing that province's place within Canada. Elsewhere, many English-speaking Canadians viewed it as a set of maximalist demands that would recognize Quebec as a "distinct society" within Canada and therefore would inexorably lead to a special status for the province.

Meech Lake thus crystallized a debate between two fundamentally incompatible views of Canadian federalism that Canadian politicians of every stripe had frequently attempted to fudge: the view in Quebec that the province deserved special recognition and particular powers because of its French-speaking identity; and the view elsewhere that all provinces must be constitutionally equal. The debate also demonstrated that the old idea of Canada as an ongoing arrangement between two large groups no longer reflected adequately the entire Canadian reality. This outdated idea left behind both multicultural Canadians, who now represent nearly a third of the population, and Canada's aboriginal peoples, who felt excluded from the debate. And the debate further demonstrated that an accommodation among political elites, often made behind closed doors, no longer satisfied interest groups and individual citizens who felt empowered by a written charter of rights and freedoms. The 1982 charter, which has added distinctly American attitudes toward authority to the Canadian political culture, has emboldened private citizens and interest groups to seek court remedies in the pursuit of rights rather than relying on participation in political parties with all their messy

compromises. In the charter era, elite accommodation, which lies at the heart of federal-provincial negotiations, is seen as exclusive, secretive, and fundamentally undemocratic.

At one level, the debate was carried on with customary enthusiasm by constitutionalists, lawyers, academics, and government officials experienced in a legal lexicon after a generation of intermittent constitutional debates. At the level of the general public, the debate centered on symbols, impressions, biases, hopes, and aspirations. A poll by the *Globe and Mail* of Toronto and the Canadian Broadcasting Corporation taken four months before the collapse of Meech Lake showed that 71 per cent of respondents knew little or nothing about the accord, yet a similar number professed strong or very strong views about it. A poll by the same organizations just after the accord's demise showed that, despite months of media saturation, 62 per cent still knew little or nothing about the accord but a similar number had strong or very strong views about it. So despite a widespread basic ignorance about the contents of Meech Lake, Canadians saw fit to pour out their grievances and frustrations about each other. Some of these grievances related to Meech Lake; others did not.

Meech Lake had its political roots in a 1984 campaign speech given by Mulroney, then the opposition leader. He promised to bring Quebeckers into the Canadian constitution with "honor and enthusiasm," a reference to the constitutional changes of 1982 that gave Canada a charter of rights and freedoms. Those changes were approved by the federal government of then Prime Minister Pierre Trudeau and the nine English-speaking provinces. Quebec refused to approve the changes. At the time it was governed by the Parti Québécois, which had lost a 1980 referendum on sovereignty-association but remained committed to an independent Quebec.

A mixture of statesmanship and partisan considerations led Mulroney to his 1984 promise. He correctly sensed that in the wake of the bruising referendum fight, the majority of Quebeckers wanted a respite from constitutional debates. For more than 20 years before the referendum, Quebeckers had been debating their role in Canada; the referendum seemed to clinch their adherence to federalism. Mulroney perceived that if certain modest constitutional changes were made, moderate French-Canadian nationalists, including many who had campaigned for sovereignty-association, could be reconciled to federalism for a very long time.

Mulroney also had to consider his Conservative party's dismal history in Quebec, long a fiefdom of the Liberal party. By promising to offer Quebec constitutional changes, he made the Conservatives the preferred party for almost all French-Canadian nationalists. His overwhelming majority, in Quebec and all of Canada, confirmed for the prime minister the desirability of constitutional changes.

When the Parti Québécois was defeated in the 1985 provincial election, the federalist Liberal government of Premier Robert Bourassa immediately began developing and circulating to other provinces a series of proposed constitutional changes. These changes became the heart of the Meech Lake accord as the other provincial premiers delayed debate on additional constitutional issues.

To a majority of English-speaking Canadians, Meech Lake represented yet another demand for concessions from a province perpetually unhappy within Canada.

Quebec presented five basic demands. First, the constitution should recognize Quebec as a "distinct society" within Canada with suitable recognition for the English-speaking minority in that province and the French-speaking minorities elsewhere in Canada. Second, Quebec should be given a veto over constitutional changes affecting federal institutions such as the Senate, the Supreme Court, and the House of Commons. Third, Quebec should be given additional powers over immigration in recognition of the province's low birthrate and its challenge of retaining a French-speaking character in North America. Fourth, provinces should be allowed to opt out of federal spending programs in areas of provincial jurisdiction, provided they establish a comparable program that meets "national objectives." Finally, provinces should be given a role in nominating members of the Supreme Court—where already three of the nine justices must by law be from Quebec and thus trained in the civil code rather than the common law.

With a few adjustments required to secure the approval of other provinces, Meech Lake was duly signed by the prime minister and the ten provincial premiers in the early spring of 1987. Under the 1982 constitutional changes, amendments to the constitution must be ratified within three years of action by the first legislature. When Quebec's National Assembly became the first legislature to approve Meech Lake on June

23, 1987, the three-year time clock began ticking.

At the time of Meech Lake's negotiation and for some time thereafter, the accord scarcely touched the nation's consciousness. In Quebec, Meech Lake was considered dry, necessary business in harmony with the prevailing political climate favoring accommodation of Quebec within Canada. Elsewhere, Meech Lake was little understood or noticed. But the prime minister and premiers, the so-called First Ministers, had agreed that the entire Meech Lake accord must be ratified by all governments. This requirement of unanimous consent, coupled with the three-year time period for ratification, provided the straightjacket from which Meech Lake would not be able to break free.

The first blow against Meech Lake was delivered by the father of the 1982 constitutional changes, former Prime Minister Pierre Trudeau. In a series of scathing public criticisms, he tore into the accord, claiming it would eventually grant Quebec special status, feed the demands of French-Canadian nationalists, and ultimately dismember Canada. For three decades, as teacher and politician, Trudeau had scorned French-Canadian nationalism as a trap for imprisoning the French language and culture within Quebec. Federalism, he always argued, offered nationwide breathing space for the French language and culture in Canada. During his years in office the federal government began operating in French and English and funding dramatically increased for French minorities across Canada. Although three years removed from active politics, his criticisms resonated across English-speaking Canada and especially within his own Liberal party.

Subsequent provincial elections in Manitoba, New Brunswick, and Newfoundland brought to power premiers who had not signed the original Meech Lake accord. These new premiers demanded changes, in some cases wholesale changes, before they would seek legislative ratification. Attempts were made for a year to find a solution to the impasse through public debate and federal provincial meetings culminating in a marathon six-day, closed-door meeting in June 1990. Quebec's Bourassa, supported by the federal government and the six other premiers who had signed Meech Lake, insisted no changes were possible; the three recalcitrant premiers continued to demand them, though the premier of New Brunswick eventually switched sides. But in the end, Meech Lake collapsed in a heap of recriminations.

Meech Lake failed in large part because it was loaded down with grievances and perceptions

If Quebec does decide to leave Canada, there will be bitterness, even shock, in the rest of Canada.

unrelated to its actual content. Nothing was more damaging in English-speaking Canada than a decision by the Quebec government in December 1988 to ban outdoor signs with advertising in both English and French.

Quebec's language legislation, passed under the Parti Québécois, required that only French appear on public signs in the province. This section of the law was appealed on the grounds that it impaired freedom of expression. Two Quebec courts and the Supreme Court of Canada struck down the legislation. However, the Supreme Court hinted that a law that gave French a predominant position on outdoor signs, with another language less-prominently displayed, was acceptable.

In the United States, such a ruling by the Supreme Court would be implemented automatically. But the 1982 Canadian constitutional changes incorporated a clause that allows provincial legislatures to override court rulings for a period of five years. Bourassa, worried about an upsurge of nationalist sentiment, invoked this "notwithstanding clause" and offered the English-speaking minority the meager solace of displaying their language only inside public buildings—and even there in a subordinate position.

The premier's decision brought about the resignation of three respected English-speaking cabinet ministers and set off a storm of protest around Canada. The decision provided fresh ammunition for anti-French elements in English-speaking Canada; but, more important, it discouraged moderate English-speaking Canadians who felt betrayed by Quebec's unwillingness to abide by the Supreme Court's ruling. To them, the decision signaled Quebec's apparent indifference to attitudes elsewhere in Canada, an indifference that hardened attitudes against what Quebec was seeking: the Meech Lake accord.

A number of small Ontario municipalities and two medium-sized cities—Sault Ste. Marie and Thunder Bay—passed resolutions declaring their jurisdictions unilingual. These measures were ostensibly directed at attempts to provide additional services to French-speaking minorities, but their underlying purpose was to send a message to all politicians that citizens were tired of compromising with French Canada.

With Meech Lake the focus of Canadian attention, old grievances toward Quebec were aroused. In Manitoba, citizens bitterly recalled a decision of the Mulroney government to grant an aircraft maintenance contract to a Montreal company, despite a less costly and technically superior bid from a Winnipeg firm. In Newfoundland, citizens remembered a reprehensible hydroelectric deal by which Hydro Quebec took power from the rivers of Labrador for a pittance, then resold it at a huge profit to the United States. Meech Lake reminded English-speaking Canadians that Quebec always seemed to be demanding, and often receiving, special consideration in the decisions of successive federal governments dependent upon that province's political support for reelection.

Since 1968, with two very brief exceptions, prime ministers have come from Quebec and their governments have boasted overwhelming strength in that province. The next election will also be between parties led by Quebeckers: Mulroney and Jean Chrétien, the new leader of the opposition Liberal party. Some of the popular resentment in English Canada can be explained by imagining the reaction in America if every president since 1968 had come from the northeastern part of the country. People in the south, west, and midwest would undoubtedly claim the political deck was stacked against them. Many English-speaking Canadians chafe at this sense that any government, regardless of political orientation, is beholden to Quebec.

What Does English Canada Want?

For nearly 30 years, English-speaking Canadians struggling to understand Quebec have asked: What does Quebec want? Quebec responded with the Meech Lake demands, which were widely popular in that province. Now the more interesting and difficult question is, What does English Canada want?

The mutual misunderstanding that often bedevils relations between French- and English-speaking Canadians reflects the traditional, and quite erroneous, view in Quebec that the rest of Canada—le Canada anglais—resembles Quebec: a relatively homogeneous bloc of people that can easily come to a national consensus on important matters. English-speaking Canada is nothing of the sort. It features such strong regional rivalries as those between western Canada and Ontario, and between the four Atlantic provinces and Ontario. In the large urban centers, a polyglot ethnicity has become an important characteristic. Approximately 50 per cent of the children in the Vancouver elementary school system are of

Asian descent; in Toronto white Anglo-Saxon Protestants are now a minority.

In addition to the global changes that are buffeting people everywhere, Canadians face three concerns that have plunged English-speaking Canada into a crisis of identity—or at least a kind of existential debate—that focuses on the question, What does English Canada want? First, the Mulroney government has pursued an agenda of deficit-reduction, privatization of crown corporations, and trimming of social programs. All these policies aim to make the Canadian economy more competitive internationally and to reduce a federal deficit and national debt larger on a per capita basis than the American ones. This course of action has shaken many traditional English-Canadian views of appropriate state activity. Since many English Canadians have typically defined their identity through contrasts with the United States in state institutions and state-funded programs such as universal medical insurance, publicly financed broadcasting, and generous unemployment schemes, the Mulroney government's agenda has struck at that distinct character.

Second, the free-trade agreement with the United States severely divided English-speaking Canadians. In the 1988 election, the pro-free trade Conservatives won solid majorities only in Alberta and Quebec. A slim majority of English-speaking Canadians opposed free trade, many of them bitterly and passionately. They threw themselves into the fight, believing free trade would inevitably lead to the Americanization of Canada. As then leader of the Liberal party John Turner argued to Mulroney in a televised debate, free trade would inevitably erode Canadian political sovereignty because so many economic levers would be turned over to the stronger partner in the deal. The Mulroney government's victory thus deflated English-Canadian nationalists. Some of them attributed their defeat to the overwhelming popularity of free trade in Quebec, where the French-speaking population harbored no fears of cultural assimilation or loss of political sovereignty. When the time came to support Quebec's Meech Lake demands, the majority of English-Canadian nationalists either refrained from debating the accord or opposed it outright. They had typically favored a strong central government capable of resisting American influence. Free trade seemed to deliver one blow against this conception of Canadian government by restricting future interventionist policies; Meech Lake dealt the second blow by contemplating a further decentralization of power from Ottawa to the provinces.

Third, Meech Lake once again forced English Canadians, already angered by the Mulroney government's agenda and divided by free trade, to accommodate themselves to proposed constitutional changes beneficial to a province whose chronic restlessness and indifference toward the rest of Canada made it a source of profound irritation. Moreover, some of the premises of Meech Lake—like those of free trade—struck at English Canada's self-definition. If all provinces are constitutionally equal, argued Meech Lake critics, then there could be no recognition of Quebec as a "distinct society." If provinces could opt out of federal-provincial programs and establish their own, meeting only vague national objectives, then what hope remained for new social programs binding all Canadians together? If Meech Lake passed, many English Canadians concluded, Quebec would simply use the accord to demand even more powers and gradually achieve sovereignty-association.

Formally, Meech Lake died because two provinces, Newfoundland and Manitoba, failed to ratify it before the expiration of the three-year deadline. In Manitoba, the three party leaders in the province's minority government returned from the marathon negotiations in Ottawa with enough commitments on other constitutional issues to grudgingly submit the accord to the assembly for ratification. But the accord never came to a debate, let alone a vote. One politician—Elijah Harper, the only aboriginal politician in the legislature—used procedural tactics to prevent debate.

Harper, like other native Canadians, felt betrayed by Meech Lake because it did not deal with aboriginal demands, including a recognition of their inherent right to self-government. Harper's stance made him a hero to aboriginal Canadians, who reveled in their newfound sense of political power. No matter how Canada evolves in the years ahead, the grievances of aboriginal Canadians and their demands for quasi-autonomous status within Canada have now been placed squarely on the agenda.

Looking for Answers

The defeat of Meech Lake has changed Canada's future. The constitutional status quo is finished, though no one knows what will take its place. Government commissions studying the future shape of Canada are already at work in Alberta, New Brunswick, and Quebec, and the federal government has launched its own nationwide consultations looking for answers.

In Quebec, the demise of Meech Lake and the

resentments the pact elicited in the rest of Canada have given *indépendentistes* an opportunity. Eight members of parliament—six Conservatives and two Liberals—resigned from their parties to form *le Bloc Québécois* in the House of Commons, and a candidate from the new bloc trounced the old-line parties in a summer by-election in Quebec. Public opinion surveys depict a sharp swing away from the federalist option. The Quebec government has formally withdrawn from virtually all the myriad federal-provincial meetings in the Canadian system.

A year may pass before the political battle lines are formed in Quebec. The Parti Québécois will continue to favor outright independence. The governing Liberals, who are currently revising their constitutional position, will likely defend the retention of limited links with the rest of Canada, especially in economic fields such as monetary policy and trade. The reaction of Quebec's business elite will be critically important. This group emerged in the 1980s as the most trusted and respected element of Quebec society, taking over that role from the bureaucrats and academics who had led the fight for sovereignty in the 1970s. During the referendum campaign of 1980, the overwhelming majority of business leaders in Quebec were hostile to sovereignty. Many are now willing to accept whatever political option Quebec chooses. Indeed, the success of Quebec's entrepreneurial class and the development of some multinational business firms based in the province have given Quebeckers a confidence that they can go it alone politically. Yet despite this self-confidence, polls indicate a majority would still prefer an economic association with the rest of Canada as a kind of security blanket.

The free-trade agreement has encouraged Quebeckers to believe they are no longer dependent upon the existing Canadian federal system for economic prosperity. Access to the U.S. market, now guaranteed by the trade agreement, offers opportunities beyond what Quebec businessmen find in the rest of Canada. The agreement was admittedly signed between the United States and Canada; but Quebeckers assume that if they opt for independence, they could easily negotiate a similar deal with Washington or persuade Washington and Ottawa to extend the agreement to an independent Quebec.

The business community also understands the fiscal predicament of the federal government, which is running deficits of nearly US$25 billion. After nearly 15 years of deficit-financing, the country's national debt consumes about one-third of every tax dollar sent to Ottawa. Under these circumstances, the federal government's ability to assuage regional discontent with massive new spending is severely circumscribed, further dimming the attractiveness of the federal system.

Canada's prospects after Meech Lake are complicated by the erosion of the national parties' ability to build bridges between the two major language groups and among far-flung regions. Mulroney's Conservatives retain respectable support in Quebec, where they are viewed as having tried honorably to achieve a constitutional settlement. But elsewhere in Canada, no government has ever been held in such low esteem. This poor rating stems partially from policies such as tax reform that have nothing to do with Meech Lake, and partially from the prime minister's opening of a Pandora's box of Quebec nationalism. Jean Chrétien, the Liberal leader who opposed Meech Lake, is widely reviled as "yesterday's man" in his own province of Quebec. But in the rest of Canada, his pan-Canadian patriotism plays well, as did his attacks on the Meech Lake accord. And as le Bloc Québécois is grabbing nationalist votes in Quebec, a new formation called the Reform party is making important gains in Alberta and British Columbia. The new party feeds upon traditional western Canadian grievances against the central government dominated by Ontario and Quebec. So in a country where the institutions of national integration are often weak, the decline of the national parties is a further indication of the loosening bonds of nationhood.

Meech Lake failed in large part because it was loaded down with grievances and perceptions unrelated to its actual content.

Little can be predicted accurately about Canada's future except that nothing will happen immediately. Quebec will require a year or two to sort out its political options, and the next provincial election may not occur until 1992 or 1993. The next federal election is also two or three years away. In the meantime, Canadian politicians will be struggling to restore a sense of common purpose to a sorely divided country.

The failure of Meech Lake represented a tragic missed opportunity for Canada to marry moderate French-Canadian nationalism to federalism. Those such as Trudeau and the accord's fiercest critic among provincial premiers, Newfoundland's Clyde Wells, were dreaming when they argued that the rejection of Meech Lake would leave Canada unshaken. Meech Lake was the most moderate constitutional proposal emanating from Quebec in a generation and a half; its defeat will ensure that Quebec never demands less. No matter how hard Wells and other Meech Lake critics insisted that their opposition to Meech Lake did not mean a rejection of Quebec by the rest of Canada, Quebeckers did not buy the argument. A solid majority of Quebeckers have now given up on the existing federal system. All that remains is for them to decide how much additional sovereignty they desire, and whether any merit exists in a much more limited partnership with the rest of Canada.

The odds are now better than even that the forces of national disintegration are so strong that the future will bring a far looser political arrangement between Quebec and the rest of Canada. The new order will likely be either an even more decentralized federation or a European-style superstructure in which two sovereign countries would delegate certain defined powers to a common parliament.

The path to one of those new arrangements, however, will be fraught with pitfalls. Framing a looser federation will involve endless haggling between the federal government and the provinces and between the English-speaking provinces and Quebec.

If Quebec does decide to leave Canada, there will be bitterness, even shock, in the rest of Canada. What remained of Canada would take a long time to decide how to organize itself, let alone what relations it wanted with Quebec. The negotiations for dividing Canada's assets and liabilities would be nightmarishly complicated. The prospect of splitting Canada geographically—the Atlantic provinces separated from the rest of Canada by an independent Quebec—is a chilling one given the short and troubled histories of other similarly divided countries. Although polls consistently show that the vast majority of Canadians have no desire to join the United States, the long-term option might be more palatable in western parts of the country should the Canadian federation fail. In Atlantic Canada, the disintegration of the Canadian experiment would lead many to wonder whether economic security lay with New England, and, through it, with the rest of the United States. After all, the free-trade agreement has reinforced north-south economic links; and with the absence of a durable political superstructure on an east-west axis, those links might reorient political thinking.

Canada, in its own modest way, has represented a noble political experiment that a country could be formed in defiance of the enormous economic and cultural pull of the United States. Apart from the French language, the differences between Canada and the United States are often difficult for Americans to fathom. But the accumulation of a multitude of small differences has made for a country whose distinctiveness was something of a miracle in North America.

At the core of that distinctiveness lay an accommodation between French- and English-speaking Canadians and a mixed economy in which government plays a more interventionist role in society than it does in the United States. The pressures of the global economy, with its fierce imperatives for improved competitiveness, and the free-trade deal with Washington have eroded the state's capacity to intervene; the country's huge deficit and debt leave the federal government crippled even when it wishes to act. And the Meech Lake accord shattered, probably irrevocably, the possibility of a harmonious accommodation between French- and English-speaking Canadians.

However the next few years unfold, Americans will have to revise their traditional stereotype of Canada as a country where nothing of interest or consequence ever happens. Successive American administrations, from that of John Kennedy to George Bush, have always refused to intervene publicly or privately in Canadian debates about national unity. The three pillars of U.S. policy toward Canada, enunciated again in 1990 by Bush, are that the United States values its relations with Canada, it prefers a united Canada, and it will leave internal Canadian debates to Canadians. Nothing would be gained for any American administration in the turbulent years ahead for Canada to shift from these positions until some new political arrangement emerges north of the border. Americans, after all, must live with whatever outcome emerges in Canada. They would prejudice their chances of maintaining harmonious relations with Canada, or whatever emerges from the Canada of today, by taking sides in an essentially Canadian problem. All regions of Canada wish to remain on friendly terms with the United States anyway. The American government will likely be invited by Canadian or Quebec leaders to tilt U.S. policy, at least rhetorically, to favor their particular aims. Americans, acting in their own interests, should politely decline.

Earlier in 1990, the *New Republic* lamented how dull things were in Washington under George Bush, complaining that "it's positively Canadian around here." To that remark, Canadians these days would say: Give us a little of that dullness.

Don't Write Off Japan

Could Paul Kennedy be right about America but wrong about Japan?

Ronald A. Morse

Ronald A. Morse, a Japan specialist, is executive vice president of the Economic Strategy Institute in Washington, D.C. and former director of the Asia Program at the Woodrow Wilson International Center for Scholars.

In the current environment of Japan bashing, American assessments of Japan have to be taken with a stiff dose of reality. Americans are fed up with hearing about excellent Japanese education, manufacturing, and quality control. What they welcome is any news about the downside of Tokyo's miracle. There is a big market in the U.S. media for stories about Japan's sexist society, its poor "rabbit hutch" housing, its stinginess with foreign assistance, and its wimpiness when it comes to standing up to a bully like Iraq's Saddam Hussein. The reason the Japanese buy up so much of Hawaii and Los Angeles, the pessimist scenario goes, is because they want someplace decent to live. Or, to push the logic, the Japanese supposedly can thank the United States for everything. If it weren't for our protection, they would be dead in a minute. And worst of all, if they couldn't steal their ideas from our universities and didn't cheat on trade, we could beat them in a minute in any arena.

Most Japanese would agree with the facts, if not the tenor, of this assessment. They would add that it was the United States that wrote Japan's postwar constitution and initiated the reforms that gave Japan a single national mission—peaceful economic recovery and growth. The Japanese are great students. They accept new ideas readily, give them their own twist, and then, unfortunately for their mentors, often improve on the imported idea with a vengeance. Like overzealous students, they just don't know when to cool it. So now we have what Peter Drucker calls "adversarial trade."

The Japanese readily accept ideas, but they do not like having many foreigners around to mess up their tidy little all-Japanese world. They find it convenient and easy to control a nation where everyone is the same race, goes to the same schools, and tends to think the same things about politics, religion, sex, and the outer world. Uniformity is great for doing business and makes all kinds of coordination and consensus-building easy. The Japanese are also happy with their "no surprises" politics: The Liberal Democratic Party (LDP) has been in power since 1955. The opposition communist, socialist, and numerous religious parties can bark and scream, but they are not taken seriously in conservative, high-growth Japan.

If that weren't bad enough, the Japanese are the Calvinists of Asia, working like little beavers to prove themselves to each other and the world. I remember vividly the petite Japanese lady—nearly 90 years old—telling me atop Mount Fuji to hang tough and not give up because the top of the mountain was only another hour away. If nothing else, the Japanese are resilient.

All of this would be fine if we could take exception to their rudeness or ingratitude. Then we could dislike them. Unfortunately, they are not very helpful on this score. We are all familiar with the sight of nicely dressed Japanese visitors bringing some small, homemade Japanese souvenir and bowing deeply for no reason. They are orderly, polite, and unfailingly considerate.

Still, it would be great if they would be more like us, if they became mass consumers and got sloppy and weak. After all, good cars and smart people are not all that important to having the good life—or so the American scenario goes. But no one ever accused the Japanese of being stupid. They watch every move Americans make the way a scientist studies a specimen with a microscope.

Rising Stars

Hiroyasu Tomaru

"When in Rome, do as the Romans do," said a Japanese policymaker who will most likely head Japan's trade negotiations in the latter half of this decade and beyond. In a clear message to Americans, Ichiro Ozawa, secretary-general of the ruling Liberal Democratic Party, does not hesitate to say that Americans should stop being so demanding abroad, particularly in dealing with the Japanese.

Ozawa, the No. 1 rising star in Japan's political world, said that while U.S. negotiators denounce tenders by specified bidders in Japan, they tolerate a nearly identical system in Britain and European countries. He noted that the United States engages in a similar practice itself.

The 28-year-old conservative politician also criticizes Jap-

Toshiki Kaifu or former Premier Yashuhiro Nakasone, he is not a newcomer to the political arena. When he was deputy chief cabinet secretary for the Takeshita government, Ozawa made many contacts in Washington during the negotiations over such problems as the opening of the Japanese construction market, joint development of the FSX superfighter, and Motorola's entry into the Japanese cellular telephone market. U.S. officials held him in high esteem for his decisiveness. At home, he is already the undoubted champion among the so-called new leaders in the political world.

"Unlike docile Kaifu, Ozawa is a difficult man for Washington to deal with," says a political observer. Kaifu, the most popular premier in post-

tious policy toward the Soviet Union. On this point too, he is in sharp contrast with Kaifu, who promised President Bush he would follow U.S. leadership in setting policy on the Soviet Union, East Europe, China, and Asia as a whole. Through all of these viewpoints and statements, Ozawa may be making the Bush administration nervous. Nevertheless, he is planning to visit Moscow, possibly this fall. "To contain Ozawa," says a Japanese analyst, "Bush may have to praise Kaifu even more."

Ozawa is the archetypal fixer—the latest in a long line who have influenced Japanese politics since World War II. He is also a political thoroughbred: His father was a cabinet minister in the late 1940s and early 1950s with a talent for securing the regional interests of his constituency.

What makes Ozawa a rising star is his negotiating ability. He recently said that he wants to realize a "true, international, partnership" with the United States.

U.S. lawmakers should pay more attention to Ozawa than to nationalist Shintaro Ishihara, who tries to keep Japan and the United States at a distance. Ozawa is a tough but able politician who inspires trust. Unlike Ishihara, who writes controversial best-sellers such as *A Japan that Can Say 'No'*, Ozawa is viewed as more mainstream.

Hiroyasu Tomaru is Tokyo correspondent for the Bureau of National Affairs and the **New York City Tribune.**

Tracking Japan's Baby Boomers

Dates	Events	The Boomers
1947–49	New Japanese constitution	Born
1960–62	Start of income doubling plan	Entered high shcool
1963–65	First Olympics held in Japan	Entered college
1966–68	Japan's GNP becomes No. 2 in World	Started work
Mid '70s	Japan starts to go international	Married
Early '80s	Reversal of U.S.-Japan trade flow	Became mid-level workers

anese negotiators. He says that the Japanese "must abandon their dependency and think about what they should do in the international community; it is my job to forge a framework for this in the Diet."

While Ozawa is not yet as famous as Prime Minister

war Japan, claims that the Japanese and American peoples have come to share a common viewpoint through the Structural Impediments Initiative (SII) talks on bilateral economic issues.

Ozawa also recently criticized the Foreign Ministry's cau-

3. AMERICAN ALLIES: Japan

Just starting to get tough

The Japanese, generally speaking, share the views of those American writers who see the United States as being in terminal decline. Paul Kennedy, who wrote *The Rise and Fall of the Great Powers*, predicting the collapse of America due to military overextension and neglect of infrastructure, is a hero in Japan. Not only did he tip them off to the logic of decline, but he gave them ideas about how to beat the seemingly inevitable laws of historical decline. There must be at least 500 Japanese books about surviving safe and sound into the twenty-first century. They admire the United States, but they know they are different. And if all their projects work well, they might even think they are superior.

The Japanese are relativists about everything—as distinct from Americans, taught by the Cold War that you either win or lose. In the courts, in life, and in their foreign dealings, the Japanese are always willing to compromise and cut a deal. Life for them is not a zero-sum game. The trick is to create advantage, not to win. They have a saying that "in the leftovers from a meal, there is fortune." They always leave something on their plates for the gods. Put into trade terms, they have no desire to dominate America economically. They just want 20 percent of everything.

While the Japanese don't like winner-take-all situations, they certainly don't like to lose. Losing World War II left them with a strong desire to do economically what they could not achieve militarily. The past is still vivid in their memories. The Japanese may not care if Americans ever love them, but they certainly want our respect.

It should be obvious by now that I am not a member of the crowd that thinks the Japanese sun has already begun to set. Rather, I would argue that they are just about ready to get tough. The sunset theory would have it that the Japanese have already started getting lazy. They play more, and their society is getting old fast. There is a rising demand for social services. Once the Japanese start spending like we do, the sunsetters argue, they will be just like us and then we've got them. Because the Japanese don't have a large landmass, a large, multiethnic population, and all the creative scientists that we have in New York, Dallas, and elsewhere, they really can't compete.

Though there is a grain of truth in the sunset critique, these factors are not likely to bring Japan to its knees in the near future. Even if these developments have an impact over the long haul, they are not likely to slow Japan down much over the next 20 years. In any event, the United States can't simply hope for Japan's decline. Behind Japan is Korea, Taiwan, and a host of other little Japans, all ready to step in and continue the struggle. In my view, the United States should target the optimistic scenario and prepare to compete at the highest level.

Still, within the optimistic context of my scenario for the longer term economic and basic trends analysis of Japan, it must be admitted that all is not roses. Japan's uniform culture keeps it from being able to mix easily with foreigners and places severe con-

World's Richest Man

The Japanese public sees a dynamo, but company insiders say he is a prudent businessman. Either way, it all adds up to one fact: Yoshiaki Tsutsumi, president of the Seibu railways group and owner of the Seibu Lions professional baseball team, is the world's wealthiest person for the fourth straight year.

Hanging on to extensive holdings in real estate, hotels, ski resorts, and tourism, Tsutsumi netted earnings of an estimated $16 billion, up about $1 billion from last year, according to *Forbes* magazine. His conglomerate comprises more than 100 companies.

The superactive executive resigned early this year from his "prestigious" position as president of the Japan Olympic Committee after criticism of his aggressive resort development projects, which some described as being against environmental protection and the Olympic spirit.

Yet, Tsutsumi, 56, ranked first in a recent survey of 47 Japanese prefectural governors asked to select business leaders whose management strategy is instructive in the running of local governments.

"If Tsutsumi should join the political world, he would immediately become the leader of a big faction. But I would prefer that he become a coordinator of the political world, because he has the influence and ability to play a fixer's role," says a ruling Liberal Democratic Party lawmaker in the middle echelon of power.

Because he is a multitalented personality, nobody is sure of Tsutsumi's ultimate ambition. By the standards of Japanese business and political communities, he is still very young; however, nobody can predict what he might achieve in 10 or 20 years' time.

—*H.T.*

straints on the ability of its managers to operate effectively in multinational firms. Japanese receptivity to multicultural situations has been slow—too slow to keep pace with the needs they have for managing their economic success.

It might help to examine a few of these issues. What about the domestic work force? Will Japan have to employ large numbers of foreign workers over the next two decades, thereby upsetting the ethnic homogeneity of the country? Will Japan be able to keep its crime rates low as its society is woven into the fabric of international relations?

Demographically, there seems little to worry about. By their own estimates, in the year 2005 the Japanese will need six million more workers than currently available. But they are optimistic that they can pick up the equivalent of four million workers annually by employing more women, extending the current retirement age, and making more effective use of currently underemployed blue-collar workers. That means only a small need for foreign workers in Japan. Also, by 2005 most of the labor-intensive jobs will have moved offshore. As Japan's workers move into knowledge-intensive and service-sector jobs, its educated population will be more productive.

In the year 2000, the number of persons 65 years and over will be about 16 percent of the total Japanese population, compared to 7 percent of the U.S. population. By the year 2025, the gap will close—the United States will be at 20 percent and Japan at 23 percent.

One politically-sensitive element of economic and social change to which they have not given enough attention is how quickly and smoothly the leadership will be able to deal with the opening up and nationalization of the rice and agricultural markets. Once the decision to stop or re-

duce subsidies to rice farmers takes effect and impacts on Japan's multilateral commitments for trade and tariff agreements, there could be a sudden depopulation of all the small farms in Japan that are run largely by older folks. The drop in farm values will echo throughout the Japanese land-price scheme and even impact on Tokyo's real estate prices. Then it can't help but affect the stock market values that are linked to inflated land-asset values.

They have the business leaders

If the West is hoping for a lazy bunch of Japanese managers over the next two decades, it will be disappointed. In a society as status conscious as Japan, it is little wonder that Japan's first baby boom generation has been the object of considerable study. Anyone trying to figure out what we can expect of Japan in the years ahead must understand this generation. They were born between 1947 and 1949; the 1990s will be their decade. They fought hard to get where they are. Because of their numbers—about 15 million—the competition for good schools, good jobs, and fast advancement on the job has been keen. Now in their early 40s, they know that their turn to rule has come. As the data show, they have a big investment in Japan's continued success. An amazing 75 percent are happy with their work.

The baby boomers see themselves as the intermediaries between the older, prewar crowd that managed Japan's rise and the younger generation that most enjoys the fruits of Japanese success. They are conscious that at each stage in their lives they have been pacesetters. Specially recorded songs have documented their youth, their family-oriented interests, their competitive instincts, and their frustrations. They view themselves as being more individ-

ualistic than their elders but still team players. They are more leisure-oriented than their bosses, and they will spend more money on themselves and their families. They are at ease with computers, see themselves as technocrats, and would probably feel free to switch companies if a good opportunity arose. They are comfortable with women in the workplace and confident around foreigners. About a third of them want to continue working after retirement.

These baby boomers will be in charge, but they are still going to have a tough time keeping the next generation of affluent, easygoing youngsters in line. There has always been a strong hedonistic tradition in Japan. With no sense of national purpose (now that economic success is at hand), no requirement for public service, and no military conscription, younger Japanese may not prove to be the good economic warriors that the baby boomers and their parents were.

They have the economic machine

In 1987, Japan's GNP of $2.3 trillion was about 53 percent of the $4.5 trillion U.S. GNP. Estimates by Japan's Nomura Research Institute and other groups say that by the year 2000 Japan's GNP will be $4.05 trillion, about two-thirds of the U.S. GNP of $6.5 trillion. Assuming a 4 percent growth rate for Japan and a 2 percent growth rate for the United States, by the year 2010 Japan's per capita GNP will be the same as the United States'. Japan's GNP could exceed that of the United States by then if Japan's savings rates remain high, investments keep pace, and the government retains its informal role of catalyst for Japan's economic growth. At present, only 5 percent of Japan's productive manufacturing capacity is offshore, compared to 20 percent for the United States. It will take Tokyo a decade to reach U.S. levels.

If the Japanese economy grows as projected, will Japanese consumers really benefit from it? Again, the predictions look good. American trade negotiators have just convinced Japan to spend 9 percent of its GNP on infrastructure investments—sewage, urban parks, housing, sports facilities, and high-tech communications networks—over the next decade. This will provide the groundwork for the next domestic spending boom in Japan.

The Japanese government's new vision calls for a satisfying and prosperous 1990s. The Ministry of International Trade and Industry plan calls for nothing less than the dawning of an industrial "age of Aquarius." The goal is to improve the quality of all aspects of Japanese life. And just in case the consumption boom doesn't work, the Japanese have been investing heavily for four years in all areas of their industrial sector—new plants, equipment, research and development. In 1989 Japan spent $750 billion, or about 24 percent of its GNP, on capital investment. The Japanese economy is about 60 percent the size of the U.S. economy, which allotted only $500 billion, or about 20 percent of GNP, on capital investments (*New York Times*, April 11, 1990). Moreover, Japan's research and development expenditures in areas other than defense exceed those of the United States, and most of the expenditures are in the private, productive sector.

Will the Japanese be able to translate this economic success into a global financial capability? The indications so far are good. How have they done it, given the fact that this is a whole new area for them? The answer is that they have either hired the necessary foreign talent or entered into close business alliances with major securities houses, financial firms, and banks. The Wall Street financial wizards have proven themselves as cooperative as the Washington, D.C. lawyers and lobbyists who push political issues for the rich Japanese. Mergers, acquisitions, real estate, and now even leveraged byouts are part of the Japanese style of international finance. In the same way that their banks are now the largest in the world, their financial houses are equally formidable—for example, Nomura Securities has assets ten times those of Merrill Lynch.

They have the political stability

Neither America nor Japan would have been successful but for close coordination between the public and private sectors. In the United States, the G.I. Bill, space spending after *Sputnik*, land grant colleges, agricultural subsidies, the highway system, and other programs gave the private sector the boosts needed to reach world-class levels. In Japan, the government has played an even more important role, largely for historical reasons. The Confucian tradition, featuring respect for government, was blended with a British-style senior civil service run by the elite graduates of the national universities.

The Japanese people defer to government as a positive force for the common good. That is why there are no consumer or environmental movements of consequence in Japan. The Japanese have been convinced that they should pay higher prices for gasoline and electricity because national well-being and security require investigating alternatives to oil and developing new technologies. Public policy overrides consumer-oriented, free-trade economic policies. Until recently, Japan has concerned itself with production, not consumption.

The governing LDP has set the guidelines, represented the private-interest groups, and moved the Japanese economy forward swiftly. Politics—political stability—it could be argued, is largely responsible for Japan's dramatic economic success.

Will this change in the next decade? Can politics continue as the backbone of the Japanese system? Will a wave of deregulation and free-trade principles sweep this Japanese elite and shake up the entire system? Not likely. To be sure, political corruption, sex scandals, and badly planned tax increases have caused the ruling party to lose its majority in the upper house of the Diet. Still, the LDP held its own in the lower-house election earlier this year. With a popular, youthful prime minister only in his 50s, the LDP is likely to make the transition from a rural, farm-based party to an urban, more consumer-oriented one.

Although many commentators point out that the Japanese private sector has grown and that parliamentarians have become less dependent on the bureaucracy, these shifts are still marginal. Japan's politicians will continue to set the nation's goals, coordinate cooperation between businessmen and policymakers, and keep defense spending at a modest level.

Foreigners might not like the closed nature of Japan's body politic, and they may feel the Japanese national interest often clashes with broader concepts of free world interests. But despite real concerns that Japan, though wealthy and prosperous, is unwilling to bear the costs of world leadership, the Japanese do not want to be No. 1—yet.

Japan still wants to figure out the magic formula of human, technological, and capital instruments that will cause the deterministic economic-decline model of development to be revised in Japan's favor. Kennedy could be right about America, but he could well be wrong about Japan. With such an ambitious agenda and such a successful track record to date, the Japanese cannot be written off easily.

AMERICAN-JAPANESE-EUROPEAN RELATIONS:
A View from Washington

". . . Without mutual respect, political support for common principles of democracy, and economic openness among Japan, America, and Europe, the world may never know what a peaceful and prosperous future it really could have."

Clarence J. Brown

Mr. Brown, former Deputy Secretary, U.S. Department of Commerce, heads a Washington, D.C., consulting firm.

TRADE negotiations between the U.S. and Japan may become increasingly difficult because they now involve partners who are more equal than they ever have been in the past. The big question is whether that equality makes them stronger allies or sets them more at odds.

In an article in the Oct. 21, 1989, *National Journal*, Bruce Stokes suggests that Japan now has the economic muscle to resist American pressures to pursue courses of action the U.S. wants and increasingly will chart an independent course, economically, politically, and militarily. He notes that Japan no longer will do what it did for Pres. Reagan and go along with American policy. Rather, he thinks, Japan may follow Mrs. Reagan's advice and "just say no." For Americans who do not think the world has changed since 1945, this is a disturbing article, as it is for those of us who recognize that the world is changing at an alarming pace.

Stokes also suggests that forces within both the U.S. and Japanese political economies are at work to push the two greatest economic powers in the world onto separate and perhaps conflicting paths. He points to Japan's rapidly accelerating prosperity and the stubborn U.S. trade deficit as the most obvious problems and predicts that the Japanese Gross National Product on a per capita basis may soon be 50% greater than the U.S.'s. That means Japan has increasing financial strength in world markets to buy, loan, or give, independent of U.S. policy. As a result, the criticism of Japan which was valid half a decade ago—that it was a rich nation failing to exercise its social responsibility in the world and leaving the burden to others who had carried it for so long—no longer is true. The new fact, that Japan is now the world's largest foreign aid donor, gives it the right to be independent of the U.S. in the exercise of policy options on where that aid goes.

Japan also now has the second highest military budget in the world. A recent book by Sony's Akio Morita and right-wing politician Shintaro Ishihara states that the time has come for Japan to tell the U.S that it does not need American protection and will defend itself because the American nuclear umbrella is just an illusion as far as the Japanese people are concerned.

Japan's former vice minister of finance, Toyoo Gyohten, in a recent issue of *The International Economy*, suggests that the overwhelming attraction of U.S. Treasury bonds is waning. Such a view, and the fact that the U.S. share of Japan's overseas investment portfolio has declined from 50 to 40% in the past three years, raises the threat of a withdrawal of Japanese financing of U.S. Federal debt with all that implies for interest rates in the U.S. and our domestic economy.

The availability of surplus financing also has implications in the race between Japan and the other industrial powers to develop new technology. Japan now can buy not only the industrial capacity to flood foreign markets with high-quality goods, it can invest in the research to originate new products or more competitive old ones, thus strengthening its economic position even further.

Disadvantages of the new prosperity

However, all these advantages may create some disadvantages. The financial power, if exercised too brazenly, can trigger reactions like the flurry of xenophobic concern caused by the acquisition of Rockefeller Center by a Japanese company. While most Americans approve of the establishment of new Japanese-owned factories in the U.S., which bring new jobs to localities, the purchase of real estate landmarks stirs a more negative reaction.

This new Japanese prosperity and its international financial power do not necessarily make for worldwide political popularity, as the U.S. learned in the decades immediately following World War II. When the new financial power can be exercised independently by Japanese companies and individuals, it also tends to break down the traditional policy unity between public and private institutions. Capitaliza-

Reprinted from *USA Today Magazine*, July 1990, pp. 38-39. Copyright © 1990 by the Society for the Advancement of Education.

tion of the Tokyo stock market is half again larger than the New York Stock Exchange and is now the major source of industrial financing in Japan.

A decade and a half ago, major Japanese companies were still in debt and beholden to the government for subsidized bank financing. Today, most Japanese firms are solvent and doing business in many parts of the world, sometimes under more beneficent laws than in their own country. In some cases, more of their corporate economic success comes from outside Japan than from Japan-based production or sales. They may be thinking of themselves as more global than Japanese companies. That has happened to many European and American companies, and could be either the salvation or the ruin of the world in the 21st century.

If these new industrial profits can be devoted to research and technical development, Japan has the financial resources to become the new center of world technology. However, as Japanese companies become increasingly internationalized, they also may find that the social pressures which have required firms in Europe and the U.S. to offer expanded employee benefits and socialized systems to aging populations will cut into their industrial priorities.

Perhaps most significantly, the new prosperity of Japan makes it an alternative market for producers all over the world, just as the prosperous and larger U.S. market attracted Japanese sellers and, then, Japanese investments in American production. Japan can not afford to leave any impression that it is not, for whatever reason, as open a market to world products as the rest of the world would want it to be. Japan increasingly has been confronted with this worldwide *quid pro quo*. The U.S. is such a large market that it has been able to afford its failure to be more competitive while still maintaining the openness of its market and to absorb its large trade deficit with Japan. It is to be hoped that America is relearning how to compete, as Japan is learning to be a generous world leader. Meanwhile, smaller European economies have been less gracious historic competitors. The larger European economy which will exist after the integration of the 12 nations in the European Community (EC) in 1992 may not be as open to Japan and the U.S. as has been the U.S. economy to Japan and Europe.

An economically integrated EC will be the largest single market in the world, with 325,000,000 people having an average per capita income of $13,000. The U.S. will have only 250,000,000 consumers with an estimated per capita income of $18,500, so the markets will each have Gross National Products of about $4.5 trillion. At the moment, ours is still slightly ahead of that of the EC. With the recent free trade arrangement between Canada and the U.S. as a single market, we have the largest GNP, but not by much.

The long-range prospect for economic integration of the EC goes beyond the present 12 nations (West Germany, France, the United Kingdom, Italy, Spain, the Netherlands, Belgium, Denmark, Greece, Portugal, Ireland, and Luxembourg). Outside the EC, but close in economic activity to it, are the so-called EFTA nations and others which bear a special relationship to the EC. These include 10 additional democracies in the Council of Europe (Austria, Cyprus, Finland, Liechtenstein, Malta, Norway, San Marino, Sweden, Switzerland, and Turkey). Their participation in an integrated Europe would bring it to 400,000,000 people and put the combined GNP ahead of the U.S. and Canada.

The Europeans generally have supported the General Agreement on Tariffs and Trade. They have provided statesmanlike leadership, along with the U.S., in reducing or removing tariffs and less forthright trade barriers, not only among European nations, but, to a lesser degree, worldwide. The Europeans also have backed U.S. efforts to reduce the overproduction and consequent market disrupting dumping of such products as steel. Maturity on trade matters has been a pattern for Europe much longer than it has in the U.S. or Japan, in spite of the internal political, social, and economic conflicts that sprang from long-standing frictions of religion, language, and culture.

European monopolies

Historically, European nations have been less sensitive than has the U.S. political/economic system about corporate monopolies in products and services. National monopolies have been common in all European countries, particularly in basic industries such as steel, autos, pharmaceuticals, and energy. Favored domestic companies were provided with a protected base in their native land and its colonies. The transition from royalty to socialism didn't chill acceptance of national monopolies. Royal Dutch Shell, British Steel, Fiat automobiles, and Bayer chemicals have been given strong national bases from which to compete abroad in other European countries and to penetrate markets in the U.S., Latin America, and Asia.

What will happen when Europe integrates economically and Shell fights it out with British Petroleum for dominance in the EC, or Fiat, Saab, and Renault go after each other? In the auto industry, it looks as if a solution tried in America in 1982 by the Democratic majority in the House of Representatives may be tried by Europeans. Some there have asked that autos made and sold in Europe after 1992 must have a 70-80% domestic content. Take that, Chrysler, Toyota, and Hyundai!

Even in the midst of recession, the Reagan Administration, the GOP Senate, and most progressive American corporations rightly opposed that approach in 1982. It would have meant such operations as the brand new Honda manufacturing plant would have been obliged to close. Today, Honda's production in the U.S. has a domestic content as high as Chrysler's. With a 97% American workforce of over 10,000 employees, Honda is manufacturing in the U.S. more than half the cars it is selling here. It also is selling abroad cars made in Ohio.

If Europe attempts similar exclusionary tactics against American and Japanese firms—say, the French demand protection because Renault is being squeezed out of Europe—the result surely will be bad for the international trading system. A reaction not unlike that of the U.S. Congress to a persistent trade deficit with Japan quickly could develop into a new U.S. isolationism against Europe as well as Japan.

It is essential that North America and Japan stick together in their attitudes about Europe '92. If the three largest economies in the world maintain an open trading and investment system, the international relationships they established could maintain a prosperous worldwide economic system that could preclude the need for massive national military expenditures. After economic unification, the EC should discover that the old rivalries between nationalistic Germany, France, Britain, and Italy will fade into the new integrated Europe.

The break-up of the communist bloc can be beneficial or harmful in this regard. An integrated Europe can absorb a Poland, Hungary, or East Germany, but European nationalism could be made nervous by the reunification of East and West Germany.

America grew and prospered when the various colonies united politically in 1787 because economic unity quickly followed political unification. We now see Europe attempting economic union, with the possibility of a political union to follow. Increased prosperity already has come to Europe from the steps taken toward openness and economic unity. Open economic relationships and trading since World War II between Europe and the U.S. have helped both prosper, just as Japan and the U.S. have from increasing economic ties and improving openness in investment and trade. It should follow that other parts of the world similarly can benefit from open economic trade and investment.

However, without mutual respect, political support for common principles of democracy, and economic openness among Japan, America, and Europe, the world may never know what a peaceful and prosperous future it really could have.

JAPAN AS COMPETITOR

Edson W. Spencer

EDSON W. SPENCER, *former chief executive officer and chairman of Honeywell International, is chairman of the Commission on U.S.-Japan Relations for the Twenty-first Century.*

From a global point of view, it is clear that the world's two largest economic powers should work together to contribute to the solution of the world's problems. Today, however, the ability of the United States and Japan to maintain a cooperative relationship is being questioned widely. U.S. relations with Japan are going through a difficult time, caused in no small part by the success of American policies toward Japan since 1945. The United States is no longer the dominant partner in the alliance, even though it remains economically and militarily more powerful.

American attitudes toward Japan are affected greatly by the trade deficit figures. Even an approximately 50 per cent devaluation of the U.S. dollar since 1985 has failed to reduce the U.S. deficit with Japan to the levels at which the deficits with the European Community (EC) and Canada now stand. The cheaper dollar has enabled the Japanese to buy U.S. assets at favorable yen prices. Some U.S. experts on Japan now argue that Japan is an economic predator, unwilling or unable to change its ways. When Japan makes even modest concessions in trade negotiations, they appear to come only after the United States has repeatedly pressed and threatened.

To Japanese, this pattern of behavior may seem like shrewd negotiating, but to Americans the Japanese appear more than a little reluctant to fully join the world trading system. They are seen as unwilling to open up their markets sufficiently in return for the access to the United States Japanese products, services, and investments enjoy. To Americans, it is particularly troubling to see Japan

continue the kind of cooperation between government and industry that limited the access of American companies to Japanese markets and assets from the 1950s through the 1970s—years when the Japanese economy was becoming a strong competitor.

Japanese, on the other hand, look at the United States increasingly as a country that has grown soft and complacent, that has lost its competitive industrial edge, and that is calling for protection from the pressures of the international marketplace because it is unwilling to deal with its own shortcomings. Japanese criticize Americans for their low savings rate, for being too greedy for short-term economic gains, and for being unwilling to make the long-term commitments and sacrifices that are necessary to maintain their international competitiveness.

The criticism each country is leveling at the other threatens to drive a wedge into the bilateral strategic relationship, which until now has been extraordinarily close and mutually beneficial. This criticism could poison relations in areas where more cooperation between the two countries is needed to maintain a growing world economy, and where it is crucial that the Japanese increase their commitment to share the burden the United States has borne since World War II for raising living standards in less-developed nations. The conflict between the United States and Japan comes at a time when the political and economic system of liberal capitalism, which in different ways both embrace, has proven its superiority in competition with the statist communist system, which is in complete disarray everywhere.

Presented with the opportunities these developments create, the United States and Japan should cooperate to reinforce their political and economic successes. Instead, their policies are diverging largely because of problems in their trading relationship. Yet observers in both countries are well aware that future problems between the two countries may be even more difficult to manage than the recent frictions. The policy dialogue between the two countries is now turning to trade impediments that arise from cultural, historical, and structural differences. These are much harder to negotiate than tariff levels or quotas.

Meanwhile, balance-of-payments difficulties and trade competition between the two countries notwithstanding, there are many areas where Japan and the United States can cooperate in their mutual self-interest as well as contribute to a stable and more prosperous world. But before this can happen, the United States must recognize that Japan is a powerful, increasingly nationalistic state disposed, like the United States itself, to act in its own self-interest. Americans must learn to think of Japan not as a war-devastated country that it helped rebuild in its own image, but as an equal with which it is necessary to cooperate whenever respective self-interests converge. By contrast, when there is no convergence, the two sides must negotiate their differences in ways that meet the needs of both without destroying the vast advantages of cooperation. To succeed in this endeavor will be a sign that the U.S.-Japanese relationship has matured along the lines of the U.S. relationship with its West European allies.

The Protectionist Wall

How has the U.S.-Japanese relationship developed in recent years? From the end of World War II through the mid-1960s Japan was creating an export economy sheltered behind a wall of protectionism and buoyed by a pattern of cooperation between government and industry that was designed to stimulate growth in jobs and gross national product (GNP) and to provide export earnings to finance imports of raw materials and food that the resource-starved island economy needed to survive. Despite the high walls of protectionism, the United States enjoyed a trade surplus with Japan throughout this period.

Today some observers describe this goal-oriented government-industry alliance as mercantilism. What Japan has considered necessary for economic growth—indeed, for economic survival—foreigners view as a predatory export effort designed to raise the Japanese standard of living at the expense of jobs lost in other countries. Perhaps, however, con-

sumers have preferred Japanese products because they are priced right, styled appealingly, and offer excellent quality.

The trade deficit figures illustrate the magnitude of the problem from the American point of view. America's worldwide merchandise trade balance turned decisively negative in the mid-1970s, reaching a nadir of $152 billion in 1987. Japan represented $60 billion—about 40 per cent—of that figure. In 1989, notwithstanding a much-weakened dollar, the total deficit was still in the range of $100 billion, almost half of which was with Japan. Imports of cars and auto parts from Japan alone account for well over one half of the trade deficit with Japan. America's own auto exports to Japan are minimal.

Japan's propensity to import has not risen commensurately with the decline in import prices brought on by a sharp appreciation in the value of the yen. The principal reason is that an inefficient distribution system has not passed along lower prices to the Japanese consumer. Similarly, the American propensity to import has not declined along with the fall in the value of the dollar. Here the reason is that most Japanese exporters have been more interested in maintaining their market share and, knowing that Americans now need and like Japanese products, have not raised dollar prices.

Meanwhile, the impact of the dollar's devaluation on U.S. trade with other major countries has been enormous. The U.S. deficit with Canada was more than halved between 1985 and 1989 and the balance with the EC has changed from a $22 billion deficit in 1985 to a small surplus today. Because many developing countries are restricting imports and pushing exports to pay the interest due to foreign banks on their enormous debts, the dollar devaluations did not have the impact on trade with the Third World that monetary theory might suggest; the United States thus continued to have a substantial negative trade balance with less-developed countries in 1989. At the same time, Japan continues to export slightly more to those countries than it imports from them.

Even these numbers fail to tell the whole story. During the years when American industry enjoyed world leadership in technology and a capital base undamaged in World War II, the United States provided the capital and goods that war-ravaged Europe and Japan needed to rebuild. Unfortunately, Americans became complacent in the 1960s and 1970s. They suffered from a cost structure that was increasingly uncompetitive; the savings rate slumped as did growth in investment and productivity. American industry paid too little attention to quality, and government policies paid too little attention to the industrial sector's declining international competitiveness. Then, in the 1980s, the federal government allowed its budget deficit to get out of hand, absorbing domestic savings and requiring the import of foreign capital—much of it from Japan—to finance its overspending. An overvalued dollar in the first half of the decade, and high interest rates throughout, further weakened U.S. international competitiveness compared to Japan and West Germany.

The frugal and hard-working Japanese, goal-oriented and supported by a government-coordinated industrial policy, began to cut into the U.S. market share in the United States itself as well as in third countries. Trade friction first began in the 1960s in the form of increased competition from Japan in textiles and steel and a consequent loss of American jobs. In the 1970s Americans watched their television, automobile, and machine tool industries decline in the face of Japanese competition. By the 1980s Japan and then South Korea and Taiwan came to dominate the U.S. consumer electronics market. Also in the 1980s, Japan's increasingly competitive high-technology industries started to threaten America's major semiconductor and computer firms.

The question for the future is whether Japan will take over other high-technology markets such as supercomputers, medical equipment, telecommunication switches, aircraft, satellites, and biogenetic products. Fortunately, American industry has learned a lot about competing internationally in recent years. On a cost and quality basis it is better equipped to meet the Japanese now than it was in the 1970s and early 1980s.

Washington had hoped that Japan, reflecting its new success, would move quickly to accept new responsibilities in the international economy. Instead, Japanese officials have worked to maintain a relatively closed market much longer than trade surplus figures indicate was in Japan's best interest. Japan continues to ask for foreign understanding of the internal political problems it must solve before opening its markets further; meanwhile, it has gratefully used the advantage of a relatively open American market to continue to expand exports. The European countries have been far less reluctant than the United States to hold back the wave of Japanese exports through market-sharing agreements and quotas.

New Trade Talks

The U.S. and Japanese governments are now engaged in the Structural Impediments Initiative (SII) negotiations. Each government is telling the other what it thinks should be done to bring down the U.S. trade deficit with Japan. The objective is to address structural differences between the two countries—Japanese practices that the Americans say interfere with growth in Japanese imports, and U.S. practices that the Japanese say make U.S. industry less competitive. Unfortunately, expectations in Washington of changes that will reduce the U.S. trade deficit fairly quickly may be running too high. From the Japanese side, structural changes in the Japanese distribution system and reform of exclusionary business practices and relationships—the American requests—do involve measures the Japanese government wishes to take. In fact, Japanese consumers will be the major beneficiaries. Even so, changes will come slowly and the impact on the U.S. trade deficit of a more open Japanese import market will take several years to show meaningful progress. From the American side, a reduction in the federal budget deficit, an increase in savings, or a change in short-term pressures on firms to maximize their financial return to shareholders—all of which the Japanese are requesting—will not occur in time to have an immediate impact on the U.S. trade deficit.

The issues on both sides are ones that the citizens of each country should be telling their own governments to correct. If the SII were implemented, the Japanese would gain cheaper, more competitive imports, and the Americans would develop a more competitive industrial base.

Not enough has been said in the United States about one area where Japan enjoys a strong competitive advantage that is unlikely to change. Japanese industry enjoys the benefits of lower capital costs because of a significantly higher savings rate. The yen is strong, savings are high, inflation has been tamed, and interest rates are markedly lower than in the United States. The result is low-cost, low-risk financing supported by the stability of the industrial group to which a company belongs, and backed by intragroup share holdings and the financial resources of the group bank. Any steps to improve U.S. competitiveness in this area will have to come from reform within the United States itself.

There are also differences in the financial measurement systems between the two countries that bestow additional competitive financial advantages on Japan. The United States has become obsessed with the quarterly investment performance of pension and endowment funds; this in turn puts new pressures on corporate management to perform well in each quarter. U.S. management is also preoccupied with what Wall Street estimates to be the breakup value of companies when and if sold piecemeal, and with what are termed hidden asset values or unrealized shareholder values. Shareholders may look for a short-term payoff but the consequence may be the unintended one of a heavy debt load or even the sale or breakup of a company. Japanese businesses, in contrast, are able to ignore short-term earnings and stock price pressures and focus more of their management energy, as well as their investment capital, on longer-term objectives. In fact, the American attention to short-term financial objectives is the area where Japanese observers are most critical of U.S. business performance.

The United States today has a trade deficit with Japan that refuses to decline. There is growing concern in the United States that what Americans perceive as unfair Japanese trading practices will threaten more American industries in the 1990s and that the United States will not be able to increase exports to Japan. Nonetheless, American politicians seem unwilling to reduce the federal budget deficit, which is the leading cause of the trade deficit. Defense spending cuts in an era of international relaxation may relieve some of the pressure but demands for domestic social programs will continue to make deficit reduction politically problematic. Meanwhile, the latent Japanese consumer movement has yet to raise a loud enough cry for lower prices and more efficient distribution of both domestic and imported products to compel political action. In short, solutions that would have an immediate and major impact on the U.S. trade deficit with Japan are not apparent.

Yet, at the same time that the U.S.-Japanese relationship has become increasingly troubled by trade frictions, other aspects of the relationship remain extremely productive. Both Japan and the United States as well as Japan's neighbors have benefited from the U.S. decision to provide a defense umbrella for Japan. Neither Tokyo nor Washington has wanted to encourage the rebirth of Japanese militarism, and neither has wanted to trigger alarm among Japan's neighbors. Because of the defense arrangement, Japan has been quite willing to support U.S. strategic directions and has been freed from the cost of building its own military establishment.

Postwar Japan has never wanted the burden of a major defense industry; nevertheless, because of its wealth, it now has the world's third largest defense budget. Only the United States and the USSR spend more. Rising voices of nationalism in Japan are calling for building a Japanese defense industry independent of American technology. The FSX dispute at the beginning of the Bush administration illustrated this trend. There are no signs yet that Japan is moving away from sharing with the United States a common strategic view of the USSR and the People's Republic of China (PRC). Indeed, Japan remains very cautious regarding its political relationships with the two communist giants even if it tends to be more aggressive than the United States in its trade relations with both.

The end of the Cold War and reductions in U.S. and Soviet defense forces will put new strains on the U.S.-Japanese security relationship. Pressures will mount in Japan for withdrawal of U.S. military forces stationed there, emotionally a very sensitive issue. The leadership of both countries will have to work hard to construct a new security relationship, perhaps using 1990, the 30th anniversary of the present security treaty, as an opportunity to do so.

There is also change in the financial field. Japan and the United States share a common interest in encouraging economic growth and debt relief in less-developed countries. But Japan's official development assistance to less-developed countries now surpasses that of the United States and is continuing to grow. And Japan is the leader in pushing for regional development in South and Southeast Asia, which will certainly help Japanese exports and overseas investment. While the memory of World War II remains alive, however, Asian countries desire the continued involvement of the United States in the area as a counterweight to Japan.

In such sectors as research and development, manufacturing technology, and management expertise, Japan has evolved from heavy dependence on the United States to a position of equality or even superiority in many fields, with increasing opportunities for a flow of technology and expertise back to the United

States. Yet at the same time that Japan has quite naturally become stronger and more independent of U.S. leadership, it remains more dependent than ever on the United States and other industrial countries for export markets and investment opportunities, and hence for its economic growth and prosperity. Since World War II the strength and growth of the U.S. economy have helped fuel the economic development of Japan, and to this day the United States remains the largest single market for Japanese exports. Japan is also heavily dependent on American food, coal, and wood products.

The dependence is increasingly mutual. Japanese capital is an important source of funding for the U.S. federal budget deficit. Japanese electronics are the sole source of critical components for some weapons systems. Growing Japanese private manufacturing investment in the United States provides badly needed jobs.

With the increasing interdependence of the world's economies, no major country today can implement domestic economic policy without paying careful attention to the policies of others. Loss of confidence by any major industrial power in the policies of another can have a devastating effect on the economies of all. American policies, along with the hard work of the Japanese people, stimulated the recovery of Japan in the occupation years and then during the 1950s and 1960s. Americans should take full credit for the success of those policies. They have to recognize, however, that with the rebuilding of Japan—and of Europe as well—they now face strong economic rivals with comparable levels of economic development and standards of living. As competition between the United States and Japan is growing, the two nations are becoming increasingly interdependent politically and economically.

It is unfortunate that disputes over the trade deficit overshadow this strategic and economic interdependence. It is unfortunate also that significant cultural and structural barriers to opening Japanese markets to imports remain at a time when Japan has removed many of the legal barriers. At the same time, the United States, reacting to the towering U.S.-Japanese trade deficit, has also been taking unhelpful steps. It has been raising protectionist barriers to protect jobs, to save the critical industrial base in America, and to try to manage trade rather than letting market decisions prevail. The question for the 1990s is whether U.S.-Japanese trade disputes can be solved without

causing a rupture in the many critical areas of mutual dependence.

Three Scenarios

What are the possible scenarios for U.S.-Japanese relations? Some trends in the 1990s seem fairly certain and affect all possible scenarios. After 1992, as intra-European companies continue to become stronger and more efficient, both the United States and Japan will face a more competitive Europe. But they will not face a Fortress Europe; as the EC leadership has indicated, closed markets are not in the best interest of the Community. Communications and the flow of information will become even faster and more efficient. International flows of capital in search of the best returns will accelerate. Even the strongest economies will not be able to pursue policies that ignore the reactions of other major countries. The developing countries—which must now include the Soviet Union, Eastern Europe, and the PRC—will continue to struggle to balance imports of capital needed to finance development with the cost of their debt and debt servicing to the industrial countries and the international financial institutions. One or more times during the 1990s there probably will be a temporary slump in economic growth, but the overall trend in the decade should be upwards. Another major probability is an energy crisis triggered by a squeeze on oil availability, a continuing rise in the world's consumption of energy, and a rise in oil and gas prices. Because of the sensitivity of the trade issue to their relationship, the United States and Japan should be preparing to deal with the effects of a substantial increase in oil prices on their respective balances of payments.

Under any scenario, it is likely that relations between the United States and Japan will be even more difficult in the next decade than they have been in the last one. Past problems have been largely in the trade field, with friction growing as a result of increasing Japanese investment in the United States. The problems of the future are likely to be more subtle and subjective and less suited to confrontational negotiations.

An optimistic scenario for the 1990s, from the U.S. point of view, would bring a favorable turn in the U.S. trade balance with Japan: A decline in trade disputes smooths negotiations in other aspects of the relationship; a more competitive U.S. industry oriented toward the longer term develops; increases in U.S. savings and productivity occur; and a reduction in the federal budget deficit takes place. Japan's flexibility and ingenuity are then tested as Japan increasingly faces the problems of all advanced industrial countries: an aging population (in Japan's case faster than in other industrial powers), rising social security costs, more consumerism and environmentalism, mounting demands for quality housing at affordable prices, more spending on physical infrastructure, and a great increase in the penetration of competitive imports. In this scenario Japan also encounters the problems of a high-valued currency, a shrinking labor force, an oil price rise, and less competitive exports.

In this optimistic scenario, the U.S. trade deficit with Japan declines in the 1990s, though it is unlikely that it could be eliminated, and the security and other policies of the two countries remain closely linked. The two nations work together closely to assist economic development around the world. Regrettably, the main reason this scenario is improbable is that the Americans are unlikely to be able to deal with their own structural weaknesses quickly enough. On the Japanese side, the scenario also assumes that the Japanese ability to adjust to major structural changes will be less in the future than in the past.

Because of its wealth, Japan now has the world's third largest defense budget.

A pessimistic scenario is also possible. In this case, the United States is not able to control the federal budget deficit even in the medium term; investment remains oriented toward the short run; and savings and productivity rise slowly, if at all. Japan fails to increase imports and continues to have large trade surpluses not only with the United States but also with Europe and the developing countries. In this scenario the dollar continues to fall against the yen, bringing Japan ever larger capital surpluses that it uses to buy assets and to finance federal and corporate debt in the United States.

The pessimistic scenario is unfortunately nothing more than a continuation of present trends, which are likely to bring an increase in hostility and eventually a breakdown in the productive aspects of the U.S.-Japanese relationship. Following this scenario means a closing of U.S. markets to Japanese products and investments, a wave of reciprocal protectionism in other countries, and serious political consequences. The United States might well return to a policy of isolationism, which was so detrimental to world order in the 1930s and so painstakingly replaced by a more internationalist consensus after 1945.

Neither Japan nor the United States can allow this scenario to become reality. Assuming each will recognize the dangers of drift, the future is most likely something between the optimistic and pessimistic scenarios. But even a suboptimal course will require a great deal of attention from leaders in both the United States and Japan so that difficult problems can be tackled in time and the U.S.-Japanese relationship can prosper to the benefit of both countries and the rest of the world.

In the 1990s, in this third scenario, economic trends and Japan's own self-interest will most likely propel Japan along the economic path that other advanced industrial economies have followed. It will experience a higher level of imports and its exports will become less competitive. Consumerism will become an important issue in electoral politics, creating pressures for modernizing the distribution system, enhancing competition by enforcing antitrust laws, and opening space for competitively priced imports. But the noted Japanese ability to adapt quickly to changing circumstances may well lead to continued increases in productivity and thus may keep Japan's trade surplus from declining as rapidly as the United States would like. And a strong yen will enable Japan to continue to invest in overseas manufacturing and to acquire foreign assets at favorable exchange rates. Consequently, the slowly declining trade surplus will be offset by rising returns on overseas investment. Japan will enjoy a strong positive current payments account. Finally, the Japanese financial system will not change. This system allies business and government in developing long-term plans that are in the interest of both and lead to rapid economic growth; it has worked well and the Japanese will see no need to change it.

In this most likely scenario, which has both positive and negative aspects, the United States will nonetheless begin to show the benefits of its own industrial restructuring. The capital gains tax will probably be modified to encourage long-term holding of assets. Investors will then become more patient. Savings will grow as will productivity. There may even be production expansion in some domestic industries where employment was lost to Japanese imports in the 1980s. The dollar will continue to be weak in relation to the yen in the early part of the decade. Congress and the administration at last will have an opportunity to slash the federal budget deficit as defense spending declines and rising GNP leads to greater tax revenues.

Increasing competition between the United States and Japan in the emerging high-technology industries will continue to cause tension, with Japan investing more to establish a competitive advantage in this sector as its older industries decline. Expanding Japanese investment in the United States will also be a contentious issue. The problems will be solved by negotiation; but in part progress will be possible because Japan, as recent history suggests, will become far more sensitive to the loss of goodwill and markets in the United States, where its trade and investment practices will continue to be viewed as predatory and insensitive.

As the United States gets its own economic house in order, and as Japan reacts faster and more sensitively to dislocation in other countries caused by its trade and investment policies, trade frictions will first become manageable and then decline in the 1990s. On investment, the United States will remain relatively open and easy for foreign companies to start business, establish factories, and buy assets. The Exon-Florio amendment demanding that incoming investment be screened will be used only in a few cases of bona fide national security. Japan will become significantly more open, legally as well as culturally, to foreign investment on the basis of equal national treatment.

Japan may occasionally appear to grow tired of buying U.S. bonds, but will continue to purchase them nevertheless because U.S. interest rates will continue to make the investment attractive. Japan will also retain a strong self-interest in access to growing U.S. markets for its exports and investments, as these allow its own economy to keep expanding. Japan will use its strong domestic government finances—which show a surplus if social security payments are added to state and local government revenues—to invest in improving social security, housing, and public infrastructure, and to create a dramatically greater demand for imports.

As time passes, within the United States the idea that the U.S. government is capable, by establishing overall targets, of managing trade of the magnitude now taking place between the United States and Japan will lose credibility.

Nonetheless, from time to time there will be steps to restrict imports from Japan. Washington will continue to explore all options available within the General Agreement on Tariffs and Trade (GATT) framework to press Japan to export fairly and to raise imports. Such pressure will make use of sections 201, 232, and 301 of the U.S. trade laws, most recently amended in the 1988 Omnibus Trade and Competitiveness Act. These sections provide measures to protect domestic industries from imports during competitive restructuring, to protect strategic industries, and to protect U.S. manufacturers from unfair trading practices in general.

U.S.-Japanese overall economic cooperation will expand, although a United States-Japan free trade agreement will not be reached. Such an agreement will not be in the interest of either country, since other trading nations would look upon it as a threat. (In any case, tariffs between the two sides are already very low.) The United States-Canada free trade agreement is not an appropriate model; but parts of it, such as the mechanisms for dispute resolution, may be studied for applicability to trade disputes with Japan.

A return to the protectionism of the 1930s also will not occur. None of the major trading areas or individual countries can afford a trade war in a world where the economies are so closely interrelated. Cooperation such as that in the Organization for Economic Cooperation and Development will expand within Asia from its recent start, and trade among the Asian economies will continue to increase as Japan and the newly industrialized nations draw low-cost imports from the less developed countries in the region. But the world will not turn into three protectionist trading blocs in North America, Europe, and South and East Asia.

Japan and the United States, with the European Community as the third partner, will find they have much to gain by increasing their cooperation on the items often regarded as the global agenda—for instance, managing macroeconomic relationships, solving problems of growth and debt in developing countries, and looking for solutions to global problems like AIDS, drugs, pollution, and global environmental degradation. The United States, Japan, and the EC will also be working together to share the cost of technical developments in such fields as space exploration, undersea mining, alternative energy sources, supercolliders, high-speed surface and air transport, and gene banks. Finally, Europe, Japan, and the United

States will have the opportunity to develop plans to deal with refugee flows from the South, work out converging views of human rights and policies to guarantee them, and cooperate to strengthen international organizations and financial institutions.

The Soviet Union will reach out for Japan's economic help; but for the two countries to cooperate, the political hostility between them will need to be eliminated. The Soviet Union and Japan will, therefore, reach a compromise on the four northern islands; and a Japan-USSR peace treaty will be signed. Instability in the Soviet Union and in the PRC, however, will warrant a continuation of the U.S.-Japanese security relationship, albeit at a reduced level of military strength. Security concepts will gradually shift from military to economic relationships, with a consequent strengthening of economic cooperation between the United States and Japan. A cornerstone of this relationship will be a guaranteed food supply agreement with Japan.

In sum, in the 1990s Japan and the United States will cooperate on many fronts while competing vigorously on others. Trade and investment issues will continue to plague the relationship in the 1990s, and some of the other issues will be resolved only after considerable friction and contentious negotiation. That is no different from Washington's relationships with other industrial countries, but the successful management of the relationship with Japan will require more than the usual amount of attention. American recollections of World War II and Japanese concern over protectionism, resource embargoes, dependency on food imports, and resentment from other countries about Japanese trading and investment practices will continue to cloud the relationship. In addition, both countries have an unfortunate history of racism that could make management of the relationship even more difficult than it is already. In Japan, for example, this racism is visible in displays of arrogance about what are perceived to be superior Japanese ways. In the United States racism is suggested by the double standard sometimes applied to Japanese investments in the United States as compared to West European investments. In Japan, almost complete racial homogeneity and the dominance of one language and one culture make consensus, conformity, and the accomplishment of national goals far easier than in America's diverse, multiracial, highly mobile society.

Avoiding Disaster

Success in managing the U.S.-Japanese relationship will come easier if there is recognition that while the two countries share many common values, Americans and Japanese are different and their interests sometimes diverge. It is unwise to enter the 1990s believing that the Japanese will change in ways that will make them more like Americans, just as it is unwise to assume that Americans will become more like the Japanese. America has a long heritage of democracy. In spite of recent scandals and the emergence of the leader of the Japan Socialist party, Takako Doi, as a major political figure, the Japanese system is not yet as responsive to the electorate as is that of other mature democracies. Japan is still developing as a democratic state. The task of both countries is to recognize differences and to search out common ground. There must be recognition that self-interest lies in cooperation. To work together is the essence of a mature and healthy relationship between sovereign nations.

Perhaps domestic political pressures will not permit the gradual change in the U.S.-Japanese relationship held out by the third scenario. Then the alternative is management by Japan of its imports and exports to the United States, combined with vigorous application of short-term measures under U.S. trade laws to give threatened American industries a chance to restructure. Long-term economic growth in both countries will be reduced and a process will get underway that may lead to destructive policy consequences never intended. This is not a desirable approach in a world where prosperity requires open markets and expanding international trade.

Japan, in its own self-interest, must recognize the need not to alienate its trading partners. Instead of putting the blame on others it must do more itself about its trading relations and large surpluses. Similarly, Americans must cease blaming others for a number of problems whose causes and solutions lie at home. The United States must finally act to curb its federal budget deficit, increase its savings rate, and shift its long-term investment practices—not because the Japanese tell Americans to do so, but because it is essential to America's own long-term economic strength reform.

Americans unquestionably will be competing even more directly with Japan as well as with Europe in the 1990s. That competition should be looked upon as a healthy stimulus to economic performance and as a way of assuring that consumers get the best products at the best prices, regardless of their origin. The United States and Japan have a great deal to lose if they approach the problems of the twenty-first century in growing conflict. The cost of doing so has never been greater, yet great also is the risk that this will happen. Differing strategic perceptions could arise on both sides of the Pacific. The emergence of Japan as an economic superpower, at a time when Americans are having difficulty reducing their twin deficits, is already a substantial source of friction. In addition, the cultural differences between the two countries are an ever-present obstacle to cooperation and a source of misunderstanding. A new group of political, economic, and business leaders is taking over in both countries. This new generation does not always feel the same sense of community developed by an earlier generation of leaders who forged post-war reconciliation and discovered that Japanese and Americans could be friends and allies.

The United States and Japan have much to gain by continued cooperation. The two countries cannot allow short-range disputes to impede efforts to work together in their mutual long-term interest. The peaceful resolution of disputes between nations requires compromise from all partners involved. Leaders in Japan and the United States have to redouble their efforts to bring about such compromises. One fact both the United States and Japan must recognize is that although competition between them may be inevitable, the future prosperity of both societies depends on close U.S.-Japanese cooperation. It is the responsibility of the political leaders of the two nations, and in particular of the U.S. president and Japan's prime minister, to outline publicly a vision for the future in which the current cooperation between the United States and Japan can endure and prosper.

The Disintegrating Socialist World: Eastern Europe and the People's Republic of China

- Eastern Europe (Articles 20-22)
- China (Articles 23-24)

Workers of the world, beware! You are still first and foremost members of independent nations. Your identification with an "international working class" brought you little prosperity. Exploitation of your labor continued under the guise of the Communist party and the state; but national animosities, and your rejection of the concept of an international brotherhood of workers and of Soviet domination, may mean civil strife, and even war. And only if you are willing to endure the hardships of a transitional period, including inflation and high unemployment, can you look forward to a period of prosperity and the political stability necessary for democracy.

Gorbachev, by his own policies of *perestroika* and *glasnost*, and by his refusal to support the entrenched Communist leaders of the states of Eastern Europe with Warsaw Pact troops, encouraged their peoples to overthrow entrenched Communist regimes. Gorbachev recognized that in Eastern Europe, as in the Soviet Union itself, communism had proven bankrupt. Highly centralized command economies in the hands of incompetent bureaucrats had brought continuing economic decline to most of the states of Eastern Europe. At its best, in East Germany, communism had brought "development" in terms of heavy industrial production. However, in spite of the hard work of the people, there were few consumer goods to purchase with their hard-earned wages, and even those consumer goods available were shoddy and out of date. Further, due to restrictions imposed on trade with the Communist bloc by the Western liberal democratic states during the cold war, the countries of Eastern Europe were unable to benefit from the technological revolution going on in the West since World War II.

The peoples of Eastern Europe felt overjoyed as the weights of their repressive governments were, one by one, thrown off their backs during 1989 (with Bulgaria and Albania following), but in their wake has arisen a profusion of crises, tensions, and problems. Foremost among these is the demand on the newly formed governments in the Eastern Europe states that they deliver economic and political benefits, and deliver *immediately*. The impatience of these peoples, who have at best not lived under democratic rule for the last 45 years, and at worst never, has challenged even the most high-minded of the new, more democratically inclined governments. In the case of Romania, the people's incomprehension of the need for tolerance of an opposition has led to the trashing of the headquarters of opposition parties, and efforts to murder former members of the Romanian Communist Party. Yugoslavia has almost collapsed into a state of civil war. And in East Germany (the German Democratic Republic), although successive governments promised major reforms, it was not enough to keep its citizens from emigrating to West Germany (the Federal Republic of Germany) at the rate of 2,000 per day. Now that the two Germanys are unified, what was formerly East Germany is suffering from massive unemployment. Until the issue of property ownership

claims is settled, it is unlikely that German capitalists, or anyone else, will dare to invest there.

Further, for the new governments of any one of these states to turn around its economy so dramatically in just a few years so that there are palpable improvements has been impossible. In fact, to undo the damage of long-term misguided policies of the preceding Communist governments (an inadequate infrastructure, deforestation, and the neglect of agriculture and light industry) may take years, if not decades. Removing Communist party personnel from the state administrative system, and dismantling the bloated state bureaucracies, which are themselves responsible for carrying out the very reforms that will undercut their own positions of power and patronage, impose an extraordinary burden on these states' resources. As state subsidies for food, resources, and energy have ended, massive inflation has followed. And when inefficient factories and stores, and industries that produce products nobody wants, were weaned away from state support and eventually shut down, high levels of unemployment ensued. Many of the new non-Communist governments of Eastern Europe are, therefore, faced with angry, discontented populations. They feel that they have lost the paternalism of the socialist state, yet not gained the advantages that political freedom and capitalism promised. They have shown little patience in waiting for tomorrow.

Aid from Western European states, the United States, Japan, and international institutions such as the IMF, may be crucial to these governments' ability to lessen the pain of the inevitable inflation and unemployment marking the transition from their centralized command economies to free market economies. Without sufficient support from the outside world, radical economic reforms and the political reforms that they necessarily entail may be so destabilizing that the governments will collapse, civil war ensue, and a military solution may, regrettably, follow. Unfortunately for these states, the attention, not to mention the resources, of the world's major aid donors has, since August 1990, been focused on the Middle East. And many of the funds that might have gone to support development in Eastern Europe have, instead, gone to fund the war in the Persian Gulf. This is particularly true for Germany which, in addition to helping fund the war against Iraq, must also address the costly issues associated with reunification.

In addition, the new governments of Eastern Europe have to face the specter of renewed civil violence and conflict with their neighbors, a specter that was absent during the years of Soviet dominance and enforced peace. Now that the governments of Czechoslovakia, Poland, and Hungary have demanded the removal of Soviet troops from their respective countries, a dominant outside power with an interest in maintaining the peace in Central Europe may be withdrawn. The national military left behind in each country could now come to serve as a tool of aggression if its government so chooses. Now all the submerged issues of territorial claims emanating out of World War II and before—the ill-treatment of national minorities, the recriminations involved with Nazi collaboration during World War II, or participation in the repudiated Communist parties and governments—are rapidly surfacing.

German reunification is also an issue for Eastern European states, as much as for the states of Western Europe. The possibility of the reassertion of German territorial claims, of German economic dominance, of German military power, and of the reappearance of neo-Nazi behavior and values, quickly replaced the joy over the end of Soviet control of Eastern Europe. Poland remains concerned that Germany might attempt to renegotiate its post–World War II borders—one-third of Poland is former German territory. Attitudes toward Germany remain more emotional than rational. Few seem willing to concede that the Germany of today is not only different from the Germany of the 1930s, but also that the international context is so dramatically different that Germany has far more to gain through stability in Central Europe and a stable economic and political climate than it does through military aggression.

In the People's Republic of China, protests against Chinese Communist Party rule in 1989 failed to bring about the desired change. Worse, rather than hastening the demise of the Communist regime, the protests so challenged China's leaders that they used military force to brutally suppress the demonstrators in Beijing. A repression followed and continues to this day. Regrettably, the student-led mass demonstrations against the Communist regime led to a *reversal* of many of the more liberalizing political and cultural trends within China. For example, the press and mass media have yet to recover the freedom they had before the declaration of martial law in May of 1989; culture (theater, film, music, art) is again under the thumb of the Communist party propaganda chiefs; and the universities and high schools have had to inject large doses of ideology and politics into the curriculum.

As one communist regime after another fell in Eastern Europe, the lesson China's leaders must have learned was that even a low level of tolerance for dissent could lead to the overthrow of unpopular Communist governments. Before 1988, China's Communist party leaders might have been willing to risk a more democratic polity as, with stunning economic successes visible to all, they had little to fear from rivals. But as corruption, inflation, and unemployment began to undermine these economic successes in 1988–89, China's leaders worried that they could only hold on to power by force. Although China now says that it has completed all the trials of "criminals" who participated in the "counterrevoluntary" demonstrations during the spring of 1989, the repression continues. And China's revolutionaries who successfully fought for Communist control over forty years ago continue to hold on. The urbanites of China are aware, thanks to short-wave radios and the Voice of America, of the events in Eastern Europe. Yet the message they receive is not a clear one: Could it be that their own leaders were correct? If the Chinese Communist Party were overthrown and a "democracy" replaced it, would China, like many of the Eastern European states, now be facing instability, even chaos? The Communist party-controlled press does not permit a public discussion of this

issue, and many in China seem reconciled to the need for the government to have used force to repress the demonstrations in Tiananmen Square in 1989. Perhaps worse, many seem to have become so absorbed with the stunning American military success during the war with Iraq, broadcast extensively on television within China, that the issues of the pro-democracy forces have been temporarily shelved. Nevertheless, as China's octogenarian leaders pass away one by one, there is bound to be a resurgence of efforts to being greater democracy to China and to overthrow Communist party rule.

Looking Ahead: Challenge Questions

What are the concerns that the Eastern European countries have about a united Germany? Are their concerns justified? What kinds of policies has either West Germany or East Germany had since World War II that would warrant these concerns? Does adding 18 million people to the population of West Germany give cause for concern? Why has the world not suffered from a Japan that was as aggressive as Germany during World War II but was never divided, and whose population is significantly larger than the combined population of a united Germany?

What is likely to be the economic, military, and political relationship of the Eastern European states to the Soviet Union? Is it in the interest of these states that Gorbachev should fail to move the Soviet Union away from Communist party rule and Communist doctrine? That Gorbachev be removed from power? Is a Soviet Union in a state of civil war with its republics, or in a near state of collapse, in the interest of Eastern Europe?

Is there an "inevitability" about the collapse of communism in China? Why or why not? Did the United States boycott trade and technology with the PRC help bring about a change in the politics of the Communist party leadership or simply hurt the Chinese people? Knowing what has happened in Eastern Europe, if you were among the Communist leadership of China, would you make concessions to a pro-democracy movement the next time it occurred?

Reforming the Nonreforming Regimes

The ultimate impetus for political transformation will arise from within oppressed societies.

Robert L. Pfaltzgraff, Jr.

Robert L. Pfaltzgraff, Jr., is president of the Institute for Foreign Policy Analysis and Shelby Cullom Davis Professor of International Security Studies at the Fletcher School of Law and Diplomacy at Tufts University.

The remarkable revolution of 1989 swept away nearly all communist systems in Central Europe, only bypassing Albania, followed in February 1990 by the electoral defeat of the Sandinistas in Nicaragua. What remains is a group of disparate communist states including Cuba, China, Vietnam, North Korea, and Albania. These countries share the common fate of having governments based on political elites espousing Marxist-Leninist principles and imposing on their peoples a repressive political and economic system. As such, they appear increasingly to be anachronisms —out of step with the dramatic changes that are sweeping regions extending from the Western Hemisphere to Europe and the Asia-Pacific area.

Once seen as a vanguard of Soviet power posing a threat to U.S. interests in its own front yard, Fidel Castro's Cuba now seems more a relic of a failed political-economic experiment than a model for revolutionary change. China's domestic retreat back toward the communist political orthodoxy of its early decades in the aftermath of the Tiananmen Square massacre has served only to point up the widening gap separating its present leadership and nearly all other states of the Pacific Rim. Clearly, the rising tide represented by the revolutionary forces that have altered the international landscape from Managua to Bucharest has had an unequal impact on communist structures around the world.

Those communist regimes in Europe that have been replaced by democratic forces pressing for political pluralism and market economies shared the common fate of having been occupied by the Soviet Union and its communist cadres as a result of World War II. Once Mikhail Gorbachev made clear that Moscow was no longer able or willing to make Soviet military forces available to keep them in power—as had his predecessors in the case of Hungary in 1956 and Czechoslovakia in 1968—they fell like a house of cards. In retrospect, all these regimes lacked the political legitimacy, or popular acceptability, conferred by truly free elections providing periodic tests of accountability for their leaders.

Moreover, it had proven increasingly difficult over time to isolate the peoples of Eastern Europe behind the Iron Curtain that had been erected as a barrier to what the ruling communist elites regarded as political contamination from the outside world. By the time the East German communist regime fell in late 1989, nearly all East Germans had been able for years to receive West German television broadcasts. As a result, they had undoubtedly been exposed visually to West German political figures more constantly than to their own government elites and been shown by vivid contrast the drabness of their own existence. The pace of contacts from the West elsewhere in Central Europe had quickened as well as a result of the growing impact of information and communication technologies.

An assessment of those factors that appear decisively to have contributed to the fall of communist regimes in recent months is a necessary prerequisite to developing U.S. policy toward residual Marxist–Leninist-style states whose political systems, it is hoped, will be similarly transformed.

To the extent that the United States had a coherent and constant strategy, it was that of containment, whose purpose was to thwart the expansion of communism, whether directed from Moscow itself or through intermediaries such as Cuba. In the final analysis, it was a combination of factors, including (1) the dramatic contrasts between the vibrant societies of the West shielded by the military capabilities of the United States and its allies, together with (2) the patent economic failures of the Soviet Union, which led to a growing disillusionment with communism on a global scale, and (3) a new Soviet strategy, adopted by Gorbachev, that set in motion the events leading to the collapse of communist systems.

It would be logical to expect empires first to crumble at their periphery and only subsequently at the core as they reach the limits of their expansive capacity. Such is the pattern of imperial structures from the ancient world to the recent past. In this respect, the revolutionary changes in Central Europe stand in sharp contrast, for the communist empire has crumbled at or near its central point. By the same token, it is unlikely that communist systems, having disintegrated in Central Europe, could be sustained long by the Soviet Union at the much greater distance represented by Cuba. It follows that, in the case of Soviet-sponsored states such as Cuba and Vietnam, the willingness or ability of Moscow to support such regimes could be expected to diminish, leading to consequences as dramatic as those in Central Europe.

What is different

What is different about Cuba and Vietnam, however, is that, in contrast to the Soviet-imposed governments of Central Europe, these regimes came into existence as a result of internal wars fought by indigenous forces with Soviet support. Neither Cuba nor Vietnam has relied on Soviet military power to prevent the overthrow of their regime. Therefore, the present life-support system provided by the Soviet Union for client states such as Cuba and Vietnam lies principally in the economic realm. As long as they still possess vast military and internal security forces, such regimes are likely to prove more resistant than were their Central European counterparts to reformist pressures.

Much of this antireformist profile applies to China, to which the Bush administration has made numerous approaches in an effort to mitigate the consequences of the tragic events of Tiananmen Square for Sino-American relations. In contrast to an official U.S. policy providing for minimal contact with Cuba, Vietnam, and North Korea since the early 1970s, the United States had developed a thickening web of bilateral relationships with China. Until the Chinese crackdown in June 1989, the effects of policies toward China pursued by successive administrations had seemed to bear fruit. At a state-to-state level, the United States and China have

Albania: Still Stalinist

by Nikolaos A. Stavrou

Albania remains the sole standing domino of what used to be the Eastern European bloc. Despite sporadic protests and demands by youth for basic human rights, the regime of Ramiz Alia, consisting of an aging group of Stalinists, remains in control of the domestic situation. Yet the momentous changes of 1989 had their impact. Following the bloody events in Romania, Alia and his cohorts appear increasingly concerned for their fate and have initiated a process designed to prevent their ocurrence in Albania. Cosmetic reforms and a masterful manipulation of the Western press are under way.

The Albanian reaction to events in Eastern Europe is simple and self-serving. In their view, "socialism did not fail, revisionism did." Perestroika and glasnost are, therefore, irrelevant for a "truly socialist country like Albania."

Theoretical explanations notwithstanding, the shock waves of 1989 have reached Albania's shores. In December, students in the northern city of Shkoder took to the streets to protest human rights violations and official corruption. Brutal force was used to make an example of them and to prevent the spread of protests to other cities. The regime denied the Shkoder incidents and attributed "rumors" to that effect to "evil-minded reactionaries who seek to replicate in Albania the chaos of Eastern Europe."

In the southern part of the country, where approximately 300,000 Greeks reside, protests took an ugly turn. On October 11, four brothers (the youngest only 12) attempted to cross the border into Greece. They were caught, tied behind tractors, and dragged through the villages of Malçani, Cerkovica, Partizan, and Divri to intimidate the population. When the Western press finally caught up with the story, the regime denied it and blamed provocateurs for slandering Albania. A video allegedly showing the young men celebrating the New Year with their family was produced and handed to Western newsmen. The "evidence" showed four terrified young men, all sporting identically shaven heads, typical of Albanian prisoners.

With the situation under

shared a parallel interest in preventing the extension of Soviet hegemony.

Moreover, the increasing ties between China and the outside world were accompanied in the 1980s by a remarkable rise in economic growth rates, reaching as high as 10 percent annually. China embraced reformist economic policies that included, especially in the agricultural sector, market principles. Many thousands of Chinese students were permitted to study abroad, while China actively encouraged foreign trade and investment in order to accelerate the modernization process. What the leadership of Deng Xiaoping failed to grasp, however, was that economic reform would lead inevitably to pressures for political

change that could be prevented only by force of arms.

The lessons of Tiananmen Square clearly lie in the realization that, as long as it is both possible and necessary, the Chinese leadership will employ whatever means are deemed essential to assure that it remains in power. Chinese "sticks," in the form of repression against its recalcitrant population, will be far more important to the political elite's perceived need to assure that it remains in power than will be the proffered "carrots" of outside governments, including the United States. Indeed, the lack of responsiveness and increased obduracy of the Beijing authorities to the overtures of the Bush administration has seemed to grow in direct propor-

tion to the demise of communist regimes elsewhere.

Without the action taken in Tiananmen Square, it must be reasoned in Beijing, the Chinese leadership might have suffered the same fate as Nicolae Ceauşescu in Romania. Far from being the "last hurrah" of a ruling gerontocracy, China's antireformist policies are those of a government whose premier, Li Peng, is only 61 years old. The Politburo contains other relatively young men, such as Deputy Premier Yao Yilin and the party head, Jiang Zemin, who strongly oppose reformist policies. Hence, it would be premature to suggest that the eventual passing of the Old Guard will usher in a new period of change spurred by a young reformist leadership.

---

control and the protest quashed, the government adopted a five-pronged approach to manage reforms and assure a soft landing for its leaders. It consists of: (1) implementation of cosmetic changes that in theory address the fundamental issues that caused Eastern European upheavals; (2) deflection of Western media attention from Albania proper to the Yugoslav province of Kosovo, which is inhabited by Albanians demanding autonomy from Serbia; (3) use of friendly (and eager to visit Albania) Western journalists and prominent personalities to project an image of "normalcy and stability"; (4) commencement of a process of normalization of relations with the two superpowers; and (5) intensification of a campaign to portray Albania as a "victim" scared of its neighbors and concerned for its survival.

At the Eighth Central Committee Plenum (September

19–27, 1989) Alia identified certain "ideas which merit further consideration." Among them was the introduction of multiple candidacies for elective posts of state and party organs and limited tenure for members of the Central Committee and Parliament. No similar limitation in the tenure of Politburo and Secretariat members was mentioned. At the same plenum, Alia startled his listeners with the novel (for Albania) notion that ministerial, ambassadorial, and military posts may be held by nonparty members. The latter innovation has the characteristics of power-sharing, but with a twist: "No concession will be made to bourgeois ideology in any field, either politics, arts and culture, or in economic relations," Alia stated, nor will there be any "concessions to religious ideology in any of its forms." In other words, the party retains its leading role.

The "meritorious ideas" of

the Eighth Plenum were taken a step further during the Ninth Plenum (January 22, 1990), during which formal decisions were taken to implement them. At this plenum the first secretary revived the Ministry of Justice, which had been abolished in 1967 "as any impediment in the conduct of class struggle."

Reforms on paper

On paper, these reforms seem to be a step toward democratization. In reality, the party is still in charge of implementing them and no thought was given to abrogating Article 3 of the constitution, which assures it monopoly of power. To address the problem of "bureaucratism," which Albanian theoreticians saw as the core cause of East European revolutions, more power has been shifted to local authorities. In the Albanian context, however, decentralization of power means better

Judging by the events of 1989 in China and elsewhere, China's leaders will do all that lies within their power to prevent reform in the years ahead, having seen the consequences of such change in other socialist states.

Among the policies to be pursued for this purpose will be a marked reduction of contacts between the Chinese people and the outside world, especially students sent abroad for education. Those communist states—namely Albania and North Korea—that have been most immune to the tides of reform have been most successful in imposing a largely impermeable veil of self-isolation between their peoples and the outside world. To an extent unequaled elsewhere, both regimes have succeeded in maintaining a monopoly on sources of information and news. Both are

largely untouched by the reformist forces that have swept other states.

Although Seoul, the dynamic capital of South Korea, with its rapidly growing economy based on high-tech industries and an increasingly open, pluralistic political system, lies geographically close to the Demilitarized Zone (DMZ) separating the two Koreas, otherwise it is light years away from the hermetically sealed dictatorship of the aging Kim Il Sung.

A U.S. strategy

Can one derive the elements of a strategy for the United States to pursue from a comparative survey of the remaining antireformist states? More fundamentally, to the extent that

such regimes stand in isolation from the outside world, posing little or no threat to their neighbors, should the energies of the United States be directed toward effecting change of the magnitude seen elsewhere?

Whatever their common features, the importance to the United States of these regimes differs. To the extent that their ability—by themselves or at the behest of the Soviet Union—to threaten vital interests of the United States has diminished, it follows that their importance to U.S. security has lessened. As such regimes become isolated from their outside base of support, their future rests inevitably on the durability of their military and internal security apparatus. Most vulnerable in this respect, it would appear, is Cuba. Castro's tangible links with Moscow may

control of society; more people are now available locally to spy on each other.

As a diversion from its own dismal record on human rights (Albania was singled out eight times by the UN Commission on Human Rights for "gross violations of the rights of its citizens"), the Tirana regime has been active in promoting unrest among the Albanians in Yugoslavia. There, Western television cameras and newsmen have easy access to mass demonstrations (often orchestrated) that portray Albanians as victims of "Great Serbian chauvinism."

In a twisted but masterful manipulation of the press, the Albanian regime uses Western coverage of the Kosovo events as a test to select Western journalists who might be invited to visit Albania. Ironically, newsmen who would protest any notion of "prior censorship" do not

seem offended when "samples of their work on Kosovo" are used as a criterion by Tirana authorities to grant or deny them visas. At least one radio correspondent even went as far as submitting tapes of her broadcasts to secure a visa.

In early January, the government dispatched to Western capitals Deputy Foreign Ministers Sokrat Pliaka and Muhamed Kaplani and Ambassador Xenophon Nushi to assure the world that it was in control and determined to follow its own pace of reform. Their message, not unlike other dictators, was: If reforms do not take place, it is partially your fault for pressuring us. In February, Pliaka extended an olive branch to the two superpowers, with whom relations had been broken; and recently telephone communication with the United States was established for the first time.

Efforts to project an image of internal tranquility and "normalcy" seem to be the order of the day. Major world personalities have either been invited or are under consideration for a "first" visit to Albania. Among them is UN Secretary General Javier Pérez de Cuéllar. Closer to home, prominent Albanian-Americans who have visited Tirana are actively urging major American personalities to go there. Their presence in Albania would reinforce the notion that things are changing in that Balkan country.

No single factor can explain the survival of the rigid Albanian communist regime—except one: terror. The late Enver Hoxha put in place one of the most oppressive machines known to man. Fourteen labor and concentration camps are still operational in a country of three million people. Alia has been a beneficiary of and con-

4. THE DISINTEGRATING SOCIALIST WORLD

continue to weaken as Soviet priorities shift elsewhere, and he faces a population that has never been effectively isolated from the outside world. Whatever the impact of Radio and TV Martí and other such efforts, they are likely to be resisted by the Cuban government, with its still formidable military forces and internal security apparatus.

The proper focus of U.S. strategy lies in the consolidation of those vast changes that have destroyed repressive regimes at the core of the erstwhile Soviet empire—in Central Europe —rather than the diversion of major resources to the remaining communist states whose economic and political future appears to be bleak. Nevertheless, if only as a basis for allocating limited resources among greater or lesser priorities, the United States must

develop a strategy toward nonreformist communist states.

The broad elements of such a strategy are to be found in an approach that includes an acceleration of the flow of information about the outside world from Cuba to East Asia and provides other support, to the extent politically feasible, for those reformist elements that exist in such countries.

In the case of China, the United States faces the difficult task of maintaining correct state-to-state relations with a government that will probably become increasingly unpopular both at home and abroad. On the one hand, the United States has an enduring stake in a multilateral power balance that includes China, both in the Asia-Pacific area and at a global level. On the other hand, it faces a China whose

domestic policies clearly do not accord with American values and whose foreign policy contains important elements—for example, the proliferation of missiles—that run counter to U.S. interests. This argues for a highly restrictive policy of U.S. technology transfers, combined with a greater effort to diminish the isolation of China's people from knowledge of the forces transforming the outside world.

In the four decades since the outbreak of the Korean War in 1950, North Korea has continued to pose a threat to the stability of the Korean peninsula. Periodic efforts on the part of South Korea to take steps toward reunification, dating from the early 1970s, have foundered. Meanwhile, North Korea has acquired its own armaments production capability as part of a persistent military buildup de-

---

tributor to the Hoxha terror. The fact that no Soviet troops are anywhere in the vicinity also helps explain the survival of Albanian Stalinists. Relations with Moscow were broken in 1961, and no relations were established with the United States after World War II because the communist regime refused to recognize the validity of prewar treaties and obligations. In February, Pliaka reversed a 30-year policy of "no business with the superpowers" and left open the possibility of restoration of diplomatic relations with both of them.

Finally, at the Tenth Plenum of the Central Committee held in Tirana on April 16-17, Alia irrevocably committed his country to establishing relations with the superpowers and the European Community. "Delicate negotiations with both powers" have been under way for some time in Europe and the

United States, according to senior European diplomatic sources.

No unconditional recognition

It would be a serious error on the part of the United States, however, to approach the Albanian regime with romantic notions. At this juncture, the Albanian regime has a simple objective in seeking improved relations with the United States: to tap the resources of the Albanian-American diaspora, with its considerable congressional influence.

It is obvious from reading the Albanian press and official statements that Alia is rapidly replacing Stalinism with intense nationalism. It would be an error for the United States to unconditionally recognize a country that has refused to even accede to the Helsinki Ac-

cords. Albania remains the sole European state that has not recognized the inviolability of European borders and has flagrantly violated all international treaties and obligations protecting the rights of its Greek and other ethnic minorities.

Official visits and the establishment of relations should not be treated as casual matters but must be properly framed to achieve the goals of openness and democratization. Well-meaning officials and Western journalists, eager to be the "first" to penetrate "fortress Albania," are seen in Tirana as pegs for positive stories in the Western press, which in turn are selectively replayed domestically to further demoralize the population.

Nikolaos A. Stavrou is professor of international affairs at Howard University and associate editor of Mediterranean Quarterly.

signed to provide the means to strike across the DMZ. Reportedly, North Korea is in the process of becoming a nuclear power. As North Korea obtains such capabilities, Soviet leverage over North Korea is likely to decline, despite the growing interest in the Pacific enunciated by Gorbachev. In this respect, North Korea can be expected to differ from East Germany.

At this time, North Korea combines the characteristics of increasing military independence and a tightly controlled population kept in isolation from the world beyond its largely sealed borders. Hence, compared, for example, even to Cuba, few opportunities are available to encourage its political transformation. The eventual succession of Kim Jong Il, the son of Kim Il Sung, would in all likelihood bring to power an equally repressive leadership. Therefore, the threat posed by North Korea may grow, rather than diminish, in the years ahead.

Such a prospect argues for the preservation of the security relationship between the United States and the Republic of Korea, together with efforts to probe whenever possible the limits of North Korean control of its population.

> **Those communist states that have been most immune to the tides of reform have been most successful in imposing a largely impermeable veil of self-isolation.**

The world of the 1990s will feature the emergence of regional power centers—states with growing military and technological capabilities, including the means to produce atomic weapons, missile delivery systems, and other capabilities for high-intensity warfare. It is in such a

broader context that nonreformist communist states, especially China and North Korea, as well as Cuba and Vietnam, should be considered. To the extent that the ability of Cuba and Vietnam to export military power within their respective regions is lessened, accompanied by a reduction in Soviet support, the threat that they pose to U.S. interests will thereby be diminished.

U.S. strategy toward the communist reform "refuseniks" should be designed as fully as possible to use our instruments of communications technology to penetrate closed societies. In all cases, our interest lies in the promotion of change leading to governments of the kind that have begun to be installed in most Central European countries and Nicaragua. Although the catalyst for such change can be strengthened from outside by policies beyond containment, the ultimate impetus for political transformation will arise from within oppressed societies, as events of recent months have so dramatically shown. As now in Europe and elsewhere, our task will then lie in assisting as fully as possible the formidable task of building political and economic structures capable of providing the freedom of choice sought by so many peoples and yet denied by nonreformist communist regimes.

Eastern Europe's nationalist hangover.

THE TWO FACES OF EASTERN EUROPE

Adam Michnik

WARSAW

From Romania to Germany, from Tallinn to Belgrade, a major historical process—the death of communism—is taking place. The German Democratic Republic does not exist anymore as a separate state. And the former GDR will serve as the first measure of the price a post-Communist society has to pay for entering the normal European orbit. What price, moreover, will the old Federal Republic, a normal European state with a parliamentary democracy and a market economy, pay for its absorption of a post-Communist creature? In Yugoslavia we will see a different test: whether the federation can survive without communism, and whether the nations of Yugoslavia will want to exist as a federation. (On a larger scale, we will witness the same process in the Soviet Union.)

One thing seems common to all these countries: dictatorship has been defeated and freedom has won, yet the victory of freedom has not yet meant the triumph of democracy. Democracy is something more than freedom. Democracy is freedom institutionalized, freedom submitted to the limits of the law, freedom functioning as an object of compromise between the major political forces on the scene.

We have freedom, but we still have not achieved the democratic order. That is why this freedom is so fragile. In the years of democratic opposition to communism, we supposed that the easiest thing would be to introduce changes in the economy. In fact, we thought that the march from a planned economy to a market economy would take place within the framework of the *nomenklatura* system, and that the market within the Communist state would explode the totalitarian structures. Only then would the time come to build the institutions of a civil society; and only at the end, with the completion of the market economy and the civil society, would the time of great political transformations finally arrive.

The opposite happened. First came the big political change, the great shock, which either broke the monopoly and the principle itself of Communist Party rule or simply pushed the Communists out of power. Then came the creation of civil society, whose institutions were created in great pain, and which had trouble negotiating the empty space of freedom. And only then, as the third moment of change, the final task was undertaken: that of transforming the totalitarian economy into a normal economy where different forms of ownership and different economic actors will live one next to the other.

Today we are in a typical moment of transition. No one can say where we are headed. The people of the democratic opposition have the feeling that we won. We taste the sweetness of our victory the same way the Communists, only yesterday our prison guards, taste the bitterness of their defeat. And yet, even as we are conscious of our victory, we feel that we are, in a strange way, losing. In Bulgaria the Communists have won the parliamentary elections and will govern the country, without losing their social legitimacy. In Romania the National Salvation Front, largely dominated by people from the old Communist *nomenklatura*, has won. In other countries democratic institutions seem shaky, and the political horizon is cloudy. The masquerade goes on: dozens of groups and parties are created, each announces similar slogans, each accuses its adversaries of all possible sins, and each declares itself the representative of the national interest. Personal disputes are more important than disputes over values. Arguments over labels are fiercer than arguments over ideas.

All of this constitutes a real threat to the nascent democratic order. The years of Communist oppression taught us an acquired helplessness. We are helpless in our inability to articulate our interests, to defend our values, to distinguish ourselves from others, and to coexist with what is different.

We all agree that we are returning to "Europe." But what does that mean? Here in Poland, it does not mean a reorientation of the great currents of our culture; there is no need for Czeslaw Milosz, Leszek Kolakowski, Andrzej Wajda, Witold Lutoslawski, Tadeusz Konwicki, or Zbigniew Herbert to return to Europe, because in a spiritual sense they never left. And yet the crashing down of the Iron Curtain must have its consequences in

Reprinted by permission of *The New Republic*, November 12, 1990, pp. 23-25. Copyright © 1990, The New Republic, Inc.

culture too. The language that will be used by a culture that is ridding itself of the totalitarian corset will make use of different ideas and different obsessions than a culture that has been free of this corset for the last forty-five years. This dialogue of experiences can enrich Europe. And in this dialogue we, the people of post-Communist Europe, will be the ones who give more than we take. What we will give is the experience of living in ambiguity, the experience of living on a border.

Does the return to Europe mean also the return to a market economy? All of us know how to switch from a market economy to a planned totalitarian economy. Nobody knows how to switch from a totalitarian economy to a market economy, from a monopoly of state ownership to a plurality of economic subjects. As we say in Poland, we have to distinguish between an aquarium and fish soup. The difference, of course, is that you can make fish soup out of an aquarium, but you cannot make an aquarium out of fish soup. It is impossible to return the dead to life, yet this is precisely what we have to do. We have to do it without any historical precedents, and without individuals who know how to act in a normally functioning market, and in a society that has lost all the habits of entrepreneurial activity. The road to the market must lead through poverty and unemployment. Neither the institutions of the state nor the people themselves are psychologically prepared to struggle with reality of this sort.

The enemy of this evolution will be populism. Communism put into our heads the conviction that we are equal, that each one of us has the right to the same things. It did not matter that this very communism was betraying its own egalitarian declarations. We recalled, from Communist propaganda, that we all have the same stomachs, and that these stomachs have the right to the same stuff. We remembered that the state is supposed to guarantee us work and medical benefits, and we learned to blame the state for everything and to demand everything from the state, because the state, by assuming full power over people, assumed full responsibility. The state was like a prison warden who is empowered to keep people behind bars, but is expected to provide each one of them with a bowl of soup a day. Today all these ideas are exploding around us. And the price for the past is being paid by, among others, the government that emerged from Solidarity.

We say market, we say reprivatization. But that market has many names. If, after the dogmatic faith in the benefits of the planned economy, there comes an equally dogmatic faith in the benefits of the market, then we are in trouble. Because the market is to the economy what freedom is to democracy: a primary condition. But the market is not a self-activated mechanism that can replace the economic policy of the state and the economic activity of the people. The market has several names. We know the difference between the market as it is seen by Milton Friedman and the market with a

human face as it is perceived by, say, the leaders of Swedish social democracy.

The cult of the market will lead to the great triumph of Friedmanism. But what does it mean to be Chicago Boys in a post-Communist country? It can mean a certain particular economic practice—that is, the determination to pursue a reform of relations of ownership. But it also can mean a glorification of egoism, a contempt for the weak and the poor, a disrespect for Christian options in defense of the most disadvantaged. In this, by the way, lies the paradox of the Solidarity movement. On the one hand, we opt for the market and for reprivatization. On the other, the upheaval in Poland was the creation of striking workers of precisely the huge industrial enterprises that are the least profitable, the ones that will have to be closed down.

The problem of the market is closely associated with the problem of political culture. We had no time and no place to learn this culture. Before the market, we are like barbarians. We respond to the threat with a conscious abdication of thinking, and a preference for social demagoguery. A populist is ready to promise everything to everyone, but is only able to jail everyone for everything once he takes power. Political culture, the ability to make different currents live side by side, implies the conviction that pluralism is a value in itself, that adversarial or conflicting attitudes enrich each other if the rules of the game are respected. Political culture is the ability to hold a dialogue, the renunciation of invective and hatred in political struggle, the staunch attempt to find compromises where the situation is complex.

Poland is a Catholic country. The overwhelming majority of Poles consider themselves Catholic. At the same time Poland is a pluralist society, where different ideas and perceptions coexist. Poles are indebted to the Catholic Church for saving their spiritual and national identity, for protecting them against Communist repression. But now the same Church finds itself in a totally new situation. It learned how to defend itself against communism, but it has not yet learned, because it had no time to learn, how to live with pluralism, how to exist in a democratic state.

The first answers that the Catholic Church in Poland has provided to the question of how to live in a pluralistic society make us wonder. What is the demand for an anti-abortion law, if not an attempt to inscribe in the penal code an approach derived directly from the Church's teachings? Every Catholic knows that abortion is murder, and one cannot blame the bishops for teaching what they have been taught. A bishop who renounces the struggle for God's law ceases to be a Catholic priest. But one may ask whether in a pluralist society God's law should be enforced by the police and the penal code. One may ask whether the protection of the unborn should be effected by means of discussion with the faithful or by means of discussion with a policeman and a prosecutor.

The same goes for the teaching of religion in schools. It was a totalitarian barbarity to forbid the bringing up of children in a Catholic way and to ban religious instruction in schools. Yet the attempt to impose religious instruction on all children, believers and non-believers, by means of a state decree, is also authoritarian. A post-Communist society, because it is post-Communist, is by nature not a particularly tolerant society. One may be permitted to ask whether the attempt to teach religion in schools will not lead to intolerance against the non-Catholic minority.

The argument that Catholicism is essentially tolerant, which is precisely what some bishops argue, does not convince me. I know of no examples of Catholic pulpits in Poland condemning any other intolerance except the intolerance against Catholics. Is this a repetition, then, of the situation presented in the famous formula of Montalembert: "When I am in the minority, I demand rights for myself, because you set the rules, and when I am in the majority, I deprive you of your rights, because I set the rules"? Life in a pluralist society means an ability to limit oneself, a conviction that such self-limitation is necessary, that without it an ecumenical society (to use the pointed phrase of Tadeusz Mazowiecki) cannot exist. My question is: How will our Catholic bishops manage to become part of a pluralist, tolerant, and ecumenical society? By what means will the Church limit itself and respect these limits?

For a nascent democracy, the trap is nationalism, which has exploded together with freedom. Nationalism is a deformed reaction to the need for independence, a need that was violated by communism. Nationalism is a degenerate reaction, because it rests on contempt for other cultures that is stronger than the love for one's own.

In the time immediately after communism, nationalism is a way of getting rid of the responsibility for communism. Look how easy it is to say, if you are Russian, that communism in Russia was the work of foreigners, Jews, Poles, or Latvians. How easy it is, if you are Polish, to say that it is all the fault of Russians, if you are Romanian to say that it is all the fault of Hungarians, if you are Hungarian to say that it is all the fault of Jews. Nationalism is not the idea of freedom for the individual, it is the idea of a national state: Russia for the Russians, Poland for the Poles. Nationalism means an exclusive conception of the nation, because the enemy is first of all the other nation, and then the cosmopolitans within one's own.

We should remember that the accusations of cosmopolitanism and nationalism were the two favorite tricks of Communist propaganda. The accusation of nationalism was provoked by the demand for independence and national identity; the accusation of cosmopolitanism, by the demand for universal thinking and the urge for closer links with Europe. Post-Communist nationalism also abhors cosmopolitanism, because this nationalism is an articulation of a hidden fear of European normality, of European standards of tolerance and European democracy, of an order in which you have to renounce your own xenophobia, because, like stinking shoes, it is not allowed at a European table.

One should add, however, that this dilemma now faced by the societies of post-Communist Europe—to go toward Europe or to look for one's own way according to a nationalist formula—is not by any means an invented dilemma. It is a question facing all societies that are conscious of their own backwardness. The solution still awaits all of our societies. It might turn out that the return to Europe will be as difficult as it will be costly, that Europe will not want to accept its poor relatives. And the anti-European reaction will become a nationalist megalomania, a bizarre mixture of megalomania with a feeling of not being sufficiently valued.

Simply speaking, this post-Communist Europe of ours is rent by a great conflict of two spiritual cultures. One of these cultures says, Let us join Europe and let us respect European standards, while the other says, Let us go back to our own national roots and build an order according to our national particularity. They are spiritual, rather than political, camps, and they express themselves as a dispute over culture, not politics.

Post-Communist Europe has entered the second phase of its anti-totalitarian revolution. The first phase was a struggle for freedom, for the overthrow of communism. The second phase has turned into a struggle for power and revenge. Every revolution has its logic, and every one has the tendency to devour its own children. If the logic of compromise between the main political actors prevails, a democratic order will prevail. If the logic of revenge wins, we will face the hell of dictatorship. We can choose a normal European order, a world of normal conflicts and normal human compromises, a varied world that is, because of its variety, also dangerous. Or we can choose an authoritarian state, a nationalism that rejects a pluralist culture, an order that gives up on religious tolerance, a strong quasi-dictatorial power that offers, as a solution to the common poverty, a populist envy and a chauvinism that distorts the human face with hatred.

—*translated by Anna Husarska*

Year of Economic Change Looms for Eastern Europe

Steven Greenhouse
Special to The New York Times

PRAGUE — For much of Eastern Europe, 1991 is certain to be a year of swift economic change, one that aims to keep pace with the monumental political changes the region has undergone.

So far, with the first year of Eastern Europe's post-Communist era drawing to a close, the region's economy has moved only a few steps on the road to capitalism, save for Poland.

In Czechoslovakia and Hungary, people are excited that their Governments will soon take some of the bold steps Poland took a year ago. But they worry that as the old command structure falls apart, things will get worse before they get better.

Throughout much of the region, there has been a groundswell for faster reform, with the region's 120 million people grumbling that little has changed economically. Most stores still have only a limited supply of cheerless goods; the currency black market still thrives, and most enterprises remain state-owned, with many Communist-era managers in the saddle.

'All There Has Been Is Talk'

"Until now all there has been is talk about reform," complained Pavel Chalupka, a manager at a truck factory in Prague.

On Jan. 1, that will change. Czechoslovakia will start a rapid plunge toward a market economy. The country will remove most price controls, seek

to make its currency convertible and sell thousands of state-owned stores to private owners. Hungary will begin a new wave of reforms by allowing prices on many items, including milk, meat and electricity, to jump so they better reflect supply and demand conditions.

Effect of End of Oil Subsidy

Such moves underscore that the transition to a market economy will be painful, for the process will certainly push up inflation. But the region's transition will be made far more painful, perhaps explosively so, by external developments: spiraling oil prices, an overall slowdown in the world economy, and the economic chaos in the Soviet Union, Eastern Europe's largest trading partner.

Moscow's decision to end its oil subsidies to Eastern Europe as of Jan. 1 could be the biggest blow of all. If oil costs $27 a barrel, Eastern Europe's oil bill is expected to jump by at least $9 billion a year, making it far harder for these nations to buy much-needed goods from the West and to pay interest on their debts.

"On the whole, 1991 may be the toughest year that the economies of Eastern Europe have faced in the post-World War II period," said Jan Vanous, president of PlanEcon, a Washington-based consulting group.

Poland, whose changes last Jan. 1 made it the only East European na-

Hard-Hit Economies

Inflation rates for fiscal years ending in June.

Bulgaria ▶
Romania ▶
Hungary
Czechoslovakia
'89 '90 '91(est.)
100% 75 50 25 0

800% Poland*
400
0 27.5% ▶
'89 '90 '91(est.)

*Poland is shown separately because of its extraordinarily high inflation rate.

Source: Planecon

The New York Times

tion to adopt speedy reforms, has spawned a debate of almost theological intensity about whether going fast is best.

Poland removed almost all price controls, ended almost all subsidies to industry and eliminated its huge budget deficit. These changes helped slash inflation, make its once-pitiful currency, the zloty, respectable and increase exports to the West. But according to official statistics, Poland's industrial output and wages have plummeted more than 20 percent, and economists now debate whether the program is a failure on both economic and human terms.

Elsewhere, Romania and Bulgaria have only tinkered with economic reform. "These countries are just pretending, or trying to reform the old system," said Jan Winiecki, an economist who heads the Adam Smith Institute in Warsaw.

Difficulty in Beginning

Economic Theories Unravel in Practice

In Eastern Europe, 1990 has often been characterized by small steps, half measures and false starts. The zeal of policy makers has been tempered by the daunting complexity of the reforms needed, as well as by fears of change — and of making things worse. The huge drop in output resulting from Poland's shock therapy caused officials elsewhere to think twice about tough economic reforms.

"Except in Poland, there has been a great deal of rhetoric and even more indecisiveness," Mr. Vanous of PlanEcon said.

Nonetheless, Poland's neighbors are increasingly ready to take the plunge because they recognize that their economies are steadily falling apart under the largely unchanged command structure. They are concluding that things will not improve until the structure is overhauled.

Seamless economic theories about the best way to jump from Marxism to market economics have unraveled amid the harsh realities. When Czechoslovak officials decided to close a highly polluting, energy inefficient, unprofitable aluminum plant in Slovakia, a huge public protest persuaded the Government to give the factory a year's reprieve.

In Hungary, the Privatization Minister, Istvan Tompe, was dismissed — and the nation's privatization campaign delayed — because he set a low share price on the first state-owned company to be sold through a public offering of stock.

Mr. Tompe wanted to make sure that a flood of investors bought shares in order to create publicity

An Expensive Shock

The cost of oil imports for each country, expressed as a percent of hard currency exports. Based on a world oil price of $30 a barrel.

Country	Percent
Bulgaria	120%
Czechoslovakia	90
Hungary	66
Poland	33
Romania	12

Source: Morgan Stanley

The New York Times

and momentum for private ownership. And he did attract a crush of investors. But other officials and some members of the public complained that he was selling off the people's assets too cheaply.

"This is a very complicated social process that has its own dynamics," said Vaclav Klaus, Czechoslovakia's Finance Minister. "There is no way to decide in advance what will be steps 1, 2, 3, 4, 57. It's like playing chess; you have to know the rules of the game, and you have to react."

In steering toward a free market, the region's policy makers have often changed course. Poland had originally modeled its privatization program after Britain's, selling a handful of enterprises at a time. But with 7,000 state-owned enterprises to sell, Warsaw turned to a broader brush. The Government plans to distribute stock-buying coupons to the public, which has little money to invest, and then plans to start selling scores — perhaps hundreds — of enterprises at a time.

"We are following a road that no one has ever taken before," said Waldemar Kuczynski, the Privatization Minister.

Czechoslovakia

Velvet Transition May Be Illusory

It often seems that Czechoslovakia aspires to follow its Velvet Revolution to democracy with a Velvet Transition to a market economy. Prague's perfectionist policy makers have sought to piece together a careful program that they hope will take them to

capitalism without the trauma of Poland's shock therapy.

"We shouldn't hurry up too much with reforms because we must not have a failure," said Jan Klacek, director of the economics institute at the Czechoslovak Academy of Sciences. "If we fail, we can have several years of stagnation."

Mr. Klaus, the Finance Minister, has sought to create the proper conditions for reform by, for example, restricting the money supply and slashing the budget deficit, so prices do not soar out of control when they are allowed to rise on Jan. 1.

But the Czechoslovak policy makers have also been criticized. Some economists say Prague should have done more to end monopolies in its industries and to create competition to keep prices from soaring when controls are removed. But Government officials say they have moved as fast as possible, noting that change was slowed by parliamentary bickering and by lengthy debates over Slovak nationalism that resulted in an uneasy compromise.

The biggest problem for Czechoslovaks is that they will suffer two body blows at once. On Jan. 1, price controls will be removed, and many people predict the currency will be devalued. On the same day, Czechoslovakia will start paying for its Soviet oil in hard currency, at world prices. This change is expected to cost the nation an additional $2.5 billion a year — money that could have gone to modernize factories or improve the assortment of goods in stores.

"This is a tragedy for Czechoslovakia," Mr. Klaus said.

Even with this double whammy, the Government forecasts that output will fall by 5 to 10 percent next year, far less than the drop in Poland. Czechoslovakia, they say, with a 14 percent annual inflation rate, will not have to adopt the restrictive policies, like interest rates of 40 percent a month, that Poland did to brake its hyperinflation.

Hungary

Easy Steps Taken; Hard Ones Put Off

Hungary has led the way in taking the easy steps toward a market economy. But it has dragged its feet on the more painful steps. It was the first East European nation to establish a stock exchange, and it leads the region in privatizing companies and attracting Western investment. These are important changes for modernizing industry and are relatively painless.

But Hungary's center-right coalition Government has been loath to take painful measures like removing most price controls or devaluing its money to establish a convertible currency. The convertibility is important because it makes it far easier to buy machinery, components and consumer goods from the West.

"This Government does not like to take painful steps," said Laszlo Lang, director of the Central European Research Center in Budapest.

The Government's reluctance is also shown in its refusal to slash subsidies to industry. These represent about 10 percent of the nation's gross national product, and many economists say these subsidies must be curtailed to force inefficient enterprises out of business. That would help shift investment funds and skilled labor to more promising industries.

One reason the Government vacillates is that Hungarians have not shown the same forbearance that Poles and Czechoslovaks have. When the Government raised gasoline prices in October, taxi and truck drivers blockaded roads and paralyzed the nation. The Government backed down.

With the highest per-capita debt in Eastern Europe, the Hungarian Government has little room to maneuver. Many economists worry that the 35 percent inflation rate and other economic conditions could grow far worse unless strong medicine is taken. Most Hungarians seem eager to scrap old Communist ways, even if it means more pain. But many others, who often work at three jobs to make ends meet, are enthusiastic about trauma-inducing reforms that would be likely to increase disparities in income. Besides, reform has been given a bad name because a series of changes the Communist regime began in 1968 aggravated the economic muddle.

"People are growing impatient," said Ferenc Rabar, a former Finance Minister. "They worry that this reform process is going to go on forever."

Poland

The Guinea Pig And Teacher

With the shock therapy it began last Jan. 1, Poland has served as the guinea pig, and teacher, for its neighbors in Eastern Europe. It has gone much further in sloughing off Communist ways than have its neighbors and has developed a booming private sector and a $2 billion hard-currency trade surplus. It has also slashed inflation from the 50 percent a month left by the Communists, to about 4.5 percent a month.

But many economists say Poland's policies must have been wrong, because industrial output plunged by more than 20 percent, according to official statistics, and unemployment

could soar to well above one million, or 5 percent of the work force.

"Poland's program is unsuccessful, Mr. Klacek, the Czechoslovak economist, said. "Economic output is down some 25 to 30 percent, meaning it is at 1975 levels. This is unacceptable." He added that inflation was running at well above 50 percent on an annualized rate, which he said was unacceptably high.

Many commentators say Prime Minister Tadeusz Mazowiecki's third-place finish in Poland's presidential elections showed that many and perhaps most Poles consider the economic program a failure — even though President Lech Walesa has promised full-speed-ahead reform.

Jeffrey Sachs, the Harvard economist who helped design Poland's shock therapy, insists that the program has been successful. The size of the downturn is exaggerated, he said, because the Government has measured just the foundering state sector and not the fast-growing private sector. And much of the downturn he lays at the door of higher oil prices, a regionwide recession and a sharp drop in trade with the Soviet Union and what was East Germany.

Mr. Winiecki, head of the Adam Smith Institute in Warsaw, said, "If you remember that for 30 years Poland tried to reform the Soviet system that was unreformable, then you have to say that Poland has been a success in shifting to the market system."

He credited Poland with eliminating price distortions, creating a convertible currency and building a private sector. He and others note that Poles no longer have to wait hours in line for bread, milk and other basics. Store shelves are full, they say, with a wider variety of goods than was dreamed of in Communist times.

The program's critics say shelves are full and lines are gone because incomes have been devastated by wage controls and recession and Poles simply do not have the money to buy what is being sold.

Final Lessons

A Need for Help From the West

The ideal transition to a market economy would involve little pain and no drop in output, but most economists say this is a pipe dream.

"If you want to introduce a completely new economic system, it means you have to reallocate your resources to other sectors," said Zdenek Lukas, an economist with the Institute for Comparative Economic Studies in Vienna. "During this reallocation of resources, you have to expect a decrease in output."

Some economists say the pain can be minimized through gradual approaches. They suggest removing price controls gradually and phasing out subsidies slowly. This method might dull the increase in pain, many economists acknowledge, but they say it will delay the arrival of free-market dynamism and growth. Most Western economists, and many East European ones as well, say the best transition is a fast one — to jolt nations out of their Communist torpor and to make their economies flexible that much sooner. To protect those who lose their jobs or whose wages or pensions fall far behind inflation, broad safety nets are needed, these economists say.

One of the few aspects economists agree on is the importance of a criti-

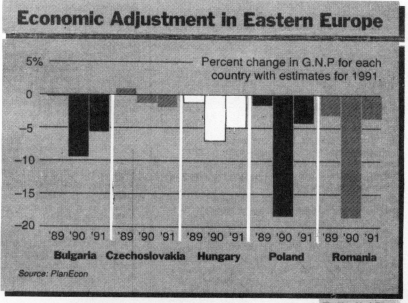

Economic Adjustment in Eastern Europe

Percent change in G.N.P for each country with estimates for 1991.

Bulgaria   Czechoslovakia   Hungary   Poland   Romania

Source: PlanEcon

4. THE DISINTEGRATING SOCIALIST WORLD: Eastern Europe

cal mass of reforms. The goal of ending price controls may be to spur enterprises to increase production, but price increases may be the only result. To spur production and efficiency, policy makers may also have to end central planning, encourage competition and convert enterprises to private ownership.

An essential step in a free market transition is to legalize layoffs, to help channel workers to growing sectors of the economy. But because Eastern Europe's housing market, still run largely by Communist rules, makes it nearly impossible to relocate to a new job, such changes may be frustrated. Little wonder that policy makers say it is essential to move on many fronts at once.

A last lesson, East European officials say, is that the region needs more Western aid — investment, debt relief and management know-how. The region's oil bill is soaring, its debt burden climbing, its social tensions and poverty increasing. Hundreds of billions of dollars are needed from the West in the next decade to avert disaster, many economists say.

"The West hasn't gotten its act together," Professor Sachs said. "There's a sense of urgency right now. We must do something."

EASTERN EUROPE ON EDGE

Starting a second year of freedom, the leaders who won it are under strain. But the outlook is far from bleak, explains an expert observer—with a little help from his liberated friends.

William Echikson

William Echikson has long covered Eastern Europe for The Christian Science Monitor and more recently The Wall Street Journal. He based this article on updating for the British edition of his book, "Lighting the Night: Revolution in Eastern Europe," coming from Pan Paperbacks.

J IŘÍ DIENSTBIER LOOKS DOWN FROM THE bathroom window of his apartment. A few days after the 1948 communist coup, the corpse of Czechoslovakia's last previous democratically appointed foreign minister, Jan Masaryk, was discovered in the courtyard three floors below. The official explanation of Masaryk's death was suicide. But ever since, the mysterious circumstances surrounding it have fueled speculation. Dienstbier, the present foreign minister, suddenly moves toward the ledge. "You see how easy it would be to fall," he says. Then his familiar chuckle returns and he reassures, "Don't worry, I won't jump."

Dienstbier's dark joke reflects how much Eastern Europe's revolutionary euphoria has evaporated. In the second year after the Berlin Wall came tumbling down, no one is dancing in the streets.

Instead of showing solidarity, the dissidents-turned-government ministers engage in party bickering; instead of offering serious plans to defend democracy, they engage in nasty innuendo and present only vague, sketchy programs. It is proving much easier to be against communism than to be "for" something. Depressed economies add to the political woes. The collapse of the Soviet market for Eastern European goods, the jolt of German unification, and the shock of higher world oil prices stemming from the Persian Gulf crisis make the shift to the market system, difficult in the best of times, look daunting. Throughout the region, newly liberated people face recession, unemployment, and insecurity.

But the outlook for Central and Eastern Europe is far from bleak. A sober observer must acknowledge remarkable progress.

The good news is that in the year following the revolutions of 1989, mostly free elections have been held at least once in every country of Eastern Europe. Almost everywhere democratic politicians have replaced the former communist tyrants. Free newspapers proliferate. Borders are open and public debate flourishes. The international environment looks favorable for consolidating this freedom. Soviet occupation troops are trekking back home in humiliation—deserting and peddling their uniforms along the way.

No one worries, as many did a year ago, that the Soviet Union will invade and crush the newfound freedom. In the 1930s and '40s Nazism and fascism overwhelmed democracy in Eastern Europe. Today Germany provides a successful democratic model.

From *World Monitor*, February 1991, pp. 60-64. Copyright © 1991 by William Echikson.

BAROQUE BUT HAPPY

Visiting old friends catapulted from jail to power, from manual worker to minister, I find them suspended between elation and despair. Power has brought undeniable changes.

In the imposing Cernin Palace, which serves as Czechoslovakia's Foreign Ministry, Dienstbier works from two immense baroque offices, full of priceless antique furniture and framed by huge tapestries. Three secretaries occupy an outside office. A chauffeured limousine awaits the minister's command.

But Dienstbier flashes the same mischievous smile as before. The formal splendor of his ministerial office has not turned him into a stiff bureaucrat. His tie is undone, his suit jacket draped over his chair.

"Let's not stay here," he says, leading the way to his private quarters. The monumental scale of the government offices vanishes and the old Jiří is again visible. His bed is unmade. Three suitcases are opened, overflowing with clothing.

Dienstbier relaxes and describes both the excitement and frustrations of his new position. Like many others vaulting from opposition to power, Dienstbier came to office believing that his most important task was to consolidate freedom from the Soviet Union. This immense task proved surprisingly simple—he went to Moscow and negotiated the withdrawal of Soviet troops from Czechoslovakia. "I get along well with Mr. Gorbachev," he says. "We have no fundamental differences."

Unfortunately, the Soviet Union's collapse into near chaos means that seeing eye to eye with the Kremlin's master isn't as important as before. Instead of fearing Soviet might, Dienstbier expresses alarm about Soviet weakness.

"You just don't know who is responsible in Moscow anymore," he complains. "If you make an agreement with the central government about oil or anything else, you don't know if the Russian Republic will cancel it the next day."

Chaos could lead to a different kind of invasion: millions of Soviet refugees fed up with the Soviet Union's economic misery pouring into Eastern Europe and plunging it into economic chaos.

I traveled to Austria to cover October's national election campaign and found that the central issue was refugees. Although Austria long has prided itself on being open to refugees from communism —more than 2 million people have fled to the country since World War II and some 600,000 have settled there—it no longer was in a welcoming mood. As thousands of refugees from liberated states poured into the country, visa requirements were reimposed for visiting Poles and Romanians. Austrian police began shipping back any refugees who arrived illegally.

The right-wing Liberal Party nearly doubled its vote. Its platform was directed in large part against immigrants and rising crime. Its candidates, dressed in traditional Austrian peasant garb, painted what they considered a nightmarish future under the slogan: "Vienna must not become like Chicago."

Similar dangerous sentiments are visible in Eastern Europe itself. The first free Hungarian elections—held in March 1990—were colored by vicious mudslinging with overtones of bitter nationalism and anti-Semitism. Brave communist reformers such as Imre Pozsgay and Rezsö Nyers were crushed.

The student group FIDESZ embarrassed all the adults by running a remarkably effective campaign and electing 22 parliamentary deputies. Their slogan was "Listen to your heart and vote for FIDESZ." Posters were plastered across the country showing, on top, former Soviet leader Leonid Brezhnev embracing former East German leader Erich Honecker and, below, a young couple kissing. The caption read, "Who would you choose?"

On election day FIDESZ found support among both young and old voters. Television showed Hungary's oldest citizen, a 106-year-old woman, casting her ballot for the youngsters. FIDESZ won 9% of the vote. In one district, FIDESZ candidate József Szájer finished more than 10% ahead of Communist leader Pozsgay.

"The youngsters are so cute," explains grandmotherly Agnes Major. "All mothers would like to have them as their children."

'I JUST WANT TO LIVE A NORMAL LIFE'

In Romania, when students protested crypto-communist Ion Iliescu's election as president, the authorities bused in mobs of miners to forcibly clear the center of Bucharest. In Transylvania street fights broke out between ethnic Romanians and Hungarians, leaving scores wounded or dead. After spending its way to popularity and election victory, the government announced some modest free-market measures, but the economy continued to shrink alarmingly, down by 15% to 20% in 1990.

Danulu Pascu, a young doctor I had known earlier, watched all these events in despair and decided there was little hope of improvement. So she left for France. "I just want to live a normal life," she explained in Paris. "That is impossible in Romania."

Bulgaria became the only Eastern European country to vote the communists back to power in a free election. Suleyman, a young Turk who had been persecuted and forced to change his name, wrote me a harrowing letter. "Kardzhali still is rife with tension," he reported. "There are nationalists trying everything they can to oppress the Turks, using new methods according to the changing conditions." Suleyman decided to flee his homeland. He applied for a visa to Sweden but informed me that he "was ready to go anywhere in search of a better opportunity."

News from Yugoslav friends also is despairing. Alexander Zigič, a young journalist, had earlier *have to be more aggressive,' said one of hundreds of thousands of East Germans laid off from their jobs. 'I must learn to sell myself.'*

found his career blocked by his refusal to join the Communist Party. More recently he received a fellowship to study journalism at Syracuse University in the United States. In the best of worlds he might later have returned to Yugoslavia and used his new-found knowledge to help train a generation of democratically minded journalists. Now he concluded that there was no future for him in his homeland. He hoped to stay in the US. His reasons were part political, part economic.

"I don't have much hope for Yugoslavia," he said. "If I return, I won't ever have my own apartment. I'll never be able to live a normal life."

THE SUDDEN-SWOOSH MISTAKE

No wonder most Western observers have concluded that Eastern Europe's year-after scorecard is negative. But I think that such a conclusion is too facile. The transition to democracy is not doomed. We simply must take a longer perspective. Those in the West who expected that communism would be replaced, in one sudden swoosh, by stable democracy and prosperity are bound to be disappointed. No magic potion exists. Democracy and prosperity must be built and solidified. That will take a generation of hard work. It is unrealistic to expect that this process will be accomplished without much pain. But it is also unrealistic to believe there are few chances of success.

In 1945 West Germany lay in ruins. In 1948 currency reform put into motion a remarkable economic recovery. Then, too, early observers focused on the pain and restructuring. Then, too, the West Germans got poorer before they got richer. But by the time of unification last year West Germany had long since become Europe's strongest economy.

Here lies the great chance for Eastern Europe. When the past is both morally and economically bankrupt, dramatic changes can be realized. Everything must be built from scratch. Postwar Germany succeeded with the moral and financial backing of the US and its allies. Eastern Europe's opportunities are just as great.

Consider the former East Germany. Abrupt monetary and political unification has resulted in a surge of bankruptcies and unemployment, a burst of inflation and poverty. Key players have often ended up unhappy and unfulfilled. Rainer Eppelmann, a Lutheran pastor and pacifist, served as East Germany's last defense minister—he gave himself the ironic title of minister for defense and disarmament. As he dismantled the East German army, many of his old pacifist colleagues criticized him for moving too slowly and for enjoying too

much the privileges of being a minister.

Bärbel Böhley, the artist-turned-leader of East Germany's New Forum, continues to fret over the transformation of her socialist homeland into a capitalist laboratory. This pessimism is understandable. But in December 1990 free democratic elections were held without a hitch in the united Germany, and no one doubts that East Germany's difficulties conceal the first painful step toward another *Wirtschaftswunder* (economic miracle).

I visited Berlin after German unification. Like hundreds of thousands of other East Germans, my friend Volker Ebermann had just been laid off from his job. He was of course anxious about the future. For the first time in his life he had to look for work. The experience unnerved him.

"I have to be more aggressive," he said. "I must learn to sell myself."

But he was not lamenting his misfortune. He had enrolled in a year-long training program that pays him three-quarters of his former salary. Since unification, he had managed to fulfill his lifelong dream of visiting England. And a new Grundig television and VCR sat proudly in his living room.

"Unification has improved my life, no doubt," he said. "Everything will work out.

THE UNRECORDED IMPROVEMENT

Do not be fooled by misleading statistics. Poland's Big Bang at the beginning of 1990 ended subsidies on basic goods, supposedly driving down real incomes by more than 30%. But before the Big Bang, most store shelves selling these subsidized goods were empty. Poles no longer spend hours standing in queues—a gain in living standards that goes unrecorded in any official index.

Improved services are another unreported bonus. Since Poland's reform, dusty neighborhoods have blossomed into colorful street markets with trucks and stands brimming with everything from beef and apples from local farms to household goods from West Germany and computers from Singapore.

Private enterprise is booming. Harvard Prof. Jeffrey Sachs, who helped foster the Polish reforms, estimates that an astounding 300,000 new private firms have sprung up in Poland over the past year, and existing ones are expanding fast. The private sector now accounts for an estimated 15% of industrial output. Competition among suppliers is driving down prices and lead times. Instead of waiting up to six months for materials and being forced to speed things up with gifts of cognac on the side, eager entrepreneurs can get supplies within days.

Admittedly, these advances mean harder work, higher prices, factory closings, and social tensions. Polish workers find themselves spending most of their paychecks on food and rent. In one year, the price of a one-bedroom apartment in Warsaw has risen by 400%. Wages have gone up less than 15%. The pain will worsen in 1991 as East German factories continue to cancel contracts with their Eastern European partners and trade with the Soviet Union switches to hard currency.

A PARADOXICAL SQUEEZE

Paradoxically, however, this squeeze will produce immense benefits. It will force companies to become competitive and begin exporting to the West. A year ago, most observers said Poland had little to sell in tough markets. But its exports to the West jumped by more than 50% in 1990 compared to 1989. Even if the overall economy shrinks, as it did in Poland, the foundations of solid export-led growth are being laid.

The great test is political. Stable, strong government is needed to implement deep and difficult reforms. Poland was able to administer its shock treatment only because Solidarity commanded broad support.

The Western democracies must send a strong message that Eastern Europe's sacrifices will pay off. They must support rigorous, consistent market reform and punish backsliders who embrace fake populist promises. How? Simply by sending strong political and economic signals: The reformers will get loans through institutions such as the new European Bank for Reconstruction and Development; the backsliders will get no money. The reformers will get debt relief from the Paris Club; the backsliders will not.

Most important, the reformers should get a promise from the European Community that Eastern Europe's emerging democracies are welcome to receive full membership. The promise should not be—and cannot be—for this year or next. Eastern Europe is not ready right now for EC membership. But the principle should be made clear: The Eastern Europeans will be welcome if they construct strong democracies and put their economies in order.

The bureaucrats in Brussels should stop moaning about the dangers of such a move and embrace it. EC membership represents the great test. The Eastern Europeans aspire above all to the kind of consumer democracy the West enjoys. If they are welcome to join the West's privileged club of prosperity, that acceptance will shape their political agenda. Instead of fighting over the ghosts of anti-Semitism and communist millionaire-making, they will face the key question: Who can best qualify for European Community membership? Skeptics may object that these are unrealistic expectations. After all, how many Western politicians are willing to stand up in front of their own electors and ask them to pay for the cleanup of Eastern Europe? Not many, judging by the paltry sums that President George Bush has asked the US Congress for.

But the example of Germany is heartening. After months of hemming and hawing out of fear of offending his right-wing supporters, Chancellor Helmut Kohl moved in November to sign a treaty guaranteeing his country's Oder River border with Poland. This was expected. But Kohl went further. He pledged visa-free travel for Poles to Germany and the right for Poles to work legally in Germany for up to three months. This was not expected. Harvard's Professor Sachs was so encouraged by the gesture that he told me that he believed the Germans finally would agree to take a lead and write off a significant amount of the Polish debt.

"Everyone said Germany was going to be so preoccupied with its own unification that it wouldn't be able to make Poland and Eastern Europe a major concern," he explained. "That's been shown not to be true."

In the future, Germany's role looks likely to grow, much more for the better than the worse. In the past, the Germans ruled and conquered Eastern Europe, first by naming kings and later by dispatching armies. Today they are peacefully providing a successful democratic example. The German democratic model is particularly valuable to the Eastern Europeans, because it was built from the ruins of dictatorship. The Czechs and Hungarians both have adopted the crucial element of the German Constitution that mandates that a party must win more than 5% of the popular vote to gain any seats in parliament.

THEIRS TO CHOOSE

In the end, of course, the Eastern Europeans themselves must choose between democracy or dictatorship. I remain confident they will choose democracy.

More than four decades of dictatorship have made Eastern Europeans impatient with the give and take of democracy. But this same oppression has left another, much more hopeful legacy of resistance to the totalitarian temptation. The Eastern Europeans, particularly in Poland, Czechoslovakia, and Hungary, did not fight so hard for freedom only to give it up upon encountering the first difficulties.

More than a year after the revolutions of '89, the incredible victory over the communist monolith remains intact, and despite the evident strains of making a transition to democracy, almost no one wants to return to life under repressive communism.

In his palace apartment, Jiří Dienstbier looks tired from staying up until 2 a.m. each morning to deal with crisis after crisis. The once voracious reader complains that, since taking office, he has not been able to read a single book.

"Sometimes I wish I was a stoker," he says. "At least then I got some sleep." A big smile breaks out over his face. "It's just a joke," he immediately adds. "Everything has happened so quickly. It still feels like a fairy tale."

Crises in Communist Reform: Lessons from Tiananmen

Harry Harding

Harry Harding, a senior fellow in the Brookings Foreign Policy Studies program, is the author of several books on Chinese domestic affairs and foreign policy. He is currently at work on a book on Sino-American relations in the 1990s.

The wave of political change that cascaded across Eastern Europe at the end of last year produced both amazement and satisfaction in the United States. Totalitarianism and tight central planning seemed to have lost their appeal, especially to those who had lived under them for more than four decades. Reform, moving in the direction of democratic politics and market-oriented economics, looked to be inevitable. The process of change, as it spread from country to country, appeared to be as irreversible as it was unexpected. American analysts understandably discussed these developments in epochal terms, describing them variously as the "end of the Cold War," the "end of communism," or even the "end of history." The contemporary era was said to be over, and a less threatening age was seen dawning before us.

The Tiananmen Incident in Peking last June should temper this optimism. In China, too, economic and political reform appeared to be an irreversible process, tracing an upward spiral toward greater liberalization and pluralism throughout the 1980s. The mass demonstrations that swept Peking between mid-April and early June of 1989 dramatically illustrated the extent of popular demands for even greater economic and political change. And the initial reluctance of the Chinese government to use force against its own citizenry appeared to prove that the demands for a more responsive government could not be resisted.

But the tragic night of June 3–4 has shown us that political and economic reform is not irreversible, at least in the middle term. Despite brave predictions that the hard-line government that emerged in Peking would stay in office for only a few weeks or months, China has subsequently witnessed a sustained suppression of dissent, a reactivation of political education, and a tightening of administrative controls over the economy. Moreover, as a direct result of these developments, U.S.-China relations, which appeared in 1987–88 to have entered a period of great maturity and stability, are now experiencing their most serious crisis since the establishment of formal diplomatic ties in 1978. In China, at least, both Leninism and central planning have gained an unexpected reprieve.

These recent developments in China bear some general lessons both for the process of reform in Communist countries and for American policy toward Communist states. Four lessons are particularly germane:

■ Attempted reform may be inevitable, but successful reform is not. Although reform may score impressive achievements during an early honeymoon period, turbulence, crisis, and retrogression are all possible at later stages.

■ The breakdowns in the reform process may be dramatic — even violent — events, serving to exacerbate the degree of retrogression at home and to magnify the impact on the international community.

■ Breakdowns in reform present the United States with troubling foreign policy dilemmas, particularly regarding the appropriateness and effectiveness of sanctions against hard-line leaders in retrogressive Communist states.

■ Finally, even if periods of retrogression and repression prove temporary, successfully liberalizing Communist systems may continue to pose challenges to their neighbors, albeit in a significantly different way than in the past.

From *The Brookings Review,* Summer 1990, pp. 47-51. Copyright © 1990 by The Brookings Institute. Reprinted by permission.

The Dilemmas of Reform

Much of the Communist world now seems to believe that political and economic reform is necessary. From Mongolia to Hungary, and from Poland to Vietnam, there is consensus on the need for less central planning and greater political openness. But there has been much less agreement on how to design the reforms: how fast to proceed, what sequence to adopt, and how far to advance.

For much of the 1980s the Chinese experience appeared promising. Under the leadership of Deng Xiaoping reform produced significant increases in growth rates, spectacular improvements in living standards, more intensive interaction with the international economy, and noteworthy gains in civil and political rights. But the balance sheet turned less favorable in the latter part of the decade, with increasing corruption, inflation, and inequality fueling sharp dissatisfaction among urban Chinese. Indeed, the Chinese case suggests that even after a strong start, economic and political reform can engender increasingly serious contradictions that can jeopardize the entire effort. Why is this so?

1. *Reform causes both pain and envy.* Clearly, the purpose of reform is to improve the performance of the economic and political systems by increasing their efficiency, productivity, and responsiveness. But these long-term benefits are accompanied by some sobering short-run costs. Eliminating subsidies and price controls will create strong inflationary pressures, at least until supply catches up with demand. Subjecting enterprises to more intense domestic and foreign competition and imposing greater financial discipline on them will most likely lead to bankruptcies and unemployment. Providing greater incentives for greater productivity and allowing the emergence of private and collective enterprises will generate new inequalities that can be perceived as unjust. And dismantling or deactivating old mechanisms of political control can lead to crime, corruption, and social disorientation, just as increasing opportunities for political participation will encounter resentment and resistance from entrenched party and government elites.

2. *Agriculture is no panacea.* The Chinese case has been frequently said to show the wisdom of starting economic reform in the countryside. And it is true that the decollectivization of Chinese agriculture in the late 1970s and early 1980s provided a great boost to the overall reform effort by stimulating economic growth, providing more consumer goods for the cities, and building a firm political base in rural areas.

But the Chinese experience also shows that such benefits may be relatively short-lived. The increases in agricultural production in the early 1980s were largely achieved through a series of one-shot initiatives that cannot be repeated: dismantling the communes, dividing the land, and reinstituting family farming. Sustain-ing the gains over time will require stimulating investment and production by increasing the prices paid to farmers for their agricultural output. This, in turn, requires either that price increases be passed along to the consumer (thus exacerbating urban inflation) or that government subsidies be provided to either peasants or city dwellers (thus increasing the financial burden on the state treasury). Once the engine of reform, agriculture can soon become a brake.

3. *Stopping reforms halfway only intensifies the contradictions.* In the 1980s Chinese leaders succumbed to the understandable temptation of implementing those aspects of reform that would produce political and economic benefits while delaying those that would impose costs. Thus, they approached the conundrum of price reform by maintaining two sets of prices for critical commodities: a lower planned price (as a subsidy for favored consumers) and a higher market price (as an incentive to stimulate production). But as the gap between the two sets of prices widened, this halfway measure gave corrupt officials an irresistible invitation to buy cheap from the plan and sell dear on the market.

Similarly, Chinese leaders gave factory managers greater autonomy over investment without making them responsible for the profitability of their decisions. At the same time, they decentralized the banking system without maintaining controls over the money supply. The result: vast quantities of unprofitable projects, an overheated economy, and growing government subsidies for enterprises in the red. Once again, halfway measures selected in hopes of painless reform generated serious economic and political contradictions.

4. *Incrementalism may prolong the agony.* Chinese leaders approached restructuring in an experimental and incremental manner, trying out different strategies in local areas and phasing in reforms over a long period of time. At first, outside observers believed that such a cautious approach was wise, for it would impose the necessary pain of reform gradually and would allow a more accurate determination of the most effective techniques of reform. Increasingly, however, the risks of such an approach became clear. Incrementalism permits the contradictions inherent in halfway measures to grow and fester. By extending the costs of reform over time, such an approach may also dissipate the political support that reform may enjoy when it first begins.

This is particularly true when, as in China, an incremental strategy involves distributing the gains of reform before imposing the costs. In such a case the public may gain the false impression that reform will be a relatively easy and painless process. Alternatively, rumors of impending price hikes and layoffs may create chronic unease and confusion. The Chinese experience therefore seems to support those who argue that economic reform should be conducted quickly, during the honeymoon period that a new government committed to restructuring may temporarily enjoy.

5. Reform requires restructuring of both the economy and the political system. One of the central issues in reform strategy involves the sequencing of political liberalization and economic restructuring. The Soviet Union under Mikhail Gorbachev illustrates the danger of undertaking political liberalization before launching significant economic change. In a more open political system, continued economic stagnation invites protest, and yet opponents of painful reform are simultaneously given greater ability to mobilize to oppose or obstruct.

China, on the other hand, exemplifies the danger of economic reform without adequate political change. The contradictions and pain inherent in economic reform produced serious social grievances. At the same time, the partial relaxation of political control and the growing independence of workers from their place of employment made it possible to turn those grievances into political action. But the political system remained authoritarian, without adequate institutions for absorbing and responding to the wave of new demands coming from urban society.

In short, the Chinese case suggests the wisdom of instituting reform rapidly and comprehensively, taking decisive action along several fronts simultaneously. Even so, the process of political and economic restructuring will still be painful. There is no guarantee that the economic situation will respond smoothly or quickly to new market forces. Nor, despite political reform, is there any assurance that reforming Communist regimes will enjoy the legitimacy they need to persuade their publics to accept economic sacrifice for a long period of time. It is very possible, therefore, that the process will bog down midway, as the growing costs of reform steadily erode its base of political support.

Possibility of Dramatic Breakdown

Before Tiananmen, it appeared that breakdowns in reform would likely occur in relatively quiet ways, such as they did in Hungary in the early 1970s. Inflation, inequality, and corruption might eventually compel a government to suspend economic reform and reimpose administrative controls over the economy. Unorthodox new ideas might lead to a reactivation of political education, and political dissent might spark the reassertion of political controls over society. But it seemed that this sequence of events would happen gradually and with restraint. In fact, China's own tortuous experience with reform — its economic austerity programs of 1980–81 and 1985–86, its campaign against "spiritual pollution" in 1983–84, and its suppression of student demonstrations in 1986–87 — suggested that periods of retrogression would be relatively muted and short-lived.

Subsequent events in China showed that breakdowns in reform can also be dramatic. Indeed, what was unexpected about the Tiananmen Incident was not the severity of the dilemmas that reform had encountered, nor the degree of retrogression that those dilemmas provoked, but the scale of the demonstrations and the brutality with which they were suppressed. The Chinese experience suggests that accumulated grievances — first from years of political repression and economic stagnation, then from the unrealistic expectations generated by the inauguration of reform — can be much larger than outsiders forecast. Partial political relaxation, especially if the national leadership is obviously divided, can encourage the expression of those grievances in intense and explosive ways. The inability of public security forces to cope effectively with large-scale demonstrations can then require the use of inexperienced military units, possibly with devastating consequences.

As dramatic as the events in China were, their international implications were further magnified by television coverage. The presence of a large international press corps in major Communist countries means that demonstrations, particularly in the capital, will be the subject of immediate and extensive reportage. The revolution in telecommunications technology — the prevalence of small videocameras, the portability of videotape, and the availability of direct-dial international telephone and facsimile service — makes it extremely difficult for Communist leaders to completely cut off news accounts to the outside world. Demonstrations for further political and economic reform are thus likely to find sympathetic audiences overseas, and any suppression of protest by the authorities will be swiftly and graphically reported.

The impact of the Tiananmen Incident on American perceptions and policy was also exacerbated by the presence of tens of thousands of Chinese students and scholars in the United States, a large proportion of whom were passionately committed to economic and political reform. The most active and articulate of them quickly learned to play a prominent role in the American political process, writing op-ed essays for major newspapers, testifying before Congress, and appearing on television news programs and radio talk shows. To be sure, no other Communist country has as many nationals in the United States as does China. But the impact of retrogression may still be magnified by the visitors who are here, as well as by the large émigré and refugee communities who settled in America in earlier years.

In sum, the Chinese case suggests the possibility that breakdowns in Communist reform movements may be sudden and violent, in ways that magnify the impact both at home and abroad. Domestically, a dramatic collapse increases the possibility that the Communist regime, now fighting for its life, will respond with sustained retrogression rather than marginal adjustment. Internationally, it increases the pressure on the United

States government to respond in ways that embody the public's frustration at seeing its expectations for peaceful and constructive change so brutally dashed.

Dilemmas for the United States

Much of the discussion of the reform in Communist states has focused on the opportunities it presents to the United States. How can the United States facilitate political and economic reform in Eastern Europe? How can Washington take advantage of the new possibilities for arms control agreements with the Soviet Union? How can the West encourage the remaining hard-line Communist states, such as North Korea and Cuba, to join the trend toward economic and political liberalization?

These questions remain important and deserve continued and careful attention. But the Tiananmen Incident also suggests the need to consider an additional, more sobering issue: How should the United States respond to breakdowns — particularly violent ones — in the troubled process of economic and political reform?

For major Communist powers, such as China and the Soviet Union, the United States must weigh its interest in promoting human rights against its interest in ending the Cold War. There is, of course, the possibility that a breakdown in reform could produce a hard-line regime that initiated a more confrontational policy toward the United States. But what if the new leadership still wished to maintain a conciliatory stance abroad, even as it pursued a retrogressive policy at home? With some exceptions, this has been the foreign policy of the Chinese government, which insists that it wants to maintain normal relations with the United States even as it represses domestic dissent. It could also be the foreign policy of a conservative leadership in the Soviet Union, preoccupied with maintaining control over restive minority republics and assertive urban intellectuals. In such a case, it might well be American policy that would be responsible for a return to international confrontation. As one Soviet intellectual recently asked incredulously, "Do you Americans really believe that Lithuanian independence is more important than maintaining a friendly relationship with the Soviet Union?"

Even if sanctions were deemed appropriate, what form should they take? The Chinese case suggests the wisdom of limiting relationships — especially symbolic ones — with hard-line leaderships in post-breakdown regimes. Restricting some kinds of contacts clearly signals American repugnance at the repression of dissent and the abandonment of political reform. But the Chinese experience also suggests that attenuating cultural, academic, and economic relationships is unwise. Indeed, it is through these channels that pressures for change and ideas about reform can enter a Communist country undergoing restructuring. That

> *In short, the Chinese case suggests the wisdom of instituting reform rapidly and comprehensively, taking decisive action along several fronts simultaneously. Even so, the process will be painful.*

explains why few intellectuals and reformers inside China are currently in favor of further American sanctions. On the contrary, they warn that substantive sanctions could enable the hard-line leadership to appeal for support on nationalistic grounds, blame economic difficulties on foreign intervention, and provide an ideal pretext for reducing further cultural and economic exchanges with the United States.

Finally, in confronting a post-breakdown Communist leadership, how effective can American sanctions be? The Chinese experience indicates that they will have an impact only if they are multilateral in character, enjoying the support of a broad range of Western nations. Otherwise sanctions will simply illustrate the isolation of the United States and will divert economic relations to countries willing to carry on business as usual with regimes where reform has been sidetracked. But the Chinese case also warns that even multilateral sanctions may not have an immediate positive effect on a regime that is fighting for its own political survival. Formal sanctions, therefore, must be sustainable for long periods of time, in the absence of any renewed movement toward economic and political reform.

Perhaps the most effective sanctions are to be found not in formal government action, but in the natural response of the marketplace. As a country experiences instability, repression, and retreat from economic reform, it becomes a less attractive partner for foreign lending, foreign investment, and even foreign trade and tourism. The net impact of these private and institutional decisions can be more severe over the longer term than the consequences of official actions taken by government.

Prospects for Renewed Reform

Given the widespread conclusion that totalitarianism and central planning are ineffective and illegitimate systems, it is tempting to assume that breakdowns in reform are temporary phenomena that will ultimately give way to renewed liberalization. In China's case, for example, many analysts predict that the deaths of Deng Xiaoping and the other octogenarians now in power will be the occasion for the resurrection of reform, perhaps in a more thoroughgoing manner than appeared possible before Tiananmen. Once again, a closer look at the situation in China evokes greater caution.

It is indeed possible that reform will revive, after the political and economic costs of retrogression became more apparent and when new leaders emerge on the political stage. But the obstacles will remain substantial. Reform will still impose significant economic, political, and social costs on powerful sectors of society. The most effective strategies for undertaking reform will remain elusive and controversial. And the difficulties China's reform encountered in the late 1980s may have weakened the political base for further restructuring. For these reasons, a mixed economy coupled with a renewed authoritarian system may endure for a long time. And if reform does revive, it may prove no more successful the second time than it was the first.

Even if reform does resume and prosper, the implications for the United States will still be mixed. It may be that successful reform in Communist systems will mark the end of the great ideological divide between capitalism and communism that characterized international politics throughout most of the 20th century. But to describe this outcome as the "end of history" is dangerously misleading. It may be more accurate to describe the implications as the "resumption of history," in which global geopolitics is once again characterized by a complex balance of power among many countries with competing claims for economic and strategic influence. A reforming China, Soviet Union, or Vietnam may no longer present an ideological or subversive threat to its neighbors, but it may continue to pose more conventional security challenges and may even provide an increasing degree of economic competition as well.

Thus, although the world is changing, it is not smart for us to engage in premature self-congratulation. Reform in Communist systems will be a difficult process, in which crises and breakdowns are highly likely. Periods of retrogression will present serious challenges to the United States and its allies. And, even if reform succeeds, the historical struggle for political influence and economic advantage among nations will not be completely abated.

The Domestic Roots of China's Post-Tiananmen Foreign Policy

Susan Shirk

Susan Shirk is Professor of Political Science at the University of California, San Diego.

In the aftermath of China's domestic political crisis in the Spring of 1989, China's stance toward the world took a sharp about-face. After more than a decade of foreign policies motivated by economic and strategic pragmatism, the People's Republic of China (PRC) revived the shrill ideological nationalism of the Maoist era. Rather than cultivating good relations with the United States, Japan and other Western nations to reduce military threats and to obtain foreign technology and funds, the Chinese Communist Party (CCP) leaders lashed out at the West. They accused Western nations of interfering in Chinese domestic affairs by supporting pro-democracy demonstrations and by pressuring China with economic and political sanctions.

Yet China's post-Tiananmen nationalist assertiveness was not expressed with equal intensity toward every part of the world. Although all the Western nations and Japan implemented economic sanctions against the Chinese government in reaction to Tiananmen, Chinese leader Deng Xiaoping treated the United States as the primary target of its anti-foreign nationalism and adopted a more conciliatory attitude toward Japan and Europe. The Chinese took tough stances in Korea and Hong Kong, areas in which the nationalist and ideological dimensions of foreign policy were prominent, but made friendly overtures to the Soviet Union and Taiwan despite strong ideological conflicts with them. Yet by the spring of 1990, China began to moderate its rhetoric and actions even toward the United States. Since then, although its domestic political rhetoric remains shrill and xenophobic, China has shown a pragmatic and flexible stance toward the world, particularly by cooperating with the US and other countries in finding solutions to the Persian Gulf crisis and the Cambodian imbroglio.

Making Sense of Chinese Foreign Policy

The roots of such trends in Chinese foreign policy over the past year lie in Chinese domestic politics and the power struggles within the CCP that resulted in the decision to suppress massive urban demonstrations with military force in June 1989. At that time, the reformist Party Secretary Zhao Ziyang and his allies who favored a conciliatory approach toward the demonstrators were kicked out of the Standing Committee of the Politburo and stripped of their power. Meanwhile, the conservative Premier Li Peng, President and Army head Yang Shangkun, economic czar Yao Yilin and the revolutionary elders who took a hard line stance toward the demonstrators strengthened their grip on the Party. Deng Xiaoping remained the pre-eminent leader, but the balance he had previously maintained between conservatives and reformists was overpowered by the weight of the conservatives. Furthermore, the protests worked to the advantage of the conservatives within the Party because Deng Xiaoping, who had been personally scarred by Red Guard street politics during the Cultural Revolution, instinctively sided with the conservatives when he saw Chinese youth taking to the streets again.

This shift in Party leadership thus resulted in a change in government policies—not a surprising outcome given the CCP's authority and tight supervision over government policy-making. The reformist foreign policy prevalent during the past decade was aimed primarily at improving relations with the West to reduce military threats and to accelerate economic modernization with infusions of foreign technology and capital. After Tiananmen, this was replaced by the conservative policy which asserted Chinese nationalism at the price of strained relations with the West and a reduced flow of foreign economic assistance.

China's relations with the United States reached their lowest point in twenty years during 1989-90 as Chinese leaders reacted with xenophobic fury to US sanctions in the wake of the Tiananmen crackdown. Their response to President Bush's overtures to improve relations reflected conspicuous intransigence, as if any flexibility would be interpreted at home and abroad as a sign of weakness. Beijing argued that the United States had interfered in China's internal affairs, claiming that American encouragement of demonstrations and imposition of

From *Harvard International Review*, Winter 1990/91, pp. 32-34, 61. Copyright © 1990, Harvard International Relations Council.

sanctions were aimed at speeding the "peaceful evolution" of China from socialism to capitalism. Negotiations over the release of prominent dissident scientists Fang Lizhi and Li Shuxian from their refuge in the American Embassy in Beijing failed to progress. The Chinese refused to release pro-democracy political prisoners or relax political repression.

The price of this intransigence toward the United States was the evaporation of American investment in China as well as the threat that Congress might revoke its most-favored-nation trading status. Indeed, the value of all foreign investment in China dropped 22 percent during the first half of 1990 compared with the first half of 1989. Yet Chinese leaders claimed the American side was responsible for injuring Sino-American relations and should be the first to make amends. The conservatives considered economic benefits to be too high a price to pay for the social and political "pollution" associated with close economic ties with the US and the West. This did not rule out relations with countries like Japan, however, which conservative Party leaders considered to be "different from the West politically and psychologically."

After the massacre in Tiananmen square, the Chinese leaders perceived their country as rejected by the West; after the dramatic renunciation of communism in Eastern Europe and even in the Soviet Union, they felt abandoned by most of their communist comrades as well. A clear expression of this sense of international isolation was China's move to reclaim its leadership of the third world, a position that it held during the Maoist era. CCP leaders, unwelcome in the West after Tiananmen, carried their flag instead to Africa, South Asia, Latin America and the Middle East.

Yet the question remains: why should the post-Tiananmen CCP leadership prefer policies that forfeited economic benefits of Western trade and investment in favor of ideological nationalism? The answer offered by most foreign analysts is that CCP leaders implemented policies designed to preserve political stability, their highest priority. I would argue that their priorities were much more narrow and short-term: they cared less about the overall stability of the socialist system and communist party rule than about retaining their own political power and defeating the reformists.

In a communist state like China with no democratic elections, a communist party monopoly on political power and no fixed terms of communist party office, the competition for power never ends and continuously pervades the policy process. During the past decade the contest has been particularly intense because everyone has known that the days of the elderly post-Maoist leadership, headed by 86-year-old Deng Xiaoping, are numbered.

Political competition is limited to the elite arena in China. Aspirants to top Party positions campaign to a "selectorate," the set of officials who are empowered to choose the Party Secretary, the Standing Committee of the Politburo and the Politburo. The selectorate consists of the officials in the Central Committee, the CCP elders, the army officers in the Central Military Commission and the pre-eminent leader himself—who certainly has a great deal of weight in choosing a successor, but cannot dictate the choice.

Thus, the policy positions of conservative party leaders have a clear political and strategic logic: they are designed to signal the strength of conservative contenders for power, to appeal to key groups within the selectorate and to weaken support for reformist rivals. In the context of communist politics, foreign policy, like policy toward intellectuals and culture but unlike most domestic economic policy, has strong symbolic and ideological elements. As elite factions contend for power, they use foreign policy to attract supporters by demonstrating the strength of their faction.

While China's relations with the European countries and Japan were strained by economic sanctions after Tiananmen, they were not colored by the same fierce ideological nationalism as were China's relations with the United States. China's positive foreign policy initiatives of 1989-90 such as strengthened ties with the Soviet Union and growing economic integration with Taiwan, despite significant ideological differences with these two countries, reflected the same domestic political logic as its intransigence toward the United States.

The Chinese decision to resume the process of normalizing relations with the Soviet Union came during the post-Tiananmen period when relations with the United States were at their lowest point in two decades and when Party conservatives were quite critical of Gorbachev and perestroika. This decision sent a clear message that Party influence had shifted toward the conservatives and away from Deng Xiaoping and the reformers, who had consistently favored putting rapprochement with the US before rapprochement with the USSR.

While Party leaders are not formally accountable to Chinese citizens through elections, neither are they free of all accountability, as dictators would be. Thus, the policy positions taken by contending leaders in China are indeed shaped by their various constituencies. Policy must win approval from the CCP selectorate consisting of central Party and government officials, provincial and municipal Party and government officials, and the military.

Conservatives like Li Peng, Yao Yilin and Yang Shangkun obtain most of their support from a "communist coalition" of central officials, heavy industrial ministries and inland provinces—groups which are favored and protected by the command economy and who have the most to lose from economic reform and openness. Since Tiananmen, the Ministry of Machine Building and Electronics, representing the industrial sectors most severely threatened by foreign competition, has spoken out to demand protection against competition from imported equipment. In addition, the inland provinces have complained incessantly about the widening economic gap between coastal and inland regions caused by a concentration of foreign trade and investment on the coast. Current Party leaders know that foreign policies which discourage foreign trade and investment from the West please many of their supporters but hurt local bureaucratic entrepreneurs, light industrial importers and exporters and coastal regions which back the reformists.

Another reason why the conservatives have been in no hurry to improve relations with the West and have sabotaged the efforts of reformist officials to improve them is that foreign governments and corporations are part of China's reform coalition. Reformist leaders like Deng Xiaoping, Zhao Ziyang, and Hu Yaobang actively cultivated the support of foreigners for the reform drive in China. Their eagerness to expand foreign trade and investment went beyond what was required for economic modernization in a country like China with a huge domestic market. It had a political rationale as well: to counter the power of groups with vested interests in central planning by adding foreign influence to the "reform coalition." When the Party conservatives, who were never enthusiastic about reform, returned to power in 1989, they naturally had an interest in reducing the role of Western governments and companies in Chinese domestic politics. For the same reason, the conservatives were prepared to drive a wedge in the flourishing economic alliance between Hong Kong and nearby Guangdong Province by taking a menacing attitude toward Hong Kong. The Hong Kong-Guangdong alliance represented the leading edge of China's reform drive, and threats to it subverted the national reform drive.

Power is not the whole story, of course. The preferences of current Party leaders also reflect their age and experience. Many conservative Party leaders are members of the Long March generation who fought for a cause in which communism and nationalism were intertwined. They undoubtedly see post-Tiananmen foreign policy issues in stark terms: China is defending socialism in a world turning toward capitalism and maintaining national independence in the face of economic temptations to become dependent on the West.

Finally, Chinese foreign policy during the past year reflects a real loss of power by CCP leaders. With the end of Cold War tensions between the US and the USSR, China has lost its leverage in the triangle. Li Peng's trip to Moscow in April 1990 may have been an attempt to pressure the US to abandon its sanctions against China, but surely Chinese leaders recognize that the effect of such a ploy is weaker than in the days when Chinese overtures toward Moscow would have been cause for serious concern in the West. Furthermore, China's sense of loss of power is exacerbated by the disintegration of international communism. With the Soviet Union and Eastern Europe abandoning communism and joining the West at the same time that the West distances itself from China, the Chinese accurately perceive themselves as isolated, with only a few small communist allies and the poor, struggling countries of the Third World to which to turn. Finally, as individuals, most of the current leaders of the CCP are elderly lame ducks; their tenure is limited by their age. From the perspective of both Chinese national interests and their own personal political interests, the conservative leaders of the Party are beleaguered. It is not surprising that their foreign policies appeared desperate and defensive.

After June 1989, the conservative leaders of the Chinese Communist Party discovered they could count on neither the support of rank-and-file Party members nor the backing of Deng Xiaoping. After the Tiananmen crackdown, CCP leaders confronted acute problems of what the Chinese euphemistically call "Party discipline." Conservative leaders were shocked to find that "among the instigators, plotters, organizers and commanders of the turmoil, there were quite a few Communist Party members." Lower-level Party leaders and members sheltered people involved in the rebellion or assumed a lax attitude toward apprehending them. This phenomenon of disobeying the orders of the Party center was fairly serious. Some Party members carried out only central decisions with which they agreed, refusing to carry out or publicly criticizing those with which they did not. Some even went so far as to insist on their right to dissent from the Party on major questions of party doctrine. The large number of Party meetings during 1989-90 devoted to improving Party discipline indicated that Party leaders were worried about dissension within the ranks.

Conservatives were also challenged from above by the efforts of 86-year-old Deng Xiaoping to shape the succession to preserve his legacy of reform. Deng may share with the conservatives a fear and abhorrence of mass protest and a determination to retain communist party rule, but he is genuinely committed to economic reforms and good economic relations with the West. So long as he is alive, he will intervene in Party politics to bolster the reformists.

In early 1990, Deng Xiaoping became alarmed by the schism between China and the United States created by American sanctions and the rigid foreign policies of CCP conservatives. He exerted himself to bring about a return to the pro-Western foreign policy of the reformists. Deng urged the Politburo to decouple foreign and domestic policy, to take a pragmatic approach to foreign policy and to avoid foreign policy polemics while staunchly defending socialist ideology in domestic policy.

Thus, a year after the Tiananmen crisis, the government released in three batches almost 900 political prisoners including several prominent intellectuals who had supported the 1989 demonstrations. On May 1, Beijing ended the martial law in Tibet that had been in effect for more than a year. The biggest obstacle to improved Sino-US relations was eliminated when the government finally agreed to allow dissident physicist Fang Lizhi and Li Shuxian to leave China in June 1990. Recognizing that Sino-American relations could not improve as long as Fang and Li remained stranded in the American Embassy in Beijing, Deng instructed the Standing Committee of the Politburo in January not to "lead our relations with the United States to a deadlock...on the question of Fang Lizhi." The Standing Committee reportedly refused to carry out Deng's instructions, with the hard-liners blocking any solution to the impasse. In fact, it made sense in terms of Party conservatives' short-term political interests to obstruct steps toward Sino-American rapprochement. Finally, in early June, Deng Xiaoping gave another instruction: "It would be appropriate to let Fang Lizhi leave the country." He may have used the upcoming US Congressional debate on China's Most Favored Nation status in persuading the conservatives to go along with him, for this time his instructions were implemented.

Simultaneous with his moves to straighten out Chinese foreign policy, Deng Xiaoping signalled his support for reformists in the succession struggle. In the spring and summer of 1990, rumors began to fly—many of them no doubt leaked by people close to Deng—that Deng was meeting with Zhao

Ziyang and was considering rehabilitating him. Encouraged by the pre-eminent leader's visible support for the reformists, reform-minded contenders were emboldened to speak out, positioning themselves to appeal to alienated Party members and to Deng. The most prominent of the reformist candidates to succeed Deng is Li Ruihuan, formerly Party Secretary of Tianjin and now member of the Standing Committee of the Politburo.

Since September 1990, Chinese foreign policy has reflected Deng's efforts to resuscitate the reformists and to repair China's tarnished image as a responsible member of the world community. China cooperated with the United Nations sanctions against Iraq, expressing its principled opposition to aggression and support for the independence, sovereignty and territorial integrity of countries like Kuwait while winning international approval for its "reasonable" and "sensible" diplomacy. China's cooperation with other countries in devising guarantees for political reconciliation in Cambodia also "were acknowledged by the international community." At the same time, China restored diplomatic relations with Indonesia, established diplomatic relations with Saudi Arabia and was on the verge of establishing diplomatic relations with Singapore. At Deng Xiaoping's personal urging, China invited Vietnamese leaders to Beijing to discuss the improvement of Sino-Vietnamese relations. Even on the Korean peninsula, China signalled its return to international pragmatism by agreeing to an exchange of trade offices with South Korea. This drive for international respectability was obviously motivated by the desire to end sanctions imposed after the crackdown in Tiananmen.

With Deng Xiaoping blocking their attempts to use foreign policy to wage domestic power struggles, conservative Party leaders have been left holding only their domestic ideological weapons. In October 1990, they took the innocuous campaign against pornography initiated by reformist Politburo member Li Ruihuan and began to turn it into a struggle against foreign subversion. According to the *People's Daily* of October 26, 1990, foreign forces were using pornography, gambling and drugs to advance the "peaceful evolution" of China away from communism. The code words "peaceful evolution" signalled that although Deng Xiaoping had temporarily neutralized the conservatives' influence on foreign policy, the conservatives were still a force to be reckoned with in domestic politics. As a result, China in fall 1990 was characterized by "internal strictness and external relaxation."

Implications for US Policy

Accordingly, foreign statesmen and investors should not expect a resumption of easy relations with China unless the reformers return to Party power and the conservatives are defeated by natural or political attrition. Recent foreign policy changes in a flexible direction can be interpreted either as a sign that the reformers are making a comeback or merely as further evidence of Deng Xiaoping's ability to prevail in the foreign policy arena.

There is indeed little that foreign countries can do to influence the outcome of Chinese domestic power struggles. However, international sanctions may have helped the reformists build support within the Party and shorten the reign of the

conservatives by raising the cost of the conservatives' intransigence to the country as a whole. The reformists can use issues such as the loss of Western economic cooperation to make political points against the conservatives; they can argue that China has paid a high price for its conservative reaction against the demonstrators and against foreign nations afterwards.

Foreigners who oppose sanctions toward China argue that they evoke a unified nationalistic response from the Chinese and drive them into hostile isolation. Yet with no systematic data on public opinion in China, we can have no way of knowing whether the xenophobic nationalism articulated by Party conservatives still resonates with the public today as strongly as it did in the earlier days of the communist era. It would seem that anti-foreign nationalism no longer has such a broad appeal in China because so many people at every level, from top officials to ordinary citizens, have benefitted from China's opening to the world. Furthermore, because Party conservatives like Li Peng and Yang Shangkun have blood on their hands from Tiananmen, people place little credence in anything they say.

International sanctions against the Chinese government are less likely to be interpreted by elites and masses in China as neo-imperialist aggression than as the price the entire Chinese nation must pay for continued rule by Party conservatives. Now that this price has been felt, Deng Xiaoping and perhaps the Party membership to relax their international intransigence and even to release most of the political prisoners from the Tiananmen protests.

At this point, eighteen months after the crimes of Tiananmen, the utility of strengthening sanctions by not renewing US most-favored-nation trade status for China is questionable. Concerted action to pressure China has become less feasible since the Houston Summit when the Japanese announced their intention to lift sanctions against China. Furthermore, American refusal to renew most-favored-nation trade status would not only escalate pressure on Chinese domestic politics, it would deviate from our prior standards for treatment of China. If unsupported by our allies, such a move could expose us to broad-based anti-Americanism in China. Indeed, there is little to be gained at this point by having the US "pummel and penalize" China. Neither is the answer, in *New York Times* columnist William Safire's language, to "forgive and forget" by extending unrestricted most favored nation status to China. Rather, the solution most likely to have the desired effect on Chinese domestic policy is one that Safire describes as "induce and incentivize." We should tie the renewal of most-favored-nation trade status to improved human rights conditions—an approach originally proposed by former US Ambassador to China Winston Lord and that is now embodied in a Congressional bill sponsored by Representative Donald Pease (Democrat, Ohio). For now, the best American policy toward China is one that rewards China's relaxation in both foreign and domestic policy while allowing the US to maintain its distance from the current conservative Party leadership. Too friendly an attitude toward these leaders could diminish the credibility of the United States in the eyes of future generations of Chinese leaders.

The Newly Industrialized Countries and the Less Developed Countries

The complexity of the conditions within the less developed countries (LDCs), often referred to as the Third World, continues to make solutions to their problems elusive. The LDCs, a group of over 100 countries that have little in common beyond their poverty and inability to sustain economic growth, have until recently seemed unable and unwilling either to help themselves or each other. Those national elites most capable of contributing to their own countries' development choose instead to invest in the industrialized states, where there is less political risk to endanger their investments. Burdened by external debt, high birth rates, low levels of literacy, and corrupt, incompetent elites, these countries eat despair as the main course in their daily diet. In Africa, one country after another faces massive starvation, the AIDS epidemic spiraling out of control, or internal rebellion. Few are truly "developing."

National, ethnic, religious, and sectarian conflicts contribute to the drain on the LDC's already scarce economic and financial resources. And all too many LDC governments choose to use their scarce resources to purchase military weapons, which they use to oppress their own populations or to attack their neighbors. The case of Iraq's eight-year war with Iran, followed by Iraq's invasion of Kuwait in August 1990, exemplifies how LDC governments choose to expend their scarce resources.

These countries have, as a result of their mutual animosities, exhibited a limited capacity to unify themselves as a bloc even for the purpose of demanding changes in the international economic system that would benefit their position within it. Their political clout is undercut by their political disunity. Most are easily bought out by countries from the developed "North" on which they have grown dependent for aid and investment.

Third World development is also hindered by environmental problems, the end results of extreme poverty—desertification, deforestation, erosion, and salinization of the soil. The abuse of the environment, either because the peoples and governments of these countries are unable or unwilling to protect it, are both the cause and the effect of poverty. As a result, "natural disasters" occur far more frequently in Third World countries than elsewhere, precisely because the environment is ripe for disaster.

All this is not to say that Third World countries should be treated as an undifferentiated whole. On the contrary, the unique combination of political, historical, economic, geopolitical, and cultural factors in each country makes it incumbent upon aid donors and investors to be sensitive to the particular needs of each individual country.

Nevertheless, developmental aid, loans, and investment have not resulted in development for most Third World countries. This has recently led to a rethinking of the best approach to development. Apart from the significant efforts of the International Monetary Fund and the World Bank to bring about a fundamental restructuring of the economic (and even political) systems of those governments trapped in poverty by indebtedness, there are now new efforts among the LDCs themselves to help each other. This is most notable on a regional basis, but the "newly industrialized countries" (NICs) of Asia, especially Taiwan, Korea, and Hong Kong, are now also investing in LDCs outside of Asia as a way of securing resources and markets. Were the oil-rich countries of the Middle East not so involved in conflict with each other, they too might emerge as major investors in the Third World, even though they themselves are in most respects underdeveloped.

The international economic system itself seems, however, to be the major obstacle to achieving sustained growth in the LDCs. Most of these countries are producers and exporters of commodities whose prices are determined at the whim of an undisciplined and erratic international economy governed only by the marketplace. Prices for commodities are at their lowest levels since the early 1930s. Those countries that are now attempting to industrialize at this point in history discover that their manufactured goods are competing in an international marketplace already glutted by overproduction. It is the most difficult time in history thus far for an underdeveloped country to be trying to find a niche in the developmental cycle.

As of 1990, the LDCs faced yet one more problem: the collapse of Communist regimes in Eastern Europe meant that the United States and some other aid donors, already at the limits of their foreign aid budgets because of their own international indebtedness (an indebtedness augmented in 1991 by the war with Iraq), are switching a portion of their aid from the LDCs to Eastern Europe. Combined with the fact that the Soviet Union is facing an economic and political crisis of its own at home, and is no longer disposed to confront the capitalist West through massive foreign aid to poor developing countries, former beneficiaries of the cold war struggle between communism and Western liberal democracy/capitalism now see their aid drying up.

Looking Ahead: Challenge Questions

In your opinion, are most of the problems that Third World countries face of their own making, or are they largely the products of unequal bilateral relations and the "international system"? What can be done to support the LDCs in their

developmental efforts? What can they do for themselves? Is it in the interest of the industrialized world to have Third World countries develop? Why? What would be the impact on the environment and the world's resources if just one country, China or India, succeeded in achieving the living standards of the Western world?

Examine one major conflict in Latin America, Asia, the Middle East, and Africa and indicate what factors have fueled these conflicts. Of what consequence are the outcomes of these conflicts for the East-West rivalry? How much control over these conflicts do outside states have?

How did the massive indebtedness of so many states within the Third World occur? What is the root cause of these countries' inability to repay their debts? What obligations do other states have to help out countries suffering from serious balance of payments deficits? Are the kinds of solutions to indebtedness that the International Monetary Fund and the World Bank are now offering effective in addressing issues of indebtedness? What kinds of problems have governments in the LDCs had to confront when they have tried to reform their political and economic systems in line with the conditions set out by the IMF and World Bank?

129

Black Africa:

from aid dependence to self-sustaining growth

Tony Hawkins

The adage that in economics only the answers change, the questions are the same, is disturbingly applicable to Africa in the 1990s. The problems of African development have been analysed ad nauseam since the World Bank's sober assessment of the sub-Saharan economy, *From Crisis to Sustainable Growth*, was released towards the end of 1989. The subsequent debate has generated little heat and even less light. Few have faulted the Bank's analysis. So widespread and deep-rooted is Afro-pessimism that it is now impossible to read anything on regional economic prospects without being subjected to a litany of dismal economic statistics. Whether the authors be from the World Bank, the United Nations, the Economic Commission for Africa (ECA) or Western politicians, academics or businessmen, the effect is the same.

There is broad agreement on the nature of the problems, though deep-seated disagreement as to its causes. Africans, on the whole, continue to blame the external environment for the region's economic failure, supported by the interventionists and apologists for socialism. Bankers, businessmen and, increasingly, the donor community, while accepting that reduced protectionism and strong growth in the industrialised countries are necessary preconditions for economic revival in Africa, argue—pragmatically—that the solution lies in policy reform in Africa itself.

The problems are obvious: the population is growing too fast; the foreign debt burden is unmanageable; exports, investment and employment have stagnated or fallen; agriculture has under-performed. For many, the most disturbing aspect of Africa's economic decline is the absence of serious new policy initiatives to deal with the crisis. The depressing news is that a decade of policy-based lending has left the continent poorer than it was before structural adjustment medicine was first administered. The ECA blames this on inappropriate adjustment strategies and the foreign debt burden. But it seems clear that without structural adjustment the situation would have been far worse. Structural change takes time—decades rather than years. It is still too early to ask for the jury's verdict.

A loss of nerve at this juncture is just what Africa does not

need and cannot afford. The search for new prescriptions in a deteriorating situation is both laudable and understandable but it is also dangerous, since those African policy-makers who have embraced the Western solution with varying degrees of enthusiasm and conviction are already under pressure at home. To suggest that the policies they have fought to implement against often bitter opposition from doctrinal hardliners should now be changed would destroy their credibility altogether.

To be fair, the World Bank has not suggested that. Structural adjustment is alive, even if it is not very well. A major reason for its lacklustre performance is the lack of political commitment on the part of many—if not most—African governments forced against their better judgment to swallow Washington's medicine. A second is operational—the difficulties of sequencing and implementing structural adjustment policies.

In the search for strategies to make structural adjustment work faster and more effectively, some grasping after straws is apparent. It is difficult to read the Bank's 1989 Report without concluding that the prospects for informal sector development are being oversold; that the savings and investment targets are unrealistically high; that the resource-inflow targets are out of reach, and so on. The Report's credibility is undermined, too, by the Bank's unwillingness to acknowledge the seriousness of the Aids crisis, certainly in so far as East, Central and Southern Africa are concerned, while the exclusion of the region's most powerful economy—South Africa—is a measure of political expediency rather than logic.

It is a sign of the times that the Bank's courageous call for improved 'governance' attracted so many adherents so quickly. Scarcely was the ink dry on the Report when Western donors, who in the past had preferred discreet silence on so sensitive an issue, began to suggest that in future economic aid might be withheld from countries that failed to meet the 'good governance' test. There are few better examples of the 'thundering herd' syndrome.

But this sudden conversion to a cause, ignored for 30 years, was largely fortuitous. It arose partly from a growing sense of desperation over the African economy, but more pertinently from the demise of superpower rivalry in Africa. So long as the

From *The World Today*, November 1990, pp. 205-208. *The World Today*, published by the Royal Institute of International Affairs.

Russian or Cuban threat existed, the end of defeating Communism justified the means of bolstering corrupt dictatorships. Indeed, even with Moscow and Havana retreating in disarray, President Mobutu's regime in Zaire still commands aid, if not support, because of its perceived contribution to the resolution of the Angolan crisis.

The 'chattering classes' of the media and the political, diplomatic and academic communities have been quick—too quick—to conclude that political revolution in Eastern Europe will be replicated in Africa. Street protests in Francophone Africa, President de Klerk's bold initiatives in South Africa and unrest in Kenya and Zambia in the first half of 1990 certainly lend support to this assessment. But unlike Eastern Europe, no government has yet fallen. Admittedly, leaders in some one-party states—Presidents Houphouet Boigny in Ivory Coast, Mobutu Sese Seko in Zaire, Haile Mariam Mengistu in Ethiopia and Joachim Chissano in Mozambique—have been reluctantly forced to accept multi-party democracy, but the yawning gulf between words and deeds, characteristic of so many of Africa's economic reform programmes, will manifest itself in the political field during the 1990s.

Not only are there good grounds for questioning the sincerity—and capacity—of those who have promised change to achieve it, but for every leader who has embraced multi-partyism there are two who have flatly rejected it. President Robert Mugabe insists that one-party states are more democratic than pluralist ones; in Togo, President Eyedema says his people do not want it. President Mwinyi of Tanzania rejects it.

The initial reactions of Presidents Daniel Arap Moi in Kenya and Kenneth Kaunda in Zambia to street unrest in their two countries was to intensify repression. Under pressure from Western donors both have since softened their positions, but tactics should never be confused with strategy. In a continent where in the past 30 years there have been only one or two examples of ballot box-determined political change, those who believe that democracy is about to break out will be proved wrong.

In any event, the fact that political unrest in some African countries has closely followed the Eastern European revolutions is an inadequate explanation. Political ferment in Africa has a far longer pedigree. It is the result of a combination of economic failure and political paralysis.

The twin pillars of post-colonial Africa—the command economy and the one-party state—were viable only as long as economic growth kept ahead of population growth so that living standards were improving. Until the first oil price shock in 1973–74 African economies had just about managed to keep their heads above water. Immediately thereafter, economic decline was cushioned by foolish bankers and well-intentioned, though largely unsuccessful, aid agencies.

The full cost of externally-funded, largely unprofitable investment became apparent only in the 1980s, by which time it was obvious that, between them, the bankers and the donors had saddled the region with an unmanageable debt burden. Worse still, much of the foreign capital was poorly invested. Tanzania, one of the region's top aid recipients, recently embarked on a $1.2bn road rehabilitation programme designed to regain the standards existing in the mid-1970s. During the 1980s, sub-Saharan Africa received nearly $100bn in official development assistance. During that time income per head fell by more than 1 per cent a year. There can be no more stinging indictment of the aid community.

In 1990, living standards throughout the region are no higher than they were at independence 30 years ago. The seeds of

political change were sown, not when protesters took to the streets in Prague, East Berlin and Budapest in the autumn of 1989 but in the preceding 10 to 15 years—a period of sustained economic decline.

African protesters are motivated more by economic deprivation than the denial of political choice. Their hope is that by changing the government—and possibly also the political system—they will improve their economic situation. In that way Africa is no different from the West, where elections are won and lost on interest and tax rates, unemployment and inflation.

It is misleading to suggest that African leaders disregard the linkage between economic progress and political systems. They understand it very well. It is not just President Kaunda who has argued that the adoption of multi-party democracy in Zambia would not increase the price of copper or cocoa. A change of government in Zambia will help the economy only if Mr Kaunda's successor is more committed to economic reform, and more competent to carry it through.

In fact, the reverse could very well turn out to be the case. In all probability a 'popular' Zambian leader who ousted President Kaunda would abandon the harsh austerity policies necessary for the revival of the Zambian economy. The partially successful structural adjustment programmes in Ghana and Nigeria have been imposed by undemocratic military regimes. The return to civilian rule in Nigeria in 1992 could well spell the end of economic reform, since the politicians will feel obliged to reflate the economy in an attempt to win voter support.

But even if it could be demonstrated that African economies would function better with multi-party democracy (as has indeed been the case in Botswana and Mauritius, though both are essentially atypical), this assumes that the requisite political infrastructure for a multi-party system is available. It is not. The political systems the colonialists left behind when they left the continent in such haste were the fruits of expediency. There were no serious attempts to design appropriate systems.

Those who drew attention to this at the time, such as Sir Roy Welensky, Prime Minister of the Federation of Rhodesia and Nyasaland, were contemptuously dismissed by the 'chattering classes' as paternalists, racists, reactionaries. 'One man, one vote, once', said Welensky. In a continent littered with one-party dictatorships, where free and fair elections occur only when supervised from outside by the UN or the Commonwealth, that prediction, so scornfully rejected at the time by the men of Whitehall, is now grudgingly acknowledged.

Worse, not only did the colonial powers leave behind an unmanageable political system and undeveloped economies, but they compounded the felony with their adoption of a double standard of political conduct, of which perhaps the most devastating example is that of Zaire. It was Belgium's panicky scuttling of its colonial responsibilities in 1960 that created the chaos from which the corrupt Mobutu dictatorship emerged. It would be comforting to believe that Belgium's recently-expressed outrage at the conduct of the Mobutu regime, nurtured for 20 years by successive Belgian and American governments, marked a sincere policy change rather than the desire to pay lip-service to the new democracy of the post-communist world.

As the Soviet threat recedes so the West has at last found the courage to speak out against African dictatorships. Even then it was left to the World Bank to set the tone. Few dispute its commonsense assertion that 'good governance' is an essential precondition for economic development. Much more difficult is how to achieve it. The World Bank provides little guidance on this score. Donors are taking up the World Bank's challenge by threatening to add political conditions to the economic conditionalities stipulated by the Bank, the IMF and a growing number of bilateral donors, before they will disburse aid.

Unhappily, demands for political conditionality are flawed on several counts. First, the concept is undefined. African leaders are right to reject the facile distinction between multi-partyism and single-party states. Recent experience in Romania is a reminder that there is far more to a free society than multi-party elections. Zimbabwe's 1990 elections, conducted on a first-past-the-post Westminster constituency model, left the minority with hardly a voice in parliament, despite the fact that only 56 per cent of the electorate voted for President Mugabe.

African leaders justify single-party rule on the ground that it prevents the emergence of tribally or ethnically driven political parties. But one-party rule has signally failed to prevent tribalism and regionalism degenerating into civil conflict. It is now time to seek alternative mechanisms — proportional representation, decentralisation, federalism, vetoes for minority groups. All of these are ideas that will have to be investigated in the 1990s. Sadly, though, only in South Africa is there any serious discussion of a constitutional dispensation designed to counter the worst excesses of African governments.

Second, there is a problem of objective measurement. The debate over easing sanctions against South Africa illustrates the point. How much reform is enough? How far does a government have to step out of line before political conditionality is cited as justification for withholding aid?

Third, for all their sermonising on governance, donors remain reluctant to apply the yardsticks of political conditionality. Whitehall's evident embarrassment over President Moi, Nordic reluctance to pull the plug on Zambia and on American equivocation over Zaire, all reflect the fact that conditionality decisions are far from unidimensional. Verbal sabre-rattling by the British and American governments over aid to Kenya has still to be translated into any sort of action, while the French have reportedly agreed to sell arms to Mr Moi.

Then there is the aid lobby's complaint that it is wrong to punish a country's poor and underprivileged for the misdeeds of its government—unless, of course, that country is South Africa. The aid lobby holds that President Moi's repressive policies do not justify withholding aid from 25m Kenyans. This argument would carry more weight had aid programmes been more successful in channeling assistance to the world's needy than they have, as shown in the World Bank's 1990 World Development Report. It is unconvincing, too, since there are many ways in which aid can be provided to a country in a manner that expressly demonstrates disapproval of the ruling regime—as in the South African case.

The self-interest of the aid lobby itself is a potent consideration, too. Exporters, consultants, academic researchers, university research foundations, research institutes and educational institutions all have a vested interest in maintaining aid flows. They, like businessmen with fat export contracts with Iraq, have no sympathy with political conditionality.

In one of the most positive and constructive contributions to the sterile debate over African economic development, Sir William Ryrie, Executive Vice-President of the International Finance Corporation, the private-sector arm of the World Bank group, suggested that 'the gigantic misuse of aid funds' might have something to do with the fact that almost all of them were transferred by methods that avoided the discipline of the market.

Unfortunately, this valuable comment begs the question: how to increase the use of market mechanisms to channel aid to Africa's indigenous private sector, as distinct from its benefits being appropriated by exporters, consultants, and 'researchers' in the donor countries? The weak link in the proposal is the assumption that viable private sectors exist in recipient countries.

This emphasis on the role of the private sector—the argument that self-sustaining growth is most likely to be achieved where governments and donors between them create an 'enabling environment'—falls short in most African countries because no private sector worthy of the name exists. There is a vibrant private sector in Nigeria, Zimbabwe, Kenya and Ivory Coast, but elsewhere non-government economic activity is largely limited to that of the informal sector.

The typical African private-sector profile is three-tiered: a handful of Western multinationals, many of whom reluctantly agreed to state participation in their African affiliates; some medium-sized 'local' firms, often owned by expatriates, especially Asians; and a huge informal sector, largely comprising peasant farmers.

Throughout the region the private sector has been a target of government policy because of its foreign links or ownership. In Kenya private-sector localisation has taken the form of increasing equity participation by local businessmen, many of whom have what are euphemistically called 'powerful political connections'. In Zimbabwe private sector 'independence' has been progressively eroded as the state or the ruling ZANU-PF party has purchased controlling equity stakes in major industrial and commercial activities. Similar patterns apply in Kenya and Malawi.

Aiding the private sector tends to take the form of bolstering the two upper tiers—multinational affiliates and the medium-sized locally-owned enterprises. Frequently, too, the IFC and similar agencies have found themselves financing joint ventures effectively controlled by African governments. There are few opportunities for financing wholly privately-owned enterprises, unless these are foreign-controlled.

This leaves the donors with the task of building not just an enabling environment but the private sector itself. The optimists believe this is less intimidating than might be thought. There is, we are told, no shortage of entrepreneurship in Africa. Unfortunately, this is another half-truth. There is no shortage of entrepreneurship in retailing, or in the import-export business—in which the export content is usually minimal—or in transport or hotels. But finding viable entrepreneurship in manufacturing, mining (other than tiny enterprises), sophisticated service industries like tourism, banking and so on is very difficult indeed.

Given the dismal performance of governments—recipients and donors—in Africa, the Ryrie argument for an enhanced private-sector role is at least worth a try, unpromising though the existing market environment might be. Like the World Bank's new-found enthusiasm for informal sector development, it may smack of grasping at straws, but the private sector can hardly do a worse job than the donors.

Official assistance should be used to relieve the debt burden, to rehabilitate the infrastructure without which there can be no sustainable growth in Africa, to train managers, technicians and—above all—trainers, not in Washington or Stockholm but on the job in their home countries or at the African training institutions. The donor community should go back to basics and undertake the functions traditionally handled by the state. This is a better way of creating an enabling environment than tying assistance to the degree of media freedom or the number of legal political parties.

The suggestion that donors with a disastrous decade of failure behind them should do more in the 1990s does not stand up. If it is right to privatise, to roll back the frontiers of the state in Europe and North America, then surely it is also right to roll back the activities of the official donors, too? Try visiting an upmarket hotel in Africa and count the number of 'official' visitors, funded by governments or donor agencies, relative to the number of businessmen there. The private sector is swamped by officialdom, not just African officialdom, but donor officialdom.

The World Bank—and others—argue that too much government smothers private initiative. So does too much aid, especially poorly targeted aid. If every dollar spent by donors on socio-economic 'research' and consultancy reports on African issues were spent on training Africans, the return on investment would be substantially higher. So high is the proportion of African imports funded by aid that export-marketing by OECD manufacturers is more about 'tapping into' aid programmes than selling Africans what they want to buy. Export salesmen do not need to know anything about market conditions in Kenya or Nigeria, as long as they know whom to contact in the relevant Ministry for Overseas Development.

Ghana, Tanzania and Mozambique are prime examples of aid dependence. Take the foreign funding away and the economic restructuring dutifully praised by IMF and World Bank teams will collapse in short order. The challenge for Africa and the aid lobby in the 1990s is to achieve what was always the intention: a self-sustaining society, rather than a poverty-stricken, aid-dependent Tanzania. Sir William Ryrie is right to champion private enterprise and investment whose neglect over the past 20 years tells us so much about the failure of African economies.

African famines

Yet again

While the world watches the Gulf, hunger stalks Africa. Our correspondents report from Khartoum and Maputo

THE rich world would love to forget Africa, but its miseries are too awful to ignore. The United Nations' World Food Programme says that more than 20m Africans will depend on food aid this year—more, by far, than during the horrors in the Horn of Africa six years ago.

The Horn is the worst of Africa's endangered regions. This is its third famine warning in four years, and the direst so far. The UN reckons it will need to get 2.2m tonnes of food from outside this year, and wants another 1.6m for the rest of black Africa (see chart on next page). That makes a total of 3.8m tonnes for all black Africa, the highest estimate the UN has ever made. It dwarfs the 1.4m tonnes the UN called for, on average, in each of the three years 1987-89.

The previous warnings in the Horn were, like the present one, prompted by severe drought. But disaster, when it came, was less severe than had been foretold. The UN's predictions of famine owe more to art than science. Aid workers use many methods. They measure rainfall. They watch markets. When grain prices rise, a seasonal shortage is developing; if the rise carries through a harvest season, serious trouble is likely. A fall in the price of meat suggests that there is no grain to feed livestock—but

by the time this happens the famine is about to begin.

Satellite photographs offer earlier warning. They show where vegetation is growing, but not what kind. To determine whether the dark patches on the computer map mean weeds, trees or crops, aid workers have to visit the spot. That is not always possible. Predictions about Ethiopia's chronically drought-afflicted highlands are particularly sketchy, because civil war makes them hard to reach. In Sudan, by contrast, forecasters claim to have visited all areas badly affected by 1990's drought.

In fact, little is known about drought's most likely victims, who often live beyond the reach of the aid workers' vehicles. Nobody is sure how many people live in each region or how much they normally eat. And peasants in areas prone to drought are good at surviving. They collect seeds and wild berries, and dig up secret hoards of grain. One bad year is rarely enough to produce famine. Donors delivered a bit less than two-thirds of what was thought necessary after Ethiopia's 1989 crop failure. It seems to have been enough, as was the amount delivered by the big but war-disrupted relief programme that followed the 1987 drought. Both the 1987 and 1989 crop failures followed good years.

Partly because of anguish that they failed to anticipate Ethiopia's 1984-85 famine, and partly to cajole rich countries into giving lots of food, aid workers do tend to err on the side of exaggeration. Yet complacency now would be wrong. For Ethiopia and Sudan, it is the second bad year in a row (and the third bad year in four). Reserves are known to be low in Sudan, and thought to be low in Ethiopia. The UN says the two together need more than 2m tonnes of emergency food, and smaller agencies agree. Even if only half that much were needed, a 20-tonne lorry would have to be loaded somewhere every eight minutes, day and night, for nine months.

No relief effort will work if war and politics get in the way. In Sudan President Omar el Bashir's government has refused to admit to the famine, declaring only a "temporary food gap" of 75,000 tonnes. It has expelled aid workers who said more was needed. Peasants in Western Sudan have already exhausted their berries and grain caches, and are starting to leave their villages in search of food. If they settle in relief camps around the big cities, they will die of cholera and other epidemics. Worse, the president promised on new year's eve to implement Islamic *sharia* law, which will probably aggravate his war against the non-Muslim rebels of Sudan's south.

Ethiopia is more hopeful, despite its civil wars. The government has allowed food to arrive at the port of Assab, which it controls, and to be moved into the rebel-held province of Tigre. Last month another group of rebels, the Eritrean People's Liberation Front, promised to be equally generous with the port of Massawa: it said it would allow food to be moved from there to the government-held town of Asmara. Yet the Eritreans have shelled Asmara's airport.

Angola's Marxist government used to be as inhospitable to aid workers as Sudan. But the ruling party's congress last month promised to establish a multi-party democracy. The past year's thaw has made it possible for at least 35 non-governmental organisations to open up offices. They have lost no time in sounding the alarm about an impending famine, which they say threatens 1.9m people. Western diplomats in Luanda scoff at that figure, though they admit that many do need help.

The UN has organised "peace corridors" to get food across the battle lines that divide the government and the UNITA rebels. They have not been respected. On December 20th the official news agency reported that rebels had destroyed a bridge in Huila province, across which 25 tonnes of relief supplies were supposed to have moved to two isolated garrison towns. The next day the Angolan government said it would allow no more food into rebel-held areas, and the UN suspended its operation.

Mozambique also wrestles with the effects of civil war. The 1m Mozambicans who have fled to Malawi are easily reachable. Inside Mozambique it is hard to deliver anything safely. In December a conference of donors pledged more than $1 billion in aid for 1991, including relief supplies for the central province of Zambezia, where at least 250,000 people were forced off their land last year by rebel or government attacks.

In December the Red Cross persuaded both sides to allow it to cross their battle lines. The UN hopes to follow this up with ceasefires in Zambezia and the north-western province of Tete. But much food aid is stolen as it is unloaded at the ports; and army-escorted convoys manage to lose up to a third of their cargoes on the way. Mozambique produces only 15% of the food it needs to keep its markets stocked; theft is rife. If a peace treaty brought those 1m refugees home from Malawi, the competition for food would get even fiercer.

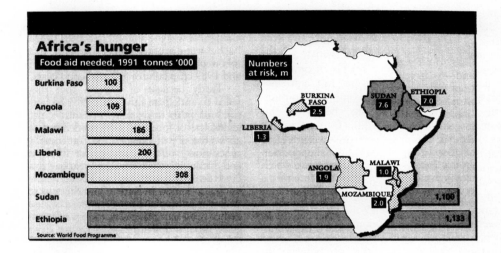

Africa's hunger

Food aid needed, 1991 tonnes '000

Burkina Faso	100
Angola	109
Malawi	186
Liberia	200
Mozambique	308
Sudan	1,100
Ethiopia	1,133

Numbers at risk, m

BURKINA FASO 2.5
LIBERIA 1.3
SUDAN 7.6
ETHIOPIA 7.0
ANGOLA 1.9
MALAWI 1.0
MOZAMBIQUE 2.0

Source: World Food Programme

Hongkong—the case for optimism

There is an ancient Chinese curse that says: 'May you live in interesting times.' The people of Hongkong have spent the last 150 years living under that curse. They have never lived in any other sort of times.

And today the curse is at its most pernicious with so many unresolved issues: the Vietnamese 'boat people', democracy, emigration, passports, inflation and the confidence crisis itself —issues which have succeeded in dividing the British and the people of Hongkong and China, creating a matrix of problems.

The Hongkong people could be seen to fall into two camps—the optimists and the pessimists. The optimists continue to hold great faith in Hongkong's future, believing that Hongkong is too economically valuable to China for the People's Republic ever to risk destroying its free- enterprise culture. The pessimists are fearful that sovereignty is too important an issue for China ever to condone 'one country, two systems'.

Let us be clear about what Hongkong could be. With Hongkong's tradition of enterprise and its continuing access to the world's largest emerging market, Hongkong could continue to be the business success story—the economic hub of the Far East. Or its economy could be destroyed through lack of business confidence and emigration. They say the difference between the optimist and the pessimist is that the optimist sees the doughnut, the pessimist sees the hole.

In discussing Hongkong's future, it is interesting to look back over the Colony's historic growth. Hongkong was inhabited from earliest times, although few people lived there until the nineteenth century. In 1841 the Treaty of Nanjing ceded Hongkong Island in perpetuity to the British. Two further treaty grants in 1860 and 1898 enlarged the territory, first through the freehold of Kowloon and Stonecutters Island and then by the leasehold of the New Territories.

Hongkong was an 'enterprise' culture long before Mrs Thatcher's Ministers popularised the concept. A gas company, electricity supply companies and tramways began and developed when Queen Victoria was on the throne. By the turn of the century, Hongkong's housing, sanitation and water conservation programmes were the envy of all Asia—and almost every other British colony. By the end of the century, Hongkong's revenues to Britain through shipping and trade were far in excess of Britain's other trading partners, most of which were ten times larger than Hongkong.

So Hongkong was 'booming' over a century ago in spite of the many setbacks the Hongkong people have suffered over the years. Fire, disease and typhoon all took their toll. The Taiping rebellion, the fall of the Manchu dynasty, the Japanese invasion of China and the Chinese civil war all brought sudden massive immigration. The Japanese occupation during the Second World War had reduced the population from 1.5m to 600,000 six years later. So Hongkong has experienced many ups and downs. Today Hongkong continues to thrive.

If there is one quality which characterises the people of Hongkong, it is resilience. That is why it is premature to pen Hongkong's obituary. Claims such as 'Hongkong is probably finished—it is like a gold town in the Yukon in the 1890s' do not present an accurate picture.[1]

When I first arrived in Hongkong 24 years ago many despaired of Hongkong's future. There were full-scale riots in progress. We witnessed an unnerving run on the banks—and in Hongkong the banks issue the currency and are not protected by a lender of the last resort. In 1967 we were in the middle of the Cultural Revolution; people were saying 'it's all over' and half the town was packing its baggage.

But the people of Hongkong, many of them refugees, are astonishingly resilient. They have an incredible instinct, not only for surviving but for prospering, too. Look at the industries Hongkong has been into and out of only to bounce back again. Maybe it is the refugee mentality that drives Hongkong forward—the search for security and a firm base.

When I arrived, those 24 years ago, everybody seemed to be making money from wigs and plastic flowers, and then it was camphor wood chests. That all went wrong somehow—the wigs disappeared overnight, like the bowler hats in London, and watches and consumer electronics were the rage, after that toys. Hongkong then progressed to shipping and was told that it was bigger than the Greeks. That all changed and somebody announced one day that Hongkong was the fourth largest finance centre in the world; banks were springing up all over the place. In 1970 Hongkong discovered the stock-market. Everybody was involved. It could take up to six months to have a shirt made because the tailors were preoccupied with their stock-market deals.

From a peak of 1770 the index fell to 152 and people were flinging themselves out of windows. Property boomed in the late 1970s and then dropped 60 per cent in 1983 almost overnight. So Hongkong has had its problems, but it has always scrambled back. Yet every time people said: 'This time it's different.'

Even today, amidst all its real and imagined uncertainties, Hongkong is still:

● the eleventh largest trading economy on earth. It exports nearly one-third of what mighty Japan exports;

● the world's busiest container port;

● one of the world's largest financial centres;

● Asia's main destination for tourism;

● the world's largest exporter of watches and second largest exporter of garments and toys.

From the Star Ferry across Victoria Harbour, you can see the single building which manufactures 10 per cent of all the watches sold in the United States. Hongkong is also the most exciting city on earth. You only have to be there an hour to feel the energy of the place: 5,5m driver-ants going for their lives. Hongkong's average per capita income in 1989 was $11,000—Britain's was $12,000. At average growth levels—not recent booms, but the growth pattern over the last 20 years—its living standards will be higher than Britain's within three to four years. Statistically, by 1997 the average Hongkong family would be taking a cut in its living standards if it were to come and live in Chelsea, let alone in Chingford. Woodrow Wyatt, Lord Wyatt of Weeford, was right when he wrote recently of the 'sublime conceit of many British' who believe that the people of Hongkong long to settle in this country.

Yet one cannot deny that underneath the bustle today Hongkong is depressed, edgy and insecure as it moves closer to 1997. The essential ingredient of this insecurity is, of course, 'fear': fear that the freedoms of its inhabitants will be curtailed, fear of retribution if they do not conform and obey, and fear of the uncertainty of it all. Uncertainty is the greatest enemy of economic progress. One contributory factor to all this uncertainty is that Hongkong was not given an equal place at the negotiating table.

Initially Britain had a strong negotiating position. I do not think that the Chinese realised that Britain would be so accommodating on the value of the 'perpetuity' rights of Hongkong and Kowloon. Britain should have insisted that Hongkong participated in the discussions on its future.

But the British government did not. In consequence, two heavyweights, miles apart, deliberated and negotiated Hongkong's future and Hongkong has been left stranded between the two, victim of melting loyalties, wondering which side is going to let it down first. From the very beginning Hongkong should have been an equal party to the discussions, which would have enabled it to feel far more confident in presenting its own united view firmly. Instead, Hongkong has been stranded high and dry, left to ponder the underlying motives of the Chinese and the British.

The huge divergence of opinion in Hongkong itself on many issues finds expression in the diverse interpretations of the Chinese and British conduct. So we are sorely wronged people at the moment, experiencing great difficulty in communicating our position because we are simply not in the show. Moreover, this relegation of Hongkong to the sidelines has led to a lack of understanding between all three parties: China, Britain and Hongkong. That is very apparent in the democracy issue.

In some ways, we in Hongkong have a clearer understanding of China's motives than those of the British. It is clear to us that China can see the positive economic value of Hongkong. We do business with them to the tune of $40bn a year—we take 40 per cent of their exports, we provide them with two-thirds of their foreign investment, we employ 25m of their people. No landlord ever had a tenant paying that kind of rent.

It is depressing for Hongkong to think that its future may in some way depend on an internal struggle about the succession of Mrs Thatcher, or assessment of electoral benefits to be gained from articulating prejudice. It is a tragedy that the future of an economy, whose enterprise and vigour puts Britain to shame, may be determined by manoeuvres aimed at winning short-term political advantage.

Hongkong boasts an historic growth rate over the last 20 years in excess of 8 per cent compounded. Given Hongkong's success record and its direct access to one of the world's largest emerging markets, the 1984 Declaration between Britain and China should be the commercial deal of the century. Hongkong nurtures talent. Its health and education records are outstanding —life expectancy in Hongkong is two years longer than in Britain or the United States. It is clear that Hongkong can be one of the world's great economic powers. After 1997, as the engine-room driving the economy of the world's largest emerging market, its capacity for growth and prosperity should be unlimited. If it remains the focus of China's trade then there can be no doubt that it could become the economic hub of Asia.

It is depressing that in this environment we are watching the outflow of Hongkong's greatest asset—and Hongkong really only has one asset—its people. They are leaving because of present uncertainty, and because they want to get passports to give them the confidence to stay. So far, in order to get those passports they have been forced to relocate and spend perhaps three years or more in the host country offering passports. Usually they do not return and, even if they do, uncertainty is compounded by the fact of their leaving—at precisely the time when they are needed.

Let me stress once more that people do not leave Hongkong because they wish to live in another country. They move to acquire foreign residential qualification because, whatever their hopes and expectations, they have anxieties about what may happen after 1997. Events in Eastern Europe suggest we should not be fixed in our assessment of the nature of any Communist government in seven years. But one cannot be surprised that parents, middle managers, skilled young people and other key individuals want an insurance policy.

Emigration today is Hongkong's biggest problem. And it is an immediate problem: 19,000 people left the colony in 1986; 30,000 in 1987; 45,000 in 1988; and 55,000 are expected to leave this year. This rate of emigration feeds on itself—the more people leave, the more the process accelerates. Nobody likes to be the last. It is necessary to stop the haemorrhaging now. It is not much good theorising about the potential beyond 1997 if the economy is shot to pieces before we get there.

Hongkong's main concern is for the departure of professional, technical and managerial staff. Many are between 22 and 40. Most are degree-holders—they are essentially tomorrow's managers.

Let no one imagine that they want to move to Chingford, Thurrock or any of the other bastions of opposition to the British Nationality (Hongkong) Bill. Their desire and their determination is to remain in Hongkong. None of the 200 senior managers of my company who have foreign passports are leaving Hongkong. It is the 280 who do not hold that insurance policy who have applied to Canada, Singapore, Australia or the United States. This is not because they wish to live there, but because only by physically moving can they secure the right to an escape-hatch if things go wrong after 1997.

It will be encouraging if France, West Germany, Belgium and Luxembourg help provide 'passports to stay'. Singapore has already introduced such a scheme. It is desirable that other European Community and Commonwealth countries do all they can to help. There is a measure before the American Congress which would raise the immigrant quota from Hongkong to

20,000 per annum, and allow beneficiaries to defer settlement until 2002—time enough to take up the 'insurance policy' or, more likely, to regain confidence in the Territory's future and let that policy lapse.

But Britain is, and Britain remains, the key to the international equation. Not only is Britain Hongkong's colonial parent. Not only are its people British subjects, who fought for Britain in two world wars—and indeed in the Falklands. But Britain has a solemn, legal obligation under the Joint Declaration to 'maintain and preserve' the 'economic prosperity and social stability' of Hongkong until 30 June 1997.

It is to Mrs Thatcher's great credit that she has never questioned that obligation. In 1984 the people of Britain gave the people of Hongkong their word. Now is the time to honour it. It has been claimed that the provision of 50,000 passports is elitist. That might be arguable if this legislation sought—as Australia's and Canada's immigration policy unashamedly seeks—to poach the best and the brightest immigrant talent.

But the British Nationality (Hongkong) Bill is not an immigration policy. It is its precise opposite: an anti-emigration policy. It is designed to reinforce Hongkong's role as the economic star of the East. It is directed principally to Hongkong's future. But that is materially as well as morally important to Britain because billions of pounds' worth of British investment is tied up in the future of Hongkong. It is open to only one 'principled' objection: the number of passports on offer is not sufficient and should be increased to improve the chances of this anti-emigration policy working.

I have spoken of the resilience of the people of Hongkong, of how they have survived stock-market crashes, typhoons and enemy occupation. Would Hongkong survive the crisis of confidence that would follow if Britain—through no fault of Mrs Thatcher's or her government—ended up reneging on its obligations under the Joint Declaration? I have no doubt that it would. The people of Hongkong would battle back, as they have before, as they will again. But what a terrible legacy it would be to a community admired internationally for its drive and tenacity—a community which has always loyally fought Britain's corner.

What a sordid end to the closing chapter of the British Empire. It would represent—in the words of a recent *Sunday Times* editorial —'A colonial trust betrayed'.

I am an optimist about the future. Our group is investing $40bn in Hongkong over the next five years. Other companies have made similar commitments. I was in China recently and I see no reason to alter that view. I think the months ahead will be quieter. There will be a process of convergence through to 1997 rather than a sudden event on 30 June 1997—what is now called 'the through-train'.

But confidence is a delicate flower. It is not often outside wartime that one society, in this case Britain, has as much potential to affect a very different society, in this case Hongkong, for good or ill. Our communities have had a long and fruitful association. Hongkong has a legal system based on English common law. Its government is run on British lines, English is the official language. Its educational system is based on that of Britain. Its flag contains the Union Jack. The Queen's head appears on Hongkong stamps and coins.

If we can only get people to stay in Hongkong, to take advantage of the opportunities to grow and prosper, Britain will reap great benefits. It will be good for the West, good for Hongkong, and good for China. If, on the other hand, this country is perceived to be the society responsible for wrecking Hongkong's economy, for triggering a crisis of confidence, there will be great bitterness towards Britain.

Recently I was in China for the brilliantly successful launching of a space satellite. The satellite is owned jointly by British, Hongkong and Chinese interests. It will have the capacity to offer sophisticated communications to a market place of 2,5bn people. I can think of nothing more symbolic of what the future holds for Britain, China and Hongkong in Asia—if we take the right steps to secure Hongkong's future.

SIMON MURRAY

[1] See Keith Colquhoun's Note of the month, 'Hongkong—the despair and the hope', in the April 1990 issue of *The World Today*.

The little Rohcomotive that could

FROM OUR MOSCOW AND SEOUL CORRESPONDENTS

"THE Soviet Union is an Asian-Pacific country," Mikhail Gorbachev declared during a visit to Vladivostok in 1986. Yet this truism—most of the Soviet Union's territory is in Asia, and Russia's Pacific coastline is longer than America's—remains untrue. Four-and-a-half years after Mr Gorbachev's speech the Soviet Union is an Asian power in a military sense alone. Its Asian neighbours think of it as a commercial joke. No deal has been struck with Japan over the islands that the Russians call the Kuriles and the Japanese call the Northern Territories. And relations with both China and India are mixed. The oddity is that one of the region's smaller and more anti-communist countries has become the Soviet Union's most promising partner: South Korea looks set to do more than anyone to help pull Russia out of its Asian sidetrack.

Relations between these two have improved with startling speed. Contacts were opened during the Seoul Olympics in 1988. In June 1990 Mr Gorbachev and his South Korean counterpart, Mr Roh Tae Woo, surprised everyone by meeting for an hour in San Francisco. Three months later diplomatic relations were established. The keystone was placed on December 13th-16th, when President Roh, accompanied by ten Korean businessmen, called on Mr Gorbachev in Moscow.

The South's aims in this have been mainly diplomatic—and President Roh has shown great skill in achieving them. The South has sought to press communist North Korea to open up to it—and to the rest of the real world—by strangling, one by one, its lines of support from other communist countries. First came a turning away by the East Europeans, then by the Russians. Now even the Chinese have agreed to formal trade relations with the South (trade between the two has been running at some $3 billion a year, around three times the value of trade between China and the North). Recently the Chinese seem to have been telling the North to look beyond brotherly socialist countries for economic support.

The South has also been playing a deeper game. It wants to maintain its links with America while using its new regional partners (China and Russia) to balance its former—and still instinctively distrusted—enemy Japan. The Russians, for their part, hope to use South Korea to prod Japan, the world's last true cold warrior, into a friendlier stance. But their main motive in reaching out to the South is economic.

For this the Russians have been ruthless with an old friend. Experts on North Korea in the Soviet foreign ministry objected to the opening of diplomatic relations with the South. The North objected even more. When Mr Edward Shevardnadze, the Soviet foreign minister, met his North Korean counterpart in September on a tour of East Asia, a Soviet observer reported that "the words 'puppet regime of US imperialism' were one of the milder expressions used." The Soviet Union has reduced cheap oil exports to the North, which in turn briefly recalled its ambassador from Moscow.

President Roh's visit to Moscow does not mean the North's complete abandonment. Mr Gorbachev declared that the Soviet Union would work with South Korea for reunification of the peninsula. Reunification as such is not controversial (it is the declared aim of the North as well), but the terms on which it takes place are. Mr Gorbachev leaned the North's way. He was careful to support its demand for a nuclear-free zone—a dig at South Korea's American protectors. Even so, the Russians plainly want to be on good terms with the richer side when Korean unification does take place.

Already the road into Moscow from its international airport, along which banners once flew proclaiming the superiority of communism, is lined with advertisements for Hyundai, Daewoo and Samsung. It makes sense. South Korea is the Asian miracle economy that offers the Soviet Union the likeliest rewards from co-operation, if not the largest. South Korea can help because, like Japan, it is long on industrial expertise but short on raw materials. Iron ore and coal from Siberia could feed Korean steel works; timber from the Far Eastern forests could be used for Korean housing.

In exchange, Korean manufacturing skills—lower, and therefore more appropriate, than Japanese—could be used to upgrade Soviet factories. If any country offers the hapless Soviet Union a remotely plausible model of development, it is South Korea, which has somehow married fast growth with a lot of government intervention. Most remarkably, Soviet goods might actually be sellable in South Korea. A recent exhibition of Soviet industrial goods in Seoul resulted in $30m in sales contracts.

Trade between the two countries in 1989 was $600m; a year later it exceeded $1 billion. An over-excited President Roh said in Moscow that bilateral trade could reach $18 billion by the mid-1990s—half as much again as the value of trade between the Soviet Union and western Germany, its biggest capitalist trading partner, in 1990.

Three Soviet container ships are being modernised in South Korean shipyards. Daewoo is to help convert arms factories to civilian production (washing machines with Korean engines in them are being produced at a military-aircraft factory). Lotte is to open a department store in Moscow. Lucky Goldstar is to build an electronics factory and a $350m office and hotel complex in Leningrad; Samsung is following suit. Even the Rev Sun Myung Moon is getting in on the act: he has given $100,000 to Mrs Raisa Gorbachev (she has handed the money over to a children's hospital).

The most enthusiastic Korean investor, though, is Hyundai. It has started a joint venture to turn rotted wood into useable chips in the Russian Far Eastern city of Svetlaya. Hyundai has opened an office in Nakhodka, the first free economic zone in the Soviet Union, has plans for a gas pipeline in the Far East and has agreed to supply car-hire firms with Korean cars. Hyundai's chairman, Mr Chung Ju Young, who tends to operate on instinct in these matters (he rushed into Middle East construction in the

From *The Economist*, December 22, 1990, pp. 39-41. Copyright © 1990 by The Economist. Reprinted by permission of The New York Times Syndicated Sales Service.

Toe in the waters

THE cold war may be over in Europe, but an after-shudder is gripping Asia. The chilling thought, particularly in north-east Asia, is that a less threatening Soviet Union—and therefore a less concerned America—could bring the region not a peace dividend but a penalty.

The penalty is that a Soviet retreat might leave room for other regional rivalries to loom larger. Nothing looms larger in most of the neighbours' minds than an increasingly powerful Japan. But Japan is not alone: China too has been gathering military clout and expanding the reach of its navy.

There are old disputes as well as potential new ones. Japan and the Soviet Union are still at loggerheads over a group of islands north of Japan. To the south, the Koreas are now on curt speaking terms, but their big armies still glare at each other at close range through gun sights.

Cold-war divisions in Asia were never as tidy as they were in block-to-block Europe. Yet, funnily enough, north-east Asia has recently seen quite a lot of arms control, even if not the tidy European sort. Since 1985 China has reduced the size of its armed forces by a quarter. Of the 200,000 troops that the Soviet Union promised two years ago to cut east of the Urals, 120,000 are to come from the military districts next to China. On both sides of the border, the troops who remain are being pulled farther back.

By 1992 the United States plans to have cut its troops in Japan, South Korea and the Philippines by 15,000 (15%). Now Japan, the world's third-largest spender on defence, is at last preparing to slow down the rate of growth of its defence budget, after

real increases that averaged a remarkable 4.3% a year for a decade.

One reason this sort of freelance arms control is less obviously reassuring is that unilateral cuts can be unilaterally restored. A sharp reminder of this came in the autumn, when the Soviet Union began preparing for its European arms-cutting deal with NATO; it quickly moved some 21,000 tanks into Soviet Asia (though well west of the Chinese border). The other reason for worry is that, the long Russia-China border excepted, the real threat of conflict in Asia's north-east comes at sea, not on land.

	Men '000	Aircraft[1]	Ships[2]	Submarines	Tanks[3]
Soviet Far East*	326	870	65	110	4,500
China	3,030	5,900	55	93	8,000
North Korea	1,111	716	3	24	3,500
South Korea	750	493	34	3	1,550
US forces in Korea	14	72	—	—	—
Japan	249	473	68	15	1,222
US forces in Japan	50	120	8	3	—
US Seventh Fleet[4]	60	250†	70-80	8	—

*Far Eastern Military District †Aboard aircraft carriers [1]Combat aircraft [2]Principal surface combatants [3]Main battle tanks [4]Before deployment in the Gulf
Sources: The Military Balance, 1990-91; G.Segal "The Soviet Union and and the Pacific"; US Pacific Command

Although the Soviet Union has reduced the size of its Pacific fleet from its peak in the mid-1980s, it is still the country's biggest. The Chinese and Japanese fleets have both been expanding, in Japan's case to enable its navy to defend the sea lanes up to 1,000 nautical miles from the Japanese coast. America's navy, squeezed by budget cuts and facing the prospect of losing its anchorage in the Philippines before the decade is out, is unlikely to volunteer for further cuts. It helps the American navy's lobby that all proposals so far for limiting the size of navies in the region have come from the Soviet Union, which is chiefly a land power and whose proposals have always been aimed at clearly denying America its offsetting sea power.

But if navy-cutting is not yet in prospect, how about something less ambitious? During a visit to Tokyo in September, the Soviet foreign minister, Mr Edward Shevardnadze, suggested talks with Japan (to match similar talks with America) about things like the prevention of incidents at sea. Perhaps in the hope that it will encourage Mr Gorbachev to hand back the disputed Kuriles when he visits in April, Japan has not said no.

Canada, a veteran of arms control in Europe, is preparing its own plan for a North Pacific Co-operative Security Dialogue, involving America, the Soviet Union, China, Japan and the Koreas. It would start with broader matters, from the environment to drug trafficking, in the hope that the habit of dialogue would eventually extend to military questions too. If it worked, it would be a way to fit Japan into a multilateral framework. The European talks bring together the landlubbers from Vancouver to Vladivostok. Time now for the seafarers to get their boots wet?

1970s, when everyone else was urging caution), says his firm is willing to invest $5 billion in natural-resource projects.

Some Korean voices are urging caution, for good reason. Korean companies are already owed past-due debts of $35m—not much compared with what German firms are owed, but a bad start. Infrastructure is lacking. It is hard enough to telephone Seoul from Moscow, let alone from some one-horse town in the Soviet Far East.

Yet something unusual is afoot. Thanks

to a new investment protection agreement, Korean businesses should be able to take their hard-currency profits out of the country. This gives Koreans the same rights as Soviet businesses—meaning they are better treated than other foreign firms. Their governments are certainly feeling pally. Talks are to start in early 1991 on the terms of a Korean government loan to the Soviet Union. It is rumoured to be worth $500m, with a $3 billion–4 billion aid-and-credit package to come.

Behind all this, for both governments, lies the great diplomatic and economic prize: Japan. The South's mistrust of Japan has been deepened by Japan's overtures to the North—confirmed this week by the announcement that the Japanese and the North Koreans will be talking in January about opening diplomatic relations. Meanwhile Mr Gorbachev visits Tokyo in April, hoping to settle his last cold-war account. South Korea's best wishes will go with him.

THE NEW & IMPROVED SOUTH AMERICA

A whole continent has swung to democracy and begun to look for partners in profitmaking. Is anybody listening? Perhaps a little North American hype is in order, as well as more of the mutual-benefit efforts begun by President Bush.

Bruce Babbitt

Bruce Babbitt, former governor of Arizona and a candidate for the Democratic presidential nomination in 1988, has lived and traveled throughout Latin America.

I N HIS NEW BEST SELLER, "THE GENERAL IN His Labyrinth," Gabriel García Márquez, winner of the Nobel Prize for Literature, applies his magic realism to the life of Simón Bolívar. The novel briefly recreates the glorious decade in which Bolívar, in one brilliant campaign after another, liberated half a continent from Spanish rule. But it quickly takes the reader on to the last years in which Bolívar faced political defeat and watched as his dream of a great continental union, counterweight to the United States, collapsed into political intrigue and civil war.

Nearing death as he drifted down the Magdalena River on a barge toward European exile, the great Liberator wrote a haunting prophecy: "South America is ungovernable, the man who serves a revolution plows the sea, this nation will fall inevitably into the hands of the unruly mob."

Up to the present, there has not been much reason to contradict Bolívar's gloomy assessment. For the history of the Latin republics has been an unending succession of military coups, human rights abuses, economic crises, and mass deprivation, symptomatic of what Venezuelan writer Carlos Rangel calls "a failed society."

DECLINING MARX

Now, suddenly, it all seems to be changing. The South American republics are reversing course and moving toward democracy and economic liberalization. This year, for the first time in history, every country on the continent is headed by a democratically elected president.

In Brazil and Argentina new presidents are selling off state-owned telephone companies, airlines, oil companies, and railroads. Bolivia, the continent's traditional worst case, is entering its fifth year of economic stabilization and democratic rule. Incomes have not yet risen, but new businesses are much in evidence, and the country shows its recovery in spruced-up streets and buildings. Chile, newly returned to democracy, is abolishing trade barriers and quotas and leading the move toward free trade. And in Peru a scholar named Hernando De Soto is driving long-dominant Marxist economists off the field with his studies of the damage inflicted by state-run economies.

Even García Márquez, an ardent Marxist and the most influential writer in Latin America, seems to be losing faith in the old quasi-Marxist orthodoxies. And therein lies the real significance of "The General in His Labyrinth." García Márquez, by delving into the formative years of the Latin republics, is showing his readers that Bolívar's political failure, and by extension the historical failures of the South American republics, resulted from internal problems—corrupt officials, vainglorious politicians, the authoritarian traditions of the Spanish crown and the papacy, and the absence of a strong work ethic and a widely shared civic culture. To the reader, it is as if a fictional Bolívar is now returning to liberate South America from itself by using history to smash Marxist dependency theories that assign external causes for those very political and economic failures.

BUT WHERE'S UNCLE SAM?

Ironically, just as Latin Americans are beginning to accept responsibility for their destiny and to undertake major economic reforms, many Washington policymakers seem to be turning out the lights. Some say that, with the end of the cold war, Latin America simply doesn't matter anymore. Who cares whether Nicaragua is governed by Daniel Ortega or Violeta Chamorro? Or whether the Argentine generals revolt or the Brazilian economy crashes?

Others complain that, whether or not South America matters, foreign aid programs simply don't seem to work, at least on that continent. President Kennedy's Alliance for Progress, the first big assistance program, achieved little except a new generation of military leaders putting the sword to democracy.

The next big aid program, the bank-lending binge of the 1970s, produced even worse results. By the time the lending was halted by the Mexican default in the summer of 1982, Latin America had received the equivalent of a bank-sponsored Marshall Plan—nearly $500 billion in all. But to little avail, for much of the money was wasted away in grandiose and inefficient government-sponsored projects.

IF BOLIVIA COULD DO IT

Political leaders skeptical of foreign aid have now been joined by economists advancing an even more pointed argument: that the best hope for reform is "to let them sink or swim." Bolivia is often cited to prove the point. In 1985 that country was comatose: It had gone through several dozen presidents in 25 years, achieved the lowest per capita income on the continent, and was swept by waves of hyperinflation that crested at an annual rate of 24,000% in September 1985.

Only then, in the depths of chaos, did that country suddenly pull itself together, adopt budget reforms, reform the tax system, abolish trade barriers, and restore democratic government.

But if past policies have seldom lived up to expectations, that is scarcely an argument for giving up. And President Bush, to his credit, has refused to do so, choosing instead to make an arduous tour of the continent, even while immersed in the Persian Gulf crisis, by way of demonstrating his commitment to Latin leaders.

As foreign aid and other forms of public investment continue to decline, whatever economic assistance remains will necessarily shift toward the private sector. Henceforth, the debate will concern how best to reinforce the movement toward market reforms with the carrots of trade and foreign investment. And, having seized the rhetorical initiative, the US president will have to follow up with concrete initiatives.

The recent collapse of the Uruguay Round of global trade negotiations now adds a note of both urgency and opportunity to economic events in this hemisphere. At least for the time being, the momentum for global trade liberalization will have to come at the regional level—in Europe, North America, and East Asia. And that situation in turn will require a concerted effort to construct a two-track hemispheric trade integration policy.

One track, now underway, is the early integration of Mexico into a true North American free trade area.

A second track will call for a parallel effort to bring South American countries into a lower-level trading tier that can gradually be incorporated into and harmonized with the core of a genuine United States-Mexico free trade area.

As daunting as the project may sound, it has been done before, and there are many instructive precedents in the development of the European Community from a small core of industrialized countries to a broader grouping including less developed countries.

PUDDING WITHOUT A THEME

While the framework for Mexican negotiations is now emerging, the concepts for South American integration are still lacking; the entire subject remains a pudding without a theme. Brazil, the economic giant of the continent, is promoting a "Southern Cone" organization taking in Argentina, Uruguay, and Paraguay. Chile, spurning Brazilian overtures, is talking with Mexico. The Andean countries, the traditional economic orphans of the continent, are raking through ashes of a failed scheme called the Andean Pact, searching for a workable scheme.

Even as they trip over each others' proposals, many Latin leaders are wondering privately whether anything will come of all the talk or whether South America is destined to become a new Atlantis, the lost continent of the world trading order.

To get the process moving toward orderly and productive negotiations, the United States will have to formulate a standard trade-liberalization package, an off-the-shelf product that opens American markets to any Latin American country willing to pay the sticker price of reciprocal market opening. There will inevitably be optional extras and negotiated discounts and terms, but to get the bargaining moving, Washington must have a product to offer.

The contents of such a package can readily be assembled from the wreckage of the GATT talks. What developing countries sought, with support from the United States, in the Uruguay Round of those global trade talks, was open markets for agricultural products, and the abolition of quotas for textiles, footwear, and steel. In return, the United States sought protection for patents and copyrights, and the opening of markets for services such as insurance and banking. It is essentially that deal, which was torpedoed by the Europeans, that should now be offered to the Latin American countries.

THE OTHER GREATEST NEED

Apart from trade, what the Latin countries most need is investment capital. Developing countries, including the United States in the 19th century and Japan in the 20th, have always looked to foreign borrowing and investment as a means of adding to domestic savings and thereby accelerating the process of development. Latin America unfortunately starts the decade of the '90s submerged in foreign debt, bereft of its own domestic capital (which has been sent abroad as "flight capital"), and reduced to searching in vain for new foreign investors.

Even as Latin countries undertake economic reforms, investors have been slow to return, preferring to wait a while longer on the sidelines to see whether those reforms will be sustained and expanded. Meanwhile, world events have intensified the competition for scarce investment capital:

West Germany is now preoccupied with assembling a dowry for its impoverished East German partner.

The other countries of Eastern Europe are providing still more new investment opportunities.

Japan is contracting its overseas investments to meet liquidity demands in its own banking and real estate sectors.

And the United States, with its persistent budget deficit, continues to soak up disproportionate amounts of foreign capital.

Investment, like trade, develops best when the rules are agreed upon—clear and followed in prac-

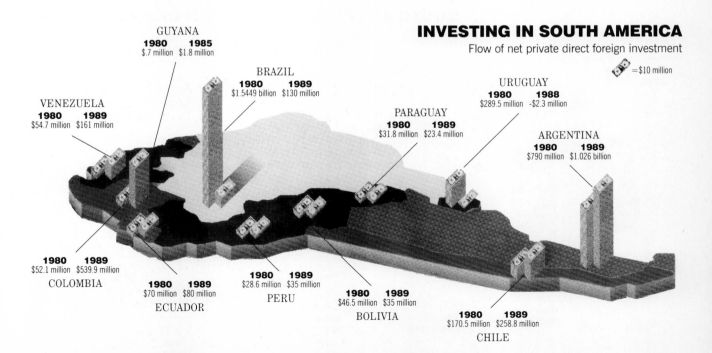

INVESTING IN SOUTH AMERICA

Flow of net private direct foreign investment

= $10 million

GUYANA
1980 $.7 million   **1985** $1.8 million

BRAZIL
1980 $1.5449 billion   **1989** $130 million

VENEZUELA
1980 $54.7 million   **1989** $161 million

URUGUAY
1980 $289.5 million   **1988** -$2.3 million

PARAGUAY
1980 $31.8 million   **1989** $23.4 million

ARGENTINA
1980 $790 million   **1989** $1.026 billion

1980 $52.1 million   **1989** $539.9 million
COLOMBIA

1980 $70 million   **1989** $80 million
ECUADOR

1980 $28.6 million   **1989** $35 million
PERU

1980 $46.5 million   **1989** $35 million
BOLIVIA

1980 $170.5 million   **1989** $258.8 million
CHILE

Map by Dave Herring

5. NEWLY INDUSTRIALIZED COUNTRIES AND LESS DEVELOPED COUNTRIES: Latin America

tice. Unlike trade, investment rules have never received much attention in the international arena—there is nothing even remotely resembling a "General Agreement on Investment and Income."

PATTERNS FOR AGREEMENT

For most of this century many South Americans, influenced by Marxist dependency theories, looked upon foreign investment as a dangerous threat to national sovereignty.

Suspicion of foreigners and their money is hardly unique to South America; if American congressmen who ought to know better can be induced to smash Toshiba products with sledgehammers on the steps of the Capitol, it may not be too hard to comprehend the sentiments that Latin nationalists harbor toward American investment. And those sentiments have all too often produced waves of expropriation, confiscatory tax and exchange rates, and endless regulations covering percentages of corporate ownership, repatriation of profits, and the like.

Now that the political climate is changing, the time may be at hand to attempt a high-profile, multi-country effort to establish pattern investment rules, just as we have become accustomed to doing with trade. (As the name implies, pattern rules set the pattern for use in a whole category of later agreements.)

A specific example that illustrates this larger problem is the uncertainty inherent in tax treatment of foreign earnings. In European countries

and Japan, the United States has long since negotiated bilateral tax treaties, which give investors and their lawyers and accountants a fixed set of tax rules on both sides of the investment transaction. For the most part such treaties do not exist in South America, partly because those countries have often viewed tax treaties as an infringement on their sovereignty and partly because the United States simply hasn't bothered to make the effort.

For example, an agreement negotiated with Brazil back in 1967 is still awaiting ratification by the Senate Finance Committee, principally because neither Brazil nor the US has ever bothered to put out the political effort to get it approved. And, in the absence of such agreements, the combined effect of uncertain and ever-changing corporate and international withholding taxes can eat up as much as 75% of foreign earnings before they ever reach American or Japanese shores.

Were it just Americans advocating these investment and tax reforms, the Latin response might well be still more resentment of gringo demands and yet another nationalistic backlash. But now, in a world short of capital and long on investment opportunities, Latin countries are learning that it is not just US investors who are insisting on clear and stable rules. For the new wave of Japanese investors, so eagerly sought by Chile, Brazil, Peru, Mexico, and others, is, if anything, even more skeptical and demanding than American investors. And to date the Japanese seem to have given a

SOUTH AMERICAN POPULATION GROWTH BY 2025

Source: United Nations Population Fund. Projections based on present trends.
Green figures represent 1990 populations,
Gold figures represent 2025 populations.

VENEZUELA **UP 93%**
1990 19,735,000
2025 38,000,000

GUYANA **UP 51%**
1990 1,039,000
2025 1,569,000

BRAZIL **UP 63%**
1990 150,367,000
2025 245,808,000

PARAGUAY **UP 115%**
1990 4,276,000
2025 9,182,000

URUGUAY **UP 24%**
1990 3,128,000
2025 3,875,000

ARGENTINA **UP 41%**
1990 32,321,000
2025 45,504,000

COLOMBIA **UP 63%**
1990 31,819,000
2025 51,718,000

ECUADOR **UP 112%**
1990 10,781,000
2025 22,909,000

PERU **UP 84%**
1990 22,332,000
2025 41,006,000

BOLIVIA **UP 150%**
1990 7,313,000
2025 18,294,000

CHILE **UP 50%**
1990 13,173,000
2025 19,773,000

Map by Dave Herring

The new economic future of South America still depends on satisfactory resolution of an old and nagging issue—the debt.

partial thumbs up signal only to Chile and, to a lesser extent, Mexico.

WHAT BUSH MUST DO NOW

For all these reasons, the touchy political task of convincing Latin American countries that liberalizing and standardizing investment rules are necessary should be undertaken as a multilateral project with Japanese cover and encouragement. As with trade, however, the Bush administration must move soon to set the tenor of the discussions, raise expectations, and maintain momentum by making a pattern proposal for hemispheric investment and tax rules.

The new economic future of South America still depends on satisfactory resolution of an old and nagging issue—the debt. "The debt" has now been with us for nearly ten years. Almost everyone, including President Bush, the banks, and the debtor countries, seems to be out of ideas and weary of talking about this seemingly insoluble problem. In Brazil Mr. Bush dismissed the debt with a comment to the effect: "Leave me out of the discussion. The debt is an issue between Brazil and the banks." No one in Latin America believes that, and neither do the banks.

Debt negotiations now have gone through three distinct stages: (1) the early years, during which the Reagan administation denied the problem and admonished debtor countries to quit whimpering and pay up; (2) the Baker plan, which requested banks to lend new money to be remitted back as interest on the old; and (3) the Brady plan, which urges the banks to discount some debt but only for those countries willing to bite the bullet of genuine economic restructuring.

Mexico, with its impressive adjustment plan, was selected for the first Brady plan negotiation. After months of haggling, the Mexicans, who were expecting a 50% reduction in debt service, received only a meager 15%. The government of President Salinas de Gortari swallowed hard and kept its silence even as the Mexican press and opposition parties began clamoring for the next round of relief. Similar plans have been worked out with Uruguay and Venezuela.

BRAZIL'S CHAPTER 11 PLAN

Meanwhile, other big debtors are falling ever further behind. Brazil, which has stopped paying altogether, owes $100 billion in principal. It also now owes another $10 billion in interest arrearages, which is more than its total foreign exchange reserves. While the Brazilians have returned to the bargaining table, they are pressing for more than a Mexican-style discount. Brazil's Finance Minister, Zelia Cardoso de Mello, argues: "They're asking for too much," adding that the bank demands "aren't consistent with our ability to pay."

What Brazil seems to be proposing is still a fourth stage of debt adjustment, something of an international Chapter 11 plan that relates annual debt payments to an ongoing measure of ability to pay. One such measure of ability to pay, frequently used in other contexts, is to calculate debt payments as a percentage of export revenues.

The recent upward spike in oil prices nicely illustrates the case for variable debt payments tied to export performance. Mexico, Ecuador, and Venezuela, as major exporters of petroleum, will have sharply increased export earnings and as a result ought to be able to pay more on their debts—just as they should be expected to pay correspondingly less when oil prices decline. The wide fluctuations in other commodity prices, such as coffee and copper, will have similar effects on the trade accounts of other South American countries and should be considered in a similar manner.

Creditor banks will resist the idea of annual payments that fluctuate somewhat unpredictably with economic performance, but it may well be the only way to obtain a lasting settlement and break the continuing cycle of crisis.

THE LIBERATOR'S SECOND CHANCE

In his novel, García Márquez recounts the night of July 4, 1817, which Bolívar spent with his officers hiding in a swamp from the Spanish Army. Suddenly, half naked and shivering in the darkness, the Liberator began discoursing about the future, explaining how he would drive out the Spaniards and telling his followers, "Then we will climb Chimborazo and plant on its snow-covered peaks the tricolor of an America that is forever great, united, and free."

That prophecy was unfortunately way off the mark. Perhaps now, with some timely international leadership, it will come true as South America at last begins the climb toward Chimborazo.

Latin America Confronts the Challenges of the 1990's

ABRAHAM F. LOWENTHAL

Abraham F. Lowenthal is currently Professor of International Relations at the University of Southern California. His latest book is Partners in Conflict: The United States and Latin America.

As the 1990's begin, history seems to be accelerating. Breathtaking change is occurring in many parts of the world and in many realms. Technological developments in computers, lasers, genetic engineering, fiber optics and superconductivity are beginning to reshape the world's economy. The striking triumph of democratic politics and market economics has prompted talk of the "end of history," or at least of the Cold War as the organizing concept of international relations.

In many world regions, rapid progress is being registered. Perestroika and glasnost are transforming the Soviet Union and Eastern Europe. Western Europe is moving quickly toward enhanced economic integration. Japan is taking its place as a major world power.

Even some of the world's most intractable problems appear to be more open to eventual solutions. Conversations have finally begun between South Africa's white minority government and black nationalist leaders. Slowly but inexorably, Israel and the Palestinians seem to be groping toward eventual compromise. In China, where 1989 saw such wrenching setbacks, one senses nonetheless that the tide of history is running toward modernization and eventual opening.

It is hard to be so optimistic, however, about Latin America and the Caribbean. After a "Lost Decade" of recession, Latin America enters the 1990's in deep trouble. Economic and social conditions are desperate in many countries, and political tensions are rising.

Just ten years ago, both the facts and the mood were very different. Latin America as a whole was still enjoying the final glow of a prolonged period of rapid economic growth. From 1950 through 1979, the region's annual rate of growth was twice that of the United States and most other OECD nations, and faster than that of all developing countries except for a very few in East Asia. In some countries—Brazil and Mexico, in particular—a generation-long drive to industrialize had produced a transformation equivalent in scope to that which occurred in the United States from 1890 to 1914. A decade ago, Latin American societies were just entering a period of hopeful transitions from authoritarian rule toward democracy.

For Latin America as a whole, the 1980's did see political opening, but also economic disaster. These past ten years saw the return of democratic politics to all the nations of South America, culminating in the last month of the decade with the first direct presidential elections since 1960 in Brazil and since 1970 in Chile. Peaceful transfers of power from incumbents to opposition movements took place during the 1980's in countries as diverse as Argentina, Bolivia, Ecuador, Peru and Uruguay—in some cases the first such democratic transitions in memory. Movement toward participatory or at least electoral politics, though less inclusive or robust, also took hold in several nations of Central America and the Caribbean. Mexico, after 60 years of one-party rule, had its most competitive and meaningful elections in history in 1988 and appears on its way, albeit by fits and starts, toward pluralist politics. At the beginning of the 1990's, Cuba is the only country in the hemisphere openly defying the regional commitment to democracy (although Guyana and Haiti are still far from embracing the commitment).

But while people in the Americas took satisfaction from the expansion of participatory politics, most countries also suffered a painful contraction of economic performance. Latin America witnessed a nearly 10 percent regional decline in per capita income and a far more severe drop in some countries and sub-regions. Unemployment and underemployment are high, inflation plagues many nations, hyperinflation is ravaging a few and socioeconomic inequalities are becoming worse almost everywhere. Latin America's share of world commerce fell during the 1980's from about 6 percent to 3.5 percent. Its terms of trade worsened markedly, with a decline in the real value of almost all of its commodity exports.

Latin America's nearly $420 billion external debt—itself partially a result of the recognition by financial markets of the region's growth and potential during the 1970's—caused a massive drain of capital, amounting to about $200 billion from 1982 through 1989. Latin American nations have had to drastically curtail imports, cut social services and reduce investments in order to service their debts. They have been caught on a treadmill, mortgaging their future in futile efforts to clear their accounts.

Translated into human terms, the statistics on Latin America's plight mean hunger, infant death, boat and feet people, stunted education, epidemics, street crime, delinquency and mounting despair. The political residue of the 1980's, in turn, is an overwhelming repudiation of incumbent governments in almost every election, increasing political polarization in many nations, incipient questioning of the democratic framework in several and growing insurgencies and terrorist violence in a few, particularly the Andean nations.

At the beginning of the 1990's, five broad regional trends

From *Harvard International Review*, Spring 1990, pp. 4-6. Copyright © 1990 by Abraham F. Lowenthal.

deserve special emphasis. First, throughout Latin America and the Caribbean, the cumulative effects of the "Lost Decade" are becoming evident. Latin America's industrial infrastructure is eroding, the results of curtailed investments in education and research are beginning to be felt, social and health problems are mounting, and there is a sense of urgent crisis almost everywhere. It is widely recognized that most of Latin America cannot count on significant external capital during the 1990's— that neither renewed foreign investments nor new commercial lending are likely to enter the region on a broad scale.

It appears increasingly improbable that the debt crisis of the 1980's will ever be "resolved" with a clear and comprehensive solution; it will more likely be managed on a case-by-case basis on terms that reflect the divergent interests and relative strengths of the various actors and will consequently leave most Latin American nations bereft. Small regional banks in the United States, as well as many European and Japanese banks, are simply withdrawing from the region to cut their losses. Large money-center banks are grudgingly reducing their expectations and are wary of new or expanded involvements. Latin American nations are bargaining individually to reduce their severe burdens at the lowest cost in terms of future economic possibilities, but it may turn out that few, if any, will be positively helped to achieve the new economic expansion that could provide the only real escape from the debt trap. The very difficult challenge faced by countries throughout the region is how to design economic development strategies that can mobilize domestic savings and re-attract flight capital without counting on external capital and without aggravating socio-economic inequalities and tensions. Without international assistance, this challenge may be overwhelming for many Latin American nations.

Second, the exhilarating progress of democratic opening throughout Latin America is giving way to preoccupation with issues of governance and governability. It is difficult for fragile democratic regimes to meet the challenges posed by economic decline, particularly when that is accompanied by prolonged insurgencies, the narcotics traffic, rampant corruption, increasing labor unrest and widespread disenchantment. After several years of strong reinforcement of Latin America's moderate center—as part of the process of *abertura*—much of the region seems now to be entering a renewed phase of polarization. Both leftist and rightist (or neo-conservative) groups and leaders are gaining greater strength, sometimes in the same countries.

Third, much of Latin America and the Caribbean—from Argentina to Mexico—is experiencing growing tension between the processes and consequences of political and economic liberalization, between opening politics and opening markets. In the United States, it is widely assumed that market economies and democratic politics necessarily accompany and reinforce each other; the parallel moves toward democratic opening and liberal economic reforms in Latin America in the late 1980's seemed to support this view. But the impressive strength in the late 1980's of Cárdenas in Mexico, Lula in Brazil, the *Frente Amplio* and *Nuevo Espacio* in Uruguay, and of MAS and *Causa R* in Venezuela raise serious questions—a

bit different in each case—as to whether more democratic participation may eventually spawn renewed populist, statist and possibly nationalist approaches and policies in the early 1990's, and whether the emergence of such challenges may produce moves to restrict democratic competition. Throughout the region, too, there are serious concerns as to whether the choices made by political actors in order to ensure the survivability of fragile democracies may make it less likely for democratic regimes to confront the fundamental problems of poverty and gross inequality. In their effort to build commitment from business and military groups that had worked to undermine democracy in the 1960's and 1970's, democratic politicians in several countries have made compromises which protect various entrenched privileges. Yet these restrictions may not only make democracies harder to sustain, but also may interfere with some of the reforms needed to foster sustainable economic development.

Fourth, the differences among the countries and subregions of Latin America and the Caribbean—always much greater than most North American policy analysis or public discussion assume—are becoming more pronounced than ever:
• Mexico and many of the islands of the Caribbean are silently integrating with the United States, in the sense that their economies are ever more closely intertwined with it, and their people are migrating to the US at an accelerated rate. Mexico, in particular, seems embarked on a course of policy that, if sustained over time, may make it increasingly a North American nation, ever more different and more removed from Latin America.
• On the other hand, Peru and to a lesser extent Colombia are showing worrisome signs of *dis*integration, with whole regions of each country under the control of insurgent movements, counter-insurgent paramilitary groups and drug traffickers, making the legitimacy and authority of the central national government even more precarious.
• Central America, the focal point of so much struggle during the 1980's, is now poised uncertainly among the possibilities of peace through utter exhaustion, the prospect of renewed and more violent confrontation or more years of low-level but deadly conflict. The FMLN offensive in El Salvador clarified that battered country's real options—another generation of brutal war, or else a negotiated peace that satisfies neither the country's establishment nor its insurgents. Guatemala's civil war simmers, ready to erupt again. Nicaragua faces, at best, a decade of painful reconciliation and slow reconstruction; no one can exclude the possibility of further violence and repression there. Panama now confronts the very tall tasks of rebuilding public order, reconstructing the institutions of national self-government and reviving a devastated economy.
• Cuba, important beyond its size in Latin America and inter-American affairs during the past generation, is receding in relevance. Isolated from Latin American political currents by its continued *caudillo* rule and virtually unique in the socialist world due to its forthright rejection of the Gorbachev reforms, Cuba seems caught in a time warp, reflecting the conditions and concerns of the 1960's more than those of the 1990's.
• Argentina, Brazil and to some extent Venezuela are internally

divided, with growing uncertainty and the possibility of quick policy reversals and even of turbulence in each case. In all three countries, proponents of market-oriented orthodoxy have dominant influence at the moment, but in each case those who espouse neopopulist heterodox formulas are strong contenders for power. In Argentina and Venezuela, charismatic political leaders Carlos Menem and Carlos Andres Perez quickly moved away from their natural populist constituencies to embrace anti-statist approaches upon taking office. In Brazil it would not be altogether surprising if the newly-elected conservative president Fernando Collor de Mello, who campaigned on a broad anti-statist platform, made something of a reverse switch in 1990 in an attempt to divide the massive following his leftist rival galvanized in last December's election. It is not at all certain in any of these three countries what policy approaches will prevail in the next two or three years, or even whether the established political rules will survive.

• Chile and Uruguay, meanwhile, enter the 1990's in relatively strong shape, as each enjoys the fruits of restored democratic politics and, in the case of Chile, of a newly modernized economy. Each country is regaining its erstwhile place as a bastion of civility and a forum for intelligent and critical political debate. Each nation has the benefit of a mature left, unlikely to repeat the excesses of the late 1960's and early 1970's that led to authoritarian repression, and of a pragmatic right chastened by the popular repudiation of military rule. In each country, however, the moderate centrists who hold power as the decade begins may soon face challenges from both sides that will make it difficult to simultaneously retain business confidence and broad popular support.

Fifth, even if there are strong reasons for concern about Latin America's immediate future, it is also important to stress some reasons for longer-term optimism about the region's overall prospects. Declining fertility rates throughout most of Latin America augur well for an improving balance between resources and population, and between economic growth and expansion of the labor market. The structural reforms already undertaken in several countries increase the likelihood that Latin America or at least part of the region will eventually be able to insert itself more fruitfully into the evolving world economy. Even during the 1980's, the region's exports expanded over 50 percent by volume. A generation of urbanization and expanded education has modernized Latin America and greatly improved the capacity of its citizens. In many countries, grass-roots and popular organizations are gaining a vibrant strength unprecedented in Latin America's history.

Furthermore, the regional commitment to human rights and democratic politics, however fragile, is also noteworthy; many Latin American countries may finally escape the syndrome of repeated military interventions.

The US-Latin American Context

With all that is happening in Latin America—and with the dramatic shifts in the overall global context—it is predictable that United States-Latin American relations will also be reshaped. After a decade of obsessive focus on Nicaragua and a year of misplaced preoccupation with Panama leading to the invasion of December 1989, Washington may finally be ready to redirect its concerns away from Central America in the 1990's. But it is by no means clear whether Washington will now focus on the nations of the Western Hemisphere where tangible US interests are most directly affected, or whether the United States will instead revert to pervasive neglect of Latin America.

With the Cold War ending, Latin America (or at least some of its subregions) may come to be recognized as increasingly significant to the United States. Mexico, a nation of 85 million persons bordering the United States, affects the daily lives of people in the United States as much as any other nation in the world. Brazil, a mega-country of some 150 million persons, is already a major economic actor with considerable political influence and potential. The Andean nations, due to the drug traffic and expanding internal convulsions, are bound to have a large impact upon the United States. So will the small islands of the Caribbean—because of their extraordinary interpenetration with this country through migration, tourism, trade and investment. If the foreign policy leadership of the United States takes heed of its citizens' primary concerns, it will turn increasingly from questions of national security (as well as national *in*security) to such problems as drugs, migration, trade and environmental protection.

If and when these "intermestic" issues—partaking of both international and domestic components and involving both foreign and domestic actors and decision-making processes—become central to US foreign policy, the United States may finally turn to building effective partnerships with its neighbors in the Americas. But it is also possible that a stagnating Latin America will instead be left without partners, increasingly marginal in a dynamic post-Malta world which has left it behind. As the 1990's open, it is by no means clear which path is more likely.

The Crisis of Leadership

*Can a new leadership emerge out of the turmoil,
fear and dissent that past rulers have brought to
the region?*

Fouad Moughrabi

Fouad Moughrabi is professor of political science at the University of Tennessee at Chattanooga. He is a writer and lecturer on Middle Eastern affairs and author of Public Opinion and the Palestine Question *(St. Martin's Press, 1987).*

In many ways, the Middle East increasingly looks like Central America, a region where the United States intervenes on occasion to shore up its interests and protect its clients. An important difference is that the Middle East has oil, a vital commodity that enables the United States to exert significant leverage over Europe and Japan.

In both regions, however, local grievances have either been ignored or subsumed under the more general rubric of the East-West conflict. In Central America, local problems were said to be the result of Soviet and Cuban interference. Similarly, in the Middle East, local and regional problems were dismissed as the results of Soviet interference in the region.

One of America's long-term objectives, enunciated in the Truman Doctrine (1947), has been keeping the Soviet Union out of the Middle East. Beginning in the early 1970s, the Middle East has been for all practical purposes an American arena. Throughout this period, the USSR played only a peripheral role in the affairs of the region, yet local and regional problems were allowed to fester. Now that the Soviet Union is uninvolved in the Middle East, these problems continue. On occasion, they flare up into intense confrontations.

Traditionally, the United States has relied on Israel as the local gendarme who intervenes in regional affairs to alter or reshape politics to suit Israeli purposes. Increasingly, however, Israel's regional interests—as defined by the Israeli extreme Right—and American global interests seem to diverge, making it necessary for the United States to intervene directly. It did so in Lebanon in 1983, and it has recently done so again in the Gulf crisis. In either case, however, whether Israel or the United States intervenes, local conflicts and contradictions are exacerbated as a consequence.

Lebanon is a classic example of a conflict made worse because of Israeli and American intervention. In the Gulf, a resolution of the conflict by force will also complicate local and regional problems to the point where the whole region may in fact become "Lebanized," as Zbigniew Brzezinski recently put it in an article in the *New York Times* (October 7, 1990). The circle of conflict is likely to expand beyond Lebanon and Israel-Palestine to engulf the Arab and Islamic worlds.

It would be unfair to blame the Middle East's problems entirely on U.S. or Israeli intervention. Local elites have allowed contradictions to go unresolved to the point where the whole area has become a political volcano. Throughout Arab history, a dynamic tension has always pitted particularistic tendencies against more universal ones. Thus, for example, the tendency of the Middle Eastern states to pursue policies that promote their own special interests has always been measured against an informal set of universal standards and Pan-Arab national concerns.

In the post–Second World War era of independence and nationalism, the charismatic Egyptian President Gamal Abdel Nasser articulated the national pan-Arab concerns. These issues included championing the Palestinian cause and freeing the region from foreign interference. Arab nationalist themes were offered in the context of the colonial era and were focused on driving British and French influence from the Middle East. Following independence, however, the political map drawn by the colonial powers reflected the growth of postcolonialism. States committed in practice to achieving their own interests at the same time rhetorically expressed pan-Arab concerns.

Pan-Arab themes began to disappear from the political lexicon after the June 1967 defeat by Israel. Only the Palestinians continued to appeal to these themes in an effort to garner support for their armed resistance against Israel. Some analysts, such as Fuad Ajami, prematurely announced the end of pan-Arabism. In reality, however, pan-Arab themes were swept from the halls of power in the Arab capitals and the official newspapers into the street. Those who benefited from the rise of the new states began to articulate pragmatic ideas limited to their own interests. Oppositional groups, submerged beneath the surface, continued to adhere to nationist themes.

The rise of petro-dollars disguised this fundamental contradiction for more than two decades. It also delayed the process of political development in the region. However, as the economies of the oil-producing states began to suffer the shocks of the Iran-Iraq War and declining oil prices, certain important trends began to appear. A reverse migration of labor from rich to poor countries led to a plunge in remittances. Egyptian, Syrian, Lebanese, and Palestinian workers began to leave the rich countries; some were even expelled. Intra-Arab aid declined sharply, and the economies of the poor countries began to suffer serious dislocations. In Jordan, for example, on the eve of the present Gulf crisis, unemployment

reached 20 percent. Now, with the influx of thousands of Palestinian and Jordanian workers expelled from the oil-rich countries, unemployment rates could be as high as 40 percent.

The myopic policies of Arab leaders in both poor and rich countries during the boom years have led to the present sad state of affairs. Nearly all the Arab countries have joined the modern world as consumers, not as producers. They have become the dumping ground for excess products from the industrialized countries. Nearly all have ignored agricultural development and have consequently become net importers of food from the outside, thereby increasing their dependence on the West. The rich oil-producing countries recycled their wealth in Europe and the United States to the point where, as in the case of Kuwait, outside earnings from investments now exceed income from oil.

Little or no investment has been made in the poorer Arab countries to create jobs and reduce reliance on the West. The net result is that Arab elites have not invested in their own region to gain legitimacy; they have preferred to invest in the West, where returns are safer and more guaranteed. As a consequence, in a moment of crisis, the West has to protect the wealthy Arabs from the people of their region, who resent them and their riches. Accusations that Arab wealth is unfairly distributed, that most of it is invested in the West or squandered at the gaming tables, find receptive ears throughout the Arab world.

Saddam Hussein's invasion of Kuwait has awakened the submerged nationalist feelings among the third estate in the Arab world. As economic conditions declined, the gap between rich and poor began to appear more and more obscene. The promise of a stronger leader who can deal a

blow to privilege and conspicuous consumption is therefore very appealing.

Islamic activism

In times of crisis and historic change, some social groups look to the past to find ways to cope with the present. In the Middle East, dissatisfaction with the present and fear about the future have led some groups to develop a restorationist image of society. The theme most often associated with this view of history and society is

> **The myopic policies of Arab leaders in both poor and rich countries during the boom years have led to the present sad state of affairs. Nearly all the Arab countries have joined the modern world as consumers, not as producers.**

what is generally called Muslim fundamentalism. The gist of this ideological current is that neither Arab nationalism nor Arab socialism has been able to deal with the challenges facing the Arab world. The only way to resist fierce attacks from the outside is to go back to the pure roots of Islam. Restoring faith and discipline, with the values associated with them, and rekindling the fervor that characterized early Islam are considered key to a revival that will restore dignity to the people of the region.

Muslim fundamentalism was invigorated by the success of revolutionary Islam in Iran. It was also strengthened by the ability of Islamic groups to force Israel out of southern Lebanon. Above all, however, Muslim reaction focused on declining social mores, an unrestrained westernization, and the spread of drugs, alcohol, and sexual promiscuity.

A similar movement occurred once in the latter part of the nineteenth century when Islamic groups in various parts of the Middle East fell back on the roots of their faith to face an onslaught from the West. This current, led by Abdou and Afghani in Egypt, was never institutionalized. Elsewhere, the same reaction led to the victory of religious revivalist movements in the Arabian Peninsula and Libya, now the two most oppressive and rigid societies.

The current wave of Islamic activism has led to pressures in countries including Algeria, Jordan, and Tunisia toward increasing democracy. Islamic groups, which are highly organized and disciplined, have so far been willing to accept their role as oppositional movements within the framework of the new democracies. However, if conditions in the region decline, especially as a result of an American attack on Iraq, Islamic groups will be positioned to mobilize the severe alienation on the street. Even those who disagree with Hussein's invasion and annexation of Kuwait will be infuriated at the sight of American warplanes bombing and killing Muslims and Arabs. Consequently, the United States may end up fighting more Khomeinis in the Arab and Islamic worlds a few years from now.

The danger resulting from an outbreak of war in the Gulf is not limited to the possible sweep of the region by Islamic groups. An equally ominous development is the fact that the nascent movement toward secular democratic reforms in the Arab world may be a casualty of a war in the Gulf. Jordan, Tunisia, Algeria, and Yemen have taken important although still tentative steps toward parliamentary democracy. This trend was accelerated by mass pressure from below at a time when major transformations were taking place in Eastern Europe and the Soviet Union. Interestingly enough, these are the countries where public opinion has been free to express itself in support of Iraq without fear of intimidation. Elsewhere in the Arab world, where governmental repression is still very high, public reaction is much more muted. Nevertheless, people are becoming bolder in expressing their frustrations. News reports show open popular dissatisfaction with Syrian President Assad's decision to join the American effort in the Gulf. The assassination of the Egyptian speaker of Parliament on October 12, 1990, is another signal of what may happen in the region in the months or years to come.

Peacemaking

Of all the problems in the region, none inflames public opinion more than the inability of Arab governments to put an end to the suffering of the Palestinians under Israeli occupation. It is indeed a measure of how important and potentially explosive this problem is that it hovers at all times over any discussion of the Gulf crisis.

The majority of people in the region blame the continuation of the problem on the United States. The latter is seen as Israel's protector because it guarantees financial and political support and refuses to pressure Israel to come to the negotiating table.

The Palestinian shift in the direction of Iraq predates the August 2 Iraqi invasion and occupation of Kuwait. It was predicated on the practical assumption that, in order to produce results in Israeli-Palestinian negotiations, the

The leadership is widely perceived to be more responsive to foreign, especially Western, interests than to indigenous demands.

Palestinians must correct the underlying imbalance to strengthen their bargaining position. It should be noted that Iraq had supported the Palestinians' peace proposal outlined in the November 15, 1988, Palestinian National Council Resolutions. Furthermore, Egyptian efforts to mediate with Israel, the Palestinians, and the United States had produced no results. The shift toward Iraq did not mean that the Palestinians had abandoned their commitment to a negotiated settlement with Israel.

Much abuse has been heaped on the Palestinians and on Jordan for siding with Iraq in the Gulf crisis. The affluent Palestinian community in the oil-producing countries is now being destroyed. Official Arab assistance to the Palestinians under occupation is likely to disappear. The truth, however, is that very few Palestinians approve of Iraq's invasion and annexation of Kuwait.

Ideally, the PLO should have taken the moral high ground and steered a mediating, peacemaking course in intra-Arab conflicts. But a careful look at how events unfurled at the hastily convened Cairo Summit reveals that such a course was out of the question. The issue, as defined by Egypt and Saudi Arabia, quickly became whether one should support U.S. military intervention. It was therefore impossible for the Palestinians or Jordan to take a middle ground—one that condemns Iraq's occupation of Kuwait and opposes foreign military intervention. An Arab solution may have eventually emerged but at the Cairo Summit it was neither possible nor desired.

The basic issues in the Israeli-Palestinian conflict have not changed as a result of the Gulf crisis. What has changed is the regional context. Israeli hard-liners are now in a stronger position; they are under no pressure to make concessions for peace. Arab governments, including Egypt, Saudi Arabia, and Syria, are not likely to pressure the United States to resolve the issue in a manner that satisfies Palestinian national aspirations. Whatever attempts are made in the direction of a settlement will be at best symbolic, designed to blunt mass furor against the United States, Israel, and their Arab allies.

From early December 1987 until now, a national uprising has

What Kind of Leader Is Saddam

Saddam Hussein received his political education from the age of twenty within the Baath Party in Iraq. This party was created by two Syrian intellectuals who had studied in Paris. Its followers were scattered throughout Syria, Jordan, Lebanon, Iraq, and among the Palestinians. Eventually it came to power in both Syria and Iraq and then quickly split into two national parties.

Virulently anticommunist, the Baath Party raised the banner of integral nationalism a la Charles Maurras. This kind of nationalism called for the exclusive pursuit of national (in this case pan-Arab) policies as opposed to regional or particularistic interests, and for the absolute maintenance of national integrity as well as the steady increase of national power. Domestically, the Baath Party subjugated the interests of the individual to those of the nation, repudiated liberal democracy, and championed political autocracy.

The second important point is that Hussein and members of the Baath Party had suffered persecution before they came to power by a coup. They were therefore paranoid about being overthrown by others, and any opposition was weeded out firmly and quickly. Under Hussein, the country became a nation of informers and was pervaded by an atmosphere of anomie, fear, and mistrust. As the army was seen as fertile ground for counterplots, its power base was eliminated and it was turned into an instrument of party policy. The party itself has witnessed numerous purges, as the regime has felt threatened by internal subversion (for example, by Syrian or Iranian agents) or external attack (as in the case of the Israeli strike against the nuclear reactor in July 1981).

In Egypt, popular culture manufactures an incredible amount of political humor. Usually, the jokes on the street show a great deal of common sense and accurately reflect the dominant political style of the leader. Humor about the charismatic Gamal Abdel Nasser focused on his authoritarian style. Jokes about Anwar Sadat usually dealt with the theme of his and his family's corruption. Now the jokes about President Hosni Mubarak nearly always focus on his ineptness as a leader.

In Iraq, no humor is tolerated about the leader. Iraqi political culture has always been known as the most violent in the Arab world. Arab schoolchildren often memorize the inaugural speech of Hajjaj ibn Yusuf, the Umayyad governor of Iraq at the end of the seventh century A.D. Al-Hajjaj used extreme brutality to subdue what was commonly known as the most turbulent province in the empire. His speech begins as follows: "I see before me heads that are ripe and ready for the plucking, and I am the one who will pluck them. I see blood glistening between the turbans and the beards." It is said that nearly 120,000 were killed before the province was finally subdued.

Hussein shares with other regional leaders some basic characteristics: a narrow political base, a lack of political legitimacy, and the need to resort to fear, persecution, and repression. He has shown that he is more efficient in his use of the instruments of coercion. But he does differ in some crucial respects: There is no evidence that he is as corrupt as the sheiks of the Gulf States; there is strong evidence that he is serious about developing his country and making it a modern, power-

All leaders lack legitimacy in the eyes of their people because in nearly all cases, leadership rests on a very narrow social base and uses the apparatus of state coercion to stay in power.

Hussein?

ful state; and there is ample evidence that he is a proud patriot who will not agree to be manipulated by outsiders, especially Westerners.

Saddam obviously wants to be treated as an equal by the leaders of the great powers and to be feared and respected by the weaker leaders in the region.

Hussein is by no means a deranged person. He believed his country was about to be strangled economically by its neighbors. His problem is that he has underestimated world reaction and did not prepare for it.

In the Middle East, arbitrary leadership depends upon the whims of the man in charge. There are no political systems at work. Hussein does not differ from his colleagues in this respect: He decides when to go to war and when to stop, what to concede, and what to do. Others simply obey. In most cases, aides are trusted loyalists or immediate relatives. This is the case in Iraq as well as in Syria, Kuwait, and Saudi Arabia.

Other leaders in the region who are calling for Hussein's head also have blood on their hands. Hafez Assad of Syria leveled an entire city when the

Muslim Brotherhood challenged his rule. The availability of sophisticated weapons make state violence all the more lethal and widespread.

Hussein is perceived by the poor of the region as a potential champion of their cause. The hatred of the corrupt rulers of the Gulf runs so deep that any strong leader who knocks them over the head will be hailed as a hero. The Iraqi president has tapped a host of latent feelings among the masses; in addition to their dislike of the oil-rich rulers, these include a generalized sense of the worthlessness of their leaders, who have failed to challenge Israel, and a barely disguised anticolonialism.

Those who destroy Saddam Hussein will not be seen as unseating a ruthless dictator. Instead, they will be widely perceived, by seculars and fundamentalists alike, as continuing the attack by the West against Arab nationalist aspirations. As a consequence, many heads of state are likely to fall, with those standing against him being some of the first, precisely because they are the most vulnerable.

—F.M.

been under way among the Palestinians in the Israeli-occupied territories. The Palestinians are demanding an end to the occupation and independence in their own homeland. The PLO adopted major resolutions in November 1988 that recognized Israel's right to exist, accepted resolutions 242 and 338 of the UN Security Council, and called for the establishment of two states in coexistence in historic Palestine.

The U.S. government was unable or unwilling to convince Israel's right-wing government to implement a plan that Prime Minister Yitzhak Shamir himself had presented for the start of negotiations between Israel and the Palestinians. U.S. State Department and National Security Council officials argued in private talks with visiting Palestinians from the occupied territories that while the intifada had changed the status quo it did not alter the strategic balance of force on the ground between Israel and the Palestinians.

It quickly became obvious to most Palestinians that the moderate approach to resolving the Israeli-Palestinian conflict had reached a dead end. Moderates in the PLO were under pressure to show results, but the U.S. government failed to reward the moderates even in symbolic ways.

A need for new leadership

The crisis in the Arab world runs deep. Its roots are political, economic, social, and cultural. Above all, however, it is a crisis of leadership.

In the Middle East, regardless of whether leadership is hereditary or usurped through military takeover, there are certain common threads. In the first place, all leaders lack legitimacy in the eyes of their people because in nearly all cases, leadership rests on a very narrow social base and uses the apparatus of state coercion to stay in power. This is as true of Saddam Hussein or Hafez Assad as it is for the monarchy in Saudi Arabia.

In the second place, a wide gap has opened between the leadership and the mass of people with the growth of education and the increase in levels of politicization: The population is now politically advanced than the leadership. This disparity contributes to a heightened state of frustration throughout the region, especially given the fact that access to power by new, sophisticated elites is blocked in nearly all cases. The case of Kuwait is perhaps the most typical. Educated and sophisticated Kuwaitis are denied access to power because the ruling family jealously guards its narrow self-interests.

In the third place, the leadership is widely perceived to be more responsive to foreign, especially Western interests, than to indigenous demands. This may be a variant of the "Khawaja complex," a syndrome commonly en-

countered in the Arab world wherein any Westerner, no matter how unqualified, commands more respect and authority than any national. Ruling elites who are more comfortable in the company of Westerners and more responsive to their interests are not likely to spend much time thinking about conditions in their own backyards. The Iranian elite under the shah, or the Lebanese elite on the eve of the Lebanese civil war, are typical examples.

The new elites produced by the oppositional movements are no less sophisticated. They are not as strident in their rhetoric as the old nationalist elites of the 1950s. More typically, they are cautious and practical because they have gained their skill and legitimacy at the ground level of the difficult struggle. They differ from the ruling elites in one important respect: They have legitimacy in the eyes of their supporters. The secular underground leadership of the Palestinian uprising and the more religious leaders emerging in Jor-

dan, Tunisia, and Algeria are perhaps typical of the new genre. In the latter case, it is a grave error

The population is now more politically advanced than the leadership.

to assume that the new leaders are fanatical xenophobes just because they are Islamic in orientation. In reality, they are sophisticated political operatives who have positioned themselves as key supporters of the new democracies.

Perhaps, out of the painful turmoil, a new era of leadership will eventually emerge in the Middle East. The best one can hope for is that the cost of replacing what has preceded them will not be too devastating.

Revolution, Reform, or Regression?

Arab Political Options in the 1990 Gulf Crisis

Yahya Sadowski

Yahya Sadowski, a research associate in the Brookings Foreign Policy Studies program, is the author of Political Vegetables: Businessman and Bureaucrat in the Development of Egyptian Agriculture *(forthcoming).*

An old Arab proverb about the romance of war goes: distant drums, sweet music. Most Washington pundits believe that the Bush administration will bring the Kuwait crisis to a close before the spring of 1991. Either Saddam Hussein's troops will bow to international pressure and walk out of Kuwait, or they will fold before an American military assault and be carried out on stretchers. After this victory America will sit back and enjoy "the new global order." But whatever transpires on Kuwaiti sands over the next few months, America will soon have to confront two painful facts. First, the Iraqi invasion of Kuwait is only one symptom of a much wider crisis in the Arab world. Second, this wider crisis is going to persist and fuel renewed instability in the region regardless of whether America claims a victory in Kuwait.

To many Americans, the Middle East in the 1980s appeared to be an unstable and violent region. The U.S. press was filled with unsettling reports about civil wars in Lebanon and the Sudan and regional wars pitting Israel against Syria and Iraq against Iran. But the truth is, the 1980s was a period of relative stability in the region.

During the 1960s the Middle East was markedly less stable — as it may be again soon. Not only were the troubles in Lebanon, the Sudan, Israel, and Iran already evident, but they were compounded by a series of conflicts that have since disappeared. The oil-rich, underpopulated, and conservative monarchies of the Gulf were threatened by republican or Marxist insurgents in the Yemen, tribal rebellions in Oman, and underground Arab nationalist parties in Kuwait and Bahrain. The poor, overpopulated, Arab nationalist regimes in countries like Syria and Iraq were wracked by a seemingly endless series of military coups d'état. A regional power struggle, which Malcolm Kerr dubbed "the Arab cold war," aggravated these domestic disputes. The struggle pitted a coalition of Arab nationalist governments led by Egypt against a rival coalition of pro-Western regimes led by Saudi Arabia.

In November 1967 King Feisal of Saudi Arabia and President Nasser of Egypt, both shocked by Israel's victory in the June war, met in Khartoum to call a truce and lay the foundations of a new Arab order. The Saudis and the other Gulf emirates began to offer billions of dollars of foreign aid to the poorer Arab nationalist regimes. In exchange, the nationalist regimes stopped supporting the insurgencies in the Arabian Peninsula and began to collaborate with the Gulf monarchies in dealing with non-Arab security threats like Iran and Israel. Military coups became less frequent because the poorer Arab states were able to buy a measure of popularity among their citizens by offering consumer subsidies, public employment programs, and lucrative state contracts.

That arrangement of buyoffs between and within

From *The Brookings Review,* Winter 1990/91, pp. 17-21. Copyright © 1991 by the Brookings Institute. Reprinted by permission.

Arab states, sometimes called the Arab state system, was criticized by both Leftists and Islamists, who claimed that it insulated the ruling elites from popular pressures, stifled social change, and fostered corruption. Their criticisms struck a chord, but most Arabs clung to the system because it provided peace, relative political stability, and a rising standard of living.

During the 1980s, however, the system became harder to sustain. The Middle East had an exceptionally fast growing population. Egypt's population, which had been 30 million in 1966, reached 50 million by 1988 and was projected to exceed 67 million by the year 2000. Jordan had the second-fastest growing population in the world (ranking just behind Kenya). The annual growth of population was higher than 3 percent in the Yemens, Sudan, Syria, Iraq, Saudi Arabia, and Kuwait.

Under the best of circumstances such growth would have taxed the local economies, but standards of living were rising too. People who had been content to eat pasta developed a taste for meat. Countries like Egypt and Iraq, which had been food self-sufficient in 1970, today import 80 percent of their basic foodstuffs. This growth of consumer demand might have been met by investing in local industrial and agricultural projects. But a large share of the petrodollar wealth was squan-

> *By the late 1980s, it was no longer possible to sustain the expenses involved in propping up the Arab state system. Just servicing debts crippled the economies of the poorer states, draining their hard currency revenues. Even the richest Gulf states began to run budget deficits and dip into their cash reserves.*

dered by corrupt elites or spent cultivating political loyalty. The few productive ventures that did receive investment were hamstrung by economic policies (such as price controls and overvalued currencies) that inhibited the growth of internationally competitive enterprises. The only sectors of the economy that typically grew faster than population were commerce and government bureaucracy.

In 1982 and again in 1985, oil prices slipped badly. The total value of Arab oil exports, which had been $212 billion in 1982, fell to $95 billion by 1987. Petrodollar aid transferred among Arab states dropped correspondingly. At first the oil-poor, heavily populated states tried to compensate by borrowing abroad. Jordan built up $8 billion in foreign debt; Morocco, $20 billion; Algeria, $25 billion; Egypt, $50 billion; and Iraq, $80 billion. But within a few years most Arab states had reached the limits of their credit with foreign lenders.

By the late 1980s, it was no longer possible to sustain the expenses involved in propping up the Arab state system. Just servicing existing debts crippled the economies of the poorer states, draining their hard currency revenues. Even the richest Gulf states began to run budget deficits and dip into their cash reserves. Across the Arab world, right-wing monarchies and left-wing military dictatorships faced a crisis of rule. Whatever popularity these regimes had acquired in the struggle against colonial occupation had long since evaporated. The lavish state patronage that had allowed them to maintain their authority was sapped by a growing economic crisis. Increasingly, the mass of Arabs saw their rulers as ideologically bankrupt, politically corrupt, and socially alien.

The Arab state system was eroded and fragile. From 1987 onward, each of the Arab countries began to react — in different ways — to that new reality. Three different styles of reaction prevailed, according to the needs and assets of each country. Kuwait, Jordan, and Iraq exemplify the three types of reaction.

Kuwait: Getting Out

During the 1970s, the Kuwaitis had been among the more imaginative of the rich Gulf states. Rather than spend the bulk of their cash on public works and subsidies, they had set aside $100 billion in two huge reserve funds to finance the needs of future generations. Many of these funds were invested in stocks abroad: British Petroleum and Hoechst metals, to name a few. In the 1980s, the Kuwaitis discovered they were actually earning more from these investments than from oil exports.

That discovery suggested a way for Kuwait to deal with the crisis of the Arab state system. Kuwait's rulers dreamed of turning their country into a Middle Eastern analogue of South Korea: economically linked to the West and defended by American power.

Economically, the Kuwaitis decided to expand and

consolidate their investments in the West. For this, they needed more cash fast. They drastically reduced the aid they dispensed to their foreign neighbors, rebuffing Jordanian requests for emergency economic assistance and notifying Iraq that they still expected repayment of more than $10 billion lent during the war with Iran. They increased their petroleum exports, exceeding their OPEC production quota and driving down the price of oil, in a frantic search for cash.

Politically, too, they began to contemplate closer ties with the West. They believed that Iraq, in the end, had failed to defend them from Iran. Instead they thought that America, through its agreement to reflag Kuwaiti tankers and its naval intervention in the Gulf, was the force that cowed Khomeini. They paid less attention to the Arab League and more to the Gulf Cooperation Council, a regional security alliance fostered by Saudi Arabia. They began to admire the Saudi "special relationship" with the United States.

The Kuwaitis, and other Gulf regimes, began to exit from the Arab state system. They began to rely more on an American security umbrella. In some ways, they were returning to the conditions of the 1960s, when Great Britain protected the Gulf states from their hungry neighbors.

The poorer Arab states were not happy about the development, and their resentment toward Kuwait and the rich states grew. They had no big cash assets; they faced an immediate economic crisis. Their choices were exemplified by Jordan.

Jordan: Economic Austerity

In 1988 conditions in Jordan were already desperate. The country needed $700 million in hard currency each year just to service its foreign debt and another $800 million to cover its trade deficit. Aid from Arab states, which had run $2 billion annually in the early 1980s, had dwindled to less than $200 million a year. The economy was slowing and the dinar was losing its value.

By early 1989 the Jordanian government no longer had enough money to keep repaying its debt. It was forced to turn to the Paris Club to arrange rescheduling. But the Paris Club would not act until the International Monetary Fund certified that the Jordanians were taking measures to strengthen their economy. So Jordan had to negotiate with the IMF, which insisted upon its usual austerity program: the currency had to be devalued, the budget cut, and consumer subsidies eliminated.

In April 1989 Jordan began to implement the austerity plan, announcing massive cuts in public spending and increases in the prices of cigarettes, gasoline, electricity, milk, and bread. The immediate result was a week of the worst rioting the kingdom had ever seen.

To halt the rioting, King Hussein sacked his prime minister and promised new elections. When the elections were held that fall, radical Islamist candidates won a clear plurality.

In most of the poorer Arab states, energetic Islamist movements wait in the wings. The oldest opponents of the Arab state system, they have developed an elaborate ideology that criticizes the ruling elites for their foreign ties, their corruption, and their injustice to their downtrodden subjects. They are experts at grassroots organizing, using mosques, medical clinics, and student organizations to propagate their program. They are not generally hidebound clerics like the Iranian ayatollahs, but young postmodernists who rejected Western culture after flirting with it. They are dedicated and effective.

The Islamists are a significant force in most Arab countries and are well positioned to exploit the anger aroused by economic adjustment programs. They prospered in Tunisia and Morocco after the bread riots of 1984, took power in the Sudan after the economic collapse of 1985, and swept the municipal elections in Algeria after the government adopted an economic austerity program in 1988.

Obviously economic adjustment is so dangerous a policy that Arab leaders have adopted it only when all other choices are closed. Some Arab states, like Egypt, Algeria, and Iraq, still have enough influence in regional affairs that they have been able to attempt a different strategy: to try to reconstruct the Arab state system. That is what Iraq has been attempting to do.

Iraq: Rebuilding a Streamlined System

Despite its domestic oil resources, Baghdad needed as much economic help as any of the poorest Arab states. Iraq had spent more than $241 billion prosecuting war with Iran (more than it had earned from oil exports since they began in the 1930s) and needed billions more to repair the damage. It had already borrowed heavily, and repayments on foreign debt consumed more than $4 billion a year. Iraqi citizens, having tolerated austerity during the war, insisted on a tangible increase in their standard of living.

Saddam Hussein desperately wanted to keep the Arab state system alive. He told his richer neighbors he still deserved their aid because his army kept Iran at bay. He began to hint that he would use his military to challenge Israel, if only the other Arab states would continue to foot his bills.

At first he put his case across peaceably. He recruited Egypt, Jordan, and the Yemen to join him in forming an Arab Cooperation Council to lobby the rich Arab states for more aid. To lend credence to his campaign, he began to cultivate ties to the poorest groups of Arabs: Palestinians in the refugee camps, Mauritanians, the Sudanese.

Saddam could have gotten most of the concessions he wanted from Kuwait through a few military maneuvers on its border and some hardball negotiations. But he knew that the process would be long and painful. He decided instead to gamble on resolving all these problems at once with a demonstration of his power: he invaded Kuwait.

But his entreaties went unanswered. The Kuwaitis and the United Arab Emirates continued overpumping oil, undercutting his revenues. The Saudis and Kuwaitis refused to forgive his debts. By May 1990 Saddam had changed his tone and suggested that if the Arab state system could not be held together voluntarily, he would hold it together by force.

Saddam could have gotten most of the concessions he wanted from Kuwait through a few military maneuvers on its border and some hardball negotiations. But he knew that the process would be long and painful and that it would be followed by slower negotiations with the Saudis, and even more laborious talks with the distant emirates. He decided instead to gamble on resolving all these problems at once with a demonstration of his power: he invaded Kuwait.

In one way, the Iraqi invasion of Kuwait eased the crisis of the Arab system: it doubled oil prices. But even in the richest Gulf states, the doubling of oil prices will not create the kind of funds that might be used to resurrect the old Arab state system. In real (inflation-adjusted) terms, the price of oil still stands below its 1980 level. Yet the price of security in the Arab World has risen dramatically.

Saudi Arabia, for example, may earn a $25 billion windfall from oil exports over the next year. But the prospect of a Gulf war has also scared off an anticipated $10 billion of foreign investment. The kingdom may al-ready have spent $8 billion to $10 billion resettling 200,000 Kuwaiti refugees, bailing out local businesses distressed by the crisis, and defraying the costs of Asian workers fleeing the Gulf. It will also spend more than $10 billion supporting the American military deployment in the region.

Since the invasion, the Saudis have wrestled with the same security dilemma that confronted the Kuwaitis. Some figures inside the royal family think that the American deployment itself foreshadows the solution of their security problems. They are trying to entice Washington into making a long-term commitment to the kingdom, involving permanent bases, more advanced weapons for the Saudi armed forces, and a formal military alliance of the two countries. To make themselves a more attractive ally for America, they have toyed with the idea of creating quasi-democratic institutions.

But a permanent American presence in the Gulf frightens many in the region. The Iranians and Syrians have already announced that, over the long run, they consider American troops more of a threat than Iraq. Many Arabs would see such an alliance as an exercise in old-fashioned imperialism, with America allying itself with local despots to preserve its access to oil. Even conservative Saudis are worried about the local social changes that might be galvanized by an intimate relationship with America.

Thus other members of the Saudi royal family would rather limit the kingdom's American entanglements and rely instead on Arab allies for its security. They have been delighted that Egypt, Syria, and Morocco have contributed troops for their defense. They note that while America can deter formal armies from invading the kingdom, other Arab states can do more to protect it from subversion by tribal guerrillas, emigré dissidents, or military cabals.

Plenty of states are willing to supply *condotierre* for the Saudis. At the beginning of 1990 Egypt was immersed in a paralyzing economic crisis and was contemplating an IMF-dictated austerity program. Cairo's solidarity with Saudi Arabia in the Gulf crisis has earned it direct aid from the Gulf and forgiveness of $7.1 billion in American military debt, and revenues from its modest oil exports have risen. But that does not mean that Egypt will enjoy the kind of prosperity it had during the heyday of the Arab state system. Its increased revenues barely offset the costs the Gulf crisis has imposed on Egypt: the loss of billions of dollars in income from emigré workers in Iraq, tourist receipts, and Suez Canal tolls.

Many of the oil-poor Arab states have been hit much harder than Egypt. A million Yemeni workers, who supplied most of their country's hard currency, have been sent home from Saudi Arabia. Jordan has been devastated. Over the next year Amman is expected to lose $660 million in Iraqi debt repayments, $250 million in transit business, $230 million in tourist business, and

$180 million in oil grants. The total bill is projected to be $2.1 billion — more than half the country's gross domestic product. Many observers fear King Hussein may lose his throne before Saddam Hussein loses his.

It is always dangerous to make any predictions about the Middle East. But in conditions of economic collapse, dissolving security arrangements, and rising domestic discontent, it seems a safe bet that the region is heading into an era of renewed turmoil. Coups, interstate feuds, and even Islamist revolutions seem likely prospects.

Potentially the most unstable state in the region is Iraq. We do not yet know how much damage the international embargo and the looming war may do to the country, but it is clear that Saddam Hussein has committed economic suicide. Baghdad has already lost its oil receipts for this year and swallowed the costs of another massive military mobilization. So long as Saddam is in power the country cannot expect rescheduling of its debts, much less new loans. And foreign firms, critical to Iraq's planned reconstruction, are unlikely to invest in a country where their employees might be made "guests by force" at any moment.

None of this bodes well for regional security. Traditionally, the Gulf states have played Iraq and Iran off against each other in a balance of power. If Iraq lapses into anarchy, who would offset the power of the Islamic Republic? If Saddam does survive, will he accept the mantle of Nasser and lead the oil-poor Arab states in another cold war against the Gulf monarchies?

The United States did not create the current crisis in the Arab World. Even if the Iraqis withdraw from Kuwait, the crisis will not be over. Yet whether or not we go to war in the Gulf will have an effect, tempering or aggravating the imbroglio. If we urge Arab to fight Arab, we may revive the Arab cold war. Every Iraqi our troops kill will provide fresh ammunition for the Islamist campaign to expunge Western influence in the region. If we demolish Iraq, we may clear the way for a resurgence of Iranian power. There is no elegant solution for the crisis of the Arab system. We had better start thinking seriously about how we are going to live with it.

It is always dangerous to make any predictions about the Middle East. But in conditions of economic collapse, dissolving security arrangements, and rising domestic discontent, it seems a safe bet that the region is heading into an era of renewed turmoil. Coups, interstate feuds, and even Islamist revolutions seem likely prospects.

Brotherly Hate

Gulf Crisis Underscores Historical Divisions In the Arab 'Family'

Geraldine Brooks
And Tony Horwitz
Staff Reporters of The Wall Street Journal

Stress Caused by Iraq Attack Renews Region's Grudges And Shifts Some Alliances

Is Arafat on a Banana Skin?

Libya's Col. Moammar Gadhafi certainly wasn't about to take the risk.

Arriving at the airport in Casablanca last summer for an Arab League summit, the colonel eyed a traditional welcoming platter of camel's milk and dates, picked up one date as if to eat it, then slipped it into his pocket. Few of the other Arab kings, presidents and emirs arriving on the tarmac were inclined to risk the untested food.

When Arab leaders gather to demonstrate brotherhood, the paradigm is Cain and Abel. Jordan's King Hussein travels with a private chef, and not just because he's a picky eater. He was 15 when he watched a Palestinian gun down his grandfather at the Al Aqsa mosque in Jerusalem. But bodyguards and food-tasters are no bar to florid proclamations that "the great Arab heart beats as one."

In speaking of the ties that bind them, Arabs constantly invoke the image of family. The current Gulf conflict, they say, is a squabble between brothers, best settled behind closed doors. "Fraternal Iraq" was how Egyptian President Hosni Mubarak referred to Baghdad at last Friday's summit in Cairo—before ordering his own troops in to protect Saudi Arabia. Saddam Hussein depicts his midnight raid on Kuwait as reuniting an Arab family shattered by colonialism.

A Different Day

To Western ears, such cant sounds cynical. But to many Arabs, it resonates back 1,000 years, to a lost age when unity and greatness were indeed real. Dreams of Arab brotherhood also feed on the resentment bred during intervening centuries, when foreign armies, from the Crusaders to the Israelis, humiliated Arabs and carved up their land.

Saddam Hussein's action has exposed these fault lines in the region, just as revolution in Eastern Europe has laid bare old feuds between nations and ethnic groups. When the sand settles on the current Gulf crisis, these historical tensions will remain, leaving the Arab world in greater flux than it has been since World War I. "Saddam," says Palestinian political scientist, Sa'eb Erakat, "may have opened the gates of hell in the Middle East."

The very notion of a monolithic Arab nation has always contained elements of Western simplification, Arab fantasy and Israeli propaganda (20 hostile nations encircling the tiny Jewish state, like Indians attacking a wagon train). While there have been flashes of modern accord—in the 1960s, under the charismatic leadership of Egypt's Gamal Abdel Nasser—the Gulf flare-up shows how deep the divisions go. A short list of Arab hates reads like an adaptation of the Tom Lehrer song, "National Brotherhood Week": The Iraqis hate the Syrians, the Yemenis hate the Saudis, the Jordanians hate the Kuwaitis—and everybody hates the Jews.

Varied Life

Such enmities are inevitable in a culture so vast and varied. Arab territory spans five time zones and is home to some 185 million people; Casablanca is closer to Boston than it is to Oman. Kuwait has a per capita income of $23,000; Yemen's is about $500.

Most Arabs are Moslem, but there also are some 10 million Christians, including the Iraqi foreign minister, Tariq Aziz, and the radical Palestinian leader, George Habash. At a synagogue in downtown Baghdad, Jews still gather in prayer, and there are thousands of Jews in Yemen, Syria and North Africa. Ethnically, the region includes blue-eyed Berbers, black Nubians, Kurdish tribesmen and fair-haired Circassians.

At its most basic, to be Arab means to speak Arabic. But while the classical, written tongue of the Koran is uniform, dialects are so varied that an Iraqi talking to a Libyan is roughly like a Scottish shepherd speaking to a Mississippi farmer. Palestinians living in Tunisia often speak to their neighbors in French, just to be understood.

For Westerners, time spent in the Arab world leaves contradictory impressions: There is the impoverished Palestinian family that piles a guest's plate with the choicest morsels; and then the handless corpse of a pregnant nurse, butchered by fellow Palestinians who said she collaborated with Israel. There are evening strolls along the Tigris River in Baghdad, where the only danger is stumbling on an embarrassed couple kissing; and then the stench of the desert battlefield as trucks driven by heedless Iraqi soldiers grind tread marks into a mass of fresh Iranian corpses.

A language that gave the world algebra also has bequeathed it the word "assassin," which originally referred to hashish-eating fanatics who murdered Christians. "Infidel" is one of the most common words in the Koran, never far from another noun, "hellfire." To die in holy war—which Saddam Hussein has called on fellow Arabs to wage against Iraq's enemies—is to gain quick entry to heaven. Yet the chances of being murdered in the Arab world are 30 times less than in America.

Saddam Hussein epitomizes the dark side of the Arab world, one which the West has too often taken for the whole. The Iraqi president doesn't make any secret of his attachment to guns, torture and poison gas. His speeches are riddled with references to plucked eyes and chopped limbs. Asked what Saddam Hussein would have become had he been born into a middle-class American family, one Iraq expert responds, "either a surgeon or a mafia don."

James Zogby, head of the Arab American Institute, likens Saddam Hussein's appeal to that of the black American preacher, Louis Farrakhan. Both speak to "a very angry, very alienated constituency," he says. Continuing the ghetto analogy, he says that for many Arabs, Saddam Hussein "is the baddest brother in town. He's tough, he's strong and nobody owns him. Many people like that." Unfortunately, in Mr. Zogby's view, "Saddam is a loose cannon, not a savior."

The Arab anger President Hussein has tapped, and the dream of a potent and united Arab world, finds its roots in the Middle East of the 7th Century. Before Allah revealed Islam to a Mecca camel merchant named Mohammed in 610, the term "Arab" referred only to the scattered tribes of the Arabian peninsula. But in the century that followed, the prophet's disciples burst out of Arabia on camel and horseback, driving east into India, and northwest as far as central France. Moslem conquests continued for centuries; pirates from Algiers even came ashore in Iceland. Though roughly one-sixth of the world's population is Moslem, only one out of five Moslems is Arab.

House of Islam

Between roughly 750 AD and 1050 AD, the Arab domain was bigger than the Roman Empire at its peak. While Saxons and Franks fought over feudal Europe, scholars in Damascus, Cairo and Baghdad translated Aristotle, and Arab doctors developed an inoculation against smallpox. Ibn Battuta, the Arab Marco Polo, traveled 73,000 miles in the 14th century without venturing much outside the Dar al-Islam, or House of Islam.

For Moslems of this period, nation and race were unimportant; the only distinction that mattered was that between believers and infidels—the sole important distinction for many Moslems today. Europeans, according to a 10th century Arab geographer, were "more like beasts than men." Europe, of course, was contemptuous of Arabs as well; in Dante's Inferno, Mohammed occupies the eighth circle of hell, not far from Satan.

The Arab world's golden age ended in feuds and foreign invasion: first by Crusaders, then by Mongols and then by Ottoman Turks, who by the mid-16th century had made most of the Arab world its vassal. It is this era of Arab history, and the European domination that followed, that created many of the tensions being played out in the Gulf today. Haunting monuments to past glory are everywhere: the pillars of the Queen of

The Roots of the Pan-Arab Dream

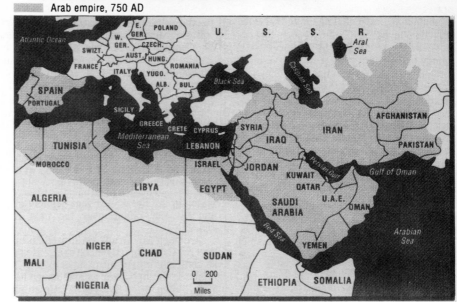

Arab empire, 750 AD

Sheba's temple in Yemen, the ruins of Babylon in Iraq, the soaring mosques of Cairo. Writes the Arabist, W.C. Smith: "The Arab sense of bygone splendor is superb."

So is the sense of betrayal. If Arabs seem uneasy at the sight of U.S. troops landing in the desert, it is because they have every reason to distrust the West. During World War I, Arabs were victims of one of history's most blatant double deals. The ruler of Mecca, great-grandfather of Jordan's King Hussein, offered to help the British against the Turks in exchange for Arabian independence. His sons set off with T.E. Lawrence on the military adventures so romantically depicted in the film, "Lawrence of Arabia."

Drawing the Map

In secret, however, Britain and France crafted a scheme to carve up the Arab world between them. In the end, France (which already held much of North Africa) took what is now Syria and Lebanon while Britain added the newly created mandates of Palestine, Jordan and Iraq to its holdings in Egypt, Sudan, Oman and Aden. Winston Churchill used to boast that he created Jordan one Sunday afternoon with the stroke of a pen.

By World War II, Jews were pouring into Palestine, fleeing Hitler. To Arabs, these Europeans looked like yet another wave of colonial usurpers. Arabs resisted the immigration in a conflict continuing to this day.

To appreciate how deeply the presence of Israel is felt, it is necessary only to turn on the television news in half a dozen Arab capitals. The land mass that the rest of the

world knows as Israel often doesn't exist, either on maps or in official parlance. In some states it is the "Zionist entity" run by "the terrorist Yitzhak Shamir." Although Jordanian and Israeli farmers gaze at each other across the narrow Jordan River, there isn't any phone, telex or postal contact between the two countries.

After King Hassan of Morocco met with Israel's Shimon Peres, Col. Gadhafi of Libya donned a white glove before greeting the King, so he wouldn't touch what he considered Zionist-tainted flesh. Even now, as Arab troops face off against Iraq, Arabs acknowledge that a single Israeli bombing raid on Iraq would force Arab nations to rally behind Saddam Hussein.

America's unwavering support for Israel pains Arabs, especially those who spent their student years in the U.S. "We get to know Americans, how fair they are, friendly and warm, and then we see all that fairness vanish when it comes to Israel," says U.S.-educated Saad Eddin Ibrahim, an Egyptian academic. Many Arabs see the Gulf conflict as yet another example of the U.S.'s double standard. They say the U.S. is resisting Iraq with a resolve never shown during the Israeli invasion of Lebanon and Israel's long occupation of Palestinian land.

Arab discomfort with the West is cultural as well. Arab students often are repelled by the crime, drugs and relaxed sexual mores of the West, and are only too happy to get home to the conservative certainties of their societies.

And certainties they are. According to the opening of the Koran, "there is no doubt in this book." Islam has never undergone a reformation. In Saudi Arabia, women aren't allowed to drive and men are herded to prayer by stick-wielding police from the "Committee for the Propagation of Virtue and the Prevention of Vice." Even liberal Egypt has banned a book by its Nobel Prize winner, Naguib Mafouz, because it indirectly questions Islam.

Mideast analysts have long focused on Islamic fundamentalism and the Arab-Israeli conflict as the big risks to peace in the region. But the current crisis wasn't provoked by either: It is about money and borders. So far, Islamic fundamentalists have divided along national lines; in Egypt, they have condemned Iraq, while in Jordan they have cheered it. However, all the fundamentalists deplore U.S. involvement in the region.

Driving a Wedge

In addition to exploiting deep-seated anti-Western feeling, Saddam Hussein is trying to inflame class tensions, which have brewed ever since drillers first spurted oil onto the Bahraini sands in 1932. That discovery would give rise to the greatest transfer of wealth in human history—from industrialized countries to desert bedouins. By the 1970s, Arabs who had eked out miserable lives on dates and camel milk found themselves able to afford jetloads of fresh Maine lobster and prime rib steak. The Persian Gulf's small ruling families were the greatest beneficiaries, and the West watched—and worried—as they amassed ever more capital.

The oil wealth divided the Arab world. In some cases, tiny city-states became the richest nations on earth while their overpopulated neighbors—many with little or no oil—remained beggars. The rich countries, such as Kuwait, imported Egyptians, Palestinians and others to do their labor and invested much of their wealth in the West, breeding further resentment and class tensions.

It isn't surprising then, that oil has aroused territorial disputes as well. One reason Saddam Hussein's land grab sent tremors through Middle East sands is that border disputes tend to proliferate here. Damascus still dreams of a "Greater Syria" that encompasses territory now belonging to Lebanon, Israel, Jordan and Turkey. Yemen claims southern Saudi Arabia, and both Oman and Saudi Arabia believe pieces of the United Arab Emirates rightly belong to them. The Emirates are so disunited that a map of the nation is a crazy-quilt of sheikdoms, some of which include pockets of land inside their neighbor's boundaries. The map is also riddled with neutral zones and lines marked "border disputed" or "boundary undefined."

A Ruling Minority

Iraq shows how arbitrary colonial boundaries can be. The north is populated by bitter Kurds, promised statehood that never materialized; the south by Shi'ite Moslems with strong links to Iran. And the area in between is home to Saddam Hussein's ruling Sunni minority. President Hussein is so wary of his own countrymen that his ruling clique is composed largely of relatives and friends from his small hometown of Tikrit.

Since the death of Egypt's President Nasser in 1970, the Arab nations, including Iraq, have jostled for his mantle. Each of the major players feels it is the rightful heir to leadership. Saudi Arabia is custodian of Islam's holy places, Mecca and Medina, and owns the world's richest oilfields. Syria has led the struggle against Israel and has as its capital Damascus, the world's oldest continuously inhabited city. Egypt has a population double that of any other Arab country and its capital, Cairo, is the traditional seat of Arab learning.

Now, Saddam Hussein is making his claim for power through military might; for added legitimacy, he says Baghdad was the historical capital of the Arab world and claims direct descent from Mohammed. He also publicly invokes the image of Nebuchadnezzar, best-remembered for sacking Jerusalem and enslaving the Jews.

In turn, Egypt's Mr. Mubarak, whose nine-year presidency has been characterized by cautious plodding, has emerged as the decisive leader of the anti-Iraq camp. If Iraq is faced down, Mr. Mubarak's unhesitating stance is likely to earn him a blank check from grateful Gulf regimes, and even firmer support from the West.

Two of the region's great survivors, meanwhile, are in trouble. The PLO leader, Yasser Arafat, is "a man standing on a banana skin," according to an Arab political analyst. "Arafat is a brilliant man, but we have a saying in Arabic: The slip-up of a brilliant man is worth a thousand deadly errors."

A Fateful Choice?

Mr. Arafat has sided with Iraq, and thereby placed himself in double jeopardy. If Iraq is smashed, Egypt and the Gulf will exact a huge price for Mr. Arafat's disloyalty. At the same time, if Saddam Hussein somehow outlasts the huge forces arrayed against him, his power and prestige could transform Mr. Arafat into an Iraqi puppet; rather than deal with him on the Palestinian issue, negotiators might well go over his head to the Iraqi leader.

Jordan's King Hussein, who has deftly weathered 38 years of crisis-ridden rule, also is playing a dangerous game, using Iraq as a deterrent against Israel and Israel as a deterrent against Iraq. After initially siding with Saddam Hussein, he now has edged toward the moderate Arab camp and risks a rebellion by his own population, which is strongly pro-Iraq.

Syria's Hafaz Assad, an archrival of Saddam Hussein, has been drawn closer to moderates such as Egypt. Syria may become, if not a U.S. ally, at least less of an enemy than it has been for decades. And Saudi Arabia's King Fahd, by making the tough decision to invite U.S. forces into his country, has shown some rare political forcefulness. The sedentary monarch has long been plagued by orthopedic problems, and whenever he failed to show up at heated Arab meetings, Arab wits blamed it on the King's "weak knees." Because he has now taken a firm stance, the King also risks appearing as a U.S. lackey, calling in infidel troops to defend Islam's holy land.

Holy War

But Saddam Hussein's call for a religious "uprising" in Saudi Arabia hasn't yet yielded much response, says Abdala Meer Mosa, a Saudi Shi'ite dissident who usually opposes the monarchy. "I don't think anyone is fooled by Saddam's 'ji'had'—everyone knows he's a butcher, a torturer, and the way he captured Kuwait is something horrible." Mr. Mosa said even dissidents recognize that Saudi King Fahd had little choice but to call for foreign help.

Still, some Arabs worry that U.S. forces, once in, will prove difficult to dislodge. They fear that Saudi Arabia will become one big U.S. base, garrisoned by Americans determined to protect future oil supplies.

These sorts of fears—and the splits they are causing in the Arab world—were apparent at Friday's hastily convened Arab summit, where just 12 of the 20 Arab League members voted to send forces to Saudi Arabia. Iraq, Libya, and the PLO rejected the proposal outright, while key states such as Jordan and Algeria wavered in a meeting so acrimonious that the Kuwaiti emir stormed out and another member of the royal family fainted. At one point an Iraqi reportedly threw a plate of food at the Kuwaiti delegation. Now, with Arab troops arrayed against each other on the Saudi border, the dream of brotherhood seems more distant than ever before.

Egyptians have long told a wistful joke about Arab divisions. A trumpeter stands outside the Arab League headquarters in Cairo. Asked why he is there, the musician says, "I'm supposed to blow my horn when Arab unity comes."

"And how much are you paid?"

"Fifteen pounds a month."

"That's nothing!"

"I know," the trumpeter says. "But it's a lifetime job."

Baghdad Formally Agrees to 'Unjust' U.N. Conditions for Permanent Cease-Fire

TRUCE NOW OFFICIAL

Peacekeepers Ready—No U.S. Order Yet on Pullout of Troops

Alan Cowell

Special to The New York Times

AMMAN, Jordan, April 6—Five weeks after the United States and its allies drove Saddam Hussein's army from Kuwait, Iraq today accepted United Nations terms for a formal cease-fire in the Persian Gulf war.

In accepting the conditions, the National Assembly in Baghdad, which follows Mr. Hussein's dictates, called the arrangement "unjust," but it acknowledged that Iraq had little choice if it was to avert further degradation.

The message of Iraqi acceptance was delivered in New York to the offices of the United Nations Secretary General and to the chairman of the Security Council by the Iraqi representative at the United Nations, Abdul Amir al-Anbari. He told reporters that Iraq accepted the terms "without conditions," but added that he considered the resolution "one-sided and unfair."

Cease-Fire Now Official

Under the terms of the resolution, adopted on Wednesday, the Iraqi acceptance automatically activates a permanent cease-fire between the opponents in the gulf war. But the Pentagon did not immediately issue orders to American forces in the Persian Gulf region proclaiming a formal end to hostilities. A White House spokesman, Roman Popadiuk, said the Bush Administration was waiting for formal notification from the United Nations.

The Iraqi acceptance clears the way for a series of steps to insure the peace. Those include the establishment of a United Nations peacekeeping force, the destruction of Iraq's biological and chemical weapons and its longrange missiles, and the payment of Iraqi reparations to Kuwait for damage suffered after the invasion last Aug. 2.

Baker Plans a Tour

Iraq's move will also clear the way for the eventual end to the economic embargo against Baghdad, and it will facilitate the withdrawal of American troops occupying 15 percent of Iraqi territory in the south of the country.

The formal acceptance of the cease-fire comes a day before Secretary of State James A. Baker 3d is to arrive in the Middle East for a new round of talks with regional leaders. The Secretary met with President Bush today in Houston, but an Administration spokesman said their talks should not be taken as an indication that some fresh diplomatic move was in the works.

The Iraqi acceptance is a major diplomatic milestone in the campaign begun by the United States and its allies last August to expel Iraqi forces from Kuwait and strip President Hussein of the military power that made his army the most feared in the Arab world.

But the allied campaign against President Hussein has not ended the Iraqi leader's hold on power. He still appears firmly in control and his army has apparently quashed rebellions by Kurds in the north of Iraq and Shiite Muslim dissidents in the south.

Hundreds of thousands of Kurds continued to flee from the Iraqi Army today fearing reprisals after the revolt in the north. In Baghdad, the Iraqi leader fired his Defense Minister and replaced him with a high-ranking son-in-law, sharpening the nepotistic profile of a government that has come to depend increasingly on clan and blood ties as the gulf crisis has unfolded.

The United States, which has declined to give the rebels direct military aid, has announced that starting on Sunday, American helicopters with Air Force cover will drop nonmilitary supplies to Kurds stranded in northern Iraq. Other Kurdish refugees continued to enter Iran, which called again today for increased international aid.

A Rubber Stamp

The vote in the 250-seat Iraqi Parliament accepting the Security Council resolution was said by Iraqi officials to be 160 to 31, although the numbers, like the assembly itself, represent little more than window-dressing for decisions of the Supreme Revolutionary Command Council, which met under Mr. Hussein's chairmanship last night.

"While declaring that this resolution is unjust, they have found there was no other choice than to accept it in order to defeat the American-Zionist plot," said the parliament speaker, Saadi Mehdi Saleh, referring to what Baghdad depicts as an American and Israeli plot to destroy Iraq. Drawing on Koranic texts, he said, "We must sometimes, for our own good, accept that which displeases us."

The allied air war that preceded the late February ground offensive into Iraq and Kuwait destroyed much of Iraq's infrastructure—including roads, bridges, oil refineries, waterpurification plants, electricity-generating stations and communications networks. To rebuild them and thus try to restore the regime's credibility, Iraq needs to free itself of the economic and other sanctions imposed after Baghdad's invasion of Kuwait.

But Security Council Resolution 687, approved by the Security Council last Wednesday and accepted by the Iraqi parliament today, makes economic regeneration conditional on the destruction of Baghdad's chemical, biological and nuclear weapons potential under United Nations supervision.

Until those capabilities are destroyed, a trade ban remains in force, and until Iraq can resume oil exports, it has no way of earning money to finance its own reconstruction. At the same time, the 20-page resolution mortgages part of Iraq's oil revenues to pay reparations to Kuwait and holds it responsible for environmental damage caused by its destruction of Kuwaiti oil wells.

The resolution also demands that Iraq withdraw support for international terrorism, respect its border with Kuwait and accept the presence of a United Nations observer force on the frontier. An arms sales embargo remains in force until the Security Council agrees to lift it.

While the terms have been widely condemned in Baghdad as a U.S. ploy to destroy Arab military potential in the fight against Israel, the Iraqi parliament's acceptance today seemed part of an effort by the Baghdad regime to build some sense of normalcy and to secure its own survival after months of crisis, war and insurrection that have brought not only destruction by allied bombing but the worst uprisings in Iraq's modern history.

The authorities say they have put down insurgencies among Shiites in the south and Kurds in the north. But the civil war has left a legacy of bitterness and fear. Iranian officials reported today, for instance, that 300,000 Iraqi Kurds had fled into Iran, braving minefields and harsh conditions to escape anticipated retribution from loyalist Iraqi units known to be vengeful.

On Friday, Baghdad offered a conditional amnesty to rebellious Kurds, but Kurdish rebel officials in Damascus dismissed the offer today as what one rebel spokesman called a "sick joke."

Panoply of Revolt

Confronted by this panoply of revolt, destruction and challenge, President Hussein has abandoned the high-flown Islamic and Arab nationalist polemics of the gulf war in favor of a series of steps and maneuvers, including today's acceptance by Parliament of the cease-fire conditions, supposed to guarantee his own survival and mollify a nation traumatized by the war he brought upon them.

At the highest levels of power, thus, the Iraqi leader has rewarded family loyalty and reinforced the power of his own clansmen. Thus, Brig. Gen. Hussein Kamel, a cousin and son-in-law from the Iraqi leader's native Tikrit region, was given the Defense portfolio today, replacing a military commander, Gen. Sadeh Tuma Abbas.

General Kamel had previously been charged with building Iraq's war machine, now likely to be destroyed under the terms of the resolution.

At the same time, he has appointed one of the few Shiite Muslims in his entourage, Saadun Hamadi, as Prime Minister, entrusting him with the propagation of promises of political reform. Official publications in Baghdad have said Mr. Hamadi will work for political pluralism, press freedoms and individual liberties.

The International Political Economy: Aid, Investment, Trade, and Finance

As we enter the 1990s, the international political economy is operating in an environment of severe stress. Some of the major industrial economies suffer from decline and serious balance of payments deficits. Economies of some LDCs (less developed countries) threaten to disintegrate into bankruptcy. Other LDCs, unwilling to use their export earnings to pay the interest on their outstanding international debts, threaten to send the whole international financial system into a tailspin by defaulting on their loans. The Soviet Union's economy continues to be plagued with inefficiency and declining productivity, and that of the United States with heavy international indebtedness. Internationally held currencies are fluctuating within a wide range against each other, resulting in massive speculation. Protectionism in developed countries continues to threaten to lead to a major contraction of the world economy and to fuel economic warfare. With the formation of the European Community in 1992 nearly complete, the fear of protectionism has been intensified. Countries dependent on the export of commodities are still subject to the dictates of an unpredictable international market system of supply and demand. Faced with lower export earnings and fewer foreign investment dollars, many developing countries have had to cut back on imports essential for economic growth.

Nevertheless, the world economy has demonstrated that it retains considerable strength and an ability to address serious international economic issues.

In 1989 the United States formulated a new approach for dealing with countries indebted to creditor commercial banks in the industrialized countries. Under this new strategy, called "the Brady Plan," the most heavily indebted Third World countries will have a percentage of their outstanding debt to private foreign lenders reduced. Mexico was the first beneficiary of this rethinking of the backbreaking indebtedness from which Third World countries have suffered. The costs of writing off the banks' bad loans will largely be absorbed by the taxpayers of the industrialized states. It is still not clear whether this highly controversial policy will be the solution to the debt problem.

The IMF's insistence on "conditionality" in order for a country to receive an IMF loan has, in a number of cases, proven too rigid and insensitive to the political conditions of the recipient state. The conditions imposed have often been severe, including austerity programs at home, major cuts in luxury consumption by government elites, and decreased consumption of imports. These conditions have, in a number of cases, notably in Africa, led to political instability so severe that governments have been threatened with revolutionary overthrow. The IMF is reviewing "conditionality" and trying to calibrate more carefully its demands with the conditions in the recipient country.

Not all economies are suffering from declining growth rates. Great Britain, for example, has recently experienced strong economic growth. The small island of Taiwan has become the twelfth largest trading country in the world, and has the third largest reserve of international currencies in its central banks. South Korea, Singapore, and Hong Kong, a short time ago considered part of the underdeveloped world, now have some of the world's strongest economies. Japan, well aware of the hostility it has generated by its successful trade practices, is attempting to address issues of concern to the international economic community: protectionism, unfair general trade practices, and the belief that Japan is doing less than its fair share in its foreign aid programs. In 1989, Japan became the world's largest aid donor. Indeed, its economic aid may prove crucial to the economic growth and stability of some of the Eastern European countries.

Which countries are doing best in the competitive international economy? Among the top performers would surely be the United States, Japan, Germany, Taiwan, South Korea, Singapore, and Hong Kong. Although a range of factors are involved, it appears that what all the successful countries have in common is a high level of human resource development (high levels of education), advanced technologies and information systems, and well-tuned financial and commercial sectors.

One problem that continues to concern developing countries is the need to repay foreign loans in internationally acceptable currencies, not local currencies. Because of this, a decision to apply for an external loan must be based on an evaluation of whether the loan will both promote development *and* generate enough foreign exchange to service the external debt. Under any circumstances, this is a gamble. The fact that the LDCs are turning toward self-help measures is certainly a positive step, however, and could do much to mitigate the relationships of dependency that tend to develop when loans are made.

Looking Ahead: Challenge Questions

What alternatives does a poor, developing country have if it wants to develop in today's world? What are the potential problems of accepting external financing and external investment? What are the environmental conditions provided by the international economy that make it so difficult for an underdeveloped and poor country to develop today? What was different forty years ago in the international economic environment that made development relatively easier?

Is there any way that poor countries can develop today without the support of foreign aid and investment? Are countries that accept aid and investment being tied into relationships of dependency with the donor countries? Why or why not? What factors have contributed to the emergence of the NICs (newly industrialized countries) of East Asia? Can the model of development in these NICs be applied in other developing countries?

What might be the impact of the formation of the European Community by 1992 on the international economy's structure? Will it cause problems for any particular countries? Why are certain countries deeply concerned about the formation of the European Community? What kinds of actions are they taking to address their concerns before 1992? Now that most of the Communist regimes of Eastern Europe have been toppled, is it likely that these countries will also be included in a united Europe? How will a united Germany fit in? Does a united Germany act as an additional source of strength for a united Europe, or a powerhouse that will dominate it?

THE EMPEROR'S NEW CLOTHES: THE WORLD BANK AND ENVIRONMENTAL REFORM

Bruce Rich

Bruce Rich is a senior attorney at the Environmental Defense Fund and the director of its international program.

On October 24, 1989, an extraordinary hearing took place in the U.S. Congress. Two and a half years after the president of the World Bank, former congressman Barber Conable, had committed the Bank to sweeping environmental reforms, activists from its most important borrower and donor countries—India and the United States—testified about the Bank's systematic violation of its own environmental and social policies in the Sardar Sarovar dam project in north-central India. The activists objected that the Bank was continuing to finance the project despite five years of noncompliance by project authorities in preparing critical environmental studies and action plans, and in the absence of a resettlement plan for the 90,000 rural poor that the dam's 120-mile long reservoir would displace. Only a month before the hearing, 60,000 people had protested against the World Bank and project authorities near the dam site—the largest demonstration against a development project in the history of India.

Conable's former colleague, James Scheuer (D-N.Y.), the chairman of the House Subcommittee on Agriculture Research, Environment and Natural Resources that called the hearing, was angry and perplexed. "It must be said that the Bank has not institutionalized Barber Conable's rhetoric and Barber Conable's demonstrated concern, both for the environment and for computing the predictable, inexorable environmental damage that these projects will cause," Scheuer stated. Indeed, the Sardar Sarovar project is only one of literally scores of ongoing and proposed World Bank ecological debacles that have come to congressional and international attention over the past two years—debacles that have occurred despite a tenfold increase in Bank environmental staff and a proliferation of new environmental policies, action plans, and task forces. "[The Bank's] written assurances don't amount to hill of beans; they don't exist for practical purposes," Scheuer charged. "Where do the pressures come from," he asked, "pressing down on the World Bank to degrade its own procedures and to bring its own integrity into question?"

How has the Bank come to such an impasse, and where indeed do the pressures come from that have led it there?

The answers to these questions have important implications for the fate of the global environment in the 1990s and beyond. Since 1987 the World Bank has been at the forefront of the most important international development institutions—the multilateral development banks (MDBs) and the International Monetary Fund (IMF)—in initiating environmental reform of its lending policies. At the same time, after a period of relative stagnation, the importance of the MDBs and the IMF as international economic and political arbiters has begun to increase dramatically. In 1988 the World Bank's lending capacity was nearly doubled by a $75 billion capital increase, and together the four MDBs are now lending more than $32 billion annually for programs whose total cost is well over $100 billion. And the IMF, in 1991, will receive the largest capital (quota) increase in its history, probably around 50 percent.

What led the World Bank to undertake environmental reform in the first place was largely the pressures from a coordinated campaign launched by nongovernmental organizations (NGOs) in the United States, Europe, and several developing nations. Starting in 1983, the "MDB Campaign" employed a variety of tactics to pressure the banks, including well-publicized case studies of World Bank-financed ecological disasters in Brazil, India, and Indonesia, congressional and parliamentary hearings in the United States and a number of European nations, and the mobilization of media attention in both the developed and developing world. [See Pat Aufderheide and Bruce Rich, "Environmental Reform and the Multilateral Banks," *World Policy Journal,* Spring 1988.] In May 1987, World Bank President Barber Conable delivered a speech in Washington in which he publicly acknowledged that the Bank had been "part of the problem in the past," and announced that the Bank would mend its ways by greatly increasing its environmental staff and by increasing lending for environmentally beneficial projects.

Environmentalists were guardedly optimistic about Conable's new-found commitment to reform at the time. Now, three years later, it is apparent that the emperor's new clothes bear only faint traces of green. Instead of becoming a leading

From *World Policy Journal,* Spring 1990, pp. 305-329. Copyright © 1990 by the World Policy Institute, 777 United Nations Plaza, New York, New York 10017.

environmental lender, the Bank has become an arena where the political, practical, and theoretical difficulties of reconciling economic development with ecological sustainability are most glaring. The Bank continues to stress its commitment to the environment, but deep institutional and political contradictions prevent it from implementing reform in any meaningful way. Unless these contradictions are resolved, they will continue to inhibit real environmental change.

The Bank's Environmental Reforms: Appearance and Reality

The Bank's environmental reform program followed in large part the outlines of Conable's May 1987 speech. First, the Bank increased its environmental staff; by 1990, some 60 new positions—representing a tenfold increase—had been created. The Bank also launched a series of environmental issues papers and environmental action plans with the purpose of reviewing and addressing environmental problems in the most vulnerable developing countries. Conable also committed the Bank to financing environmental programs of various kinds, the most important of which was a plan to address tropical deforestation through unprecedented increases in forestry lending. Finally, Conable called for greater involvement of environmental and grass-roots NGOs in both borrowing and donor countries in the Bank's operations.

On the face of it, this program reflected much of what NGOs had pushed for. The greatly increased environmental staff was particularly important, since NGOs had hoped that such a staff would finally ensure the implementation of Bank environmental policies, many of which had existed for years. Some of these policies call for the protection of wildlands and cultural sites affected by Bank projects. Others address the social impact of environmental change—for instance, the need for special measures to protect tribal populations in environments affected by development.

Yet as NGOs in the North and the South have encountered more and more Bank-financed ecological debacles, disillusionment with the Bank's environmental reform initiatives has grown. Ironically, the limits of the World Bank's reforms are becoming apparent just as the NGOs are succeeding in promoting similar institutional changes in regional development banks like the Inter-American Development Bank (IDB), and even within the IMF. In January, the IDB announced the creation of a full environmental division with 13 staff members, a change that the IDB had long resisted. Earlier, in November 1989, the U.S. Congress had enacted legislation drafted and promoted by Washington-based environmental groups that requires the secretary of the treasury to promote the creation of an environmental analysis unit in the IMF as well as the initiation of a process whereby the Fund will review prospective lending programs for their impact on the environment and natural resources. Already by February of this year, the Fund's management had indicated to NGOs its willingness to implement the measures suggested in the U.S. legislation.

Of course, creating new bureaucratic positions and producing new policies, action plans, and task forces are not difficult for centralized, Washington-based bureaucracies. But such measures by themselves do not guarantee institutional reform and substantive change. In fact, the fate to date of MDB environmental reform bears some similarity to what had hitherto been the most concerted effort to change the Bank: Robert McNamara's top-down revolution in the 1970s to make the World Bank a poverty-oriented institution. Then, as now, the Bank underwent an impressive bureaucratic reorganization and generated an avalanche of policies and papers that appeared to signal a veritable revolution in the institution's mission. When the dust settled, many researchers outside the Bank concluded that the Bank's projects were not benefiting the Third World poor to any greater degree than they had a decade before.

Beneath its self-proclaimed mission of banker to the poor, and behind its new green facade, the Bank is still essentially doing what it has always done: moving large amounts of money to Third World government agencies for capital-intensive projects or—an innovation of the 1980s—for free-market, export-oriented economic policy changes. Although in a speech delivered last September Conable claimed that a third of Bank projects approved in fiscal year 1989 had "significant environmental components," NGOs now realize that this characterization includes mainly projects whose environmental impacts were so severe to begin with that the Bank felt compelled to incorporate some mitigating measures, as well as ostensibly environmental projects whose hasty design undermines prospects for implementation or, astoundingly, are positively destructive. The few environmental projects that NGOs would commend unreservedly, such as a recent $117 million environmental protection and research loan to Brazil, are conspicuous as exceptions. To their dismay, the NGOs are realizing that their very success in promoting conventional institutional changes has resulted in a proliferation of green rhetoric that hides a reality that is largely unchanged. The Washington-based NGOs that have led the campaign fear that they have inspired the creation of a new Orwellian dialect: greenspeak.

The basis for this fear can be well seen by taking a closer look at two of the most critical areas in the Bank's environmental reform program: the Tropical Forestry Action Plan (TFAP) and the Bank's record in dealing with forced resettlement caused by Bank projects. The former is the most important example of the Bank's increased support for new environmental initiatives; the latter is a fair indication of the Bank's recent efforts to implement longstanding environmental policies.

The Tropical Forestry Action Plan. Conable's May 1987 speech emphasized that the most important focus of the Bank's new environmental lending would be to contribute to a global program to support tropical forest conservation—the Tropical Forestry Action Plan. To that end he committed the Bank to increase its forestry lending 150 percent by 1989, and in September 1989 he announced a further tripling of forestry lending through the early 1990s.

6. THE INTERNATIONAL POLITICAL ECONOMY: AID, INVESTMENT, TRADE, AND FINANCE

Tropical deforestation in the late 1980s was, in the view of many in the industrialized world, the most visible and urgent environmental crisis in the Third World. Indeed, several of the most notorious environmental tragedies of the past decade involved massive destruction of rainforests in Brazil and Indonesia, abetted by Bank-financed agricultural colonization schemes. It was not surprising, then, that the major focus of increased environmental lending announced by the Bank in 1987 would be tropical forests. The Bank's commitment to increased lending for forestry through the TFAP is unprecedented: from $138 million in 1987 to as much as $800 million annually by 1992.

The Tropical Forestry Action Plan was originally conceived in the mid-1980s by the Bank, the Food and Agriculture Organization of the United Nations (FAO), the United Nations Development Programme (UNDP), and the World Resources Institute (WRI), a Washington-based environmental think tank. The TFAP sought to alleviate pressures causing deforestation in the Third World by mobilizing $8 billion from multilateral and bilateral aid agencies over a five-year period for a variety of forestry and agricultural activities that include the building of forestry and environmental institutions, supply of fuelwood needs, conservation of protected areas and vulnerable watershed regions, and support of forest management for industrial uses.

The World Bank's involvement in the TFAP is a revealing and shocking indicator of the gap between rhetoric and reality in the Bank's self-proclaimed greening. Already by 1986, a number of Third World NGOs such as Friends of the Earth in Brazil and the Malaysia-based Asia-Pacific Peoples' Environmental Network (APPEN) were publishing urgent protests maintaining that the TFAP was basically a fraud. It had been prepared, they alleged, without any significant consultation or involvement of NGOs and local communities in tropical forest countries. Worse, it appeared mainly to be a plan to promote traditional, export-oriented timber industry investments camouflaged by small components for environmental purposes. Third World NGOs were particularly outraged because the plan seemed to blame the poor for the destruction of tropical forests while promoting investments to open up large areas of pristine forest for exploitation, rebaptizing such projects as "sustainable forestry."

WRI attempted belatedly to address many of the criticisms, but following the Bank's commitment in 1987 to increased funding of the TFAP, the plan gathered seemingly unstoppable momentum to become the most ambitious environmental aid program ever conceived. By the end of 1989, 62 developing nations had requested forestry-sector aid under the TFAP and 21 nations had already completed forestry-sector reviews (pre-investment surveys), with the World Bank as the leader or a major participant in eight. The plan is well on track to mobilize billions of dollars for forestry projects in every country in the world with remaining tropical forests.

Environmentalists around the world now fear that an ecological Frankenstein has been unleashed. The World Rainforest Movement—a Malaysia-based coalition of mainly Third World NGOs—prepared a critique in February of six completed national TFAP plans—for Peru, Guyana, Cameroon, Tanzania, Nepal, and Colombia. The study concluded that in most of these cases the forestry investments proposed would dramatically accelerate the rate of deforestation through increased logging; in no instance was it found that these investments would actually reduce deforestation. And in February, Prince Charles publicly criticized British support for the TFAP, which he said amounts to little more than a plan to chop down trees.

One of the first TFAP projects to be funded by the Bank (with a sizable contribution from West Germany) is a $23 million forestry and fisheries scheme for Guinea. Yet, as World Wildlife Fund International discovered in late 1989, the so-called "forest management and protection" component of the project actually amounts to a deforestation scheme: the Bank's money will help support the construction of 45 miles of roads in or around two humid forest reserves totalling 150,000 hectares, of which some 106,000 hectares are still pristine rainforest. Worse, hidden in the fine print of the "management and protection" section of the Bank's project document is its real thrust: two-thirds of the remaining 106,000 hectares of rainforest are to be opened for timber production. As a result of these findings, in late 1989 WWF mobilized eight national WWF organizations in North America and Europe to lobby the World Bank's executive board against the project. WWF's efforts were too late, however, and the project was approved in January, though minutes of the board meeting reveal the bewilderment of some of the Bank's executive directors. They queried Bank staff on the WWF allegations, which were mostly repetitions of what the Bank's own project appraisal report had stated. The Bank staff replied that deforestation would proceed uncontrolled without the project and that with the project logging could be controlled within "sustainable" limits.

This rationale—that the environmental situation would be worse without Bank intervention—is a particularly specious one, and has been proffered in the past to justify a number of the worst Bank-financed environmental disasters, including rainforest colonization schemes in Brazil and Indonesia. On the contrary, it is often the large infusions of foreign exchange, rapid construction of infrastructure such as roads, and an international stamp of approval provided by the Bank that ensure that a government's environmentally destructive plans become a physical reality within the shortest time possible.

Other projects in the TFAP pipeline appear, incredibly, to be even more destructive than the Guinea loan. For instance, the Bank is preparing a $30 million loan for the latter half of 1990 that will support a $167 million TFAP investment program prepared by the FAO for Cameroon. The program's principal stated goal is to make Cameroon the largest forest-product exporter in Africa by the 21st century. To accomplish this will require opening up nearly 14 million hectares (an area the size of Florida) of pristine tropical forest in southeastern Cameroon. The TFAP proposal concedes that getting the timber out will require the construction of a major penetration road to the sea, for which the Cameroon government has already approached Japanese donors. The plan provides only $4.4 million to address what it admits is the major domestic pressure on tropical forests in the country—fuelwood demand. Even more startling, it notes that given stiff international competition for timber exports, especially from Asia, the government may have to grant special tax incentives to stimulate production. This contradicts recent studies published by the World Bank and World Resources Institute that rightly emphasize the economic folly of tax holidays and subsidies for logging and deforestation.

The public pressure orchestrated by WWF and other NGOs in several countries over the Guinea loan has caused considerable concern among a number of the Bank's executive directors. The German executive director and several bilateral aid agencies have come under strong domestic attack for their support of the TFAP in general and the Guinea loan in particular. Earlier in 1989, 88 West German nongovernmental groups, including all of the country's major environmental NGOs, endorsed a "Rainforest Memorandum" to their government that condemned the TFAP.

In January, the U.S. executive director requested from the Bank's staff a copy of the draft project appraisal report for the next major World Bank forestry loan to Africa—an $80 million project for the Ivory Coast. NGOs fear that the loan will again support a national forestry sector whose main priority is to accelerate timber exports in an unsustainable fashion. The Bank's staff refused to give the report to the U.S. director—the representative of the Bank's largest shareholder—and the decision was backed by the senior vice-president for operations. This is not surprising for an institution that typically denies its executive directors—the ultimate source of authority according to the Bank's charter—access to most project documents and reports until the final appraisal report is ready, which is usually no more than two weeks before they are asked to approve a project.

In January, another troubling example of Bank efforts to fund environmental projects came to the board's attention—this time in the now infamous Polonoroeste program in northwest Brazil, where previous Bank loans totalling $457 million for road building and agricultural colonization led to the influx of 500,000 landless colonists in the early 1980s and the highest deforestation rate in Brazil. Now the Bank is preparing $317 million in new loans to control the environmental devastation in the region, which is larger than Great Britain. A Brazilian negotiating team arrived in Washington in mid-January for final consultations on the first loan, the $167 million Rondonia Natural Resources Management project.

This is one of the first Bank projects ever to be justified on purely environmental grounds, with no economic rate of return. The project finances an "agro-ecological zoning plan" for the entire state of Rondonia, setting aside large areas as Indian reserves, protected natural areas, and so-called "extractive reserves" managed by local rubber tappers that are also protected forest areas to be used for sustainable extractive harvesting of rainforest products such as Brazil nuts and rubber. A second, similar loan of $150 million is in preparation for agro-ecological zoning in Mato Grosso state. Others may follow.

Although highly commendable in theory, the Rondonia project, environmentalists argue, is actually weaker in its implementation and monitoring provisions than the original 1981 Polonoroeste loan, even though some of its environmental goals are the same. For example, the project finances the establishment of new protected areas and requires the demarcation of four natural protected areas and eight Indian reserves that were to have been fully demarcated and protected by the mid-1980s under the terms of the 1981 Polonoroeste loan agreement. While providing still more funds for the protection of these areas, the new Rondonia project lacks any specific timetable or conditions to ensure their complete establishment—timetables and conditions that the first loan required, though they were not followed. Moreover, rubber-tapper organizations complain that they were not consulted and involved in the identification of areas supposedly to be set aside for their benefit. The Bank appears to have learned little from its bitter experiences in Brazil in the 1980s. On January 10, 35 environmental and human rights groups from Brazil, the United States, and 12 other countries sent a letter to the Bank's executive directors urging them to delay consideration of the project until its implementation and monitoring provisions are strengthened.

Forced Resettlement. No single Bank activity has greater immediate social impact than the physical destruction or disruption of rural ecosystems caused by large infrastructure projects such as hydroelectric dams, power plants, and coal mines. The forced resettlement of populations that results from these projects occurs on an enormous scale: as of January an estimated 1.5 million people were being forcibly displaced by over 70 ongoing Bank projects, and proposed projects currently under consideration may displace another 1.5 million.

The World Bank policy on forced resettlement was established in 1980, predating most other Bank environmental directives. It is the most important of the Bank's environmental policies that deal with the social consequences of ecological destruction. Bank policy requires that when it finances a project that will forcibly displace populations, a resettlement and rehabilitation plan must be prepared and implemented by the borrower in a timely fashion, such that the affected population is at least put in a position where it is no worse off and preferably better off than before.

The Bank's tenfold increase in environmental staff—which includes resettlement experts and anthropologists—gave environmentalists and human rights activists hope for an improvement in implementing this policy. But a special hearing of the U.S. Congress Human Rights Caucus on the issue in September 1989 revealed a shocking fact: the Bank's own internal reviews found very few instances in which a population that has been resettled is economically better off than before or has even regained its previous standard of living.

If anything, since 1987 the situation has worsened. Over the past three years NGOs in the North and South have brought to light more and more examples of the Bank's failure to remedy the plight of populations displaced by ongoing projects, some of which are destitute or on the brink of civil disorder. In Java, where some 20,000 people have been displaced by the Bank-financed Kedung Ombo dam, more than 5,000 "development refugees" still refused to move in early 1990, after the reservoir filled, because there had been no consultations with them regarding resettlement. Rather than ensure that a fair resettlement and rehabilitation plan was being implemented, for years the Bank accepted the Indonesian government's assertion that most of the people affected by the project were volunteering to become rainforest colonists in transmigration (resettlement) sites hundreds of miles away in Indonesia's outer islands. The Bank ignored evidence of coercion and intimidation by project authorities, as reported in numerous newspaper articles and in a letter of protest from a leading Indonesian NGO to the Bank's Jakarta office in 1987.

In the case of two dam projects in Africa in the late 1980s, the Bank also ignored the plight of thousands of people aversely affected or displaced. With the Ruzizi II Regional Hydroelectric project, more than 12,500 people in Zaire and Rwanda were expropriated and forcibly resettled with inadequate compensation. Only in 1989—six years after the appraisal of the project—did the Bank acknowledge the problem and undertake to require compensatory measures, which in early 1990 were still not implemented. Similarly, with the Kenya Kiambere Hydroelectric project, 6,000 rural poor were displaced without compensation, and for the past three years the Bank again violated its most basic policies on resettlement by not requiring that the Kenyan government address the situation. As of early 1990, practical measures still have not been taken, though the Bank appears to be finally committed to demanding action from the borrower.

It is in India where popular reaction to the resettlement issue has been strongest. There a nationwide grass-roots NGO campaign has succeeded in mobilizing the public against large infrastructure projects that benefit relatively few people but that displace the poor and harm the environment on which rural communities depend. One project in particular, the Sardar Sarovar dam, located in the Narmada River Valley, has become the focus of a campaign both in India and among NGOs in the United States and Europe. The Bank committed some $450 million in 1985 to the project, whose 120-mile long reservoir, when completed, will forcibly displace more than 90,000 poor rural Indians in three different states. The Bank has also been considering funding a second dam on the Narmada, the Narmada Sagar project, which would displace another 120,000 people. Both projects are part of a series of dams on India's biggest westward flowing river to provide water for irrigation and electric power. The entire Narmada scheme, if carried out, would be the most ambitious river development program in history, involving the construction of some 30 large dams and hundreds of smaller ones, and would forcibly displace as many as 1.5 million people, mainly of tribal, outcaste origin.

The Bank has continued to disburse funds for the Sardar Sarovar project despite numerous delays, construction problems, and the noncompletion of several critical environmental impact studies and action plans that were to have been executed by December 1985. More serious, Bank funding has continued despite the unwillingness and inability of project authorities to prepare a resettlement plan for the tens of thousands of poor farmers and forest dwellers who will be displaced. In 1989, the frustration and desperation of most of the "oustees," as they are called in India, finally boiled over.

On September 28, 1989, more than 50,000 oustees as well as activists from all over India gathered in the Narmada Valley town of Harsud to protest against the Narmada dams and other large Bank-financed projects. Harsud is a settlement of 15,000 people that will be totally inundated by the Narmada Sagar project. The demonstration was timed to correspond with the annual World Bank–IMF meeting in Washington, and occurred two days after a special hearing of the U.S. Congress Human Rights Caucus on the World Bank and forced resettlement, where witnesses denounced the Bank's record in a number of projects, including Sardar Sarovar, Kedung Ombo, and Ruzizi.

Smaller demonstrations in other parts of India preceded the Harsud rally, including one staged three weeks before in downtown Bombay, where activists publicly burned a symbolic World Bank loan agreement for the Sardar Sarovar project. The Indian press views the Harsud meeting as the birth of an Indian "green" movement that consciously links international environmental issues with the local ecological, social, and economic concerns of the Indian rural poor. These poor are often tribal minorities who feel increasingly dispossessed and powerless vis-à-vis a development model that is capital intensive, export oriented, and favors urban and rural elites.

Since most of the projects that forcibly displace populations are in the energy sector—large dams and coal-fired power plants, for example—much forced resettlement could be avoided by investments in energy alternatives that are less disruptive environmentally. In fact, the World Bank itself has commissioned studies that indicate that between one-third and one-half of new demand for electricity in Brazil and India through the year 2000 could be provided through investments in energy conservation and end-use efficiency. In both countries these investments would free up the equivalent of about 20,000 megawatts—equal to the energy generated by at least 10 giant dams or giant coal-fired plants—at less than half the cost of new generating infrastructure. The need to reduce carbon emissions from coal consumption to slow global warming produced by the greenhouse effect should provide further incentive for such investments.

Over the past three years the Bank again has made rhetorical commitments to increased energy efficiency and conservation investments, but the actual changes have been insignificant. For example, in 1988 and 1989, less than 2 percent of World Bank energy and industry loans were for projects that included end-use efficiency as a component;

indeed, the proportion of conservation and efficiency loans in the Bank's energy-sector portfolio was actually higher in the mid-1980s than in more recent years. This gap between rhetoric and reality is one more example that points to deeper institutional problems at the Bank.

The Bank Beset by Contradictions

The Bank's efforts to respond to international pressures for environmental reform have exposed a whole series of contradictions that, when demands on the Bank and multilateral financial institutions were more modest, remained relatively dormant and unexposed. Some of these contradictions are largely internal, others result from conflicting pressures put on the Bank by donors and borrowers, and others appear to be rooted in the nature of the multilateral system itself—especially in its lack of accountability—as well as in current patterns of global economic development, which are often at odds with the requirements of global ecological sustainability.

Internal Contradictions. The first order of Bank contradictions are internal in origin and include a number of classic bureaucratic syndromes, such as a longstanding lack of coordination between the Bank's operations staff, who identify and prepare loans, and its policy, planning and research divisions. The 1987 environmental reforms took place in the context of a larger Bank-wide reorganization that only exacerbated this dichotomy. About half of the new environment staff (approximately 30 positions) was placed in a newly created central Environment Department, but the quality control duties that this department's predecessor had exercised over operations were assigned to four new environmental assessment units that are hampered by limited budgets and staff.

Real power is concentrated even more than in the past in country directors and project officers who actually prepare loans and who have been granted greater autonomy and authority. Thus at times during the past three years the Environment Department has taken on the appearance of a vast paper mill, while the real business of the Bank continued as if on a separate planet called Operations. The environmental policies and plans the Bank is churning out seem impressive. Environmental issues papers are being prepared for most borrowing countries, and, in accordance with one of the pledges Conable made in his May 1987 speech, environmental action plans are being drawn up for 30 nations. But the issues papers often appear to float in their own bureaucratic limbo, since the critical economic planning documents that set the outlines for Bank country lending—country strategy papers and economic memoranda—in large part do not reflect their existence.

It is in Africa where the chasm between Washington paper pronouncements and Third World reality often appears most dizzying. Africa is the Bank region responsible for the greatest volume of environmental issues papers and action plans, and though there are examples of promising projects (a $7 million IDA credit to support the protection of 295,000

hectares of endangered forests in Madagascar is one), they are overwhelmed by the scale of ecological and social atrocities posed by the Tropical Forestry Action Plan and botched resettlement in large dam projects.

The Bank's environmental effectiveness has also been undermined in some cases by the Bank's senior management, which on occasion has overruled the recommendations of its environmental staff. A decision not to incorporate environmental issues papers into country strategy papers, for instance, is said to have been heavily influenced by the Bank's chief economist. And last year, the Bank's Asia region vice-president apparently overruled objections of environmental staff and authorized the preparation of a $250 million loan to India for the Subernekha dam, even though compliance with environmental and resettlement requirements in a previous loan for the project was so abysmal that the loan was officially suspended. The project will forcibly displace 60,000 rural poor.

The lack of internal coordination that inhibits environmental effectiveness is compounded by pressures on operations staff to move money rapidly. Bank staff advance their careers by building up large loan portfolios and keeping them moving, not by slowing down the project pipeline to ensure environmental and social quality. Bank-lending priorities appear more understandable in this light. The bias toward large energy infrastructure projects, for instance, is not irrational given that efficiency and conservation loans are harder to prepare and move less money. Vested interests and government bureaucracies in borrowing countries prefer big dam projects for the same reasons. The situation has only worsened since 1988, when the Bank received a capital increase of $75 billion—the largest in its history—which has nearly doubled its total lending capacity. The Bank is now committed to increasing its annual lending by 50 percent through the mid-1990s, without any increase in its professional staff.

The Bank lobbied its major donors intensely for this capital increase, citing the growing economic and financial crisis in many Third World countries. Nothing could be more embarrassing for the Bank than to finally obtain such a capital increase and not be able to find bankable projects and programs to justify it. This was a real fear in 1989, when lending was halted or reduced for large borrowers such as China, Brazil, and Argentina because of political and economic crises—a situation that intensified pressures to keep money moving to other large borrowers such as India.

The problem of moving money will become even more acute if the Bank phases out its short-term structural-adjustment lending, as a top Bank official recently indicated it will do. Structural-adjustment loans do not finance specific projects but are transfers of funds loaned on the condition that specific macroeconomic policy measures will be adopted. These loans are the Bank's main mechanism for moving large amounts of money rapidly and account for over a quarter of all Bank lending. Thus the phasing out of structural-adjustment lending will put even more pressure on big-project lending and on the Bank's already overstretched environmental staff.

To some degree the Bank's internal contradictions are amenable to institutional reform. Already more budgetary and staff resources are being channelled into the environmental assessment divisions, which are best placed to influence operations. And with sufficient political will, greater progress could be made in integrating environmental studies and policies into country economic and sector work. But to change priorities from moving money quickly to emphasizing the environmental and social quality of projects requires more than greater political will on the part of senior management. Indeed, such efforts, though they would result in marginal improvements, would probably also have the effect of exacerbating the Bank's environmental schizophrenia. This is because of deeper problems that are linked to fundamentally contradictory pressures exerted on the Bank by its member countries.

Contradictory Pressures of Member Governments. The Bank is subject to a number of simultaneous and contradictory pressures from both its developed and Third World members—pressures that, with respect to the Bank's environmental performance, result not only in contradictory actions but in institutional paralysis.

The pressure to lend more money, for instance, is not only the consequence of the propensity of large bureaucracies to measure success in terms of their own growth and expansion. It also comes from the Bank's major donors, and especially from U.S. efforts to involve the Bank and other multilateral institutions in resolving the Third World debt crisis. As a result of this crisis, the 1980s have witnessed an unprecedented net outflow of financial resources from the Third World to industrialized countries that is now running at a rate of $50 billion a year. The United States, particularly under the Baker and Brady debt-crisis plans, has viewed increased multilateral and private lending to heavily indebted nations as a preferable alternative to forgiving large portions of private commercial debt. Thus, the United States encouraged the Bank's movement into structural-adjustment lending in the early and mid-1980s, seeing it as a way to channel more money to heavily indebted nations and at the same time impose conditions that would increase a country's ability to meet its debt-servicing obligations, at least in the short term.

In this regard, there has been a certain convergence of interest between the Bank and the U.S. government. The overall effect of this convergence, however, has been to exacerbate the Bank's tendency to ignore the environmental consequences of its lending. Some of the conditions associated with structural-adjustment loans—such as the reduction of domestic expenditures, currency devaluation, and the increase of exports—often have a negative impact on the environment. They prompt governments to reduce domestic conservation investments and they heighten pressures to exploit resources in an unsustainable fashion in order to increase exports. The Bank has recognized in theory the environmental implications of its adjustment lending, but the exclusion of substantive environmental analysis in its most

important economic planning exercises, such as country strategy papers, bodes ill for practical attempts to incorporate environmental concerns into such lending in any systematic way. In 1989, only five of the Bank's 45 adjustment loans explicitly addressed environmental concerns.

In the end, the solution is to forgive much of the debt. In this way, much of the pressure to ravage the natural resource base will be alleviated and multilateral institutions will be able to play a more constructive role than that of cash conduit to Third World regimes needing to make their next interest payments to New York banks. NGOs have maintained for years, in fact, that massive debt forgiveness would also present an unprecedented opportunity for conservation investments, if debt-relief programs were accompanied by conditions to ensure that some portion of the domestic funds freed up in developing countries were designated for environmental protection. The MDBs could act as facilitators and coordinators of such investments.

Of course borrower countries, too, bear much of the responsibility for the environmental quality of Bank-financed projects. The Bank encounters considerable resistance from some borrowing nations to conditionality of any kind, and particularly to environmental conditionality, which is viewed as both an added cost and as an imposition of the industrialized North's priorities on the South. This resistance is evident in negotiations for individual projects. It is also evident among the Bank's executive directors representing Third World countries. Although they do not have a voting majority at the Bank (the 10 leading industrialized countries control about 65 percent of the vote), some nonetheless resist as a matter of principle attempts to incorporate greater conditionality and oversight in MDB lending, which they maintain is already too heavily conditioned. Not surprisingly, the bigger borrowing nations such as Brazil, India, and Indonesia, which have been subjected to international criticism by the MDB campaign, have been the most vocal opponents of environmental conditionality.

The Bank is acutely sensitive to these pressures, and particularly with respect to its larger borrowers, is reluctant to endanger its "dialogue with host countries" by overly zealous insistence on environmental policies. The Bank's timidity in this regard is well illustrated by its approach to the recent Rondonia Natural Resources Management project. In informal discussions, some Bank directors' staff went so far as to argue that since the earlier 1981 Polonoroeste loan conditions were poorly fulfilled by the Brazilian government, less rigorous demands on the Brazilians the second time around might dispose the government to better compliance.

It is a mistake, however, to assume that either the governments or the societies of developing nations are monolithic. In many governments there are officials who advocate environmental and social measures that equal or even exceed the Bank's standards. And in the civil societies of these countries there can be found even stronger advocates among environmental and social movements, and among disadvantaged minorities such as tribal peoples in India, who suffer a disproportionate share of the adverse effects of large projects and enjoy few of the benefits. Rarely, however, are these advocates able to mount a serious enough challenge to the powerful vested interests inside and outside the government who are often the chief beneficiaries of these projects.

In the case of the Sardar Sarovar dam, for example, the Indian Department of Environment and Forests had originally refused to grant legal clearance for the project because the requisite environmental and resettlement studies had not been completed. The Bank did not allow this to stand in the way, however, and approved the loan agreements anyway. Once the loans were approved, the Environment Department was subjected to tremendous political pressure from agricultural interests in the state of Gujarat and finally from Indian Prime Minister Rajiv Gandhi himself to grant a "provisional clearance" that allowed construction to proceed even though the studies had still not been prepared. Here, as in other instances, Bank support played a crucial role in legitimizing an environmental boondoggle that might otherwise have died a natural death from divided domestic support and insufficient foreign funding.

The Bank argues that its support of projects like Sardar Sarovar is justified because Bank participation can serve to mitigate environmental destruction. In its latest environmental report to the Bank/IMF Development Committee, for instance, the Bank states that "if the project is potentially very damaging to the environment, and if Bank participation could do much to reduce the damage but would not eliminate it entirely, the net gains from participation must be the deciding factor." Over the years this rationale has been used time and time again by the Bank to justify dubious loans. Its true implications are reflected in an off-the-record comment made several years ago by a U.S. Treasury official: "There is no project too destructive, and too costly, that the World Bank will not throw hundreds of millions of dollars at to try to make it better. In fact, the worse the project, the more urgent the justification for the Bank's involvement. Is this any way to run a development institution, let alone a bank?"

Contradictions of the Multilateral System. While the conflicting pressures of member nations may sometimes hamper the Bank's environmental protection efforts, there is another explanation for its conduct that relates to the fundamental character of the Bank and of the multilateral system generally. The Bank, like other multilateral institutions, is not directly accountable to civil society within borrower and donor countries, or even fully to the representatives of its member nations. Moreover, the Bank heavily restricts access to information concerning details of its activities. These practices make scrutiny of the World Bank and other MDBs—which use *public* monies to lend for *public* purposes—extremely difficult, and place serious constraints on efforts to reform them.

The official avenue of accountability in the World Bank, other MDBs, and the IMF lies with the board of executive directors for each of these institutions. The World Bank's charter, for example, states that "all powers of the Bank are vested in the Board of Governors"—who are usually the finance ministers or central bank presidents of each of the Bank's 152 member nations—and most of the powers of the governors are delegated on a day-to-day basis to the Bank's 22 executive directors. The directors approve every loan and every major policy change.

Over the past decade, the executive directors—particularly those representing the United States and a number of European nations—have come under increasing pressure by environmental groups in their countries not only to promote institutional reforms but also to monitor and review individual projects and lending programs of the Bank more closely. But the Bank's management withholds from the executive board access to most of the documents produced by Bank staff in the identification and preparation of projects. Although a project may take over two years to prepare, the directors are given access to appraisal reports on average only two weeks before they are asked to approve a project. The U.S. executive director, E. Patrick Coady, was reminded of his relative powerlessness when, earlier this year, his request for a draft appraisal report of a proposed forestry loan for the Ivory Coast was denied.

The circulation of project preparation documents is restricted on the grounds that they are draft materials and staff would feel constrained in conducting their work impartially if their written opinions were subject to constant supervision by directors representing member countries. While this is a legitimate concern, the Bank and other multilateral institutions have grossly exaggerated its importance relative to the paramount need of the Bank's executive directors to be minimally informed about the projects they are asked to approve.

The lack of access to project documents has serious practical consequences. It means that the principal recourse for detailed information on projects are oral briefings by Bank staff. However, there is no assurance that these briefings will include any significant discussion of project risks and problems that can be found in the more candid documents in the project files—information that is obviously necessary for any critical assessment. These briefings often turn out to be little more than confidence-building sessions in which the directors nervously seek reassurances that the projects are under control, and the Bank staff gladly provides them.

The Bank's charter is ambiguous on the exact status of the directors, which in part explains management's treatment of them as well as the directors' general diffidence. Are the directors Bank officials, whose allegiance is exclusively to the Bank as an institution? Or do they represent the interests of their member countries? The Bank's directors act on the instructions of the countries they represent, but the charter states that "the President, officers and staff of the Bank, in the discharge of their official duties, owe their duty entirely to the Bank and to no other authority." The Bank's Legal Department has done little to clarify this ambiguity; it has asserted that the executive directors are Bank staff and that they owe a duty both to the Bank and to the demands of their country constituencies.

6. THE INTERNATIONAL POLITICAL ECONOMY: AID, INVESTMENT, TRADE, AND FINANCE

If there is a relative lack of Bank accountability to its directors, there is an almost total absence of accountability to the people affected by its projects and to the public in member countries. The Bank withholds all written documents prepared in the planning of projects from the public in both borrower and donor countries, despite the fact that the Bank has been insisting over the past three yeas that it recognizes the importance of involving local NGOs and community groups in its development activities. "Involving local communities in the preparation and implementation of projects that affect them is clearly of great importance for sustained development," the 1989 Bank/IMF Development Committee report states. Yet without access to information on Bank projects, meaningful involvement and participation is impossible.

In its own defense, the Bank argues that public access to information undermines its negotiating relations with borrowing governments. But here, too, the Bank is exaggerating the importance of a legitimate concern. In 1988, for instance, the Bank refused to release project documents relating to a loan to Botswana for nearly a year, even after the Sierra Club and the Natural Resources Defense Council—two U.S. environmental NGOs—produced a letter from the Botswanan government stating that it did not object to sharing the documents in question with NGOs. The Bank's Legal Department, it turns out, delayed the release of the project documents because of its concerns over the precedent this would create.

Ultimately, the World Bank and other multilateral development institutions justify their lack of transparency and accountability on the grounds that the sole legitimate interlocutor with whom they deal is the nation-state. The Bank, in fact, restricts the channels of communication even further. According to its charter, "Each member shall deal with the Bank only through its treasury, central bank, stabilization fund or other similar fiscal agency, and the Bank shall deal with members only by or through the same agencies." This leaves little room for the substantive involvement of nongovernmental entities of any kind. Moreover, the propensity to deal exclusively with finance ministries has, on occasion, helped to weaken the authority of the judicial and legislative branches of governments when conflicts over development projects have arisen.

New operational policies issued by the Bank in 1989 make some provision for consultation with and involvement of NGOs and local community organizations in Bank operations. While this can be viewed as an attempt by the Bank to promote a more participatory approach to development, in practice little has changed. In some cases (e.g. Narmada, Kedung Ombo), the Bank has been reluctant to pressure local governments that are unwilling to involve local populations in development planning, even when massive resettlement is planned. In other cases (e.g. Rondonia), participation and consultation have been pro forma: public meetings may be held simply to inform local groups of decisions that have already been reached. In either case, local groups enjoy little or no legitimacy to determine their economic, social, and

political fate. Instead, a top-down, technocratic approach prevails in which local peoples are treated merely as "project-affected populations." One need look no further than the Bank's charter to understand the basis of this tendency: the charter stipulates that officers and staff are to base their decisions and actions exclusively on economic considerations.

Environmental NGOs in the North and South are challenging these tendencies and the premises that underlie them. Sustainable development, they argue, cannot take place without greater public participation. Since the environmental impacts of a project are often manifold and widely distributed, gathering and synthesizing the information needed to formulate policy and planning decisions requires a free flow of information and inputs from local populations, as well as from nongovernmental and research organizations of various kinds. This has long been accepted in the United States, where public review and access to information have been considered vital to successful planning ever since environmental assessment procedures were established 20 years ago. And in the Soviet Union, Mikhail Gorbachev is now proposing that all major development schemes be subject to referenda by local populations.

The World Bank and other multilateral international institutions are caught in a double bind. The Bank has pledged to incorporate environmental with developmental concerns, but it is constrained to treat these as technical, apolitical matters. Its modus operandi is by definition only with sovereign governments and certain ministries within those governments, but the most crucial environmental challenges are political and social in nature, and call for planning and decision making that give much more legitimacy and empowerment to nongovernmental, civil society.

Contradictions of Global Economic Development. Finally, the World Bank's environmental quandaries are also a reflection of contradictions rooted in the Bank's attempts to reconcile ecological sustainability with global economic development. The most blatant of these contradictions relates to the very slogan that not only the World Bank but most international institutions and governments have adopted as the solution to the environmental dilemma: "sustainable development." The term was popularized by some NGOs in the early 1980s and received multilateral canonization in the 1987 Brundtland Report, the widely cited study by the U.N.'s World Commission on Environment and Development.

Sustainable development is a kind of mother-and-apple-pie formulation that everyone can agree on. The Brundtland Commission defines it as "meet[ing] the needs of the present without compromising the ability of future generations to meet their own needs." Critical to achieving sustainable development, the Commission argues, is the revival of economic growth in both the developing and the industrialized nations. Growth, it maintains, is essential to the alleviation of poverty, which intensifies pressures on the environment and as such is a major cause of environmental degradation in many Third World countries.

The World Bank and other multilateral institutions have enthusiastically embraced this aspect of sustainable development while virtually ignoring many of the Commission's other "strategic imperatives," such as the need to conserve and enhance the resource base and the need to change the quality of growth to one that is less material- and energy intensive. The Bank's emphasis on expanding the export capacities of recipient countries thus may be consistent with its own conception of sustainable development, but it is clearly at odds with the requirements of ecological sustainability.

Some of the best examples of what this contradiction means in practice are the projects that the Bank is financing under the Tropical Forestry Action Plan. The TFAP, hailed by the Bank as a model of sustainable development, places strong emphasis on export-oriented timber harvesting. This is not surprising since under current international economic conditions the most immediate option for economic growth for many Third World nations is the export of commodities. Experience has shown, however, that rainforest timber is almost always produced and logged unsustainably. Indeed, from a biological standpoint, the tropical rainforest is a nonrenewable resource, and to talk of the sustainable logging of rainforests is a contradiction in terms.

What the World Bank and, for that matter, the Brundtland Commission fail to recognize is that fundamental political, economic, and social changes are required to cope effectively with the intensive use of natural resources that is responsible for so much environmental degradation. Unequal access to natural resources, for instance, must be overcome if per capita pressures on the environment are to be alleviated. Among other things, this means redressing skewed land distribution patterns that, by forcing populations to overwork the land, have resulted in deforestation, soil erosion, siltation of waterways, and other serious environmental problems. Similarly, the Third World and industrialized economies must shift to patterns of development that are less material- and energy intensive in order to alleviate future burdens on the environment. These are matters that cannot be solved by economic or technical fixes, but require making difficult political decisions. The formulation and implementation of these decisions will require widespread public support and participation in both the North and South.

The need of nation-states and multilateral organizations to find real solutions to the global ecological crisis has thus created the conditions for, and indeed requires the empowerment of, nongovernmental and community organizations of all kinds that have a vested interest in the conservation of the world's increasingly threatened ecosystems. The global crisis is made up of myriad local ecological crises, and in most of these local situations there is a community, indigenous people, or an NGO that has a social, economic, or political interest in the conservation of an ecosystem or natural resource. Often, too, they know best how to manage natural resources in a sustainable way. In the Brazilian Amazon, for example, 500,000 rubber tappers depend for their livelihood on conservation of the rainforest; they harvest a number of extractive products for export such as natural latex and Brazil nuts. With international NGO support, they have successfully convinced the Brazilian government and MDBs to reverse development policies and support the creation of "extractive reserves" that protect the forest ecosystem, which is the basis of their livelihood.

The linking of NGO efforts in the North and South to promote environmental change has highlighted the fact that the multilateral development institutions, and many nation-states, are poorly prepared and structured to cope with the fundamental political challenge posed by the need for global ecological sustainability. These efforts on the part of NGOs have helped to globalize local, community-rooted ecological and political concerns in the Third World. They have brought the viewpoint of Amazonian rubber tappers and tribal leaders in India to the pages of the New York and London *Times,* to the board rooms of the MDB executive directors, and to First World finance ministries. Most important, they have transformed what were the obscure demands of powerless communities into international issues and have brought these issues back to Third World national capitals such as Brasilia and New Delhi.

The international media attention focused on groups like the rubber tappers or the Narmada oustees is also altering what could be called an epistemological imbalance. The political discourse and epistemological framework for multilateral development institutions has traditionally been based in the North. Third World national capitals share this conceptual framework, linked as they are to the centers of finance and multilateral power in the North as points on the outside of a wheel to a hub. By its very nature, this framework is reified and abstracted from the perceptions of social, ecological, and political reality of local Third World communities. A classic example of the distortion that results from this epistemological imbalance is the view, shared in the past by Brasilia, New Delhi, and Washington alike, of the rural Third World as consisting of relatively "empty" and "undeveloped" expanses of space awaiting planning, inputs, and infrastructure from the outside. It is precisely this view that led to the decision of the Indian government and the World Bank to build a series of coal-fired power plants in India over the past 13 years without any regard for the hundreds of thousands of people who were displaced as a consequence.

There is an inchoate but growing worldwide grass-roots green movement that is challenging these perceptual and political imbalances. Environmentalist and social groups in the Amazon, rural India, and even Siberia are changing the perception of these areas as "empty" places. As a result, the large land areas of the globe that until now have been viewed as passive fields for economic development are coming to be seen as having an ecological importance that is quite considerable. The incipient global perception of their ecological importance is providing a means for the political empowerment of at least some of the peoples of the world who have been marginalized by the past 400 years of economic internationalization.

Beyond the Contradictions

When the World Bank announced its environmental reforms in 1987, nongovernmental groups seriously underestimated the barriers to their implementation. Yet while these barriers are formidable, they are not necessarily insurmountable. The Bank's institutional schizophrenia can be remedied, but only if it is forced to choose its identity. If the Bank is truly to be a vehicle of sustainable development, it must place greater emphasis on project quality over the quick disbursement of money—a need the Bank will face even if it phases out its structural-adjustment lending. Likewise, if the Bank is to be a democratic institution committed to greater involvement of local people in development planning, it cannot continue to bar the public from access to basic project information. Institutional tinkering is not sufficient for resolving these contradictions; instead, the Bank must be pressured to sort out conflicting priorities.

The growing green movements in the North and South can play a critical role in pushing the Bank to make some of these harder choices. NGOs, for instance, can and must press for stricter Bank observance of existing environmental policies, for more far-sighted Bank leadership in the formulation of debt-forgiveness strategies, for greater transparency and accountability on the part of the Bank, and for greater substantive participation in the Bank's deliberations of those affected by its projects in the Third World.

NGO pressure, if properly targeted, can make a difference. This is evident from a number of encouraging, albeit isolated, developments since the Bank first announced its environmental reform program in 1987. For instance, NGO efforts in 1988 led the Inter-American Development Bank (IDB) to attach bold public participation conditions to an environmental and Indian lands protection plan associated with an IDB-financed road in northwest Brazil. Despite objections from the Brazilian military, the IDB insisted that local groups be granted a veto over any proposed demarcations that would affect them.

Similarly, it was largely because of NGO efforts last year that more than 30 donor nations of the International Development Association (IDA)—the soft-loan facility of the World Bank—endorsed the need for greater public access to information through the World Bank. The IDA donors, as a result, have required the Bank to consult with affected groups and local NGOs in preparing its environmental assessments, and to make the completed reports available to the public and to the Bank directors well in advance of final project appraisal.

Yet these are only isolated successes. If the World Bank and other MDBs are ever to come to grips with their environmental contradictions, such NGO efforts will need to be replicated many times over. In particular, governments must be made aware of the need for more fundamental reform of the MDBs and of development planning generally. The internationalization of Third World ecological conflicts is critically important in this regard; it is also a crucial factor for strengthening environmental and democratic movements in developing nations. Ultimately, successful MDB environmental reform depends on the growth and evolution of such movements in the Third World. Multilateral institutions like the World Bank can assist this evolution or hinder it, but they can no longer avoid the challenge it presents.

From Geopolitics to Geo-Economics
*Logic of Conflict, Grammar of Commerce*_____

Edward N. Luttwak

Edward N. Luttwak holds the Burke Chair in Strategy at the Center for Strategic and International Studies, Washington, D.C.

EXCEPT FOR THOSE unfortunate parts of the world where armed confrontations or civil strife persist for purely regional or internal reasons, the waning of the Cold War is steadily reducing the importance of military power in world affairs.

True, in the central strategic arena, where Soviet power finally encountered the *de facto* coalition of Americans, Europeans, Japanese, and Chinese, existing military forces have diminished very little so far. Nevertheless, as a Soviet-Western war becomes ever more implausible, the ability to threaten or reassure is equally devalued (and by the same token, of course, there is no longer a unifying threat to sustain the coalition against all divisive impulses). Either way, the deference that armed strength could evoke in the dealings of governments over all matters—notably including economic questions—has greatly declined, and seems set to decline further.

Everyone, it appears, now agrees that the methods of commerce are displacing military methods—with disposable capital in lieu of firepower, civilian innovation in lieu of military-technical advancement, and market penetration in lieu of garrisons and bases. But these are all tools, not purposes; what purposes will they serve?

If the players left in the field by the waning importance of military power were purely economic entities—labor-sellers, entrepreneurs, corporations—then only the logic of commerce would govern world affairs. Instead of World Politics, the intersecting web of power relationships on the international scene, we would simply have World Business, a myriad of economic interactions spanning the globe. In some cases, the logic of commerce would result in fierce competition. In others, the same logic would lead to alliances between economic entities in any location to capitalize ventures, vertically integrate, horizontally co-develop, co-produce, or co-market goods and services. But competitively or cooperatively, *the action on all sides would always unfold without regard to frontiers.*

If that were to happen, not only military methods but the logic of conflict itself—which is adversarial, zero-sum, and paradoxical—would be displaced. This, or something very much like it, is in fact what many seem to have in mind when they speak of a new global interdependence and its beneficial consequences.[1]

Logic and Grammar

BUT THINGS are not quite that simple. The international scene is still primarily occupied by states and blocs of states that extract revenues, regulate economic as well as other activities for various purposes, pay out benefits, offer services,

Reprinted with permission from *The National Interest*, Summer 1990, No. 20, pp. 17-23. Copyright © 1990 by The National Affairs, Inc.

provide infrastructures, and—of increasing importance—finance or otherwise sponsor the development of new technologies and new products. As territorial entities, spatially rather than functionally defined, states cannot follow a commercial logic that would ignore their own boundaries.

What logic then do they follow?

• Do they seek to collect as much in revenues as their fiscal codes prescribe—or are they content to let other states or blocs of states tax away what they themselves could obtain? Since the former is the reality (that is, a zero-sum situation in which the gain of one is the loss of another), here the ruling logic is the logic of conflict.

• Do they regulate economic activities to achieve disinterestedly transnational purposes—or do they seek to maximize outcomes within their own boundaries, even if this means that the outcomes are suboptimal elsewhere? Since the latter is the predominant, if not exclusive, reality, economic regulation is as much a tool of statecraft as military defenses ever were. Hence, insofar as external repercussions are considered, the logic of state regulation is *in part* the logic of conflict. As such, its attributes include the typically warlike use of secrecy and deception for the sake of surprise (as, for example, when product standards are first defined in secret consultations with domestic producers, long before their public enunciation).

• Do states and blocs of states pay out benefits and offer services transnationally—or (fractional aid allocations apart) do they strive to restrict such advantages to their own residents? Likewise, do they design infrastructures to maximize their transnational utility—or do they aim for domestically optimal and appropriately competitive configurations, regardless of how others are affected? Since the latter is the reality, the logic of state action is again *in part* the logic of conflict. (The competitive building of huge international airports in adjacent, minuscule, Persian Gulf sheikhdoms is an extreme example of such behavior, but such conduct is not uncommon in milder forms.)

• Finally, do states and blocs of states promote technological innovation for its own sake—or do they seek thereby to maximize benefits within their own boundaries? Since the latter is the reality, the logic of conflict

applies. (Three obvious examples are the obstacles that long delayed the introduction of Concorde flights into U.S. airports, Japanese barriers against U.S. supercomputers and telecommunications, and the development of rival High Definition Television formats.)

As this is how things are, it follows that—even if we leave aside the persistence of armed confrontations in unfortunate parts of the world and wholly disregard what remains of the Cold War—World Politics is still not about to give way to World Business, i.e., the free interaction of commerce governed only by its own nonterritorial logic.

Instead, what is going to happen—and what we are already witnessing—is a much less complete transformation of state action represented by the emergence of "Geo-economics." This neologism is the best term I can think of to describe the admixture of the logic of conflict with the methods of commerce—or, as Clausewitz would have written, the logic of war in the grammar of commerce.

The Nature of the Beast

WITH STATES and blocs of states still in existence, it could not be otherwise. As spatial entities structured to jealously delimit their own territories, to assert their exclusive control within them, and variously to attempt to influence events beyond their borders, states are inherently inclined to strive for relative advantage against like entities on the international scene, even if only by means other than force.

Moreover, states are subject to the internal impulses of their own bureaucracies, whose officials compete to achieve whatever goals define bureaucratic success, including goals in the international economic arena that may as easily be conflictual as competitive or cooperative. Actually much more than that is happening: *As bureaucracies writ large, states are themselves impelled by the bureaucratic urges of role-preservation and role-enhancement to acquire a "geo-economic" substitute for their decaying geopolitical role.*

There is also a far more familiar phenomenon at work: the instrumentalization of the state by economic interest groups that seek to manipulate its activities on the international scene for their own purposes, often by requiring adversarial "geo-economic" stances. No sphere of state action is immune: fiscal policy can be profitably used so as to place imports at a disadvantage; regulations, benefits, services, and infrastructures can all be configured to favor domestic interests in various ways; and, of course, the provision of state funds for domestic technological development is inherently discriminatory against unassisted foreign competitors.

The incidence of both adversarial bureaucratic impulses and adversarial manipulations of the state by interest groups will vary greatly from country to country. But fundamentally, states will tend to act "geo-economically" simply because of what they are: spatially-defined entities structured to outdo each other on the world scene. For all the other functions that states have acquired as providers of individual benefits, assorted services, and varied infrastructures, their *raison d'etre* and the ethos that sustains them still derive from their chronologically first function: to provide security from foes without (as well as outlaws within).

Relatively few states have had to fight to exist, but all states exist to fight—or at least they are structured as if that were their dominant function. Even though most of the existing 160-odd independent states have never fought any external wars, and most of those that have fought have not done so for generations, the governing structures of the modern state are still heavily marked by conflictual priorities, the need to prepare for, or to wage, interstate conflict. In how many major countries does the Minister for Telecommunications, or Energy, or Trade outrank the Defense Minister? Only—appropriately enough—in Japan, where Defense (*Boecho*) is a *Cho* or lesser department (translated as agency), as opposed to a *Sho* or ministry, as in *Tsusansho*, the Ministry of Trade. The *Boecho*'s head, while a minister, does not hold cabinet rank.

It is true, of course, that, under whatever name, "geo-economics" has always been an important aspect of international life. In the past, however, the outdoing of others in the realm of commerce was overshadowed by strategic priorities and strategic modalities. Externally, if the logic of conflict dictated the necessity for cooperation against a common enemy while, in contrast, the logic of commerce dictated competition, the preservation of the alliance was almost always given priority. (That indeed is how all the commercial quarrels between the United States and Western Europe—over frozen chickens, microchips, beef, and the rest—and between the United States and Japan—from textiles in the 1960s to supercomputers in the 1980s—were so easily contained during the past decades of acute Soviet-Western confrontation. As soon as commercial quarrels became noisy enough to attract the attention of political leaders on both sides, they were promptly suppressed by those leaders—often by paying off all parties—before they could damage political relations and thus threaten the imperative of strategic cooperation.) Internally, insofar as national cohesion was sustained against divisive social and economic tensions by the unifying urgencies of external antagonisms, it was armed conflict or the threat of it—not commercial animosities—that best served to unite nations.

NOW, HOWEVER, as the relevance of military threats and military alliances wanes, geo-economic priorities and modalities are becoming dominant in state action. Trade quarrels may still be contained by the fear of the economic consequences of an action-reaction cycle of punitive measures, but they will no longer simply be suppressed by political interventions on both sides, urgently motivated by the strategic imperative of preserving alliance cooperation against a common enemy. And if internal cohesion has to be preserved by a unifying threat, that threat must now be economic. Such a reordering of modalities is already fully manifest in the expressed attitudes of other Europeans to the new undivided Germany, and even more so in American attitudes toward Japan. Gorbachev's redirection of Soviet foreign policy had barely started when Japan began to be promoted to the role of the internally unifying Chief Enemy, judging by the evidence of opinion polls, media treatments, advertisements, and congressional pronouncements.

Should we conclude from all this that the world is regressing to a new age of mercantilism? Is that what "geo-economics" identifies, quite redundantly? Not so. The goal of mercantilism was to maximize gold stocks, whereas the goal of geo-economics (aggrandizement of the state aside) could only be to provide the best possible employment for the largest proporion of the population. In the past, moreover, when commercial quarrels evolved into political quarrels, they could become military confrontations almost automatically; and in turn military confrontations could readily lead to war.

In other words, mercantilism was a *subordinated modality*, limited and governed by the ever-present possibility that the loser in the mercantilist (or simply commercial) competition would switch to the grammar of war. Spain might decree that all trade to and from its American colonies could only travel in Spanish bottoms through Spanish ports, but British and Dutch armed merchantmen could still convey profitable cargoes to disloyal colonists in defiance of Spanish sloops; and, with war declared, privateers could seize outright the even more profitable cargoes bound for Spain. Likewise, the Dutch sent their frigates into the Thames to reply to the mercantilist legislation of the British Parliament that prohibited their cabotage, just as much earlier the Portuguese had sunk Arab ships with which they could not compete in the India trade.

"Geo-economics," on the other hand, is emerging in a world where there is *no superior modality*. Import-restricted supercomputers cannot be forcibly delivered by airborne assault to banks or universities in need of them, nor can competition in the world automobile market be assisted by the sinking of export car ferries on the high seas. That force has lost the role it once had in the age of mercantilism—as an *admissible* adjunct to economic competition—is obvious enough. But of course the decay of the military grammar of geopolitics is far more pervasive than this, even if it is by no means universal.[2]

Students of international relations may still be taught to admire the classic forms of *realpolitik*, with its structure of anticipatory calculations premised on the feasibility of war. But for some decades now the dominant elites of the greatest powers have ceased to consider war as a practical solution for military confrontations between them, because non-nuclear fighting would only be inconclusively interrupted by the fear of nuclear war, while the latter is self-inhibiting. (In accordance with the always

paradoxical logic of conflict, the application of the fusion technique meant that nuclear weapons exceeded the culminating point of utility, becoming less useful as they became more efficient.)

For exactly the same reason, military confrontations were themselves still considered very much worth pursuing—and rightly so, for war was thereby precluded throughout the decades of Soviet-Western antagonism. More recently, however, the dominant elites of the greatest powers appear to have concluded that military confrontations between them are only dissuasive of threats that are themselves most implausible. It is that new belief that has caused the decisive devaluation of military strength as an instrument of statecraft in the direct relations of the greatest powers.

Hence, while the methods of mercantilism could always be dominated by the methods of war, in the new "geo-economic" era not only the *causes* but also the *instruments* of conflict must be economic. If commercial quarrels do lead to political clashes, as they are now much more likely to do with the waning of the imperatives of geopolitics, those political clashes must be fought out with the weapons of commerce: the more or less disguised restriction of imports, the more or less concealed subsidization of exports, the funding of competitive technology projects, the support of selected forms of education, the provision of competitive infrastructures, and more.

Playing the New Game

THE DISCUSSION so far has focused on the actual and prospective role of states and, by implication, of blocs of states engaged in "geo-economic" conduct. But what happens on the world economic scene will not of course be defined by such conduct; indeed the role of "geo-economics" in the doings and undoings of the world economy should be far smaller than the role of geopolitics in world politics as a whole.

First, the propensity of states to act geo-economically will vary greatly, even more than their propensity to act geopolitically. For reasons historical and institutional, or doctrinal and political, some states will maintain a strictly *laissez faire* attitude, simply refusing to act "geo-economically." Both the very prosperous and the very poor might be in that category, just as both Switzerland and Burma have long been geopolitically inactive. In other cases, the desirable scope of geo-economic activism by the state is already becoming a focal point of political debate and partisan controversy: witness the current Democratic-Republican dispute on "industrial policy" in the United States. In still other cases, such as that of France, the dominant elites that long insisted on a very ambitious degree of geopolitical activism (ambitious, that is, in terms of the resources available) are now easily shifting their emphasis to demand much more geo-economic activism from the French state. And then, of course, there are the states—Japan most notably—whose geo-economic propensities are not in question.

Second, there is the much more important limitation that states and blocs of states acting "geo-economically" must do so within an arena that is not exclusively theirs, in which they coexist with private economic operators large and small, from individuals to the largest multinational corporations. While states occupy virtually all of the world's political space, they occupy only a fraction of the total economic space, and global political-economic trends such as privatization are reducing that fraction even further. (On the other hand, the role of states is increasing precisely in the economic sectors whose importance is itself increasing, sectors defined by the commercial application of the most advanced technologies.)

Of the different forms of coexistence between geo-economically active states and private economic operators, there is no end. Coexistence can be passive and disregarded, as in the relationship (or lack of it) between the state and the myriad of small, localized service businesses. With neither wanting anything from the other—except for the taxes that the fiscal authorities demand—the two can simply coexist without interacting or communicating.

At the opposite extreme, there is the intense positive interaction between politically weighty businesses in need of state support on the world economic scene, and the bureaucracies or politicians that they seek to manipulate for their own purposes. Or, going the other way, there is the equally intense and equally positive interaction that occurs when states seek to guide large companies for their own geo-economic purposes, or even select them as their "chosen instrument" (a specialized form of coexistence that dates back at least to the seventeenth-century East India companies, Dutch and Danish as well as, most famously, British).

Even more common, no doubt, are the cases of reciprocal manipulation, most notably in the remarkably uniform dealings of the largest international oil companies—whether American, British, or French—with their respective (and otherwise very different) state authorities. In each case, the state has been both user and used, and the companies both instruments and instrumentalizers.

Negative state-private sector interactions are not likely to be common, but they could be very important when they do occur. Geo-economically active states that oppose rival foreign states will also obviously oppose private foreign companies that are the chosen instruments of those rivals, as well as private foreign companies that simply have the misfortune to stand in the way. An era of intense "geo-economic" activity might thus become an era of unprecedented risk for important private companies in important sectors. If they invest Y million of their funds to develop X technology, they may find themselves irremediably overtaken by the X project of country Z, funded by the taxpayer in the amount of 2Y million, or 20Y million for that matter. Or private companies may find themselves competing with foreign undercutters determined to drive them out of business, and amply funded for that purpose by their state authorities. As public funding for such purposes is likely to be concealed, a victim-company may enter a market quite unaware of its fatal disadvantage. In such diverse ways the international economy will be pervasively affected by that fraction of its life that is geo-economic rather than simply economic in character (just as in the past the geopolitical activity of the few greatest powers decisively conditioned the politics of the many).

Perhaps the pan-Western trade accords of the era of armed confrontation with the Soviet Union—based on the original General Agreement on Tariffs and Trade—may survive without the original impulse that created them, and may serve to inhibit the overt use of tariffs and quotas as the geo-economic equivalent of fortified lines. And that inheritance of imposed amity may also dissuade the hostile use of all other "geo-economic" weapons, from deliberate regulatory impediments to customs-house conspiracies aimed at rejecting imports covertly—the commercial equivalents of the ambushes of war. But that still leaves room for far more important weapons: the competitive development of commercially important new technologies, the predatory financing of their sales during their embryonic stage, and the manipulation of the standards that condition their use—the geo-economic equivalents of the offensive campaigns of war.

Today, there is a palpably increasing tension between the inherently conflictual nature of states (and blocs of states) and the intellectual recognition of many of their leaders and citizens that while war is a zero-sum encounter by nature, commercial relations need not be and indeed rarely have been. The outcome of that tension within the principal countries and blocs will determine the degree to which we will live in a geo-economic world.

Notes

1. The logic of conflict is "zero-sum" since the gain of one side is the loss of the other, and vice versa. That is so in war, in geopolitical confrontations short of war, and in oligopolistic competition (as the market share of one oligopolist can only increase at the expense of another's); but not in a many-sided ("perfect") competition, wherein any two sides can both gain (or lose) market shares concurrently. The logic of conflict is paradoxical (i.e., governed by apparent contradictions and the coincidence of opposites) because all actions unfold in the presence of an adversary that reacts against whatever is being done. That is why—to give a static example—the worst of approach roads for an attack may be the best, if it confers the advantage of surprise (making the bad road paradoxically good and the good road paradoxically bad). Or, to give a dynamic example—involving the coincidence of opposites—why victorious armies that advance too far advance to their own defeat by overextension, just as weapons that are too effective are the most likely to be made ineffectual by the enemy countermeasures that their very effectiveness evokes. This same dynamic evolution toward the coincidence of opposites is operative at every level of strategy: thus the Soviet Union's accumulation of power eventually resulted in its impotence, as other states were frightened into forming a coalition against Moscow. In all dynamic manifestations of the logic of conflict there is such a culminating point, beyond which actions evolve into their opposite. In the linear logic of everyday life (and economic competition), by contrast, good is good and bad is bad, and success can facilitate further success without any necessary culminating point. For a systematic comparison, see my *Strategy: the Logic of War and Peace* (Cambridge: Harvard University Press, 1987).

2. In the train of history, the last wagons, such as the fragile states of sub-Saharan Africa, are still prebellic: they cannot yet wage war on each other, because regimes sustained only by the direct force of their armies cannot send those armies away to remote frontiers. The wagons at the head of the train by contrast are now postbellic because their ruling elites have become convinced that they cannot usefully fight one another. Only the wagons in the middle—countries such as India, Israel, Iran, Iraq, and a few others—are still capable of war with each other. But of course the train of history can not only stop but reverse its direction: in the second century B.C. the Romans already categorized prebellic societies (tribes too loosely organized to resist them) and advanced postbellic societies (of the Hellenized east) for which war could not be profitable. Things changed.

World Banking In Trouble

The U.S. savings-and-loan crisis is only a symptom

NORMAN MACRAE

The
Economist

During the 1980s, the brightest graduates from the richest countries' finest universities streamed as if on a conveyor belt into the go-go industry of financial services and banking. There had not been such unanimity of first choice since the graduating class of 1914 streamed off to France and World War I.

Both generations plunged into similarly overheated emotional nonsense. The present structure of worldwide banking has bred two endemic reasons why banks and near-banks are bound to run into continuous crises. During the 1980s, three breathtaking blunders overlapped one another.

First, up to 1982, the big banks of North America and Europe were pouring out petro-money to increase Latin American and other countries' debt—on lending criteria that were bound to make the worst basket cases worse still. Hard on their heels, another group of banks then spent the mid-1980s creating innovative (that is, unsound) sorts of borrowed money, most of which was used to bid up takeover prices of companies to levels that were increasingly megalomaniacal and destined eventually to send some of the brightest innovators and dumbest megalomaniacs to prison. The trendiest takeovers were of failing companies that were expensively sold to their own failed managers.

Today, many American, Japanese, and probably European banks are about to lose even more money on property loans. It may statistically be their biggest crash yet. One analyst has suggested that the American government, besides having to take over about 700 savings-and-loan institutions (so-called thrifts), may eventually own 1,700 failed banks, accounting for more than half of the American banking industry's assets. This is probably an exaggeration, but because banks can keep the real meaning of their accounts secret, nobody can be sure.

The worst crash will come in Japan, now the most important banking country in the world. Seven of the world's 10 largest banks, by assets, are Japanese. They

have helped property prices there to soar to levels several times more absurd than America's. So the eventual crunch in Japan will temporarily look several times worse.

Will this banking crash matter to the non-banking rest of mankind? The honest answer is, "one cannot be sure." Many people politely assumed that the appearance of unprecedented billions of bad Latin American banking debts in 1982 might damage the real world's economy. Instead, it marked the beginning of an unparalleled, eight-year-long world economic boom. The next banking weakness looks as if it will coincide with world economic weakness.

What has gone wrong? There are two unnoticed flaws in the world banking system. Call them the "damn foreigner" and the "lost cartel."

The damn foreigner. First, the present structure of world banking is ludicrously unsuited to success in international lending. This is awkward, because most lending can become international, thanks to the sudden weightlessness of both money and information, the two commodities in which bankers deal.

If, in the 19th century, some weird form of transubstantiation had suddenly made it possible to transfer the cheapest Argentine beef and Canadian grain, with no transportation costs, instantly to Europe, then the farmers of Europe would have responded by closing their own more costly farms. In this age of sending instant commands to computer screens, that transubstantiation has happened to banking products. But the banks in rich countries responded by expanding and giving their staffs more money.

The rich countries' banks argue that they have a tradition of lending abroad—indeed, that before 1914 rich countries lent abroad far more of their gross national product (GNP) than they do now. But 19th-century lending abroad was the exact opposite of today's. It is absurd to give the two the same name. From about the 1860s to nearly 1914, the British were investing annually around 5 percent of their GNP overseas, in some years 10 percent. That 10 percent today would be the equivalent of Japan's

From the newsmagazine "The Economist" of London.

running a balance-of-payments surplus of $280 billion a year and using it to buy the world. There has been quite enough fuss because, in the past 12 months, Japan has run a surplus of about $50 billion.

Yet 19th-century British investment was hugely profitable. Part of the reason for this is romantically ascribed to the character of the up-to-date Victorian banker. Two bigger reasons were probably that the Victorian bankers went hand-in-pocket with contractors and that Britain practiced complete freedom of import trade. If there is to be a return to profitable international development (of China, India, Eastern Europe, Latin America—all of the poor South), it may have to depend on the lending countries' practicing total free trade. A lot of banks will go bust before politicians understand that.

In 1914-18, the three major overseas investing countries, Britain, France, and Germany, blew their assets away in a war with no logical purpose. So the U.S. became the top manufacturing and top creditor country in 1919. It made many mistakes, all of which its successor as top banking country 60 years later—overexcited Japan—has imitated. An early mistake was that American banks started to lend abroad to aid consumption—for example, in countries in difficulties from war debts—rather than acting as watchdogs over contractors for sober empire builders' projects. Until then, contractors and banks had had every incentive to stop schemes once costs ran over budget. Today, contractors have every incentive to tell lies about cost overruns until somebody else (preferably a banker) picks up the bill.

Bankers now charge more, because, they say, they have to give more professional advice. In fact, professional advice, in the old sense, has disappeared. Today, money is whipped in through computers by young people looking at projects of which they may never have heard, in countries that they probably could not place on a map.

The lost cartel. To these problems in foreign lending have been added problems bred by unaccustomed competition. Banking in the days before computers-plus-telecommunications operated as a cartel, with national governments trying to regulate it as such—ironically, sometimes, because politicians thought that this would make it safer. Now that money can be transferred anywhere at a keystroke, these safety regulations are extremely dangerous.

The tacit offer from governments for about 30 years after 1945 was that they would allow banks a stable and high level of profit by insuring that depositors had few places other than banks in which to put their money and that borrowers would have few other places from which they could respectably borrow. Building societies and thrifts were allowed into the cartel, provided that they stuck to the role of pumping in ever more credit with which to inflate the price of second-hand houses.

The details of the cartels from 1948 to 1982 varied from the monstrous to the absurd. Some countries, including America and Japan, limited the interest paid to depositors. Others, such as Britain, let the bankers' cartel fix this among themselves. On checking accounts, the banks chose to pay no interest at all. Banks were allowed to make profits on the side by floating transactions and by

"Most rich countries have too many banks, and banks are not particularly popular."

setting high charges for every sort of service—all fixed uniformly within the cartels. In return, bankers agreed to finance irresponsible government budget deficits and even to allow governments (not competition) to decide which sorts of securities to put on the market. They cooperated with programs bound to breed double-digit inflation, which cheated those customers whose money they were using the most—those with checking accounts.

These cozy arrangements melted as technology heated up, leaving only messes behind. The costliest scandal hit America's thrifts. In the cartel days, these thrifts had a virtual monopoly on certain types of deposits and on certain types of fairly safe lending. But in the 1980s, the spread of international money-market funds and so on meant that thrifts lost many of their advantages. The alternative before a manager of a thrift was then either to close his business, and lose his job, or to woo depositors by offering higher interest rates and then invest the money in riskier ventures to earn enough to pay those rates.

A sane system would seek to steer decision makers toward the first course. Instead, the "safety-net" provisions in America steer every thrift manager into the second course, thanks to government insurance, paid for by the taxpayer, guaranteeing deposits of up to $100,000. The depositor knows that his $100,000 will be safe in the highest-interest-paying institution that is keeping its dud manager in a job by investing that money in the nuttiest operation that is most likely to lose the American taxpayer (but not the depositor) his money. In America's present expensive rescue of failed thrifts, this incentive has so far been left in place. So long as it exists, such crashes will recur.

American estimates put the income of banks and financial institutions at more than 10 percent of the gross world product, up from a fraction of that a decade or so ago. Since this computerized industry has not required similar growth in its labor force, productivity has gone up and up—which, bank economists suppose, means that profits will continue to go forward fast.

Will they? The banks' and financial institutions' present—though already fast-falling—profits might last if their computer equipment were to become more specialized, with less of it available for other people's private desks. The opposite will occur. More individuals, and certainly most firms, will be able to call up on computers an aggregation of their assets, with a menu of choices on where to hold or invest them.

Wholesale banking is now run mainly from skyscrapers in the most expensive square miles of Manhattan, Tokyo, and London. These banks will be undercut by computers at cheaper sites. Retail banks have acquired valuable sites on expensive streets, but cash withdrawal is automated, cash deposits (from small shops and so on) ought to be, and the cashless society will now approach, with credit cards being issued competitively instead of by banks.

Most people will still want guarantees of safety for deposits. Up to now, taxpayers have often paid for these guarantees, but the $200-billion-or-so bill for America's thrifts spells an end to that. Governments everywhere will surely demand bigger insurance premiums from banks to provide these guarantees. They will not just issue them to banks and building societies within a cartel but will charge each institution individually. The average return on equity of American banks is now said to be less than 7 percent. Behind the cloak covering bad debts, many banks are, in reality, losing money. A premium for insurance of deposits might push up toward that 7 percent of equity. There will be political lobbying to stop too many bank closures, but it will not get far. Most rich countries have too many banks, and banks are not politically popular.

The traditional way to rescue failed banks has been to sell them at bargain prices to stronger banks. This tradition will need to be carefully watched. There is no such thing as a bargain price for a portfolio of bad debts.

After the Wall Street crash of 1929, the world went into the Great Depression. That was because the Federal Reserve ran American banks in a cartel, in which it acted as a puritan nanny. The Fed examined bank balance sheets and then told the shakiest banks to lend less at exactly the wrong moment. Central banks will not be so foolish in the next crash. When stock markets shivered in October, 1987, all of the big countries' central banks increased the money supply instead. Many of them, especially the Bank of England, increased the supply too much, so inflation quickened. Mercifully, the Japanese authorities asked Japanese securities houses to buy equities, thus increasing the money supply naturally instead of artificially.

It would be better if other central banks responded to the next stock-market crash in this way. Even the Japanese might hesitate next time, however, because Japanese politicians have become more chary of being connected with rigged equity markets since 1989's Recruit scandal, which involved a different sort of stock rigging. But this worry depends on what sort of stock-market and property crash might happen. In 1929-32, the share price of America's General Motors Corp. fell from $73 to $8. Japan would certainly prop up the price if Nissan or Toyota fell to anything like that, to stop foreigners from buying them cheap. The coming financial troubles in Japan, therefore, will not be so damaging to manufacturing and other businesses. Remember that after 1933, America remained the world's most efficient manufacturing country, as Japan, or at least its multinationals, will after 1993.

For bankers, though, the future has to look bleak. Since 1945, the usual course in rich countries has been for everybody to say that some particular thing is going to be desperately scarce and some particular industry, limitlessly expansionary. Oversupply then drives that commodity into glut and that industry into contraction.

In 1945-50 when former Italian prisoners of war were allowed to go to work in British coal mines, the government explained that no British miner needed to fear for his job for the rest of the century. In 1950, coal mining employed about 770,000 people in Britain; today it employs about 80,000. In the 1980s, bright graduates streamed into banking and financial services. Their prospects, by the time they retire, seem on a par with those of Britain's coal miners.

TOFFLER'S NEXT
SHOCK

*A dramatic 'powershift' is coming, and all nations face
one inescapable rule—survival of the fastest.*

Alvin Toffler

*Alvin Toffler's writing on future trends in global industry,
government, communications, and learning has had wide
impact on government, business, and university leaders in
many nations. His best-selling books "Future Shock" and
"The Third Wave" have been published in some 30 languages.*

O NE OF THE GREATEST POWER IMBALANCES ON
earth today divides the rich countries from
the poor. That unequal distribution of power,
which affects the lives of billions of us, will
soon be transformed as a new system of
wealth creation spreads.

Since the end of World War II the world
has been split between capitalist and commu-
nist, North and South. Today as these old divisions fade in
significance, a new one arises.

For from now on the world will be split between the fast
and the slow.

To be fast or slow is not simply a matter of metaphor.
Whole economies are either fast or slow. Primitive organisms
have slow neural systems. The more evolved human nervous
system processes signals faster. The same is true of primitive
and advanced economies. Historically, power has shifted from
the slow to the fast—whether we speak of species *or* nations.

In fast economies advanced technology speeds production.

But this is the least of it. Their pace is determined by the
speed of transactions, the time needed to take decisions
(especially about investment), the speed with which new ideas
are created in laboratories, the rate at which they are brought
to market, the velocity of capital flows, and above all the speed
with which data, information, and knowledge pulse through
the economic system. Fast economies generate wealth—and
power—faster than slow ones.

By contrast, in peasant societies economic processes move
at a glacial pace. Tradition, ritual, and ignorance limit socially
acceptable choices. Communications are primitive, transport
restricted. Before the market system arose as an instrument
for making investment choices, tradition governed technological decisions. Tradition, in turn, relied on "rules or taboos to
preserve productive techniques that were proven workable
over the slow course of biological or cultural evolution,"
according to economist Don Lavoie.

With most people living at the bare edge of subsistence,
experiment was dangerous, innovators were suppressed, and
advances in the methods of wealth creation came so slowly
they were barely perceptible from lifetime to lifetime.
Moments of innovation were followed by what seemed like
centuries of stagnation.

The historical explosion we now call the industrial
revolution stepped up the economic metabolism. Roads and
communications improved. Profit-motivated entrepreneurs

From *World Monitor*, November 1990, pp. 34-38, 41-42, 44. From *Powershift: Knowledge, Wealth, and Violence at the Edge of
the 21st Century.* Copyright © 1990 by Alvin and Heidi Toffler. Reprinted by permission of Bantam Books.

actively searched for innovations. Brute force technologies were introduced. Society had a larger surplus to fall back on, reducing the social risks of experimentation. "With technological experimentation now so much less costly," Lavoie points out, "productive methods [could] change much more rapidly."

All this, however, merely set the stage for today's superfast symbolic economy.

The bar code on the box of Cheerios, the computer in the Federal Express truck, the scanner at the Safeway checkout counter, the bank's automatic teller, the spread of extra-intelligent data networks across the planet, the remotely operated robot, the informationalization of capital—are all preliminary steps in the formation of a 21st-century economy that will operate at nearly real-time speeds.

In due course, the entire wealth-creation cycle will be monitored *as it happens*. Continual feedback will stream in from sensors built into intelligent technology, from optical scanners in stores, and from transmitters in trucks, planes, and ships that send signals to satellites so managers can track the changing location of every vehicle at every moment. This information will be combined with the results of continuous polling of people, and information from a thousand other sources.

The acceleration effect, by making each unit of saved time *more* valuable than the last unit, thus creates a positive feedback loop that accelerates the acceleration.

The consequences of this, in turn, will be not merely evolutionary, but revolutionary, because real-time work, management, and finance will be radically different from even today's most advanced methods.

Even now, however, well before real-time operations are achieved, time itself has become an increasingly critical factor of production. As a result, knowledge is used to shrink time intervals.

This quickening of economic neural responses in the high technology nations holds still-unnoticed consequences for low-technology or no-technology economies.

For the more valuable time becomes, the less valuable the traditional factors of production like raw materials and labor. And that, for the most part, is what these countries sell.

REV UP OR DROP OUT

The acceleration effect will transform all present strategies for economic development.

The new system for making wealth consists of an expanding, global network of markets, banks, production centers, and laboratories in instant communication with one another, constantly exchanging huge—and ever increasing—flows of data, information, and knowledge.

This is the "fast" economy of tomorrow. It is this accelerative, dynamic new wealth-machine that is the source of economic advance. As such it is the source of great power as well. To be de-coupled from it is to be excluded from the future.

Yet that is the fate facing many of today's "LDCs" or "less developed countries." (The term "less developed" is an arrogant misnomer, since many LDCs are highly developed culturally and in other ways. A more appropriate term would be "less economically developed," which is the sense in which it will be used here.)

As the world's main system for producing wealth revs up, countries that wish to sell will have to operate at the pace of those in a position to buy. This means that slow economies will have to speed up their neural responses, lose contracts and investments, or drop out of the race entirely.

The earliest signs of this development are already detectable.

The United States in the 1980s spent $125 billion a year on clothing. Half of that came from cheap labor factories dotted around the world from Haiti to Hong Kong. Tomorrow much of this work will return to the US. The reason is speed.

Of course, shifting taxes, tariffs, currency ratios, and other factors still influence businesses when overseas investment or purchasing decisions are made. But far more fundamental in the long run are changes in the structure of cost. These changes, part of the transition to the new wealth-creation system, are already sending runaway factories and contracts home again to the US, Japan, and Europe.

The Tandy Corporation, a major manufacturer and retailer of electronic products, not long ago brought its "Tandy Color Computer" production back from South Korea to Texas. While the Asian plant was automated, the Texas plant operated on an "absolutely continuous flow" basis and had more sophisticated test equipment. In Virginia, Tandy set up a no-human-hands automated plant to turn out 5,000 speaker enclosures a day. These supply Japanese manufacturers who previously had them made with low-cost labor in the Caribbean.

The computer industry is, of course, extremely fast-paced. But even in a slower industry, the Arrow Co., one of the biggest US shirtmakers, recently transferred 20% of its production back to the US after 15 years of off-shore sourcing. Frederick Atkins Inc., a buyer for US department stores, has increased domestic purchases from 5% to 40% in three years.

These shifts can be traced, at least in part, to the rising importance of time in economics.

DELIVERY DELAYED IS DELIVERY DENIED

"The new technology," reports Forbes magazine, "is giving domestic apparel makers an important advantage over their Asian competitors. Because of fickle fashion trends and the practice of changing styles as often as six times a year, retailers want to be able to keep inventories low. This calls for quick response from apparel makers that can offer fast turnaround on smaller lots in all styles, sizes, and colors. Asian suppliers, half a world away, typically require orders three months or more in advance."

By contrast, Italy's Benetton Group delivers mid-season reorders within two to three weeks. Because of its electronic network, Haggar Apparel in Dallas is now able to restock its 2,500 customers with slacks every three days, instead of the seven weeks it once needed.

Compare this with the situation facing manufacturers in China who happen to need steel.

In 1988 China suffered the worst steel shortages in memory. Yet, with fabricators crying out for supplies, 40% of the country's total annual output remained padlocked in the warehouses of the China Storage and Transportation General Corporation (CSTGC). Why? Because this enterprise—incredible as it may seem to the citizens of fast economies—makes deliveries only twice a year.

The fact that steel prices were skyrocketing, that the shortages were creating a black market, that fraud was widespread, and that companies needing the steel faced crisis and bankruptcy meant nothing to the managers of CSTGC. The organization was simply not geared to making more frequent deliveries. While this is no doubt an extreme example, it is not isolated. A "great wall" separates the fast from the slow, and that wall is rising higher with each passing day.

It is this cultural and technological great wall that explains, in part, the high rate of failures in joint projects between fast and slow countries.

Many deals collapse when a slow-country supplier fails to meet promised deadlines. The different pace of economic life in the two worlds makes for cross-cultural static. Officials in the slow country typically do not appreciate how important time is to the partner from the fast country—or why it matters so much. Demands for speed seem unreasonable, arrogant. Yet for the fast-country partner, nothing is more important. Delivery delayed is almost as bad as delivery denied.

The increasing costs of unreliability, of endless negotiation, of inadequate tracking and monitoring, and of late responses to demands for up-to-the-instant information further diminish the competitive edge of low-wage muscle work in the slow economies.

So do expenses arising from delays, lags, irregularities, bureaucratic stalling, and slow decisionmaking—not to mention the corrupt payments often required to speed things up.

In the advanced economies the speed of decision is becoming a critical consideration. Some executives refer to the inventory of "decisions in process" or "DIP" as an important cost, similar to "work in progress." They are trying to replace sequential decisionmaking with "parallel processing," which breaks with bureaucracy. They speak of "speed to market," "quick response," "fast cycle time," and "time-based competition."

The increased precision of timing required by systems like "just-in-time delivery" means that the seller must meet far more rigid and restrictive schedule requirements than before, so that it is easier than ever to slip up.

In turn, as buyers demand more frequent and timely deliveries from overseas, the slow-country suppliers are compelled to maintain larger inventories or buffer stocks at their own expense—with the risk that the stored parts will rapidly become obsolete or unsalable.

The new economic imperative is clear: Overseas suppliers from developing countries will either advance their own technologies to meet the world speed standards, or they will be brutally cut off from their markets—casualties of the acceleration effect.

The likelihood that many of the world's poorest countries will be isolated from the dynamic global economy and left to stagnate is enhanced by three other powerful factors that stem, directly or indirectly, from the arrival of a new system of wealth creation on the earth.

STRATEGIC REAL ESTATE

One way to think about the economic power or powerlessness of the LDCs is to ask what they have to sell to the rest of the world. We can begin with a scarce resource that only a few countries at any given moment can offer the rest of the world: strategic location.

Economists don't normally consider militarily strategic real estate a salable resource, but for many LDCs that is precisely what it has been.

Countries seeking military and political power are frequently prepared to pay for it. Like Cuba, many LDCs now have sold, leased, or lent their location or facilities to the Soviet Union, the US, or others for military, political, and intelligence purposes. For Cuba, giving the Soviets a foothold 90 miles off the US coast and heightened political influence throughout Central America has brought in a $5 billion annual subsidy from Moscow.

For almost half a century, the Cold War has meant that even the poorest country (assuming it was strategically located) had something to sell to the highest bidder. Some, like Egypt, managed to sell their favors first to one superpower, then to the other.

But while the relaxation of US-Soviet tensions may be good news for the world, it is decidedly bad news for places like the Philippines, Vietnam, Cuba, or Nicaragua, each of which has successfully peddled access to its strategic geography. From now on, it is unlikely that the two biggest customers for strategic location will be bidding against one another as they once did.

Moreover, as logistic capabilities rise, as aircraft and missile range increases, as submarines proliferate, and as military airlift operations quicken, the need for overseas bases, repair facilities, and prepositioned supplies declines.

LDCs must, therefore, anticipate the end of the seller's market for such strategic locations. Unless replaced by other forms of international support, this will choke off billions of dollars of "foreign aid" and "military assistance" funds that have until now flowed into certain LDCs.

The US-Soviet thaw, as we'll see, is a Soviet response to the new system of wealth creation in the high-tech nations. The collapse of the market for strategic location is an indirect consequence.

Even if the great powers of the future (whoever they may be) do continue to locate bases, set up satellite listening posts, or build airfields and submarine facilities on foreign soil, the "leases" will be for shorter times. Today's accelerating changes make all alliances more tenuous and temporary, discouraging the great powers from making long-term investments in fixed locations.

Wars, threats, insurrections will arise at unexpected places. Thus the military of the great powers will increasingly stress mobile, rapid deployment forces, the projection of naval power, and space operations rather than fixed installations. All this will further drive down the bargaining power of countries with locations to let or lease.

Finally, the rise of Japanese military power in the Pacific may well lead the Philippines and other Southeast Asian countries to *welcome* US or other forces as a counterbalance to a perceived Japanese threat. Carried far enough, this implies even a willingness to *pay* for protection, instead of charging for allowing it.

UPSETTING THE LDC POWER BALANCE

New outbreaks of regional war or internal violence on many continents will keep the arms business booming. But whatever happens, it will be harder to extract benefits from the US and the Soviets. This will upset the delicate power balance among LDCs—as between India and Pakistan, for instance, or Nicaragua and its neighbors—and will trigger potentially violent power shifts *within* the LDCs as well, especially among the elites closely (and sometimes corruptly) linked to aid programs, military procurement, and intelligence operations.

In short, the heyday of the Cold War is over. Far more complex power shifts lie ahead. And the market for strategic locations in the LDCs will never be the same.

A second blow awaits countries that base their development plans on the export of bulk raw materials such as copper or bauxite.

Here, too, power-shifting changes are just around the corner.

Mass production required vast amounts of a small number of resources. By contrast, as de-massified manufacturing methods spread, they will need many more different resources—in much smaller quantities.

Furthermore, the faster metabolism of the new global production system also means that resources regarded as crucial today may be worthless tomorrow—along with all the extractive industries, railroad sidings, mines, harbor facilities, and other installations built to move these resources. Conversely, today's useless junk could suddenly acquire great value.

Oil itself was regarded as useless until new technologies, and especially the internal combustion engine, made it vital. Titanium was a largely useless white powder until it became valuable in aircraft and submarine production. But the rate at which new technologies arrived was slow. That, of course, is no longer true.

Superconductivity, to choose a single example, will eventually reduce the need for energy by cutting transmission losses and, at the same time, will require new raw materials for its use. New anti-pollution devices for automobiles no longer depend on platinum. New pharmaceuticals may call for organic substances that today are either unknown or unvalued. In turn, this could change poverty-stricken countries into important suppliers—while undercutting today's big-bulk exporters.

What's more, in the words of Umberto Colombo, chairman of the European Community's Committee on Science and Technology, "in the advanced and affluent societies, each successive increment in per capita income is linked to an ever-smaller rise in quantities of raw materials and energy used." Colombo cites figures from the International Monetary Fund showing that "Japan . . . in 1984 consumed only 60% of the raw materials required for the same volume of industrial output in 1973."

DOING MORE WITH LESS

Advancing knowledge permits us to do more with less. As it does so, it shifts power away from the bulk producers.

Beyond this development, fast-expanding scientific knowledge increases the ability to create substitutes for imported resources. Indeed, the advanced economies may soon be able to create whole arrays of new customized materials such as "nano-composites" virtually from scratch. The smarter the high-tech nations become about micro-manipulating matter, the less dependent they become on imports of bulk raw materials from abroad.

The new wealth system is too protean, too fast-moving to be shackled to a few "vital" materials. Power will therefore flow from bulk raw material producers to those who control "eyedropper" quantities of temporarily crucial substances, and from them to those who control the knowledge necessary to create totally new resources.

All this would be bad enough. But a third jolting blow is likely to hit the LDCs even harder and change power relations among and within them.

Ever since the smoky dawn of the industrial era, manufacturers have pursued the golden grail of cheap labor. After World War II the hunt for foreign sources of cheap labor became a stampede. Many developing countries bet their entire economic future on the theory that selling labor cheap would lead to modernization.

Some, like the "four tigers" of East Asia—South Korea, Taiwan, Hong Kong, and Singapore—even won their bet. They were helped along by a strong work ethic and by cultural and other unique factors, including the fact that the "containment" of China for a quarter century and two bitter wars, the Korean conflict in the '50s and Vietnam in the '60s and early '70s, pumped billions of dollars into the region.

Because of the Asian tigers' success, it is now almost universally believed that shifting from the export of agricultural products or raw materials to the export of goods manufactured by cheap labor is the path to development. Yet nothing could be further from the long-range truth.

There is no doubt that the cheap labor game is still being played all over the world. Even now Japan is transferring plants and contracts from Taiwan and Hong Kong, where wages have risen, to Thailand, the Philippines, and China where wages are still one-tenth those in Japan. No doubt many opportunities still exist for rich countries to locate pools of cheap labor in the LDCs.

But, like leasing military bases or shipping ore, the sale of cheap labor is also reaching its outer limits.

The reason for this is simple: Under the newly emerging system of wealth creation, cheap labor is increasingly expensive.

As the new system spreads, labor costs themselves become a smaller fraction of total costs of production. In some industries today, labor costs represent only 10% of the total costs of production. A 1% saving of a 10% cost factor is only 1/10th of 1%.

By contrast, better technology, faster and better information flows, decreased inventory, or streamlined organization can yield savings far beyond any that can be squeezed out of hourly workers.

This is why it may be more profitable to run an advanced facility in Japan or the US, with a handful of highly educated, highly paid employees than a backward factory in China or Brazil that depends on masses of badly educated, low-wage workers.

Cheap labor, in the words of Umberto Colombo, "is no longer enough to ensure market advantage to developing countries."

HYPER-SPEEDS

Looming on the horizon, therefore, is a dangerous de-coupling of the fast economies from the slow, an event that would spark enormous power shifts throughout the so-called South—with big impacts on the planet as a whole.

The new wealth creation system holds the possibility of a far better future for vast populations who are now among the planet's poor. Unless the leaders of the LDCs anticipate these changes, however, they will condemn their people to perpetuated misery—and themselves to impotence.

For even as Chinese manufacturers wait for their steel, and traditional economies around the world crawl slowly through their paces, the United States, Japan, Europe and—in this case the Soviets, too—are pressing forward with plans to build hypersonic jets capable of moving 250 tons of people and cargo at Mach 5, meaning that cities like New York, Sydney, London, or Los Angeles will be two-and-a-half hours from Tokyo.

Jiro Tokuyama, former director of research for Nomura Securities and now a senior adviser to the Mitsui Research Institute, heads a 15-nation study of what are called the "Three T's"—telecommunications, transportation, and tourism. Sponsored by the Pacific Economic Community Commission, the study focuses on three key factors likely to accelerate the pace of economic processes in the region still further.

According to Tokuyama, Pacific air passenger traffic is likely to reach 134 million . . . at the turn of the century. The Society of Japanese Aerospace Companies, Tokuyama adds, estimates that 500 to 1,000 hypersonic jets must be built. Many of these will ply Pacific routes, speeding further the economic development of the region and promoting faster telecommunications as well. In a paper prepared for the Three T's study, Tokuyama spells out the commercial, social, and political implications of this development.

He also describes a proposal by Taisei, the Japanese construction firm, to build an artificial island five kilometers (three miles) in length to serve as a "VAA" or "value-added airport" capable of handling hypersonics and providing an international conference center, shops, and other facilities to be linked by high-speed linear trains to a densely populated area.

AIRPORT ASSEMBLY LINES

In Texas, meanwhile, billionaire H. Ross Perot is building an airport to be surrounded by advanced manufacturing facilities. As conceived by him, planes would roar in day and night bearing components for overnight processing or assembly in facilities at the airport. The next morning the jets would carry them to all parts of the world.

Simultaneously, on the telecommunications front, the advanced economies are investing billions in the electronic infrastructure essential to operations in the super-fast economy.

The spread of extra-intelligent nets is moving swiftly, and there are now proposals afoot to create special higher-speed fiber optic networks linking supercomputers all across the US with thousands of laboratories and research groups. (Existing networks, which move 1.5 million bits of information a second, are regarded as too slow. The proposed new nets would send 3 billion bits per second—i.e. three "gigabits"—streaming across the country.)

The new network is needed, say its advocates, because the existing slower nets are already choked and overloaded. They argue that the project merits government backing because it would help the US keep ahead of Europe and Japan in a field it now leads.

This, however, is only a special case of a more general clamor. In the words of Mitch Kapor, a founder of Lotus Development Corp., the software giant, "We need to build a national infrastructure that will be the information equivalent of the national highway-building of the '50s and '60s." An even more appropriate analogy would compare today's computerized telecom infrastructures with the rail and road networks needed at the beginning of the industrial revolution.

What is happening, therefore, is the emergence of an electronic neural system for the economy—without which any nation, no matter how many smokestacks it has, will be doomed to backwardness.

For the LDCs, as for the rest of the world, power stems from the holster, the wallet, and the book—or, nowadays, the computer. Unless we want an anarchic world—with billions of poverty-stricken people, unstable governments led by unstable leaders, each with a finger on the missile launcher or chemical or bacteriological triggers—we need global strategies for preventing the de-coupling of fast and slow economies that looms before us.

A study of "Intelligence Requirements for the 1990s" made by US academic experts, warns that in the years immediately ahead the LDCs will acquire sophisticated new arms—enor-mous firepower will be added to their already formidable arsenals. Why?

As the LDCs' economic power diminishes, their rulers face political opposition and instability. Under the circumstances, they are likely to do what rulers have done since the origins of the state—reach for the most primitive form of power: military force.

But the most acute shortage facing LDCs is the shortage of economically relevant knowledge. The 21st-century path to economic development and power is no longer through the exploitation of raw materials and human muscle, but, as we've seen, through application of the human mind.

KNOWLEDGE IS WEALTH

Development strategies make no sense, therefore, unless they take full account of the new role of knowledge in wealth creation, and of the accelerative imperative that goes hand in hand with it.

With knowledge (which in our definition includes such things as imagination, values, images, and motivation, along with formal technical skills) increasingly central to the economy, the Brazils and Nigerias, the Bangladeshes and Haitis, must consider how they might best acquire or generate this resource.

It is clear that every wretched child in northeast Brazil or anywhere else in the world who remains ignorant or intellectually underdeveloped because of malnutrition represents a permanent drain on the future. Revolutionary new forms of education will be needed, ones that are not based on the old factory model.

Acquiring knowledge from elsewhere will also be necessary. This may take unconventional—and sometimes even illicit—forms. Stealing technological secrets is already a booming business around the world. We must expect shrewd LDCs to join the hunt.

Another way of obtaining wealthmaking know-how is to organize a brain drain. This can be done on a small scale by bribing or attracting teams of researchers. But some clever countries will figure out that, around the world, there are certain dynamic minorities—often persecuted groups—that can energize a host economy if given the chance. The overseas Chinese in Southeast Asia, Indians in East Africa, Syrians in West Africa, Palestinians in parts of the Mideast, Jews in America, and Japanese in Brazil have all played this role at one time or another.

Transplanted into a different culture, each has brought not merely energy, drive, and commercial or technical acumen, but a pro-knowledge attitude—a ravenous hunger for the latest information, new ideas, skills. These groups have provided a kind of hybrid economic vigor. They work hard, they innovate, they educate their children, and, even if they get rich in the process, they stimulate and accelerate the reflexes of the host economy.

We will no doubt see various LDCs searching out such groups and inviting them to settle within their borders, in the hopes of injecting a needed adrenalin into the economy. (During World War II the Japanese military actually drafted a plan to bring large numbers of persecuted European Jews to Manchuria, then called Manchukuo, for this purpose. However, the "Fugu Plan," as it was known, was never implemented.)

NEGLECTED MEDIA

Smart governments will also encourage the spread of nongovernmental associations and organizations, since such groups accelerate the spread of economically useful information through newsletters, meetings, conferences, and foreign travel. Associations of merchants, plastics engineers, employers, programmers, trade unions, bankers, journalists, etc., serve as channels for rapid exchange of information about what does, and does not, work in their respective fields. They are an important, often neglected communications medium.

Governments serious about economic development will also have to recognize the new economic significance of free expression. Failure to permit the circulation of new ideas, including economic and political ideas, even if unflattering to the state, is almost always prima facie proof that the state is weak at its core, and that those in power regard staying there as more important than economic improvement in the lives of their people. Governments committed to becoming part of the new world will systematically open the valves of public discussion.

Other governments will join "knowledge consortia"—partnerships with other countries or with global companies—to explore the far reaches of technology and science and, especially, the possibility of creating new materials.

Instead of pandering to obsolete nationalist notions, they will pursue the national interest passionately—but intelligently. Rather than refusing to pay royalties to foreign pharmaceutical companies on the lofty ground that health is above such grubby concerns, as Brazil has done, they will gladly pay the royalties—provided these funds stay inside the country for a fixed number of years, and are used to fund research projects carried out jointly with the local pharmaceutical firm's own experts.

Profits from products that originate in this joint research then can be divided between the host country and the multinational. In this way, the royalties pay for technology transfer—and for themselves. Effective nationalism thus replaces obsolete, self-destructive nationalism.

Similarly, intelligent governments will welcome the latest computers, regardless of who built them, rather than trying to build a local computer industry behind tariff walls that keep out not merely products—but advanced knowledge.

The computer industry is changing so fast on a world scale that no nation, not even the US or Japan, can keep up without help from the rest of the world.

FREEDOM FOR COMPUTERS

By barring certain outside computers and software, Brazil managed to build its own computer industry—but its products are backward compared with those available outside. This means that Brazilian banks, manufacturers, and other businesses have had to use technology that is inefficient compared with that of their foreign competitors. They compete with one hand tied behind them. Rather than gaining, the country loses.

Brazil violated the first rule of the new system of wealth creation: Do what you will with the slowly changing industries, but get out of the way of a fast-advancing industry. Especially one that processes the most important resource of all—Knowledge.

Other LDCs will avoid these errors. Some, we may speculate, will actually invest modestly in existing venture capital funds in the US, Europe, and Japan—on condition that their own technicians, scientists, and students accompany the capital and share in the know-how developed by the resulting startup firms. In this way, Brazilians—or Indonesians or Nigerians or Egyptians—might find themselves at the front edge of tomorrow's industries. Astutely managed, such a program could well pay for itself—or even make a profit.

Above all, the LDCs will take a completely fresh look at the role of agriculture, regarding it not necessarily as a "backward" sector, but as a sector that, potentially, with the help of computers, genetics, satellites, and other new technologies, could some day be more advanced, more progressive than all the smokestacks, steel mills, and mines in the world. Knowledge-based agriculture may be the cutting edge of economic advance tomorrow.

FARMING FOR MORE THAN FOOD

Moreover, agriculture will not limit itself to growing food—but will increasingly grow energy crops and feedstocks for new materials. These are but a few of the ideas likely to be tested in the years to come.

But none of these efforts will bear fruit if a country is cut off from participation in the fast-moving global economy and the telecommunications and commuter networks that support it.

The maldistribution of telecommunications in today's world is even more dramatic than the maldistribution of food. There are 600 million telephones in the world—with 450 million of them in only nine countries. The lopsided distribution of computers, databases, technical publications, research expenditures, tells us more about the future potential of nations than all the gross national product figures ground out by economists.

To plug into the new world economy, countries like China, Brazil, Mexico, Indonesia, India, as well as the Soviet Union and the East European nations must find the resources needed to install their own electronic infrastructures. These must go far beyond mere telephone services to include up-to-date, high-speed data systems capable of linking into the latest global networks.

The "gap" that must be closed is informational and electronic. It is a gap not between the North and the South, but between the slow and the fast.

The Arms Race, Arms Control, and Disarmament

Since 1989, the explicit and mutual threat that fueled the arms race between the capitalist and Communist blocs has slowly dissipated. Put another way, with the Soviet-led Warsaw Pact formally dissolved (1991), with the countries of the former Communist bloc concerned only with promoting economic development and political democracy and not with threatening Western Europe, and with the Soviets continuing to dismantle the massive conventional military forces and nuclear arsenal they assembled after World War II, the Western bloc must either quickly identify a new enemy, or admit that none are adequate—at least not in Europe—to justify burdensome military budgets any longer.

If there were ever a time in history to test the hypothesis that because states arm themselves out of fear for their security, they will disarm when their security is no longer at risk, this is it. Of course, if the first assumption of this hypothesis is not true, then it will make little difference to a particular state if others no longer threaten them. A state's goal in arming itself may, for example, be to dominate other states through the threat or actual use of military power, or to acquire prestige through the acquisition of higher levels of military power. If the second assumption of this hypothesis is not true, either because states continue to believe their security is *still* at risk regardless of what other states say and do to diminish that perception, or because their own internal political forces have a vested interest in sustaining the arms race, then the hypothesis will also fail.

Gorbachev's repeated exercises in preemptive disarmament and his willingness to compromise and make concessions have been a challenge to NATO in general, the United States in particular. If the Communist bloc laid down its arms, how could the United States not do the same? If the Communists were the aggressors and the democratic liberal regimes of Western Europe and the United States the defenders—if defense was in fact the West's only goal—then why hesitate to slash the military budget?

To be sure, the United States was barely able to sustain the pace of Gorbachev's breathtaking initiatives in disarming a major empire. Between 1991 and 1993, in compliance with the Conventional Forces in Europe (CFE) Treaty, the Soviet Union will destroy all sorts of military equipment, including over 100,000 aircraft, artillery pieces, tanks, and other armored vehicles. Although the United States has gone ahead with its decision to demobilize a substantial part of its NATO forces, the war with Iraq abruptly torpedoed any idea that the United States could simply disarm worldwide. Without a clear sense of just *who* the next enemy will be, or when a former ally will suddenly enter "the enemy" category, disarmament by the former superpowers cannot go below a certain level. One thing is clear: if the arms exporters of the world do not curb their greed, the potential that many small or otherwise improverished countries may start a major international war, such as Iraq did, will be greatly strengthened. It is thanks to military aid programs and military sales that today 20 countries possess missiles, and a growing number of these are suspected, if not known, to possess nuclear weapons. As more countries develop their own weapon production capabilities, however, export controls become steadily less effective in curbing the growth of substantial military establishments.

Thus the leading industrial powers must all be prepared for a new enemy, presumably from among the LDCs, and perhaps from among former allies among those countries, to suddenly emerge and threaten world peace. Regrettably, Iraq's aggression gave pause to the developing sentiment that at last the time had arrived to convert swords into plowshares.

The leadership of every country is concerned that it not be hoodwinked by devious ploys on the part of its adversaries. Further, regardless of Gorbachev's sincerity, the very real dismantling of the Warsaw Pact forces in Eastern Europe, and the birth of non-Communist regimes in Eastern Europe, Gorbachev's political future in the U.S.S.R. is in grave doubt. It is entirely conceivable that he will be replaced with men who think about the West and defense in a different and more hostile manner. History has repeatedly shown that one man can make a difference; and it behooves the West to be wary of disarming itself to a dangerously low level before Eastern Europe and the Soviet Union are more stabilized. It is a sad denouement to the liberating events of 1989–1990, and to the replacement of authoritarian Communist regimes with more democratic political systems that the net result has been the emergence of ethnic and national hatred that threatens to destabilize the countries of Eastern Europe and the Soviet Union.

The Soviet Union's motivation for initiating the process of disarmament was complex. Its domestic context was crucial. It included the drain of a massive military budget on economic development and social programs; the inability of the Soviet Union, even after 45 years of nearly intolerable sacrifice by the Soviet peoples, to get ahead in the military technology race with the United States; domestic unrest; a failure to win a war in Afghanistan after nine years; and the isolation of the communist bloc from the international mainstream of economic growth and technological development because of policies of confrontation that fueled the arms race. Had these factors not been enough, Gorbachev was aware that, were nuclear weapons ever used, the Soviet Union as well as the rest of the world would be the loser in the "nuclear winter" to follow.

The motive for the United States to respond positively to Gorbachev's initiatives sprang from some of the same roots: the drain of a massive military budget on domestic social programs, the awareness that nuclear weapons could not be used without acknowledging the possible end to civilization as we know it, and the failure to achieve a technological breakthrough for "Star Wars" (or "strategic defense initiative") to work. But the final straw was the collapse of "the enemy": the fall of the Communist regimes of Eastern Europe and the efforts of Gorbachev to bring about a more peaceful world. The United States simply had to respond. Could it really justify amassing military forces to overrun the governments and peoples led by Walesa in Poland, Havel in Czechoslovakia, or even those overseeing the dismantling of the communist system in East Germany, Romania, and Bulgaria?

With all the above factors to consider, it is likely that arms control and disarmament efforts will plateau for the time being.

In fact, the war with Iraq was responsible for yet one more major delay in a final agreement on the Strategic Arms Reduction Treaty (START). Perhaps more important than the war was Washington's concern about Gorbachev's inability to gain public support for this policies, and his resort to a dogmatic coercive style in response to public challenges to his policies and authority. The United States has tried to be supportive of Gorbachev, the single most important person in bringing the cold war to an end. It sees the difficulty of Gorbachev's position vis-à-vis various nationalities demanding autonomy and citizens impatient with the lack of results from the economic reforms embodied in *perestroika*. The United States realizes that Gorbachev needs all the support he can get in liberalizing the economic and political system without the Soviet Union's disintegrating into civil war. Yet Gorbachev's repeated resort to coercive measures since 1990 to suppress legitimate public dissent, to prevent secession movements, and to put down ethnic strife has given Washington pause.

An additional reason for delay in agreeing to START is the desire by START negotiators to *convert* rather than destroy the designated missiles to peaceful space-launch vehicles. This debate is accompanied by efforts to convert military production facilities and other military hardware scheduled to be destroyed into civilian use. Most military hardware cannot, in fact, be converted to civilian use, but the factories can be converted to civilian production—or should be shut down. The truth is that the hoped-for results of reducing weapon inventories of the two superpowers will be undercut if all the major industrial countries continue to produce weapons they do not need for their own security and to export arms to other countries. Countries in the Third World continue to buy arms even when it means their people lack enough to eat, and many countries are trying to build their own nuclear (or chemical or biological) weapons so that they can try to get what they want with military threats, just as Iraq tried.

The superpowers should retain a strong defense—military power that is strictly defensive. By definition, it would lack offensive capability, the ability to project the use of military force beyond its own territory. The United States and many other countries, however, define "national security" in a way that goes far beyond the defense of their own territory to include the assurance of an uninterrupted supply of strategic resources. The solution to this dilemma could, in part, be an energy policy that would make these countries less dependent on the foreign supply of energy resources. The other major part of the solution would be attention to confidence-building measures rather than to the technicalities of arms control and disarmament. Confidence-building measures are essentially security-building measures, ones that would allow countries to feel secure enough to put their resources into economic development rather than the arms race.

Looking Ahead: Challenge Questions

Imagine that you were the chief arms control negotiator for either the Soviet Union or the United States. What factors would you have to consider while negotiating disarmament? As a

negotiator under the present circumstances, would you feel sure that you knew enough about the future disposition of European and Soviet affairs to make major decisions to disarm your country? Given the demonstrated inability of either the Soviet Union or the United States to control their Mid-Eastern "allies," how would an awareness that some of them might be acquiring, or might already have, nuclear weapons capabilities affect your willingness to disarm? How would it affect your reconceptualization of your defense needs?

Does the continuing development of chemical and biological weapons affect the willingness of the Soviet Union and the United States to continue to negotiate away nuclear weapons? Why do some countries believe that nuclear weapons have actually stabilized the post–World War II world so that a major war has not occurred again? Why has the existence of nuclear weapons inhibited the willingness of either NATO or U.S.S.R. to use conventional weapons in Europe? Can you imagine a future situation in which the reign of nuclear terror will be seen as a period preferable to what followed its demise?

STARTing Over

Adam Garfinkle

Adam Garfinkle is coordinator of the Political Studies Program at the Foreign Policy Research Institute and contributing editor of the institute's journal, ORBIS.

EVER SINCE THE Soviet concession on SDI at Jackson Hole, Wyoming in mid-September 1989, expectations for a reasonably quick completion of a START Treaty have run very high. Judging from the pace of negotiations so far in 1990, these expectations are justified. In all likelihood, sometime this year the Bush administration will set a completed treaty before the Senate for ratification.

This rapid progress has struck most people as a wonderfully good thing and it is not hard to see why. START would be the first strategic nuclear arms agreement to reduce nuclear weapons, an achievement ardently promised but left unrequited in both SALT I and SALT II Treaties. START would also be seen as adding critical momentum to the improving state of relations between the superpowers—an appearance of no small political importance to both Gorbachev and Bush.

But a closer look raises other possibilities. Even if completing an agreement turns out to be relatively easy, securing ratification may not be. Intoxicating as the present U.S.-Soviet mood may be, it cannot divert scrutiny from anything as critical as a major agreement on strategic weapons. The START ratification process will not resemble the ca-sual cakewalk over the INF Treaty in early 1988. To the contrary, the administration is headed into a political hornet's nest of debate about strategic doctrine and programs. Indeed, despite vast changes in the last decade, START's ratification may resemble nothing so much as the SALT II ratification process of 1979.

Here We Go Again?

IT IS NOW standard political wisdom that SALT II was sacrificed on the altar of Washington politics. Attacks from both the Left and Right on the treaty, and related disputes over other issues such as the size and composition of the defense budget, were too much for a weak Carter administration to parry. The result was a debacle. The Senate refused to ratify SALT II, and to avoid political embarrassment during the year before a presidential election, President Carter removed the treaty from consideration, using the Soviet invasion of Afghanistan as a pretext.

But politics alone did not kill SALT II. The main reason that SALT II was not ratified is that between the time negotiations began in earnest in 1974 and the time they concluded in 1979, a sea change had occurred in U.S. strategic doctrinal thinking and in U.S. views of the concordance (or lack thereof) between U.S. and Soviet conceptions of arms control and strategic liability. Had SALT II been ready for the Senate in 1975, or even 1977, it would have passed easily. But by 1979, new technological developments pertaining mainly to counterforce ballistic accuracies and new intelligence about how the Soviet Union was deploying that technology convinced a majority of observers that key U.S. assumptions about the very nature of strategic stability were no longer valid.

Specifically, Soviet deployments beyond numerical parity that had been thought to compensate for general American technological superiority were now seen instead as components of a war-winning first strike counterforce doctrine. If that were so, then post-SALT I expectations—that after the achievement of rough parity, the arms race would find a natural equipoise—were unwarranted. Also put in doubt was the assumption that Soviet accession to the ABM Treaty reflected a strategic viewpoint consanguine with that of the United States. Instead, the belief gained ground that Soviet interest in the ABM Treaty had more to do with limiting U.S. technological momentum and with guaranteeing a free ride for new Soviet counterforce systems.

This huge conceptual shift doomed SALT II. The Carter administration, whose own views on these issues were diverse, could not argue for the treaty with one voice. Officials were thus caught between the floors, so to speak, as the doctrinal debate evolved, and the deal went down.

Much has changed over the last ten years, but some things have not. In 1979, U.S. foreign and security policies were in deep malaise, while an aggressive Soviet geopolitical offensive and arms build-up proceeded unabated. In 1990, Western fortunes are waxing and it is the Soviet empire that finds itself in deep trouble. This shift gives rise to at least two ironies about the politics of arms control.

First, while improved U.S.-Soviet relations have opened up a host of opportunities for arms control, the reasons for pursuing them are both different and diminished. The new U.S.-Soviet detente, built as it is on Soviet weaknesses, has made arms control politically less important in the United States. In the popular mind, the Soviets are less a threat than a defeated basket case deserving of U.S. political advice and economic charity. The popular impulse, there-fore, is to ask: Why split hairs counting warheads when peace is breaking out all over? So while agreements may be easier to get, we have less need of them politically than we have had for some decades.

Second, the conceptual divide about deterrence, strategic doctrine, and arms control that shaped the SALT II debate will return, but in a new form. Adherents of minimal deterrence who believe that only a few weapons are needed to deter one's opponents can now seize upon the calm of the early 1990s to argue that even if Soviet strategic doctrine once called for aggressive preemptive counterforce strikes, it does so no longer. Instead of "the empire isn't evil," we now hear "the empire isn't *still* evil." Such advocates will insist that Soviet doctrine is now reformulated as a "defensive strategy" in fact as well as in theory; that continuing Soviet counterforce deployments would cease if only ours did; and that the strategic balance itself has become virtually irrelevant.

One might have thought that we would have learned our strategic lessons by now, and that these old arguments would have been settled at last by experience and common sense. But some things never change. Democracies have short memories and American democracy, in particular, when allowed by normal times to be itself, has an almost unlimited appetite for circumscribing its military forces and commitments. The irony is that in seemingly calmer times, vigilance is undermined and exactly the kinds of "soft" positions that got us into trouble in the first place can return. And so, the doves are back, arguing for a general demobilization of deterrent U.S. military power. Such thinking followed virtually every other war the United States has fought; why should the end of the Cold War be different?

This is not to suggest that the Soviet Union itself remains unchanged. When the Soviets say that they *no longer* think a nuclear war can be won, they probably mean it. But the Soviet military has not abandoned counterforce for purposes of damage limitation. Damage limitation does not require the mix and size of forces that a war-winning strategy requires, and that is good. But the strategic balance has not become irrelevant; a nuclear war has not become impossible; nuclear weapons still cast political shadows; and deterrence has not somehow become self-regulating.

Prelude to Cacophony

ONE WAY OF thinking about the coming debate is to examine the travails of a certain infamous phrase: "the window of vulnerability." The phrase works like a catalyst: dropped into any argument about strategic affairs and arms control, it soon separates any intellectual mixture into its basic axiomatic assumptions. The notion also serves as a kind of transparent palimpsest; through it one can trace the evolution and debasing of a variety of arguments and the partisan designs of their advocates.

Since at least the mid–1970s, Americans concerned with arms control have been divided about basic premises concerning strategic nuclear deterrence. At the heart of this disagreement lies the disputed significance of the ballistic counterforce imbalance, depending in turn on disputes about Soviet strategic doctrine and policy. The imbalance is what gave rise to the "window of vulnerability" thesis itself. Even to refer to it is to conjure the strategic divide that separates one school of American strategic thinkers from another.

In plain English, the difference comes down to whether it is more effective to deter war by credibly threatening to destroy Soviet cities and people no matter what they do or when they do it; or whether it is more effective to confront the Soviets with the prospect that their relative military situation would be far worse after a nuclear exchange than before it. The former approach only requires that the United States have enough fairly accurate, but survivable, weapons systems capable of targeting enough Soviet cities to inflict "unacceptable damage," however that may be defined. The latter one requires a substantially larger number of survivable systems capable of accurate attacks against a range of Soviet military assets.

These doctrinal questions remain unsettled, and politics will again shape the arms control debate. For those who adhere to the more minimal view of deterrence, SALT II was defensible from a military perspective. For those who believe deterrence rests on more exacting strategic capabilities, SALT II was either a bad deal or a meaningless one. This dispute still matters. Those who liked SALT II will like START even if it leaves the relative Soviet advantage in prompt hard-target ballistic systems unchanged, or even if it enhances it. Those who opposed SALT II, other things being more or less equal, will also oppose START if it does not redress the counterforce imbalance.

As before, doctrinal disagreement will mix with peripheral but emotional arguments about the size of the defense budget and the level and types of strategic modernization to be sought. Clearly, if the administration cannot find a way to pull enough liberal Democrats behind its preferred modernization program and is forced to settle for less, it will lose conservatives when it comes time to count votes for START. And the collapse of communism notwithstanding, it still only takes a third of the Senate plus one to spoil the party.

Your "Window" or Mine?

IN ORDER to argue that the strategic balance is essentially irrelevant, many Democrats will insist that the counterforce imbalance is a bogeyman from bygone days. What vocabulary will they choose? They will claim that the "window of vulnerability" has been closed, and that President Bush's own adviser on national security, General Brent Scowcroft, was himself the one who closed it in April 1983 with the Scowcroft Commission report.

The assertion that the Scowcroft Commission closed the "window of vulnerability" in 1983 is one we are bound to hear repeatedly as soon as the treaty is completed and the White House begins to circle the wagons for the ratification debate. Indeed, this notion has become an indelible part of the Common Knowledge, but, like many other aspects of the Common Knowledge, it is quite wrong.

What treaty opponents said in 1979 was that SALT II would countenance the theoretical vulnerability of the *land-based* leg of the U.S. strategic triad. In its original formulation, the "window of vulnerability" never meant that the vulnerability of U.S. land-based missiles was tantamount to the literal vulnerability of the entire U.S. strategic force. But because the land-based force was the only leg of the triad capable of a counterforce response to a Soviet first-strike, its vulnerability was deemed crisis-unstable (such is the jargon), unhealthy for the credibility of extended deterrence, and therefore worth worrying about.

The original "window of vulnerability" idea was thus part of a serious debate about the dynamics of the then-new mutual counterforce strategic world. What were the implications of counterforce inequality—even amid overall rough numerical parity—on crisis dynamics? Would a superpower with a counterforce advantage be inclined toward great risk-taking at lower levels of violence? SALT II opponents had no monopoly of wisdom on these questions, and doubtless some of the fears they expressed ten years ago were exaggerated. Nevertheless, the problems encapsulated by the phrase "window of vulnerability" were real and so difficult that we are discussing them still.

Clearly, the "window of vulnerability" was shorthand for one approach to the bedeviling issues of stability in a counterforce imbalanced world, *not* a simple-minded notion that the Soviet Union would initiate a nuclear war "out of the blue" just because Minuteman was theoretically vulnerable. Opponents of SALT II never claimed that nuclear war was at hand because of the proposed treaty or for any other reason; such fearsome tactics instead became a staple of the Left and the nuclear freeze movement. SALT II was not undone, as some latter day pundits would have it, by a band of hysterical Cold Warriors whose views had not changed since the days of the 1948 Berlin crisis. On the contrary, it was the views of proponents of finite deterrence that were stuck in the rut, ignoring the implications of the on-going revolution in strategic technology.

The core argument over SALT II, revolving around the "window of vulnerability," was a serious one, but a funny thing did happen to the "window" on the way to the Reagan administration. President Reagan, as is well known, lacked a solid grasp of such esoteric matters; his strengths lay in other domains. One of them was political savvy, so when he came upon the evocative notion of a "window of vulnerability" through his advisers in the 1980 campaign, he took it with him into the presidential election season. As often happens with complex ideas spun out into a partisan environment, nuance gave way to the requisites of polemics. The "window of vulnerability" exited the campaign a simple-minded caricature. Suddenly, the vul-

nerability of Minuteman was tantamount to decisive Soviet military superiority as construed in the flattest and most primitive sense of the phrase.

Once this had happened, the "window of vulnerability" became easy prey for those who wanted to discount the very real problem it had originally described and who wanted to frustrate the Reagan administration's plans for modernizing U.S. land-based strategic forces. This explains how much of the erroneous Common Knowledge on this matter came about. It also helps to explain the strange notions about what the Scowcroft Commission did and did not do to the famed "window." As a result, the partisan battle over the "window of vulnerability" as a piece of strategic vocabulary was waged continuously between 1980 and April 1983, and when the Scowcroft Commission report was issued, it set off a stampede into print by those committed observers who were determined to make the report mean what they wanted it to mean. In the process, the truth was trampled still further.

The Scowcroft Commission report affirmed the vulnerability of the land-based leg of the strategic triad, and it did say early on that the vulnerability of U.S. land-based forces was not the same as the vulnerability of the entire U.S. strategic triad. But, as noted earlier, this was hardly news, for SALT II's opponents had never made such claims. Nevertheless, a lot of people, seeing what they wanted to see, threw down the report and picked up their pens. To give one of many examples of what happened next, the senior editors of the *New Republic* wrote in May 1983 that the report

. . . should be satisfying to certain critics of the Administration's strategic thinking as it should be embarrassing to the Administration. Some of the Administration's most fundamental strategic axioms—which the president has put to good political use, in the form of such slogans as "the window of vulnerability"—do not survive the Scowcroft Commission's scrutiny. . . . The vulnerability of America's land-based forces, in other words, is not the vulnerability of America. Or, to put it differently, we, without a first-strike force, are deterring them, and they, with a first-strike force, are deterred.

The scribblers did not read far enough. The Scowcroft Commission *supported* the fundamental strategic axioms of the Reagan administration; it affirmed rather eloquently the "window of vulnerability" argument as it existed in pre-Reagan 1979. If the window were really closed, why would the commission have insisted that the United Stated develop a mobile missile? Even though it is more than seven years old, it is worth quoting the report at some length because so many people seem never actually to have read it:

> Effective deterrence of any Soviet temptation to threaten or launch a massive conventional or a limited nuclear war. . . requires us to have a comparable ability to destroy Soviet military targets. . . . A one-sided strategic condition in which the Soviet Union could effectively destroy the whole range of strategic targets in the United States, but we could not effectively destroy a similar range of targets in the Soviet Union, would be extremely unstable over the long run. Such a situation could tempt the Soviets, in a crisis, to feel they could successfully threaten or even undertake conventional or limited nuclear aggression in the hope that the United States would lack a fully effective response. A one-sided condition of this sort would clearly not serve the cause of peace.

In the report's conclusions, the critical issue of extended deterrence was addressed:

> The serious imbalance between the Soviet's massive ability to destroy hardened land-based military targets with their ballistic missile force and our lack of such a capability must be redressed promptly. Our ability to assure our allies that we have the capability and will to stand with them, with whatever forces are necessary. . . is in question as long as this imbalance exists. . . . [W]e must have a credible capacity for controlled, prompt, limited attack on hard targets ourselves. . . . Consequently, in the interest of the alliance as a whole, we cannot safely permit a situation to continue wherein the Soviets have the capability promptly to destroy a range of hardened military targets and we do not.

Now, that is exactly what Paul Nitze and Eugene Rostow and Alexander Haig and Senators Henry Jackson and John Tower meant by a "window of vulnerability" during the SALT II hearings, as even a cursory review of their testimonies and statements from 1978 to 1979 makes plain. The Scowcroft Commission never closed the "window of vulnerability"—it only closed the ill-constructed shutters affixed by the Great Communicator, who was, in this instance at least, a "window of vulnerability" in his own right.

Closing the Window of Vulnerability

THE ORIGINAL "window of vulnerability" is still open, at least judging by the usual numbers and ratios. For all the Reagan administration's huffing and puffing, the ratio of Soviet to U.S. counterforce warheads actually *grew* over the eight years of Reagan's tenure. While the United States has fumbled around for more than ten years trying to bring to full operational capacity a new ICBM, arguing inconclusively between deploying a mobile MIRVed MX or a single-warheaded Midgetman, the Soviet Union—poverty, glasnost, perestroika, wild-eyed Lithuanians, and all—has designed, developed, and deployed *both* the SS–25 and SS–24. In addition, it has deployed what Moscow calls a modified version of the monstrous SS–18, but which is in fact qualitatively improved to the point that it is in essence a third new Soviet ICBM.

These three additions contribute considerably to the already daunting Soviet strategic advantage. Even with the 50 percent reduction in heavy ICBMs required by START, the Soviets will be able to maintain, indeed improve in relative terms, their prompt hard-target capabilities. Increased mobility, combined with improvements in missile guidance, will result in a more accurate, survivable, and dangerous Soviet strategic force. This effort is not born of absent-mindedness. On the contrary, now that the Soviet security perimeter in Eastern Europe has collapsed, and given the enormous expense of conventional forces, nuclear weapons are more important to the Soviet sense of security and superpower status than ever before. Soviet doctrinal adjustments notwithstanding, this continuing build-up simply must not go without an answer, and START, no matter how benign it might (or might not) be in other ways, cannot substitute for one.

Reducing warheads by half, even down to numerically equal levels, would not thereby create equal capabilities and equal risks that are conducive to deterrence. The mix of weapons would remain significantly different between the two powers, yielding different operational capabilities favoring the Soviet Union. There would also be two other related and important asymmetries. One is that if war begins, the Soviets will start it; the other is that, overall, the number of targets inside the Soviet Union is larger and better defended that ours. If available U.S. retaliatory warheads diminish dramatically relative to the Soviet target set—which includes some 3,000 buried and hardened command posts—we will find ourselves unable to do what our strategic integrated operating plan (SIOP) would have us do. We must then confront two questions: Does a reduced likelihood of war, thanks to the presumed political benefits of START, compensate for a reduced ability to prosecute war should deterrence fail? And does a diminution in relative capabilities drive us for better or worse to a redefinition of our strategic doctrine? These are crucial questions, and no ratification debate will be able—or should be allowed—to avoid them.

Arms control cannot substitute for military competition; it is rather *a part* of military competition. If the Bush administration tries to ignore these questions, those who led the attack on SALT II will lead an attack on START. The administration must find a way to modernize and reconfigure U.S. strategic forces effectively within a START-constrained context, or it will be undercut from the Right, perhaps decisively so.

If the administration does tend to business, however, it will face even stronger attacks from the Left. These will be easier to manage, but to do so, General Scowcroft and his associates will need to invest in a couple of cases of Windex to restore the "window of vulnerability" to its pristine condition circa April 1983.

GOODWILL MISSIONS FOR CASTOFF MISSILES

ANN M. FLORINI and WILLIAM C. POTTER

Ann M. Florini is a senior researcher at the University of California at Los Angeles Center for International and Strategic Affairs. William C. Potter is a professor of international policy studies and director of the Center for Russian and Soviet Studies, Monterey Institute of International Studies.

U.S. and Soviet arms control negotiators were able to agree, with relative ease, on the general outline for deep reductions in strategic arms (START). But it has proved more difficult for them to decide what to do with all the missiles that will be decommissioned as a consequence of the treaty. Neither the United States nor the Soviet Union is inclined to follow the INF Treaty precedent in which all the costly intermediate-range missiles were destroyed—a wasteful, if straightforward and readily verifiable, approach. Instead, START negotiators are considering plans to convert treaty-prohibited missiles into peaceful space-launch vehicles. To date, however, the two sides have been unable to agree on what constitutes peaceful uses.[1] An increasingly sharp dispute has arisen over whether the START missiles should be used only for civilian purposes, or whether some military uses would be permitted.

There is little doubt about the technical and economic feasibility of conversion. Converted missiles have carried non-weapons payloads into space from the dawn of the space age. The first U.S. satellite, Explorer I, was launched in January 1958 on a modified Army Redstone missile called Jupiter C, while the first Sputnik was launched on a virtually unmodified Soviet liquid-fueled intercontinental ballistic missile (ICBM), the SS-6. Since then, payloads have frequently ridden into space atop deployed or surplus missiles pulled from their silos or storehouses and turned into space boosters. [See boxes.]

Despite the extensive experience both superpowers have in converting military missiles to space launchers, no missile conversion has yet been undertaken as a consequence of any arms reduction accord. Even the INF Treaty, which allowed each side to destroy up to 100 missiles by launching them, effectively ruled out their use as space launchers by specifying the areas where the missiles must crash to earth. Most INF missiles, in any case, lacked the thrust to be very effective space boosters.

The larger missiles on the table in the START negotiations, however, are much more promising candidates for conversion. Although neither government has announced specifically which missiles it plans to cut, it is not difficult to make an educated guess about where the brunt of the cuts is likely to fall. On the U.S. side, the older land-based Minuteman II and III missiles and the sea-based Poseidons head the list of likely targets. On the Soviet side, the draft START treaty explicitly requires the destruction of half of the big SS-18s. In addition, the Soviets will probably scrap their older SS-11s, SS-13s, and SS-17s, as well as some SS-19s, to make room for newer SS-24s, SS-25s, and SS-18 Mod 5s.

Compared to most dedicated space-launch vehicles these missiles have very small payload capabilities, ranging from a few hundred to about 1,300 kilograms. Even the largest, the Soviet SS-18, can boost a payload at best one-half to one-third the size carried by standard U.S. space boosters such as the Delta or Atlas. But the converted missiles are also substantially cheaper. Officials of Lockheed Corporation, which makes all of the U.S. family of submarine-launched ballistic missiles (SLBMs)—the Poseidon, the Trident I, and the new Trident II—estimate that customers could expect to pay about $12 million per launch for any of these missiles if they were converted. This is competitive with the costs of NASA's small Scout booster. The much larger Titan III space booster, by contrast, costs over $100 million per launch.[2]

Although cost estimates are very rough approximations which depend on assumptions

INF missiles weren't powerful enough, but missiles retired under START will be good candidates for delivering small payloads into space.

From *The Bulletin of the Atomic Scientists*, November 1990, pp. 25-31. Copyright © 1990 by the Educational Foundation for Nuclear Science, 6042 South Kimbark, Chicago, IL 60637, USA. A one-year subscription is $30.

Converted missiles could be used for scientific and humanitarian projects.

LIFTING SATELLITES INSTEAD OF WARHEADS

Weight of payload, in kilograms, that converted ballistic missiles could loft into polar low-earth orbit.

U.S.

Minuteman III	260
MX	1,320
Poseidon	225*
Trident I	360*
Trident II	725*

Soviet

SS-25	260
SS-19	1,140
SS-24	1,320
SS-18 Mod 4	2,900
SS-18 Mod 5	3,200

*payload for orbital height of 400 nautical miles. All other payloads are calculated for 300-nautical-mile orbits.

—A.M.F., W.C.P.

about the number of missiles to be procured, the extent of the refurbishment required, how much reliability is sought, and so on, it appears that converted missiles will at least be competitive in terms of cost per pound of payload. The small size and low cost would make the converted missiles suitable for a variety of both military and civilian missions to low-earth orbit, especially given the rapidly advancing technical capabilities of small satellites.

At least four options exist for disposing of the decommissioned START missiles:

■ **Destruction is still the simplest option.** It is easily verified, whereas missiles converted into space-launch vehicles might be converted back into military missiles carrying nuclear warheads. And it eliminates the danger of adversely affecting the nascent private launch industry in the United States by flooding the market.

But verifying conversion is not likely to be much harder than verifying destruction of missiles. The danger that either side could suddenly break out of the treaty can be reduced by linking the conversion schedule to the disarmament schedule, thereby preventing the accumulation of a large stockpile of idle launchers. As long as the missile launch platforms are destroyed, the breakout potential is not likely to be a serious problem.

■ **Convert to alternative military use.** U.S. and Soviet negotiators are stalemated over conversion provisions in the treaty largely because the United States wants to use missiles such as the Minuteman II and Poseidon in Strategic Defense Initiative research, to launch space weapons or to serve as targets for testing SDI weapons.[3] The U.S. Air Force also seems interested in acquiring some of the START missiles to supplement its depleted stockpile of Minuteman I and II boosters, which it uses to space-test warheads and ICBM subsystems.[4] In addition, the START missiles are attractive to proponents of the view that the United States should be able to launch on short notice large numbers of light-weight, cheap, simple satellites, known as Lightsats, for military purposes. Missile conversion is especially appealing to the U.S. Air Force, which already controls the missiles and has extensive experience in converting them to space boosters.

But the Soviets have less to gain from conversion to alternative military use. They have plenty of launch vehicles. Most of the proposed U.S. military uses of converted small launch vehicles would benefit the United States in the case of a conflict with the Soviet Union. Moreover, introducing a primary military element to missile conversion would destroy the swords-into-plowshares symbolism that makes the conversion

proposal so attractive. Not surprisingly, Soviet START negotiators have opposed using decommissioned missiles for purposes other than launching non-weapon payloads.

■ **Transfer missiles to the private sector.** Decommissioned START missiles, minus warheads, could be made available to commercial launch firms through sales to the highest bidders or free distribution. Either approach is likely to reduce launch costs and expand space-launch capabilities. There is no consensus in either country, however, on the demand for boosters of the START missile variety or the effects that their availability would have on the commercial space-launch industry.

One U.S. company has bet on greatly increased demand: Lockheed wants to purchase decommissioned SLBMs from the navy and convert them to carry small satellites for NASA and other customers. It maintains that its plan could save taxpayers millions of dollars, provide income to the U.S. government, and cut space launch costs.[5]

Other companies in competition for the commercial rocket business are less enthusiastic. Orbital Sciences Corporation, for example, the co-producer of an innovative small-winged launch vehicle called Pegasus, charges that conversion would amount to "government dumping" and would place it at a disadvantage in the highly competitive space-launch business.

The debate is similar in the Soviet Union, where the major resistance to the idea of missile conversion has come from Glavcosmos, the civilian space agency. In recent interviews, Glavcosmos officials maintained that they could provide commercial launch services on new launch vehicles more cheaply than could be obtained through converting ballistic missiles to peaceful space launchers. This argument may well be self-serving: conversion would produce competition for Glavcosmos at a time when the agency is hard pressed to find customers for its rockets. It must be acknowledged, however, that Glavcosmos has offered launchers for as little as $20 million.

■ **Dedicate the missiles to scientific and humanitarian purposes.** Converted missiles could promote international cooperation in space, assist efforts to monitor global environmental change, and facilitate Third World economic development. A combination of technical and political factors now makes conversion of the START missiles an attractive prospect for a new group of potential users including nonprofit organizations and developing nations.

Advances in microelectronics and other technologies have made it possible to build satellites weighing as little as 10 kilograms and costing as little as $1 million each. If a few hundred satellites of the same design were made, the cost per satellite would probably drop to a few hundred thousand dollars. Thus, it is now possible to undertake meaningful space missions with a budget that is, by space program standards, quite small. The START missiles, with their relatively small payload capacities, might be appropriate candidates to launch this type of satellite.

Several nonprofit organizations are now working to launch small satellites for a variety of worthy causes. Satelife, a private international venture run largely by American and Soviet specialists, is working on a small, cheap communications satellite that would give physicians in remote areas of developing countries access to major centers of medical information located in industrialized countries. A physician on the ground would use a small work station, about the size of a suitcase, to plug into the system and retrieve electronic mail or send messages. Users would have access to the system six to eight times a day. Satelife expects to have the first "Healthsat" satellite built some time in the early 1990s, and the Soviet Union has offered to launch it. Although the design is still under review, the spacecraft will probably weigh about 45–70 kilograms.

A nonprofit U.S. development organization called VITA has a similar project called Pacsat, based on two small satellites in polar orbit with the capability to pick up messages from a ground station, store them, and transmit them to ground stations in any part of the world. In its demonstration phase VITA hopes to show the value of cheap, satellite-based communications for development programs. Appropriate projects could include communications with isolated refugee camps, tracking locusts in Africa, or identifying droughts and other disasters in their early stages. If successful, VITA plans to launch two operational satellites in the early 1990s, each weighing 50–60 kilograms and costing about $1 million.

In response to the growing concerns over environmental degradation, especially global warming, the world's space agencies have banded together to begin a monitoring program called Mission to Planet Earth, aimed at providing, for the first time, a relatively detailed and accurate picture of the changes and interactions occurring in the planet's ecosphere. As currently structured, the program will be carried out largely by the United States, Japan, and a dozen West European countries cooperating under the auspices of the European Space Agency. They plan to launch a set of four large platforms (two U.S., one Japanese, and one European), weighing 15 tons each and carrying 12–14 instruments. In time, the planners hope to launch additional instruments.

Although the program has drawn a generally enthusiastic response from scientists and policymakers who recognize the urgent need for information about climate change, the reliance on a few very large platforms has sparked concern. The broad range of instruments needed to monitor the biosphere and geosphere have to be placed in different types of orbits and at different altitudes. As one leading scientist said, "The whole thing should be better and less expensive, I think, if we had a multitude of instruments on smaller platforms."[6]

One Soviet proponent of missile conversion, an economist, has proposed that SS-18s be modified to lift satellites into orbit to perform a vari-

Revamped Atlases and Titans

The U.S. Air Force Atlas E and F ICBMs were built between 1960 and 1965. In the early 1970s, many were scrapped, but the air force also began the Vandenberg Atlas Modification Program (VAMP) to transform the ICBMs into space launch vehicles. The first VAMP launch took place October 2, 1972. Few Atlases remain available, and the last will probably be launched in the next few years.

Atlas missiles are taken out of storage at Norton Air Force Base near San Bernardino, California, and shipped to General Dynamics in San Diego, where the cone that formerly housed the nuclear warhead is removed and the ringweld modified to allow a spacecraft and upper stage adapters to be attached. The rockets are then shipped to the launch site at Vandenberg Air Force Base, also in California.

In response to a series of failures, the air force undertook an overhaul program called Canoga in the early 1980s. The troublesome booster engines undergo a complete overhaul by Rocketdyne in Canoga Park, in the San Fernando Valley, and are then shipped to Vandenberg to be reinstalled in the vehicle. At Vandenberg, new guidance, destruct, telemetry, electrical, and hydraulic systems are installed; wiring is replaced; necessary structural repairs are accomplished; and all systems are tested. Since the Canoga overhaul program was instituted, Atlas E launchers have enjoyed a perfect success record.

The conversion, including the extensive Canoga overhaul, averages about $8 million per vehicle. Another program will convert at least 14 of the 55 existing deactivated Titan II ICBMs into space launch vehicles. The first converted Titan was launched September 1988. As currently configured, the Titan II, the largest ICBM the United States has ever deployed (not to be confused with the even larger Titan III space rocket), can put up to 1,900 kilograms into a 110-mile polar orbit. According to *Military Space* (May 8, 1989), it is being used to launch Defense Department and civil weather satellites, naval surveillance satellites, and a Landsat civil remote-sensing satellite.

Because these boosters are used to launch costly military payloads that are frequently more expensive than the launch vehicles themselves, the air force has been willing to pay for extensive refurbishment to insure that they work properly. Even so, the converted missiles are economically competitive with rockets now being offered by private firms. The cost of using a Titan II ($35–40 million per launch), is less than the $50 million being charged by McDonnell Douglas to launch payloads on the slightly larger Delta.

—A.M.F., W.C.P.

ety of environmental observation tasks, including monitoring the dynamics of cloud and snow cover, volcanic activity, and forest fires.[7]

In addition to yielding scientific and economic benefits to developing nations, a missile conversion plan could show countries often critical of the superpowers that they too can benefit from progress in East-West arms control. A demonstrable link between disarmament and development may be especially important in securing support for stopping the spread of nuclear weapons and ballistic missiles.

The United States and the Soviet Union have found it difficult to agree on what to do with the START missiles because the two countries have very different needs. The United States is short of small, cheap launch vehicles, especially for military purposes, but it is also trying to encourage the development of a private launch industry to meet those needs. The Soviet Union has a bigger stable of launch vehicles, and it is eager to make money, but its efforts to market space boosters, in some cases allegedly at less than market prices, represent potentially unfair competition for U.S. industry.

To break the current deadlock over conversion, START negotiators need to find a common interest, and the most attractive one is cooperation for scientific and humanitarian purposes. This approach not only preserves the political appeal of conversion, but would create projects that would increase the demand for small launch vehicles. The impact on the fledgling U.S. space-launch industry would therefore be minimized. In fact, by creating new demand that could persist after the START missiles were expended, such a program could actually bolster the industry. Both countries also stand to gain in the long run from scientific cooperation and from economic development of poor countries.

To avoid further complicating the START negotiations, the treaty should simply state that the converted missiles will be used only for mutually agreed purposes, with all missiles to be destroyed by a certain date if no mutually acceptable use is found. The United States and the Soviet Union have an opportunity to demonstrate a space-age version of beating swords into plowshares.

Boon for Soviet space business

The Soviets have used a number of ballistic missiles as the basis for space-launch vehicles. The SS-6, which did not materialize as an operational weapon, for example, spawned a stage-and-a-half booster version that was used for nearly 1,000 space launches through 1983, including Sputnik I. In a modified form, it is still used for manned and military-observation space missions. The SS-4 and SS-5 intermediate-range ballistic missiles and the SS-9 heavy ICBM also spawned a variety of Soviet space-launch vehicles.

Soviet space scientists indicate that the Soviet Union, prior to the INF Treaty, experimented with actual conversion as well, and last year, the Soviets proposed to build a small new launcher using engineering plans and some parts of the SS-20 intermediate range ballistic missiles which were banned by the treaty. The new launcher, confusingly called "Start," would add a small-launch capability to the already substantial stable of launch services the Soviets are trying to market in the West in a series of joint ventures with a Houston firm, Space Commerce Corporation.

More than hard currency is at stake, however. The Soviets generally are trying to find ways to convert parts of their military industry to civilian uses. The Soviet side of the new joint venture is represented by a Soviet consortium called Technopribor, whose function is to export previously secret technology declassified as part of perestroika. In this case, the Soviets also want to avoid throwing the SS-20 factory employees out of work.

American officials have expressed concern about the proposal, noting that the new launcher will be similar to the Soviet SS-25 ICBM. Thus, not only could the new launcher provide a covert means of stockpiling SS-20s; it could also complicate the current START negotiations and might have to be counted under START limits. Soviet and Space Commerce officials note that American inspectors are already permanently stationed at the former SS-20 factory; that the new rocket will not use any of the SS-20 parts, such as rocket motors, required to be destroyed by the INF Treaty; and that the treaty's Special Verification Commission provides a forum for addressing questions related to treaty compliance.

Oleg Shishkin, head of the ministry which has overall responsibility for production of ballistic missiles, says the ministry has begun to compete with the United States, France, and China in launching commercial satellites (*Insight*, May 21, 1990). U.S. restrictions on delivering satellites that use modern U.S. technology to Soviet launch sites have hampered these efforts, but the ministry's negotiations to build a commercial satellite-launching facility in Australia, to be operated by Australians, appear to have paid off. In July 1990, President Bush announced that satellites containing American technology could be launched from the Australian spaceport on Soviet launchers.

—*A.M.F., W.C.P.*

---

1. R. Jeffrey Smith, "Strategic Arms Talks at Virtual Halt," *Washington Post*, Aug. 5, 1990, pp. 8, 11, 13.

2. Edmund L. Andrews, "Intelsat Is Suing Marietta," *New York Times*, Sept. 5, 1990, p. C1.

3. "Minutemen 'Could Have SDI Role,' " *Jane's Defense Weekly* (April 8, 1989), p. 587.

4. James W. Canan, "The Dangerous Lull in Strategic Modernization," *Air Force Magazine* (Oct. 1988), pp. 72–3.

5. John H. Cushman, "Two Companies, Big and Little, Clash over Plan on Missiles," *New York Times*, Aug. 8, 1990, p. B8.

6. Thomas M. Donahue, quoted in William K. Stevens, "NASA Plans a 'Mission to Planet Earth,' " *New York Times*, July 25, 1989, p. B7.

7. A Kireyev, "Perestroika—Test by Deed: Conversion to Economic Accountability," *Ogonyok* (July 1989), pp. 6–7, 26–27.

IS THE SOVIET UNION PREPARED FOR PEACE?

Cuts in military spending could help save the nation's economy, but the transition to a peacetime footing may not be as easy as it seems.

MICHAEL G. RENNER

Michael G. Renner, a senior researcher at the Worldwatch Institute, specializes in disarmament issues. He is the author of Worldwatch Paper 96, Swords Into Plowshares: Converting to a Peace Economy.

Five years into Mikhail Gorbachev's top-down transformation of the U.S.S.R., Soviet citizens' expectations of better living standards are skyrocketing past the capacity of an economy that could barely keep up with less extravagant desires. Store shelves remain bare, serious social needs are going unmet, and tempers are rising. The reasons for the malaise of the Soviet economy are numerous, but among the most significant is the lingering burden of excessive military spending.

President Gorbachev has stated repeatedly that ending the arms race with the United States is a prerequisite to invigorating the Soviet economy. At the 28th Communist Party Congress held in early July, Foreign Minister Eduard Shevardnadze claimed that "in the current five-year period, the sum-total peaceful dividend...can make 240 billion to 250 billion rubles." At official exchange rates, this would be equivalent to $380 to $400 billion, clearly a significant infusion of resources. Yet, so far, the fruits of Gorbachev's disarmament initiatives are not apparent.

Moscow faces a dilemma: While the eventual economic gains of disarmament promise to be sizable, they will no doubt be diminished in the near-term by costs associated with destroying military hardware, verifying arms treaties, demobilizing and housing soldiers, and reorienting military enterprises toward civilian objectives and retraining employees for that purpose. According to Valentin Smyslov, a high-ranking official with *Gosplan,* the state planning agency, the retooling of factories alone may cost some 40 billion rubles ($64 billion) over the next five years.

The Superpower Burden
The political liberalization under Gorbachev has spawned a fierce debate over the burden of heavy military spending. However, determining the extent of this burden is difficult, even in the heady days of *glasnost.* Soviet leaders say they spent 77.3 billion rubles (about $120 billion) on the military in 1989. But certain items—foreign military aid, military space programs, and parts of the defense research and development budgets—almost certainly are excluded from this figure. Additionally, the contribution of labor, machinery, and materials to arms

production probably is undervalued to a considerable degree.

Because uncertainty surrounds the size of both the military budget and the total Soviet economy, verifying the relative burden of defense spending seems an impossible task. If the officially stated numbers are correct, then military outlays absorb about 9 percent of the gross national product (GNP). Estimates by the U.S. Central Intelligence Agency run in the 15 to 17 percent range, but economist Oleg Bogomolev, a member of the Congress of People's Deputies, asserts the real burden is as high as 20 to 25 percent of GNP (the world average is about 6 percent.)

A more telling picture of military spending might emerge by measuring the share of goods and services devoted to military purposes. Unfortunately, complete up-to-date figures are not available. David Holloway of the University of Edinburgh estimated in the early 1980s that one-fifth of the Soviet Union's total industrial output was absorbed by the arms sector, including two-thirds of the aircraft and shipbuilding industries. This is a much higher share than in other industrialized countries. A little over 6 percent of total U.S. economic output went to the military in 1989, although the military portion came to 53 percent in aircraft manufacturing and virtually 100 percent in shipbuilding.

Although the true extent of military spending in the Soviet Union is not clear, it is readily apparent that the country's leaders must shift resources from guns to butter, a process known as economic conversion. Along with the enormous shortage of quality consumer goods, numerous other pressing needs in Soviet society underline the need for such a policy. There is a serious housing shortage. One-third of all schools have no running water, and the Soviet Union has infant mortality and life expectancy rates closer to those of the Third World than the West.

Spending on environmental protection—currently at 1.3 percent of GNP, according to *The Economist* in London—is a pressing need but remains clearly insufficient. By the government's own reckoning some $56 billion will be needed to prevent the complete disappearance of the Aral Sea. Some scientists think double that amount, or roughly the equivalent of one year's military expenditures, will be required. Dealing with the effects of the Chernobyl nuclear accident, meanwhile, is now estimated to cost as much as $46 billion, and perhaps more. These, of course, are just the two most publicized of the Soviet Union's many ecological disasters.

The easing of Cold War tensions has allowed the Soviets to take the first steps toward rescuing their economy; cutting weapons production and troop deployments will help rein in military spending. According to official statements, by 1991 total military spending will be 14 percent below 1988 levels. Prime Minister Nikolai Ryzhkov has said he expects the military budget to be trimmed by a third to a half by 1997.

Part of the savings derives from the withdrawal from Afghanistan. Unilateral force reductions in Europe amounting to 500,000 troops and 10,000 tanks will free up additional resources. The 1987 Intermediate-Range Nuclear Forces (INF) Treaty with the United States yielded a comparatively small net savings of $480 million, though that sum is large enough to build 30,000 to 40,000 apartments.

The remainder of projected savings in the military budget will come from a 19.5 percent reduction in arms production. Statements by various officials disagree somewhat about the specifics, but it appears that during the first half of the 1990s, tank production is to be cut by 50 percent, aircraft by 12 percent, helicopters by 25 or perhaps even 60 percent, and ammunition by 20 to 30 percent.

Although channeling these savings into civilian use would do wonders for the cash-short Soviet economy, much hard work remains before any gains will come. Military hardware needs to be adapted for peaceful purposes where possible; demobilized soldiers must be reintegrated into society; and, most important, military production facilities must be retooled for civilian use. In addition, supply-related and financial arrangements among individual factories (and the ministries to which they belong) need to be recast. These difficult steps, central to the process of economic conversion, have only just begun.

As it embarks on the conversion process, the Soviet Union joins China as the only other major power to do so in the post-World War II era China headed down this road a decade ago (see "Swords Into Consumer Goods," *World Watch*, July/August 1989).

Military Recycling

Options for adapting military hardware to civilian applications are often limited. In some cases, pieces of equipment might be refashioned and reused, in others, valuable components, such as engines, electronics equipment, or precious metals, might be salvaged and recycled. Of 10,000 battle tanks that are being withdrawn unilaterally, half are to be destroyed, some used for training purposes, and the rest converted to bulldozers and other equipment for civilian purposes. Meanwhile, Kranlod—an Odessa-based joint venture with West Germany—has begun to transform several hundred launchers for the SS-20 missiles banned by the INF accord into self-propelled hoisting cranes.

Unilateral military cutbacks turned some military equipment into surplus. Supplies worth a half-billion rubles, including motor vehicles, ships, transistors, and navigational equipment, were put up for sale to the public in 1989. Some 60 military transport planes, roughly 10 percent of the total fleet, have been made available for civilian tasks.

Unfortunately, most military hardware simply has no use in the civilian world. Scrapping missiles, tanks, and warplanes will save on maintenance and operating costs, but the expense associated with their destruction, treaty verification measures, and, in many cases, environmental cleanups takes a substantial bite out of any savings. In any event, the cost to society of building these weapons in the first place cannot be fully recouped.

Reintegrating Soldiers

Moscow's decision to demobilize 500,000 troops has led to some transitional problems. Conscripted soldiers generally return to their civilian jobs without much difficulty, but problems arise in reintegrating officers into civilian society, primarily because they need jobs and housing. By the end of the year, some 100,000 officers and 50,000 *praporshchiki* (non-commissioned officers) will have been discharged—primarily those of advanced age, judged incompetent or unmotivated, and those serving as reserve officers.

A number of measures have been taken to smooth the transition of demobilized soldiers to civilian life, including the provision of higher pensions. The Ministry of Defense

and *Goskomtrud* (the State Committee for Labor) have also established a joint retraining program; in conjunction with local authorities, they are responsible for job place-

---

Early Soviet attempts at conversion produced washing machines that cost twice as much as civilian models and television sets that exploded and caught fire.

---

ment. It is too early to tell, however, whether these programs are working as intended.

Perhaps the most critical aspect of successfully decommissioning officers is finding housing. According to Alexei Izyumov of the Institute of the U.S.A. and Canada in Moscow, more than 20,000 officers' families had no permanent homes even before the current troop cuts, and the Defense Ministry will be able to provide no more than 7,500 apartments during 1990-91. The housing shortage is particularly acute in Moscow and other large cities in the European part of the Soviet Union, where most discharged officers wish to return.

These problems will soon balloon. Gorbachev has already agreed to reduce Soviet troops stationed in Europe from the current level of 565,000 to 195,000. Soviet forces are in the process of pulling out of Czechoslovakia and Hungary. They still remain in Poland and East Germany. But with the Warsaw Pact disintegrating rapidly, Moscow may have no troops left in Eastern Europe by the turn of the century. East Germany used to foot the bill for the 360,000 Soviet soldiers stationed there, and West Germany agreed to shoulder that burden, at over $700 million a year. But once these troops return home over the next four years, Moscow will have to pay for their upkeep.

If the soldiers are successfully reintegrated

Figure 1.

Distribution of 100 Arms Producing Enterprises in Economic Regions of the Soviet Union

Arms Producing Cities in the Central/Ural areas

1 Smolensk	9 Kirov
2 Voronezh	10 Votkinsk
3 Volgograd	11 Perm'
4 Saratov	12 Sverdlovsk
5 Kuybyshov	13 Chelyabinsk
6 Ul'yanovsk	14 Kurgan
7 Gor'kiy	15 Orenburg
8 Kazan	

Number of Soviet Defense Industry Enterprises (out of 100)

☐ 0 - 5
▨ 6 - 10
▧ 11 - 15
▦ 16 - 20

Source: National Technical Information Service; Julian Cooper, *The Soviet Defence Industry and Conversion, Disarmament and Employment Program*, Working Paper No. 10, International Labor Office, Geneva, 1988; U.S. CIA, *The Soviet Weapons Industry: An Overview*, Washington, D.C., Sept. 1986, S.2.

into Soviet society, they can be a boon to an economy characterized by continuous labor shortages. If the effort fails, however, there could be serious political implications. In January 1960, for example, then-Premier Nikita Khrushchev announced a troop reduction of 1.2 million soldiers, coming on top of an earlier demobilization. Yet the policy was implemented with little preparation or regard for those affected. The military's dissatisfaction with the entire undertaking was an important factor in Khrushchev's downfall in 1964. The Gorbachev leadership is well aware that misgivings within the armed forces, of which there are already indications, could lead the military to oppose additional reductions.

Missiles into Baby Carriages

The most crucial element of conversion concerns the retooling of factories that produce war matériel. Successful retooling involves several steps: identifying alternative civilian products, conducting engineering studies to determine the feasibility of producing these goods, retraining employ-

ees and refashioning machinery where needed, organizing adequate supplies of energy and materials, and preparing marketing studies.

The factories that once produced missiles now proscribed by the INF accord have shifted part of their capacity to civilian production. The Votkinsk machine tool plant in the Udmurt Autonomous Republic, the Petropavlovsk facility in Kazakhstan, and a third factory in Volgograd are now manufacturing metal-cutting machines, drilling rigs and other oil industry equipment, washing machines, bicycles, and even baby carriages. Several missile design laboratories have also been reoriented toward civilian work, including the development of a rocket to carry meteorological equipment into orbit.

At Votkinsk, some 5 percent of the total number of skilled workers were retrained. Due to high production targets, the changeover to civilian output occurred without loss of employment. While the facility had already been involved in civilian production to some degree, the adjustment would have been smoother if conversion planning had been done in advance. To compensate for a drop in the plant's profits (and thus in its fund for wages and fringe benefits), the government allocated extra money during the transition period of 1988-90.

Retooling for Peace

The Soviet military sector has a long history of producing both military and civilian goods. The civilian share of military industry enterprises' output has doubled to about 40 percent between 1965 and today (see Table 1). Although official Soviet statements are contradictory, it appears that the defense industry now produces nearly 8 percent of all Soviet consumer goods. In 1989, some 345 military plants and 200 defense-related scientific research institutes and design bureaus were involved to varying degrees in civilian production.

According to plans approved by the Council of Ministers, the Kremlin cabinet answerable to Gorbachev, the portion of defense industries' output devoted to civilian purposes is to rise from the current 40 percent to 50 percent in 1991 and more than 60 percent by 1995. Put differently, the country's overall production of civilian goods is to rise by 5 percent through these measures. For 1990, a rather paltry sum of $6.4 billion has been budgeted to facilitate the changeover.

The additional civilian output of military enterprises will be targeted primarily toward the food-processing industry. Nearly half the $59 billion of planned new equipment deliveries to the food industry under the investment plan for 1988-95 is to be provided by defense industry enterprises. The military sector has also been directed to produce $11 to $13 billion worth of goods for light industry, as well as to increase the output of construction materials, medical equipment, and plumbing supplies.

No More Lethal TVs

If previous experience is any guide, however, simply increasing the civilian share of military industries, without proper reorientation, is likely to spawn price and quality problems. Earlier Soviet attempts at conversion produced washing machines that cost twice as much as civilian models and television sets that exploded and caught fire. Similar problems exist today.

So far, the items selected for production have not always been well-matched with the

Table 1.

Share of Total Output of Selected Civilian Goods Produced by Military Industry Enterprises, 1965-1988

	1965	1975	1985	1988
		(percent)		
TVs, Radios, VCRs, Cameras	100	100	100	100
Sewing Machines	na	na	100[1]	100
Tape Recorders	95	95	95	98
Vacuum Cleaners	49	46	75[1]	77
Washing Machines	41	32	27	69
Motorcycles & Scooters	73	68	63	61
Tramcars	72	65	60[2]	na
Refrigerators	48	48	48[2]	na
Bicycles	44	39	40	45
Watches	12	11	19	22
Tractors	13	14	15	na
Metal-cutting Machine Tools	14[3]	14	13	na
Passenger Cars	11[3]	10	12	na

[1] 1987 [2] 1980 [3] 1970

Sources: Julian M. Cooper, *The Scale of Output of Civilian Products by Enterprises of the Soviet Defence Industry*, CREES Discussion Paper, University of Birmingham, 1988 (for 1965-1985 data); John Tedstrom, *Is the Contribution of the Defense Complex to Civilian Production Growing?*, Report on the USSR, June 16, 1989 (for 1987-1988 data).

factories targeted for conversion. Of 585 consumer goods scheduled to be manufactured in 1988-89 by all military factories, only 126 were successfully produced. The target for 1989-90 was scaled down to 126 products, but by the end of 1989 only 23 of these were actually being produced.

Part of the explanation is that the conversion endeavor is proceeding hastily, more improvised than properly planned and prepared. There are efforts at the factory level and attempts to direct the process from above, with the latter tending to neglect local conditions and capabilities in deciding what alternative products individual military enterprises should produce.

Defense industries, for their part, are accustomed to working with little regard for the costs involved, a practice that if simply transferred to the civilian sector could have disastrous results. Soviet observers agree that the civilian goods produced by military firms are often too expensive for their customers. As long as these factories remain in the orbit of the defense bureaucracy, some critics charge, they will never accord priority to civilian needs and principles.

Despite these dangers, the Soviet leadership has decided to enlist the services of the military industry (with its superior access to skilled labor, materials, equipment, and technologies) in its campaign to boost the production of consumer goods. The civilian industry is seen as too backward and hamstrung to realize the hoped-for rapid improvement in living standards. Thus, the civilian Ministry of Machine-Building for the Light and Food Industries was disbanded in 1988 and many of its 260 enterprises transferred to defense ministries. While it is uncertain whether this quick-fix approach will yield the expected results, there is a definite danger that it will backfire.

A debate is currently under way between those who want to keep the military sector as a separate "economy within the economy" and retain the capability to switch back to defense production, and those who favor its breakup. The outcome is crucial to the nature of Soviet economic conversion.

Out of Military Orbit?

Defense factories still have little incentive to switch to civilian production. Many engineers, along with blue-collar workers, see civilian production as clearly secondary in priority, temporary in nature, or imposed on them. As an inducement for defense factories to produce more civilian goods, the Council of Ministers decreed in September 1988 that factories could retain profits from above-quota production of consumer goods during 1989 and 1990.

Perhaps more important than ideological preference is the fact that wages, as well as housing, child care, and other social benefits available to military industry employees and their families are closely linked to the fortunes of defense factories. At least in some cases, profit margins and wages have dropped as factories have moved from military to civilian production. Unless the situation is remedied, it may sow the seeds of resentment, and possibly resistance to conversion. On the other hand, military enterprises may seek to compensate for lower profits by charging higher prices for their civilian products, endangering the success of this transformation.

At the same time, however, Alexei Izyumov argues that remaining in the military orbit is becoming less attractive for leaders of military-industry enterprises, especially now that the defense establishment is being put on a self-financing basis. Some seem prepared to accept the loss of privileges in return for greater independence from the constraints and pitfalls of rigid centralized planning.

Likewise, the military sector has lost a good deal of its earlier attraction for the non-managerial work force, according to Izyumov. During the past few years, virtually all of the superior wage and fringe benefits have evaporated for the rank and file, while the negative aspects of military industry employment—rigid discipline, overtime, unhealthy conditions, strict quality control, and limitations on travel abroad—have remained in place.

Wanted: Military *Glasnost*

Many Soviet analysts agree that the lack of military *glasnost* is a serious obstacle to successful conversion. According to Sergei Blagovolin, an economist writing in the magazine *Moscow News*, there are still no

O_f 585 consumer goods scheduled to be manufactured in 1988-89 by Soviet military factories, only 126 were successfully produced.

reliable data on the number of military enterprises, their location, the number of people employed, worker skills, the quantity and characteristics of the equipment, and the raw materials and supplies used.

A sample of 100 arms-producing enterprises, assembled by Julian Cooper of the University of Birmingham in Great Britain, sheds some light on the regional distribution of military factories. He shows that the overwhelming majority of these enterprises are located within the Russian republic—particularly in the Urals, in the central economic region around Moscow, in the Volga region, and around Leningrad (see Figure 1, which shows the distribution of factories in Cooper's sample by republic and, within the Russian Republic, by economic region). But much more far-reaching and detailed information is needed to assess both the problems and the potential of conversion.

The potentially most serious impediment

to conversion is the lack of any adequate system to account for the enormous resources devoted to military purposes. As Paddy Ashdown, a member of the British Parliament, put it recently: "The army simply said what it wanted and industry supplied it. There were no overall budget limits, no effective costings system, and only the most rudimentary methods of cost control."

The revitalization of the Soviet economy depends crucially on a successful conversion of defense industries. But that success is in turn inextricably linked to the fate of Gorbachev's *perestroika*. Only with a meaningful set of costs and prices, rather than an arbitrary and unaccountable bureaucratic system, can a realistic conversion program be created. Reliable indicators are needed to assess the military's real drain on the economy and the possibilities for converting defense industries to civilian uses. Without such information, it may be impossible to decide whether to convert a given facility or close it and start from scratch, or to determine the success of any conversion undertaking.

To date, Soviet conversion has proceeded on an ad hoc basis. For example, the government's decision in early 1989 to slash the volume of arms production came out of the blue, leaving military factory managers with neither sufficient orders nor an alternative plan. There has been no overall integration of measures to promote greater civilian production.

To move beyond this haphazard stage, a National Commission to Promote Conversion has been formed—with representatives from *Gosplan*, the military-related ministries, the Academy of Sciences, and various universities—to design a proper long-term program. In addition, a draft economic conversion law has been submitted to the Supreme Soviet that, among other things, would provide a two-year allowance and a job information system for military workers who lose their jobs.

Although current conversion plans are directed from the top, there is growing public discussion and appreciation of the concept, and Soviet conversion proponents are seeking to share their insights with their counterparts abroad.

Gorbachev's Appeal

President Gorbachev's foreign and military policies have so far yielded far more political than economic dividends. While the domestic benefits of trimming the Soviet military apparatus will materialize only in the medium- or perhaps even the long-term, the country needs to mobilize considerable funds now to smooth the social and economic effects of disarmament.

The success of conversion depends on

Soldiers successfully reintegrated into Soviet society could be a boon to an economy characterized by continuous labor shortages.

more than technical factors, as crucial as they may be. Just as important is the constellation of political concerns. Gorbachev needs to convince the military leadership that his unilateral military concessions are yielding returns that make the gamble worthwhile. In other words, he needs tangible evidence that less military spending and fewer weapons do not translate into less security. And he needs to transform guns into butter fast, or else the rising tide of unmet expectations may drown his entire undertaking.

As open debate has increasingly replaced old taboos, the Soviets have become preoccupied with internal matters. But while the fate of Soviet conversion is of obvious domestic relevance, there is an important international dimension as well. The Soviet case is important because the country is a global leader in arms production. It demonstrates that conversion is a realistic option, even in a world that has barely begun to consider alternatives to the arms race seriously. If the West follows suit with its own demilitarization and conversion measures, the arms race may at long last be transformed into a "peace race."

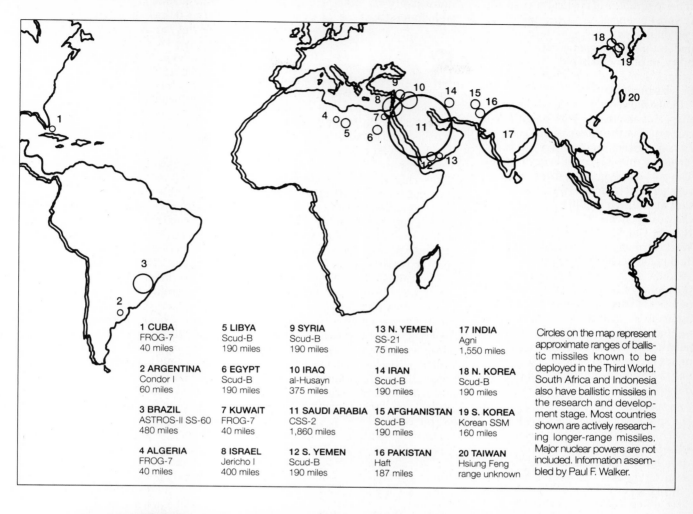

1 CUBA FROG-7 40 miles	**5 LIBYA** Scud-B 190 miles	**9 SYRIA** Scud-B 190 miles	**13 N. YEMEN** SS-21 75 miles	**17 INDIA** Agni 1,550 miles	Circles on the map represent approximate ranges of ballistic missiles known to be deployed in the Third World.
2 ARGENTINA Condor I 60 miles	**6 EGYPT** Scud-B 190 miles	**10 IRAQ** al-Husayn 375 miles	**14 IRAN** Scud-B 190 miles	**18 N. KOREA** Scud-B 190 miles	South Africa and Indonesia also have ballistic missiles in the research and development stage. Most countries
3 BRAZIL ASTROS-II SS-60 480 miles	**7 KUWAIT** FROG-7 40 miles	**11 SAUDI ARABIA** CSS-2 1,860 miles	**15 AFGHANISTAN** Scud-B 190 miles	**19 S. KOREA** Korean SSM 160 miles	shown are actively researching longer-range missiles. Major nuclear powers are not
4 ALGERIA FROG-7 40 miles	**8 ISRAEL** Jericho I 400 miles	**12 S. YEMEN** Scud-B 190 miles	**16 PAKISTAN** Haft 187 miles	**20 TAIWAN** Hsiung Feng range unknown	included. Information assembled by Paul F. Walker.

MISSILE MANIA
SOME RULES FOR THE GAME

JANNE E. NOLAN

Janne E. Nolan, a visiting fellow at the Brookings Institution in Washington, D.C., is the author of Guardians of the Arsenal: The Politics of Nuclear Strategy *(1989)*

Efforts to control the trade in military technology have traditionally focused on preventing Western technology from flowing east, and on preventing the

> **Any system of control must respect the developing nations' struggle for independence.**

spread of nuclear materials. But in the late 1980s, ballistic missiles became the currency of a new international security environment, as a number of developing countries heralded their entry into the missile age. Not coincidentally, most of the new missile producers are in regions of chronic tension where the interests of the great powers intersect.

For now, the significance of these programs may be more political than military. At a minimum, however, they demonstrate the developing nations' drive for military independence, some-

From *The Bulletin of the Atomic Scientists*, May 1990, pp. 27-29. Copyright © 1990 by the Educational Foundation for Nuclear Science, 6042 South Kimbark, Chicago, IL 60637, USA. A one-year subscription is $30.

times regardless of political or economic consequences. And the fact that regional rivals have little common understanding of what constitutes stability, or of how to avoid provocation, suggests that the new missile age will be a turbulent one.

Industrialized nations have observed these developments with heightened concern. Yet the international consensus on controlling military exports, including missiles, is still very fragile. The only existing agreement is a consensual cartel of eight Western nations that manufacture ballistic missiles or their components—the United States, Britain, Canada, France, Italy, Japan, West Germany, and Spain. The Missile Technology Control Regime (MTCR), established in 1987, reflects the traditional view that the technical characteristics of ballistic missiles make them inherently destabilizing. But the regime has weak enforcement mechanisms, lacks an international agency to monitor compliance, and represents only a few of the current suppliers of missile technology.

It may already be too late to control the spread of ballistic missiles. Export controls are efforts by great powers to assert their prerogatives, and the foundations for those prerogatives are eroding quickly. Emerging regional powers are becoming less susceptible to coercion as they develop their own defense production capabilities. They see the denial of exports as discriminatory, and they accuse industrialized nations of hypocrisy when they denounce the legitimacy of ballistic missiles (or chemical or nuclear weapons). The new missile arsenals are obviously dwarfed by those of the five major nuclear powers. "It is fashionable among industrialized nations to deplore acquisition of high-technology weapons by developing nations," noted one Indian analyst recently, "but this moralistic stand is akin to drug pushers shedding tears about the weaknesses of drug addicts."[1]

Efforts to restrain missile programs are more likely to be effective if they are part of initiatives to end or contain regional conflicts. And these must be part of a broader effort to build a genuinely interdependent international system with codified, reliable means of resolving disputes peacefully. But how to encourage Third World countries to adopt nonaggressive and

defensively oriented postures is not well understood.

Superpower-style arms control—limiting numbers and ranges of weapons, for example—seems an unpromising way to contain the threat of ballistic missiles in the Third World. The East-West military competition is relatively abstract, in contrast to the diffuse, highly volatile political and military conditions in those regions where missile proliferation is of most concern. And negotiated limitations depend on a measure of political accommodation among adversaries which does not exist in these regions.

To establish numerical ceilings, for example, the sides must agree on rough equivalencies among different weapon types, or agree to accept asymmetries, and they must agree that lower levels of weapons would improve stability. Negotiated limits derive from a common understanding of what is needed for overall military parity and stability, and these conditions must be within reach.

Defining regional balances in the Third World is extremely difficult. In the Middle East, for instance, Israel counts the inventories of the Arab and Persian Gulf states as a collective threat to its security. But the Arab states believe Israel's nuclear and missile capabilities vastly outweigh their own superiority in numbers. Both sides seek qualitative capabilities to offset the perceived threat. The problem is exacerbated by the Arab world's lack of political consensus, which would preclude any agreement requiring its forces to be counted collectively. Even defining the framework for negotiations can be complicated. Saudi Arabia, for example, sees both Iran and Israel as regional threats. In South Asia, India sees China as more important to its military calculus than Pakistan.

Negotiating numerical limits might seem more promising in Latin America, to mitigate the military and economic rivalry between Brazil and Argentina. Because these countries are producing missiles largely for export, however, economic or trade incentives may be more appropriate than arms control.

Range limits are also difficult to envisage. Israel, India, and Saudi Ara-

bia already possess missiles that exceed the limits imposed by the U.S.-Soviet Intermediate-Range Nuclear Forces Treaty. And missile ranges can be increased by adjusting payloads or altering rocket engine efficiency. Restraints on such conversions would be difficult to enforce.

Instead of pursuing technical arms control measures, it would be more profitable to explore confidence- and security-building measures, including information and intelligence exchanges, on-site inspection of defense production and space launch facilities, and prior notification of missile tests. These mechanisms could help ease unwarranted suspicions about missile programs, limit their political and military consequences, and possibly reduce incentives to expand them. Although confidence-building measures only indicate political will and can be violated at any time, they can begin the process of broader accommodation. They can reduce tensions by taking the mystery out of rivals' military activities and providing channels for routine interaction.

Some regional measures have already been instituted or proposed: India and Pakistan have agreed not to attack each other's nuclear facilities and to begin negotiating a nuclear test ban. Argentina and Brazil inspect each other's nuclear facilities and have declared their nonhostile intent. And the United States has informally proposed encouraging Middle Eastern countries to abjure first use of ballistic missiles and to give prior notification of missile launches.

Other confidence- and security-building measures might be included in a missile restraint regime:

■ International safeguards could be applied at space launch facilities to insure that they are not being used to develop missiles.

■ An international space launch agency could grant nations access to space in return for giving up missile programs.

■ Missile forces might be kept unarmed and unfueled during peacetime, subject to monitoring.

■ Tests could be conducted only after notification, and away from rival territory.

■ Routine bilateral military exchanges could document the extent and pace of missile development plans and provide a forum for discussing security concerns.

Declarations of intent would not endure in a crisis, but they are important signs of political conciliation. On-site visits alone will not stop missile programs, but they can help reduce the reciprocal fears that fuel arms races.

Significant curbs on the demand for missiles will depend on reducing regional tensions, but incremental measures to enhance confidence will also help the broader objective. The great powers can encourage regional adversaries to pursue confidence-building measures. The United States and its allies could begin by helping countries develop routine consultative mechanisms, with which Third World governments are often genuinely unfamiliar. But the initiatives must come from the governments themselves and must reflect local realities.

It is even more important for the United States and Soviet Union to cooperate to stem conflict between nations they support. As the influence of both superpowers over their clients weakens, bilateral agreements will not be sufficient to contain future wars, but they are nevertheless vital. And, with the reconciliation of the superpowers, they now seem possible.

In June 1989 the chairman of the Joint Chiefs of Staff, Adm. William Crowe, and Soviet General Staff chief Sergei Akhromeyev signed an agreement to prevent and resolve crises arising from provocative activities by their respective armed forces. Although this was a technical accord, not a regional security agreement, it was inspired in part by the experience of the Iran-Iraq War, when, as one analyst put it, "American and Soviet forces sometimes operated in proximity to each other, leading both sides to recognize the need for a mechanism to coordinate their activities."[2] The nuclear risk reduction centers, established in Washington and Moscow in 1987, could be used for such communications.

But in the future, international agreements must elicit the support of both developing and developed states. An effort to broaden the Missile Technology Control Regime into an international treaty seems quixotic, at best. Developing countries would object to its discriminatory nature, and it does not cover other destabilizing weapons such as nonballistic missiles and aircraft. In fact the regime's success, such as it is, has derived from its modest goals and from the fact that it was negotiated out of the glare of the international spotlight.

Most proposals to restrain missiles show little sensitivity to developing states' ambitions to become equals in the international system. A first step might be to convene an international missile conference, under neutral auspices, to permit a full airing of all countries' views and to set a framework for cooperation. Modest agreements on some confidence- and security-building measures outlined here might be possible in the near future, and these might build momentum for more ambitious efforts.

The spread of ballistic missiles is a harbinger of future weapons proliferation. Industrial nations may find they are no longer able to use technological superiority to influence international events, and the quest for technological advantage will become ever more elusive. New generations of weapons may spread which could have even more adverse effects on international stability—precision-strike systems, biotechnologies, and antisatellite capabilities.

The developing countries must be taken seriously, and their interests must be recognized as enduring as well as diverse. Realism need not be the pretext for fatalism, however. The great powers must understand that although their leverage is limited, using it judiciously is as urgent as it is difficult.

1. C. Raja Mohan and K. Subrahmanyam, "High Technology Weapons in the Developing World," in Eric Arnett, ed., *New Technologies for Security and Arms Control: Threats and Promises* (Washington, D.C.: American Association for the Advancement of Science, 1989), p. 230.
2. Barrus M. Carnahan, "Decreasing the Danger in Military Activities: The Meaning of a New U.S.-Soviet Agreement," *Arms Control Today* (Aug. 1989), p. 13.

International Organization and International Issues

Contradictory trends in the arena of world politics have grown ever more apparent in the 1990s: both internationalism and nationalism are striving to be the dominant force of the last decade of the twentieth century, with neither predicted to be the winner. Instances of extremely harsh nationalism hold our attention: efforts by strongly yet often narrowly defined national groups to establish greater autonomy or even independence rage on in Canada, the U.S.S.R., Yugoslavia, and elsewhere throughout Eastern Europe. In more authoritarian states, such as China and Burma, the government subdues such incipient movements with force—precisely what the governments of Eastern Europe and the U.S.S.R. did until 1989, when Communist party regimes were either undermined or overthrown. When governments more tolerant of freedom of expression replaced them, spokesmen for the various nationalities within these countries did not hesitate to demand concessions to their respective national identities. They vehemently protest against governmental policies geared toward integrating all national groups within a common polity under what they believe are the cultural values and interests of one dominant national group. And, of course, the nationalism of the already existing nation-states of the world, which often aggressively asserts itself at the expense of the interests of other nation-states, whether through war, trade, the arms race, or politics, is a form of nationalism that exerts its power in the world on a daily basis.

In the meantime, the growing strength of internationalism is, quite simply, stunning. In its various manifestations, internationalism is reshaping how nation-states and their citizens view themselves and the world. The European Community, within which national borders are virtually disappearing; multinational corporations, whose "national" origin is ever less significant as they adapt to the various national values and practices of those countries in which they operate; and the United Nations, whose Security Council resolutions actually formed the framework within which decisions were made to fight and to end a major war in the Middle East; the various "international regimes" that now virtually govern international commerce, finance, and communication—all these internationalist trends simultaneously coexist with and fight for dominance over the forces of nationalism.

At present it appears that internationalism will become still stronger, but that strong nationalist forces will continue to provide the basic framework, if only because of the issue of governance: the more heterogeneous and larger an entity, the more difficult it is to govern as a single, undifferentiated whole. This would explain why national governments will continue to be in charge of certain basic policies within the European Community, and why massive entities such as the U.S.S.R. and China threaten to disintegrate into small nation-based units. As for the divisional trends in the smaller states of the world, such as in the countries of Eastern Europe or Burma, they too will continue until their respective governments succeed in greater integration into a multicultural, multinational polity.

The development of a body of international law that covers issues from the law of the sea and tariffs to human rights and the allocation of international radio wave frequencies has helped define the rights and responsibilities of states. Their creation suggests a willingness on the part of states to relinquish their sovereignty for the greater good of the international community, which is also for their own greater good. Insistence on absolute sovereignty over a state's internal and external affairs, based on a zero-sum perception of the world in which one state's gains are viewed as another state's losses, has gradually been eroded. States now are increasingly likely to realize that they can all gain or lose together.

The rules, organizations, regulations, and patterns of behavior among states that have developed over the years have come together to form "international regimes" that have created a framework within which states can address their problems.

Thus, while the United Nations seems helpless to address effectively such highly politicized issues as arms control and disarmament, the major nuclear powers have constructed an international nonproliferation regime. This regime deserves most of the credit for limiting the proliferation of nuclear weapons to a mere handful of countries in the more than 40 years since atomic weapons first made their appearance. A fledgling international sea regime addresses the issues of access to resources and transit, and determines what kinds of things can be dumped or located in the oceans. The international economic regime is one of the most diverse and complicated, with institutions such as the World Bank and the International Monetary Fund (IMF) playing major roles in the complex issues of debt restructuring, development, trade protectionism, and currency regulation. Commercial banks, individual governments, and multinational corporations also participate in the international economic regime through investments, loans, aid programs, and technology transfers.

International regimes address issues that are functionally specific to what are considered apolitical areas, although, in any real sense, most are highly political. By building agreement block by block in those areas of international action that *must* be regulated if anarchy is not to reign, it is hoped that countries will become so interdependent that they will not want to risk war. More positively, they want to maintain the relationships within these various international regimes because their own national interests are advanced by them. Eventually, states which have reached agreement and built interdependency in functional areas such as in fighting environmental pollution, AIDS, and drug trafficking will, presumably, be able to more easily reach agreement on highly sensitive political issues.

Those who hope for world integration believe that states will prefer adhering to the restrictive rules of the General Agreement on Tariffs and Trade (GATT) to insisting on their sovereign rights to erect trade barriers, and prefer adhering to the Nonproliferation Treaty to selling nuclear weapons technology for a profit. Greater international integration and interdependence cannot guarantee the elimination of war or the pursuit of national interests at the expense of other states, but the accomplishments of internationally coordinated efforts in creating mutually shared interests are growing.

On the issue of protecting human rights, it is not entirely clear which provides the better mechanism: the nation-state or an international organization. Although some "human rights" are universal (such as the right not to be tortured or imprisoned without cause), other human rights are culturally defined. How

can an international organization make *universal* standards that cross cultures, that anticipate, incorporate, and are sensitive to culturally specific values? Are standards that accommodate cultural diversity, or universal standards, to be the goal? Is it any more appropriate for an international body to tell the Saudi Arabians that their treatment of women is a derogation of their human rights than it is for it to tell other countries that not allowing national minority groups to be taught in their own language is a derogation of their human rights? Or that an insistence on policies that favor the public good over the rights of the individual is a derogation of human rights? And who, in the end, will set these universal standards?

While in some countries, such as South Africa, the U.S.S.R., and those in Eastern Europe, the human rights situation has improved dramatically, in others, it remains oppressive. In still others it has even regressed. China is an example of a country that had, in the ten years leading up to 1989, given its people more freedom than they had had at any time since the Communist takeover in 1949. With the military crackdown on June 4, 1989, and the repression that followed, this was reversed. Freedom of the press has been eclipsed, student demonstrations are prohibited, and dissidence is again treated as a criminal offense. In Saudi Arabia, there are beheadings; in El Salvador people disappear; and throughout much of the developing world, arbitrary arrest and torture are commonplace.

States that have a bilateral relationship with countries where human rights violations occur have sometimes used the withholding of aid, trade boycotts, or diplomatic withdrawal as instruments to pressure the government toward better human rights policies. Such instruments have, however, proven far more effective when the intervening country does not need the cooperation of the target government for access to a strategic location, military base, or important natural resource. The best way for peoples to achieve greater human rights is to demand these rights of their own government. This strategy is, unfortunately, accompanied by great risks to those who dare to challenge authoritarian and repressive governments; but when they do succeed, they are at least certain of gaining respect for those human rights that are important to themselves and not for those important to individuals living within a completely different cultural context.

Looking Ahead: Challenge Questions

How much credit can we give to international organizations, such as the United Nations, for bringing about an improvement in the human rights environment throughout the world? What role have the leaders of particular states played in improving human rights for their own countries and others? Who are they? Which countries have witnessed the greatest improvement in human rights over the past year? Which countries have suffered from greater repression? What should be the next major steps taken to improve human rights worldwide? What role has the foreign policy of individual countries played in forcing governments to improve their internal human rights policies? Has the withholding or giving of foreign aid proven to be a useful tool in advancing the protection of human rights in particular countries? Can you give some examples?

Does the United Nations provide a democratic forum in which major progress on international problems can be made through discussion among nations? What diminishes the effectiveness of the United Nations as an organization for promoting the peaceful resolution of issues? What types of issues has the United Nations proven most effective in addressing and why? If you could construct an international organization that would be successful in serving as both a forum for discussion and a tool for resolving major economic, social, political, and security questions, what would it be like?

THE STIRRINGS OF HISTORY

A new world rises from the ruins of empire

John Lukacs

The historian John Lukacs writes frequently for Harper's Magazine. *His most recent book is* Confessions of an Original Sinner *(Ticknor & Fields).*

Very soon after the Second World War most Americans began to believe that the twentieth century was dominated by the struggle between communism and capitalism, one of these rival faiths incarnated by the Soviet Union, the other by the United States of America. For more than forty years this belief has governed American politics. Despite its ceaseless assertion and repetition, the belief is false. The history of the twentieth century has been dominated not by this ideological strife but by the two world wars. The Bolshevik revolution in Russia, the establishment of communist governments in Eastern Europe, the atom bomb, the end of the colonial empires, the rise of the United States as the superpower of the world, the Cold War— all these phenomena have been the result of the two world wars, a chapter in world history that now has ended.

The so-called struggle of classes has amounted to little when compared with the struggles of states and of entire nations. More than fifty years ago an English wit, upon receiving the news of the Nazi-Soviet pact, was supposed to have said, "All the isms are wasms." He was entirely right. All the isms *are* wasms—except one, the most powerful ism of this century, indeed, of the entire democratic age, which is nationalism.

Nationalism appeared in Europe during and after the Napoleonic Wars, and as a consequence of the French Revolution. People have attributed enormous importance to the three revolutionary shock waves that trembled across Europe in 1820, 1830, and 1848. But these internal upheavals mattered far less than the unification of Germany achieved by Bismarck. In the forty-five years after Napoleon the political map of Europe changed little. With the unification of Germany, and of Italy, it began to change drastically. The unification of Germany in 1871 proved to be a more important event than even the French Revolution, just as the new political map now emerging in Europe is a more important event than the final (and it is a final) end of communism.

Bismarck was not directly responsible for the two world wars that turned out to be so different from the wars that he had arranged. Neither will Gorbachev be responsible for a Third World War that, if it comes (note that I write *if*, not *when*), will be very different from the twentieth-century wars to which we, and our memories, have become accustomed.

THE VICTORS OF THE SECOND WORLD WAR WERE BRITAIN, Russia, and the United States, but during the forty-five years following the utter defeat of their enemies in 1945, their victory and their gains have dissipated. By now they can be described as declining powers—in just about every sense of the word. The accepted wisdom relates the decline to economics. In fact, the decline has little or nothing to do with economics: It is the result of waning national cohesion, discipline, and will.

Again there is an obvious historical precedent. France was a victor of World War I. After the war her army remained the largest in Europe. Her alliance system was the greatest on the continent, extending to both sides of Germany. Even during the worldwide Depression of 1929–1933 France was less affected by the economic crisis than Germany or Britain or the United States. Yet, by 1933, when Hitler became the untrammeled dictator of Germany, the decline of France was evident. Her government, her politicians, her people were deeply divided, unwilling to accept those risks and potential sacrifices that were needed to halt the swift rise of the Third Reich—whose leader benefited mightily from his disdain for economics. Hitler knew that what mattered was force and not money; that the power and the wealth of his nation would result from the rise of its national confidence and not the reverse. When someone asked him whether he would nationalize the industries, he said,

"Why should I nationalize the industries? I shall nationalize the people." When, a few years later, Hitler began to change the political map of Europe by force, it became evident that France's alliance system was a frayed paper structure. Its effectiveness had dwindled to nothing—a condition not entirely dissimilar to the present condition of the Warsaw Pact and NATO.

After the victory in 1945 the British Empire was the first to dissolve. During the war Winston Churchill said that he did not become prime minister to preside over the liquidation of the British Empire. The phrase continues to tarnish his reputation—unfairly so. Long before the war the British people had become unwilling to carry on with some of their imperial tasks. The hard Victorian carapace (and discipline) of their imperialist convictions had already cracked after World War I. Again, this had little to do with economics. The architects of that devolution were not British bankers or even Churchill (when for a time he was chancellor of the exchequer in the 1920s). The failure of will had many causes, ranging from the domestic politics of David Lloyd George and the Lib-Labs through the business mentality of the Chamberlain conservatives to liberal intellectuals such as E. M. Forster (to wit, his *Passage to India*).

The Second World War for Britain had not much to do with the empire. It had everything to do with the survival of Britain, and of Europe. Churchill understood the awful options as early as 1940, well before Pearl Harbor and before Hitler's invasion of Russia. If the alternative to surrendering to Hitler was the transfer of large portions of the empire to the tutelage of the United States, so be it. Surrendering to Hitler would not—as Churchill rightly understood—necessarily mean a German occupation of the British Isles; but it would mean an acceptance of German domination over Europe and the reduction of Britain to a junior, vassal partner in such an arrangement. As early as 1940 Churchill recognized that, as far as Europe went, there might be only two alternatives: either all of Europe dominated by Germany, or the eastern—faraway—portion of Europe dominated by Russia. Half of Europe was better than none.

As far as the empire went, it gave way to the "Commonwealth": But that Commonwealth was (and is) a fiction even greater than that of a "united" Europe. There was (and is) no national cohesion between Pakistanis, Canadians, Tanzanians, Englishmen. With regard to Europe the situation was different. It was true that Britain was exhausted economically in 1945. But at that moment, and for some years thereafter, her prestige in Europe was tremendous. She could have had the leadership of Western Europe for a song. Nothing was further from the mind of the Labour government that came to power in 1945. Its abdication of European responsibilities had consequences worse even than its abandonment of much of the empire

(which was about to happen anyhow). When in 1947 Britain turned to the United States to sustain its traditional Mediterranean ally, Greece, the Labour government said that Britain could not afford that task. In the lives of nations, as in the lives of individuals, when people say they cannot afford something they usually mean that they really don't want to afford it. The Conservative governments that have ruled Britain for nearly thirty of the last forty years have not behaved very differently. At the same time it is not only Britain's economic but her political influence throughout Europe that has been eroding. Whether Britain will join "Europe" in 1992 or not no longer matters much. In nearly every sense the power and the influence of Germany are already stronger than Britain's. This is especially applicable to Eastern Europe, which is close to Germany and—politically—very far from Britain.

A MUCH MORE PAINFUL AND DISTURBING DEVELOPMENT—and not only for Russians—is the dissolution of the Russian Empire. It is now obvious that the Russians have lost not only the Cold War but also the fruits of their victory in the Second World War. Their victory in the Second World War forty-five years ago had nothing to do with communism. They defeated the Germans in what they—not improperly—have called the Great Patriotic War. Because they had to carry the fight all the way to the middle of Germany and Berlin, their army took control of much of Eastern Europe and of eastern Germany.

In 1945 the Americans (and to a lesser extent the British) were not willing either to contest that Russian predominance or to question Stalin seriously about its conditions. Stalin could have done what he and his successors eventually consented to do with Finland: to allow the states bordering the Soviet Union on the west to be ruled by more or less free and democratic governments, whose foreign and military policies would remain coordinated with Russian national and security interests. Stalin did not choose to do so, for three reasons. The Americans did not really press him on the point. The formula was not applicable to Germany, the largest and most valuable portion of which was occupied by the Western Powers. Thirdly, and most important: Stalin preferred communists in the Eastern European states because they were the only functionaries he could count on. The prospect of these nations following a pro-Russian foreign policy while they maintained all other kinds of connections with the West did not appeal to him. Under such conditions Russian influence would, naturally and inevitably, decrease. His was the ancient conservative preference for the bird in one's hand—in his case, rather, in his fist. Stalin was not a revolutionary; he had no intention to spread communism into Western Europe. The communist governments in Eastern Europe did not come into power because of communist revolutions. They were imposed by the presence of Russian troops.

When Gorbachev came to power in Russia five years ago, he was deeply troubled by what he, an insider, knew only too well: the corruption and inefficiency of the Communist Party machine within the Soviet Union proper. We do not know whether this honest recognition was accompanied by a recognition of the explosive force of nationalism. Certainly he recognized that the Soviet Union's relation with its democratic neighbor, Finland, was much preferable to the messy and troublesome relations with the other, still largely communist-ruled, Eastern European nations. What he may not have recognized, at first, was that the Moldavians or Armenians or Lithuanians are not like the Finns; and that once nationalism in Eastern Europe was approved by Moscow, there was nothing to stop it from bubbling up and flooding component parts of the Soviet Empire itself.

The extent of the Russian conquest of Eastern Europe forty-five years ago was so unnatural that it could not last. The Russian retreat from Eastern and Central Europe began soon after 1945. As early as 1948 Yugoslavia broke away from the Russian orbit. In 1955 Khrushchev gave up the Russian naval base in Finland. In the same year the Russians withdrew from their occupation zone in Austria. That was thirty-five years ago, when the winding down of the Cold War through a mutual withdrawal of Russian and American forces and alliances from the middle of Europe was a realistic possibility. That possibility was denied and sabotaged by Dwight Eisenhower and John Foster Dulles; and it is both melancholy and ironic to consider that these Russian retreats occurred at the same time that the hysteria of American anticommunism reached its peak. But that is another story.

What is important to remember is that for the past thirty-five or forty years the Russian and communist influence in Eastern Europe has been slackening—in some places more rapidly, in others more slowly, but generally tending toward weakness. Today the Russians cannot and will not restore anything even remotely resembling their political control over the region that they established in 1945. Their traditional empire—perhaps the last of the great multinational empires—is dissolving under the pressures of democratic and populist nationalism. The same pressures exist within the frontiers of the Soviet Union, and the Russians will be lucky if they can preserve a substantial part of their inner empire. Only God knows what will be left when the process of disintegration is finally halted.

There is an ironic paradox here. The great revolutionary of the early twentieth century was not Lenin, who ignored the force of nationalism and insisted upon his narrow-minded dogma of class struggle. It was the no less narrow-minded Woodrow Wilson, with his insistence on the—potentially disastrous—principle of self-determination. Lenin lost the western portion of the Russian Empire and was obliged to accept the independence of Finland, the Baltic States, Poland: the price for maintaining his power in the rest of the Russias. Lenin believed that from Russia communism would soon spread westward. He was wrong. For more than twenty-five years the Soviet Union remained the only communist state in the world—until, after World War II, the Russian army imposed communist regimes in Russia's neighbor states. The occupation lasted for forty-five years. Wilson's achievements were more enduring. In 1918 he insisted not only on a German surrender but on the abolition of the German monarchy; and he was the principal advocate of the dissolution of the Austro-Hungarian Empire too—the only great state between Germany and Russia. From these achievements Adolf Hitler (and a slew of minor Hitlers in the future) would profit mightily. More than seventy years later the end is not yet at hand—for the principle of self-determination remains the most explosive force at large in the world, to the detriment not only of the Soviet Union but, eventually, of the United States too.

TOGETHER WITH THE BRITISH AND THE RUSSIANS, THE third power that has fallen into decline is, alas, the United States. In 1945 the United States was the greatest power in the world. Yet it is at least questionable whether the zenith of American power was not 1918 rather than 1945; for at the end of World War I the United States (and its Western allies) did not have to share the victory with Russia. At the end of World War II, with Russian troops as far east as Germany, there was no other choice. The result was the Cold War, during which American governments, politicians, and people often misread the intentions of their Russian adversaries.

The Cold War burdened the American economy with enormous military expenditures, but those expenditures (although often excessive and irresponsible) did not—alone, or even mostly, and contrary to the conventional *liberal* wisdom—cause the decline of the United States. The principal cause of the American decline is the changed character of the nation that has in turn deeply affected its institutions—educational, legal, commercial, and political institutions whose operations and procedures have become less and less capable of functioning as instruments of proper regulation and reform. These institutions—foremost among them the American presidency—have become grossly inflated. A principal element in this malignant growth, very much contrary to the accepted, *conservative* wisdom, was the degeneration of American patriotism into an ideological nationalism, equating global anticommunism with *the* American credo. As early as 1956 the platform of the—so-called isolationist and conservative—Republican Party called for nothing less than the extension of American air and naval bases "strategically dispersed . . . around the world." There followed the quarter-century rise of the "conservatives" in the Republican Party, until in the 1980s their hero Ronald Reagan extended this American aspiration of ruling the globe into space: the Cosmocrat of the Universe. (This "conservative" and "traditionalist" president of the United States was a Hollywood actor who admitted that his interest in Star Wars had been inspired by the movie of that name—a movie made expressly for a juvenile audience.)

The sources of American decline, like those in Britain, have not been economic. More precisely, the economic problems of the United States follow from the confusion of a people in whose mind image has become not merely a component of reality but its substitute. The loss of self-knowledge and self-discipline expresses a devolution in the character of a nation whose youthful leaders at its birth were (at times precociously, at times priggishly) exceptionally serious and mature. Two hundred years later, the expressions, the gestures, the acts, and the preferences of the recent presidents display the traits not of maturity but of puerility.

What matters now is that in 1990—unlike in 1945 and for some time afterward—other people in the world have become aware of the American predicament. The power of a nation, like that of a person, is inseparable from the unquantifiable asset of its prestige. A nation whose prestige is considerable will withstand a temporary, or even lengthy, erosion of its power better than a nation whose prestige is weak. American—unlike Soviet—prestige is still considerable, but its erosion has already begun. After 1945 the greatest contribution of the United States to the benefit of the world (and especially to that of Western Europe) was not the Marshall Plan. It was the American example of a mass democracy capable of maintaining a high level of prosperity and of freedom; of functioning traditional institutions of law and order; of giving credit to the masses. This has led to the adoption of many American practices and institutions in the democracies abroad, ranging from social security and income tax withholding through extended opportunities for higher education to the emulation of American forms of art and advertising.

Four decades later most nations have subtly reshaped these matters for themselves. Economic statistics tell us that in the 1980s the material possessions of French or German or Japanese workers had become very similar, if not identical, to those of an American worker, including cars, color televisions, etc.; they also tell us that, for the first time in this century, the per capita income of Americans is less than that of the Swiss, Germans, or Swedes. Real experience (which is not the same thing as economic statistics) also tells us

that while twenty years ago the American dollar was worth something like four German marks or Swiss francs, it is now worth less than half of that. But all of these matters are consequences of the deteriorating confidence of other peoples in the quality of American leadership—and, for the first time, in the quality of American products too. In 1945 the quality of American everyday life—those shining towers of Manhattan—was the wonder of the world. By 1990 that example is less than inspiring, to say the least.

Of course, nothing is irreversible, including decline; and one of the engaging, and positive, marks of the American national character is the American ability to reform and change. Nor is there much reason to worry about America becoming something other than "Number One" (a vulgar phrase whose assertion by a recent American president—Richard Nixon—in itself suggests a want of self-confidence). Still, with all of the monstrous instruments of power at its disposal, the United States—as the last of the great victorious powers of the two world wars—can no longer control events in Europe, even at this time of the dissolution of its once great adversary, the Second Superpower, and at a time when its presidents have felt compelled to arouse national cohesion and enthusiasm by military victories in . . . Grenada or Libya or Panama. And without really recognizing something that the American people have begun to feel in their bones—that both America and Russia are threatened not by each other but by the increasing pressures from the so-called Third World.

IF, THEN, GREAT BRITAIN, RUSSIA, AND THE UNITED States have lost the advantage of their victories in World War II, does that also mean that the erstwhile losers, Germany and Japan, have become the winners? Yes and no.

Yes, because their prosperity already has defied all materialistic logic, including that of the population experts. For some time now Japan and West Germany have enjoyed the rank of economic and financial superpowers. The most prosperous nations on earth, they are also among the most densely inhabited. After 1945 West Germany, conquered and occupied by many millions of foreign soldiers, its cities bombed into ruins, had to accommodate 12 million German refugees: an accretion amounting to one fourth of an impoverished population. The forced crowding had the making of an unprecedented catastrophe. The very opposite happened. The newly arrived citizenry became an asset, not a liability. A similar revival took place in Japan, which, in 1945, found itself under foreign occupation, powerless, its cities destroyed, reduced to its small islands, crowded with refugees. What mattered was not overpopulation, not the *quantity* of people. What mattered was their *quality*: their ability and willingness to work. These matters are not quantifiable. They are national characteristics. The Germans were able to absorb, and benefit from, the presence of millions of incoming Germans. They have not been able to absorb a million Turkish immigrants. Nor have the Japanese assimilated immigrants from the Asiatic mainlands.

Now a new condition has arisen in Germany. That a reunited Germany, with 80 million people, will become the greatest economic and financial power in Europe need not be argued. The question remains as to whether the character of the German people has changed so much that they will be satisfied with the possession and consumption of material goods. The recent disinclination of West German Chancellor Helmut Kohl to ratify the German-Polish frontier (for the purpose of gaining political support from the not altogether suppressed currents of German nationalism) is but one disquieting example of an old trait. It may be true that the great majority of the German people stand willing to accept the present frontiers of Germany; the majority may also believe in the "European" future of Germany. But history and human nature abhor a vacuum, as does physical nature. In the aftermath of the great Russian retreat in Eastern Europe a great vacuum is opening up again. That vacuum will be filled, not by the United States, not by "Europe," but by Germany. Economically and financially the Germans already have begun to fill it. The cultural and political (and perhaps even military) consequences will follow.

I do not mean that sooner or later panzer divisions will assemble along the Oder, or that the reputation of Hitler will be wholly rehabilitated. What I mean is that the collapse of Russian power, and of communism in Eastern Europe, makes the Germans (and also some other people) think and feel that the accepted idea of their unique responsibility for some of the crimes of World War II is invalid or, at best, relative and now definitely a thing of the past. The assumption that World War II is, finally, ended will correspond to the inclinations of other peoples in Eastern Europe, and it will persuade some of their nationalist and populist parties to seek, eventually, the active support of Germany (and not of the United States). It is true that the Germans of today are not the Germans of 1938. No German is, or will ever be, interested in a Fourth Reich—in dominating all of Europe. But one half of Europe—its eastern half—is better than none. The famous French proverb *Plus ça change, plus c'est la même chose*—that things and people never really change—is only a half-truth. But that other French proverb *L'appétit vient en mangeant*—that appetite rises with the meal—is more than a half-truth, alas.

Something similar is already occurring in a Japan that sees its great World War II enemies, the United States and the Soviet Union, in decline. Hence the natural Japanese tendency will be to seek a close association with China, eventually at the expense of America and of Russia. We ought to know that before 1945 Japan's aim was not the conquest of all China but the establishment of a pro-Japanese regime in China: anti-Russian as well as anti-Western. China as a great power was an illusion cherished by Franklin Roosevelt; that China could be a superpower, an American ally balancing the Russian superpower, was an illusion dear to Richard Nixon and, it seems, even now to George Bush. Even one billion Chinese do not a superpower make. But if and when a Japanese-Chinese alliance—and not merely an economic one—comes about, then, for the third time, America and Russia must be allied again: a not necessarily remote contingency for which the present American government as well as our international experts are leaving the American people entirely unprepared.

But history remains unpredictable, after all. That, after fifty years, which *is* a fairly long time, the British and the Russian and the American empires have lost most of the fruits of their victory in World War II is not arguable. At the same time Germany and Japan, the losers of World War II, are not the superpowers of the world. They have not yet been willing to translate their economic prestige into political and military power—more precisely, into that willingness to use force that is as much a component of power as is prestige. That willingness, in this democratic age, depends on the inclinations of their peoples. They may remain content with their present circumstances of material well-being, satisfied with their present reputations, without feeling constrained by their political and military desiderata still imposed on their states by the declining superpowers. Or they may not.

YET, IN THE SUMMER OF 1990, THE MOST FATUOUS OF THE illusions confusing the public discussion is the one about the return, or the rebirth, of liberal parliamentary democracy and of capitalism, which, given world enough and time, will become everywhere triumphant.

Parliamentary democracy belonged to the nineteenth century. Its existence in Western Europe was restored with the help of the Anglo-American victory in World War II, and its survival depended on a social structure in which the bourgeois and upper classes furnished the majority of political representatives. In Eastern Europe such a social structure does not now exist. What are rising there are not liberal parliamentary democracies but nationalist and populist ones: quite another kettle of fish—or can of worms, depending on how you call it.

To believe that what we are witnessing in Eastern Europe is a rebirth of traditional capitalism is even more of an illusion. That, too, belonged to the nineteenth century. Traditional capitalism is gone in the West too, even from the United States. The universal attribute of every country in the world is the welfare state, administered by large bureaucracies. We are all socialist now, whether we call ourselves that or not. It is only that international socialism is a mirage. The dominant reality is that of a variety of nationalist socialisms. What the Eastern European peoples are reacting against is the deadening, and ineffective, rule of their nominally communist ruling classes. But anti-communism does neither capitalism nor liberal democracy make. The communist bureaucracies will be succeeded by another kind of national bureaucracy; and the rise of modern bureaucracy is a worldwide phenomenon, something quite different from the Roman or czarist or Prussian bureaucracies of the past.

What we have learned (or should have learned) during the last few decades is that Adam Smith was as wrong as Marx—not only because of his utopian notions about free trade but also because of his insufficient understanding of human nature. The "market economy" as well as "supply and demand" are myths. When Ralph Waldo Emerson said that all men have to do is to invent a better mousetrap, he was mouthing nonsense. The inventor of the best mousetrap in the world will profit nothing until the availability of the aforesaid mousetrap is broadly publicized and advertised, that is, widely known. Just as in the history of American politics the devolution of elections to popularity contests in the nineteenth century was followed in the twentieth century by a further, and more insidious, degeneration from popularity contests to publicity contests, so also in the history of commerce the same process has involved devolution not only of goods but also of intellectual achievement, the so-called marketplace of ideas, and of art itself. It is absurd to speak of a free and independent "market," of a true "supply and demand," independent of the massive interventions of promotion and publicity, of self-fulfilling prophecies, hypes, and fixes. Economic Man is a myth.

History is not determined by economics—which is why it is absurd to assume that the economic and administrative arrangements in 1992 will amount to a real political union of Europe. The best we can hope for—especially in the Western world—is that the wars of the past will not occur again, at least not in their prior incarnations. But war is only one form of communal violence; and certainly there are no signs in the world—certainly not within our supposedly civilized cities—that violence, indeed savagery, has disappeared. Where and when the exercise of law and order has been corrupted or weakened, the prestige of brutal power rises. Those who think (or who make themselves think) that such abstractions as the gross national product amount to real wealth, or that credit structures provide the principal guarantees of freedom against violence or savagery, are fools. Wealth may be an instrument of power, but it is no more than one of its instruments—and sometimes not even that. And the more wealth is computerized, the more abstract it becomes—a commonsense truth that escapes the minds only of those who believe that the human mind is a computer and that history may be computed.

Near the end of the twentieth century—indeed, near the end of the so-called Modern Age—two dangerous circumstances threaten the world. One is the institutionalized pressure for material and economic "growth"—contrary to stability and threatening nature itself. The other is the existence of the populist inclinations of nationalism—contrary to a greater and better understanding among peoples. One is the thrust for increasing wealth; the other, for tribal power. One issues from the presumption that the principal human motive is greed; the other, that it is power. To imagine that the former is morally superior to the latter is at least questionable; but to think that the progress of history amounts to the triumph of money over force is stupid beyond belief.

Nationalism is not necessarily the path to a democratic world

FRED HALLIDAY/*NEW STATESMAN & SOCIETY*

Across much of the contemporary world, we are witnessing a supposedly welcome revival of nationalism. Nationalism, it is said, is the driving force behind the new political movements in Eastern Europe, responsible for the unification of Germany as well as for the likely breakup of the USSR. Flags, languages, cultures long suppressed (or supposedly forgotten) have now been revived.

There are two welcome aspects of this phenomenon. First, what we are seeing in Eastern Europe and the USSR is the development of democracy, increased freedom for peoples who have long been denied it. Because nationalism asserts the rights of distinct peoples to independence, it plays an important role in democratic politics.

The changes in Eastern Europe are also reasserting a cultural diversity—in language, writing, music—that draws on the richness of traditions among these peoples. Insofar as "internationalism," as imposed by the USSR, denied these two things, the world is well rid of it. But to welcome greater democracy and self-determination, and the extension of cultural diversity, is not to welcome nationalism itself. Nationalism may well incorporate such positive forces, but it is not identical with them and is itself beset with myths and dangers.

For all the emphasis that nationalism in its various forms places on uniqueness and special character of a country, nationalism in different countries is in many respects all the same, and it rests on three recurrent ideas, each of which is unfounded.

The first is that nations have existed for a long time. Peoples, cultures, communities—with varying degrees of continuity and homogeneity—have existed for centuries and more. But nations, in the sense of communities practicing the right to self-rule, are all less than 200 years old. It is only since the French Revolution that the values and ideology of nationalism have become part of political life.

The second myth of nationalism is that in some way nations correspond to something real—to a history, a tradition, a common race, language, territory, fate, and, in some cases, a divine order. All this is nonsense. Counting newly independent Namibia, there are now 170 sovereign entities in the world that we dignify with the term *nation-state*. But there is nothing "given," by history, God, or anything else, that makes our contemporary political map correspond with the diversity of peoples in the world. Language, the first try of anyone trying to define a nation, defines very few—not just in the Third World, but in many parts of Europe too, not least Switzerland and Belgium. There are more than 4,000 languages in the world. Perhaps there should be 4,000 states?

Race, the other most common criteria for what constitutes a nation, is a dangerous concept at best. Even if it were not, it would not get very far with most of the nations in the world. None of the societies created since the year 1500 make much sense in terms of race. The United States, Australia, Brazil, and dozens of others actually represent a vigorous mingling of races. Even in more settled continents, the dividing lines of the contemporary international system fell haphazardly, with little respect for existing communities and peoples.

The third myth of the nation is that in some way we all belong to one. But many people in the world have more than one national identity. My father was a Yorkshire Quaker, my mother an Irish Catholic. Having lived in England and Ireland, I find much in each that I like, and feel a refreshing degree of non-belonging in both.

From *Utne Reader*, November/December 1990, pp. 99-100. Originally from *New Statesman and Society*, March 30, 1990.
Reprinted by permission.

In many nation-states of the world, the official nationalism is that of one dominant group using its

True internationalists must question the terms on which the world is being internationalized today.

supposed legitimacy to enforce the subordination of others. It is conventional to say that this is true of Third World states, but it is equally true of the United Kingdom, a multinational state forged by conquest and long maintained by force.

But even for people who qualify, the idea of belonging is equally bogus. For what is the entity to which they are supposed to belong? How is its identity defined? Here the ready answers of nationalism draw upon tradition in one form or another, as if what constitutes the nation is handed down by earlier generations. This is an absurdity. Tradition is an artifact, a selective collection of myths and inventions made for contemporary purposes; and what constitutes tradition is defined by those with power.

It is these myths that underlie all nationalism. In themselves these myths might be seen as innocuous, necessary for identity and a sense of security in the modern age. Yet once accepted they provide a basis for oppressing those within the community who dissent, and they provide an excuse for arrogance (or worse) toward those seen as foreign or alien.

The dangers of nationalism are not confined to oppressor states. Other peoples, including those currently or recently oppressed on national and ethnic grounds, may well reply in kind, and often against other oppressed peoples. The current upheavals in the USSR and Eastern Europe have already unleashed their own crop of ethnic and communal conflicts in Bulgaria, Romania, Armenia, and Azerbaijan as well as the rise of anti-Semitism in Russia and Poland.

In recent years many political activists around the world have abandoned the idealistic notion of internationalism. I believe that internationalism is still relevant in the contemporary world, particularly in two respects: the rejection of nationalist myths (whether these be the myths of "others" or of one's "own" people) and support for democratic forms of international cooperation in the face of international trends that are neither.

Yet true internationalists must question the terms on which the world is being internationalized today. A question arises: On whose terms is this internationalization taking place? In the media, for instance, we can see a growing concentration of power at the international level. The same thing is happening in many other sectors of our world economy. The release of Eastern Europe from Soviet political domination may be replaced by the less overt but equally tenacious economic domination by West German capital. The questions that arise with regard to both nationalism and internationalism are the same: How far do they lead to greater or lesser democracy, and how far do they promote or preclude cultural diversity? On their own, both can be instruments of control by social classes, states, genders, or dominant ethnic groups.

With all her faults, she is my country still

The nation-state, that worldwide triumph of political, social and economic organisation, is barely 200 years old. It is also, many people now say, on its deathbed. They are wrong

THE signs of decay are everywhere. The Soviet Union, which was in part a heroic effort to unite many nationalities under one state, is cracking. French-speaking *Québécois* talk about parting company with the mainly-Anglophone rest of Canada. Hindus run riot in officially secular India, hinting that Indian-ness should be more closely identified with Hinduness. Yugoslavs argue violently over national differences so fine that Chicago neighbourhoods could become countries on the basis of them.

At the other end of the scale, Mrs Margaret Thatcher is toppled as prime minister partly because of her entrenched resistance to the idea of surrendering some British sovereignty to a prospective European currency and central bank. At the Uruguay round of talks in the General Agreement on Tariffs and Trade, countries negotiate about freeing trade in services, which would involve each of them admitting far more foreign people and foreign ways of doing business—quite a different matter from admitting mere foreign goods—into its territory. More bizarrely, America and Japan, in their bilateral trade talks, agree to snoop into each other's national habits, like savings rates and retail-distribution systems.

Even the meat-and-potatoes of the nation-state diet, the power to wage war, is no longer quite what it used to be. The struggle between George Bush and Saddam Hussein involved the American president in a complicated alliance-building exercise that has relied to a surprising degree on decision-making by the UN Security Council and the nation-state-smudging concept of collective security. Is that it for the nation-state?

First Italy, then Italians

If so, the world will not be losing some long-standing and deep expression of the nature of human society. In a fine recent book called "Nations and nationalism since 1780", Mr E.J. Hobsbawm shows that the nation-state, in any version that would be recognisable to twentieth-century man, is no older than the American constitution and the French revolution, both born in 1789.

Even nationality, in its modern sense, is surprisingly new. In most of Europe, until the nineteenth century, "nation" meant little more than "place of birth" or "where I come from". In Spain, which, together with Britain and France, is one of Europe's older and most natural nation-states, it was only in 1884 that the dictionary of the Royal Spanish Academy stopped referring to *nación* as "the aggregate of the inhabitants of a province, a country or a kingdom", or, just as good, "a foreigner". In that year the dictionary at last made the link that now sounds so inevitable: "the aggregate of the inhabitants of a country under the direction of a single government".

The nation-state, even national consciousness, is the result of a deliberate effort to mobilise economic and social resources in the pursuit of large political aims. This was obviously the case with the creation of Germany and Italy, neither of which had existed in even rudimentary form before the nineteenth century. ("We have made Italy," Massimo d'Azeglio said at the first sitting of the Italian parliament, "now we have to make Italians.") But the effort of the will is there, too, in the virulent, often racist, European and Japanese nationalisms of the years 1910-45. And it also characterises the great revolutionary states of the eighteenth century, the United States and France: especially America, whose nationhood has been defined almost entirely by acts of will rather than accidents of history. "Americans are those who wish to be," as Mr Hobsbawm puts it.

What man has created, particularly so recently, man can re-create, or even demolish. The medieval world was a world of local and personal allegiances, with great sway being held by often tiny places: city-states like Lübeck and Venice were global powers. The world could become such a place again in the twenty-first century—provided that the purposes which the nation-state has served for the past couple of centuries can now find a better servant.

What countries are for

Those purposes can be summarised under three or four headings. One is the organisation and use of social violence. Modern technology has brought this to an astonishing pitch of sophistication and destructiveness, but the tendency of human societies—or of the people whom they allow or choose to lead them—to try and exert power over others is deeply entrenched. If "national" defence and security are to be a thing of the past, something else will be needed to keep order between societies.

A second purpose of the nation-state has been to express a sense of political and social identity. It may be a very new-found identity, as Mr Hobsbawm's book argues, compared with family, local, religious, ethnic or linguistic attachments, but the awareness of being the citizen of a country does seem strong in much of the world. A closely

A different measure

Conventional and "ownership-based" trade balances, US (1986) and **Japan (1983)** — All figures $ billion

Exports			Less intra-company transfers		Plus local sales to foreign multinationals		Plus sales by home-owned multinationals abroad		Equals total "foreign sales"	
224	146		122	60	400	3	865	150	1,367	239
Imports			Less intra-company transfers		Plus local purchases from foreign multinationals		Plus purchases by home-owned multinationals abroad		Equals total "foreign purchases"	
368	114		190	65	617	58	558	90	1,353	197
Trade balance -144 42									**Ownership-based trade balance** 14 32	

Source: DeAnne Julius

related function of the nation-state has been to legislate: to write and then execute the rules by which a society chooses to govern itself (and, not incidentally, to define the sort of society it is going to be).

The people who think the nation-state is fading do not often mention matters like law-making and identity; defence and security, too, still seem strongly rooted in the national system, despite alliances like NATO and whatever bigger role the United Nations wins as a result of the Gulf saga. But the one thing in which the nation-state's grip seems visibly to be loosening is the organisation of economic life.

One world, one economy

However much power over commerce and finance the newly rising states of the nineteenth century actually had—and this article will argue later on that it was not much—the leaders who built the early nation-states, from Hamilton in America to Bismarck in Germany to the Japanese in charge of the Meiji restoration, all wanted to use national economic activity to put muscle behind their political ambitions. Their modern counterparts do not find it so easy.

With information and money both as weightless as the electronic impulses that carry them down wires or beam them through space, a government's ability to shape business and financial decisions is limited. Companies and money alike are ever freer to move to wherever they find the best returns—which means that governments are being shorn of the power to set the economic rules within their borders, let alone outside them. France's President Mitterrand discovered this in 1982, when the markets forced him to reverse the socialist economic policies that his government had been elected to carry out.

World economic integration is being speeded up by growth in trade (trade in goods and services amounted to some $4 trillion in 1990, up 13-fold in real terms since 1950), financial flows, and the migration of people and companies. A look at companies alone suggests how quickly the world is being knitted together.

In the last three years of the 1980s, the flow of direct foreign investment measured in 1980 dollars was more than $100 billion a year, ten times as much as it had been in the first three years of the 1970s (again in 1980 dollars). Once installed, direct foreign investment begins changing economic calcula-

tions in ways that leave policymakers scratching their heads. Take the item that people have spent so much time worrying about in recent years, America's trade deficit.

By the book, the American deficit was $144 billion in 1986. But if, like Ms DeAnne Julius, the chief economist at Shell International Petroleum, you then take account of the activities of American-owned firms abroad and foreign-owned firms in America, you find that this huge deficit becomes a surplus of $14 billion (the two measures for Japan, whose companies have invested far less than America's in the outside world, are much closer, see the table). An "ownership-based" measure of American trade raises basic questions about how international transactions should be thought of. It certainly puts fears about American competitiveness in a sharply different light.

If "American" competitiveness means anything at all these days. Mr Kenichi Ohmae, who heads the Japan office of McKinsey, a management consultancy, has long argued that the nationality of companies is an irrelevance—and tried to prove it in a recent book book, "The Borderless World". Big firms, at least, have to operate in many different markets around the world and, if they are to succeed, have to behave like locals wherever they find themselves. They may be headquartered, or most of their shares owned, in one country, but employ more people and pay more taxes somewhere else. What can their "nationality" really count for?

Mr Michael Porter, a business professor at Harvard, produced a 900-page answer in 1990, called "The Competitive Advantage of Nations". Mr Porter says that a company's home determines much of its (and thus of the home's) competitiveness: education, industrial structure, consumer sophistication, and the fierceness of the competition at home. Two of his most interesting examples, though, are highly localised Italian industries, footwear and ceramic tiles. Italy again. Why not "The Competitive Advantage of Provinces and City-States"?

Thatcher, Delors and Macrae

The European Community's 1992 single-market experiment is testing many of these ideas. Optimists say that both Mrs Thatcher, who until she lost office was the nation-state's most outspoken defender in the debates, and Mr Jacques Delors, the

commission president who is the champion of a supranational Europe, are wrong about the way the EC is headed. Europe, they say, is going to be remade by a gradual competitive deregulation of its governments.

It could work like this. Even with a single European currency, individual countries will remain in charge of their own fiscal policies and most of the laws that regulate companies, professions, health standards and the like. Because the EC will be not only a free-trade zone, but also a place where people can move freely, along with services and the firms that provide them, some way will have to be found to allow, say, German lawyers to set up shop in Bordeaux.

One way would be to gather in rule-making powers to Brussels and Strasbourg. A likelier approach is for Community members to agree on a few minimum standards for rule-making ("lawyers cannot be licensed without at least two years of professional training") and then start giving full marks to the regulatory approvals of other members. That German lawyer, once the German authorities had pronounced him fit to practise law, could set up shop without further ado in Bordeaux—even though he had not satisfied the requirements France imposes on its own would-be lawyers.

This might lead to a gradual interweaving of Europe's economies and societies, while avoiding the Delorsian threat of supranational government. It would also start putting competitive pressure on member governments to run similar fiscal policies. With a single European currency, a British company that faced British corporate-tax rates substantially higher than those in France would have good reason to think that being incorporated in France was not a bad idea at all.

The idea that, once a certain level of economic integration is reached, the pressure on governments to pursue policies that will attract rather than repel people and companies can be applied far beyond the EC. Mr Norman Macrae, *The Economist*'s former deputy editor, wrote in a piece of futurology called "The 2024 Report" that in the second quarter of the next century the world will be run with a single currency under the control of Centrobank, a global central bank answerable to no politicians.

With people pretty much free to move where they want, local governments will be the ones that matter (and even they will not count for much). Tax rates long since hav-

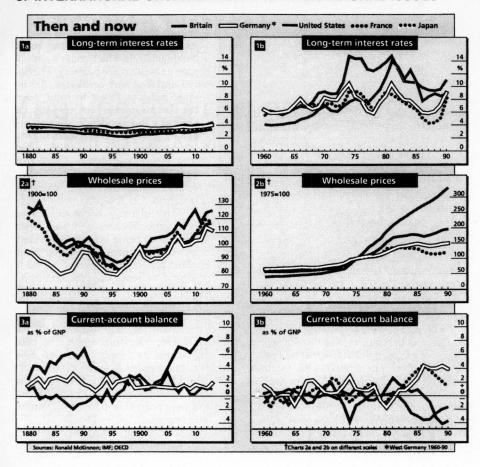

Then and now — Britain — Germany* — United States •••• France •••• Japan

1a Long-term interest rates
1b Long-term interest rates
2a† Wholesale prices (1900=100)
2b† Wholesale prices (1975=100)
3a Current-account balance as % of GNP
3b Current-account balance as % of GNP

Sources: Ronald McKinnon; IMF; OECD
†Charts 2a and 2b on different scales   *West Germany 1960-90

ing been equalised by competitive pressure, public spending will amount to 10% or so of gross world product; and national defence spending, having proven its economic uselessness, will have been unilaterally abandoned, world order being secured by a small force under international control. Even welfare spending will be on its way to being equalised, which will at last finish off the nation-state.

It sounds like an appropriate end—except that this world, in many of its essentials, already existed once. It was called the nineteenth century.

The golden years

The years 1870-1913, when the world was on the gold standard as administered by the Bank of England, were a period of remarkable economic integration. Mr Ronald McKinnon, an economist at Stanford, has compared this period with the years 1960-88, the last 11 years of the dollar-dominated Bretton Woods system and the first 17 years of the floating-rate system. Some of his findings are shown in charts 1-3.

Because the gold standard was so rigid, and the rules were so widely adhered to (anybody who suspended convertibility, as the United States did during the civil war, felt compelled to return to the gold standard as soon as its crisis had passed), for all practical

purposes there was a single world currency. The first result was that long-term interest rates were low and uniform throughout the world, especially compared with the past 30 years (chart 1).

Second, price levels in the big economies were unstable, moving sharply up or down, but moving the same way everywhere; now they move only up, and at quite different rates in different countries (chart 2). Third, current accounts (and hence the flows of long-term capital) were volatile but were also, by modern standards, astonishingly large in relation to GNP (chart 3). In the decade before the first world war, Britain ran a current-account surplus that averaged 8% of GNP (and was investing that amount elsewhere in the world)—compared with a range of 2-4% for the West German and Japanese surpluses (and the American deficit) in the mid-1980s.

Immigration was freer in the nineteenth century. There were almost no restrictions on the movement of people, and move they did. In the 80 years beginning in 1845, 50m people, mostly Europeans, migrated to the western hemisphere: this in days when the world's population was less than a fifth of its present level. In the years 1900-13 alone, 10m Europeans left for the new world.

Long-term money and goods moved in larger relative volumes too. Governments

controlled little spending (10% of GNP or less), there were no quantitative barriers to trade and few to capital flows, and most countries had low or non-existent tariffs. The world was so tied together by trade and investment in the late nineteenth century that, despite the glorious years of growth in trade and GNP from 1950 to 1973, it took most countries nearly 70 years for merchandise trade as a proportion of their GNP to overtake the levels it had achieved in the years before the first world war.

The first lesson of these decades is that even a high degree of economic integration does not necessarily spell trouble for the nation-state. The gloomier lesson is that strong economic ties will not in themselves restrain countries bent on furthering other aims. The period of the gold standard ended with an appallingly destructive bout of nationalism that killed 75m people in the years 1914-45 and reduced the total GNP of the OECD countries by nearly 20% in 1929-32. Unless the nation-state fails to satisfy its other purposes as well—defence, social identification, rule-making—the global economy will not be in a position to pronounce its obituary.

Supra and infra, dubious twins

This might or might not be unfortunate. It all depends on what form of political and social organisation is best placed to make possible, worldwide, the kind of thing that chart 4 shows happened in the United States over the past 60 years. In 1929 the United States had large discrepancies in personal income from one region to another. Over the next seven decades they were practically eliminated. It is not too fanciful to believe that the technologies of production, information and communication have now entered a phase that would allow the same sort of convergence to happen worldwide by the year 2100.

This will come to pass only if the fewest possible restraints are placed on the movement of people, companies, money, goods, services and ideas. Letting these things find their right rates of return is what both raises and equalises incomes. The reason regional incomes could converge in the United States, once technology had become advanced enough, is that Americans enjoyed a single currency, and a set of laws and institutions that guaranteed them the right to move themselves and their property as they liked around their country.

The obvious analogy, on a global basis, is a world government. This is so implausible over the next century that it is not worth talking about. Besides, a world government is not necessary: the gold-standard years clearly showed that a great deal of freedom of movement is compatible with a strong system of independent states. The real question is about the size of the governing units, and the principles on which they operate.

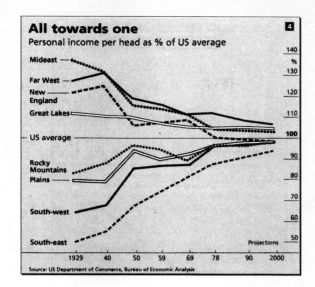

All towards one
Personal income per head as % of US average

Mideast
Far West
New England
Great Lakes
US average
Rocky Mountains
Plains
South-west
South-east

Projections

1929   40   50   59   69   78   90   2000

Source: US Department of Commerce, Bureau of Economic Analysis

These units are at least as much an expression of values, beliefs and experience as they are an instrument for making policies or delivering public services. Perhaps this is irrational. What made a true nation of America was a horribly bloody civil war which established, among other things, the principles that slavery is wrong even if most people in some places prefer it; and that, once those places had joined the United States, they could never leave it even if they democratically decided they wanted to.

Yet such things matter: they define whole societies. It therefore matters, too, who makes the laws and what the laws say, and who runs the public institutions. The link between a government and the society it governs needs to be a natural one. For the sake of peace and economic sense, it should also be a relaxed and tolerant one.

The nation-state has hardly been ideal at satisfying either of these aims. But would either supranationalism or infranationalism be any better? The trouble with supranationalism—which can be defined as the collection of several of today's largish and well-defined nation-states under a single government—is that it is hard to see how a true supranation could be put together. Not every state needs a civil war to forge its people's values. But every state does need something to make people feel comfortable with it and attached to it. The United States and Canada are more closely linked economically than many regions within America itself, and their recent free-trade agreement is drawing them closer together still. Yet the Canadians are fierce about wanting their own identity, their own government and their own country.

The likelier alternative is a breakdown of the nation-state into smaller units: call it infranationalism. A modern version of the pre-nineteenth-century world of unprej-udiced local attachments sounds good, but that does not seem to be the direction in which today's nation-state unbuilders are pointing. The Soviet and Yugoslav breakups, the revived religious fervor in India, even the language-based movement for Quebec's independence: they all are aiming towards states based not on tolerant and fairly open little countries, but on the blinkered view that what should hold people together is ethnic, religious or linguistic sameness.

This is a step backwards. Some homogeneous states work well (Japan and Korea being obvious examples). Most of the ones now being clamoured for are much likelier to end in bigotry, violence and protectionism. So where is the nation-state going to end up? In the short term, meaning the next few decades, in much the same place it now is. Some countries, like Yugoslavia or the Soviet Union, may disintegrate into near-warring ethnic or religious enclaves. Elsewhere, organisations like the EC, the GATT and the United Nations will continue to promote internationalism, and start becoming the scenes of a slow pooling of societies and sovereignties.

The basic unit, though, is going to remain the nation-state. Nothing else can govern whole societies without toppling, one way, into the infranationalist error of tribalism or, the other way, into the supranationalist sterility of rule by bureaucrats. If the world is lucky, the next era of nation-states will operate under a free-trading, fixed-exchange-rate (maybe even single-currency) regime. It will be liberal and open, with power more or less peacefully balanced. But most of the same flags will still be snapping on the poles outside the United Nations, and it will still be nations, and not something else, that are united.

What next? The post-Cold War world

WOLFGANG SACHS
NEW PERSPECTIVES QUARTERLY

In his 1949 inaugural address, President Harry S. Truman changed the world: With one conceptual stroke, he created a vision in which all the people of the globe were moving inexorably along the same track—toward industrial development. Never mind the respective aspirations of Kikuyus and Sicilians, Filipinos and Peruvians. With Truman's pronouncement, these groups suddenly became "underdeveloped," and the road they were to follow lay clearly before the president's eyes: "Greater production is the key to prosperity and peace." The world's nations fell easily into place under Truman's all-encompassing definition of development, with one clearly leading the field: "The United States is preeminent among nations in the development of industrial and scientific techniques." The front runners, it was announced, would be generous. They would offer assistance that would relieve suffering through "industrial activities" and a "higher standard of living." The shift from colonialism, which held occupied territories under an iron political rule, to developmentalism, which called for the competition of independent nations in a global economic arena, is the principal novelty of the world order after the Second World War. Truman's world view was inspired by two very different forces: First, he urgently needed a vision that could guide the United States, as the new world power after the downfall of Europe, in creating a new world order. Drawing on the experience of his own country, he projected onto the rest of the globe the 18th-century drive to subordinate all society to the rationality of the market.

Secondly, the threatening expansion of communism forced him to offer emerging nations an alternative to communist revolution. Truman, after all, was probably the man most responsible for starting the Cold War. Truman promised young nations an industrial utopia, but warned that it was not to be reached through the state's seizure of the instruments of production but through private accumulation and free trade.

Though the means were different, capitalism and communism both promised rapid industrialization to the newly emerging nations of the Southern Hemisphere. During the Cold War, the confrontation between East and West obscured their profound similarities: The superpowers were rivals not only because of differences in their two political systems but also because a good deal of common ground lay beneath their respective economic aspirations.

Both camps were deeply rooted in a 19th century imagination that saw salvation from the problems of the human condition through ever-increasing technical capabilities. Further, they both

Now that the Berlin Wall has crumbled, the West may turn its back on the South.

From *Utne Reader*, November/December 1990, pp. 90-92, 94-98. Excerpt from *NPQ*, New Perspectives Quarterly, Spring 1990. Copyright © 1990 by the Center for the Study of Democratic Institutions.

embraced a ferocious productivism that strove for a society in which everyone was either a willing producer or an eager consumer.

The Promethean urge to destroy the present in favor of a utopian future, and to squander the treasures of culture and nature along the way, dominated both sides. Socialism and capitalism were like hostile brothers that jealously insisted on their respective pre-eminence, while they were driven by the same family imperatives.

In 1989, however, the socialist track was abandoned. State despotism, instead of leading to material utopia, led toward social paralysis and economic regression. What was once celebrated as the liberating alternative to capitalism ended in mass demonstrations, as people demanded liberation from the state yoke. From Estonia to Romania, citizens found themselves locked in societies that were not free, equal, or prosperous. Private initiative, in conjunction with political pluralism, had proven far more versatile in furnishing society with goods and services.

Such political and economic conversion in the East will have far-reaching consequences: Now that the Berlin Wall has crumbled, the West may finally have a way to turn its back on a Third World stuck with debts, drugs, and depression. Looking toward the near future, it is inevitable that as investment opportunities open in the East, the West will turn much of its attention away from the nations of the South.

The emerging indifference toward the South, however, reinforces a trend that has been looming for years. Since the rise of high-tech industries, many Third World countries have lost the bargaining power of their raw materials in the international marketplace: Microprocessors trim energy consumption, new synthetic materials replace copper and steel, and biotechnology drives soybeans and raw sugar from the market.

As industry grows less dependent on raw materials, the demand for traditional export products from the developing countries slackens. Even those countries that offered cheap labor for the production of export-bound manufactured goods are not protected against this trend; as automation proceeds, the comparative advantage of low-wage labor diminishes.

In other words, the Third World has become irrelevant in the eyes of Western economic planners. As a result, the base for export-oriented development envisioned by Harry Truman has crumbled. This situation, combined with the lingering debt crisis, means that many Southern countries are not only falling behind but are sliding backward. With the Northern countries competing among themselves and the Southern countries struggling against the crash, the world is rapidly splitting into a two-track economy.

Though Truman's rallying cry was "development" for all nations, the lead of advanced countries never slackened; they outdistanced the field by ever-increasing margins during the last 40 years. Despite tremendous effort and unspeakable sacrifice on the part of developing nations to pull within reach of the GNP-hefty countries of the North, the gap inexorably grew.

The reason is simple: In this kind of race, the rich countries will always move faster than the rest. Certainly, exploitation plays a role, but far more important is the built-in capacity of advanced societies to continuously outpace others with the latest technology—to win at the game of competitive obsolescence. The rich countries drive hard to continuously degrade and discard the achievements of yesterday in order to make room for a "new, improved" version. Zooming ahead with consumer novelties keeps people's demand for goods ever-increasing. The creation of scarcities is capitalism's elixir.

In the South, the drive toward "development" often undercuts people's deep desires to avoid addiction to modern institutions: The peasant who is forced to buy his seeds each and every year, the mother who enjoys neither the assistance of a hospital nor the care of traditional women healers, the clerk who has been laid off as a result of cost-cutting measures are all like refugees who have been rejected and have no place to go. Shunned by the advanced sector and cut off from the old ways, they are expatriates in their own country, forced to get by in the no-man's-land between modernity and tradition.

As Eastern Europe seeks to join the global economic arena, the shadow of the world market will fall on it as well. Though certain industries will leap ahead, there is no reason to believe that most of the Eastern countries will ever catch up, simply because the West is so adept at creating new scarcities.

Burdened by foreign interference, technological dependence, accumulated debts, and glaring inequalities, Eastern Europe will most likely join the ranks of the South. Indeed, why should Romania, Bulgaria, Poland, or even the Soviet Union escape the destiny of Egypt, Thailand, or Brazil? The more they unconditionally expose themselves to the world market, the harder the stiff wind of competition will blow against them.

To be sure, in Truman's time, the founding fathers of development policy were inspired by the vision that a globalized market for goods would guarantee world peace. Instead of violence, the spirit of commerce would reign; instead of firepower, productive power would rule competition between nations.

Indeed, in the decades after World War II, events gave some credence to this conception: The conquest of foreign territories by bellicose states yielded to the conquest of foreign markets by profit-seeking industries.

Yet recent decades have shown that unrestrained competitiveness easily becomes a self-defeating exercise. Once brandished as a weapon against political despotism, the world market has

If all countries followed the Western model, five or six planets would be needed to serve as mines and dumps.

itself become a closet dictator under whose dominion both rich and poor countries tremble. The fear of falling behind in international competition has become the predominant principle of politics North and South, East and West.

Business enterprises and entire states see themselves trapped in a situation of relentless competition, where each participant is dependent on the decisions of all the other players. What falls by the wayside in this hurly-burly is the possibility for self-determination. The demands imposed by world market competition repeatedly thwart all attempts for a society to determine its own needs and future in a creative way: Some countries cannot do without agricultural exports, others cannot drop out of the high-tech race. There is scarcely a country today that seems able to control its destiny. In this respect the differences between countries are only relative: The United States certainly enjoys more control over its own fate than India, but also feels intense pressure from Japan.

Probably the most insidious effect of the development era has been this worldwide loss of alternatives. Not only is much of the Third World geared to the development idea, but the mental space in which people dream and act is largely occupied by Western imagery. It has become difficult to honor communal traditions in Third World villages when individual property is introduced; difficult to keep the value of individual enrichment in perspective when *Dallas* flickers on the screen; difficult to resist deforestation when economic pressures from outside insist it is necessary; difficult to be generous with time when speed is the order of the day. In fact, the global standardization of people's dreams is likely to be the most obstinate legacy of the Cold War period.

Yet despite the overall impact of the development idea promoted over the last 40 years, people worldwide are beginning to rediscover their own paths: In order to protect their livelihood in a dignified manner, many countries have discovered that insistence on rampant modernization can be quite reactionary, while attention to tradition can be a creative force.

For instance, Third World countries often recognize that what was indiscriminately denounced

as "poverty" during the period of development in fact contained elements of a social system that tried to keep the impact of the money economy at bay.

After all, frugality—one meaning of the word *poverty*—was once the mark of cultures free from the frenzy of accumulation. Though people in these cultures had rather meager possessions, everyone usually enjoyed access to fields, rivers, and woods, while family and community provided services that were paid for in other cultures with hard cash.

This indigenous "anti-capitalism" has been eroded by the development strategy of fighting poverty through accelerating growth. As a result, people have often been driven to destitution—the second meaning of *poverty*—as they were deprived of their land and communities. Or they were forced to live under the regime of scarcity—the third meaning of *poverty*—as they became urban dwellers forever wrestling with their insufficient purchasing power.

In many spots around the world, villages, neighborhoods, and associations are attempting to restore community-based non-economic relations as a way to shelter themselves against the pressure of a failing economy. In part renouncing the race that leads nowhere, these people are trying to stitch together a patchwork of the traditional and the modern experience.

Until now, the West has followed Truman's logic in reacting to the downfall of communism. With an air of self-righteousness, Western governments lure Eastern countries into the world market. If the experience of developing countries is any indication, it is likely that a number of Eastern countries will find themselves near the periphery of the world economy as Europe's South America.

When applause for the entrance of the Eastern countries into the competitive market economy has passed, the disquieting suspicion may arise that the entire race is leading in the wrong direction.

The advanced countries are wealthy, prosperous, and far ahead of the rest of the pack, but they may well be heading toward an abyss. What Truman could not have imagined has long since come into focus: The impressive achievements of modern technology have, to a considerable extent, revealed themselves as self-deception.

For more than a century, technology carried the promise of ending unnecessary sweat, toil, and tears. But technologically induced euphoria cannot be enjoyed by everyone. After all, we consume in one year

The global standardization of people's dreams is the most obstinate legacy of our era.

what it took the earth one million years to accumulate. Further, much of our glorious productivity is fed by the gigantic exploitation of fossil fuels; the earth is being excavated and permanently scarred at the same time as a steady stream of harmful substances rains down from the sky and seeps up from the ground. If all countries successfully followed the industrial example, five or six planets the size of ours would be needed to serve as mines and garbage dumps. Unfortunately, the advanced countries still follow the mental map of the 19th century. Now captives of competition, these countries long ago destroyed not only much of their precious natural resources but also those treasures of meaning that could have given them peace of mind outside the development track. They can no longer afford to decelerate.

Fortunately, however, the future cannot be foretold. It is also possible that, as the East-West competition falters, the left-right framework, which still dominates political perceptions, will also dissolve. A new constellation of conflicts, focusing not on which development track to join but on how to get off the development track altogether, may emerge.

Both "redistribution" and "revolution," the principles of the Cold War era, implied imitation, leaving the dynamics of the rich countries unquestioned. The emerging concept of "regeneration" will have to center on a politics of self-limitation in the rich countries. As Aristotle said: "The greatest crimes are committed not for the sake of necessities, but for the sake of superfluities. Men do not become tyrants in order to avoid exposure to the cold."

Abbreviations

ABM: Antiballistic missile
ACDA: Arms Control and Disarmament Agency (USA)
ACP: African, Caribbean, and Pacific Countries
AID: Agency for International Development (USA)
ALCM: Air-Launched Cruise Missile
ANC: African National Congress (South Africa)
ANZUS: Australia, New Zealand, and the United States
ASAT: Anti-satellite
ASEAN: Association of Southeast Asian Nations
ASW: anti-submarine warfare (DOD)
AWACS: Airborne Warning and Control Systems
bbl: barrel
BMD: Ballistic Missile Defense
C³ (C-cubed): command, control, communications
C3I: command, control, communications, and intelligence
CBW: chemical and biological weapons
CCD: Conference of the Committee on Disarmament (UNO)
CCP: Chinese Communist Party
CD: Committee on Disarmament (UNO)
CIA: Central Intelligence Agency (USA)
CIEC: Conference on International Economic Cooperation
CMEA: Council on Mutual Economic Assistance
COCOM: Coordinating Committee for Multilateral Export Control
COW: Committee of the Whole (UNO)
CPE: Centrally Planned Economies (communist industrial)
CPSU: Communist Party of the Soviet Union
CSCE: Conference on Security and Cooperation in Europe
CTB: Comprehensive Nuclear Test Ban Treaty
CW: Chemical warfare
DC: developing country
DIA: Defense Intelligence Agency (DOD)
DOD: Department of Defense
DTA: Democratic Turnhalle Alliance (Namibia)
EC: European Community
ECDC: Economic Cooperation among Developing Countries
ECOSOC: Economic and Social Council (UNO)
ECU: European Currency Unit
EEC: European Economic Community
EFTA: European Free Trade Association
EMS: European Monetary System
END: European Nuclear Disarmament
FAO: Food and Agriculture Organization (UNO)
FBS/FOBS: Forward based systems (strategic)
FDR: Revolutionary Democratic Front (El Salvador)
FMLN: Farabundo Marti National Liberation Front (El Salvador)
FRG: Federal Republic of Germany (West Germany)
G-77: Group of 77
GATT: General Agreement on Tariffs and Trade
GCC: Gulf Co-operation Council
GDP: Gross Domestic Product
GDR: German Democratic Republic (East Germany)
GLCM: Ground-launched cruise missile
GNP: Gross National Product
GWP: Gross World Product
IAEA: International Atomic Energy Agency
ICA: International Communication Agency (USA)
ICBM: Intercontinental Ballistic Missile
ICJ: International Court of Justice
ICNT: Informal Composite Negotiating Text (UNCLOS)
IDA: International Development Association (World Bank)
IEA: International Energy Agency (OECD)
IFC: International Finance Corporation (World Bank)
IGO: Inter-governmental Organization
IISS: International Institute for Strategic Studies (London)
ILO: International Labor Organization
IMF: International Monetary Fund
INF: Intermediate-Range Nuclear Forces
IRBM: Intermediate Range Ballistic Missile
JCS: Joint Chiefs of Staff (DOD)
KT: Kiloton
LDC: Less Developed Country

LLDC: Least Developed Countries
LOS: Law of the Sea
LRTNF: Long-range theatre nuclear forces
MAD: Mutual Assured Destruction
MARV: Maneuverable Re-entry Vehicle
MBD: Million of barrels per day (oil)
MBFR: Mutual and Balanced Force Reductions
MDB: Multilateral development banks
MFN: Most Favored Nation
MIRV: Multiple Independently Targetable Re-entry Vehicle
MNC: Multinational Corporation
MRBM: Medium-range ballistic missile
MSA: Most Seriously Affected Countries
MTN: Multilateral Trade Negotiations
MX: Missile Experimental
NATO: North Atlantic Treaty Organization
N-bomb: Neutron bomb
NGO: Non-governmental (international) organization
NIC: Newly Industrializing (industrialized) country
NIE: National Intelligence Estimate
NIEO: New International Economic Order
NIO: New (international) Information Order
NPT: Non-Proliferation Treaty
NSC: National Security Council
NSM: National Security Memorandum (NSC)
NTB: Non-tariff barrier
OAPEC: Organization of Arab Petroleum Exporting Countries
ODA: Official development assistance
OECD: Organization for Economic Cooperation and Development
OPEC: Organization of Petroleum Exporting Countries
OSD: Office of the Secretary of Defense
PD: Presidential Directive
PGM: Precision-guided munitions
PLO: Palestine Liberation Organization
PQLI: Physical Quality Life Index
PRC: People's Republic of China
PZPR: Polish United Workers (Communist) Party
RDF: Rapid Deployment Forces
RV: Re-entry vehicle
SAC: Strategic Air Command (DOD)
SALT: Strategic Arms Limitation Talks
SDI: Strategic Defense Initiative
SDR: Special Drawing Rights
SIPRI: Stockholm International Peace Research Institute
SLBM: Submarine-Launched Ballistic Missile
SLCM: Submarine-launched cruise missile
SRBM: Short-range Ballistic Missile
SSBN: Submersible Ballistic Nuclear (Nuclear Ballistic Submarine)
START: Strategic Arms Reduction Talks (Reagan)
SWAPO: South-West African People's Organization
TCDC: Technical Cooperation Among Developing Countries
TNE: Transnational Enterprises
TNF: Theatre Nuclear Forces
UN: United Nations
UNCLOS: UN Conference on the Law of the Sea
UNCTAD: UN Conference on Trade and Development
UNDP: UN Development Programme
UNEF: UN Emergency Force
UNEP: UN Environment Programme
UNESCO: UN Educational, Scientific, and Cultural Organization
UNGA: UN General Assembly
UNHCR: UN High Commissioner on Refugees
UNICEF: UN Children's Fund
UNIDO: UN Industrial Development Programme
UNITAR: UN Institute for Training and Research
UNO: United Nations Organization (the whole UN system)
UNRWA: UN Relief and Works Agency for Palestine Refugees
UNSC: UN Security Council
UNU: UN University
WHO: World Health Organization
ZPG: Zero population growth

Glossary

This Glossary*contains primarily technical, economic, financial, and military terminology not usually defined in most World Politics textbooks.

—A—

Absolute poverty: The condition of people whose incomes are insufficient to keep them at a subsistent level. If affects some 800 million people who are without adequate food intake (calories and proteins), water safe from disease-carrying organisms and toxins, minimum clothing and shelter, any kind of education, health care or employment. They are concentrated in certain areas such as the Sahel and the Horn of Africa, and Bangla Desh, but they also exist in almost all LDCs, including *middle-income countries.*

African, Caribbean, and Pacific Countries (ACP): Fifty-eight countries associated with the European Community through the *Lome Convention.*

Airborne Warning and Control System (AWACS): Flying radar stations that instantaneously identify all devices in the air within a radius of 240 miles and detect movement of land vehicles.

Air-Launched Cruise Missile (ALCM): A cruise missile carried by and launched from an aircraft.

Antiballistic missile (ABM): A missile that seeks out and destroys an incoming enemy missile in flight before the latter reaches its target. It is not effective against MIRVs.

Apartheid: A system of laws in the Republic of South Africa that seeks to preserve for the white minority population the absolute political, economic, and social control over non-whites who are variously classified as Coloureds (of mixed blood), Asians and Bantus (native Africans). Bantus are forced to settle in reservations known euphemistically as homelands or Bantustans. They must always carry passes to be appropriately stamped for work outside their area of domicile.

Appropriate technology: Also known as intermediate technology. It aims at using existing resources by making their usage more efficient or productive but adaptable to the local population.

Arms control: Any measure limiting or reducing forces, regulating armaments, and/or restricting the deployment of troops or weapons.

Arms race: The competitive or cumulative improvement of weapons stocks (qualitatively or quantitatively), or the build-up of armed forces based on the conviction of two or more actors that only by trying to stay ahead in military power can they avoid falling behind.

Association of Southeast Asian Nations (ASEAN): A regional regrouping made up of Indonesia, the Philippines, Singapore, and Thailand.

Atomic bomb: A weapon based on the rapid splitting of fissionable materials thereby inducing an explosion with three deadly results: blast, heat, and radiation.

Autonomy talks: Intermittent negotiations between Egypt and Israel, as provided in the *Camp David Agreements,* with the USA as intermediary and with as an objective the development of self-rule among Palestinians of the West Bank and the Gaza Strip. These autonomy talks are considered a sham by the Arab world, as Israel rules out a national homeland, not to say a state, for Palestinians.

—B—

Backfire: US code name for a Soviet supersonic bomber that has a range of 5,500 miles and can carry nuclear weapons. US experts disagree as to whether or not Backfire should be classified as a strategic weapon.

Italicized terms are defined elsewhere in the glossary.

Balance of Payments: A summary of the international transactions of a country over a given period of time, including commodity, service, capital flows, and gold movements.

Balance of trade: The relationship between imports and exports.

Ballistic missile: A payload propelled by a rocket, which assumes a free-fall trajectory when thrust is terminated. Ballistic missiles could be of short range (SRBM), intermediate range (IRBM), medium range (MRBM), and intercontinental (ICBM).

Barrel: A standard measure for petroleum, equivalent to 42 gallons or 158.86 liters.

Basic human needs: Adequate food intake (in terms of calories, proteins, and vitamins), drinking water free of disease-carrying organisms and toxins, minimum clothing and shelter, literacy, sanitation, health care, employment, and dignity.

Bilateral: Between two nations.

Binary (chemical) munitions/weapons: Nerve gas canisters composed of two separate chambers containing chemicals that become lethal when mixed. The mixing is done when the canister is fired. Binary gas is preferred for its relative safety in storage and transportation.

Biosphere: The environment of life and living processes at or near the earth's surface, extending from the ocean floors to about 75 kilometers into the atmosphere. It is being endangered by consequences of human activities such as air and water pollution, acid rain, radioactive fallout, desertification, toxic and nuclear wastes, and the depletion of non-renewable resources.

Brandt Commission: An independent commission on international economic issues created in September 1977 and headed by former West German Chancellor Willy Brandt.

"Broken arrows": Pentagon code word for accidents involving US nuclear weapons.

Buffer Stocks: Reserves of commodities that are either increased or decreased whenever necessary to maintain relative stability of supply and prices.

—C—

Camp David Agreements/Accords: Agreements signed on September 17, 1978 at Camp David—a mountain retreat for the US President in Maryland—by President Anwar al-Sadat of Egypt and Prime Minister Menachem Begin of Israel, and witnessed by President Jimmy Carter of the United States of America. They are "A Framework for Peace in the Middle East" and "A Framework for the Conclusion of a Peace Treaty between Egypt and Israel."

Cancun Summit: World leaders' meeting on October 22-23, 1981, in the Mexican resort of Cancun to discuss global economic issues—a major event that could make or break the North-South dialogue. The agenda item: whether to launch a new round of *Global Negotiations.*

Centrally Planned Economies (CPEs): As distinguished from free-market economies, countries generally included in this category are industrialized Communist countries: the USSR, East European countries, and the PRC.

Circular error probable (CEP): The radius of a target circle within which half of the enemy weapons are projected to fall.

Cold war: A condition of hostility between the USA and the USSR in their struggle to dominate the world scene since the end of World War II.

Commodity: The unprocessed products of mining and agriculture.

Common Fund: A fund to finance 18 commodity buffer stocks as proposed in the 1976 Nairobi *UNCTAD* IV integrated program for *commodities.*

Common Heritage of Mankind: 1970 UN declaration states the "seabed and ocean floor, and the subsoil thereof, beyond the limits of national jurisdiction. . ., as well as the resources of the area, are the common heritage of mankind."

Common Market: A customs union that eliminates trade barriers within a group and establishes a common external tariff on imports from nonmember countries.

Compensatory Financing Facility: An IMF program established in 1963 to finance temporary export shortfalls, as in coffee, sugar, or other cyclically prone export items.

Concessional loans: Loans given to LLDCs by MBDs which can be repaid in soft (non-convertible) currencies and with nominal or no interest over a long period of time.

Conditionality: A series of measures that must be taken by a country before it could qualify for loans from the International Monetary Fund, such as: (1) devaluing its currency, in an attempt to boost exports and restrain imports; (2) controlling the rate of expansion of the money supply in order to dampen inflation; (3) reducing government spending, especially human services expenditures; (4) imposing wage controls, while eliminating price controls; (5) raising interest rates in order to encourage savings; (6) increasing taxes; (7) reducing or dismantling barriers to foreign private investment and to free trade in general.

Conference on International Economic Cooperation (CIEC): A conference of 8 industrial nations, 7 oil-producing nations, and 12 developing countries held in several sessions between December 1975 and June 1977. It is composed of four separate commissions (energy, raw materials, development, and financing). It is the forum of the *North-South dialogue* between rich and poor countries.

Conference on Security and Cooperation in Europe (CSCE): See *Helsinki Agreement.*

Confidence-building measures (CBMs): Understandings (called for in the Final Act of Helsinki) to give advance notice of NATO or Warsaw Pact military maneuvers and major troop deployments.

Consensus: In conference diplomacy, a way of reaching agreements by negotiations and without a formal vote.

Contact Group: See *Western Five Contact Group*

Coordinating Committee for Multilateral Export Controls (COCOM): Composed of representatives of 14 NATO countries and Japan, it sets restrictions on the transfer of Western technology to communist nations with direct or "end use" military applications.

Council on Mutual Economic Assistance (CMEA OR COMECON): Founded in Moscow in 1949 as a counterpart of the Marshall Plan (European Recovery Program), today it is comprised of the USSR, the countries of Eastern Europe, Mongolia, Cuba, and Vietnam.

Counterforce: The use of strategic nuclear weapons for strike on selected military capabilities of an enemy force.

Countervalue: The use of strategic nuclear weapons for strike on an enemy's population centers.

Cruise missile: A small, highly-maneuverable, low-flying, pilotless aircraft equipped with accurate guidance systems that periodically readjusts its trajectory. It can carry conventional or nuclear warheads, can be short-range or long range, and can be launched from the air (ALLUM), the ground (GLCM), or the sea (SLCM).

—D—

Declaration of Talloires: A statement issued in 1981 by Western journalists who opposed the UNESCO-sponsored *New World Information and Communication Order,* at a meeting in Talloires, France.

Delivery systems or Vehicles or Launchers: Land-Based Missiles (ICBMs), Submarine-Launched Missiles (SLBMs), and long-range bombers capable of delivering nuclear weapons.

Democratic Turnhalle Alliance (DTA): A party in the Namibian dispute, set up by South Africa as a political alternative to SWAPO. The DTA is considered as a puppet creation of South Africa by the United Nations. Its leader is Dirk Mudge.

Denationalization: A policy of the government of South Africa to declare certain reserved areas as "homelands" or "Bantustans" which it then recognizes as separate "national states." The black population is forcibly transferred into one of these "independent homelands" and declared to be its citizens, whether they like it or not. Once that is done, Blacks are no longer considered as citizens or nationals of South Africa, and thus become, in effect, foreigners in their native land.

Detente: A French term meaning the relaxation of tensions or a decrease in the level of hostility between opponents on the world scene.

Deterrence: The prevention from action by fear of the consequences.

Developed Countries: (DCs): Countries with relatively high per capita GNP, education, levels of industrial development and production, health and welfare, and agricultural productivity; 24 OECD members and 6 centrally planned economy countries of Eastern Europe, including the USSR.

Developing Countries (LCDs): Also *Less Developed Countries;* these countries are mainly raw materials producers for export with high growth rates and inadequate infrastructures in transportation, educational systems, and the like. There is, however, a wide variation in living standards, GNP's, and per capita incomes among LCDs.

Development: The process through which a society becomes increasingly able to meet basic human needs and assure the physical quality of life of its people.

Disappearance: Government kidnapping of individuals without leaving a trace. A violation of human rights occurring in alarming proportions under various dictatorial regimes, whereby individuals would be taken away by government agents, unbeknownst to their family, friends, or co-workers. Where they are detained, what they are charged with, whether they are still alive or are dead is not known. Usually attempts to inquire about their fate are futile or result in the disappearance of those making inquiries.

Disinformation: The spreading of false propaganda and forged documents to confuse counter-intelligence or to create political confusion, unrest, and scandal.

Dumping: A special case of price discrimination, selling to foreign buyers at a lower price than that charged to buyers in the home market.

Duty: Special tax applied to imported goods, based on tariff rates and schedules.

—E—

East (as in the East-West Struggle): (a) A shorthand, nongeographic term that includes non-market, centrally planned (communist) countries; (b) In a more restricted sense, the Warsaw Pact (military)/ CEMA (economic) bloc of the USSR and Eastern European countries under its sway.

East-West conflict: The military, economic, political, and ideological worldwide struggle between the communist countries and the industrial democracies. Also known as the Cold War.

Economic Cooperation among Developing Countries (ECDC): Also referred to as intra-South, or South-South cooperation, it is a way for LCDs to help each other with *appropriate technology.*

Escalation: The stepping up of the level of conflict, either qualitatively or quantitatively.

Essential equivalence: Comparing military capabilities of two would-be belligerents, not in terms of identical mix of forces, but in terms of how well two dissimilarly organized forces could achieve a strategic stalemate.

Eurodollars: US dollar holdings of European banks; a liability for the US Treasury.

Euromissiles: Shorthand for *long-range theatre nuclear forces* stationed in Europe or aimed at targets in Europe.

European Community (EC): Composed of the nine European Economic Community (EEC) members; it has a Council of Ministers, an elected European Parliament, a European Court of Justice, a European Investment Bank, and a European Monetary System.

European Currency Unit (ECU): The common unit of valuation among the eight members of the European Monetary System (EMS).

European Economic Community (EEC): Also known as the European Common Market. Founded in 1957 by France, West Germany, Italy, Belgium, the Netherlands, and Luxembourg for the purpose of economic integration. It was joined in 1973 by the United Kingdom, Ireland, Denmark and in 1981 by Greece. Spain and Portugal have also applied for membership. Its main features include a common external tariff, a customs union on industrial goods, and a Common Agricultural Policy. Full economic and monetary union remains an objective.

European Free Trade Association (EFTA): Austria, Finland, Iceland, Liechtenstein, Norway, Portugal, Sweden, and Switzerland. Each member keeps its own external tariff schedule, but free trade prevails among the members.

European Monetary System (EMS): Established in 1979 as a preliminary stage toward an economic and monetary union in the European Community. Fluctuations in the exchange-rate value of the currencies of the participating countries are kept within a 2¼ percent limit of divergence from the strongest currency among them.

Exclusive Economic Zone: As proposed in *ICNT,* a belt of sea extending 200 nautical miles from coastal state. In this area coastal state would have rights and jurisdiction with respect to the resources of seabed, subsoil, and superjacent waters.

Exports: Products shipped to foreign countries.

Export subsidies: Special incentives, including direct payments to exporters, to encourage increased foreign sales.

—F—

Farabundo Marti National Liberation Front (Frente de Liberacion Nacional Farabundo Marti; (FMLN): The unified guerilla command of El Salvador, comprising five groups; Popular Forces of Liberation.

Finlandization: A condition of nominal neutrality, but one of actual subservience to the Soviet Union in foreign and security policies, as is the case with Finland.

First strike: The first offensive move of a general nuclear war. It implies an intention to knock out the opponent's ability to retaliate.

Fissionable or nuclear materials: Isotopes of certain elements, such as plutonium, thorium, and uranium, that emit neutrons in such large numbers that a sufficient concentration will be self-sustaining until it explodes.

Foreign policy: The process and the substance of preserving one's national interests in the tangled maze of global relations that are constantly changing.

Forward based system (FBS or FoBS): A military installation, maintained on foreign soil or in international waters, and conveniently located near a theatre of war.

Fourth World: An expression arising from the world economic crisis that began in 1973-74 with the quadrupling in price of petroleum. It takes the least developed countries (LLDCs) and the most seriously affected countries (MSAs).

Front-line states: As regards to Namibia, the expression refers to Black African states immediately adjacent to it, namely Angola, Zambia, Zimbabwe, Mozambique, and Tanzania. Nigeria and Kenya, being leading states of Black Africa, also consider themselves part of this anti-South Africa group, even though they are located over 1,500 miles away from Namibia.

—G—

General Agreement on Tariffs and Trade (GATT): Created in 1947, this organization is the major global forum for negotiations of tariff reductions and other measures to expand world trade. Its 83 members account for four-fifths of the world's trade.

Generalized System of Preferences (GSP): A system approved by GATT in 1971, which authorizes DCs to give preferential tariff treatment to LCDs.

Global: Pertaining to the world as a whole; worldwide.

Global commons: The Antarctic, the ocean floor under international waters and celestial bodies within reach of planet Earth. All of these areas and bodies are considered the common heritage of mankind.

Global Negotiations: A new round of international economic negotiations started in 1980 over raw materials, energy, trade, development, money, and finance.

Golan Heights: Syrian territory adjacent to Israel that occupied it since the 1967 war and that annexed it on Decemer 14, 1981.

Gross National Product (GNP): The total value of all goods and services produced by a country in a year.

Gross world product: The sum of all gross national products.

Group of 77 (G-77): Initially a group of LDCs which issued a "Joint Declaration of 77 Developing Countries" at *UNCTAD I* in 1976 in Geneva. Now, made up of 122 countries, it remains the caucus of LCDs. Synonymous with the "South" in the North-South dialogue.

—H—

Hegemonism: Any attempt by a larger power to interfere, threaten, intervene against, and dominate a smaller power or a region of the world.

Hegemony: Domination by a major power over smaller, subordinate ones within its sphere of influence.

Helsinki Agreement: A declaration adopted on August 1, 1975 by 35 nations, including the USA and the USSR, participating in the *Conference on Security and Cooperation in Europe* that started in Helsinki, Finland, on July 3, 1973. Its main document is the Final Act in which signatories pledged to respect each other's sovereign equality and individuality, to promote detente, fundamental human rights, economic and social progress and well-being for all peoples. They also pledged not to use force or the threat of force and subversion in relations among themselves and with other nations. Three follow-up conferences took place in Belgrade in 1978 and in Madrid in 1980 and 1982. They have provided a forum for diplomatic confrontation between the USA and the USSR.

Horn of Africa: The northeast corner of Africa which includes Ethiopia, Djibouti, and Somalia. It is separated from the Arabian peninsula by the Gulf of Aden and the Red Sea. It is plagued with tribal conflicts between Ethiopia and Eritrea, and between Ethiopia and Somalia over the Ogaden desert. These conflicts have generated a large number of refugees who have been facing mass starvation.

Human rights: Rights inherent to human beings, including but not limited to the right to dignity; the integrity of the person; the inviolability of the person's body and mind; civil and political rights (freedom of religion, speech, press, assembly, association, the right to privacy, habeas corpus, due process of law, the right to vote or not to vote, the right to run for election, and the right to be protected from reprisals for acts of peaceful dissent); social, economic, and cultural rights. The most glaring violations of human rights are *torture, disappearance,* and the general phenomenon of *state terrorism.* The basic documents of human rights are: the Universal Declaration of Human Rights (1948), the Genocide Convention (1951), Convention on Political Rights of Women (1952), the International Covenant on Civil and Political Rights (1966), the International Covenant on Economic, Social, and Cultural Rights (1966), the International Convention on the Elimination of All Forms of

Racial Discrimination (1969), the European Convention for the Protection of Human Rights and Fundamental Freedoms (1954), the [Inter-]American Convention on Human Rights (1969), and the Declaration on Protection from Torture (1975). An international covenant against the use of torture is near completion in 1981.

Hu Yaobang: Chairman, Chinese Communist Party, succeeding Hua Guofeng.

—I—

Imports: Products brought into a country from abroad.

Informal Composite Negotiating Text (ICNT): Prepared in July 1977; officially only a procedural device serving as basis for negotiations, but functions as draft law of the sea treaty.

Innocent Passage: In a nation's territorial sea, passage by a foreign ship is innocent so long as it is not prejudicial to the peace, good order, or security of the coastal state. Submarines must surface and show flag.

Intercontinental Ballistic Missile (ICBM): A land-based, rocket-propelled vehicle capable of delivering a warhead to targets at 6,000 or more nautical miles.

Interdependence: An increasingly obvious characteristic of current world politics and economics whereby no country, however powerful, is totally immune from the consequences of actions and events happening in other countries, no matter how small and weak.

Intermediate Range Ballistic Missile (IRBM): A missile with a range from 1,500 to 4,000 nautical miles.

Intermediate-Range Nuclear Forces: Nuclear arms that are based in Europe with a deployment range that easily encompasses the U.S.S.R.

Intermediate-Range Nuclear Forces Treaty (INF): The treaty between Russia and the U.S. that limits the dispersion of nuclear warheads in Europe.

International: Between or among sovereign states.

International Development Association (IDA): An affiliate of the World Bank that provides interest free, long-term (50 years) loans to developing countries in support of projects that cannot obtain funding through other existing sources. Its lending may be curtailed if the USA, as announced, reduces its contribution from $3.2 to $2 billion for the 1983 fiscal year.

International Energy Agency (IEA): An arm of *OECD* that attempts to coordinate member countries' oil imports and reallocate stocks among members in case of disruptions in the world's oil supply.

International Finance Corporation (IFC): Created in 1956 to finance overseas investments by private companies without necessarily requiring government guarantees. The IFC borrows from the *World Bank*, provides loans and invests directly in private industry in the development of capital projects.

International Monetary Fund (IMF): Conceived of at the Bretton Woods Agreement of 1944 and in operation since 1947, its major purpose is to encourage international cooperation in the monetary field and the removal of foreign exchange restrictions, to stabilize exchange rates and aid in balance-of-payment problems.

Interstate: International, intergovernmental.

Intra-South: See *Economic Cooperation among Developing Countries.*

—J—

Jaruzelski, General Wojciech: Succeeded Jozef Pinkowski as Poland's Prime Minister, then succeeded Stanislaw Kania, as First Secretary of the Polish United Workers (Communist) Party. A pragmatic and moderate leader, he was caught in the middle by hardliners within the party's Central Committee on one side, and by the hard-liners in the Solidarity independent trade union on the other. Due to the ultimatum adopted by the Executive Committee of Solidarity on December 12, 1981, Jaruzelski imposed martial law on Poland on December 13.

—K—

Kampuchea: The new name for Cambodia since April 1975.

KGB: The Soviet security police and intelligence apparatus, engaged in espionage, counterespionage, anti-subversion, and control of political dissidents.

Khmer Rouge: Literally "Red Cambodians," the communist organization ruling *Kampuchea* between April 1975 and January 1979 under Pol Pot and Ieng Saray.

Kiloton: A thousand tons of explosive force. A measure of the yield of a nuclear weapon equivalent to 1,000 tons of TNT (trinitrotoluene). The bomb detonated at Hiroshima in World War II had an approximate yield of 14 kilotons.

—L—

Launcher: See *Delivery Systems*

Least Developed Countries (LLDC): Countries that in 1979 had a per capita income of $370 or less and where the basic human needs cannot be met for the bulk of the population.

Less Developed Countries (LDC): (Previously called underdeveloped countries, and later, developing countries.) Countries where the basic human needs are not fully met, yet are well on their way to development.

Linkage: Putting together two separate issues in diplomatic negotiations.

Lome Convention: An agreement concluded between the European Community and 58 African, Caribbean and Pacific countries (ACP), allowing the latter preferential trade relations and greater economic and technical assistance.

Long-Range Theatre Nuclear Forces (LRTNF): Recently developed nuclear weapon systems with a range greater than 1,000 kilometers (or 600 miles) such as the US Pershing II missile or the Soviet SS-20.

Low-income countries: According to the World Bank there are 36 such countries with per capita income ranging from 80 to 370 US dollars per year. They account for 2.26 billion people, of which 1.62 billions are in China and India.

—M—

Maneuverable Re-entry Vehicle (MARV): A ballistic missile re-entry vehicle equipped with its own navigation and control systems capable of adjusting its trajectory during re-entry into the atmosphere.

Medium-range Ballistic Missile (MRBM): A missile with a range from 500 to 1,500 nautical miles.

Megaton: The yield of a nuclear weapon equivalent to 1 million tons of TNT (approximately equivalent to 79 Hiroshima bombs).

Microstates: Very small countries, usually with a population of less than one million.

Middle-income countries MICs): According to the World Bank, there are 60 such countries, with annual per capita income (PCI) ranging from 380 to 4,380 US dollars. Twenty-five of these countries have an annual PCI of less than $1,000; 23 of these countries have a PCI ranging from $1,000 to $2,000; and 12 countries have a PCI ranging from $2,000 to $4,380. This is a most unsatisfactory classification, as the highest PCI of MICs is $4,380 while its lowest PCI is only $380, which is only $10 more than the highest PCI in the low-income country group.

Ministates: Small countries, usually with a population of less than five million.

Missile experimental (MX): A mobile, land-based missile that is shuttled among different launching sites making it more difficult to locate and destroy.

Most Favored Nation (MFN): In international trade agreements, a country granting most-favored-nation status to another country undertakes to make available to that country the most favorable treatment in regard to tariffs and other trade regulations that it makes available to any other country.

Most Seriously Affected Countries (MSA): Low-income countries that import their energy needs and that were hurt the most by the OPEC price increases in 1973.

Multilateral: Involving many nations.

Multilateral Development Banks (MDBs): These are the World Bank Group that include the *International Development Association* (IDA) and the *International Finance Corporation* (IFC), the Inter-American Development Bank (IDB or IADB), the Asian Development Bank (ADB), and the African Development Bank (AFDB).

Multinational: Doing business in many nations.

Multinational corporation: *See* Transnational enterprise.

Multiple Independently Targetable Re-entry Vehicle (MIRV): Two or more warheads carried by a single missile and capable of being guided to separate targets upon re-entry.

Mutual and Balanced Force Reductions (MBFR): The 19-nation Conference on Mutual Reduction of Forces and Armaments and Associated Measures in Central Europe that has been held intermittently since 1973.

Mutual Assured Destruction (MAD): The basic ingredient of the doctrine of strategic deterrence that no country can escape destruction in a nuclear exchange even if it engages in a pre-emptive strike.

—N—

Namibia: African name for South-West Africa.

National Intelligence Estimate (NIE): The final assessment of global problems and capabilities by the intelligence community for use by the National Security Council and the President in making foreign and military decisions.

Nautical mile: 1.852 kilometers.

Neocolonialism: A perjorative term describing the economic exploitation of Third World countries by the industrialized countries, in particular through the activities of multinational corporations.

Neutron bomb: Enhanced radiation bomb giving out lower blast and heat but concentrated radiation, thus killing people and living things while reducing damage to physical structures.

New International Economic Order (NIEO): The statement of development policies and objectives adopted at the Sixth Special Session of the UN General Assembly in 1974. NIEO calls for equal participation of LDCs in the international economic policy-making process, better known as the *North-South dialogue*.

New World Information and Communication Order: A highly controversial proposal made in 1980 by the UNESCO-sponsored Commission for the Study of Communication Problems (McBride Commission) to promote a "free and balanced flow of information and news" through "effective legal measures designed to circumscribe the action of transnationals by requiring them to comply with specific criteria and conditions defined by national development policies." The "transnationals" referred to here are the West's Big Four news agencies, namely the Associated Press and the United Press International (USA), Reuters (UK), and Agence France-Press, plus major Western broadcasting companies. This attempt to legitimize state censorship of foreign media by Third World countries provoked a response by Western journalists known as the *Declaration of Talloires*.

Nonaligned Movement (NAM): A grouping of nations that have deliberately chosen not to be politically and militarily associated with either the West or the Communist bloc. Started with Bandung in 1955, six nonaligned summit meetings have been held—Belgrade (1961), Cairo (1964), Lusaka (1970), Algiers (1973), Colombo (1976), and Havana (1979). Interim leadership of the nonaligned countries rests with the country that last hosted a summit meeting. There were 94 members in the NAM in 1981.

Non-alignment: The concept or policy of remaining neutral in the cold war; not taking sides with either the USA (West) or the USSR (East).

Non-nuclear (weapons) state: One not possessing nuclear weapon.

Non-proliferation of Nuclear Weapons Treaty (NPT): Under this Treaty, the non-nuclear-weapon states pledge not to manufacture or acquire nuclear explosive devices and agree to international verification. Nuclear-weapon states, party to the NPT, pledge not to transfer nuclear explosive devices to any recipient and not to assist any non-nuclear-weapon state in the manufacture of nuclear explosive devices.

Non-tariff barriers (NTBs): Subtle, informal impediments to free trade designed for the purpose of making importation of foreign goods into a country very difficult on such grounds as health and safety regulations. Japan as of 1981 had 99 categories of NTBs.

Normalization of relations: The reestablishment of full diplomatic relations, including de jure recognition and the exchange of ambassadors between two countries that either did not have diplomatic relations or had broken them.

North (as in North-South dialogue): (a) A shorthand, non-geographic term for the industrialized countries of high income, both East (the USSR and Eastern Europe) and West (the USA, Canada, Western Europe, Japan, Australia and New Zealand.) (b) Often means only the industrialized, high-income countries of the West.

North Atlantic Treaty Organization (NATO): Also known as the Atlantic Alliance, NATO was formed in 1949 to provide collective defense against the perceived Soviet threat to Western Europe. Its members are Belgium, Denmark, France, the Federal Republic of Germany, Greece, Iceland, Italy, Luxembourg, the Netherlands, Norway, Portugal, Turkey, the United Kingdom, Canada, and the United States. France has an independent striking force not integrated into NATO. Greece intends to withdraw militarily from NATO.

North-South dialogue: A wrangling between the industrial Western countries (North) and the LDCs (South) for trade preferences, and economic and technical assistance taking place in Conferences on International Cooperation (CIEC). The Soviet Union and its allies generally remain aloof from the North-South dialogue, arguing that LDC problems are the result of past colonialism and capitalism and, therefore, are the sole responsibility of the West. It was started in 1974 with the *Third World's* call for a new international economic order.

Nuclear free zone: A stretch of territory from which all nuclear weapons are banned.

Nuclear Non-Proliferation Treaty (NPT): A treaty that, among other things, binds those non-nuclear countries adhering to it to forgo the acquisition or production of nuclear weapons and forbids the transfer of such weapons to a non-nuclear state.

Nuclear proliferation: The process by which one country after another comes into possession of some form of nuclear weaponry, and with it develops the potential of launching a nuclear attack on other actors.

Nuclear reprocessing: The separation of radioactive waste (spent fuel) from a nuclear-powered plant into its fissile constituent materials. One such material is plutonium, which can then be used in the production of atomic bombs.

Nuclear terrorism: The use (or threatened use) of nuclear weapons or radioactive materials as a means of coercion.

—O—

Oestpolitik: Literally, Eastward politics, it is the West German foreign policy of *détente* aiming at cooperative relations with the Soviet Union and East European communist countries, with the intermediate goal of normalization of relations with East Germany and the ultimate goal of reunification of the two Germanys.

Official Development Assistance (ODA): Government contributions to projects and programs aimed at developing the productivity of poorer countries. This is to be distinguished from private, voluntary assistance, humanitarian assistance for disasters, and most importantly from military assistance.

Ogaden: A piece of Ethiopian desert populated by ethnic Somalis. It has been a bone of contention between Ethiopia and Somalia, a war that contributed significantly to the refugee and starvation problems in the Horn of Africa.

Organization for Economic Cooperation and Development (OECD): Composed of 23 Western countries plus Japan. All have democratic political systems and, except for a few, have high-income industrial economics. Also referred to as the "North" as in the North-South dialogue.

Organization of Arab Petroleum Exporting Countries (OAPEC): A component of OPEC, with Saudi Arabia, Kuwait, the United Arab Emirates, Qatar, Iraq, Algeria and Libya as members.

Organization of Petroleum Exporting Countries (OPEC): A producers' cartel setting price floors and production ceiling of crude petroleum. It includes members of OPEC plus Venezuela, Iran, Ecuador, Gabon, Nigeria and Indonesia.

Osirak: Site of the Iraqi nuclear power plant near Baghdad that was destroyed by Israeli bombings on June 7, 1981. The site was constructed with the assistance of France, which has pledged to rebuild it.

Overkill: The capability of the USA and the USSR to kill not only each other's population several times over, but the world's population as well.

—P—

Palestine: "Palestine" does not exist today as an entity. It refers to the historical and geographical entity administered by the British under the League of Nations mandate from 1918 to 1947. It also refers to a future entity in the aspirations of Palestinians who, as was the case of the Jews before the founding of the State of Israel, are stateless nationalists.

Palestine Liberation Organization (PLO): A coalition of Palestinian groups united by the dedication to the goal of a Palestinian state through the destruction of Israel as a state.

Payload: Warheads attached to delivery vehicles.

People's Republic of China (PRC): Communist or mainland China.

Pershing II: US MRBMs to be deployed in Western Europe to counteract Soviet SS-20s.

Petrodollars: US dollar holdings of capital-surplus OPEC countries; a liability for the US Treasury.

Physical Quality of Life Index (PQLI): Developed by the Overseas Development Council, the PQLI is presented as a more significant measurement of the well-being of inhabitants of a geographic entity than the solely monetary measurement of per capita income. It consists of the following measurements: life expectancy, infant mortality, and literacy figures that are each rated on an index of 1-100, within which each country is ranked according to its performance. A composite index is obtained by averaging these three measures, giving the PQLI.

Polisario: The liberation front of Western Sahara (formerly Spanish Sahara) that is fighting against Morocco claims over that territory. The USA supports King Hassan of Morocco in this war in return for staging rights of Rapid Deployment Forces in the Middle East/North African area.

Polish United Workers Party (PZPR): Poland's communist party's name since 1948.

Post-industrial: Characteristic of a society where a large portion of the work force is directed to non-agricultural and non-manufacturing tasks such as servicing and processing.

Precision-Guided Munitions (PGM): Popularly known as "smart bombs." Electronically programmed and controlled weapons that can accurately hit a moving or stationary target.

Pre-emptive strike, attack: To attack an enemy before one is attacked. A nuclear attack launched in the expectation that an attack by an adversary is imminent, and designed to forestall that attack or to lessen its impact.

Proliferation: Quick spread, as in the case of nuclear weapons.

Protocol: A preliminary memorandum often signed by diplomatic negotiators as a basis for a final convention or treaty.

—Q—

Quota: Quantitative limits, usually imposed on imports or immigrants.

—R—

Rapprochement: The coming together of two countries that had been hostile to each other.

Recycling: As used in recent international finance, it means the flow of money from capital-surplus OPEC countries (Saudi Arabia, Kuwait, Libya, and Iraq) into private or *multilateral development banks* (MBDs) for relending to poorer countries. Recycling resulted from the capital surplus accumulated by certain OPEC countries due to the quadrupling of oil prices in 1973-74 and subsequent price hikes.

Re-entry Vehicle (RV): That portion of a ballistic missile designed to carry a nuclear warhead and to re-enter the Earth's atmosphere in the terminal portion of the missile trajectory.

Regionalism: A concept of cooperation among geographically adjacent states to foster region-wide political (OAS, OAU), military (NATO, Warsaw Pact) and economic (EEC, EFTA) interests.

Rejectionist Front: In the context of the Arab-Israeli conflict, the front consists of Arab countries that reject any solution to the Palestinian question short of the establishment of a Palestinian state in place of the state of Israel. It is made up of the PLO, Syria, Libya, Algeria, and to a lesser degree all other Arab states except for Egypt and the Sudan. They also rejected the Camp David Agreements.

Reprocessing of nuclear waste: A process of recovery of fissionable materials among which is weapon-grade plutonium.

Resolution: Formal decisions of UN bodies; they may simply register an opinion or may recommend action to be taken by a UN body or agency.

Resolution 242: Passed by the UN Security Council on November 22, 1967 calling for the withdrawal of Israeli troops from territories they captured from Egypt (Sinai), Jordan (West Bank and East Jerusalem), and Syria (Golan Heights) in the 1967 war, and for the right of all nations in the Middle East to live in peace in secure and recognized borders.

Resolution 435: Passed by the UN Security Council in 1978, it called for a cease-fire between belligerents in the Namibian conflict (namely SWAPO, Angola and other front-line states on the one side, and South Africa on the other) and an internationally supervised transition process to independence and free elections.

—S—

SALT I: The discussions between the US and the USSR on the limitation of strategic armaments that have been under way since 1970. They have resulted in (1) a treaty limiting the deployment of anti-ballistic missile (ABM) systems; (2) an agreement setting ceilings on intercontinental ballistic missiles (ICBMs) and sub-marine-launched ballistic missiles (SLBMs) for a five-year period; and (3) the Vladivostok Accord, setting ceilings on all strategic nuclear delivery systems (including heavy bombers) and on MIRVs (multiple independently-targetable reentry vehicles).

SALT II: The SALT II agreement consists of three parts: (1) A treaty, to last through 1985, which, inter alia: sets initial equal aggregates of 2,400 on the total of strategic nuclear delivery vehicles: mandates further reductions in the overall ceiling down to 2,250 before expiration of the treaty; sets equal subceilings on several key categories of systems; restricts the number of warheads that are allowed on each missile; and limits each side to one new type of ICBM. (2) A protocol to last through 1981, which covers issues not ready for longer term resolution. (3) A joint statement of principles and guidelines for subsequent SALT negotiations. SALT II never went into effect, as it was not ratified by the US Senate.

Second strike: A nuclear attack in response to an adversary's first strike. A second-strike capability is the ability to absorb the full force of a first strike and still inflict unacceptable damage in retaliation.

Shatt al Arab: The body of water located between Iran and Iraq, and claimed by both. The dispute over Shatt al Arab was one of the causes of the Iran-Iraq war.

Short Range Ballistic Missiles (SRBM): A missile with a range up to 500 nautical miles.

Solidarity: Independent self-governing trade union movement started in Poland on August 22, 1980 and terminated on December 13, 1981 after radical members of its Presidium passed a resolution on December 12 calling for a national referendum to see whether the communist government of Poland should continue to govern. Individual members of the Presidium also called for the establishment of a provisional government.

South (as in North-South dialogue): A shorthand, non-geographic term that includes economically less developed countries, often represented by the Group of 77.

South-South: see *Economic Cooperation among Developing Countries*

South-West African People's Organization (SWAPO): The guerilla organization fighting against South Africa's illegal occupation and exploitation of Namibia. SWAPO is recognized by the United Nations as the authentic representative of Namibia.

Sovereignty: The ability to carry out laws and policies within national borders without interference from outside.

Special Drawing Rights (SDRs): Also known as paper gold. A new form of international liquid reserves to be used in the settlement of international payments among member governments of the International Monetary Fund.

SS-17, 18, 19: Soviet ICBMs.

SS-20: New mobile Soviet medium-range nuclear missiles aimed at Western Europe.

Stabex Program (stabilization of export receipts): An EEC program that provides financial assistance to selected developing countries that experience temporary export earnings shortfalls.

State: Regarding international relations, it means a country having territory, population, government, and sovereignty, e.g. the US is a state, while California is not a state in this sense.

State terrorism: The use of state power, including the police, the armed forces, and the secret police to throw fear among the population against any act of dissent or protest against a political regime. Such state power includes extraordinary measures such as martial law (military rule), revolutionary or military tribunals ("kangaroo courts"), summary executions, mass killings either by face-to-face firings or indiscriminate use of artillery, and bombings against wide areas that contain civilian settlements. It also includes the use of physical, biochemical, medical, and psychological torture on political prisoners or prisoners of conscience. State terrorism is a phenomenon of modern technology, practiced by totalitarian and authoritarian regimes, by communist and non-communist regimes alike.

"Stealth": A code name for a proposed "invisible" aircraft, supposedly not detectable by hostile forces, and that would be the main US strategic fighter-bomber of the 1990s.

Strategic Arms Limitation Talks: See *SALT I* and *SALT II*

Strategic balance or parity: A concept used in nuclear planning and debate to determine the equivalence of forces between two armed blocs, e.g. the US vs. the USSR, NATO vs. the Warsaw Pact. Opposite of strategic imbalance that could be either superiority or inferiority.

Strategic consensus: An elusive objective of forging an anti-Soviet alliance pursued by the Reagan administration in the Middle East. It would link together such entities as Israel, Egypt, and Saudi Arabia, except that Israel and Saudi Arabia consider themselves enemies. Jordan, which was also courted by the Reagan administration, would have no part of it.

Strategic Defense Initiative (SDI): A space-based defense system designed to destroy incoming missiles. First advanced by President Reagan in 1983 and promptly dubbed "Star Wars," the technological possibility of such a system, not to mention paying the enormous cost, is still very much in doubt.

Strategic minerals: Minerals needed in the fabrication of advanced military and industrial equipment. Examples are uranium, platinum, titanium, vanadium, tungsten, nickel, chromium, etc.

Strategic nuclear weapons: Long-range weapons carried on either intercontinental ballistic missiles (ICBMs) or Submarine-Launched Ballistic Missiles (SLBMs) or long-range bombers.

Strategic stockpile: Reserves of certain commodities established to assure that in time of national emergency such commodities are readily available.

Submarine-Launched Ballistic Missile (SLBM): A ballistic missile carried in and launched from a submarine.

Superpowers: Countries so powerful militarily (USA, USSR), demographically (PRC), or economically (Japan) as to be in a class by themselves.

Supranational: Above nation-states.

—T—

Tactical nuclear weapons: Kiloton-range weapons for theatre use. The bomb dropped on Hiroshima would be in this category today.

Tariff: A tax levied on imports.

Technetronic: Shorthand for technological-electronic.

Technical Cooperation Among Developing Countries (TCDC): A clearinghouse and a coordinating body through which less developed countries (LDCs) may help each other solve similar problems by low-capital, appropriate technology applications.

Territorial Sea: The territorial sea, air space above, seabed, and subsoil are part of sovereign territory of coastal state except that ships (not aircraft) enjoy right of *innocent passage.* As proposed in ICNT, a coastal state's sovereignty would extend 12 nautical miles beyond its land territory.

Terrorism: The systematic use of terror as a means of coercion.

Theatre: In nuclear strategy, it refers to a localized combat area such as Europe, as opposed to global warfare involving a US-USSR nuclear exchange.

Theatre Nuclear Forces (TNF): Nuclear weapons systems for operations in a region such as Europe, including artillery, cruise missiles, SRBMs, IRBMs, and MRBMs.

"Thinkables": Nuclear strategists who believe that one should plan in terms of nuclear war actually occurring, and for its aftermath.

Third World: Often used interchangeably with the terms *less developed countries, developing countries,* or the *South,* its two main institutions are the *nonaligned movement* (which acts primarily as the political caucus of the Third World) and the *Group of 77* (which functions as the economic voice of the Third World).

Tokyo Round: The sixth and latest in the series of GATT trade negotiations, begun in 1973 and ended in 1979. About 100 nations, including nonmembers of the GATT, participated.

Torture: The deliberate inflicting of pain, whether physical or psychological, to degrade, intimidate, and induce submission of its victims to the will of the torturer. It is a heinous practice used frequently in most dictatorial regimes in the world, irrespective of their ideological leanings.

Transnational: An adjective indicating that a non-governmental movement, organization, or ideology transcends national borders and is operative in dissimilar political, economic, and social systems.

Transnational Enterprise (TNE) or **Corporation (TNC):** Synonymous to *Multinational Corporation* (MNC). An enterprise doing business in more than one country.

Triad (nuclear): The three-pronged US strategic weapons arsenal, composed of land-based *ICBMs,* underwater *SLBMs,* and long-range manned bombers.

Trilateral: Between three countries or groups of countries, e.g. USA, Western Europe and Japan; USA, USSR, and China.

—U—

Unilateral: One-sided, as opposed to bilateral or multilateral.

United Nations Conference on Trade and Development (UNCTAD): Was convened in 1964 in response to growing concern among LDCs over their effort to bridge the standard-of-living gap between them and DCs. Meetings were held in 1968, 1972, 1976, and 1979 and have focused on North-South economic issues.

"Unthinkables": Nuclear strategists who believe that a nuclear war, once begun, is likely to create a disaster of such magnitude that it is not meaningful to plan in terms of its actual occurrence.

—V—

Venice initiative: The Declaration by the European Community foreign ministers, on June 12, 1980, backing Palestinian "self-determination" and participation in Middle East negotiations; calling for an end to Israeli occupation of the Gaza Strip and the West Bank and to Israeli settlements there; and condemning Israel's proposed change in the status of Jersualem.

Verification: The process of determining that the other side is complying with an agreement.

Vulnerability: As used in strategic planning, it refers to the condition under which US silo-based ICBMs can be targeted for pinpoint hits by Soviet missiles.

—W—

Walesa, Lech (pronounced vah-wen-sah): Was leader of the independent trade union movement known as Solidarity, which came into existence in August 1980 and was dissolved on December 13, 1981 by the martial law decree imposed. He was elected president of Poland in December 1990.

Warhead: That part of a missile, projectile, or torpedo that contains the explosive intended to inflict damage.

Warsaw Pact or Warsaw Treaty Organization: Established in 1955 by the Soviet Union in response to the inclusion in NATO of the Federal Republic of Germany (West Germany). The members are the Soviet Union, Bulgaria, Czechoslovakia, Hungary, Poland, and Romania. It is expected that the alliance will not survive the reforms among member nations that occurred in 1989–90.

West (as in the East-West conflict): A short-hand, nongeographic term that means (a) in economic matters, the *OECD* countries; (b) militarily, *NATO,* France, and *ANZUS.* Basically the market-economy, industrialized, and high-income countries that are committed to a political system of representative democracy. The three main anchors of the West today are North America, Western Europe, and Japan, also known as the Trilateral countries. Australia and New Zealand are also parts of the West.

Western economic summits: Annual meetings of the leaders of seven Western industrialized nations (the USA, the UK, France, West Germany, Japan, Italy, and Canada) with the president of the Commission of the EEC in attendance. These meetings were first held at Rambouillet, France, in 1975. The latest was the Ottawa Summit in 1981.

Western Five Contact Group (re Namibia): Five Western countries acting as intermediaries between South Africa, SWAPO and Frontline States to work out procedures for the independence and future government of Namibia. They are Canada, the Federal Republic of Germany, France, the United Kingdom, and the United States. The European nations are more pro-SWAPO while the USA is more pro-South Africa.

"Window of vulnerability": An expression often used, but not consistently defined, by Ronald Reagan and his associates since the Presidential campaign of 1980. Military specialists use the word to refer to a period of time in the future (in the late 1980s) when US silo-based ICBMs can be accurately hit by Soviet missiles while the mobile MX system (now scrapped) will not yet be operational, and when the aging B-52 bombers are no longer serviceable while the *Stealth* aircraft will not yet be operational. Mr. Reagan approved a plan to close this "window" by MIRVing the silo-based ICBMs, by hardening their concrete covers, and by building B-1 bombers.

World Bank (International Bank for Reconstruction and Development-IBRD): Makes loans, either directly to governments or with governments as the guarantors; and through its affiliates, the International Finance Corporation and the International Development Association.

World Politics: The sum of all those actions and interactions of some 160 nation states and scores of non-national and transnational actors in terms of political, diplomatic, military, and economic policies.

—X—Y—Z—

Yield: The explosive force, in terms of TNT equivalence, of a warhead.

Zero option: President Reagan's proposal made on November 19, 1981, that the US would cancel its plan to deploy MRBMs (Pershing II and GLCMs) in Western Europe if the USSR agreed to remove those it has already emplaced in Eastern Europe and Western USSR.

Zhao Ziyang: Head of government, People's Republic of China.

Zimbabwe: Formerly Rhodesia.

Index

Credits/ Acknowledgments

Cover design by Charles Vitelli

1. The United States
Facing overview—Congressional News photo by K. Jewell.

2. The Soviet Union
Facing overview—United Nations photo.

3. American Allies
Facing overview—AP/Wide World photo.

4. The Disintegrating Socialist World
Facing overview—United Nations photo.

5. Newly Industrialized Countries and Less Developed Countries
Facing overview—United Nations photo.

6. The International Political Economy
Facing overview—WHO photo.

7. The Arms Race, Arms Control, and Disarmament
Facing overview—United Nations photo by Yutaka Nagata.

8. International Organization and International Issues
Facing overview—United Nations photo by Yutaka Nagata.

PHOTOCOPY THIS PAGE!!!*

ANNUAL EDITIONS ARTICLE REVIEW FORM

- NAME: _____ DATE: _____
- TITLE AND NUMBER OF ARTICLE: _____
- BRIEFLY STATE THE MAIN IDEA OF THIS ARTICLE: _____

_____
_____
_____
_____

- LIST THREE IMPORTANT FACTS THAT THE AUTHOR USES TO SUPPORT THE MAIN IDEA:

_____
_____
_____
_____
_____
_____

- WHAT INFORMATION OR IDEAS DISCUSSED IN THIS ARTICLE ARE ALSO DISCUSSED IN YOUR TEXTBOOK OR OTHER READING YOU HAVE DONE? LIST THE TEXTBOOK CHAPTERS AND PAGE NUMBERS:

_____
_____
_____
_____
_____
_____

- LIST ANY EXAMPLES OF BIAS OR FAULTY REASONING THAT YOU FOUND IN THE ARTICLE:

_____
_____
_____
_____

- LIST ANY NEW TERMS/CONCEPTS THAT WERE DISCUSSED IN THE ARTICLE AND WRITE A SHORT DEFINITION:

_____
_____
_____
_____
_____

*Your instructor may require you to use this Annual Editions Article Review Form in any number of ways: for articles that are assigned, for extra credit, as a tool to assist in developing assigned papers, or simply for your own reference. Even if it is not required, we encourage you to photocopy and use this page; you'll find that reflecting on the articles will greatly enhance the information from your text.

ANNUAL EDITIONS: WORLD POLITICS 91/92
Article Rating Form

Here is an opportunity for you to have direct input into the next revision of this volume. We would like you to rate each of the 46 articles listed below, using the following scale:

1. **Excellent: should definitely be retained**
2. **Above average: should probably be retained**
3. **Below average: should probably be deleted**
4. **Poor: should definitely be deleted**

Your ratings will play a vital part in the next revision. So please mail this prepaid form to us just as soon as you complete it.
Thanks for your help!

Rating	Article	Rating	Article
	1. Finding America's Place		25. Black Africa: From Aid Dependence to Self-Sustaining Growth
	2. Look Homeward		26. African Famines: Yet Again
	3. Coping With Victory		27. Hong Kong—The Case for Optimism
	4. U.S. Foreign Policy and Europe, 1990–2000		28. The Little Rohcomotive That Could
	5. Crisis in the Soviet Union—The Historical Perspective		29. The New & Improved South America
	6. The New World Disorder?		30. Latin America Confronts the Challenges of the 1990s
	7. Brzezinski on the Breakup of the USSR		31. The Crisis of Leadership
	8. Russia vs. the Soviet Union		32. Revolution, Reform, or Regression?
	9. Toward a New Russian Federation		33. Brotherly Hate: Gulf Crisis Underscores Historical Divisions in the Arab 'Family'
	10. Europe's Extremes		34. Baghdad Formally Agrees to 'Unjust' U.N. Conditions for Permanent Cease-Fire
	11. Several Germanys Since 1871, But Today's Is 'Very Different'		35. The Emperor's New Clothes: The World Bank and Environmental Reform
	12. Germany: The Uncertain Colossus		36. From Geopolitics to Geo-Economics
	13. A United Germany Shoulders New Responsibilities		37. World Banking in Trouble
	14. NATO's Identity Crisis		38. Toffler's Next Shock
	15. The Two Canadas		39. STARTing Over
	16. Don't Write Off Japan		40. Goodwill Missions for Castoff Missiles
	17. American-Japanese-European Relations: A View From Washington		41. Is the Soviet Union Prepared for Peace?
	18. Japan as Competitor		42. Missile Mania: Some Rules for the Game
	19. Reforming the Nonreforming Regimes		43. The Stirrings of History
	20. The Two Faces of Eastern Europe		44. Nationalism Is Not Necessarily the Path to a Democratic World
	21. Year of Economic Change Looms for Eastern Europe		45. With All Her Faults, She Is My Country Still
	22. Eastern Europe on Edge		46. What Next? The Post–Cold War World
	23. Crises in Communist Reform: Lessons From Tiananmen		
	24. The Domestic Roots of China's Post-Tiananmen Foreign Policy		

(Continued on next page)

ABOUT YOU

Name_____ Date_____

Are you a teacher? ☐ Or student? ☐

Your School Name _____

Department _____

Address _____

City _____ State _____ Zip _____

School Telephone # _____

YOUR COMMENTS ARE IMPORTANT TO US!

Please fill in the following information:

For which course did you use this book? _____

Did you use a text with this Annual Edition? ☐ yes ☐ no

The title of the text? _____

What are your general reactions to the Annual Editions concept?

Have you read any particular articles recently that you think should be included in the next edition?

Are there any articles you feel should be replaced in the next edition? Why?

Are there other areas that you feel would utilize an Annual Edition?

May we contact you for editorial input?

May we quote you from above?

ANNUAL EDITIONS: WORLD POLITICS 91/92

BUSINESS REPLY MAIL

First Class   Permit No. 84   Guilford, CT

Postage will be paid by addressee

The Dushkin Publishing Group, Inc.
Sluice Dock
DPG **Guilford, Connecticut 06437**

No Postage
Necessary
if Mailed
in the
United States